GERD THEISSEN is Professor of New
Testament at the University of
Heidelberg.

PSYCHOLOGICAL aspects of PAULINE THEOLOGY

GERD THEISSEN
Translated by John P. Galvin

FORTRESS PRESS   PHILADELPHIA

Translated by John P. Galvin

This book is a translation of *Psychologische Aspekte paulinischer Theologie* (FRLANT 131). Copyright © 1983 by Vandenhoeck & Ruprecht, Göttingen, Federal Republic of Germany.

Biblical quotations, unless otherwise noted, are from the Revised Standard Version of the Bible, copyright 1946, 1952, © 1971, 1973 by the Division of Christian Education of the National Council of the Churches of Christ in the U.S.A. and are used by permission.

English Translation Copyright © 1987 by Fortress Press

Library of Congress Cataloging-in-Publication Data

Theissen, Gerd.
  Psychological aspects of Pauline theology.

  Translation of: Psychologische Aspekte paulinischer
Theologie.
  Bibliography: p.
  1. Bible. N.T. Epistles of Paul—Psychology.
I. Title.
BS2655.P88T4613 1986   227'.06'019   86-45196
ISBN 0–8006–0789–9

2102D86   Printed in the United States of America   1–783

Contents

Contents   vii

Preface

Completion of this book requires that I express thanks in several directions. The influence of many people is reflected in it.

As early as my years of study in Bonn, I came into contact with Hans Thomae's synthesis of humanistic and modern theoretical approaches in psychology. His synthesis has been a model for this work. During my year at St. Augustin (1977–78), I came to know in Y. Watanabe an original Japanese approach to the analysis of religious experience and behavior. This strengthened my preference for "cognitive" theories.

In Copenhagen (1978–80), while working on the Scandinavian psychology of religion of the Uppsala School, I came upon the idea of bridging the gap between the psychology of religion and an exegesis concerned with the history of traditions with the aid of Hjalmar Sundén's approach of role theory and perception psychology.

A decisive impulse came from Kiel, although I have never lived in that city (though I came very close to doing so). In the spring of 1979, Joachim Scharfenberg delivered guest lectures in Copenhagen. His nondogmatic, hermeneutic variant of psychoanalysis opened anew for me access to this approach.

It was in Denmark that I was able to work out the basic conception of this book and presented it for discussion in classes and lectures. I would like to express explicit thanks for the critical tolerance of new ideas among both students and pastors. Antipsychological prejudices may be the rule in other places, but in Denmark they were the exception.

In Heidelberg, where I have taught since 1980, I have come into contact with the Jung school's psychology of religion, which is influential in southern Germany. Conversation with students marked by this approach has certainly contributed to having this tendency considered more positively than was originally intended. The chapter on glossolalia was published internally in our seminar in a Festschrift for the fiftieth birthday of C. Burchard. This chapter is dedicated to him—in part as thanks for my friendly reception in Heidelberg. I owe more thanks to my wife than to any of those already mentioned. Her professional knowledge has opened up to me learning theory and cognitive conceptions of psychology; I have her to thank for a critical distance on the psychodynamic currents that dominate almost exclusively in theology. She mediated my acquaintance with newer approaches in psychotherapy. I discussed each chapter of the book with her. Yet I cannot hold her responsible for my mistakes; I am myself responsible for the application of psychological theories to religious texts and phenomena.

I am grateful to Wolfgang Schrage and Rudolf Smend, the coeditors of Forschungen zur Religion und Literatur des Alten und Neuen Testaments, for accepting this book in this series. The work stands deliberately in the tradition of this series; it seeks not to replace but to deepen the tested historical-critical methods. I am aware that some readers will find desirable a more thorough systematic theological reflection on exegesis conducted from the perspective of the psychology of religion. I sketched my theological position in a brief book published in 1978, *Argumente für einen kritischen Glauben* (ET: *A Critical Faith: A Case for Religion* [Philadelphia: Fortress Press, 1979]), and would refer to what I said there about the psychological critique of religion.

H. Kohns and M. Hoffmann have assisted me with the preparation of the German manuscript. W. Stegemann has checked it for clarity. All are due my sincere thanks.

GERD THEISSEN
Heidelberg, December 1982

Translator's Preface

This book is a translation of Gerd Theissen, *Psychologische Aspekte paulinischer Theologie* (Göttingen: Vandenhoeck & Ruprecht, 1983). The German text is volume 131 in the series Forschungen zur Religion und Literatur des Alten und Neuen Testaments. Minor corrections have been made in several of the references.

Unless otherwise noted, biblical citations are from the Revised Standard Version. Citations from the Septuagint are taken from Lancelot C. E. Brenton, *The Septuagint Version: Greek and English* (Grand Rapids: Zondervan Pub. House, 1970). An asterisked biblical citation indicates that I have altered the translation in order to preserve the nuances of Prof. Theissen's German rendering of the text.

In the translation of psychological terminology I have been influenced by the argument of Bruno Bettelheim, *Freud and Man's Soul* (New York: Alfred A. Knopf, 1982); I am grateful to Rev. Walter J. Edyvean for reference to this work.

A passage originally published in Danish was translated by Prof. Leo A. Connolly of Memphis State University.

For suggestions concerning the translation I am indebted to Prof. Leo A. Connolly, Mr. Thomas F. Coronite, Rev. Christopher J. Coyne, Mr. Joseph M. Hennessey, Mr. Joseph T. MacCarthy, Mr. Timothy J. MacGeorge, Rev. Laurence W. McGrath, Jr., Rev. Frank J. Matera, and Mr. James A. Smith.

The translation is dedicated to Edmund and Rosemary O'Rourke.

JOHN P. GALVIN
Boston, August 1985

PART ONE

Theoretical Problems of Psychological Exegesis

Every exegete has learned that psychological exegesis is poor exegesis. It interpolates between the lines things that no one can know. It inserts modern categories into ancient texts. Because of its interest in personal problems behind the text, it does not let the text come to speech. Above all, however, it relativizes the text's theological claim through appeal to factors that are all too human. The lengthy catalogue of the sins of psychological exegesis is imposing; the rejection of any combination of psychology and exegesis is often presented with such disarming obviousness that it is almost an offense against the good manners of historical-critical tradition that an attempt at psychological exegesis is nonetheless presented here.

What does psychological exegesis seek to accomplish? What can it achieve with favorable sources? It seeks to describe and explain, as far as possible, human behavior and experience in ancient Christianity.[1] Its foundations are early Christian texts, whether it concludes from them to human behavior and experience or interprets the texts themselves as psychic acts—as acts of praying, appealing, thinking, interpreting, and evaluating. Under the rubric of psychological exegesis we include all attempts to interpret texts as expression and occurrence of human experience and behavior.[2]

1. Cf. the definition of Thomae and Feger: Psychology "seeks to grasp human behavior and experience as appropriately as possible, that is, to describe and if possible measure its constancy and variability, to determine the conditions of constancy and variability, and to predict their future course as much as possible" (*Hauptströmungen*, 1). Measurements and predictions are not part of psychological exegesis. There remain the task of describing experience and behavior and analysis of their conditions.
2. Further differentiation is possible if necessary. A psychological evaluation of texts is conclusion from the texts to experience and behavior. Psychological exegesis would then be interpretation of the texts themselves as forms of experience and behavior.

1

No one will deny that ancient Christian faith elicited changes in human behavior and experience. The goal of describing these changes will scarcely meet with rejection, though there may be doubt that the sources permit well-founded statements about psychic processes. Psychological exegesis's goal of explaining religious behavior and experience to a certain extent will, however, remain controversial, for there are in psychology explanations of religious phenomena that blatantly contradict religious self-understanding. But controversial attempts at explanation can be found in every science—not to mention theology. What is decisive is whether one ventures the fascinating attempt to explain religious experience and behavior with reference to its conditions.

The proposal presented here stands in a tradition in which individual psychological approaches to explanation are relativized in favor of a comprehensive understanding—the tradition of a hermeneutically oriented psychology. The hermeneutic orientation offers no independent approach to explanation on the same level as learning theory, or as psychodynamic and cognitive models. It is on the one hand a corrective in the exegetical use of these models, and on the other hand a general framework that becomes concrete and fruitful only through assumption of explanatory models. This general framework consists of five premises that are characteristic of a hermeneutically oriented psychology.[3]

1. Human experience and behavior are mediated interpretively; that is, psychic processes are decisively conditioned by the interpretations one gives one's inner and outer world. Intrinsic and extrinsic causes have effects not "by themselves" but rather as interpreted causes and circumstances. Psychic life is interpretable because it occurs in interpretations itself. The foundation of understanding human existence, in other words, is human self-understanding.

2. Human experience and behavior are historically conditioned. The interpretations that determine behavior and experience derive from tradition; they are constantly newly applied to situations and are modified in the process.[4] This interplay of tradition and situation emerges from a particular historical context but cannot be deduced from this context as from a cause. It is individual and singular.

3. The programmatic text of hermeneutical psychology is Dilthey, *Ideen*. A brief summary is provided by Thomae, *Hauptströmungen*, 89–95.
4. Dilthey undoubtedly underestimated the dependence of psychic processes on the history of tradition. His hermeneutic psychology is oriented on the great "geniuses," who usually appear as conquerors of traditions.

Ultimately, therefore, psychic life can only be described "ideographically," though general categories are indispensable in doing this.

3. Human experience and behavior can be objectified in texts (or other signs). The interpretations that determine our experience and behavior are structured in communicable sign systems—works of art, rites, and institutions, for example—but above all in texts. Later generations can tell from them what interpretations of world and of self once determined psychic life. This is true not only of the great literary and philosophical texts but also of the texts of "lesser people." The New Testament goes back to social levels and groups that otherwise remained mute.

4. Human experience and behavior form a unified whole. While we find it necessary in the case of physical occurrences to reconstruct the total context of nature through hypotheses, the unity of psychic life is certain for us a priori from personal experience—prior to all dismemberment, explanation, and construction of hypotheses.[5] Understanding therefore takes place in the light of a preunderstanding of the full context that is to be understood. With regard to texts, this means that understanding occurs in the hermeneutic circle between part and whole.

5. Human experience and understanding are marked by content. They cannot be fully grasped in isolation from the contents to which they relate. It is therefore insufficient to investigate general forms and conditions of psychic events independently of the contents of human life. Psychic life is marked in specific ways in the respective contexts of religion, art, science, politics, and the economy. The psychology of religion is more than an application of general psychology.

Let it again be emphasized that these principles of a hermeneutical psychology are not a particular explanatory model but rather a framework within which various models will be drawn upon. Three approaches will be discussed in the following pages: learning theory, psychodynamic models, and cognitive models. Each will be drawn upon to the extent that it can make religious experience and behavior

5. This was a basic idea of Dilthey: "In psychology, the whole is originally and continually given in experience; life is always present only as a whole" (*Ideen*, 144). It is said to be true of the natural sciences, on the contrary, "that in them nature as a whole is present only through complementary conclusions, by means of a combination of hypotheses" (p. 143). Does this not fail to recognize that there is a prescientific experience of nature as unity, and that scientific research presupposes this unity? Without being able to prove it, we presuppose that natural laws do not change, and that what holds true today will also hold true tomorrow.

in a historically limited context intelligible as an event mediated by interpretation.

It must be frankly conceded that a hermeneutical psychology stands apart from the main streams of contemporary psychology. At the present time, however, a convergence between psychological and hermeneutical approaches can be noted.

On the one hand, there is a "trend to cognitive theories" within psychology.[6] Cognitive processes, that is, all acts of perception, interpretation, thought, judgment, and evaluation, are increasingly assessed as decisive factors of psychic life. Even learning theory and psychodynamic approaches appear today in cognitively or hermeneutically modified form. On the other hand, the interpretive sciences have become open to social-scientific models of explanation. History is not only narrated, described, and interpreted, but also to a certain degree explained.

Understanding and explanation today no longer appear as the sharp opposites familiar to us from philosophical tradition. New connections appear between natural sciences, which explain, and human sciences, which understand: nature and history are not absolutely separate. An evolutionary interpretation of the whole of reality can relate them to each other without having to deny their distinction.

We shall now discuss in detail the three theoretical approaches of psychological exegesis. After this, we must ask anew how these three approaches are inserted into the framework of a hermeneutically oriented psychology, and to what extent they transform this framework. In the last chapter of Part One, we shall therefore discuss again the five premises of a hermeneutical psychology.

6. Thus Thomae, *Psychologie*, 183.

Chapter 1

Learning Theory: Religion as Socially Learned Experience and Behavior

The fundamental idea of psychology of religion based on learning theory is that religious experience and behavior are socially learned.[1] In this context, "learning" means changes in behavior and experience on the basis of occurrences, not, in other words, through maturation or physical influences. According to learning theory, the environment has a threefold effect on human experience and behavior. First, in associative learning, environmental stimuli that previously were neutral become determinative of behavior and experience. Second, in operant learning, the frequency and direction of behavior and experience are influenced by their consequences. Third, in imitative learning, ready-made forms of behavior are observed in models, appropriated, and imitated.

In what follows, any interpretation of human behavior and experience that operates with these three principles of learning will be subsumed under the concept "learning theory." The concept of learning theory will be understood more broadly than it is in behaviorism. This will become even more clear as we discuss the three principles of learning in detail.

ASSOCIATIVE LEARNING IN RELIGION

Associative learning[2] is based on the connection of two stimuli, of which stimulus A always provoked a reaction but stimulus B was

---

1. There is no psychology of religion oriented on learning theory. In what follows I am independently applying the general principles of learning theory to various religious phenomena. A good introduction to these principles is offered by K. I. Bredenkamp, "Was ist Lernen?"

2. The terms "classical conditioning" and "respondent conditioning" are also used

originally neutral. If both stimuli constantly occur together, the reaction to stimulus A will soon also occur in response to stimulus B.

While this sounds trivial, it is of great importance in religion. We almost always hear organ music, for example, in connection with liturgies. It is therefore understandable that emotional reactions to liturgies are also transferred to organ music—whether they are feelings of familiarity or of repugnance. In itself, organ music is something neutral.

The example of organ music is characteristic inasmuch as it is above all emotional reactions that are learned through associative learning. No one will dispute that emotional reactions to particular signals and signs have great importance in religion. Just consider all the classifications of objects into the categories of pure and impure, or think of all that is condemned as demonic or glorified in positive terms. All of these rest on associative learning. Originally neutral objects and forms of behavior become "triggers" of religious efforts to approach or avoid them. And this process is historically conditioned: things considered sacred in one culture are profane elsewhere. What is venerated in one place is condemned in another. The historical diversity of religion cannot be explained without learned connections of triggers and forms of religious reaction.[3]

In order to make the concept of associative learning fruitful for an exegesis from the perspective of a psychology of religion we must take two further steps.[4] First, it must be noted that emotional religious reactions are caused not by external stimuli "in themselves" but rather by stimuli experienced as religiously significant in the light of a culturally formed history of learning. Even the designation of a stimulus as demonic is culturally conditioned. In other words, it is not the world in itself but the interpreted world that affects us through stimuli.

The second step is even more important. Religious experience and

instead of "associative learning." The discovery and experimental investigation of associative learning are associated with the names of Pavlov and Watson. Cf. Thomae, *Hauptströmungen*, 35ff.

3. This raises the question whether there are originally religious reactions to reality. In *Argumente*, 23–29, I have sketched the thesis that religious reaction to sacred objects is a human transformation of the animal reaction to improbable and simple stimuli.

4. I proceed in what follows on the basis of the cognitive modification of classical learning theories. A summary of this may be found in Mahoney, *Cognition and Behavior Modification*. In this approach the stimulus-response schema (i.e., the connection between stimulus and reaction) is modified in two ways. First, external stimuli, reinforcements, and models have effects through cognitive mediators, i.e., depending on how they are interpreted in each instance (cf. pp. 169–93). Second, parallel to external behavior there are a (hidden) internal behavior and corresponding inner stimuli, reinforcers, and models (pp. 61–122).

behavior can occur independently of external stimuli. They can be connected with internal conceptions, images, and symbols. Behaviorist learning theory, which excludes all internal (mental) processes from consideration, can have no understanding of this. But a cognitively modified learning theory, which views inner images and fantasies as stimuli that determine experience and behavior just as much as external stimuli, differs on this point. Since the inner processes cannot be observed, people speak of "hidden behavior" in this connection. Religion opens itself to analysis from the perspective of learning theory only when hidden processes are recognized.

What we find in religious texts are precisely those symbols and images that have effects through inner representation. Of course they are not independent of external realities, such as sacred places and times, buildings and rites. Even a word has to be heard! But precisely in biblical religion there is an emancipation of religious experience and behavior from external stimuli. The prohibition of images was enforced in the Old Testament. And Jesus said that pure and impure are not external qualities connected with specific stimuli; they are exclusively inner qualities—hidden stimuli (Matt. 7:15).

OPERANT LEARNING IN RELIGION

Like all human behavior, religious behavior and experience can be influenced by operant reinforcers.[5] "Operant learning" means the influencing of behavior through its consequences—in popular terms, through reward and punishment. Positive consequences increase the probability that specific behavior and experience will occur. Lack of reinforcers quenches them. Negative sanctions can suppress them in short order. Consequences can be material reinforcers (like food and drink), social reactions (like praise and blame), and symbolic reinforcers (e.g., fantasies about heavenly rewards).

It is beyond question that religious behavior is conditioned by material reinforcers. Religious feasts are a good illustration. For centuries a joyous common meal followed the religious rite of slaughter ("sacrifice"). The bloody performance of sacrifice was so thoroughly reinforced by the sequence "cultic rite–consumption of meat" that it survived into late antiquity despite all intellectual criticism and was abolished only through Christianity. It is clear from 1 Corinthians how strong the motivation to participate in sacrifices was. It was

5. Research on operant learning is associated above all with the name of B. F. Skinner; cf. Thomae, *Hauptströmungen*, 51–52.

difficult especially for poorer Christians to refrain from cultic celebrations that included distribution of meat. The material reinforcement of (undesired) religious behavior could be balanced only by massive counterconditioning (cf. 1 Cor. 8—10).[6] Even today the popularity of Christmas is due not least to the fact that as children we were all reinforced on this occasion by gifts, so that even in contemporary secularized people rudimentary religious forms of behavior and experience are reactivated at Christmas.

Material reinforcers are almost always joined to social reinforcers. In ancient Christianity the poor did not receive only material support. Even a slave was addressed as "brother." In Christ the slave was free. Even the foreigner was a fellow citizen in the heavenly city. All could consider themselves loved and chosen by God. Preachers, sacraments, and community life constantly strengthened this certainty.

These social reinforcers were supported by symbolic reinforcers. It is a paradox for orthodox behaviorism that future reinforcers that are never experienced in reality have a powerful force in motivating behavior, that people will even sacrifice everything for the future.[7] But the cognitively modified approach can explain this too. Expectation of the Lord's Parousia has effects like a real reinforcer if it is constantly repeated in words, feasts, and confessional formulas, if one constantly relives in one's fantasy that the "last things" occur—the Lord comes, the elect receive their reward, and the damned go away empty. The gospel's effects in changing experience and behavior can only be made intelligible within the framework of an eschatological—symbolically present—system of reinforcement.

IMITATIVE LEARNING IN RELIGION

Human experience and behavior are marked by models.[8] We need not be reinforced ourselves in order to learn a form of behavior. It often

6. Cf. my reflections in Studien zur Soziologie, 272–89.
7. Kraiker (Psychoanalyse, 160) shows this by the following example: "The statement 'At the end of his life, Emperor Charles V entered a monastery in order to attain eternal bliss' would certainly not be translated by Skinner into the statement 'At the end of his life, Emperor Charles V entered a monastery because eternal bliss had frequently followed his earlier visits to monasteries.' That is certainly objectively false, if not semantic nonsense." Explanation through hidden operant learning would, however, in my opinion be less foolish. Charles V entered a monastery because his cultural environment in its imagination constantly connected monastic life and eternal bliss, and because this idea took control over him. Consequences anticipated in imagination have the same effects as real consequences if they are imagined frequently enough and socially reinforced.
8. Research on learning from models is associated above all with the name of A.

suffices to see successful behavior in others. Vicarious models have a greater effect if they do not dominate the situation from the start but rather overcome only after meeting resistance. We identify more readily with models that overcome opposition than with those which dominate from the start.

The ancient world already knew that religious behavior and experience were highly dependent on models. In his *Laws* (887D–E), Plato explained the development of religious convictions as an act of imitative learning. Children hear of the gods in myths. In addition to this,

> their own parents they saw showing the utmost zeal on behalf of themselves and their children in addressing the gods in prayers and supplications, as though they most certainly existed; and at the rising and setting of the sun and moon they heard and saw the prostrations and devotions of all the Greeks and barbarians, under all conditions of adversity and prosperity, directed to these luminaries, not as though they were not gods, but as though they most certainly were gods beyond the shadow of a doubt.[9]

Here Plato mentions two types of models: real models like parents, and symbolic models like Greeks and non-Greeks, of whom the children only hear. Both forms of imitative learning can be shown to exist in religion everywhere.

Paul was a real model of religious experience and behavior for his communities. It is only for this reason that he was able to instruct them to imitate him as he imitated Christ (1 Cor. 11:1). The symbolic model of Christ was brought close to the communities through Paul's behavior as a real model; the life and death of Jesus became manifest in Paul's life (2 Cor. 4:10–11).

In this text, as in many others, Paul appeals to symbolic models; he himself soon became the model of the converted persecutor. The unique significance of the Bible rests in part on the fact that it contains a large selection of realistic models, from Adam to Paul. The Bible was able to become one of the most important textbooks of human behavior and experience precisely because in it "dominating" models recede and models that first fail but then overcome are so numerous. For Paul himself, for example, Abraham and Christ had exemplary significance.

In conclusion, it must again be emphasized that learning theory

---

Bandura. He went beyond classical learning theories in holding that learning through observation presupposes cognitive acts. An overview is provided by Zumkley-Münkel, *Imitationslernen*.

9. ET: R. G. Bury, *Laws*, vol. 2 of 2 vols. (LCL, 1926), 307.

becomes fruitful for the analysis of religion only when it is modified
in a cognitive manner, that is, when the principles of associative,
operant, and imitative learning are applied not only to real stimuli,
reinforcers, and models, but also to symbolic—internally represented—
ones. It is these stimuli, reinforcers, and models that we also encounter
in religious texts.

One question remains open. What is specific to religious experience
and behavior? How can particular stimuli, reinforcers, and models
achieve religious character? We can at most suggest an answer. Religious
symbols wish to place the human being in a relationship to the whole
of reality. A stimulus achieves religious character when the whole
becomes present in it and a reaction to it is perceived as an emotional
response to the whole. The same is true of reinforcers. Religious faith
is a search for certitude that life is ultimately "worthwhile"—despite
all its negative aspects. Reinforcing elements in the symbolically
interpreted world attain religious character when they give expression
to this basic conviction. Something similar can be said of imitative
learning. Religious faith senses behind our limited life-world a fullness
of meaning that serves as model and impetus for meaningful personal
action.

Fortunately, within the framework of our studies, we can leave open
the question of the specific characteristic of religious experience and
behavior. A psychology of ancient Christian religion is primarily
interested in the new patterns of experience and behavior that appeared
with ancient Christianity. From the perspective of learning theory, it
inquires into new stimuli and combinations of stimuli, new reinforcers,
and new models that occur in the symbolic world of ancient Christianity.
Even at first glance new manifestations are apparent. Cross and
resurrection, for example, are "associated"—an extremely negative and
an extremely positive stimulus. The eschatological reinforcement
symbolism is radically transformed. Even the godless is justified. There
is an unconditioned positive reinforcement despite guilt and sin. And
with Christ there comes into the center of the interpreted world a
model in whom failure and victory, being judged and judging, power
and impotence are joined in unique fashion.

Chapter 2

The Psychodynamic Approach: Religion as Confrontation with the Unconscious

---

Learning theory explains changes in experience and behavior as the construction or extinguishing of reactions to the environment. Only a relatively undirected, general activity is presupposed in the human being itself. Classical learning theory even deliberately abstracts from everything that takes place within the human being. If, for example, a reaction is extinguished, within this theoretical framework it no longer exists.

What is located solely on the periphery of (classical) learning theories becomes the central theme of psychodynamic approaches.[1] Their great discovery is that the inner world of the human being has depth dimensions that escape consciousness. According to psychodynamic theory, for example, when a mode of conduct ceases, the energy that lies behind it is not simply extinguished but transformed, that is, sublimated, transferred, or suppressed. It continues to have an effect, even if it remains unconscious.

According to the psychodynamic conception, changes in experience and behavior occur through movement of the boundary between consciousness and the unconscious. It is above all in (therapeutic) dialogue that this movement is steered in a constructive direction. An emotionally accepting partner helps through interpretations to bring to consciousness previously unconscious aspects of the person and to integrate them. The factors that have effects in the unconscious and the function of the unconscious in life are specified differently in the two classical psychodynamic approaches.[2]

---

1. An overview is offered by Wyss, *Die tiefenpsychologischen Schulen*, and by Wiesenhütter, *Grundbegriffe*.
2. An instructive comparison of the two conceptions is offered by Fetscher, *Grundlinien*.

11

Psychoanalysis (Sigmund Freud) seeks to achieve constructive change in experience and behavior by overcoming dysfunctional unconscious traumas and fixations that derive from early childhood experiences within the family. The unconsciousness is seen as a swamp that must be drained. The goal is a realistic adaptation to reality through reduction of tension within the human being.

Analytic psychology (C. G. Jung) seeks, on the contrary, constructive changes through integration of functional structures of the unconscious. Lying ready in the collective unconscious are inherited types of behavior and experience to which we can entrust ourselves. The unconscious appears less as a swamp to be drained than as a vivifying spring from which one has far too long been separated. The primary goal is "adaptation" to this collective interior world. Integration of this world makes it possible to handle the external world better as well.

Hermeneutical processes play a major role in all psychodynamic approaches. The dialogue between therapist and client is a hermeneutic event that, as the many schools of psychodynamic orientation show, is historically conditioned. Nonetheless, the hermeneutic character of psychodynamic theories is not always conscious. In view of the development of psychodynamic theories, it is justifiable to speak of a "hermeneutic" turn, such that, in sum, psychodynamic theories envision three factors of human experience and behavior: (1) genetic predispositions (above all, in analytic psychology); (2) early childhood imprinting (above all, in orthodox psychoanalysis); and (3) cultural interpretations (above all, in theories that have been modified hermeneutically). These three factors will be discussed in order.

GENETIC PREDISPOSITIONS (ARCHETYPES)

Jung concluded from continually recurring motifs in expressions of the unconscious—dreams, myths, and fantasies—to universally distributed foundational structures of experience and behavior.[3] He called these structures archetypes. Unconscious, unimaginable, and formal, archetypes belong to the collective genetic heritage. They may be compared to a magnetic field, which no one can perceive but which becomes visible through its effects. The effects of archetypes are the recurring motifs, images, and symbols in our "interpreted world."

The doctrine of archetypes enjoys a certain degree of probability.

3. The best introduction is the summary in Jacobi, *Komplex*, which was authorized by Jung. Mann, *Einführung*, stands in the tradition of this school.

The human being is the current end product of a lengthy evolution. We must expect in human beings as in all living beings, genetically preprogrammed dispositions—adaptive structures that correspond to an archaic phase of our existence but that are now unconscious since adaptation to the changed conditions of the contemporary environment requires conscious acts of a completely different type. It is important that such preprogrammed predispositions never work automatically. They are always shaped by cultural influence and can be reinforced, modified, or even suppressed by cultural factors. They explain only a certain probability that culturally variable tendencies of experience and behavior will occur.[4]

How can one uncover such archetypes? What criteria are at our disposal to enable us to recognize a common "heritage" behind all the cultural variations? Three criteria are to be noted.

1. Archetypal structures may be presumed when biological research establishes the existence of comparable reactions in human beings and in animals, although comparable behavior is in no way a certain indication of genetic predisposition.[5]

2. Archetypal structures can be presumed where neurophysical research has found indications of a neural basis of specific structures of experience and behavior.[6] Here we enter a sphere in which the human being is fundamentally different from its animal relatives—the sphere of the brain.

3. Finally, archetypal structures can be presumed where intercultural comparison consistently finds comparable forms of experience and behavior.[7] Since archetypal structures never establish themselves automatically, they need not be universally demonstrated in manifest appearances.

It must be conceded that the methodological basis for concluding to the existence of archetypes is still rather weak. Yet there are plausible

4. The psychology of Jung must, in my opinion, be made more precise and limited by the results of biological behavior research. This goal lies behind the collection of Heusser, ed., *Instinkte.*

5. Distinctions must be made between predispositions for behavior (e.g., smiling), for processes of knowledge (e.g., sensibility for the "child schema"), for drives (e.g., sexuality), and for learning processes; see Eibl-Eibesfeldt, *Der vorprogrammierte Mensch,* 13–74. The fact that biological behavior research often concludes prematurely from animal behavior to human behavior (see Thomae, *Psychologie,* 154–63) ought not lead to rejection of this entire direction of research.

6. See d'Aquili, "The Neurological Bases."

7. Intercultural religious phenomena have been presented above all in the so-called phenomenologies of religion, e.g., in Eliade, *Patterns in Comparative Religions.*

examples. The symbol of the "divine child" occurs in many cultures and is also found in the infancy narratives of the Gospels. It probably addresses relics of "instinctive nest-care behavior" in us, like the "child schema" in other living beings. The symbol of the divine child thus receives inner reinforcement from a very general behavior disposition, which could explain its widespread occurrence.

The father symbol is also demonstrably intercultural. It occupied a central place in ancient Christianity. Nowhere else is God so emphatically called Father. This symbol too may possibly address relics of childlike "begging behavior" with respect to parents who provide care—relics which were transformed into a general feeling of trust and emotional security.

Reference should also be made to symbols that derive from the relationship of friend and enemy. In the New Testament, Christ is represented as a ruler who triumphs over his foes (1 Cor. 15:25; Col. 2:15). The victoriously triumphant God is a widespread phenomenon in the history of religion. He is usually represented in a way corresponding to a widespread imposing stance among living beings, with outthrust breast and abnormal size. Such symbols can address rudimentary tendencies of behavior and experience within us.

Symbols from the area of sexuality may be found in almost all religions. Even mystical union with Christ has sexual overtones. The gnostic sacrament of the bridal chamber[8] makes clear the metaphorical connection between sexual union and Christ mysticism. It is characteristic that the sexual symbols are directed not toward sexual behavior but toward religious experience.

The examples above all derive from areas in which there are analogies (and perhaps homologies) between animal and human behavior—the parent-child relationship, the friend-enemy relationship, and the union of sexual partnership. At the center of Jung's psychology of religion, however, there stands an archetype for whose effects there can be no analogies in the animal kingdom—the archetype of the self, which grounds the striving for wholeness and self-realization. To my mind there is no doubt that only human beings can be grasped by this striving for "individuation." Only in them do we find a consciousness that can distance itself from the unconscious and that longs for more comprehensive unity, for the integration of conscious and unconscious, of masculine and feminine, of ideal image and "shadow." Yet even this

8. *The Gospel of Philip* 61, 66–68, 73, and passim.

tendency toward wholeness has an organic foundation. Even in the biological realm we can detect tendencies toward inner equilibrium: a homeostatic tendency rules all the processes in an organism. We see the organism become active in order to resolve tensions of need. Similarly, we strive in our psychic and intellectual life toward an inner equilibrium; psychic life is a dynamic equilibrium that, like a bicycle that tips over when it stops going forward, can retain its balance only as long as it continues to develop. Possibly there are neural structures that steer this equilibrium—an understanding of "wholeness" and "unity" located in the nondominant hemisphere of the brain. Whatever the case may be, we are always engaged in balancing present imbalances and discrepancies; there may even be within human beings a preexistent tendency toward self-realization which actively seeks out dissonances and attempts to integrate them.[9]

Jung's psychology of religion interprets religious symbols chiefly as objectification of an archetypal tendency toward self-realization. Christ is a symbol of the self.[10] In him the polarities of conscious and unconscious, of ideal and shadow,[11] of masculine and feminine are integrated into a comprehensive unity. What appears in learning theory as a model of human experience and behavior becomes here a symbol of an archetypal reality. Christ does not simply have effects as a vicarious symbolic model—because it is reinforced in our place. Rather, the Christ symbol undergoes inner reinforcement by a preprogrammed human tendency. A preexistent tendency toward self-realization incarnates itself in Christ; even more, in Christ this tendency arrives at consciousness of itself.

It must be conceded that this sounds rather speculative, but the most plausible currently available solution to a historical problem lies here. Within a surprisingly brief time, the historical Jesus was interpreted as a preexistent divine being. Theories that explain this

9. Even less speculative psychologists allow for such a tendency toward self-realization. By "self-actualizing tendency," Carl Rogers means the general tendency of an organism "to use all its abilities for the preservation or advancement of the organism. This tendency is innate. All other drives and motivations are merely partial aspects or manifestations of this 'master motive.' Only the organism as a whole evokes this tendency" (so presented in the account of Bommert, *Grundlagen*, 22).

10. Jung offers a summarizing interpretation of the Christ symbol in "Versuch," esp. in the section entitled "Christus als Archetypos," 166–72.

11. Jung does criticize the Christ symbolism as lacking "the nightside of spiritual nature, the darkness of the spirit and sin" (*Gesammelte Werke* 11:170; cf. also "Aion," in *Gesammelte Werke* 9:469). To this extent, the Christ symbolism is for him not a perfect symbol of the self.

occurrence as derivative from other religions can provide only an inadequate explanation.[12] Even the classical proponent of theories of derivation from the history of religion, Wilhelm Bousset, emphasized that such derivations are occurrences "in the unconscious, in the uncontrollable depth of the overall psyche of a community."[13] The psychological doctrine of archetypes can make this occurrence partially intelligible. The effects that went forth from the historical Jesus addressed preexistent tendencies within human beings. In the experience of the first Christians, there appeared with Christ a reality that had always existed but that had just then entered consciousness. Christ was therefore experienced immediately as a preexistent being that had just emerged from its concealment.

Not only the historical Jesus but also the archetypal reality was "reinterpreted" through the connection of archetypal tendencies with the historical Jesus. The effects that went forth from the historical Jesus marked the archetypal reality in a historically unique way. The process of individuation was interpreted as the most painful experience of a man with himself. It can be experienced only through conversion from one's previous manner of life. It is death and rebirth. The cross symbolizes the necessity of conversion through crises from one's previous life. The human being is confronted with the nightside of reality. Only through its integration does one achieve wholeness, "salvation."

With these reflections we have modified the psychological doctrine of archetypes hermeneutically. According to Jung the archetype is the cause of the religious symbol. The two are related as a seal is related to its imprint. This one-sided causal relationship must be loosened and replaced by acceptance of a mutual causality. The starting point should be the symbolic world that is historically given. Archetypal structures explain why this world finds resonance deep in human hearts, why it encounters inner reinforcement that contributes to its historical expansion and consolidation. Yet the reality in human hearts that confers resonance on religious symbols is in no sense joined to them in necessary causal relationship. Over the course of history, the human unconscious has reacted "in a reinforcing manner" to very

12. "Theories of transfer from the history of religions" are understood as the assumption that more or less fixed conceptions of the redeemer were taken from the environment of ancient Christianity and applied to Christ. It makes no difference whether the pagan or the Jewish environment of ancient Christianity is chiefly envisioned.

13. See Bousset, *Kyrios Christos*, 99. For similar comments, see 74, 90.

different symbolic systems. The archetypal structures of experience and behavior that are innate in human existence are of themselves open. They are modified and formed in a historical learning process. They do not exist "in themselves" but always only in historically variable interpretation.

EARLY CHILDHOOD IMPRINTINGS

Psychoanalysis (Freud) also interprets the Christ symbolism as correspondence to and unveiling of a dynamism of which the human being is unconscious; but it interprets this unconscious dynamism as a dark resonance of early childhood conflicts, not as a striving for wholeness and self-achievement.[14]

In doing this, Freud inserts religion into an anthropology that sees human beings as determined more by early childhood imprintings than by genetically preprogrammed structures. This foundational idea of psychoanalysis enjoys a certain plausibility. We find analogies to early childhood imprintings in nest-fleeing animals, which assume an irreversible relationship to their parents in a short phase that is sensitive to learning. The process of imprinting presupposes both innate structures and an astonishing flexibility. It makes it possible for an organism to recognize a particular individual among many others. The individual image of the mother or the father (or of a surrogate) cannot have been preprogrammed in the brain. An arena receptive to relatively arbitrary imprints—as wax is to a seal—must be present.

Although Freud scarcely used the concept of imprinting, he did in fact regard early experiences with one's parents as imprints with almost irreversible character.[15] It is in fact necessary to hold that foundational linguistic, cognitive, and emotional forms of behavior and experience are imprinted in phases sensitive to learning, and that they can be "made up" later only with difficulty, even if these phases do last much longer than in the animal realm and surpass all analogies in flexibility.

---

14. The best introduction is Freud's *Vorlesungen* (1916–17) and *Neue Folge der Vorlesungen* (1932). Vergote, *Religionspsychologie;* Faber, *Religionspsychologie;* Heimbrok, *Phantasie;* and Scharfenberg and Kämpfer, *Mit Symbolen leben* are among the more important works on the psychology of religion within this tradition. An overview is provided by the collection of Nase and Scharfenberg, eds., *Psychoanalyse und Religion.*

15. An interpretation of psychoanalytic knowledge with the aid of the concept of imprinting may be found in Görres, *Methode,* esp. 68–70, 237–39. Jung's doctrine of archetypes has also been interpreted in this fashion; see Portmann, "Das Problem."

But as plausible as this idea is, it has up to now been impossible for psychoanalytic theory to formulate it in a universally valid way.

With regard to religious experience and behavior, Freud held to two "imprinting processes" that stood in tension with each other: a pre-Oedipal imprinting by parents who fulfill wishes and an Oedipal imprinting by parents who deny wishes.

First, religion is interpreted as fixation at a stage of unproblematic wish fulfillment. The long dependence of the child on the parents is said to be never fully overcome by a religious person, who is said to seek over an entire lifetime for the omnipotent figures who radiated safety in need and abandonment, and guaranteed fulfillment of basic needs. Since these figures are no longer to be found on earth, they are sought in heaven—and this all the more when a real-life situation approximates early childhood's situation of dependence. Religion is said to be a regressive renewal of early childhood dependence in view of the frustrations of life, an illusory revival of early childhood satisfaction and security.[16]

The second root of religion lies in the confrontation with parents who deny desires. In an Oedipus conflict (in boys), sexual desires directed toward the mother and corresponding aggressive death wishes directed against the father are overcome through identification with the father. The child renounces the effort to take the place of the father physically as the mother's sexual partner, because he identifies himself morally with the father. He speaks to himself the father's prohibition "Thou shalt not!" and internalizes it as his "superego." Internalization of the command exacts a high price. From then on the son can torture himself with guilt feelings when absolutely no external punishment is to be feared, even when he has not performed any deviant actions but only fantasized them. He has, however, already carried out one crime in his fantasy—rebellion, to the point of a death wish, against his father. The superego, with the help of which the Oedipal fantasies were suppressed, originated as reaction to this death wish. But the superego knows of these fantasies. It punishes drives that are no longer conscious and burdens human life like a inexplicable shadow—and this leaves its deposit in consciousness of an obscure "original sin."[17]

Thus, according to Freud, religious experience and behavior are

16. A compact summary of this aspect of psychoanalytic psychology of religion may be found in Freud, "Eine Kindheitserinnerung," 146.
17. Cf. the summary in Freud, *Totem und Tabu*, 437.

relics of early childhood imprinting through parents, marks both of wish-fulfilling and wish-denying parents. Both have imprinted themselves deeply in the soul of the child and leave indelible traces, particularly a longing for imaginary parents in heaven who offer reconciliation and peace beyond all conflict.

The significance of early Christian religion lies in the fact that it reveals the essence of all religion with particular clarity. On the one hand, an infinite trust in the heavenly Father is regressively renewed; on the other hand, the punishing Father emerges with archaic strictness and kills *the Son* vicariously for all sons. This ingenious interpretation of early Christian symbolism can neither be ignored nor accepted uncritically. Freud himself had doubts about his interpretation. Since, in his judgment, early childhood experience did not suffice by itself to explain religious experience and behavior, he postulated a prehistoric event in the infancy of the human race—patricide in the primeval tribe. In doing this, he showed himself to be not only a genius in interpreting myths but even more of a genius in creating myths. His construction is untenable from a historical-critical perspective. Yet it does express the truth that imprintings by empirical parents are not able to explain the depth of religious consciousness of guilt and reconciliation. The question is whether this cannot be interpreted less speculatively.

Here we recall a simple anthropological recognition. In human beings, the instinctive system of direction is replaced by moral norms. Commandments take the place of signals provoking behavior. Two things are changed by this. On the one hand, the connection between moral commandment and corresponding behavior is loosened. Human beings can escape the commandment; they follow it only conditionally. On the other hand, an archaic tendency to "unconditioned reaction" continues to exist in them—a tendency to the quasi-automatic readiness to react which is absolutely essential for an animal when an encounter with an enemy is a matter of life and death and the whole organism must be activated quickly. Human beings too have within themselves the preparedness for such total activation. It is, however, not coupled to specific situations; through learning processes it can be joined to other situations that call it forth, and even be generalized to a groundless anxiety.

This means that human beings can experience fear of death even outside situations in which their existence is threatened; they can unnecessarily talk themselves into "stress situations" if they consciously or unconsciously interpret a situation as a challenge to "total inner mobilization"—which includes activating latent preparedness to kill. For this reason, one can also experience moral requirements as threats to existence and connect the death of the self with the coming of the commandment (Rom. 7:9–10). Parents are the first representatives of the moral system of guidance. When a child reacts to their commands with the unconditional archaic readiness for activation, the commands acquire an absolutist overtone. It is a matter no longer of an "offense" but of the possibility of boundless rejection. The command becomes a hostile signal that unleashes unconditional anxieties. This unconditioned readiness to react can be connected with the most varied contents in the course of individual and historical development—concrete persons, standards of performance, expectations of the future, social authorities, etc. There is nothing on earth that cannot become a trigger of unconditioned readiness to act through a historical learning process. Religious symbolism confronts "all powers in heaven and on earth."

Freud's thesis can therefore be reformulated as follows. The father, interiorized as superego, can through learning processes become the trigger of an unconditioned activating tendency that can be connected to all sorts of figures independently of its archaic roots. Religion is confrontation with this archaic heritage—not only with the "father" but with all authorities, institutions, and ideas with which that archaic readiness to react is bound up. For Paul, this readiness to react was connected with the law, as the quintessence of the norms of his sociocultural world. The encounter with the figure of Christ helped him to freedom from these norms, in the sense that they lost their absolutist, threatening character.

So far we have considered only one aspect of Freud's theory of religion. The security offered by caring parents lives on in religion beside early childhood imprinting by demanding parents. Here too it is necessary to ask if this security is exclusively an echo of early childhood experiences with one's empirical parents. Psychoanalytic theory went beyond this. With its theory of a "primary narcissism" it postulated an original unity with all things, in which self and outside world were undivided. This experience of unity was said to be the basis of humor, creativity, sensitivity, and reconciliation with death.[18] It was held to continue in a mystical feeling of solidarity, which again

18. At the present time, attempts to revise the psychoanalytic theory of religion take the concept of narcissism as their point of departure. See Scharfenberg, "Religiöses Bewusstsein," 10–16; and Heimbrock, *Phantasie*, 94ff.

and again flooded through religions. Here too psychoanalytic theory itself gives indications that the sense of security points beyond one's empirical parents. Ought one not pick up on such indications?

Just as there is in human beings an unconditioned tendency toward activation which is imprinted by historical learning processes, so too is there an unconditioned tendency toward relaxation which sets in after successful satisfaction of needs. It is first experienced with reference to one's parents. They imprint our sense of security for our entire lives. It becomes a value in itself, for human beings do not live only from the satisfaction of physical needs but seek to experience the entire interpreted world as home. Their inner preparedness for relaxation can be bound to new situations, and even with the world as a whole. They experience in the world moments in which they feel absolutely secure. There is no doubt that religion is a search for such a world. In an unending learning process, the world is combed for valid triggers of that inner peace which the nearness of our parents once conferred on us.

It is time to summarize our modification of the psychoanalytic psychology of religion. Religion is more than the echo of our first experiences with caring and demanding parents. Parents imprint a tendency toward activation and relaxation which exists independently of them. They are the first "environment" of the search for a world in which we can experience unconditioned motivation and security without feeling threatened.

When we pursue the confrontation of early Christian religion with the superego, we need not conceive of its voice as an echo of the paternal voice. It is superfluous to know the story of the childhood of the authors of the New Testament. The superego is rather the internalized voice of all normative systems of the culture of that period, that is, of all control mechanisms to which a human being can potentially react with absolutist readiness for activation.[19] Nor need we consider an expression of profound security simply an echo of childhood, even though metaphorical references to fathers and to childhood are richly present in the New Testament. A readiness for unconditioned relaxed

19. A similar generalizing of psychoanalytic concepts may be found as early as Fromm, "Die Entwicklung des Christusdogmas." Fromm interprets the Oedipus conflict with reference to the class struggle. In this way it is desexualized (the ruling class deprives the son of all chances of life, not only of the mother) and made historically controllable (social conflicts leave traces in sources; dramatic family events in childhood usually do not). Fromm's psychoanalytic interpretation of Christology is therefore much less speculative than Freud's.

reaction to the whole of reality is conveyed by these images, so that even the lilies of the field and the birds of the sky become triggers of unconditioned security.

But the family and other socializing institutions have a great significance independently of this—even where the sources do not make this visible. They pass on to the succeeding generation the historical interpretations of reality with which the impulses of the world that evoke anxiety and relaxation are ordered, interpreted, and handled. Here too the basic principle of a hermeneutically oriented psychology comes into play: Nothing affects a human being by itself; everything is mediated by human interpretations. These interpretations are neither arbitrary nor absolutely fixed. They are historical; that is, they are simultaneously the product of a continuous development and contingent, inconfusable, and unpredictable.

CULTURAL INTERPRETATIONS

At first glance, psychodynamic theories seem radically to dethrone human consciousness, deny the historical change of symbolic inter-pretations, and reduce their meaning to natural factors. A second look shows that at least in the therapeutic process itself, historically conditioned interpretations of meaning occupy a central place. Here changes in behavior and experience occur through hermeneutic acts—through interpretation of meaning by means of symbols taken in part from ancient tradition, in part from the tradition of a particular school. Every therapeutic dialogue constructs a symbolic world common to each partner; this world is as variable as the wide-ranging multiplicity of psychotherapeutic tendencies. While psychodynamic *theories* rely on models from natural science, therapeutic *practice* has always been hermeneutic. Sooner or later, this contradiction between theory and practice had to lead to a hermeneutic revision of psychodynamic theory. This can be seen most clearly in the history of the concept of symbol.

Jung was the first to break with the reductive understanding of symbol in orthodox psychoanalysis. Instead of reducing symbols to drives in a naturalistic manner, he clarified them "in an amplifying fashion" with the help of the cultural tradition. What came to consciousness in private dreams was clarified and interpreted with symbols from all the cultural regions to which he had access. What Jung granted to hermeneutic consciousness with one hand, he took away with the other. For him, all of these historically variable symbols

were expressions of genetically inherited archetypes—an explanation
that again "reduced" them to natural factors. Belief in universal
archetypes gave him a good conscience in drawing symbols from the
most widely varied cultural regions and periods in order to enrich
them mutually ("amplify")—a procedure he often handled so arbitrarily
that it found little welcome among interpreters with schooling in
historical-critical method.

An even more profound revision of the concept of symbol within
orthodox psychoanalysis came later.[20] While classical psychoanalysis
saw the symbol as a symptom of repressed content, with the aid of
which the repression was maintained, people today see symbols as a
language of the unconscious, with which unconscious content can be
rescued from repression and brought into public communication.
Joachim Scharfenberg has concisely expressed this hermeneutic shift
in the psychoanalytic understanding of symbol: "It is not repression
which occasions the necessity of symbolization, but refraining from
using symbols which causes repression."[21]

The common element in the revised understanding of symbols is
that symbols are not only object of interpretation, they are interpretations themselves. They are not only caused by inner psychic
dynamics, they are cognitive structures that actively influence the
psychic process. It would take extraordinary arrogance for psychologists
to claim that the structuring of psychic processes through symbols
occurs only in therapeutic dialogue, as if psychologists had a monopoly
on interpretations that modify behavior and experience. Such structuring takes place wherever people interpret their experiences and
conflicts. It occurs particularly in religious symbol systems, which for
centuries were the most important net of communication for psychic
processes.

The development of learning theory and of the psychodynamic
approach shows an instructive convergence at this point. Both approaches have been modified by the incorporation of cognitive elements.
It is not the outer and inner world in themselves, but their interpretations that determine human experience and behavior. Interpretations

20. It is understandable that the hermeneutic shift in psychoanalysis was inspired or
developed especially by philosophers and theologians. The influence of Jürgen Habermas
may be found in Lorenzer, *Kritik*. Foundational is the work of Ricoeur, *Freud and
Philosophy* and *The Conflict of Interpretations*. This hermeneutical shift is represented in
theology especially by Scharfenberg's three works *Sigmund Freud*, *Religion*, and *Mit
Symbolen leben*, esp. 46–70.

21. Scharfenberg, *Symbole*, 67.

are not to be traced back causally to archetypal programming or early childhood imprinting; they are active cognitive processes of structuring, in which cultural tradition is a factor.

The question of the function of religious symbols can also be raised anew in the context of the hermeneutical understanding of symbol which has just been sketched. The interpretations of orthodox psychoanalysis (symbols of conflict) and of analytic psychology (symbols of goals) complement each other. Religious symbols can reveal profound conflicts, because they are supported by the certainty that they can be addressed and overcome. Interpretations of symbols with reference to goals presuppose conflicts that have been overcome.

Psychoanalysis interpreted the Christ symbolism as an expression of ambivalence with regard to a loving and punishing father, and between rebellious insurrection and longing for security on the part of the son. The rebellion reaches its goal, for the son takes the place of the father. But the father also achieves his goal, for in the son he vicariously punishes the rebellion of all. Does this not suggest saying that early Christian symbolism aims at a reconciliation of son and father in which no one loses?[22]

Conversely, the interpretation of Christology in "goal symbolism" as incarnation of the "self" presupposes profound conflicts. The self is the overcoming of basic human conflicts—not only of the conflict between rebellious autonomy and security but also of that between norm and antinomian tendencies, between masculine and feminine aspects, between power and impotence, between life and death.[23]

Interpretations of Christology with regard to symbols of conflicts and goals can be combined if Christology is not retraced to different psychic causes. If it is explained causally as an expression of a genetically preprogrammed archetype or as a deposit of a universally distributed Oedipus conflict, the two explanations are mutually exclusive. But if the Christ symbolism is seen as a historically developed reality by which people are placed in a position actively to interpret and deal with their basic problems, then this symbolism can definitely be related to different psychic factors. This is especially true if these psychic factors are interpreted as open tendencies—as tendencies toward wholeness, activation, and relaxation which can be joined to historically variable content and which can scarcely be grasped apart from their historically variable form.

22. See Ricoeur, "Fatherhood: From Phantasm to Symbol."
23. On such basic conflicts, see Scharfenberg, *Symbole*, 170–97.

It would be impossible, in my opinion, to understand the historical power of the Christ symbolism without any reference to inner psychodynamic tendencies. It was not fortuitous that this symbolism found such profound resonance in many human hearts and simultaneously reformed the experience and behavior that are rooted in the human heart. The symbolism had effects in a depth dimension we still do not fully penetrate.

It is no coincidence that psychodynamic—especially psychoanalytic—explanatory models are the foundation of most psychological interpretations of Pauline theology. They concentrate on six themes: consciousness of sin, conflict with the law, devaluation of the body, the message of justification, Christ mysticism, and Paul's social relationships.

1. *Consciousness of sin in Paul.* According to Freud, Pauline theology brought to light a previously hidden truth; it makes rebellion against one's father conscious. The unconscious intention of killing one's father can be atoned for only by the death of the son. It is true that the primordial assault on the father is mentioned only in allusions. But Paul was "in the strictest sense a religiously inclined man; the dark traces of the past lurked in his soul, ready for the breakthrough into more conscious regions."[24] Here theology appears as the opening of the unconscious, not as a repressing power. According to Freud, this revelation of the unconscious took place in ritual activity, not only in theological ideas. The Lord's Supper was said to be a repetition of the totem meal, in which rebellion against the father was symbolically enacted and atoned. It is noteworthy in all of Freud's observations on Pauline theology that he does not trace it back to biographical factors. He is interested in its objective statement—and he agrees with it, although in a completely different theoretical frame of reference.

2. *Conflict with the law in Paul.* An initial biographical interpretation of Paul from a psychoanalytic perspective was presented by a friend of Freud's, Oskar Pfister.[25] Pfister was a pastor and psychotherapist. He explained Paul's fanaticism for the law in his persecution of Christians as a compulsive neurotic symptom with which Paul reacted to an inner conflict that is depicted in chapter 7 of Romans. Repressed sexuality led to severe self-accusations, so that Paul had to persecute compulsively every transgression of the law by himself or by others. Only through his conversion outside Damascus was he freed from this complusion. But later effects of his neurotic conflict are recognizable throughout his entire life (e.g., in his devaluation of sexuality, or in glossolalia).

More recent psychoanalytic interpretations of Paul's conflict with the law

24. Freud, *Der Mann Moses*, 534–35. On Freud's interpretation of Paul, see the accurate remarks of Taubes, "Religion."
25. O. Pfister, "Die Entwicklung."

limit themselves to clarifying structural and dynamic relationships between law, ego, and flesh with the aid of psychological categories. G. Créspy finds the three-tribunal model of superego–ego–id reflected in Romans 7.[26] A. Vergote offers correctives to this interpretation and shows how the conflict is overcome in Romans 8, as Christians moved by the Spirit can once again say "Father."[27]

A third variant of psychoanalytic interpretations (besides recourse to depths of the past in collective and individual history) shows itself here—the uncovering of structural connections in the present. Genetic explanations can recede into the background in this context.

3. *Devaluation of the flesh.* The work of Hermann Fischer stands in the tradition of Pfister's biographical interpretation of Paul.[28] Fischer's new idea is that Paul was forced throughout his life to repress latent homosexual tendencies. Devaluation of the flesh is said to generalize defense against a particular "fleshly" inclination to everything pertaining to the body. Paul's strong judgment on homosexual behavior in Rom. 1:25–27 is also held to be a reaction to this inclination. Even before Fischer, S. Tarachow had postulated in more general form a passive homosexuality in Paul.[29]

4. *The doctrine of justification.* A more positive view of Pauline theology is attained by those who take Paul's criticism of the law—man is justified without the works of the law—as their point of departure. R. Scroggs assesses the Pauline doctrine of justification as liberation from a repressive principle of performance; it promises present fulfillment instead of projecting needs into the future.[30] J. J. Forsyth even interprets Paul's theology as the solution to all the obscure problems that give Freud's late work a pessimistic tinge: life in the Spirit and in love make possible normative regulations that do not serve the death wish.[31] D. Stollberg offers a third possibility of translating the doctrine of justification into psychoanalytic categories: liberation from the power of the law is a transition from an ethic based on the superego to one based on the ego.[32] Not the person but the theology of Paul is analyzed psychologically, as overcoming of the principle of performance, of the death wish, or of ethics based on the superego.

5. *Christ mysticism.* From the very beginning, Jung's school of depth psychology had greater appreciation than classical psychoanalysis for the mystical elements of Pauline theology. Jung interpreted the Damascus experience as the breakthrough of an unconscious archetype.[33] Since Christ is a

---

26. "Exégèse et psychoanalyse."
27. "Der Beitrag."
28. H. Fischer, *Gespaltener christlicher Glaube.*
29. "St. Paul and Early Christianity."
30. "The Heuristic Value."
31. "Faith and Eros."
32. "Tiefenpsychologie."
33. "Die psychologischen Grundlagen." This position was picked up by Inglis, "The Problem."

representation of the self, the Christ mysticism could be interpreted, following Jung, as a symbolic presentation of the process of individuation; Christ "in me" became a new psychic center that overcomes division within us. D. Cox's comparison of faith in Christ and individuation showed that in the process of individuation the goal is unknown, yet confidence in one's own power to achieve it is high; conversely, while Christ is known as a goal, confidence in one's own powers is negative.[34] J. G. Bishop emphasizes that Christ is only a possible symbol of the self—though the only true symbol for faith.[35]

Since the theory of narcissism has enjoyed a renaissance within psychoanalysis, a new appreciation for mystical experience has also been present in these circles. The committed interpretation of Paul presented by the Jewish theologian Richard L. Rubenstein sees in Paul's sacramental mysticism an overcoming of the distance between the unconditionally demanding God and rebellious human beings. They are forbidden direct identification with divine omnipotence, but an indirect identification is possible; narcissistic desires of omnipotence are fulfilled through identification with Christ.[36] Stollenberg also notes that fantasies of omnipotence are addressed in Christ mysticism, but observes that Christ mysticism is a dying with Christ. The cross is the symbol of a renunciation of omnipotence.[37]

6. *Paul's social relationships.* Although the social relationships of Paul do not belong to Pauline theology, they do shed a light on it. S. Tarachow seeks to establish that Paul showed a consistent ambivalence with regard to paternal authorities. On the one hand, he was dependent on them; for this reason he sought recognition from the Sanhedrin, from Barnabas, and from the original apostles. On the other hand, he rebelled against the authorities he had chosen, so that his life was a chain of conflicts.[38] A. Schreiber investigates the ambivalent stance of the community in Corinth to Paul as a paternal authority; his departure had the effect of a sudden withdrawal of authority on the Corinthian community, with the group's rebellion and regression as consequences.[39] Erich Fromm had already examined the relationship of early Christianity to authority structures on an even wider scale; when the first Christians proclaimed the crucified as Lord of the universe, they carried out in heaven the revolution the Zealots had sought on an earthly plane.[40]

As this summary overview shows, there are numerous ideas for interpreting Paul from the perspective of depth psychology. But the results are mutually contradictory. Pauline theology can be evaluated as expression of a neurotic defensive stance or as liberation from neurotic compulsion, as fulfillment or as overcoming of fantasies of omnipotence, as revelation of universal truth or

34. *Jung and St. Paul.*
35. "Psychological Insights."
36. *My Brother Paul.*
37. "Tiefenpsychologie."
38. "St. Paul and Early Christianity."
39. *Die Gemeinde in Korinth.*
40. "Die Entstehung des Christusdogmas."

of personal idiosyncrasies. All the interpretations are far removed from methodical security. They are on the whole isolated contributions that make little reference to one another. Mediation with historical-critical methods occurs only rarely and is often inadequate even when present. Nonetheless, I am of the opinion that something worth investigating lies hidden in all these presumptions and speculations. The goal of historical-critical exegesis is to make texts intelligible on the basis of their context in life. Do not these psychological interpretations also seek to contribute to this aim? Can the life context of religious texts be clarified without consideration of psychic factors and aspects?

Chapter 3

The Cognitive Approach: Religion as Construction of an Interpreted World

Learning theory and the psychodynamic approach are at first glance diametrically opposed, yet they have one thing in common from their origin—devaluation of consciousness. Psychoanalysis attributed decisive influence on human experience and behavior to the unconscious, and orthodox behaviorism rejected mentalist assumptions as academic superstition. In the course of their development, both approaches have conceded greater rights to human consciousness, either by assuming mediating cognitive processes between stimulus and reaction or by attributing to symbols a more active role in psychic dynamics.

The step from cognitively modified learning theory and psychodynamic approaches to a cognitive psychology takes place when all interpreting processes are understood as expressions of human activity, that is, as conscious interaction with the environment, and when they are recognized as having a tendency toward construction of a coherent "interpreted world." It occurs, in other words, when it is seen that interpretations form a structured whole all the parts of which are mutually dependent, the whole being in constant exchange with the environment—in part, in that it accepts the environment into itself and "assimilates" it into its present schemes and categories, in part, in that it adapts itself to the environment and "accommodates" its own forms of interpretation to it. The most comprehensive proposal of a cognitive psychology of this sort stems from Jean Piaget, who investigated the construction of the intellectual world with reference to generally valid universals and laws of development.[1] He thus created a new theoretical paradigm that was just as inspirational for further

---

1. Piaget does not use the adjective "cognitive" to characterize his psychology, but it captures his position well; cf. Wetzel, *Kognitive Psychologie*.

research as the paradigms of classical psychoanalysis or learning theory. His model does, however, have limitations, for it is interested only in the universal structures of the interpreted world and not in individual or historical life-worlds of the sort with which we are concerned in this book. We will therefore sketch the cognitive approach to the psychology of religion in such a way that it is from the start open to the hermeneutical task of interpreting a historically singular life-world.[2]

In accordance with the two criteria of a cognitive approach mentioned above, we must attempt, first, to view religion as a contribution to the construction of an "interpreted world," and second, to describe individual techniques of interpretation as active confrontations with the environment.[3]

THE INTERPRETED WORLD

All human beings are occupied daily with integrating through interpretation their experiences, desires, and conflicts into an "interpreted

2. Characterizing a third approach—beside learning theory and the psychodynamic approach—as cognitive could lead to misunderstandings, since frequently only cognitively modified learning theory and behaviorist approaches are understood under the rubric of cognitive theories. Between behaviorism and depth psychology there have always been third ways that are to be understood much more on the basis of philosophical tradition. This third way can be called humanist (in an evaluative sense) or hermeneutical or phenomenological (from a methodological perspective): hermeneutical, with reference especially to the interpretation of expressions of life by others; phenomenological, with reference to introspective description of the content of one's own consciousness. The investigations presented here stand in the tradition of this third way. (We abstract completely from a fourth approach, factor analysis.) The term "cognitive" was chosen for the following reason. Since Piaget, there has been a convincing new paradigm of psychological research within which cognitive categories are decisive. They occur as explanatory categories, and to this extent compete with behaviorist and depth-psychology approaches. Proximity to the models of the natural sciences is unmistakable, for the concepts of assimilation and accommodation are derived from biology. The terms "hermeneutical" and "phenomenological" would, however, imply clear distance from explanatory nomothetic categories. In my opinion, humanistic, hermeneutical, and phenomenological approaches are not so much competing efforts at explanation as the basis of a critical consciousness with which differing explanatory models are related. This critical consciousness insists on reconnecting all abstract psychological concepts to the everyday world of immediate experience, on the embedding of all psychic processes in their historical context, and on the responsibility of the human being and of the psychologist whose interpretation of a human being itself has effects on that human being. An exemplary model of a psychology that is open to all approaches toward explanation, yet supported by a critical consciousness, is in my opinion the work of Hans Thomae. The material that follows owes much to Thomae, *Das Individuum und seine Welt.*

3. Allport, *The Individual and His Religion*, is a psychology of religion written from a hermeneutical tradition.

world," in which a dynamic equilibrium holds sway.[4] We do not cease
from doing this even at night; dreams seem to be the continuation of
this work of interpretation. We can describe this tendency toward an
interpreted world under various aspects—first as the construction of a
topical structure and order, then as regulation of a dynamic moving
equilibrium that gives direction and goal to life.

The Topical Structuring of the Life-World

Without interpretation, the experienced world of a human being is
chaotic. A first order consists in arranging regions of human life
according to proximity and distance, accessibility and inaccessibility,
so that the chaos of the stream of life becomes manageable and
orientation is possible.[5] We distinguish between regions we connect so
closely with ourselves that they become part of our self and other
regions that form various zones of proximity and distance, familiarity
and accessibility—up to a background of our life-world, always present
but beyond our access by the usual techniques and means. Every
human being senses such a "depth dimension of his life-world," for
no one lives in his world like a spider in its web. An individual knows
that his world is limited and that reality is deeper, more mysterious,
and more unsettling than all historically developed interpretations
assure him. Religion is consciousness of the depth dimension of our
life-world. Religious experience restructures the everyday field of life.
What was previously the unexpressed background of the everyday life-
world becomes the foreground, while the rest of the world recedes in
significance or even fades. This restructuring of the experienced world
is comparable to the perception of silhouettes, which allow different
forms to be recognized through change in base and background.

In biblical texts, the depth dimension of the life-world is structured
through mythical narratives. Beyond the life-world stands, for example,
the primeval event of creation or—in the opposite temporal direction—
the last judgment. We notice in the New Testament how this depth
dimension is "inserted" into the world with which we are familiar—
the new Adam appears in the midst of this world. Definitive judgment
takes place in the present. What protological and eschatological myths
report of a beyond behind our life-world becomes a present "form" on
the basis of which the everyday world is seen in an entirely new

4. My conception of a "symbolically interpreted world" goes back to Langer, *Philosophy
in a New Key*.
5. Cf. the expansion of Kurt Lewin's field theory in Thomae, *Individuum*, 219–81.

manner. Similar processes of restructuring are to be found in all religions.

The Dynamic Regulation of the Life-World

Life is not a static structure but a current that acquires structures only by being in constant movement forward. The dynamic equilibrium of life is threatened equally by excessive disturbances and by the absence of tensions. We are therefore constantly occupied with either reducing or seeking tensions. For purposes of comparison, we could think of a system of regulation that corrected departures from the norm in different directions—although life is far more complicated than a thermostat for psychic tensions.

The regulation of the current of life encompasses both reduction of cognitive dissonances and their "induction." The model of "cognitive dissonance theory" can serve as an example of the phenomenon of reduction of dissonance.[6] Decisions between two alternatives leave behind a postdecisional conflict in which the decision that has been made must be defended against the attractiveness of the unsuccessful alternative. Cognitive dissonances also occur when our expectations are refuted by the course of events; disappointed eschatological expectations were one of the first fields to which the theory of cognitive dissonances was applied.[7] Cognitive dissonance can often be resolved through reinterpretation of an event: all the elements consonant with a decision and an expectation are reinforced and stressed in one's consciousness, while all dissonant elements are repressed. That religion is concerned with reducing cognitive dissonance hardly needs to be demonstrated. Religion thematizes the notorious contradiction between norm and behavior and offers means to reduce this contradiction in the forgiveness of sins, rites of penance, and sacrifices of atonement. The contradiction between our expectations and actual world events is also one of the great themes of all religions. The theodicy question is a phenomenon of cognitive dissonance.

It would, however, be too one-sided to see the equilibrium dynamic of life only under the aspect of reducing dissonance. Without tensions there is no current of life. Without movement, the structure of life dissolves; it loses its direction, its motive. Cognitive discrepancies are necessary to give us motivational impulses again and again—provided

---

6. A brief summary is offered by Festinger, "Die Lehre." A discussion of the research that has developed from this theory may be found in Oerter, *Struktur*, 43–69.

7. On early Christianity, see Gager, *Kingdom and Community*, 43ff.

that they do not overtax us.[8] It can in general be said that "dosed discrepancies" would be optimal—but it depends completely on the individual who experiences the discrepancies whether a specific amount is experienced as the proper dose or as terrifying. The only certain thing is that we experience the world as more meaningful and more motivating if we are able to experience even stronger tensions as motivating impulses. It is precisely here that religion is active. Religion constantly attempts to restructure even extreme situations with high tensions into meaningful challenges. We can observe in the New Testament how even the hopelessly ill were healed and how even the greatest suffering "will not be able to separate us from the love of God" (Rom. 8:39*). We also see how ecstatic experiences, which at first stood unconnected to the everyday world, were transformed through cognitive restructuring into an impulse for a more profound experience of the world. This aspect of the matter will concern us in our investigation of glossolalia.

Religion appears so far as a regulatory system whose function consists in maintaining the equilibrium dynamic of life. All regulatory processes presuppose norms with reference to which deviation from the "normal state" is measured. Without such norms there would be no dissonances and discrepancies. These norms, however—unlike those of a thermostat—are subject to change; they differ both historically and in individuals. They are to be sought in the basic concerns of an individual—in the individual's motives and thematics.[9] The thematics of an individual life determine what is experienced as discrepant or consonant, what elicits positive or aversive motivation, which dissonances are actively sought and which ones are reduced through reinterpretation. It is impossible to present a valid timeless list of such life thematics. They are different in every historical life-world and must constantly be described anew. Yet there are beyond doubt recurring themes—the motif of dominance, a wish to make others dependent on oneself; a normative thematics, striving for correspondence with rules and commandments; a thematics of social annexation, that is, the embedding of one's life in the security of a group; a thematics of competition, competing in pursuit of comparable goals; the creative thematics, etc. One who investigates the major symbolically

8. Cf. Oerter, *Psychologie des Denkens*, 453ff.
9. Thomae (*Individuum*, 311ff.) distinguishes seven thematic units: regulative thematics, anticipatory regulation, enhancement of existence, social integration, social separation, creative thematics, and normative thematics.

interpreted life-worlds of different religions will frequently discover that they are dominated by only a few thematics. Judaism and early Christianity, for example, lack the motif of the "jealousy of the gods"—a thematics of competition which determines the relationship between God and man.

It is important that thematics can change over the course of a life. Motifs that at first were subordinate techniques can become a goal in themselves. Others can lose their dominant position and sink to the level of secondary techniques. Still others can be changed radically.[10] Paul would seem to be a classic example of change in life thematics. He describes his pre-Christian period retrospectively as a phase of life determined by a thematics of competition and performance (Gal. 1:15). As a Christian, however, he sees the highest way in "love" (1 Corinthians 13). Here a thematics of love has taken the place of the thematics of competition without completely suppressing the latter. As a Christian missionary, Paul does repudiate "works" as an occasion for self-glorification before God. His message is directed toward rejection of justification through works. But in the service of this message Paul picks up without hesitation his old thematics of competition: he has worked harder, he says, than anyone else (1 Cor. 15:10). He is proud of his own work—and says this with an evident jab at others (2 Cor. 10:11–12). A life thematics became a technique—and it did so in service of a message that emphatically opposed the old life thematics.

INTERPRETIVE STRATEGIES IN
THE CONSTRUCTION OF THE
"INTERPRETED WORLD"

How does an individual proceed in structuring a life-world, maintaining its dynamic balance and giving life a thematic direction? He interprets the experienced world. Four of the many techniques of interpretation will be described in more detail here since they have proved themselves in the analysis of religious texts—causal attribution, anticipation, self-assessment, and assumption of roles. These cognitive strategies of interpretation are related to some psychodynamic "defense mechanisms"—projection, sublimation, rationalization, and identification, for

10. Thomae (*Individuum*, 329–400) distinguishes the following techniques: techniques related to performance; adaptation; evasive and aggressive techniques. He stresses that themes can become techniques and, conversely, techniques themes. The recognition that motives can acquire weight of their own independent of their origin—the so-called functional autonomy of motives—derives from Allport, *Personality*, 190–212.

example. It would nonetheless be one-sided to subsume all human cognitive strategies under the general heading of defense.

Causal Attribution

We are constantly engaged in attributing life's stream of experience and action to different causes, since our future behavior is largely determined by what factors we take into account.[11] What is important in this regard is not only which causes we accept but also what relationship to ourselves we place them in—whether we locate them in or outside ourselves, and whether they appear to us as constant or variable factors. Since the two distinctions overlap, there are four forms of possible causal attribution (see fig. 1).

FIGURE 1

	Stable	Variable
Internal	inalterable aspects and factors within us	alterable aspects and factors within us
External	inalterable factors outside us	changing factors outside us

In such attributions of causality it is not so important whether a given cause is really stable or variable, internal or external—although, clearly, false attributions can be ruinous. What is decisive is how they are assessed by an individual. We draw different conclusions depending on whether we retrace an unhappy experience to our stupidity or lack of effort (i.e., to internal factors) or to the unalterability of conditions or simple bad luck (i.e., external factors). It follows from this that the ability to reattribute events and actions also increases the range of possible reactions. If we are not committed to a particular causal attribution, we are also not committed to particular consequences. At this point we encounter one of the most important functions of religion. Religious interpretations of events and actions are restructurings of one-sided causal attributions. Although religious persons perceive the "earthly" causal chain of an action or an event just as anyone else does, they can simultaneously assume a different perspective from which everything is seen from another, all-determining causality that lies beyond the distinctions of internal and external, stable and variable.

11. The causal-attribution theory stems from F. Heider; cf. Görlitz et al., *Bielefelder Symposium*. A brief overview is offered by Heckhausen, "Lehrer-Schüler-Interaktion," 559–73.

This makes it possible to see the unchangeable as changeable, what one has caused oneself as fate, external experience as inwardly willed. One can evaluate one's own achievement as gift, the fortuitous as not fortuitous. Typical examples of such religious reattribution are 1 Cor. 15:10, where Paul boasts, "I worked harder than any of them, though it was not I, but the grace of God which is with me"; Rom. 7:17, "So then it is no longer I that do it, but sin which dwells within me"; and Gal. 2:20, "It is no longer I who live, but Christ who lives in me." In such assertions we grasp immediately the possibilities of reattribution that distinguish religious interpretations of the "experienced world." A greater freedom of behavior is established in them—in good conduct and in bad.

Anticipations

Causal attributions primarily interpret events and actions that have already taken place; still, they are directed toward the future, since they are inseparable from the question of how an individual should behave. Anticipations play an important role in decisions about future conduct.[12] They recede in unimportant decisions. Whether one takes a ten-minute walk or drinks a cup of coffee seems insignificant. "Ambitendencies" of this sort become decisions only if larger convictions are inserted into the interpretation of the situation—if, for example, walking is evaluated as promoting health and one's health is viewed as problematic. Conversely, situations are also relieved by "exclusion" of more general convictions. We tell ourselves that "once doesn't count" in order to convince ourselves that a decision will have no relevant consequences. The reaction to a given situation thus depends on whether and to what extent more comprehensive systems of conviction are included or excluded. A situation is interpreted in the light of such systems of conviction until it corresponds to a projection of the future that has been accepted by the individual. The decision is made when a possible mode of behavior is experienced as corresponding to dominant convictions. But we do not always succeed in bringing together the situation, our convictions, and our anticipations of the future. An individual can then drift into a fundamental crisis of orientation in which not only the accomplishment of previously valid convictions is up for discussion but the system of convictions itself is called into question so that it will either be replaced by a new normative

12. The following treatment is dependent on Thomae, *Konflikt*, esp. 80ff.

direction of life or affirmed anew in a conscious decision. A distinction must therefore be made between normative and existential decisions.[13] In normative decisions, the dominant system of convictions remains untouched; in existential decisions, it is drawn into the process of decision and either rejected or confirmed. Most situations of decision are first interpreted according to the model of normative decisions. Only in the course of cognitive confrontation with the situation does it emerge that the individual is forced to make an existential decision. It is understandable that pluralist societies with competing systems of conviction exert pressure for existential decision on many people, while traditional societies with a stable consensus in basic existential questions place a person chiefly before normative decisions. Roman-Hellenistic antiquity was surely the first culture in world history with a clearly formed pluralism. One of the theses to be developed in the following chapters will be that Paul took the step from a normative to an existential decision—and that he became the paradigm of a larger historical process in which structures of existential decision gradually developed. For the issues here are not timeless constants of human life.

Self-Assessment

Causal attribution and anticipations are closely connected with self-assessments. The attribution of failures to external causes unburdens one's feeling of personal value; bagatellizing or inflating a situation of decision can have a self-confirming function. But all acts with which we form our self-image and evaluate ourselves are also to be seen in a third dimension. We always evaluate ourselves in comparison with others, whether with real reference groups or with ideal roles from our cultural tradition. Our self-evaluation is always an echo of the evaluation of others, which is presented to us or which we create for ourselves through comparisons. Y. Watanabe sees in religions attempts to overcome a fundamental human uncertainty about self-value, which always occurs when an individual determines his value in comparison with others.[14] An individual will always have only a relative value— on the basis of relative norms. Buddhism and early Christianity seem to Watanabe the most consistent solutions to the problematic that this causes. In early Buddhism, the human self is totally devalued as an illusion. It is thus unburdened of every problematic about self-value

13. Ibid., 117ff., 152ff.
14. "Selbstwertanalyse und christlicher Glaube."

and unthreatened by any evaluative comparison with others. In early Christianity, conversely, unconditioned value is attributed to each human being—independently of the social reference group. The parable of the laborers in the vineyard shows this new evaluation of human beings most clearly; despite differing periods of work all receive the same pay (Matt. 20:1–16). The same trait is present in Paul's doctrine of justification; justice before God is independent of the "works of the law," so that boasting of oneself before God in comparison with others is excluded.

Assumption of Roles

Attribution, anticipation, and self-assessment are individual strategies of interpretation in the construction of an "interpreted world." But religions offer us holistic models of possible self-interpretation and self-assessment, not isolated techniques of interpretation. An individual can understand himself as "child of God," as a wandering nomad in search of the promised land, as an exile in a foreign country, or as the lamenting and praying subject of the psalms, to mention just a few examples of what Hjalmar Sundén calls "the religions' storehouse of roles."[15] Just as we restructure our perception in assuming everyday social roles—we see the same landscape differently as a tourist than as a businessman—so too does identification with traditional religious roles enable religious perception of the world through cognitive restructuring. Because of the changed frame of reference, the experiential material pouring in on us is no longer interpreted according to the structures of everyday reality or the categories of scientific interpretations—as fields of waves or of corpuscles—but as the expression of a universally present and authoritative power. Sundén's role-theoretical psychology of religion is of great significance for exegesis. It overcomes the false opposition of tradition and experience: by offering roles, religious tradition becomes a condition of the possibility of religious experience. The relationship of Paul to his tradition, that is, to the Old Testament and the oldest early Christian confessions, can also be determined from this approach. Paul relates to preestablished roles both positively and negatively. Thus he interprets his pre-

15. Sundén, *Die Religion* and *Gott erfahren*. Sundén combines two psychological theories. He derives the concept of role from social psychology, and theoretical Gestalt concepts from the psychology of perception. The two elements are combined in his central thesis that the identification of roles enables an active restructuring of the field of perception. In doing this, Sundén broadens the concept of role: in addition to social roles it includes symbolic roles from the cultural tradition.

Christian life in the light of the roles of Adam and Moses, but the new life in faith in the light of the roles of Abraham and Christ. We shall have to ask to what extent this acceptance of roles cognitively restructured his perception of himself and his world.

One final observation. Attributions, anticipations, self-assessments, and assumption of roles take place in a constant dialogue that a human being conducts with himself and with others. The external dialogue takes place in religion, for example, through homilies, songs, confessions, and reading. The most developed form of internal dialogue is prayer. It is characteristic of this inner dialogue that a "Thou" can constantly be inserted into it. The inner dialogue takes place in the presence of another who can be addressed directly in individual moments, not only as a conversation with oneself. Whatever one thinks of the power of prayer, it can activate within persons possibilities of resolving problems which otherwise remain latent.[16]

Summary. What is religion from a cognitive perspective? Religion is the cognitive restructuring of the human life-world through opening of its depth dimension. This depth dimension can lie within the human being itself; then religion is confrontation with unconscious dimensions within us. Or it can lie in the surrounding reality; then religion is confrontation with the reality behind our everyday world. The opening to the depth dimension of the experienced world occurs through processes of attribution, anticipation, and self-assessment, but especially through the assumption of preestablished roles into which we grow through social learning.

As is evident from this attempt at specifying what religion is, the cognitive approach can be combined very well with other approaches. It is more amenable to traditional hermeneutical consciousness than are learning theory and psychodynamic models of explanation. A hermeneutical psychology of religion will therefore rely especially on cognitive approaches, or draw upon cognitive modifications of learning theory and psychodynamic approaches. But integrating the three approaches for the purpose of the exegesis of texts raises in addition special problems, which will be discussed in a separate section.

16. On the inner dialogue, see Meichenbaum, *Cognitive-Behavior Modification*, 201–14.

Chapter 4

The Problem of a Hermeneutical Integration of the Three Approaches

A hermeneutically oriented psychology of religion can make use of various models of psychological explanation without accepting their premises in every respect. When they are used in the framework of text interpretation their character is changed—not through new elements of theoretical content but through the new context. But the opposite is also true. A hermeneutical psychology changes character when it opens itself to explanatory approaches. A "new" hermeneutical psychology is developed. To describe this novelty more precisely, we shall once again run through the five characteristics of hermeneutical consciousness that were sketched at the beginning.

THE INTERPRETIVE MEDIATION
OF PSYCHIC LIFE

It is a basic principle of every hermeneutical psychology that all scientific interpretations of psychic life rest on the fact that life itself takes place in interpretations. Nevertheless, in what follows we shall also work with explanatory models that wish to call human self-understanding—especially religious self-understanding—into question. Is that not an insoluble contradiction?

It should first be reemphasized that a movement toward hermeneutical consciousness has taken place in "explanatory" psychologies, as the trend to cognitive theories shows. It is true that cognitive theories are not per se hermeneutical. In principle, all cognitive acts can be viewed as additional "mechanisms" within a complicated "psychic apparatus." But it is progress when cognitive acts are inserted between stimulus and reaction, between a drive and the carrying out of a drive. Even if these insertions are determined by the model of a psychic apparatus, still a small place has become free in this apparatus, in which historical and culturally conditioned self-understanding can have an effect on human experience and behavior.

Conversely, in my opinion, a hermeneutical psychology is also required to open itself to explanatory approaches—precisely when it takes its own program seriously and views psychological theories as further development of immediate experience and behavior. The axiom that "all psychological interpretations have their foundation in the self-interpretation of life" must be complemented by a second axiom, that "all psychological explanations have their foundation in the fact that psychic life itself takes place in explanations." We do not experience ourselves only as "understanding" subjects; we are always occupied with "explaining" our own experience and that of others. Causal attributions belong to the most elementary realities of our consciousness—and that not only today, but all along. The only thing new in the present is that elements of the explanatory psychological models that have been sketched above have entered the causal attributions of modern people.

Perhaps it would be more correct to say that these elements have not secondarily become components of modern self-understanding but rather that they are themselves merely further developments of pre-scientific explanatory customs. This is evident in learning theory. When we speak in everyday language of the atmosphere of a room, of reward and punishment, of examples and patterns, we are speaking of stimuli, reinforcers, and models without using those terms. What psychological research has brought to light in this regard can easily be retranslated into our everyday consciousness.

The same is true of cognitive approaches. Even methodically, they are based on description of one's own experience. Everyone is familiar from personal experience with the question of causes. Everyone knows what "cognitive dissonance" is—the poor feeling after a decision, which can extend as far as contrition and shame. We all conceive images of ourselves in the future, assess ourselves in comparison with others, and understand ourselves with the aid of predetermined roles. All of this stems from everyday experience—and everything that science says about it can be retranslated into everyday experience without difficulty.

Psychodynamic approaches are a problem, for they represent precisely the claim of explaining everyday behavior and experience on the basis of unconscious processes. In my opinion, this is a pseudoproblem, for it is precisely the basic concepts of psychodynamic theory that today belong to the psychological lingua franca of the educated. No other current in psychology has informed prescientific human self-understanding as firmly as has depth psychology. Being dependent on unconscious factors, having to repress or sublimate energies, and assuming the presence of frustrated sexuality behind all sorts of problems—even when this seems scarcely probable—belong to the self-understanding of modern human beings.

Summary. It belongs to the basic facts of psychic experience that we are occupied with attribution of causes. We not only understand ourselves and one another, but also explain. In doing this we do not miss what is "authentically human"; on the contrary, human tact presupposes the ability to make intelligible the bizarre behavior, sore points, and personal limitations of others through causal attribution. Anyone who wants to "understand" another only in the full sense that a hybrid hermeneutics calls "genuine understanding," anyone who wishes to see in everything an expression of meaningful intentions, does not understand the full human being whose intentions are crossed causally by many factors, for example, by the human being's own body or by the environment. Understanding and explaining form a unity in experience. A hermeneutical psychology that departs from human experience should not play the two off each other.

THE HISTORICITY OF PSYCHIC PROCESSES

Anyone with a background in the historical sciences who reads psychological books is constantly astounded at how rudimentary their historical consciousness is, although psychology in its multiple branches is an unmistakably historical phenomenon that cannot be understood apart from its historical context.[1] For a hermeneutical consciousness, precisely the plurality of psychologies competing successfully with one another is an indication that there are no psychic processes in themselves but only interpreted processes that run differently in accordance with historically variable human self-understanding.

Learning theory and psychodynamic and cognitive approaches can thus be understood as differing human self-interpretations whose correctness lies in the fact that they illuminate partial aspects of human life in a plausible manner. As a rule, "plausible" means "in accordance with the historical life-world of the groups that present and receive

1. The historicity of psychology is shown by Thomae in his report on a century of psychology, *Psychologie in der modernen Gesellschaft*.

psychological theories." Learning theory, for example, sees the human being as an organism that seeks to control its environment effectively and successfully; the environment is usually seen as, in principle, promising success. A vapor of Anglo-Saxon optimism hovers above such theories. Psychodynamic approaches see the human being as an organism limited by archaic elements of its collective and individual past. The European catastrophes of this century resonate in such theories. Cognitive approaches correspond to a general renaissance of Enlightenment traditions in the period of economic and social stabilization of Western democracies between 1950 and 1980. Today they form a counterbalance to an emotionally "frayed" psychoculture in which crises of these societies have left their mark. The connections hinted at here may be seen differently, but there can be no doubt that our particular psychological pre-understandings are historically conditioned.

That psychological theories are historically conditioned could be adduced as an argument against psychological illumination of ancient texts. But apart from the fact that there is no access at all to the past "in itself," preliminary stages of the psychological theories foundational in this book are found even in antiquity. A first interpretation of religious experience and behavior from the perspective of learning theory lies in a fragment of Critias that is critical of religion; religion appears here as a cleverly devised system of reinforcement and sanction that serves social adaptation through promise of reward and punishment.[2] We have already seen in Plato an initial assessment of imitative learning for religious socialization.[3]

Echoes of psychodynamic theories of religion are found in Augustine. For him religious experience and behavior are determined from "within." Desire for God is innate in us. "For thou hast created us for thyself, and our heart cannot be quieted till it may find repose in thee."[4] But there are also very different tendencies within us—content stemming from the pre-Christian past that comes forth in dreams but that we resist with our reason.[5] There is no doubt that Augustine was aware of unconscious processes within.

Cognitive theories have a significant precursor in Epictetus. His

2. Diels, *Die Fragmente der Vorsokratiker*, vol. 2, Kritias no. 25; ET: Freeman, *Ancilla to the Pre-Socratic Philosophers*, 157–58. The fragment perhaps stems from Euripides, who need not for this reason have supported the critique of religion it contains.
3. *Laws* 887D-E.
4. *Confessions* 1.1; ET: William Watts, *Confessions;* vol. 1 of 2 vols. (LCL, 1912), 3.
5. Ibid., 10.30.

central doctrine was that our opinion of things, not things in themselves, determine behavior and experience. But our opinion of things depends on whether we attribute them to internal or external causes, that is, whether we count them among the things "under our control" or "not under our control."[6] With this observation, Epictetus became the first to formulate clearly the theory of attribution.

It is one of the great advantages of Greco-Roman antiquity that it places at our disposal the rudiments of the concepts with the aid of which we analyze its phenomena. Those who insist as a matter of principle that modern psychological categories are inapplicable to the ancient world have the self-interpretation of ancient authors against them.[7]

It is possible to conclude from the historicity of our understanding of psychic processes to the historicity of the processes themselves. "Understanding" is not something attached secondarily to the psychic processes; it is a part of these processes from the start. It follows from this that if our historically conditioned pre-understanding rings true in an entirely different historical situation, this need not necessarily be traced back to an unchanging human nature. It could also be that some structures of human experience and behavior were first formed in antiquity, and even that the modern subject has its historical origin there. The investigations that follow seek to show this with reference to two important psychological categories—the categories of the unconscious and of decision. Both emerge in our texts more clearly than they ever had in the past. Both stand within a theological framework of interpretation. This framework of interpretation is the historical presupposition for structuring the corresponding psychic processes.[8]

This recognition has implications for the methodical conduct of the following investigations. Before the Pauline texts are interpreted psychologically, they are always illuminated from their context in the history of tradition. These analyses from the perspective of the history of tradition are not preludes to a psychological interpretation but part of it: historical traditions are conditions for the possibility of human experience and behavior.

A second implication rests in making a fundamental point more

---

6. *Enchiridion* 1.1; ET: W. A. Oldfather, *Epictetus;* vol. 2 of 2 vols. (LCL, 1928), 483.

7. A history of ancient psychology is offered by Siebeck, *Geschichte.*

8. A historical psychology is much to be desired; cf. the beginnings in van den Berg, *Metabletica.*

precise. Hermeneutical psychology is "ideographic"; it describes irreplaceable and unique realities. One may not infer from this that it is oriented exclusively on the individual. On the contrary, a hermeneutical psychology enlightened from the perspective of the history of tradition recognizes that individual experience and behavior are determined by common models of interpretation received from the past. It is ideographic in the sense that each historical situation and constellation is singular—including early Christianity as a whole, its typical models of experience and behavior, and ultimately the whole of antiquity.

This expansion of the ideographic aspect of hermeneutical psychology is also of importance for Pauline exegesis. Of course Paul must be numbered among the great individuals. But everything we know of him is contained in letters to communities—and only what these communities received was passed on. Even in Paul, the models of experience and behavior typical of the early Christian movement as a whole are more interesting than purely personal traits, however unmistakable these are.

THE EXPRESSION OF PSYCHIC PROCESSES IN TEXTS

Human experience and behavior leave their marks in objectifiable semiotic structures. Neither experiment nor dream is the royal road to human experience and behavior; sign systems—texts and expressive conduct—are. It is to be remembered that there are no psychological experiments without texts (i.e., without oral directions, questions, answers) and that even dreams enter science only in the form of texts. The problem is only how one can interpret and evaluate texts psychologically.[9]

In principle, only cognitive modification of psychological theories makes controllable methods in psychological exegesis possible. The texts themselves contain what is psychologically decisive according to a cognitive approach—interpretations. They can be assessed in a threefold manner—descriptively, analytically, and comparatively.

Descriptive processes describe the interpretations contained in the texts with the aid of psychological categories. They do not attempt to

9. On the methodological problematic of interpreting ancient texts on the basis of depth psychology, see Schmidbauer, *Mythos*. As far as biblical texts are concerned, see Niederwimmer, "Kerygmatisches Symbol" and "Tiefenpsychologie und Exegese," and Wink, *The Bible in Human Transformation*.

expose something hidden behind the texts. Instead, they rely on the texts to say on their own what a psychological frame of questioning seeks in them; here clear questions also receive satisfying answers. The greater portion of the psychological exegeses presented in this book proceed from such psychological aspects in the texts, drawn forth descriptively. This is true above all of the analysis of the texts from the perspective of learning theory and cognitive methods.

Analytic procedures, which proceed from the principle that psychic processes are only inadequately symbolized in the texts and can be uncovered from them only through special reasoning processes, seem more problematical. The search for unconscious processes seems almost hopeless. Unlike a psychotherapist, a historian cannot obtain additional information and have interpretations confirmed by the patient. It is nonetheless possible to assess the unconscious dynamics contained within religious symbols if one proceeds on the basis of a cognitively (or hermeneutically) modified concept of symbol. Religious symbols are a language in which the unconscious becomes capable of consciousness. We must therefore look for statements containing semantic layers—a level close to consciousness and one distant from consciousness, or to put it better, a level near the self and a level distant from the self—for it is hardly likely that anything of psychic processes will be deposited in the texts unless the processes themselves reach a shadowy level of consciousness. On the whole, there are six forms of statement that reflect the desired semantic structure: metaphors, exegeses, homologies, displacements of motif, contradictions, and overreactions.

1. *Metaphors* combine (*a*) an area of offering an image with (*b*) an area of receiving one. Since consciousness is concentrated on the recipient of the image, the associations and connotations evoked by the one who offers the image can bring to expression content and orientations that are less conscious, more distant from the self. When God is addressed as Father, the conscious intention of the statement is directed toward the reality addressed, God. Yet the image of father awakens associations with childhood. Such associations affect the connotations of the entire family of words and can be examined philologically.

2. *Exegeses* likewise have a double semantic structure. Above the text which is to be interpreted (*a*) lies an interpretation (*b*), which can be interpreted like a projective test. Interpreters always put something of themselves into the text to be interpreted. This occurs unconsciously,

for the interpreters think they are letting only the text come to expression. Such projections are unmistakable when texts are reinterpreted against their evident meaning. Paul offers numerous examples. In 2 Cor. 3:6–18 he places his ambivalent attitude to Moses into the Old Testament text: on the one hand, he distances himself from Moses in sharp contrasts; on the other hand, he sees in Moses a model of conversion to Christianity.

3. *Homologies* consist of (*a*) the depiction of an objective (mythical) event and (*b*) a parallel description of inner processes. Gal. 4:4–6 is an example of this psychomythical parallelism. Juxtaposed are the statements that "God sent forth his Son" (4:4) and that "God has sent the Spirit of his Son into our hearts" (4:6). The first mission involves an objective event, the sending of the Son into the world; the second involves an event that changes the subject, the sending of the Spirit into our hearts. The question forces itself on us, Are not the two processes ultimately aspects of one and the same event? Do psychic aspects that are always implicit in mythical statements become incipiently tangible in psychomythical parallelisms?

4. *Displacements of motif* occur when (*a*) a motif that is objectively to be expected within a complex of motifs is omitted and (*b*) that motif appears in a completely different context. Paul offers an interesting example of this. Although he occupied himself intensively with the figure of Abraham (Romans 4; Galatians 3), in contrast to contemporary Jewish and Christian sources he does not mention the binding of Isaac—the most important sign of Abraham's faith. Paul is silent about Abraham's willingness to sacrifice his son. He attributes precisely this readiness to God in Rom. 8:32, in words that must remind every reader familiar with the Bible of Gen. 22:16. Does this not suggest the interpretation that God has taken on the sacrifice that the model believer no longer has to perform? Faith and readiness to kill are separated.

5. *Contradictions* between different texts can likewise draw attention to two different levels of consciousness, if (*a*) one text brings to expression the meaning that dominates consciousness, while (*b*) the contradictory text reveals a contrary unconscious orientation. As an example of this kind of contradiction we shall examine the relationship of Romans 7 to Philippians 3. On the one hand stands an unbroken pride in the law which lives from the consciousness of fulfilling the law without reproach (Phil. 3:6); on the other hand there is despair at inability to fulfill the law (Romans 7). In the text closer to himself,

Paul uses a personal "I," while in Romans 7 a typical "I," intended to include everyone, is speaking.

6. *Overreactions* can also be interpreted as formation of reactions if other indicators point in the same direction. It is presupposed (*a*) that the reactions contained in a text can be compared with other reactions in the text and (*b*) that this comparison shows they exceed the range of reactions that is to be expected. Paul's reaction to the problem of women's head covering (1 Cor. 11:2–16), for example, strikes one as notably excessive when it is compared with the tolerance for different sociocultural norms promoted even in 1 Cor. 9:19–21, with the overcoming of differences in sex roles in the early Christian communities (Gal. 3:28), or with very different statements on the themes of "veils" and "veiling of the head" (2 Cor. 3:18). The possibility that here Paul is reacting to unconscious tendencies that are symbolized in this symbol of sexual roles is not to be excluded. It is not necessary to think in this regard of tendencies within Paul; it could be a matter of unconscious tendencies in the whole group, tendencies Paul sensed intuitively. The first possibility would be difficult to examine methodically; the second is more readily accessible.

Thus we obtain six possibilities of drawing analytic conclusions from religious texts. As figure 2 suggests, the juxtaposition of semantic layers closer to and more distant from the self makes possible glimpses of the unconscious.

FIGURE 2

	Semantic Layer Close to the Self	Semantic Layer Distant from the Self
Metaphors	image-receiving sphere	image-giving sphere
Exegeses	text to be interpreted	interpreting text
Homologies	psychic event	mythic event
Shifts of Motif	new context of motifs	traditional complex of motifs
Contradictions	text near the self	text distant from the self
Overreactions	texts with normal reactions	texts with striking reactions

Comparative conclusions form a third group of evaluative procedures in the psychology of religion. As in all historical-critical research, texts must constantly be adduced for comparison. Only what comes from the context of that period is freed from the suspicion of being a retrojection of modern ideas. Comparative texts can be factual analogies or traditions. Traditions must not be drawn on psychologically only in the sense that their modification is considered psychologically relevant while the content of the tradition is considered psychologically unproductive. On the contrary, traditions contain "religions' storehouse of roles"—conditions for the possibility of religious experience. Factual analogies are to be investigated with the same descriptive and analytical procedure as all other texts. They are especially enlightening when they permit the emergence of a phenomenon's psychic aspects that can at most be presumed in comparable New Testament texts. Factual analogies from differing cultural spheres form a special problem. In what follows, this problem will become acute with regard to glossolalia, which has again emerged during the last twenty years. The question is whether it is permissible to conclude from modern glossolalia to ancient phenomena. At the very least, modern research on glossolalia can serve as a heuristic starting point—abstracting from the fact that it probably illustrates the early Christian phenomenon better than the general headshaking about glossolalia in historical-critical research.

Summary. The "symbolic" character of human experience and behavior which is postulated by a hermeneutic psychology makes it possible to read psychic phenomena from objective sign structures (especially texts), to detect even processes distant from the self in which what is unconscious is rendered capable of consciousness.

THE HOLISTIC CHARACTER OF EXPERIENCE AND BEHAVIOR

The different psychological models of explanation receive a new framework from the hermeneutic postulate of wholeness. A hermeneutical psychology is not absolutely committed to integrating different competitive theoretical approaches into a unified general psychology. It is aware of its unity in another way—through the reference of all interpretations to the connection of all psychic phenomena directly given in experience. This is true even if psychic life is divided into unconscious and conscious elements. Precisely psychoanalysis interprets putatively foreign expressions of life, which have little to do with the conscious self, as expressions of one's own person. It is hermeneutical inasmuch as it establishes a meaningful connection with the whole person even in places where this at first seems to be lacking.

Just as our experience of self is holistic, so too is our understanding of others. Texts and expressions of life are intelligible only as a whole. This leads to both an expansion and a limitation of explanatory approaches in a hermeneutical psychology.

The expansion consists in the fact that explanatory models usually investigate only individual phenomena. Even where they can justifiably be applied to texts, the aspects of the text that they illuminate are placed by the whole context in a broader framework from which it would be artificial and one-sided to abstract. It is doubtless correct, for example, that an extremely negative and an extremely positive symbolic stimulus—cross and resurrection—are combined in early Christian texts. But this observation says little in isolation. Cross and resurrection are the center of an interpreted world. The whole of this world must also come into focus if parts of it are to be understood correctly. This has consequences for the accounts that follow. Particular text phenomena are illuminated by the specific explanatory models, yet it is not only legitimate but also necessary to pursue all the contexts of meaning that the texts impose—even if they lead into regions where the given psychological approach is not applicable at all. The decisive criterion within a hermeneutically oriented psychological exegesis is the correspondence of an interpretation with the whole of the text, not the consistency of theories.

The hermeneutical task requires not only that one constantly move beyond the limits of the individual approaches to explanation with reference to the overall context to be interpreted. The individual explanatory models are also relativized and corrected through this overall context. They are to be measured exclusively by the extent to which they make parts of the text more intelligible in the context of the whole or deepen the picture of the whole through newly discovered connections. The whole can be a document, the entire corpus of an author, or even the literary remains of an entire group.

"Coherence of the whole to be interpreted" is a vague criterion, but it is indispensable. It is not to be confused with an unmediated sensation. It depends on disciplined self-immersion in the sources. Only in this way does there emerge the sense of what is historically possible and what corresponds to the sources, a sense that is lacking in many psychological efforts at exegesis. In such cases, the texts too quickly become illustrations of preconceived theories.

Summary. Because a hermeneutical psychology has its fixed point of reference in expressions of life that are to be interpreted and that in themselves form a context, it can begin its work without a finished theory of religion. It is another question whether it need not work toward such a theory. If the different approaches to explanation throw factually new light on the texts, it is necessary to inquire about their interconnection—precisely from the standpoint of a hermeneutical psychology, which presupposes as given the overall context of psychic life. Let me sketch an attempt at this.

Psychodynamic approaches, learning theory, and cognitive approaches can be ordered to one another if they are placed in a context of the history of evolution. Psychodynamic approaches thematize archaic aspects of human behavior and experience that we have in common with other organisms—genetic programs and early childhood imprintings. Religion appears as confrontation with the unconscious archaic elements within us.

Learning theories investigate higher forms of individual learning through experiences with the environment. We also have these learning processes in common with other forms of life. Associative and operant learning can be detected in comparatively primitive animals. Imitative learning can be found in some higher animals, especially in primates, but it is only in human beings that it becomes the decisive foundation of the nongenetic communication of information between generations. From the perspective of learning theory, religion appears as a result of social learning, a socially mediated manner of reacting to reality.

Religion is not only formed by archaic relics within us and social factors around us. It is active confrontation with the archaisms of the unconscious and the influences of society. The ability to confront the given conditions of life actively and consciously, to transform them and integrate them into an interpreted world, is found only in human beings. From the perspective of the history of evolution, what cognitive approaches grasp is the most recent aspect of religion—its specifically human dimension.

In this way we reach a type of "layer model" of religious experience and behavior. It encompasses the heights and depths of humanity, its most archaic atavisms and its most progressive powers. Strong tensions are balanced and developed in religion. This leads to the hypothesis that religion is a regulative system that cares for the equilibrium dynamic of life through balance and tension among the various layers of human nature. Heights and depths should be able to develop, but they should not overburden us through unbearable tensions. In this regard, the function of religion seems to differ in different historical epochs.

Religion occurs in past history as revolution in human beings' interpreted world. The breakthrough of monotheism in Israel led to strong tensions with the archaisms in human nature. The new faith had to assert itself against tendencies to regression into more archaic forms of religion.

Today, with regard to society as a whole, religion seems to have more regressive functions. Its central problem is the separation between modern cognitive interpretations of the world and human emotional and motivational needs. The religions seem to exert themselves to bring into harmony with the modern interpretation of the world human archaisms—functional and dysfunctional—that have only apparently been overcome.

Even though the application of different explanatory models legitimates itself chiefly through its hermeneutical contribution to the illumination of the whole reality that is to be interpreted, this procedure is not at all an arbitrary eclecticism; on the contrary, an evolutionist interpretation of man can demonstrate elements of an integration of the three competing explanatory models. In this matter as in others, understanding and explaining are not ultimately opposed to each other. Both presuppose the total context of reality.[10]

THE ORIENTATION OF PSYCHIC
LIFE TOWARD CONTENT

We cannot analyze human experience and behavior independently of the objects to which they are related. A psychology of religion must allow for the fact that general forms of experience and behavior are modified by the specific object of religious experience, and even that some phenomena come into existence only through religious experience—for example, glossolalia, which occurs almost exclusively in religious contexts. The psychology of religion is therefore more than general psychology applied to religious phenomena. Its task is not to make religion intelligible within the framework of an already established anthropology; on the contrary, it can open new dimensions of general

10. For elements of a new evolutionist theory of religion, see Burhoe, "Religion's Role"; Hardy, *The Biology of God;* and von Ditfurth, *Wir sind nicht nur von dieser Welt.*

anthropology and psychology. For what has one understood of man if one has not understood man's religion?

The only problem is that the object of religious experience and behavior is disputed. A secularized society, at least, finds itself perplexed here. Experience and behavior related to content exempt from methodical control is a foreign body in such a society. Religion is pushed to the fringe of general consciousness. It is from this situation that psychodynamic theories of religion draw their plausibility; the more consciousness is free of religious bonds, the easier it is to interpret any remaining attachment to religion as a consequence of unconscious bonds, whether by evaluating these bonds as atavistic relics or by hoping to receive creative impulses from them. Religion and the unconscious was therefore rightly the great theme of psychology of religion. It corresponds to this state of the question when in the following investigations texts are selected in which confrontation with the unconscious is visible—not to demonstrate that psychodynamic interpretations of religion are correct but to show that precisely confrontation with the unconscious requires a comprehensive hermeneutical psychology that makes use of various explanatory approaches.

But the factual problem remains. If religious behavior and experience are marked by their object, is this object a consciousness-transcending sphere within the human being or outside it? Does the "beyond" lie within or in reality outside the subject? Here the self-understanding of religion and theories critical of religion arrive at different statements. Can their opposition be bridged?

It can first be shown that both experiences—that of the unconscious within us and that of transcendence outside us—are based in the human condition. The two can be thought of together with an evolutionist image of the human being. We must assess human organic, motivational, and intellectual structures as specific forms of adaptation to reality. These adaptive structures are not timeless givens but the product of a long evolution that is far from complete. Relics of archaic adaptive structures are therefore preserved in the human being; they stand in tension to present adaptive requirements and either remain unconscious or are repressed. This is the unconscious within man. But even the present adaptive structures do not correspond to reality in itself. What we call reality is only reality as it appears on the basis of our organic composition, our current technical instruments, and intellectual strategies of thought. It is only one specific life-world—beside other possible life-worlds. A fundamental difference exists between the human life-world and the world in itself, and human beings are conscious of this difference. They know that a (still?) inaccessible "unconscious" exists outside themselves.

The experience of both internal and external transcendence thus corresponds to the human condition. The human being comes from the depths of an evolution that leads a ghostly afterlife in the human unconscious; and we move with constantly new adaptive structures toward an as yet inaccessible reality that we sense even beyond our most advanced interpretations of the world as something "wholly other."[11] It is a priori probable that we do not separate objective and subjective transcendence in our experience. Is what human beings fantasize about this nonsubjective transcendence deception, because it often comes from inside themselves? Or would that be a false psychological conclusion?

Like every science, psychology proceeds from the premise of a unified reality. This unity is described vaguely as "reality," "objective reality," or "nature." All experience and behavior can be described as appropriation of this reality and as adaptation to it. Whether we proceed from psychodynamic approaches, learning theory, or cognitive approaches, this "objective reality" always appears as a power determining from without.

Genetically preprogrammed forms of behavior and experience have come about through mutation and selection. Only things compatible with reality can preserve themselves. Even on a very foundational level, reality shows itself as a power determining—often gruesomely selecting—from without, a power that constructs and destroys and that produces a surprising multiplicity of structures through the constant process of mutation and selection in an endless sequence of generations. It follows from this that if we conceive of our unconscious as residue of the evolutionary pre-stages of our current life, it too would ultimately be marked by nonsubjective reality.

Cultural learning programs are subject to selection of a different sort. Modes of behavior can be abandoned and changed without having the subjects of behavior die (individually or as a species). Human beings can turn around and "repent." But it is possible only with

11. Here my thoughts touch those of Ricoeur, who wishes to attribute both an "archaeology" and a "teleology" to religious symbols (cf. *Freud and Philosophy*, 459–93 and passim). In Ricoeur, psychoanalytic theories illuminate their "archaeology"; their orientation toward something new is elucidated with the aid of Hegelian categories. In my work the doctrine of evolution takes the place of Hegelian philosophy.

difficulty to escape from socially established patterns of behavior and experience, even if it is evident that they lead to historical catastrophes that signify the end of entire cultures. Again we are confronted with an objective power that makes behavior systems possible and lets them collapse when they are incompatible with the conditions of reality—the objective power that the great prophets of doom called on as "Yahweh" in the historical crises and catastrophes of their people. Religious experience and behavior also belong to these social behavior systems. Even if we view them as socially learned, they have in each instance developed in lengthy confrontation with reality and were produced by that reality.

But what individuals experience most intensively is the failure of their self-interpretations and of their symbolically interpreted world. The pressure of reality shows itself here in identity crises, in which philosophies of life collapse as lies of life or as conviction systems hostile to life—a process often accompanied by bodily collapse. Again we receive a noticeable reply from surrounding reality, which seems to say, "That doesn't work!" And again religious consciousness articulates these crises as a call to repentance, and sees even in the collapse of old forms of life a chance of a new beginning.

Behind the pressure of reality in selection, historical catastrophes, and crises of identity, we experience a given central reality that places clear limits on human self-will, that imposes a harsh education toward reality, and that often proceeds gruesomely and inexorably—but that simultaneously makes possible and permits an infinite multiplicity of organisms, cultural patterns, and self-interpretations, so that we are as astonished at its apparently boundless liberality as we are appalled at its severity. This central reality is ultimately the "creator" of our life-world. Everything found within us is an experiment attempting to correspond to it. All organic, psychic, and intellectual structures are attempts to adapt to it.[12] Is it so inexplicable that some human beings intuitively sense this, become conscious of it, and wish to lead their life as an echo of this hidden transcendent reality? Is it unjustified to call this reality God?

12. Cf. the comments of Burhoe: "But I shall make a special point of the central notion of the major religious doctrines or theologies that is far ahead of contemporary secular thinking and more in keeping with evolutionary theory for understanding man's place in the scheme of things. This is the notion of man's dependence upon the system of objective requirements posed by a nature that is much more than human, to which all living systems must adapt, the ultimate reality system, whether we call it nature or God" ("Religion's Role," 158).

PART TWO

The Secrets of the Heart: The Disclosure of Unconscious Motives Through Pauline Theology

The "unconscious" is a central theme of the modern psychology of religion. But the reality itself is old. Paul is familiar with the idea of unconscious impulses within human beings. In order to articulate this idea, he has recourse to elements in the biblical-Jewish tradition but he changes them in characteristic fashion. Three traditional elements of thought are involved: (1) faith in the omniscient God, who probes even inner motives and thoughts (God's knowledge of the heart); (2) conviction that human insight with regard to oneself is limited, that one does not fully probe even one's own being; (3) recognition of an autonomous inner reality in which, in addition to the remembrance of past actions, motives and impulses are also real and significant.

The combination of these three elements of thought makes it possible to imagine an unconscious human dimension. The decisive issue here is whether the idea of God's knowledge of the heart—clearly present in 1 Cor. 4:1–5; 14:23–25; and Rom. 2:15–16—is joined to the consciousness of limited human self-knowledge; only then is the content God sees in the depths of the human being removed from the consciousness of the individual concerned, and not only from that of others. If in addition inner processes are assessed as an autonomous reality, then there is present a concept of the unconscious whose theological framework of interpretation differs from the modern conception, but which is comparable to that conception in content.

Chapter 5

Text Analyses:
1 Corinthians 4:1–5;
Romans 2:16;
1 Corinthians 14:20–25

The Revelation of Unconscious Intentions in the Last Judgment: 1 Cor. 4:1–5

The three conceptual presuppositions of a conception of the "unconscious" are found within a coherent section of text in 1 Cor. 4:1–5. We therefore begin with this text.

Conflicts between different parties in Corinth stand in the background of 1 Cor. 4:1–5. In 3:18–23 Paul had just warned against overestimation of the teachers to whom the parties appealed. The parties were said to be subordinate to the community, not superior to it. In 1 Cor. 4:1–5, Paul de facto retracts this statement. Confronted with accusations of the Corinthians, he retreats to the formal legal position that he does not owe the Corinthians any accounting. They are not superior to him. Unfortunately, we are not told what accusations were brought against Paul. We do sense, however, that Paul was by no means as indifferent to these accusations as he claimed (4:3), for in 1 Cor. 9:3–5 he sets in again with an extended "apology" addressed to the Corinthians.[1] In 4:1–5, however, he discusses only the question of the formal competence of a judgment passed upon him:

> This is how one should regard us, as servants of Christ and stewards of the mysteries of God. Moreover it is required of stewards that they be found trustworthy. But with me it is a very small thing that I should be judged by you or by any human court. I do not even judge myself.

---

1. In 1 Cor. 4:1–5 Paul probably already had in view the charges he addresses in chap. 9. The term *anakrinein* occurs in both texts (cf. 9:3). In both texts Paul appeals to his being *oikonomos* (1 Cor. 4:1) or to the *oikonomia* entrusted to him (1 Cor. 9:17), and connects to this the words *pistos* (4:2) and *pepisteumai* (9:17), which have related roots. Above all, 9:3 gives the reader the impression that it refers to a theme that has already been mentioned.

I am not aware of anything against myself, but I am not thereby acquitted. It is the Lord who judges me. Therefore do not pronounce judgment before the time, before the Lord comes, who will bring to light the things now hidden in darkness and will disclose the purposes of the heart. Then every man will receive his commendation from God.

The text forms a unit grounded in the metaphor of stewards. The background that provides the metaphor is the steward, often a slave, who has received a command from his master and who must render an account of its fulfillment; the image is familiar to us from the synoptic tradition (cf. the parables of the unjust steward, Luke 16:1–9; and of the two stewards, Luke 12:41–48).[2] Our text develops this image in three parts:

(1) 4:1–2: Basic information on the role of Paul.
  (a) Paul has the role of a servant and steward of Christ: he administers divine mysteries.
  (b) The decisive criterion of conduct in this role is fidelity.[3]
(2) 4:3–4: The competence of different tribunals of judgment to judge Paul (the term *anakrinein* occurs three times).
  (a) Incompetent tribunals.
    1. Men and human courts (v. 3).
    2. Paul and his conscience (v. 4a).
  (b) The only competent tribunal.
    The Lord (v. 4).
(3) 4:5: The time of judgment. Judgment must be postponed until the coming of the Lord.

The text forms a unit. The image of the steward is introduced in v. 1 and ends with the coming of the Lord in v. 5.[4] Verse 2 names the criterion by which a steward is measured. A slight jump in thought

2. In Luke 12:41–46, *oikonomos* and *doulos* are synonymous. Luke 16:1–9, on the contrary, presupposes a free steward, who must seek a new position after his dismissal. Paul presumably thinks of the role of a slave, for in 1 Cor. 9:16–18, he connects his *oikonomia* with concepts of servile existence, especially with the concept of *anagke*. In Homer's *Iliad* (6.458) slavery is designated as *anagke*. (See further, Marshall, *Enmity*, 460.) That Paul works without pay also suggests the role of a slave. In addition, he says explicitly, "I have made myself a slave" (1 Cor. 9:19). There were, obviously, also high-ranking civil offices, such as that of the *oikonomos tes poleos* (the city treasurer; Rom. 16:23). But the emphasis on the exclusive dependence of the steward on his master suggests thinking of a slave in 1 Cor. 4:1–5. For an opposing view, cf. Reumann, "Stewards of God."

3. The association of *oikonomos* and *pistos* is also to be found in Luke 12:42; 16:8–12.

4. The coming of the Lord belongs to the metaphorical picture; cf. the servant parables of Luke 12:43, 46; 19:15; Mark 13:35.

then follows. In vv. 3–4, this criterion is not applied, but rather tribunals that are or are not authorized to judge Paul are listed: only the Lord can judge his steward. From this follows, in v. 5, an eschatological reservation. No one is authorized to judge before the time. Then, however, the Lord will come, and God will distribute to each his praise.[5]

Thus Paul contrasts two illegitimate tribunals of judgment with the sole legitimate one. He connects this contrast with the opposition of consciousness and the unconscious. For Paul himself is conscious of no guilt: *ouden gar emauto sunoida*.[6] He is convinced that he is faithful, but he does not therefore venture to assert his innocence: *all' ouk en touto dedikaiomai*. Even this claim of innocence contains the acceptance of a possible unconscious guilt. Precisely this idea of a—theoretically possible—unconscious guilt is then underlined by the concluding eschatological reservation. The eschatological judge will bring to light not only hidden deeds (as in 2 Cor. 5:10) but also the hidden intentions of the heart (*tas boulas ton kardion*)[7]—precisely what, in view of the preceding claim of innocence, must have been unconscious. If the text is taken literally, it allows for the possibility of unconscious forces and impulses within us.[8] Precisely the three basic elements that are the

5. On the analysis, see Mattern, *Das Verständnis*, 179–86; and Synofzik, *Die Gerichts- und Vergeltungsaussagen*, 42–43.

6. The concept of conscience developed from the verbal expression *sunoida emauto* (see Maurer, s. v. *sunoida*). The concept of a pure conscience was at first described negatively; Plato (*Republic* 1.221A) wrote that "on him who is conscious of no wrong that he has done a sweet hope ever attends" (ET: Paul Shorey, *Plato: The Republic*, vol. 1 of 2 vols. [LCL, 1930], 17, 19). In our text Paul draws on Job 27:6* LXX: "ou gar sunoida emautou atopa praxas," a passage in which the Hebrew "heart" is translated freely under the influence of the Hellenistic Greek expression. "My heart does not reproach me for any of my days" becomes "I am conscious of no improper deeds." That Job insists on his innocence is instructive. It does not occur to him that against the judgment of his consciousness he might be unconsciously guilty. Paul allows for the possibility of unconscious guilt.

7. Cf. the comments of Weiss (*Der 1. Korintherbrief*, 99): " . . . since it is a matter of impulses of the will which were not put into practice and which therefore remain hidden, the terms 'projects' or 'recommendations' are almost a bit too strong; perhaps 'inclinations,' or 'impulses.' "

8. This exegesis has a long tradition. After Augustine had cited 1 Cor. 4:3 ("I do not even judge myself") at the end of *Confessions* 10.4, he continued as follows in 10.5: "For thou, O Lord, dost judge me: because, that although no man knows the things of a man, but the spirit of man which is in him; yet is there some thing of man, that the very spirit of man that is in him knoweth not. But thou knowest all of him, who hast made him" (ET: William Watts, *St. Augustine's Confessions*, vol. 2 of 2 vols. [LCL, 1912], 85). In Protestantism, 1 Cor. 4:4 was later interpreted with reference to unconscious guilt; cf. the survey of the history of interpretation in Althaus, *Paulus und Luther*, 88–

presupposition of uncovering the unconscious within human beings are combined in this text: God's knowledge of the heart; the limited nature of human self-knowledge; and the significance of inner reality. Nonetheless, it is appropriate to doubt if the text needs to be understood in this way. Three objections will be discussed. They amount to (1) relativizing the reservation with regard to the claim of innocence in 4:4; or (2) relativizing the invocation of the eschatological judge in 4:5; or (3) determining the inner connection of the two statements in a different way. All the objections contain an element of truth, yet instead of refuting the thesis that in 1 Cor. 4:1–5 Paul thought of an unconscious dimension within us, they rather specify more precisely what is involved.

1. The first objection charges that Paul is only speaking purely theoretically about a guilt of which he is unconscious. When he invokes the eschatological judge he mentions only the possibility of praise in judgment, not the possibility of punishment. He does not seriously allow for unpleasant surprises. He does express the reservation that his conscience does not justify him. But is he not surprisingly sure that his conscience tells the truth?[9] Is not the reservation about his own consciousness purely theoretical? Does it say any more than "I still await the objective confirmation of what I already subjectively know surely"?

This conception could appeal to v. 5 if one were to emphasize "then every man will receive his *commendation* from God," while overlooking the fact that *everyone* is to receive this praise.[10] Paul is speaking not

---

107. In this, Protestant consciousness of sin was undoubtedly projected into the passage, as, e.g., by Moe: "Paul will in fact reserve that God's eye sees hidden sins that escape Paul's view and remain unconscious" ("Zur Frage," 488). That the Paul who persecuted Christians had an astonishingly good conscience is even today difficult for Protestant piety with its guilt culture to understand. As Krister Stendahl ("The Apostle Paul") has rightly emphasized, we must not read Paul in the light of this culture of guilt and conscience. What we find in Paul is that he recognizes unconscious motives—but even so does not feel guilty!

9. According to Weiss (*Der 1. Korintherbrief*, 98), the reservation with regard to his own conscience is not due to any "capability of error." Paul says only "that his conscience is not authorized to award him complete unburdening." But this does not include everything. First, in other places Paul clearly has command of the notion of an erroneous conscience; conscience can be weak and eat meat offered to idols as sacral meat (1 Cor. 8:7). Second, Paul recognizes the possibility of self-condemnation; according to 1 Cor. 11:32, Christians anticipate the judgment of the Lord. Third, Paul bases his renunciation of self-assessment first of all on lacking consciousness of guilt. "I am aware of nothing" is connected by *gar* with the previous sentence as its foundation. His positive certitude is all the more astonishing!

10. Weiss (*Der 1. Korintherbrief*, 98) wishes to think only of the apostles here. Com-

only of himself but also of others. He explicitly mentions Apollos, to whom he applies what has been said just as he applies it to himself (4:6). Paul cannot subjectively anticipate the eschatological judgment for other missionaries (and other people)! This is all the more true since according to 3:15 he allows for competing missionaries to be "punished" in the judgment. Paul's conscience can only testify to himself. But even this testimony is not sufficient for Paul. When in 4:5 he puts himself on the same level with others and relates the revelation of what is hidden to "everyone," he says indirectly that he is concealed from himself just as others are concealed from him.

There is also another reason the reservation with regard to one's own conscience is not merely rhetorical. To say it is would be to underestimate the gravity of the idea of judgment for Paul. The "fear and trembling" with which Christians should work their salvation (Phil. 2:12) would not come to bear.

And yet the objection does hit on something essential. Paul does allow for unconscious intentions that could stand in tension with his consciousness. But he is convinced that these unconscious intentions can no longer existentially endanger him in the judgment. He is "reconciled" with the unconscious which is unknown to him. He no longer experiences the relationship of consciousness and unconscious as a painful contradiction. It is therefore illegitimate to read into this passage a consciousness of sin expanded to the unconscious.[11]

2. The second objection proceeds from the traditional character of the theme of God's knowledge of the heart. According to 1 Cor. 4:5, it is God "who will bring to light the things now hidden in darkness and will disclose the purposes of the heart."

The parallelism in this text could be assessed as an indication that traditional material, perhaps even a citation, is present here.[12] In any

mendation could hardly be accorded to every Christian. But first, *hekastos* is to be found in connection with general statements about judgment in 2 Cor. 5:10 and Rom. 14:12; there it means every Christian, as the synonymy with *pantes*, "all," shows. Second, Paul goes on to say that he has applied this to himself and Apollos (1 Cor. 4:6). He is envisioning a more general situation, which he subsequently wishes to apply to the relationship of two apostles.

11. This is rightly criticized by Mattern, *Verständnis*, 181 n. 579.

12. The indications of traditional material are the following: (1) relative connection with *hos;* (2) the parallelism; (3) the vocabulary (this is the only text in which Paul uses *photizein*, and the only occurrence of the expression *ta krupta tou skotous* in the New Testament); (4) the tension between this verse and the context (what is hidden is to be understood negatively, while Paul assumes a positive result of the judgment); (5) parallels to the opposition of light and darkness and to the divine knowledge of the heart in the

case, it is said, Paul is relying on well-known formulations, and
formulations taken from other sources must not be taken too seriously.

Against this interpretation we may note that the correct reference
to the presence of a traditional theme says absolutely nothing about
how serious Paul is about this topic. The confession of the Lord Jesus
(Rom. 10:9) is also traditional, and yet it is the foundation of Pauline
existence. Anyone who attributes significance only to what is entirely
original will hardly be able to understand ancient literature. Traditional
material can again and again acquire a central character in new contexts.

The tradition that appears in 1 Cor. 4:5 is well anchored in its
literary and historical context. The possibility of unconscious guilt was
already alluded to in 4:4, when Paul said that he was conscious of
nothing yet not for that reason justified. Something well integrated
into the context's train of thought can hardly be purely ornamental.
In addition, the theme of God's knowledge of the heart could also be
very well anchored in the historical context if Paul had been charged
in Corinth with having improper motives hidden behind his declared
intentions.[13] In that case, the invocation of one who probes the depths
of the heart would certainly not be purely rhetorical.

But this second objection also strikes on something essential. A
tension is recognizable between the Pauline statement and the tradition.
First, the theme of God's knowledge of the heart is transferred to
Christ. The tension in relation to the tradition is also tangible when
Paul attributes to the coming Lord (i.e., Christ) penetration and
disclosure of hearts but, immediately after that, ascribes to God the
conferral of praise.[14] Second, the tradition relates chiefly to sins against

---

Old Testament and in other Jewish literature; (6) the modification of the traditional
theme of God's knowledge of the heart (this knowledge is transferred to Christ, but it
is God who distributes commendation!). On the assumption of traditional material, cf.
Weiss, *Der 1. Korintherbrief*, 99; Lietzmann, *An die Korinther*, 19; Conzelmann, *Der erste
Brief an die Korinther*, 103; and Synofzik, *Gerichts- und Vergeltungsaussagen*, 42–43.

13. In 2 Corinthians it is quite clear that Paul was accused of having improper
motives. For this reason he emphasizes that he lived among the Corinthians in "holiness
and godly sincerity" (2 Cor. 1:12), that he had "taken advantage" (2 Cor. 7:2) of no one,
that he is no "deceiver" (2 Cor. 12:16–17*). When he avows in 2 Cor. 4:2 that he has
renounced the *krupta tes aischunes*, this is immediately reminiscent of the *krupta tou skotous*
of 1 Cor. 4:5. Now, it is not legitimate to draw immediate conclusions from 2 Corinthians
to 1 Corinthians, since new charges have arisen in the meantime. But the theme of
"renouncing support" persists. In this connection things in 1 Corinthians could have
already reached the point of imputing hidden "improper motives."

14. Even in 1 Cor. 4:1, Christ and God are juxtaposed as the two masters of Paul,
the servant and steward. On the basis of the whole text, it is therefore logical that both
have a function in the rendering of account.

a norm.[15] The things hidden in darkness (1 Cor. 4:5) shrink from the light just like the "works of darkness" (Rom. 13:12). But Paul does not fear the revelation of what is hidden. The presumption that the two modifications of the tradition are closely related lies near at hand: the relationship to Christ makes possible a transformed attitude to the unconscious. This point will be examined later. Here let it be noted that demonstration of the presence of a traditional theme underlines the importance of the idea for Paul. The theme is not only well anchored in the context, it is also modified by Paul individually.

3. Last, there remains the possibility of determining in a different way the inner connection between the protestation of innocence in v. 4 and the eschatological outlook in v. 5. It is said that Paul is primarily concerned in both verses to deny the Corinthians competence to pass judgment on him. The accent does not lie on what is psychically unconscious, withdrawn from personal assessment, but rather on what is socially hidden, inaccessible to external assessment by the Corinthians. Paul invokes two witnesses against them—his conscience and God. Even if the Corinthians do not believe his conscience, what Paul could now—consciously—conceal will come to light at the latest in the last judgment.[16]

This interpretation is also one-sided. In contrast to Rom. 9:1 and 2 Cor. 1:12, here Paul does not appeal at all to his conscience as judge but rejects conscience as a competent tribunal of judgment. For this reason he also cannot invoke the future divine judgment as confirmation of his present statement. The divine judgment appears rather as a possible corrective of that statement. In order to exclude this idea, one would have to dispute any inner connection between the protestation of innocence and the idea of judgment. But that is impossible. Not only is v. 5 a conclusion from the preceding, introduced by "therefore," but, in addition, the concluding eschatological outlook repeats decisive terms of the preceding protestation of innocence—(*ana*)*krinein*, "to judge," and *kurios*, "master, Lord." The metaphorical framework remains the same. The servant must render account. The only disputed points are whether this should occur before a human court or before

15. See the tradition analysis, pp. 81–95 below.
16. Thus, e.g., Althaus (*Paulus und Luther*, 90): 1 Cor. 4:5 "does call to mind the limitation of all human ability to judge, but here only in view of judgment of *others*, hardly in view of *self-assessment*. Paul raises against the critique of the Corinthians the objection that they cannot look into his heart, the apostle's heart." But Paul not only says, "You cannot judge me"; he also says, unmistakably, "I cannot judge myself."

God, and whether it should take place now or only when the Lord comes. The unity of the text cannot be challenged.

This last objection, which envisions the text consistently as defense against the Corinthians and subordinates all its elements to this purpose, also has a legitimate core. Paul transforms the dialogue with his addressees into an inner dialogue. He can probe into himself no more than the Corinthians can probe into him. His inner dialogue is an echo of his dialogue with his addressee. Paul assumes with regard to himself the role of an "outsider." This is true even of the concept of conscience as such: conscience is the interiorized other human being as co-knower. Paul goes a step further: conscience can stand over against one's own interior in just as foreign a fashion as one person stands over against the interior of a fellow human being.

Summary. In my opinion, the text admits the conclusion that Paul possessed a conception of an unconscious dimension within the human being. Within this dimension lie not only repressed unconscious deeds but also unconscious plans and motives. Paul no longer experienced the relationship of consciousness and unconscious as a contradiction, although he knew theoretically of a possible contradiction. This possible contradiction was defined forensically: the unconscious is that which no human court—not even one's own conscience—can bring to light but which is revealed only in the divine judgment.

THE "SECRETS OF MEN": ROM. 2:16

The notion that God will judge the "secrets of men" on the last day occurs also in Rom. 2:16. The term "secrets" refers to the context. A little later Paul speaks of "a Jew in secret" (Rom. 2:29*) who receives praise only from God, not from men. Now to the train of thought in Rom. 1:18—3:20:

> 1:18—2:11: Just as the gospel is valid for all, first Jews, then also Gentiles, so too is the revelation of the wrath of God (cf. 1:16 and 2:9). Paul develops this thesis in two trains of thought.
> 1. The immanent effect of the wrath of God on mistaken veneration of God is shown in the decay of human life (1:18–32). Paul is thinking of pagan modes of behavior, as the connection of idolatry and homosexuality shows, but he also has Jews in view when he alludes to the golden calf (1:22–24).
> 2. The transcendent effect of the wrath of God is condemnation at the last judgment without partiality (2:1–11). Now Paul is thinking

more clearly of the Jews, who condemn pagan behavior (2:1), but he also has pagans in view: all are inexcusable (2:1).

2:12—3:8: The thesis that there is no partiality before God (2:11) must be defended against the Jew, insofar as the Jew appeals to the law (2:12–24), to circumcision, (2:25–29) or to God's promises (3:1–8).

1. The law establishes no preference before God (2:12–24). As a matter of principle, it is not hearing but doing that is decisive (2:12–13).

   (a) In the case of Gentiles (*hotan gar ethne* . . .), this means that they can keep the law and bear witness to it in a conflict of conscience. Judgment of a Gentile is reserved to God alone (2:14–16).

   (b) In the case of Jews (*ei de su Ioudaios* . . .), it means that they can boast of the law yet break it. For this reason, the Gentiles judge negatively about God (2:17–24).

2. Circumcision creates no preference before God (2:25–29). As a matter of principle, circumcision is of value only if the law is fulfilled.

   (a) In the case of Jews (*ean de parabates nomou es* . . .), this means that if the law is broken, circumcision is equivalent to being uncircumcised (2:25b).

   (b) In the case of Gentiles (*ean oun he akrobustia* . . .), it means that those who, while uncircumcised, keep the law will be judged like those who are circumcised; they will even condemn the Jew who disobeys the law in the last judgment (2:25–27).

   In a different sequence than in 2:12–24 there now follow foundational reasons that were touched on only briefly in v. 25. What is decisive with regard to a Jew is not outward circumcision but "circumcision of the heart" (2:26–29).

3. The promises of God are indeed an advantage, but this advantage is not based on human behavior. God is faithful, even if some were unfaithful. Yet it would be illegitimate to conclude that one may do evil in order to bring about good (3:1–8).

3:9–20: The thesis that all men are sinners can therefore be maintained and supported by reference to the law (3:10–18). The law established no preference but creates knowledge of the sin that is common to all.

The structural analysis shows that the treatments of the law and of circumcision are parallel to each other. The goal of the treatment is in each case to interpret a concept originally connected only with Jews in such a way that it no longer applies only to Jews. "Law" and "circumcision" are therefore used in a metaphorical sense. The "work of the law" is inscribed in the hearts (2:15). It is an inner law.

Circumcision is circumcision of hearts (*kardias*), an inner circumcision (2:29).[17] What takes place within is hidden: the revelation of secrets (*krupta*) in the last judgment (2:16) corresponds to the Jew in secret (*ho en to krupto Ioudaios*, 2:29). What is secret is accessible only to God. He will judge it (2:16); only he, not man, can assess it (2:29). In both contexts (2:14; 2:27) the term *physis*, "nature," also occurs. In each passage it is applied to Gentiles, who were not brought up in Judaism but nevertheless have the chance to do "on their own," without law and circumcision, what law and circumcision really intend. The parallels in structure and content suggest interpreting both passages along the same lines.[18] The point in each case is that concepts that were originally used in an ethnocentric way are redefined in a universalist manner.[19]

This result is not achieved by abstraction of common traits of Jews and Gentiles from a neutral perspective but through confrontation of the norm and the behavior of each group from the perspective of the other group. Paul first views the Gentiles from the perspective of the Jews, then the Jews from the perspective of the Gentiles.

In 2:12–16, Paul begins with statements of principle in two chief sentences, formulated antithetically, which are spoken completely from the perspective of Judaism: "For it is not the hearers of the law who are righteous before God, but (*alla*) the doers of the law who will be justified" (2:13). This is followed by a conditional clause with resultative or iterative sense, in which the behavior of the Gentiles is made

17. An alternative that is not this sharply present in Paul is often read in here—the idea that it is either a matter of (timeless) opposition of internal and external or one of (temporal) opposition of the old and new eons (cf. Käsemann, *An die Römer*, 70–71). For Paul, however, the "inner man" is one who "renews" himself. Spatial and temporal categories overlap here.

18. Of late, 2:12–16 is often related to Gentiles, and 2:25–29 is related to Christians; cf. Wilckens, *Der Brief an die Römer*, 133, 157; Käsemann, *An die Römer*, 60, 71. But Paul would then have had to work the transition out more clearly in order to be understood by a reader. The train of thought is rather as follows. Even Gentiles keep the law. But can this truly be said if they do not have themselves circumcised? In order to preserve for 2:12ff. the possibility of keeping the law without knowledge of the law, it is necessary to show that circumcision and fulfillment of the law are not simply identical.

19. This occurs in each instance through combination of Jewish ideas and those of popular philosophy. In Rom. 2:14–15, Paul makes use of Stoic ideas (*phusis, suneidesis, nomos agraphos*) and combines them with the Jewish-apocalyptic idea of judgment. (On the Stoic terms, cf. Bornkamm, "Gesetz und Natur.") In Rom. 2:25–29, he picks up the opposition of true human nature and socially measurable external existence—an idea that can also be found in Epictetus (cf. Fridrichsen, "Der wahre Jude")—and combines it with the Old Testament–Jewish theme of circumcision of the heart.

thematic (vv. 14–15).[20] A look forward toward the judgment concludes the section (v. 16).

In 2:17ff., on the contrary, Paul criticizes Jewish conduct from the viewpoint of the Gentiles. The Jews transgress even the law. For this reason, God is blasphemed among the Gentiles (v. 24). Transgression of the law makes circumcision worthless. This point is formulated in two conditional sentences (vv. 25b–26). A look toward the judgment, in which the Gentile will judge the law-breaking Jew, follows. Only after this (Rom. 2:28–29*) come the decisive formulations of principle, which define the "true Jew" in two antithetic main sentences:[21]

> For he is not a Jew who is one visibly, nor is that which is visible in the flesh circumcision, but [alla] he is a Jew who is one secretly, and circumcision is of the heart in the spirit, not the letter; his praise is not from men but from God.

The discovery of the hidden true Jew appears within the text as a result of the effect of the gentile critique of Jews in the present (v. 24) and as a result of the anticipated gentile critique in the future judgment (v. 25).

The apparently insignificant variation in structure—requirements in principle stand at the beginning or at the end—indicates a shift in perspective. First, gentile conduct is judged from the perspective of Jewish norms with—in contrast to Rom. 1:18ff.—a positive result. Fulfillment of the law can also be found among the Gentiles. Such fulfillment of the law among the Gentiles is presupposed in vv. 26–27. Conversely, this now sheds new light on Judaism. If noncircum-

---

20. The constantly renewed interpretation of *ethne* as gentile Christians (e.g., Flückiger, "Die Werke des Gesetzes") collapses on 2:14. It is true that in v. 14a*, *phusei* can out of necessity be related to the preceding words "But if the Gentiles, who do not have the law by nature [but then received it through the Christian proclamation] . . . " But the main clause " . . . they who do not have the law are a law to themselves" (v. 14b*), which follows, would then have to speak of those who *did* not *have* the law. As Christians they do possess and know the Old Testament.

21. Wilckens (*Der Brief an die Römer* 1:157) holds that "the true Jew in the sense of v. 28 is not to be found among the empirical Jews, for all these are sinners." With regard to Rom. 2:12–16, however, Wilckens does accept that Paul allows not only hypothetically —for the possibility of a "good" Gentile, even though for Paul all Gentiles are sinners. What was conceivable for Paul among the Gentiles must also be true of Jews. The separation of *sarx* and *pneuma*, to which allusion is made in Rom. 2:28–29, runs right through Israel (Gal. 4:29). Patriarchs like Abraham (Rom. 4:1ff.) and Isaac (Rom. 9:10– 13), prophets like Elijah (Rom. 11:1ff.), and even Moses as prototype of a convert (2 Cor. 3:13ff.) would seem to belong to the true Jews. In Rom. 3:3, Paul speaks only of some Jews who became disobedient. That "now" they are all disobedient (Rom. 11:31) is another issue—for Paul, a transitory state.

cision can be equivalent to circumcision, then the true circumcision cannot be the external circumcision. The true Jew is circumcised on the heart.

From the perspective of the other group, a picture of the model Gentile and the true Jew is sketched, in which the characteristics "law" and "circumcision" are interiorized. The good Gentile has the law within, and the true Jew is circumcised in an invisible manner. The confrontation of the two groups and their systems of norms leads to emancipation from socially measurable social characteristics. Inner law and circumcision of the heart remain in the realm of the secret (*krupta*).[22]

This is even more clear in the assessment of negative behavior. It is well known that people see in others precisely what they do not wish to admit in themselves. Paul formulates this principle as a general rule in Rom. 2:1–3. In 2:17–24 he illustrates this rule with the example of the Jew, proud of the law, who will not admit his lawbreaking conduct. Paul sees in the opposition between norm and conduct one of the roots of anti-Jewish prejudices among the Gentiles. "The name of God is blasphemed among the Gentiles because of you" (2:24).

Conversely, in 1:21ff., Paul depicts gentile conduct as it appears from the Jewish perspective. Here too it is clear that those involved assess their own behavior differently. They approve of it (1:32). Only one who is familiar with the demands of the true God knows that it is a matter of offenses that merit death.

Negative aspects that people do not notice, as well as their positive possibilities, are illumined from the perspective of the opposite group. It is certain that Paul is thinking of actual conduct in his description of the negative types of behavior, however conventionally they are depicted. Here he is not speaking only hypothetically. But may one conclude from this that he is also thinking of real instances with regard to the positive possibilities? Are the pious Gentile and the true Jew only hypothetical constructions?[23] In 1:18—3:21, Paul's theme is the universal guilt of human beings, not their hidden positive qualities.

---

22. Interiorizing the law and circumcision has precedents in Judaism. On circumcision of the heart, cf. Lev. 26:41; Deut. 10:16; 30:6; Jer. 4:4; 9:25; Ezek. 44:7, 9; *Jubilees* 1.23; 1QS V,5; 1QH 18,20; Philo *On the Migration of Abraham* 92; *On the Special Laws* 1.6.305; *Odes of Solomon* 11.1–3; Justin *Dialogue with Trypho* 114. The liberal Jew Ananias (Josephus *Jewish Antiquities* 20.41) stresses, as does Paul, that keeping the law is more important than circumcision; the more strict Galilean Eleazar (*Jewish Antiquities* 20.44) insists that one must not only read (*anaginoskein*) the laws but do (*poiein*) them.

23. So esp. Lietzmann (*An die Römer*, 40, 44). Kuss (*Der Römerbrief*, 70–71, 91–92) is more cautious. It is to be noted that Paul speaks of the positive conduct of the Gentiles

Nonetheless, we must suppose that Paul is thinking of real instances of hidden pious people among Jews and Gentiles. If the good Gentile of v. 14 were only a theoretical postulate, then the conflict of conscience in v. 15 would also be construed. As far as the secret Jew is concerned, Paul knows Abraham, at least, as a model believer—in the midst of the Old Testament.[24] But does he not then fall into a logical contradiction of his thesis that no one is just before God and that all are redeemed only through Christ? Three arguments are to be considered here.

First, the criteria of being a hidden pious man are in principle exempt from public measurement. They are *krupta* (secret). Only God, no human being, can decide whether they are present. But God's judgment occurs "through Christ." That someone achieves salvation while bypassing Christ is therefore not possible.[25]

Second, we must not imagine the hidden pious among Jews and Gentiles as justified by works. It is precisely the Gentile who fulfills the commandment that is affected by a conflict of conscience. He is not self-justified. And the Jew who allows himself to be circumcised in the heart is one who repents.[26]

Third, it is only when proper behavior is in principle possible that actual guilt can be charged. The hidden pious man, whom no human being can identify, is the bright background against which determinable guilt appears all the greater.

Thus far we have established that it becomes clear from the opposite social perspective that there are in the other human being "hidden" things that escape social measurement. They are relatively independent of the given system of social norms. Our further question is whether the "secrets of men" are unconscious to the individual himself. Or are they only inaccessible to the public, to other human beings? The answer to this question depends in large part on where the conflict of

---

in a main clause, not only in conditional clauses like 2:14 and 2:26: in 2:15, as in Rom. 1:25, *hoitines* introduces a main clause. Nor are the statements on the true Jew formulated conditionally (cf. 2:28–29).

24. Cambier ("Le jugement," 203) refers to this.

25. For Paul, Christ already has effects in Old Testament history; see 1 Cor. 10:1ff. God's definitive judgment on man does not bypass Christ; cf. Rom. 2:16.

26. Circumcision of the heart is repentance; cf. *The Book of Jubilees* 1.23: But after this they will return to me in all uprightness and with all of (their) heart and soul. And I shall cut off the foreskin of their heart and the foreskin of the heart of their descendants. And I shall create for them a holy spirit, and I shall purify them so that they will not turn away from following me from that day and forever (ET: O. S. Wintermute, *The Old Testament Pseudepigrapha*, ed. Charlesworth, 2:54).

conscience in 2:15 is located temporally. One possibility is to envision v. 15 as a parallel statement to v. 14. Just as the Gentiles now perform good works, so too does their conflict of conscience occur in the present. The present tense of *endeiknuntai* (v. 15) speaks in favor of this interpretation. Against it speaks the fact that the following v. 16 clearly speaks of the future day of judgment and seems on this interpretation to be appended without logical or grammatical connection, unless one inserts an intermediary thought or strikes the entire verse as a gloss.[27]

Another possibility consists in keeping the specification of time "on the day of judgment" (v. 15) in mind from the start.[28] On that day the Gentiles will bear witness to the existence of the law by their conflict of conscience. The present tense *endeiknuntai* would then be a logical future. This would correspond better to the overall context. In 2:12–16 Paul wishes to defend a thesis about the future judgment, that is, that God will judge without partiality. The future *krithesontai* (v. 12) and *dikaiothesontai* (v. 13) refer to the last judgment. The outlook toward the future in v. 16 is therefore in no way disruptive but consistent. In fact there are some arguments in favor of drawing v. 15 closer to v. 16:[29]

1. The conflict in conscience in v. 15 is a postdecisional conflict. Testimony, accusation, and defense refer to prior misconduct. It does not follow from this that the review takes place from the standpoint of the law, but it does follow that there is a structural similarity between conflict in conscience and retrospective judgment.

2. A clear shift in accent occurs between vv. 14 and 15, since the first point of departure is the possibility of fulfillment of the law (v. 14), whereas the conflict in conscience presupposes consciousness of transgression of the law.

3. In the conflict in conscience, there are witness, accuser, and defender present. But the judge is missing. In Philo (*On the Decalogue* 87), on the contrary, conscience is both accuser and judge. In Paul, a place is still waiting to be occupied in the trial. The court will not be complete until the last day.

27. Thus Bultmann, "Glossen im Römerbrief," 282–83. Against this, rightly, Saake, "Echtheitskritische Überlegungen."
28. Thus Käsemann, *An die Römer*, 62–63; and Wilckens, *Der Brief an die Römer*, 137.
29. The parallel in *Testament of Judah* 20 also speaks in favor of this. Here the conflict of conscience develops only in the eschatological judgment. Appealing to *Testament of Judah* 20, Agersnap (*Paulusstudier*, 101–36) understands the "works of the law" as completed works of the law which have left their traces within man. But the accusing thoughts also presuppose missing works of the law in Rom. 2:15.

The conflict of conscience refers to the day of judgment.[30] Yet the eschatological orientation of the conflict in conscience does not exclude its present aspect. If conscience is to appear as witness on the last day, it must be present and active even beforehand, since witnesses must be present at the events to which they testify. Conscience is therefore a present phenomenon like the law written in the heart, on the basis of which Gentiles can fulfill the law. They are unconscious of the fact that through law and conscience they are already confronted with the eschatological judge. The conflict of conscience depicted in v. 15 begins, therefore, in the present but has unconscious aspects that far exceed what the Gentile senses and knows. The uncovering of these "secrets of men" includes, among other things, a becoming conscious before the forum of God.[31]

That those addressed in Rom. 1:18—3:21 are not yet enlightened about themselves can be seen from the total context. The section begins with the words "For the wrath of God is revealed from heaven against all ungodliness and wickedness of men who by their wickedness suppress the truth . . ." (1:18). It concludes by establishing that knowledge and admission of guilt are accomplished by the law (3:20). Both statements include the idea that the addressee still lacks a complete consciousness of sin; otherwise there would be no need for a "revelation from heaven" in order to effect knowledge of sin. Consciousness of one's own guilt is, therefore, still lacking. Those addressed in part

30. Thus Käsemann (*An die Römer*, 63): "The process depicted in 15 cannot possibly remain without a final clarification and crisis, in which the judge who has until then remained concealed steps forward." It can hardly be said that in addition to the model "current concealment–eschatological revelation," there is also a model of "eschatological reversal"—the judgment turns prevailing conditions into their opposite. This is against Saake, "Echtheitskritische Überlegungen," 487–88.

31. This has been elaborated convincingly by Käsemann (*An die Römer*, 57–64). Käsemann speaks of the "secret day of judgment in our existence," under the "force of a judge still hidden from us," confronted with whom each individual will become conscious that "precisely within himself he is not his own master" (p. 62). Surely "apocalyptic is projected into anthropology" (p. 63) here. In view of this, I find incomprehensible the polemic against "psychological misunderstanding of this anthropology" in which no distinction is made between psychological state and its eschatological meaning. Where, then, is this eschatological meaning manifest? According to Käsemann, it is manifest in the fact that the psychological phenomena themselves pertain to the "secrets of man" and must still be deciphered (p. 63). But does this contradict the possibility of interpreting them psychologically? It would, of course, if one were to identify psychology with psychology of consciousness! But is there not also a psychology of the unconscious, which seeks to decipher what is hidden within man? A psychology aware that man is not master of his own house? A psychology that uncovers the force of the hidden judge? All of the exegetical observations that have just been cited could be accepted by such a psychodynamic interpretation of Rom. 2:15–16!

positively approve of the misconduct described by Paul (1:32) or condemn in others what they are unwilling to admit in themselves (Rom. 2:1–3, 17–23).

Thus, we can also find in Rom. 2:12–16 the three elements of thought that historically made possible discovery of an unconscious within man. First, God's omniscience is presupposed. There can be no doubt of the ability of the judge to bring to light even unconscious processes. Second, it is furthermore clear that "secrets" refers to inner processes. The thoughts within human beings which accuse and defend all revolve around what is secret. The third element, the limitation of human insight into oneself, is not directly formulated, but it is to be inferred from the context.

Beyond this, it has become clear that in chapter 2 of Romans the uncovering of what is "secret" is connected with the confrontation of two different systems of norms.

THE DISCLOSURE OF SECRETS THROUGH EARLY CHRISTIAN PROPHECY: 1 COR. 14:20–25

According to 1 Cor. 4:1–5 and Rom. 2:12–16, the "secrets" of men will be revealed only in the last judgment. In 1 Cor. 14:20–25, however, they are already disclosed in the present by early Christian prophets. The section contains some obscurities, which emerge as soon as the train of thought is sketched:

14:20: Paul begins with an *admonition*. The Corinthians should be perfect in understanding. Intelligible forms of speech are to be preferred to glossolalia.

14:21: The *biblical citation* (Isa. 28:11)[32] assesses glossolalia as the language of God, which nonetheless remains inefficacious among "this people."

---

32. It may be presumed that this citation of Isaiah has a prehistory. It is found in the Qumran community, in order to brandmark foes (1QH 2.18–19) and lying prophets (1QH 4.16) who seduce the people. The "strange tongue" in which they propagate their errors could concretely be the Greek language, which could have been widespread among the Hellenizing enemies of the Qumran community. These passages are scarcely thinking of speaking in tongues. The same is true of 1QIsᵃ, where—as in Paul, the masoretic text, and Aquila—Isa. 28:11 is presented in the first-person singular as a statement of God's (this against Harrisville, "Speaking in Tongues," 45). Since the citation played a role in the confrontations between conflicting Jewish currents, it is possible that even prior to Paul it was used to defend early Christian speaking in tongues against criticism (thus Sweet, "A Sign for Unbelievers," esp. 243–44). But this is not certain.

The abnormal special language has achieved nothing. Even then (*oud'*
houtos) the people do not listen.

14:22: The *conclusion* from the biblical citation is introduced by *hoste* and
states in two antithetic main clauses that

(*a*) speaking in tongues has a function with regard to unbelievers, not
believers;

(*b*) prophecy, on the contrary, has a function with regard to believers,
not unbelievers.

In this verse, the function of glossolalia is described as *einai eis semeion*,
that is, "to serve as a sign." In the statement on the function of
prophecy this specification is not explicitly repeated.

14:23–25: A *contrast example* is meant to support the assertion (*oun* is a
particle that leads the thought further). The two examples are
formulated in conditional sentences, the first as a rhetorical question,
the second as a declarative sentence.

(*a*) Speaking in tongues evokes an impression of madness (*mania*) on
the part of outsiders and unbelievers.

(*b*) Prophecy, on the contrary, discloses the secrets of the hearts of
unbelievers and outsiders—the sequence of the two terms is now
reversed—and leads to the confession that God is truly at work in
the community.

The crucial problem for interpreters is that the general conclusion
(v. 22) does not correspond to the illustrating examples in vv. 23–25.
The conclusion holds, first, that speaking in tongues is a sign for
unbelievers and, second, that prophecy is for believers. The illustrating
contrast example, however, says first that speaking in tongues scares
unbelievers away and, second, that prophecy has a positive effect on
unbelievers. Previous efforts to resolve this problem are not convincing.

In one such attempt, the concept of a sign has been understood in
the sense of a negative sign of warning.[33] Glossolalia is said to be
witness against unbelievers: they become hardened. In this fashion one
can harmonize the first instance of the example with the first part of
the conclusion, but not the second. Prophecy is certainly not a warning
sign directed against believers, intended to harden them. Prophecy has
a positive effect. The unity of the concept of *semeion* (sign) in v. 22 is
thus lost—apart from the fact that this notion of sign (sign = hardening
sign of warning) is not otherwise attested in Paul.

33. Thus Weiss (*Der 1. Korintherbrief*, 332–33), who sees clearly the difficulty that the
negative concept of sign does not fit prophecy. Stendahl (*Paul Among Jews and Gentiles*,
115–16) is of the opinion that "sign" in Paul never means something unambiguously
positive.

A second approach is to expand the concept of believers, so that the "believers" of v. 22 can be identified with the unbelievers of vv. 23–25. A believer is one who is on the road to faith.[34] In this way one harmonizes the second instance of the example with the second part of the conclusion. Prophecy has a positive effect on believers: it brings unbelievers to faith. But in doing this one burdens the concept of believers with an improbable ambiguity.

A third solution states that the general premises and the conclusion are not related as primary statement and illustration. On the contrary, v. 22 is to be understood as a rhetorical question, Is then speaking in tongues a sign for unbelievers? A negative answer to the question then follows: an unbeliever who comes into the assembly of the community is rather repelled by it. This interpretation is logically satisfying but philologically untenable. The contrast example is not attached by an adversative particle, but by a *oun*, "therefore," which continues the train of thought.[35]

Our effort at interpretation is based on the consideration that Paul wishes to replace speaking in tongues in its social function with prophecy. We can therefore conclude from the function of prophecy to the function of speaking in tongues. Prophecy has two effects: it has a juridical function, when it convicts, judges, and reveals secrets, and it has a missionary function, when it leads to faith. The one who is convicted exclaims, "Truly, God is in you!" The second function is not the only decisive one, for prophecy exercises its function with regard both to unbelievers and to outsiders. The outsider is a participant in the liturgy. Theoretically, he could speak the Amen at the end of prayer (1 Cor. 14:16). He is therefore already on the road to faith. But something is still lacking—a sign for believers. A clear sign that enables recognition that this person has come to faith is missing. If he were to begin to speak in tongues or to understand them, that would be an

34. Thus Héring (*La première épître de Saint Paul aux Corinthiens*, 129): "ceux qui sont en train de devenir chrétien."

35. Johanson, "Tongues." In addition to the missing adversative particle, the following four points speak against this thesis, which is initially very appealing. First, apart from Gal. 4:16, *hoste* always introduces a conclusion, not a rhetorical question; see Rom. 7:4, 12; 13:2; 1 Cor. 3:7; 7:38; 2 Cor. 4:12; 5:16–17; Gal. 3:9; 4:7. Second, after a rhetorical question one would expect a declarative statement as rebuttal, but Paul continues with a rhetorical question (v. 23). Third, Johanson has to relate "this people" in the citation of Isaiah to the Christian church. But could Paul seriously assert that the Christian community does not hear God even through speaking in tongues—that, in other words, it does not hear at all? Fourth, if v. 22 were a rhetorical question, Paul would deny that prophecy is for believers, although in the entire chap. 14 he elaborates the positive function of prophecy for the community.

unambiguous indication to the Corinthians that he truly belongs to the community. Here Paul offers a new assessment: speaking in tongues is no sign for the community. Isaiah 28:11–12 attests rather that speaking in tongues is directed to people who do not wish to hear— thus, certainly not to the community. Prophecy, on the contrary, accomplishes what the Corinthians expect from speaking in tongues: it discloses the secrets of man. Prophecy can achieve a sure judgment about new entrants to the community. To this extent, it is a "sign for believers."

The following arguments also speak in favor of this interpretation. First, the interpretation of "sign" as equivalent to "sign enabling recognition" yields no conflict between the general premise (v. 22) and the contrast example. An unbeliever who comes is judged prophetically. If his innermost dimension is thus revealed, this is a far more reliable sign for the community than active or passive participation in ecstatic speech. Glossolalia, on the contrary, is a sign of demarcation and recognition toward those outside. But something that distinguishes from those outside need not be a sufficient criterion of belonging to the community.[36]

Second, Paul says not that glossolalia and prophecy are "signs" but that "they serve as signs" (eis semeion einai). There are in the Septuagint instructive parallels to this expression.[37] God places, for example, the rainbow as sign of his covenant: kai estai eis semeion diathekes ana meson emou kai tes ges ("it shall be a sign of the covenant between me and the earth," Gen. 9:14). Even here it is more a matter of juridical confirmation than of spectacular miracle. The concept of semeion as personal sign of recognition was not unknown in Corinth.[38] In 2 Cor. 12:12*, Paul formulates the Corinthians' expectations of him: they seek

36. According to Roberts ("A Sign"), glossolalia, as an ecstatic phenomenon, was for outsiders a divine manifestation. "Sign," he holds, here means "a sign of divine or spiritual activity" (p. 200). But in Paul the accent does not lie on this. That glossolalia is directed toward outsiders is something Paul took from the citation. His intention is to show that it is not directed toward the community.

37. The expression einai eis semeion occurs in Gen. 9:13; Exod. 13:16; Isa. 19:20; 55:13; and Ezek. 20:20; there it means a sign of remembrance or a witness. The function of recognition emerges most clearly in Ezek. 20:20: the Sabbaths are to be a sign "between me and you, that you may know that I the Lord am your God." Comparable expressions (a verb plus eis semeion) are found in Gen. 1:14; Num. 17:3; Deut. 6:8; 11:18; Josh. 4:6. The value of the sign as witness, not the miraculous dimension, is always stressed. Semeion can also mean "password" (Josephus Antiquities 19.54).

38. That semeion in the New Testament can mean "sign of recognition" is shown by Luke 2:12; Matt. 26:48; and 2 Thess. 3:17. The idea of miracle is of course not excluded by this; it is a miracle when the secret thoughts of a new arrival's heart are disclosed and that individual comes to faith.

in him the "signs [*semeia*] of the apostle." These *semeia* surely consist in miracles; even prophecy, after all, is a miracle. But their function is identification of the office, legitimation of the person.

Third, in some places in the Acts of the Apostles, glossolalia has precisely the function that, according to our conjecture, was attributed to it in Corinth. Speaking in tongues is a sign that even Gentiles have the Spirit and can be accepted fully into the community (Acts 10:45–46; 11:15). This ability distinguishes from the community the disciples of John in Ephesus, who stand close to the Christians (Acts 19:1–7).

From all this we conclude that the early Christian prophets' disclosure of secrets stood as a sign of recognition for the community.[39] Our guiding question, however, is whether the *krupta tes kardias* (secrets of the heart) include unconscious contents. We must again test to see if the three conceptual elements that made disclosure of the unconscious historically possible are present. First, it is beyond doubt that God's knowledge of the heart is presupposed. It is only conferred upon the early Christian prophets. They enact already what God will do on the last day. They probe man even into the hidden recesses of his heart. Because they enjoy this divine power, the new entrants can exclaim that "God is truly among you." Second, it is beyond question that it is a matter of interior content. What comes to light is what is hidden in the heart. This could of course include the hidden remembrance of past deeds, which have been forgotten or "repressed." The juridical concepts *elegchein* and *anakrinein* (convict and judge) do not refer arbitrarily to content of any sort but to what one would like to conceal from the public. It is difficult to judge whether, third, a limited insight of man into himself is also presupposed. If the interpretation proposed above is correct, prophecy reveals not only hidden individual details[40] but the situation of an individual before God. The individual's faith

39. In *To the Philadelphians* 7.1–2, Ignatius offers an example of the revelation of secrets through the Spirit. "The spirit . . . tests secret things [*ta krupta elegchei*]. I cried out while I was with you, I spoke with a great voice,—with God's own voice,—'Give heed to the bishop, and to the presbytery and deacons.' But some suspected me of saying this because I had previous knowledge of the division of some persons: but he in whom I am bound is my witness that I had no knowledge of this from any human being" (ET: Kirsopp Lake, *The Apostolic Fathers*, vol. 1 of 2 vols. [LCL, 1912], 245, 247). Here too the Spirit reveals whether believers really belong to the community. It is not concrete details that are disclosed but Christians' "state of faith."

40. Gunkel (*Die Wirkungen des heiligen Geistes*, 24), Weinel (*Die Wirkungen des Geistes*, 183), and Dautzenberg (*Urchristliche Prophetie*, 247ff.) think much more concretely of skill at reading minds. Paul certainly means more than this, even if he does not exclude such paranormal skill.

and unbelief come to light. But how could the unbelieving visitor to
the community already be conscious of what is disclosed in this regard?
It is only through the community that such an unbeliever is confronted
with God. If our interpretation of prophecy as a sign of recognition
for the community is correct, it must also disclose unconscious contents.

Two supplementary observations point in the same direction. First,
ta krupta tes kardias is an abbreviated formula for what is said in 1 Cor.
4:5. In that passage, the "things hidden in darkness" and the "purposes
of the heart" are placed in parallel to each other. The expression
"secrets of the heart" (1 Cor. 14:25*) combines both elements of the
sentence. Since 1 Cor. 4:5 thinks of unconscious elements, they cannot
be excluded as far as 1 Cor. 14:25 is concerned. Of course it cannot
be asserted with certitude either; after all, the two passages are separated
from each other by several chapters.

The second observation is based on the immediate context, the
confrontation with Corinthian glossolalia. As we shall see later,
glossolalia can be interpreted as the language of the unconscious, which
becomes capable of consciousness through interpretation. It follows
from Paul's statement that "he who prophesies is greater than he who
speaks in tongues, unless some one interprets, so that the church may
be edified" (1 Cor. 14:5) that, taken together, speaking in tongues and
interpretation are of equal value to prophecy. This suggests the
conclusion that if interpretation of speaking in tongues is making the
unconscious conscious, then prophecy can also be understood as making
the unconscious conscious.[41] Yet this conclusion is not compelling. It
is not possible to conclude with certitude from the equal value of two
phenomena to their equivalence.

Thus the idea of the unconscious cannot be postulated for 1 Cor.
14:25 with the same certitude as for the texts previously discussed.
There is, however, a certain probability that the "secrets of the heart"
also include unconscious contents, which are brought into the light of
day by prophecy, against the will of those concerned.

An important difference stands out when the three texts are viewed
in retrospect. Where Paul speaks of the disclosure of secrets with
regard to Gentiles and unbelievers, he clearly allows for a conflict

41. Paralleling speaking in tongues and prophecy finds support in Irenaeus (*Adversus
haereses* 5.6.1): "In like manner we do also hear many brethren in the Church, who
possess prophetic gifts, and who through the Spirit speak all kinds of languages, and
bring to light for the general benefit the hidden things of men, and declare the mysteries
of God" (ET: Alexander Roberts and James Donaldson, ANF 1:531). Here the prophetic
gift includes glossolalia and disclosure of what is hidden.

between unconscious contents and normative standards. With regard to himself, however, he exudes the certainty that he is beyond this conflict in fact though not in principle (1 Cor. 4:1–5). Had he achieved a new "peace" with himself? What are the new accents as far as he is concerned? In order to determine this, we must interpret his statements against the background of the tradition.

Chapter 6

Tradition Analysis: Divine Omniscience and Human Unconscious

Belief in the omniscient God is a historical presupposition of discovery of the unconscious. Such belief is older than the Old Testament. Even simple pastoral cultures believe in a highest God of heaven who sees all human actions by virtue of his luminous nature and punishes human misdeeds with meteorological means—thunder, lightning, storms, floods, and drought. Raffaele Pettazoni has demonstrated the existence of this type of omniscient God among the Egyptians, Babylonians, Phoenicians, Hittites, Persians, and Greeks, as well as in India, China, Africa, and America.[1] Yahweh is a variant of this type of deity. His monotheistic revolution consists in the fact that he imposed himself as omniscient God against all other gods.

The path from the idea of the omniscient God to the disclosure of the human unconscious is long. It presupposes three steps. God's omniscience must (a) be confronted with the limited insight of human beings. It must (b) be expanded to the processes within human beings; in fact, inner human motives must appear as the most important object of divine omniscience. The decisive step to the disclosure of unconscious motives within human beings then (c) consists in transposing the confrontation between the omniscience of God and the limited insight of man into the human interior and interpreting that confrontation as an intrapsychical conflict.

DIVINE OMNISCIENCE AND LIMITED HUMAN SELF-KNOWLEDGE

Confrontation of divine omniscience with limited human self-insight is found long before Paul. The place to start is with a phenomenon

---

1. Pettazoni, *The All-Knowing God.*

widespread in the history of religion—sin committed unknowingly. In the ancient east, it is found among the Hittites, Babylonians, and Assyrians even more emphatically than it is in the Old Testament.

In a Hittite prayer, a seriously ill man begs for help. He insists on his innocence and claims that he has never transgressed a commandment of his god. Nonetheless, he is sick. He therefore prays to the god,[2]

> [Now] may my god freely open his heart and his soul and t[ell] me my sins, so that I may know them. May my god either speak to me in a dream—indeed, may my god open his heart to me [and] tell [me] my [sin]s, so that I may know them—or may a prophetess speak to me or may a seer of the sun god tell me (my sins) from (inspecting) a liver. Indeed, may my god freely open his heart and his soul and tell me my sins, that I may know them. [And] do you, my god, bestow upon me new [health] and [stren]gth!

The text seems practically to demand a psychological interpretation. The man who is praying knows that he could have sinned unconsciously, and hopes to obtain information about his unconscious sin from a dream (or from another revelation). But caution is in order with regard to such interpretations. That the text is concerned with "repressed sins" that reveal themselves in a dream is not excluded—but it could simply be a matter of unintentional objective violations of sacred norms. A later Sumerian "lament for every god to console the heart" makes clear how external these unknown offenses could be. The decisive point is that they were not intended. Whether an unconscious intention was involved lies outside the range of vision:[3]

> The sin which I committed I do not know,
> the omissions which I committed I do not know,
> the abomination which I ate I do not know,
> the abomination on which I stepped I do not know.

This statement is then generalized. In principle, man is poorly informed of his actions:[4]

> Men are deaf, and know nothing;
> men, as many as bear names, know nothing;
> they do not know if they dissipate or do good.

2. Cited according to Beyerlin, ed., *Near Eastern Religious Texts*, 169.
3. Falkenstein and von Soden, *Sumerische und akkadische Hymnen und Gebete*, no. 45, p. 226.
4. Ibid., 227. Jastrow (*Die Religion Babyloniens und Assyriens* 2.1:92) sees the function of the frequent allusions in Babylonian prayers to "unknown sins" in suppressing doubt about the justice of the gods.

"Sins of error" can be the fortuitous touching of an unclean object one had not noted, but they can also be deeply rooted within one. Thus, in an Akkadian penetential psalm, inner motivation—wrath—is included in the confession of guilt:[5]

In the wrath of my heart I denounced your divinity; again and again I committed conscious and unconscious sin.

The conception of such sins of error could be pursued further. I refer here only to atonement inscriptions from Asia Minor,[6] and also to Oedipus, the classical example that one can fall into serious guilt unintentionally. It is worth reflecting on the fact that Oedipus could become the model for shedding light on the modern unconscious.

Like its environment in the ancient east, the Old Testament is also familiar with the idea of unconscious sins. The Septuagint speaks of *hamartanein akousios* (Lev. 4:2). At issue are those sins that can be atoned for by a sin offering (Lev. 4:1–5, 13; Num. 15:22–29). It is astonishing how seldom the idea is found in the Psalms. There is an exception in Ps. 19:12:

But who can discern his errors?
Clear thou me from hidden faults.

Is this connected with the fact that the Old Testament believers lived in the certitude of knowing the will of God? That they were able to distinguish good and evil (Gen. 3:22)? The entire Book of Job can be read as a protest against the imputation of unconscious sins. And yet, the Old Testament also knows that one can be in the wrong without knowing it. Examples are Prov. 21:2 and Jer. 17:9* LXX:

Every way of a man is right in his own eyes,
but the Lord weighs the heart.

The heart is deep beyond all things,
and it is human.[7]
Who can know it?
I the Lord try the hearts, and prove the reins,
to give to every one according to his ways.

---

5. Falkenstein and von Soden, *Sumerische und akkadische Hymnen und Gebete*, no. 19, p. 173.
6. Cf. Steinleitner, *Die Beichte*, regarding sin *(ex) eidoton kai me eidoton* (no. 11) and sin *kat' agnoian* (no. 14).
7. Actually "feminine," for here *anthropos* is feminine, and related to *kardia*.

Here divine omniscience and limited human self-knowledge are clearly confronted with each other. But it is a conflict between God and man, not an intrapsychic conflict, in which the former conflict results.

THE EXTENSION OF GOD'S OMNISCIENCE INTO THE INTERIOR

Logically, the idea that the Deity knows everything implies that he also probes the human interior. We must, however, be clear as to how disputed the idea of omniscience was even where we find assertions of omniscience. Socrates, for example, affirmed God's omniscience but emphasized that his opinion deviated from the view of the crowd. He was consistent enough to include in this omniscience human thoughts.[8] The Old Testament cites the fool and the sinner who ask how God can see through clouds (Job 22:13–14) and in darkness (Sir. 23:18–20). Omniscience was understood in a comprehensive fashion only gradually.[9] Four objects of divine omniscience are mentioned: "everything," "secrets," the future, and the "heart."

1. Linguistic reference to the God who knows *everything* occurs relatively seldom in the Old Testament and in early Christian literature. According to 2 Sam. 14:20, the angel of God knows "all things that are on the earth." God knew everything before he created it (Sir. 23:20); he looks upon everything,[10] knows everything (Bar. 3:32), sees everything (Job 34:23 LXX), observes everything (2 Macc. 9:5; 12:22; 15:2). Everything is known to him.[11] References in early Christianity are scarce. God knows everything (1 John 3:20) in advance.[12] Everything is near him and before him.[13] Only after the New Testament period does the omniscience of God become a fixed theological theme—for

8. Cf. Xenophon *Memorabilia* 1.1.19: "For, like most men, indeed, he believed that the gods are heedful of mankind, but with an important difference; for whereas they do not believe in the omniscience of the gods, Socrates thought that they know all things, our words and deeds and secret purposes; that they are present everywhere, and grant signs to men of all that concerns man" (ET: E. C. Marchant *Xenophon*, vol. 4 of 7 vols. [LCL, 1923], 13). Cf. also 1.4.17.

9. Cf. Pettazoni, *The All-Knowing God*, 97–114; and Hempel, *Gott und Mensch im Alten Testament*, 168–73. According to these works, the conception of a knowledge of God that penetrates everything is found primarily in the wisdom literature, which in turn is rooted in ancient eastern traditions.

10. Sir. 15:18; Philo *On the Creation* 69.

11. Philo *On Dreams* 1.87.

12. *The Shepherd of Hermas: Mandates* 4.3.4.

13. *1 Clement* 27.3.6.

example, in Clement of Alexandria (*Stromata* 7.2.5), who speaks of
God as "seeing all things, hearing all things, knowing all things."[14]
The relatively late emergence of linguistic reference to the God who
knows "everything" may be due to its having penetrated from Greek
tradition into the Jewish-Christian texts.[15] As early as Homer, the
gods are said to know "everything,"[16] although in fact they often know
little. Xenophanes defines his monotheistic God as the one "who sees
and hears everything."[17] Zeus is the all-seer (*pantoptes*).[18]

2. What is *secret* appears much more frequently in the Old Testament–
Jewish tradition as the object of divine omniscience. As a rule, this is
a matter of hidden human deeds. Only in a few cases are inner
processes envisioned. The "secret" is what is inaccessible to the public.
Thus the "secret sins" in Josephus (*Jewish War* 5.402) are theft, assault,
and adultery.[19] In contradistinction to human beings, God also sees
and reveals what is secret. Deuteronomy 29:29 formulates it as a
principle: "The secret things belong to the Lord our God; but the
things that are revealed belong to us and to our children." This
conception also is to be found most frequently in late writings.[20] It
occurs in the New Testament (Rom. 2:16; 1 Cor. 4:5; 14:25) and
probably stands behind the Synoptic logion (Mark 4:22) that states,
"For there is nothing hid, except to be made manifest; nor is anything
secret, except to come to light." It is noteworthy that the secret deed
is not always evaluated negatively: what is "secret" is usually a matter
of actions that shy away from the light of publicity. The Sermon on

14. ET: Mr. Wilson, ANF 2:524.
15. Cf. the survey in Pettazoni, *The All-Knowing God*, 145–62.
16. *Odyssey* 4.379, 468, 12.139–40; *Iliad* 2.485.
17. Fragment 24 (Diogenes Laertius 9.19).
18. Aeschylus *Supplices* 139, *Eumenides* 1045; Sophocles *Antigone* 184. In Jewish
literature, this attribute of God first occurs in 2 Macc. 9:5 (cf. 7:35); here, as in other
texts where *ta panta* is the object of divine omniscience, its presence is probably due to
Hellenistic influence.
19. ET: H. Thackeray, *Josephus*, vol. 3 of 8 vols. (LCL, 1928), 327. Epictetus (*Discourses*
3.22.14–15) designates as *ta krupsonta* what is committed behind closed doors, while the
Cynic who lives in the open has only his sense of shame as protective wall between
himself and the public.
20. See Jer. 16:17; 30:4 LXX; Susanna 42 (Theod.) (God is *ho ton krupton gnostes*);
and Sir. 1:30 (God reveals *ta krupta sou*). Cf. Sir. 16:17; 17:15, 20; 39:19; 42:19; *Epistle
of Aristeas* 132; *1 Enoch* 9.5; cf. 9.11; 2 Macc. 12:41; Josephus *On the Jewish War* 5.413,
Jewish Antiquities 9.3; Philo *On the Cherubim* 16–17, *On the Special Laws* 3.52. The following
early Christian texts should be mentioned: Rom. 2:16; 1 Cor. 4:5; 14:25; Polycarp *To
the Philippians* 4.3; Ignatius *Letter to the Philadelphians* 7.1. A nonbiblical reference is
Dionysius of Halicarnassus *Antiquitates Romanae* 10.10.2: providence brings to light *ta
kekrummena bouleumata*. But something different is meant by this.

the Mount, on the contrary, advises one to give alms, to pray, and to
fast "in secret" (Matt. 6:4, 6, 18): good works also occur in secret.

3. God's omniscience extends not only into hidden regions but also
into hidden times, namely, the future. While what is secret could also
be known by human beings, only God knows the *future*. Here human
beings reach an insuperable barrier to their knowledge. In many texts,
advance knowledge of the future is placed next to knowledge of the
interior and secret. Can one conclude from this that what is interior
and secret is just as inaccessible as the future? More than an associative
connection cannot be demonstrated. Susanna, calumniated, calls out
(Sus. 42–43):

> O eternal God, who dost discern what is secret, who art aware of all
> things before they come to be, thou knowest that these men have borne
> false witness against me.

According to Sir. 42:18–20, God knows past and future and probes
the heart. According to Philo (*On Dreams* 1.90–91), God sees all things,
"even those which are perpetrated invisibly in the recesses of the
understanding. . . . Nothing is withdrawn from His sight, but . . . all
things are ever known and manifest to Him, not only those which
have been done already, but the far greater body of those which are
but contemplated in the future.[21] In the following citations, knowledge
of the future and probing of the interior are juxtaposed in a comparable
way:

> He not only sees the acts that are done, but clearly knows even the
> thoughts whence those acts are to come.[22]

> But not so are sinners and criminals, who love (to spend) the day in
> sharing their sin.[23]

> Hast not thou, O Lord, examined the heart of all generations before
> thou formedst the world?[24]

> For the Lord knows the heart, and knowing all things beforehand he
> knew the weakness of man.[25]

21. ET: G. H. Whitaker, *Philo*, vol. 5 of 10 vols. (LCL, 1934), 343, 345.
22. Josephus *Jewish Antiquities* 6.263; ET: H. Thackeray and R. Marcus, *Josephus*, vol.
5 of 8 vols. (LCL, 1934), 297.
23. *Psalms of Solomon* 14.5; ET: R. B. Wright, *The Old Testament Pseudepigrapha*, ed.
Charlesworth, 2:663.
24. *Biblical Antiquities* 50.4; ET: James, *The Biblical Antiquities of Philo*, 215.
25. *The Shepherd of Hermas: Mandates* 4.3.4; ET: Kirsopp Lake, *The Apostolic Fathers*,
vol. 1 of 2 vols. (LCL, 1912), 85.

For he has knowledge of all things beforehand, and knows the things in our hearts.[26]

Of course, the concept of the unconscious is not present in such texts. It is sensed. God can foresee thoughts man does not even know, because they have not yet "risen in his heart." Then God would also know thoughts that have not yet entered human consciousness. Yet this is never said explicitly. Whether the knowledge of inner thoughts is concerned with future intentions or with plans that already exist usually remains an open question.

4. God's omniscience extends above all to the human *heart*. This idea occurs relatively early. In connection with the anointing of David, when Samuel sees the tall Eliab, God says to Samuel (1 Sam. 16:7):

Do not look on his appearance or on the height of his stature, because I have rejected him; for the Lord sees not as man sees; man looks on the outward appearance, but the Lord looks on the heart.

Comparable formulations are found frequently in the Old Testament, Judaism, and early Christianity.[27] The conception of God who tries hearts and loins is well known. This must be a characteristic trait of the biblical tradition, for early Christianity developed in this regard a new title for God, *kardiognostes*, "knower of the heart," which up to now is not known outside Christian sources.[28] The new word indicates a new experience or at least a characteristic experience. The idea that a deity searches the human heart is not new; it is also attested outside the biblical writings.[29] What is new is that this is the sole God, to whom man is delivered everywhere. As a psalm (Ps. 139:1–2, 5, 7) makes clear, no other deity relativizes his power:

26. *2 Clement* 9.9; ET: Lake, *The Apostolic Fathers* 1:143.
27. 1 Kings 8:39; Ps. 26:2; 44:22; 94:11; 139:23; Prov. 15:11; Jer. 17:9–10; 20:12; Wis. 1:6; Sir. 42:18–20; *Psalms of Solomon* 14.6 (17.25); *Biblical Antiquities* 22.7; 50.4; 1QM 16.15; 1QH 12.34; 18.24; Luke 16:15; Rom. 8:27; 1 Thess. 2:4; Heb. 4:12; 1 John 3:20; *2 Clement* 9.9.
28. Acts 1:24; 15:8; *The Shepherd of Hermas: Mandates* 4.34; *Acts of Paul and Thekla* 24; *Acts of Thaddaeus* 3 (here predicated of Christ); *Didascalia* 7, 15, 18, 24; Clement of Alexandria *Stromata* 14.96.4; *Pseudoclementine Homilies* 4.13; *Constitutiones Apostolorum* 2.24.6; 3.7.8; 6.12.4; 8.5.6. Cf., however, already *Biblical Antiquities* 22.7 and 50.4!
29. Cf. Pettazoni, *The All-Knowing God.* References to the gods' knowledge of the heart may be found for Thot (p. 51), Enlil (p. 77), the Hittite sun god (p. 115), and Tezcatlipoca (p. 409). With regard to Zeus, cf. Archilochus (*Fragment* 13): "Thus Zeus perfects retribution! Completely different from man, for the god never punishes an individual deed in violent rage. No one who plans secret disorder in his heart remains hidden long; time eventually exposes him." However, this passage need not be interpreted

> O Lord, thou hast searched me and known me!
> Thou knowest when I sit down and when I rise up;
> thou discernest my thoughts from afar. . . .
> Thou dost beset me behind and before,
> and layest thy hand upon me. . . .
> Whither shall I go from thy Spirit?
> Or whither shall I flee from thy presence?

When Paul attributes to the early Christian prophets a marvelous knowledge of the "secrets of the heart" (1 Cor. 14:25*), he is combining three traditions—that divine omniscience discloses secrets, that it searches the heart, and that it relates to the future. The relationship to the future is implied in the concept of prophet.

The decisive question is whether the presuppositions in the history of the tradition for the Pauline assertion imply that the "secrets of the heart" are inaccessible not only to the public but to the individual concerned as well. Where, before Paul, are "secrets" and the "heart" brought into close connection?

It is unmistakable that initially what is kept hidden in the heart is only inaccessible to the public. The "things hidden in my heart" (*Testaments of the Twelve Patriarchs, Reuben* 1.4)[30] are words that one hides in the heart (cf. Job 23:12; Ps. 118:11 LXX). The step toward uncovering the unconscious is undertaken where the interpersonal limit of understanding becomes an intrapersonal limit, where one stands over against oneself in as strange a manner as to a strange person, without projecting this strangeness outward as a mythical reality, but rather accepting it as part of oneself. Such transposition of interpersonal experiences within one can be observed well on the basis of other concepts: conscience is the interiorized "co-knower."[31] So we ask, then, where does the "hidden" become something internal? In this regard,

---

as referring to the god's knowledge of the heart; it may simply mean that what is planned within will at some time become outwardly discernible. A more certain reference is Theognis (375): Zeus "knows the intention and heart of every man." Epictetus (*Discourses* 1.14) develops this idea in a tract.

30. ET: H. C. Kee, *The Old Testament Pseudepigrapha*, ed. Charlesworth, 1:782.

31. Cf. Epictetus *Fragment* 97: "When we are children our parents deliver us to a paedagogue to take care on all occasions that we suffer no harm. But when we are become men, God delivers us to our innate conscience . . . to take care of us" (ET: Long, *The Discourses of Epictetus*, 425). In this spurious fragment of Epictetus it is clear that antiquity already saw the analogy between the interior and the exterior "guardian." That conscience is among other things the result of interiorizing of other people who know and examine us is still far from view. Conscience is considered innate. But it replaces the external guardian.

two stages of development are to be distinguished. First, there are statements about a current omniscience of God, which also includes the secrets of the heart. Second, there are eschatological statements about the judge of the last days, who will bring all things into the public light.

We begin with the noneschatological statements. In Ps. 44:20–21 LXX, the secrets of the heart (*krupsia tes kardias*) consist preponderantly in external actions, namely, in idolatry. But this naturally has an inner side:

> If we have forgotten the name of our God, and if we have spread out our hands to a strange god; shall not God search these things out? for he knows the secrets of the heart.

Something similar applies to Sir. 1:30. What is "secret" is associated with the "heart," and therefore refers to an inner reality, but this seems to be a matter of what is socially "secret":

> Do not exalt yourself lest you fall, and thus bring dishonor upon yourself. The Lord will reveal your secrets [*ta krupta sou*] and cast you down in the midst of the congregation, because you did not come in the fear of the Lord, and your heart was full of deceit.

The interiorization of what is "secret" is even more clear in the following text (Sir. 42:18–20*, Hebrew text):

> He searches the abyss, and the heart, and has insight into all their nakedness; for the Most High possesses knowledge; he looks at the coming events of the age. He makes known what has been and what is to be; he reveals the searching of hidden things. Knowledge of any sort is not lacking to him; nothing escapes him.

When the primeval flood (the *abyssos*) and the heart come to stand next to each other, each is as bottomless as the other; one could ask if the primeval flood has not here become a symbol of the unconscious depths of the human interior.[32] The interiorization of what is "secret" is also tangible in the *Letter of Aristeas* (132–33). Here God's omniscience

32. Cf. Prov. 15:11: "Sheol and Abaddon lie open before the Lord, how much more the hearts of men!" In *1 Clement* 20.5, the abyss is viewed as impenetrable; in 59.3, on the other hand, God is the one who searches the abyss. It need not be the case that the chaos of the id is envisioned everywhere that reference is made to the chaotic primeval flood. This thought is close, however, where the ancient authors themselves associate the primeval flood and the human heart. On this problematic, cf. Arndt and Schulz, "Individualpsychologische oder kollektivistische Interpretation?"

first relates to socially hidden deeds but is then extended to inner intentions and plans:

> (Eleazar) began first of all by demonstrating that God is one, that his power is shown in everything, every place being filled with his sovereignty, and that none of the things on earth which men do secretly are hidden from him, but rather that all the deeds of any man are manifest to him, as well as that which is to come to pass.[33]

What is said here in simple language appears in Philo (*On the Cherubim* 16–19) on a higher level of reflection. He comments on the law that a woman suspected of adultery is to be placed before God without head covering (Num. 5:18 LXX). For him, this ordinance becomes a symbol of the uncovering of the interior by the all-knowing God:

> Now words spoken openly and deeds done openly are known to all, but the inward thought which prompts them in either case is not known. We cannot tell whether it is wholesome and pure, or diseased and stained with manifold defilement. No merely created being is capable of discerning the hidden thought and motive. Only God can do so, and therefore Moses says "things hidden are known to the Lord God, but things manifest are known to the Creature" (Deut. xxix. 29). Now we see the cause why Reason, the priest and prophet, is bidden to set the soul "over against the Lord" with her head uncovered (Numb. v. 18), that is with the dominant principles, which constitute her head, laid bare, and the motives which she has cherished stripped of all their trappings, so that, being judged by the all-penetrating eye of God the incorruptible, she may either like counterfeit coinage have her lurking dissimulation revealed, or being innocent of all evil may, by appealing to the testimony of Him who alone can see the soul naked, wash away the charges brought against her.[34]

In some places, Philo even achieves formulations that approximate conceptual grasp of unconscious dimensions within the human being. In *On the Creation* 69, he transfers to the soul the idea that God sees everything without being seen himself. Here too the idea could initially be that the soul does perceive everything but is not perceived by other people:

> For the human mind evidently occupies a position in men precisely answering to that which the great Ruler occupies in all the world. It is

33. ET: R. J. H. Shutt, *The Old Testament Pseudepigrapha*, ed. Charlesworth, 2:21.
34. ET: F. H. Colson and G. H. Whitaker, *Philo*, vol. 2 (LCL, 1929), 19.

invisible while itself seeing all things, and while comprehending the substances of others, it is as to its own substance unperceived.[35]

It is unambiguously clear from another text (*On the Cherubim* 115), however, that Philo is also thinking of not knowing one's own soul. The idea of the context is that the soul, like everything else, is a creature of God and not our property. This shows itself in the fact that we can neither examine it completely nor search it completely:

> Even now in this life, we are the ruled [by the soul] rather than the rulers, known rather than knowing. The soul knows us, though we know it not; it lays on us commands, which we must fain obey, as a servant obeys his mistress.[36]

What is important is that here the consistent idea of creation makes possible the recognition that one is partially inaccessible to one's own self-knowledge—without tracing this being withdrawn from oneself back to mythical powers outside oneself.

The idea of divine omniscience received new impulses with the emergence of apocalypticism. Each individual had to render account of his deeds before the divine judge. There was always the possibility that things the individual had forgotten would come to light in the judgment. Expectation of judgment was at least a great incentive to self-examination—and thus also an occasion for sensing the limits of such self-examination. Yet this was clearly expressed only rarely. The Syrian text of the *Apocalypse of Baruch* (83.1–3) speaks in a very general fashion of the disclosure of what is "secret" in the last judgment:

> For the Most High will surely hasten his times, and he will certainly cause his periods to arrive. And he will surely judge those who are in his world, and will truly inquire into everything with regard to all their works which were sins. He will certainly investigate the secret thoughts and everything which is lying in the inner chambers of all their members which are in sin. And he will make them manifest in the presence of everyone with blame.[37]

The recognition that God judges the objective deeds of persons—independently of their subjective consciousness—is expressed even more clearly in the *Testaments of the Twelve Patriarchs, Judah* 20. These deeds are written on the breast of each individual:

35. ET: F. H. Colson and G. H. Whitaker, *Philo*, vol. 1 (LCL, 1929), 55.
36. ET: Colson and Whitaker, *Philo* 2:77.
37. ET: A. F. J. Klijn, *The Old Testament Pseudepigrapha*, ed. Charlesworth, 1:649.

So understand, my children, that two spirits await an opportunity with humanity: the spirit of truth and the spirit of error. In between is the conscience of the mind which inclines as it will. The things of truth and the things of error are written in the affections of man, each one of whom the Lord knows. There is no moment in which man's works can be concealed, because they are written on the heart in the Lord's sight. And the spirit of truth testifies to all things and brings all accusations. He who has sinned is consumed in his heart and cannot raise his head to face the judge.[38]

The human deeds objectively inscribed on the breastbone are attested by the "spirit of truth," not by the individual himself. This leaves the possibility that objective deeds might differ from one's subjective consciousness of them. In the text just cited, whether unconscious (repressed and forgotten) deeds also come to light remains an open question. In the *Testament of Abraham* 10 (recension B) this idea is expressed clearly. Abraham saw a woman led before the divine judge. The woman pled for mercy, but the judge turned the plea aside. He was unable to have mercy, since she had not had mercy on her daughter but rather killed her. The woman denied this. Then the judge called for the heavenly books in which all deeds are recorded. The "recording angel" opened the books,

> and sought out the sin of the woman's soul, and he found (it). And the judge said, "O wretched soul, how can you say that you have not committed murder? Did you not, after your husband's death, go and commit adultery with your daughter's husband and kill her?" And he charged her also with her other sins, including whatever she had done from her childhood. When the woman heard these things, she cried aloud, saying, "Woe is me, woe is me! Because I forgot all my sins which I committed in the world, but here they were not forgotten." Then they took her too and handed (her) over to the torturers.[39]

Here the idea that even our repressed deeds become revealed before the eschatological judge is expressed clearly. Judgment discloses the unconscious. This applies not only to deeds, but also to inner thoughts and motives. According to the Syrian text of the *Apocalypse of Baruch* (83.1–3), it is precisely "secret thoughts" that come to light in the judgment. Hebrews 4:12–13 emphatically invokes the all-revealing

38. ET: H. C. Kee, *The Old Testament Pseudepigrapha*, ed. Charlesworth, 1:800.
39. ET: E. P. Sanders, *The Old Testament Pseudepigrapha*, ed. Charlesworth, 1:900.

character of the divine judgment—not as a future event but as one that is already taking place in the present:

> For the word of God is living and active, sharper than any two-edged sword, piercing to the division of soul and spirit, of joints and marrow, and discerning the thoughts and intentions of the heart. And before him no creature is hidden, but all are open and laid bare to the eyes of him with whom we have to do.

The *Letter of Polycarp* 4.3 points in the same direction. Here it is said of God that

> [n]othing escapes him of reasonings or thoughts, or of "the secret things of the heart [*ti ton krupton tes kardias*]."[40]

The "secrets of the heart" have doubtless become an internal reality. The idea that what is "secret" is also hidden from the individual involved is close everywhere, but it is not expressed clearly.

THE CONFRONTATION BETWEEN CONSCIENCE AND SIN WITHIN HUMAN BEINGS

Discovery of the unconscious presupposes that the confrontation between divine omniscience and sin be transposed into the human interior. This happened in only one text prior to Paul. Interiorization of the conflict was made possible by acceptance of the concept of conscience. In Jewish literature, it occurs for the first time in Wis. 17:11, within a psychological interpretation of the "Egyptian darkness," which appears as a symbol of the unconscious. Here for the first time the idea of the unconscious is clearly expressed, though with the aid of biblical images rather than in abstract concepts. In Wis. 17:20–21, the Egyptian darkness is interpreted as an inner darkness which enveloped only the Egyptians:[41]

> For the whole world was illumined with brilliant light,
> and was engaged in unhindered work,
> while over those men alone heavy night was spread,
> an image of the darkness that was destined to receive them;
> but still heavier than darkness were they to themselves.

---

40. ET: Lake, *The Apostolic Fathers* 1:288–89.
41. On Wis. 17, see Reese, *Hellenistic Influence*, 21ff., 100–101, 102.

What oppressed the Egyptians was their "secret sins." According to Wis. 17:3, these sins led to the inner darkness with its plagues:

> For thinking that in their secret sins they were unobserved
> behind a dark curtain of forgetfulness,
> they were scattered, terribly alarmed,
> and appalled by specters.

In principle it would be possible to think of the public with regard to the "curtain of forgetfulness" (*lethes parakalumma*): not the sinners themselves but others had forgotten their misdeeds. But, first, there is a reference to secret sins (*epi krupsaiois hamartemasin*), precisely to deeds, in other words, which in any case were unknown to the public. Second, in Wis. 16:11 the concept of "forgetting" is related also to one's own consciousness (and not only to others'). Third, the context also speaks in favor of an inner boundary of forgetting. As Wis. 17:9–12 indicates, the external horrors are merely an occasion for internal turmoil:

> For even if nothing disturbing frightened them,
> yet, scared by the passing of beasts
>   and the hissing of serpents,
> they perished in trembling fear,
> refusing to look even at the air,
>   though it could nowhere be avoided.
> For wickedness is a cowardly thing,
>   condemned by its own testimony;
> distressed by conscience, it has
>   always exaggerated the difficulties.
> For fear is nothing but surrender
>   of the helps that come from reason.

If the terror ultimately comes from within, the "curtain of forgetfulness" must also represent an inner border—the border between conscious and forgotten contents. Breaching this boundary causes panic and chaos. There can be no doubt that this passage is speaking exactly of what in our language we call the unconscious—repressed contents, whose sudden breakthrough destabilizes the conscious order of life.

It should also be noted that the Egyptian darkness is simultaneously an image of the future night that will envelop all sinners (Wis. 17:20–21). The last judgment is foreshadowed in the Egyptian darkness. As in Paul, *suneidesis* (conscience) appears as precursor of the eschatological judgment. Thus Wisdom 17 is structurally related to the Pauline statements. Yet there is an important difference. Paul formulates with regard to himself, saying that he does not scrutinize himself fully. The author of Wisdom observes the limits of self-knowledge in others: he sees in the Egyptians the breakthrough of what has been repressed.

The analysis of the history of the tradition has shown that the "unconscious" is not a modern discovery. The idea of an unconscious region within the human is already approximately expressed in ancient texts. It results from specifically ancient presuppositions—belief in the omniscience of God, knowledge of the limitedness of human self-knowledge, and a growing consciousness of inner processes. These three elements of thought promoted human self-examination, especially where they were intensified by the expectation of an eschatological judgment that would reveal everything. It is therefore no coincidence that in Wisdom 17 and in Paul we find the idea of the unconscious clearly expressed in connection with an expectation of judgment, while prior to this we could usually demonstrate only the presence of individual elements of thought in which the idea of the unconscious was contained more implicitly. In this Paul goes beyond Wisdom 17. He not only notes unconscious guilt in others but also asserts with regard to himself that his own consciousness does not encompass all the depths of the human heart. Only the eschatological judgment will reveal everything.

In conclusion, we emphasize that the unconscious was discovered in antiquity in a completely different cognitive framework than in modernity. Where modernity speaks of an unconscious dimension within us, antiquity spoke of transsubjective powers that uncovered the unconscious; more precisely, it spoke of God's all-knowing and all-scrutinizing gaze where moderns attempt to analyze themselves. But antiquity was in a position to experience the unconscious as intrapsychic potential for conflict—especially where the confrontation between God and the human was transposed into the human interior by the concept of conscience.

Chapter 7

Psychological Analysis: The Unconscious

The discovery of the unconscious in modernity is closely connected with psychodynamic theories. It would seem appropriate to study its "discovery" in early Christianity, among other things, in the light of these theories. Yet precisely the phenomenon of the unconscious shows that it is necessary to connect different approaches from complementary perspectives. From the approach of learning theory, the way in which unconscious processes become conscious can be retraced to competing environmental conditions; from a psychodynamic approach, they can be retraced to an intrapsychic transformation. From a cognitive approach one will place in the center of the analysis human self-exploration before the all-knowing God. The restructuring of one's own self-perception opens the view to the unconscious.

ASPECTS OF THE "SECRETS WITHIN MAN" IN LEARNING THEORY

If we examine the texts that most clearly presuppose an unconscious dimension in human beings—the Pauline texts and Wisdom 17—we note that two social groups in competition with each other appear in all these texts. The discovery of the unconscious is probably connected with the competition of two systems of reference. Let us look at the most important texts.

In Rom. 2:12–16, 24–29, the confrontation between Jewish and gentile norms leads to the disclosure of what is hidden within man, whether it be disclosure of an unconscious guilt that manifests itself in a conflict of conscience, or disclosure of the true Jew and true Gentile, who have in secret interiorized circumcision and law. In each instance, what is "secret" is seen and postulated from the perspective of the other group. This section of Romans (1:18—3:21) could only have been formulated by someone who stood between the two groups, someone who could observe Jews with the eyes of Gentiles and Gentiles with the eyes of Jews.

Two different groups of reference also encounter each other in 1 Cor. 14:20–25: unbelievers come into the community assembly. The disclosure of the "secrets of the heart" occurs when early Christian prophets confront them with the Christian system of convictions and "convict and judge" them. What the newly arrived experience here is something they could not have said to themselves within the framework of their previous system of convictions. Their "secret" is revealed through their coming to stand between two groups.

In 1 Cor. 4:1–5, Paul sees himself confronted with the expectations of the Corinthians. We do not learn what the content of these expectations was. In any case, they did not correspond to Paul's standards. Paul knows that he is innocent by his own standards but does not exclude the possibility of unconscious guilt. Here too the confrontation with a deviant system of norms leads to recognition of a possible unconscious.

Prior to Paul, Wisdom 17 gives clear expression to a consciousness of unconscious guilt. This occurs through confrontation of Egyptians and Jews. The Jews live in light, the Egyptians in darkness of their own making. The Egyptians do not comprehend what implants anxiety in them, but the Jews see in all the factors which evoke fear the power of conscience, behind which God's judgment ultimately stands. The discovery of the unconscious again stands in connection with the competition of different systems of norms.

How is this connection between competing environmental conditions and the discovery of the unconscious to be interpreted from the perspective of learning theory? One who emerges from the network of inherited norms and is confronted with strange norms experiences stimuli and reinforcers for modes of behavior that played no role in one's previous system of norms, or were even "repressed," that is, superimposed with negative sanctions. In this way there are evoked within one forms of reaction that strong inhibitions previously opposed and that one was not at all accustomed to in oneself. Often the new tendency of reaction will not reach the stage of manifest behavior; it will remain at the level of impulse, drive, and fantasy. But if the tendencies of reaction that have been evoked are not completely suppressed, one will experience how something unknown erupts within one, something to which one can react in different ways. One can, for example, condemn it sharply. Or one can experience it as an enrichment of one's life, even as the disclosure of a hidden positive "germ" that was previously unable to unfold. Or one can push the manifest differences of norm systems aside as superficial variations, and sense and postulate behind them, for example, the "pious Gentile" or the "true Jew"—as Paul does in Rom. 2:12ff. Competing environmental conditions, that is, mutually exclusive stimuli, reinforcers, and models, can thus facilitate the emergence of "unconscious" modes of reaction. This is an experience each of us can have during a stay in a foreign country, where the unaccustomed environment can "reveal" unaccustomed aspects of ourselves.

But the competition of different cultural environmental stimuli does not explain everything. It is perhaps a necessary condition, but scarcely a sufficient one, for the disclosure of unconscious aspects within us. The confrontation of different cultures can also lead to heightened self-righteousness and self-defense, to, for example, the intolerant mobilization of received convictions. According to his own statements, this was the case with Paul. He had made more progress in Judaism than all his contemporaries, and had been zealous "for the traditions of my fathers" (Gal. 1:14), so that even as a Christian he could proudly assert that we "are Jews by birth and not Gentile sinners" (Gal. 2:15). It was only the gospel that enabled him to appropriate constructively the competition of different environmental conditions. How was that possible?

Paul formulates his decisive new insight in Gal. 2:16, among other places. The demarcation between Jew and Gentile, between the just and "sinners," is surpassed by the recognition that "a man is not justified by the works of the law but through faith in Jesus Christ" (Gal. 2:16). Expressed in the language of learning theory, this means that a new system of reinforcement, independent of the then current and competing systems of reinforcement, was introduced with the gospel; faith in Jesus "justifies" independently of specifically Jewish or gentile norms and creates what is for Paul the most positive conceivable consequence—eternal life.

We want to make clear what this means. In many respects, religions are interiorized continuations of the general social system of reinforcement. Where social controls do not suffice, religious convictions of divine reward and punishment assume control of human behavior.[1] In

1. Cf. the fragment of Critias that is critical of religion, in Diels, *Die Fragmente der Vorsokratiker*, vol. 2, Kritias, no. 25.

extended stretches of the history of religion, the "all-knowing god" is an instrument of social control: he oversees the valid norms and distributes reward and punishment corresponding to human behavior. In the early Christian message, on the contrary, an independence in principle of the religious reinforcement system from the social norms is asserted, not only in the sense that new norms are defined, but in the much more radical sense that even the transgressor of norms may hope for grace. Thus the gospel offers an unconditional reinforcement. Every social reinforcement system, in contrast, has only conditioned reinforcement to offer: one who behaves well will be rewarded, one who trangresses the norm will be punished. According to Paul, on the contrary, God justifies the godless (Rom. 4:5), and Paul places only one condition: one must accept the offer of unconditional positive reinforcement in faith. Thus the competition of Jewish and gentile systems of conviction is relativized by a new system of convictions.

The transformed attitude to the unconscious aspects of human life can then be explained as follows. Anyone exposed to different systems of norms will constantly experience that what is a "sin" according to one system is tolerated or even required by the other. Here there are always unconscious sins—according to the other system of reference. But if there emerges in this situation the belief that the true system of norms is identical with none of the systems of reference, then the possibility of unconscious sin becomes conscious in a much more foundational sense. This is especially true if the new system of norms is experienced not as threat but rather as "gospel," as acquittal, reconciliation, and acceptance.

What is decisive is therefore not simply the competition of two learning environments. What is decisive is how an individual appropriates the competition of different learning conditions on the basis of inner transformation. Before we interpret this inner transformation psychodynamically, the distinctive characteristic of interpretation of the unconscious on the basis of learning theory should be emphasized by way of conclusion. According to learning theories, the unconscious emerges less from inner conflict between nature and culture—as all psychodynamic approaches hold—than from conflict between different culturally conditioned and externally elicited tendencies to reaction, not all of which come to bear. The more variegated the learning environment is, the greater are the possibilities of competing behavior tendencies. The more pluralistic the culture is, the greater the sphere of what is not actualized, of what is "repressed." It would then not— or not only—be strict cultural prohibitions that lead to processes of repression. Precisely differentiated cultures with competing value systems would promote the consciousness that there exist in human life unrealized "unconscious" elements of both positive and negative sorts. The experience of the unconscious, and even the unconscious itself, would then be historically conditioned. Its discovery would be tied to pluralistic cultures. Before modern times, Roman-Hellenistic antiquity was the first truly pluralistic culture. Paul occupied a special place in this pluralism, for he stood on the boundary of two cultures. According to his origin, he is a Jew; but according to his task, missionary to the Gentiles. We probably owe to this boundary position of Paul one of the first conceptual formulations of the "unconscious" within us. Something similar may be true of Augustine.

PSYCHODYNAMIC ASPECTS OF THE "SECRET WITHIN MAN"

From a psychodynamic perspective, the unconscious is the result of a conflict between internal tribunals and drives. For the unconscious to become conscious presupposes an internal transformation of the individual—that the opposed tribunals of the id and the superego or of the ego and its shadow draw closer together. Only then can contents opposed to the norm be perceived. According to the psychodynamic conception, internal processes of transformation are reflected in dreams, sagas, and religious symbols. Changes in the symbolic world therefore permit us to conclude to internal transformation. This is especially the case when there are references in the texts themselves to a parallelism between occurrences in the symbolic world and those within.

Two parallel tendencies can be seen in the Pauline symbolic world: (a) Christ assumes the role of the heavenly judge. Divine predicates—for example, God's knowledge of the heart—are transferred to him. (b) At the same time, Christians are also occasionally mentioned as the agents of divine judgment. Thus early Christian prophets also have at their disposal the gift of divine knowledge of the heart. Both events can be interpreted as a homology: both represent a restructuring of the superego. The superego receives accepting traits; the ego participates in its competence. In both cases the objects of judgment become agents of judgment.

Christ as Agent of Judgment

Expectation that messianic figures appear in the role of the eschatological judge was available to Paul from his tradition.[2] What is new in early

2. In the similitudes of *1 Enoch* a chosen eschatological judge gathers the elect and

Christianity is that a condemned man assumes the role of judge. Must not the role of the judge of the world change with this development? Can the expectation of judgment continue as it was before? Despite all the traditional statements (often juxtaposed without being harmonized), new accents can be found in Paul: for him Christ has chiefly saving and revealing functions in the last judgment. A penal judgment of sinners is not attributed to him.[3] It is found only in 2 Thess. 1:7ff., in a Pauline letter whose authenticity is seriously disputed.

Paul consistently holds to the conception that all are really subject to the wrath of God, a conception in which "wrath of God" means the definitive condemnation in the judgment. Christ has the function of saving from this judgment. Paul stands on ancient Christian tradition when, in 1 Thess. 1:9–10, he reminds the Thessalonians of their pre-Christian days,[4]

> how you turned to God from idols, to serve a living and true God, and to wait for his Son from heaven, whom he raised from the dead, Jesus who delivers us from the wrath to come.

Paul also mentions the judgment elsewhere in thanksgivings, wishes of prayer, and praises[5]—yet always in the certitude that Christ "has delivered [the community] from the present evil age" (Gal. 1:4*) and will preserve it until the final judgment (cf., e.g., 1 Cor. 1:7–9). This certitude, which is expressed in traditional formulations, is of course called into question by concrete transgressions in the Christian communities. Is Christ even with regard to such transgressions the merciful judge who saves from the wrath of God?

Twice Paul speaks of the judgment of Christ in view of concrete transgressions.[6] At the Lord's Supper, some Corinthians exhibit socially

destroys the sinners (51.3; 62.1ff; 69.27). Comparable things are said of the Messiah (cf. 4 Ezra 12.32–33; Psalms of Solomon 17.24ff.).

3. Paul knows the statement of judgment as a "theme of polemic against enemies" (cf. Synofzik, Gerichts- und Vergeltungsaussagen, 31–38). But in none of these threats of judgment is Christ named as judge; cf. Rom. 3:8; 1 Cor. 3:17; 14:38; 2 Cor. 11:15, Gal. 5:10; Phil. 1:28; 3:19; 1 Thess. 2:16. Usually an explicit agent is not mentioned at all. Only in 1 Cor. 3:17 is God explicitly named as the punishing judge.

4. Cf. Friedrich, "Ein Tauflied."

5. On this, cf. Synofzik, Gerichts- und Vergeltungsaussagen, 16–30. With regard to the thanksgivings that introduce letters, cf. 1 Cor. 1:7–9; 2 Cor. 1:14; Phil. 1:6, 10–11; 1 Thess. 2:19–20; 3:13 (and Phlm. 6). Romans 16:20 and 1 Thess. 5:23–24 may be mentioned as concluding wishes of prayer and statements of praise. Much of this is previously formulated material.

6. Synofzik (Gerichts- und Vergeltungsaussagen, 49–53) rightly summarizes both passages under the theme of the "current medicinal judgment as substitute for the eschatological judgment."

unconcerned behavior. Paul threatens that they are eating judgment to themselves. But in 1 Cor. 11:31–32 he also refers to another possibility:

> But if we judged ourselves truly, we should not be judged. But when we are judged by the Lord, we are chastened so that we may not be condemned along with the world.

Here the idea of judgment is modified. As soon as Christ enters the role of judge, judgment becomes a punishment that is ultimately intended to save us. "Judgment" becomes "chastisement." The much disputed statement of 1 Cor. 5:5 has the same meaning. Here the community together with the apostle assumes judgment in the present, in order that the sinner be saved on the "day of the Lord." The evildoer is "to be delivered to Satan for the destruction of the flesh, that his spirit may be saved in the day of the Lord" (1 Cor. 5:5*). The evildoer is condemned "in the name of the Lord Jesus" (5:4) in the present, but the current judgment is directed toward eschatological salvation.[7] The day of the Lord—traditionally a day of terror—shall mean no destruction for him.

Besides this saving function, Christ has above all a revelatory function. In 1 Cor. 4:5 he assumes partial functions of the judge. He "will bring to light the things now hidden in darkness and will disclose the purposes of the heart." But God appears as the one who assesses in a judicial way the things that have been revealed. He distributes to each his praise.

In 2 Cor. 5:10 Christ has grown fully into the role of God. He assumes the office of judge. But again it is his revelatory function that is stressed:

> For we must all appear before the judgment seat of Christ, so that each one may receive good or evil, according to what he has done in the body.

Being revealed before Christ is simultaneously being revealed before God. Paul continues by saying, "Therefore, knowing the fear of the Lord, we persuade men; but what we are is known to God" (2 Cor.

---

7. A different view is expressed by Donfried ("Justification," 107–10). According to Donfried, it is not the spirit of the sinner but that of the community which shall be saved in the last judgment; it is for this reason that the possessive pronoun *autou* is missing from "spirit." But, first, this pronoun is also missing from *sarx*, which clearly means the flesh of the sinner. Second, the saving of the spirit occurs on the day of the Lord, but the preservation of the community's holiness must take place in the present.

5:11). Even beyond this, Paul wishes that eschatological revelation between him and the Corinthians take place right now: "I hope it is known also to your conscience" (2 Cor. 5:11). Here too—despite the mention of the good and bad works—the tenor is confident: "We have become in Christ the righteousness of God" (5:21*).

In Rom. 2:16* the division of judicial functions between God and Christ is unclear. God, it is said, judges the secrets of men "according to my gospel" and "through Christ." Here Christ has in part an instrumental function (cf. *dia*, "through"), in part a normative significance: the gospel of Christ determines the judicial process.

But Paul can also speak of the final judgment independently of Christ. In Rom. 14:10 he speaks exclusively of God as eschatological judge: "For we shall all stand before the judgment seat of God." Here Paul even applies to God a citation from Isaiah that he had applied to the exalted Christ in the hymn of Philippians: "Every knee shall bow to me, and every tongue shall give praise to God" (14:11). But here too Paul says nothing about condemnation. He insists only on responsibility: "Each of us shall give account of himself to God" (Rom. 14:12).

Take note that where only God is mentioned, the revelatory aspect recedes (Rom. 14:10). Where Christ enters the role of eschatological judge, two aspects are emphasized. First, his saving function: he rescues from the future judgment of wrath, and when he punishes, it is only to chastise. Second, his revelatory function: he reveals what is secret. Above all, however, Christ is a judge who himself was a victim and was judged (cf. 1 Cor. 11:24–25 with v. 32; 2 Cor. 5:10 with v. 14). There would seem to be a close connection between these different aspects of Christ's role as judge and the disclosure of the unconscious; because Christ is the saving judge, Paul can allow for the possibility of unconscious guilt without feeling himself threatened existentially (1 Cor. 4:5).

Now we will attempt to translate these processes in Paul's symbolic world into psychodynamic categories. Christ symbolizes an internal transformation of man. He represents, on the one hand, all within man that is condemned, whether one calls that the id, the shadow, or anything else. Christ himself was *sarx* and *harmartia*. He himself was condemned as "flesh" and "sin" (Rom. 8:3; 2 Cor. 5:21). He represents on the other hand all the tribunals that judge man—the superego, consciousness, the norm, for he is the eschatological judge. But he removes from the superego its archaic severity and overcomes the wrath of God that aims toward the death of the sinner. He reforms the condemning aspect of human life through an accepting model. When he as the one who is judged becomes the judge, portions of the id are assumed into the superego. The shadow is integrated. Aspects of man that are opposed to each other are drawn closer together. A coincidence of opposites occurs in the symbol of the "judged judge."

Christians as Agents of Judgment

An event on earth corresponds to the exchange of roles in heaven; in some texts, Paul attributes to Christians the eschatological judicial competence he otherwise attributes only to God and Christ. With regard to the restructuring of the superego we can therefore note not only a growth of Christ into the role of the eschatological judge (with the judicial function of God remaining in force) but also a growth of the ego into the role of judge (with permanent distance from the divine judicial competence). We shall first discuss the statements that bring to expression an identification with the eschatological judicial competence.

Paul attributes to Christian prophecy the capability of disclosing even now the secrets of the human heart. When an unbeliever comes into the community, "he is convicted by all, he is called to account by all, the secrets of his heart are disclosed" (1 Cor. 14:24–25). Thus he is forced to recognize that "God is really among you" (1 Cor. 14:25). Christian preaching anticipates the eschatological event of judgment.

Other texts refer not to the present but to the future; that is, in them the transferral of eschatological judicial competence to Christians is promised. In 1 Cor. 6:1–8, Paul criticizes the legal proceedings of the Corinthian Christians against one another. He sees in this a contradiction of the juridical competence that is promised to Christians. For this reason, in 1 Cor. 6:2–3, he cries to the litigants, "Do you not know that the saints will judge the world? And if the world is to be judged by you, are you incompetent to try trivial cases? Do you not know that we are to judge angels?"

The Christians' consciousness of authority is grounded in their possession of the Spirit. In 1 Cor. 2:15*, Paul says clearly, "The spiritual man judges everything, but is himself to be judged by no one." The verb *anakrinein* is the same as in 1 Cor. 4:4 and 14:24 (cf. also 9:3). It is a concept with forensic associations. Through the Spirit of God the spiritual man participates in divine judicial competence and applies this to everything. The statement about judging everything (*panta*) is unmistakably a transferral of divine predicates to the Christian.

If Christian judicial competence encompasses everything, it also includes the Christians themselves. Paul formulates this in 1 Cor. 11:31*: "But if we judge ourselves, we shall not be judged." Here it becomes completely clear that judgment of oneself is an anticipation of the eschatological judgment and that it can therefore mitigate the eschatological judgment. "But when we are judged by the Lord, we are chastened so that we may not be condemned along with the world" (1 Cor. 11:32). When the ego has the power to judge itself, it becomes free of the severity of the superego, which now no longer categorically condemns but rather "chastens."

A provisional summary. A process in which the ego of a Christian receives an enhanced judicial competence becomes visible in a few texts of Paul. The ego receives divine judicial competence through the gift of the divine Spirit and of prophecy. For the spiritual, the last judgment thus becomes an event in which one is involved not only as object but also as agent. In psychological terms, an ego has come into being where a superego once was. But this is only one side of the process.

Beside the cited statements that attribute to the Christian an almost superhuman judicial competence, there stand statements that clearly limit this competence. These are statements in which the expectation of divine judgment is to prevent mutual human condemnation.[8] The Corinthians have no right to judge Paul, because only the Lord himself can judge him (1 Cor. 4:1–5). They are in the wrong when they even now play the missionary work of different missionaries against each other, for this will be definitively tested only in the eschatological judgment (1 Cor. 3:5–17). The Jews have no right to judge Gentiles, and mutual condemnation in general is of the evil one, for God will bring the secrets of man to light in the judgment (Rom. 2:1–16). The strong should not judge the weak, for each will be judged by his own Lord (Rom. 14:1ff.).

The contradiction between these statements and those previously cited is in my opinion easily made comprehensible. In each case a greater independence is attributed to Christians. Despite their different content, the statements show a comparable tendency. That Christians are not only objects but also agents in the judgment points in the direction of greater autonomy of the ego, just like the repudiation of human judicial competence in the condemnation of others. Man is

---

8. Cf. Synofzik, *Die Gerichts- und Vergeltungsaussagen*, 39–49, on the "prevention of interhuman judgment by the idea of the eschatological judgment."

released from the pressure of the environment through appeal to the exclusive competence of the divine judge. He receives increased independence.

Nevertheless, the statements of Paul are not to be understood only in the sense of a greater autonomy of the ego; in the judgment, the Christian encounters the judge. There are limits to human judicial competence. Yet it can still be said of the spiritual man that he judges everything! How are such tensions to be understood?

Remember that these tensions also occurred in the statements about the exchange of roles in heaven. Christ grows into the role of the eschatological judge, but Christ does not supplant the divine judge. On the one hand, we must all be revealed before the judgment seat (*bema*) of Christ (2 Cor. 5:10); on the other hand, we must render account before the judgment seat (*bema*) of God (Rom. 14:10). Something similar is true of the corresponding "anthropological" process. On the one hand, the full divine judicial competence is transferred to the Christian; he judges other men (1 Cor. 14:25), the world and angels (1 Cor. 6:2–3), absolutely "everything" (1 Cor. 2:15). On the other hand, other men, even he himself, are withdrawn from his judgment (cf. Rom. 14:1ff.; 1 Cor. 4:1–5).

These tensions in "Christology" and "anthropology" parallel each other. The restructuring of the superego through Christ corresponds to the conferral of eschatological judicial competence on Christians; the remaining judicial function of God corresponds to the reservation with regard to human judicial competence. The occupation of the superego with models that steer and measure behavior encompasses both identification and distancing. The conferral of the role of judge on Christ, that is, on one who was himself condemned and crucified, is a humanization of the superego. The irrational divine wrath is overcome where Christ enters the role of judge. An ego comes to be where a strict superego was. But this identification is never complete. There remains within the individual an obscure region that, just like the behavior of one's fellows, remains withdrawn from the individual's judicial competence. And this too is an humane characteristic: the human being is not God. One is not fully transparent to oneself. Even when one, as *homo religiosus*, has experienced an enormous expansion of consciousness with regard to oneself and others, even when the "Spirit of God" has been conferred on one, even then, yes, precisely then, does one become conscious that this does not exhaust matters.

COGNITIVE ASPECTS OF THE
"SECRETS WITHIN MAN"

The concepts of the unconscious in learning theory and in psycho-dynamic thought can be combined in the framework of a cognitive psychology. The internal and external world is unconscious insofar as it has an effect on the subject but is excluded from the subject's interpretation of self and world because the excluded aspects of reality would elicit too great a cognitive dissonance. Opening to previously unconscious contents occurs through cognitive restructuring of our perception of self and others; a new view of self and of the world enables us to accept into our "experienced world" and our self-image contents we would otherwise have to repress as dissonant and threatening. This process presupposes that the experienced cognitive discrepancies are dosed in such a way that they do not threaten the moving equilibrium of life but rather keep it in motion and make it possible. Restructuring of self-perception means above all transformation of the inner dialogue with oneself. This inner dialogue is an interiorization of the external dialogue; for this reason, it is open to the "insertion" of dialogue partners. Modern forms of modifying behavior and experience systematically take advantage of this possibility: the therapist is inserted into the dialogue of an individual, as a helpful person of reference. For millenniums, however, it was above all the gods whom man inserted in his "inner dialogue" in critical situations, by turning to them in petition, praise, and thanksgiving. Prayer cannot be removed from the evolution of the inner dialogue.

In connection with our topic, four epochs of this inner dialogue may be distinguished. The idea of an "all-knowing god" must have originated in prehistoric times—a figure invoked by an oath because he had the power to punish even secret transgressions. This faith in an all-knowing god was a latent threat to one's own equilibrium. Yet cognitive equilibrium was easily sustained, for the all-knowing god was only one god among many, joined positively to one's own group. In the treaty between Jacob and Laban, Jacob swears by the "Fear of his father Isaac," Laban by, among others, the "God of Nahor" (Gen. 31:53). Each swears by his god, who he is convinced is positively connected to his own tribe, as is shown by the motif of promise which is connected with such "gods of the fathers."

The monotheistic revolution brought an intensification of the inner dialogue. Now one was exposed to one and the same God everywhere. No longer were there other gods to relativize the power and the demands of the all-knowing God. The ethical severity of the all-knowing God contributed further to expanding the region of the unconscious. The stricter the norms became, the more necessary it was to exclude from one's own self-perception anything that could endanger belief in one's fundamental correspondence with them.

It is therefore no coincidence that consciousness of sin also increased with the monotheistic revolution. In the priestly document, the purification of Israel, which included conscious and unconscious sins, became the central purpose of the cult.[9] On the other hand, consciousness of election also increased with monotheism. The increase of possible cognitive dissonance is counterweighed by the fact that cognitive consonance is also raised: the uniqueness of one's own election is emphasized with the uniqueness of God. It is probable that Israel was able to test itself so uncompromisingly with reference to the commandments of Yahweh only because the consciousness of election balanced the threat to equilibrium posed by the ethical severity of the commandment.

In the intertestamental period, a further important step was taken in apocalypticism. The sole, all-knowing God became the eschatological judge before whom all men would have to render account. But if each person is tested individually, it becomes uncertain if collective realities as such are "chosen." The apocalyptic preacher of penance, John the Baptist, disputed this: descent from Abraham is of no help in the judgment (Matt. 3:9ff.). Other groups restricted the circle of the chosen: not all Israel is chosen but only a portion of the Israelites, a "remnant" of the truly pious. Thus we find in the Qumran literature the self-understanding of a group that claimed election by Yahweh exclusively for itself. This extreme consciousness of election was combined with equally extreme consciousness of sins.[10] The two elements balance each other. Together they form a cognitive equilibrium.

Dialogue with the all-knowing God, the only God, and finally with the eschatological judge, forced man to constantly more extensive self-exploration. The insertion of the divine partner into one's inner dialogue with oneself is an essential element of this self-exploration. One needs a strong opposite, in order to be able to see oneself as a stranger and to come to the recognition that one is no less concealed from oneself

9. Cf. Koch, "Sühne und Sündenvergebung."
10. Cf., e.g., 1QH 4.29–40.

than another person is concealed from one. Every hidden human thought will be disclosed before the all-knowing eschatological judge, beside whom there is no competing power. A sense of an unconscious region within thus imposes itself. But a clear concept is still lacking.

For this a fourth step is presupposed. The eschatological judge must have a temporary representative within the human being, so that the confrontation of the human being with God leads to an inescapable confrontation with oneself, and the interpersonal boundary between God and us becomes an intrapersonal boundary between consciousness and unconscious. In other words, the eschatological judge must be "internalized." The internalization of judgment took place in Judaism with the help of the Hellenistic concept of *suneidesis:* conscience became the precursor of the eschatological judge.

Presupposed is the interiorization of behavior-directing tribunals; this can be observed in Greek antiquity. In Homer, human action is determined either by social shying from the reaction of others (*aidos*) or by irrational impulses in persons, which they do not ascribe to themselves but interpret as the effects of gods and strange powers.[11] But soon social shame (*aidos*) was interiorized. Democritus (*Fragments* 84; 244; cf. 264) requires that one have "shame" before oneself, not before others.[12] Similarly, the co-knower of the deed is interiorized to conscience; in fact, conscience is nothing other than the interiorized Other. This is clear also from the metaphors with which conscience is described—as pedagogue, enemy, accuser, and judge.[13]

By itself, however, the development of the concept of conscience does not suffice to reach the boundaries of human consciousness. Seneca, for example, gives an imposing depiction of the phenomenon of conscience (*On Anger* 3.36.1–2):

> Sextius had this habit, and when the day was over and he had retired to his nightly rest, he would put these questions to his soul: "What bad habit have you cured to-day? What fault have you resisted? In what respect are you better?" Anger will cease and become more controllable if it finds that it must appear before a judge every day. Can anything be more excellent than this practice of thoroughly sifting the whole day? And how delightful the sleep that follows this self-examination—how tranquil it is, how deep and untroubled, when the soul has either praised

11. Cf., e.g., respectively *Iliad* 13.122ff. and 19.86ff.
12. Cf. Freeman, *Ancilla*, 102, 244, 264.
13. Epictetus *Fragment* 97 (pedagogue); Josephus *Jewish Antiquities* 2.25 (enemy); Philo *On the Decalogue* 87 (accuser and judge).

or admonished itself, and when this secret examiner and critic of self has given report of its own character![14]

In this connection Seneca does not show the slightest inclination to presume that something could have escaped his conscience. To the contrary, he insists explicitly, Nihil mihi ipse abscondo, nihil transeo ("I hide nothing from myself, I pass over nothing"). He is convinced that he is hiding nothing from himself. His reason is, "For why should I shrink from any of my mistakes. . . ?" (3.36.3).[15]

But this changes when one is confronted with both God and one's own conscience. The possibility that the two tribunals will not overlap completely in their judgment is then present from the start. Precisely this happens in Judaism, which connects the Old Testament tradition's theological conception of omniscience with the Greek-Hellenistic tradition's anthropological conception of conscience, without identifying God and conscience. The two are distinguished in human self-interpretation. They do stand parallel to each other, but this does not make them identical. One text (*Testaments of the Twelve Patriarchs, Reuben* 4.3–4) speaks in parallel fashion of the pangs of conscience and the wrath of God:

> Even now my conscience harasses me because of my impious act. And yet my father consoled me greatly and prayed to the Lord in my behalf so that the Lord's anger would pass me by—which is just how the Lord treated me.[16]

In Wisdom 17, God's plagues in Egypt are interpreted as plagues of conscience. The darkness that cast the Egyptians into panic is nonetheless only an image of the future darkness that will envelop them (Wis. 17:20). For Paul, the shadow of the eschatological judgment stands behind the inner tribunal of thoughts that accuse and excuse (Rom. 2:15–16).

It is no accident that the conception of the unconscious emerges for the first time in the same place in which the noun "conscience," *suneidesis*, is first attested in Jewish literature—in Wis. 17:11.[17] The opposition between the omniscient God and sinful man is located in

14. ET: John W. Basore, *Seneca*, vol. 1 of 10 vols. (LCL, 1928), 339, 341.
15. ET: ibid., 341.
16. ET: H. C. Kee, *The Old Testament Pseudepigrapha*, ed. Charlesworth, 1:783.
17. The Septuagint otherwise uses this term only in Eccl. 10:20, but there it means "consciousness," not "conscience." In view of Democritus (*Fragment* 297), it can hardly be claimed that this is its first occurrence in Greek literature (against Georgi, *Weisheit Salomos*, 463).

man himself with the aid of the concept of conscience, without the omniscient God relinquishing his sovereignty over man. A region of "inner darkness," with reference to which the Egyptian darkness is symbolically interpreted, originates only in this way. As precursor of God, conscience here spreads panic—a true contrast to the inner rest and balance that Seneca promised from daily examination of conscience. In fact, the threat to cognitive equilibrium grows when the God who judges is interiorized in conscience. One can conceal oneself before another person, or hope to find mercy. But no one can escape his own conscience. It can become a plague! The author of the Wisdom of Solomon did not find it difficult to handle this problem; he judged a strange group, a group to which he did not belong. He knew himself to be in the light. He belonged to the chosen. Only with regard to others did he perceive the enormous tensions between interiorized "omniscience" and sinful man.

Paul was the first to take the decisive step of allowing for the possibility of unconscious sin in himself. But he gives new accents to the tradition of omniscience. In the tradition, the "secret" is as a rule something negative. Secret deeds are actions that shy from the light. Where inner reality is opposed in a positive way to outward appearance, the term "heart" usually appears instead (cf. 1 Sam. 16:7). Paul speaks of what is "hidden in darkness," an expression that would have to release negative associations; but he trusts that this "darkness" will survive in the light of the eschatological judgment. He expects a commendation from God.

How did Paul sustain his cognitive equilibrium? How can he concede the possibility of hidden guilt without feeling threatened? The answer is simple. Paul inserts into the interior human dialogue a new reference person, Christ. This person opens unconscious depths within him without making him feel threatened.

This cognitive restructuring of self-perception through relationship to Christ is clear, for example, in Rom. 8:26–27, 33–34. In Rom. 8:26–27, Paul writes:

> Likewise the Spirit helps us in our weakness; for we do not know how to pray as we ought, but the Spirit himself intercedes [huperentugchanei] for us with sighs too deep for words. And he who searches the hearts of men knows what is the mind of the Spirit, because the Spirit intercedes [entugchanei] for the saints according to the will of God.

A few lines later (Rom. 8:33–34*), parallel to this, we read:

Who shall bring any charge against God's elect? It is God who justifies; who is to condemn? It is Christ Jesus, who died, yes, who was raised from the dead, who is at the right hand of God, who also intercedes [*entugchanei*] for us.

The three elements that are decisive for the disclosure of the unconscious within the framework of Jewish–Old Testament tradition are present in Rom. 8:26–27. First, God is omniscient and searches hearts. God's knowledge of the heart is taken over from the tradition. Second, we do not understand our own intentions. We do not know what we should pray; our self-knowledge is limited. Third, the sigh that comes from the depth of the heart is a significant inner reality. It has cosmic dimensions and joins man to the whole of creation (cf. Rom. 8:18ff.). It is instructive that God understands the "inexpressible sigh" that we ourselves cannot probe sufficiently. God exposes a dimension within us of which we ourselves are not fully conscious.

The text also gives a clear indication of what expresses itself in the cosmic sigh. In 8:20, there is an unmistakable reference to the Fall. Through this event, creation became subject to decay. It is a lament over sin, at first inaccessible to rational insight, that expresses itself in an "inexpressible sigh" that transcends consciousness. At this point the eschatological judge understands us better than we understand ourselves.

How did the opening of this dark dimension of a guilt and need that has been burdening creation since primeval times come about? Here the parallel between Rom. 8:26–27 and 8:33–34 is decisive. What is said at first about an event in the human heart is later transposed into heaven. The intercession of the Holy Spirit occurs in the depth of the human heart. From the heart comes the inexpressible sigh that stands in an obscure connection with the guilt that subjected all creation to decay. The Spirit vicariously articulates our sigh and thus intercedes before God. The intercession of Christ before the divine court in heaven above, where the Risen One sits at the right hand of God, occurs parallel to this. There is a parallel in the luminous heights of heaven to what occurs in the dark and impenetrable depths of human beings. Between the two processes there is no contradiction but rather "cognitive consonance." Ultimately, it is one and the same process on two different levels. But if one has an intercessor in heaven, then one need no longer persuade oneself that one is "blameless according to the law" (Phil. 3:6*). Then one can perceive in oneself the obscure lament over human perdition and guilt, even if one must admit to oneself that one does not penetrate it fully. One finds oneself in agreement with God in this lament; God's Spirit vicariously formulates it for one. As Spirit, God is agent of the lament; as judge, he is its addressee. But Christ mediates between human beings and God. Here we can discern the revaluation of what is "secret" in man even more clearly than in 1 Cor. 4:5. What at first had to be repressed as something negative—unconscious guilt—is now experienced as the provocation of spiritual "sighing" in which the divine Spirit is active.

Paul does not stand alone in early Christianity with this restructuring of self-experience. The tradition of omniscience is also modified in a paradoxical manner in 1 John 3:19–21. In place of the contradiction between God's condemning omniscience and our positive self-con-sciousness comes the opposition between human self-condemnation and God's forgiving omniscience:

> . . . and [we shall] reassure our hearts before him whenever our hearts condemn us; for God is greater than our hearts, and he knows everything. Beloved, if our hearts do not condemn us, we have confidence before God.

The numerous exegetical problems of this text derive from the fact that the traditional theme of the all-knowing God actually tends in a different direction, toward God's disclosure of hidden sins.[18] But the train of thought in 1 John undoubtedly sets a new accent. The human heart accuses itself, while God is sovereign above all such self-accusation—not because he overlooks sins but precisely because he knows everything. Here too the range of what is known by God is greater than what is grasped by human consciousness.

Texts from 1 John (3:19–21) and 1 Corinthians (4:5) show that the disclosure of the unconscious in early Christianity was not conditioned by heightened anxiety about unknown sins. Paul's ability to allow for the possibility of unconscious guilt despite his conviction of his innocence and the Johannine community's belief in innocence before the all-knowing God despite consciousness of guilt had the same basis— a cognitive restructuring of self-perception that was rooted in confidence that God does not impute guilt to the sinner. This confidence makes transformed causal attribution possible for us as well: we too need no longer impute guilt to ourselves. Another bears our guilt for us.

In Romans 8, the restructuring of self-perception stands in close

---

18. Cf. Schnackenburg, *Die Johannesbriefe*, 201–4.

connection with a fundamental restructuring of the Pauline life-world. Before Christ, this life-world was determined by the theme of the law, that is, by a normative thematic that caused the relationship to fellow human beings, world, and God to be experienced entirely under the aspect of fulfillment of norms. Through Christ, however, Paul's life-world was determined by a universal thematic of love. As Paul asks in Rom. 8:35, "Who shall separate us from the love of Christ?" When the all-knowing God is no longer exclusively experienced in the framework of a normative life-thematic, the "unconscious" in us, latently present along with divine omniscience, can be seen and recognized. The thematic restructuring of the Pauline life-world, however, is a consequence of faith in Christ—the transformation of the inner dialogue through a central new reference person.

Summary. The opening of the unconscious in Pauline theology was facilitated by its historical location between competing systems of conviction. Pluralist cultures often stimulate the same psychic tendencies they repress in another place. This can lead to rigid defensive postures, as was perhaps the case in the pre-Christian Paul. But faith in the one who was crucified placed Paul at a distance from the systems of conviction available to him. The cross contradicts both Jewish and Greek expectations: it is a scandal to Jews, folly to Greeks (1 Cor. 1:23). For precisely this reason it frees the view to a region within man which lies beyond historically formed systems of conviction—or in psychodynamic terms, beyond the contents of the respective superegos.

A transformation thus takes place in the human interior. Christ occupies the place of the previous contents of the superego. As judge and judged, he is the symbol of superego and id, of the ideal of the ego and its shadow. A drawing together of inner tribunals is symbolized in him, one that enables the opening, appropriation, and transformation of previously unconscious processes.

The assumption of an intensive emotional and motivational relationship to Christ achieves an "inner dialogue" in which the previously unconscious dimensions within one can be explored without endangering life's equilibrium dynamic. Even threatening aspects of the unconscious can be experienced in consonance with the judging tribunals. Even the "inexpressible sigh" at the basic perversion of life no longer separates from the judging God, but joins to him, for it is the sighing of the divine Spirit. Consciousness of overcome guilt makes cognitive consonance possible—even with an opening for those obscure unconscious dimensions from which the "inexpressible sigh" derives.

PART THREE

The Veil of Moses and the Unconscious Aspects of the Law

In part 2, we saw that the restructuring of the superego through the Christ symbolism expanded Paul's consciousness; he accepted the possibility of unconscious guilt in himself without feeling threatened. The expansion of his conscious life-world will now be pursued in a different direction. The blindness of the ego relates not only to its own failures but also to all the norms that direct and assess behavior— to the "law," as Paul names the sociocultural norms and rules of Judaism. These norms mark the superego aspects of his self. His new insight consists in recognizing that prior to his conversion he had perceived these superego aspects falsely. His consciousness had connected with them the promise of life. Unconsciously, however, they had exercised an aggressive-destructive function. In my judgment, the symbols and images of 2 Corinthians 3, which are difficult to interpret, give expression to this recognition.

Chapter 8

Text Analysis:
2 Corinthians 3:4—4:6

In 2 Cor. 2:14—6:10, Paul speaks in a twofold way of his office as apostle, first with concepts of a *theologia gloriae*,[1] then with the paradoxical statements of a *theologia crucis* (2:14—4:6 and 4:7—6:10). In the first section, Paul depicts his activity as part of a triumphal procession (2.14), in the second as a chain of sorrows (cf. 4:8–12). In 4:6, Christ occurs as "image" resplendent in the light of creation; in 5:21, however, he is atoning sacrifice. In the first section, the glory is present (3:18); in the second, it is future (4:17). In the first part, Christians all have access to the vision of the Lord (3:18); in the second, they live by faith, not by sight (5:7). Paul makes the transition between the two parts with the declaration that "we have this treasure [the previously developed knowledge of the glory of God] only in earthen vessels [i.e., in the fragility of apostolic existence that is yet to be described]" (4.7*). Here we shall be concerned only with a portion of the first part, but the overall context must not be lost from view.

After Paul has described his task in triumphalistic images, he poses the question, "Who is capable of these things?" (2:16*). In emphatic contrast to the "many" who are not capable, he underlines his qualifications with the aid of two images—the metaphors of the letter and of the stone.[2] Even though his opponents can exhibit letters of

1. Friesen (*The Glory of the Ministry of Jesus Christ*) rightly interprets the entire section of 2 Cor. 2:14—3:18 on the basis of the motif of glory.
2. Lietzmann (*An die Korinther I.II*, 110) emphasizes the incongruence of the two images. A letter is written with ink on papyrus, while an inscription is hewn into stone. But, first, the letters of inscriptions were often painted in color (cf. Meyer, *Einführung in die lateinische Epigraphik*, 21). Second, certain texts that were intended for the public, such as decrees and laws, were often fixed in inscriptions, and Paul is concerned with witness to the public. Third, the real reason Paul associates letter and inscription is his desire to demonstrate a contrast between himself and the old covenant and to associate his enemies with the old covenant.

recommendation, Paul possesses a much better letter of recommendation—the Corinthian community that is written in his heart (or that
represents a living letter of recommendation) and which recommends
him to all. This reality also characterizes what is new in his message.
In contrast to the Mosaic service, Paul brings no "stone tablets of law"
but a message that transforms the heart. The community itself is the
letter of Christ that Paul has to deliver. Thus Paul determines his
qualifications first through his relationship to the community, and
second through his relationship to the old covenant.

These qualifications are then unfolded in three further sections.
Each section is introduced by a "have formula" (cf. *echomen* and *echontes*,
3:4, 12; 4:1).[3]

In the first part, the issue is the legitimation of the Pauline diakonia.
This lies in the fact that the service of the new covenant far surpasses
service of the old covenant (3:4–11). In the second section the accent
is on carrying out the diakonia: it occurs with *parresia*, that is, with an
openness that has nothing to hide (3:12–18). The third part treats the
ambivalent effect of the Pauline diakonia: the preaching is rejected by
those blinded, but is enlightenment by God for the converted (4:1–6).
The status of Paul, his "conduct in office," and the success of his
activity are thus treated in succession. We shall first outline the train
of thought in 2 Cor. 3:4—4:6:

> 3:4–11: The status of the Pauline diakonia.
>
> The introductory "have formula" refers to what preceded it: "We
> have this confidence [namely, that our message transforms hearts]
> through Christ toward God" (3:4*).
>
> Paul asserts the thesis that this confidence is grounded in the fact
> that God has established a new covenant, one that is no longer
> determined by the "killing letter" but rather by the "life-giving Spirit"
> (3:4–6). The status of Paul is superior to that of Moses. Paul has a
> higher rank.
>
> The foundation for this occurs in three parallel conclusions from
> the lesser to the greater. In each case, a conclusion is drawn from
> the lesser glory of the old covenant to the greater glory of the new
> covenant:
>
> (*a*) The first conclusion (3:7–8) confronts the old and new covenants
>   as "service of death" and "service of the Spirit." An interposed

---

3. The term "have formula" comes from Prümm, *Diakonia Pneumatos* 2.1:36–37. For
additional examples, cf. 4:7, 13; 17:1. Less to the point are 5:12 and 6:10.

consecutive *hoti* clause underlines the glory of the old covenant.
Its splendor was so great that the community could not bear it.

(*b*) The second conclusion confronts the "service of condemnation"
with the "service of justification" (3:9). A parenthesis (3:10) breaks
the ascending thought pattern: in comparison with the splendor
of the new covenant, that of the old is nothing.

(*c*) Drawing on this, the third conclusion (3:11) can conclude from
the relative splendor of the "corruptible" to the surpassing splendor
of the "permanent"; a corruptible splendor is one that fades in
view of a new splendor.

3:12–18: The carrying out of the Pauline diakonia.

Again a "have formula" picks up on the preceding material. Because
we have such a hope—namely, the hope of life, justification, and
"something permanent"—Paul is able to speak openly.

The thesis is that Paul is distinguished from Moses by this openness.
Moses concealed under a veil the corruptibility of his splendor, which
was unable to give hope of life and justification.

The foundation for this follows in two symbolic interpretations of
the "veil" of Moses, in which first the existence of the covering and
then its removal are interpreted:

(*a*) The existence of the covering refers to a veil over the reading of
the old covenant, ultimately to a veil over the heart of the listeners.
Only in Christ is the veil removed (3:14b–15).

(*b*) The removal of the covering occurs whenever Moses turns to the
Lord. All converted Christians stand without a covering before
the Lord. While the Israelites could not bear even the splendor
of Moses, in the new covenant all are changed into eternal glory
(3:16–18)

4:1–6: The ambivalent effect of the Pauline diakonia.

With *dia touto*, the introductory "have formula" refers in general
fashion in what has been said previously.

Paul defends the thesis that his preaching of the gospel reaches the
conscience of men through revelation of the truth (4:1–2).

The foundation is provided negatively and positively:

(*a*) Negatively: where the Pauline preaching remains inefficacious,
hardness of heart and blindness prevail (4:3–4).

(*b*) Positively: where the Pauline preaching is efficacious, it mediates
illumination through the Creator God (4:5–6).

The train of thought is antithetical throughout. The Pauline diakonia
is developed as a contrast to the Jewish diakonia, and the contrast is
expanded in the third part. Reference is made there to all unbelievers,
whose senses have been blinded by the god of this world; this section

is not concerned only with the Israelites. What is the point of comparison in each of these contrasts?

1. In the first part, the old and new covenants are compared with respect to their "splendor." The parallelism of the three conclusions from the lesser to the greater (subordinate clause with *ei*, main clause with *pollo mallon*) is interrupted in only two places—by a consecutive clause in v. 7 and a parenthesis in v. 10. In the first place, the point of comparison is developed positively: the splendor of the old covenant is emphasized.[4] This splendor established distance. Here it is necessary to keep in mind the opposition to the new covenant: the new covenant is written in the heart and eliminates the distance. The second interruption of the parallel conclusions points in exactly the opposite direction. Compared with the splendor of the new covenant, even the strongly emphasized splendor of the old is vacuous. Formally, the entire section is aimed at a gradual ranking of splendor; in content, however, the gradualist pattern of thought is overlaid by a contrast scheme. The new covenant is not only superior to the old in degree, it is its direct opposite.

2. In the second part (2 Cor. 3:12ff.), the veil is the point of comparison between the old covenant and the new.[5] Here there is no enhancement but only contrast. Moses concealed his head under a veil; the apostle, on the contrary, has nothing to hide. This idea stands in logical tension to the first section: if, namely, the splendor of Moses was unbearable, how much more terrifying would the glory of the new covenant be! If even Moses had to cover his countenance, how much more reason would Paul have had to do this![6] But these logical

4. According to Schulz ("Die Decke des Mose," 3–4), Paul, or the pre-Pauline tradition, goes beyond the Septuagint in three places. First, according to Schulz, the degree on unbearability is increased; according to the Septuagint, the Israelites see the splendor but cannot bear it, whereas according to 2 Cor. 3:7, they could not even look on. But *atenizein* means "observe intensively." Even according to the Septuagint, the Israelites could not do this. Second, Paul speaks of splendor as a noun, but the Septuagint uses the verbal form "being glorified" (Exod. 34:35*). Third, Paul adds the words *me dunasthai*. That there is really an increase beyond the Septuagint here is hard to prove.

5. Van Unnik (" 'With Unveiled Face' ") explains the connection of *parresia* and *kalymma* through an association that can be made only in Aramaic: in Aramaic, "to uncover one's head" means openness and freedom. While Paul wrote in Greek, he thought, according to van Unnik, in Aramaic. But, as the following citation shows, this is surely a generally intelligible image. Cassandra's intention of giving a clear oracle is expressed as follows in Aeschylus (*Agamemnon* 1178–81): "Lo now, no more shall my prophecy peer forth from behind a veil [*ek kalymmaton*] like a new-wedded bride; but 'tis like to rush upon me as a fresh wind blowing against the sun's uprising" (ET: Herbert Weir Smyth, *Aeschylus*, vol. 2 of 2 vols. [LCL, 1926], 101).

6. So, rightly, Hooker, "Beyond the Things That Are Written," 297ff.

tensions do not cause disturbance, because Paul reinterprets the motif of the veil in a threefold way.

(*a*) First, Paul departs from the literal meaning that Moses put on a covering so that the Israelites could not see the splendor. Paul imputes a brand-new motive. The veil no longer conceals the splendor of the radiance but now conceals its corruptibility. A deceptive function is thus attributed to the veil.[7] If Paul preaches the gospel with unveiled face, this is not because he has no splendor to hide or because the splendor of the new covenant is less than that of Moses. The missing cover is rather an advantage; it signifies the overcoming of an objective deception.

(*b*) In the second interpretation, the veil becomes a symbol. The specification of time ("to this day," v. 14; cf. v. 15) makes clear that the veil is not a past reality but a present one. A veil lies over the reading of the old covenant. In general, this interpretation is considered artificial. Curtains and covers do occur in various forms in the synagogue liturgy,[8] but Paul does not seem to be thinking of any of these covers. There are three types:

(1) The area in which the shrine of the Torah stands is marked off by a curtain. The curtain can be seen clearly in the floor mosaic of the synagogue in Beth-Alfa.[9]

(2) The shrine of the Torah itself is covered with a veil that is pushed aside, as the floor mosaic in Hammath-Tiberias shows.[10]

(3) The Torah scrolls are rolled in covers in order to protect them. The same thing is done with other books.

None of these curtains and covers fits what Paul says. During the reading of the Torah, the Torah room and container are open, and the rolls are removed from their coverings. Yet Paul speaks of a veil over the reading of the old covenant.

The problem can perhaps be solved with the help of the frescoes from Dura Europos. The reading of the Torah is depicted in them to the right of the Torah niche.[11] Who the reader is—Moses, Esra, or

---

7. Attempts to deny the motive of deception fail owing to the context; in 4:1ff., Paul defends himself against the charge that he "cunningly tampers with God's word" (4:2*) and says that his gospel is "unconcealed." Paul himself associates concealment and falsification. On the various apologetic attenuations of the motive of deception, cf. Schulz, "Die Decke des Mose," 10–11.

8. Cf. Krauss, *Synagogale Altertümer*, 376–84.

9. Cf. Avi-Yonah, ed., *Encyclopedia of Archaeological Excavations in the Holy Land* 1:189.

10. Ibid 4:1179

11. See the illustration in Kraeling, *The Synagogue*, pl. 87; and Goodenough, *Jewish Symbols*, pl. 5 and p. 326.

the lector in the synagogue liturgy—can be left open here.[12] To the left of the reader stands a covered, caselike object—either the Torah shrine itself or a *capsa*, in which the scroll or several scrolls were transported from the Torah shrine to the synagogue room.[13] It is striking that the scroll container is covered, although taking the scroll from the container would presuppose removing the cover. The covering is even more noteworthy if the container should be the Torah shrine itself. The Torah shrine, or the ark of the covenant, which corresponds to it, is a consistent leitmotif in the middle row of pictures in the frescoes of Dura Europos. The cover is missing in almost all the portraits; it is found only in connection with the reading of the Torah. Here there is in fact a veil over the old covenant—precisely during the reading. It is therefore possible that Paul has a concrete practice in view when he speaks of this veil.

(c) The third interpretation, on the contrary, is free of spatiotemporal illustration from the start. Here the veil moves once again. Now it lies over the "hearts" of the listeners; it is, in other words, thoroughly interiorized. Those who listen to the Torah do hear the words, but they do not grasp their real meaning. The veil of Moses and the veil over the hearts form an unmistakable parallel. They permit the conjecture that the veil of Moses is a symbol for an inner boundary of understanding.

In the last part of the section, Paul again has recourse directly to the Moses story. Now it is not the placing of the veil but its removal that is interpreted. When Moses turns to the Lord, the veil is removed.[14] Moses' turning is interpreted as conversion. The astonishing thing is that here Moses becomes the prototype of the convert. While he had just been a negative foil, to distinguish the service of the new covenant

12. Cf. the discussion in Gutmann, "Programmatic Painting in the Dura Synagogue."

13. On the interpretation as a *capsa*, cf. Wendel, *Der Thoraschrein*, 9–10, 25.

14. The subject of v. 16 is Moses (as asserted by, among others, Schulz, "Die Decke des Mose," 15–16 and Moule, "2.Cor 3,18b," 235). First, that Exod. 34:34 is picked up here is difficult to dispute. Anyone thinking of the pericope in Exodus has to think of Moses, especially since "Moses" is the only personal subject in the preceding sentence and "turn around" presupposes a personal subject. Second, the other possibility, that "heart" is the subject of v. 16, seems improbable (against Allo, *Saint Paul seconde épître aux Corinthiens*, 92). Hearts are indeed "converted," but they do not appear as the subject of *epistrephein* (cf. Luke 1:17 = Mal. 3:24; 1 Kings 8:47; 18:37; 2 Chr. 6:37). Or one is converted with the heart (cf. Matt. 13:15 = Isa. 6:10), or from the whole heart (*1 Clement* 8.3). Third, the addition of "Israel" as subject is equally improbable (against Windisch, *Der zweite Korintherbrief*, 123; Bultmann, *Der zweite Brief an die Korinther*, 92). Israel is mentioned only in the plural form "sons of Israel" (2 Cor. 3:7, 13). Since v. 15 still speaks of "their hearts" (in the plural), one would have to expect a plural in v. 16 as well.

all the more gloriously against a dark background, he now becomes the symbol of the convert. The interpretation occurs in two steps. First it is made clear that the "Lord" to whom Moses turns is the Spirit who grants freedom. Second, it is emphasized that all Christians stand before the Lord with uncovered countenance. All grow into the role of Moses and are changed into a form marked by splendor.[15]

3. The third section abandons the comparison between Moses and Paul, between old covenant and new. Paul now goes back directly to creation as an analogy. This section goes beyond the preceding ones through a stronger generalization and interiorization. The generalization lies in the fact that Jews and Gentiles are no longer opposed to each other, but rather unbelievers and believers. The interiorization consists in the fact that not only the veil, but also the process of transformation after elimination of the veil, is interpreted as a symbol of an inner reality. Even the splendor into which the Christian is transformed is an inner light. The text of 3:18 spoke, on the contrary, of objective vision and metamorphosis; that of 4:6 speaks of an inner process. Where the gospel does not remained covered, inner illumination occurs. A light shines in the heart. "For it is the God who said, 'Let light shine out of darkness,' who has shone in our hearts to give the light of the knowledge of the glory of God in the face of Christ" (4:6). But then the removal of the veil over the heart can be nothing other than the illumination of darkness within us. Previously unknown and obscure regions of the interior are suddenly illumined. The transformation of man—unveiling the face, seeing the splendor, being transformed into the image—all of this occurs in this shining of light in the interior of man.

We can go one step further. The "we" in 2 Cor. 4:5 is unquestionably an apostolic "we."[16] At least Paul includes himself in it. The inner illumination, however, can only refer to his conversion. At that time a veil fell from Paul's heart. At that time he discovered a dark side to the law, a side he had denied up to then. At that time he had an experience that he considered representative and that he developed and appropriated intellectually over the course of his activity. There

15. As in 2 Cor. 5:10, "we all" means all Christians. The omission of "all" in *Papias* 48 and some manuscripts of the Vulgate is intended to limit the statement to the apostle. It understands the "we" in the sense of the apostolic "we" of 3:12 and 4:1. On this problematic, cf. Carrez, "Le 'Nous' en 2 Corinthiens," esp. 476ff.

16. Bultmann (*Der zweite Brief an die Korinther*, III) relates *elampsen* to the conversion of Paul. But if Paul were thinking exclusively of his personal conversion, he would more likely speak of "our heart" than of "our hearts." Here Paul is depicting against the background of his personal experience an event typical of all Christians.

is not a presentation of the process of conversion in 2 Cor. 4:5. Instead, this passage seeks to describe something generally valid that was contained in the event of conversion.

Here we come to a provisional hypothesis from the perspective of the psychology of religion. The veil is a symbol of the boundary between what is conscious and the unconscious. In its three parts, the text bears witness to a progressive interiorization of objective realities into symbols of interior events. In the first section, splendor and veil are still understood objectively; in the second, the veil becomes a symbol of an inner boundary; in the third, splendor becomes a symbol of inner illumination.

Before we draw further conclusions, we must inquire about alternative possibilities of interpretation. The motif of the veil, for example, could also be conditioned by the situation. The charge had probably been raised against Paul that his gospel was veiled (4:3). To this he responds, "Even if our gospel is veiled, it is veiled only to those who are perishing" (4:3). Here he speaks not of the gospel in general but of his gospel. Since he already had to defend himself in the previous sentence against charges that are also well attested elsewhere,[17] it is probable that 4:3 is also an echo of concrete charges.[18]

The uncertainty of the exegesis is in part due to the fact that we do not have a clear picture of the overall situation of the section 2:14—7:4. If 2 Corinthians is a literary unit, it would be necessary to conceive of 2:14—7:4 as part of a letter of reconciliation, that is, as an echo of the good reports Titus had brought from Corinth (2 Cor. 2:12–13; 7:5ff.). Profound conflicts and misunderstandings would then be overcome. All polemical elements of 2 Corinthians would be a mild echo of the conflict.[19]

To others, however, the polemical tone of 2:14—7:4 seems so clear that they do not see these parts of the letter as a component of the letter of reconciliation after the conflict, but rather find in this and in the last four

17. For the term *panourgia*, cf. 1 Cor. 3:19; 2 Cor. 11:3; 12:6. For the term *dolos*, cf. 1 Thess. 2:3; 2 Cor. 12:16.

18. There are three possibilities of polemic-apologetic interpretation of 2 Cor. 4:3. First, most exegetes assume a concrete charge, either that his gospel is unintelligible in form or that he does not develop important elements of his preaching (cf. the survey in Windisch, *Der zweite Korintherbrief*, 134). Second, the possibility that it is a hypothetically constructed charge is weighed here and there (thus, ibid., 134). The fact that a comparable charge occurs nowhere else speaks in favor of this. The third possibility, the idea that Paul's opponents were proud of the fact that their gospel was veiled and that Paul attacked them for this, is improbable (against Georgi, *Die Gegner des Paulus*, 209).

19. E.g., Kümmel, *Einleitung*, 249–55. The unity of 2 Corinthians has most recently been defended by Hyldahl, "Die Frage."

chapters of 2 Corinthians portions of the "letter of tears," mentioned in 2:4, which was written at the height of the conflict.[20]

Still others distinguish between the polemical allusions in 2:14—7:4 and the vehement attacks of chapters 10 to 13. Because of its milder tone, our portion of the letter is said to have been written prior to the climax of the conflict, at a stage when Paul had already heard of charges raised against him but still deceived himself about their serious character.[21]

How difficult must it be to understand completely a text that people have been able to understand both as expression of a growing conflict and as confirmation of later reconciliation. We can be certain of only one thing. Every part of 2 Corinthians reflects a vehement conflict, whether it is one developing, reaching its climax, or resolved. We are therefore required to take into account the possibility of concrete charges against Paul.

A great deal of conjecture has surrounded the question as to what the charge of being veiled might mean. Methodically there is in my opinion only one way of coming to well-founded assumptions. It is necessary to make historically intelligible on the basis of Paul's previous working in Corinth—that is, on the basis of 1 Corinthians—how this charge could have come about, or how such a charge could have found response in Corinth. In 1 Corinthians there are two sections that could be understood as if access to the full "truth" was denied to a group among the Christians. In 1 Cor. 2:6–16, this group is the "psychics"; in 1 Cor. 11:3–16, it is the women. The gospel is in fact "veiled" with respect to both.

Paul says that the wisdom for the perfect is "hidden." The "hidden wisdom" of 1 Cor. 2:7 and the "veiled gospel" of 2 Cor. 4:3* are reminiscent of each other.[22] There are also other terminological connections between the two texts. That the rulers of this world resist the Lord of glory in 1 Cor. 2:6–8 corresponds to the passage in 2 Cor. 4:4 in which the "god of this world" does not permit the gospel of glory to come to bear among unbelievers. That the hidden wisdom of God penetrates into the hearts of men in 1 Cor. 2:6ff. corresponds to the divine light of creation, which in 2 Cor. 4:6 illuminates the hearts of men. All these associative ties point toward a factual connection. In both cases, the issue is a radical restructuring and expansion of consciousness through the gospel. In both cases, demonic resistance, which comes from the "world," is overcome in the process. There could in addition have been historical connections between the two

20. Thus, e.g., Vielhauer, *Geschichte*, 150–55.
21. Above all, Bornkamm, "Die Vorgeschichte."
22. The participles *apokekrummenen* and *kekalummenon* are related in meaning; cf. the shift from *kekalummenon* to *krupton* in Matt. 10:26.

texts. It is conceivable that the Corinthians, proud of wisdom, were irritated at Paul's explanation that he had withheld from them the perfect wisdom because of their inability to grasp it. They could have objected that his gospel was "hidden," that he had kept back the most important things.[23] And even if they did not directly raise this charge against him themselves, they would still have had sympathy for any charges in this direction.

The theme of the "veiled gospel" could have entered the discussion through the confrontation over the "veil" on the head of a woman. In 1 Corinthians 11, Paul sought with contradictory arguments to require head covering of a woman as a sign of her subordination to a male, but in the process had come into contradiction with the equality of male and female in Christ. Even in 1 Cor. 11:11, he has to retreat—in the Lord there is neither the woman without the man nor the man without the woman—though this did not prevent him from continuing to insist on a head covering. In 2 Cor. 3:18, he emphasizes on the contrary that we all stand before God with unveiled face. No longer is a distinction made between male and female. Even if Paul did not mean it in this way, some in Corinth must have understood this statement as complete retreat from the position represented in 1 Corinthians 11.

Thus we can make intelligible from the prehistory of 2 Corinthians 3 how the charge of a "veiled gospel" could have come about; with great probability it can be established why this charge was able to find so much response that Paul had to confront it. Directly or indirectly, 1 Cor. 2:6ff. and 11:3ff. played an important role in this. The motif of the "veil of Moses" is anchored in the historical situation. Does this preclude interpreting it from the perspective of the psychology of religion? Not at all! An understanding of 1 Cor. 2:6ff. and 11:3ff. is not possible without psychological analysis. For this reason, both texts will be examined later. In anticipation of these studies, we need to say that if the polemic behind the motif of the "veil" has a psychological dimension itself, the polemic interpretation of the motif can hardly be an alternative to its psychological evaluation. The psychological analysis rather serves to shed light on the historical context, and the investigation of the historical situation, pursued consistently, leads to psychological analysis.

23. Thus Windisch, *Der zweite Korintherbrief*, 134, as a possibility.

Chapter 9

Tradition Analysis:
2 Corinthians 3

Derivation of the motif of Moses' veil from the history of tradition could be brought into the picture as a further alternative to interpretation from the perspective of the psychology of religion. In 2 Corinthians 3, Paul is interpreting the Old Testament; perhaps he is dependent on a traditional picture of Moses. But here too analyses from the perspective of the psychology of religion and traditional exegetical methods are not alternatives. Insofar as Paul applied to his own situation a tradition upon which he drew, one can ask what principles of learning theory determined experience and behavior in the tradition and led to a cognitive structuring of the situation. Insofar as Paul revised the tradition, however, one will ask what psychic dynamics stood behind the reinterpretation of the Old Testament texts and how their cognitive restructuring in Paul's "exegesis" was conditioned. Psychology and tradition history are dependent upon each other.

THE EXEGESIS OF EXOD. 34:29–35
IN 2 CORINTHIANS 3

In English translation, the Septuagint version of the pericope Exod. 34:29–35 reads,

> And when Moses went down from the mountain, there were the two tables in the hands of Moses. When he went down the mountain, Moses knew not that the appearance of the skin of his face was glorified, when he [God] spoke to him. And Aaron and all the elders of Israel saw Moses, and the appearance of the skin of his face was made glorious, and they feared to approach him. And Moses called them, and Aaron and all the rulers of the community turned towards him, and Moses spoke to them. And afterwards all the children of Israel came to him,

and he commanded them all things, whatsoever the Lord had commanded him in the mount of Sinai. And when he ceased speaking to them, he put a veil on his face. And whenever Moses went in before the Lord to speak to him, he took off the veil till he went out, and he went forth and spoke to all the children of Israel whatsoever the Lord commanded him. And the children of Israel saw the face of Moses, that it was glorified; and Moses put the veil over his face, till he went in to speak with him.

The original narrative is probably an etiology of priests' masks, which are known from the environment of the Old Testament but seldom occur in the Old Testament itself. With the aid of such masks, the priest assumes the countenance of his deity and identifies himself with it.[1] But the mask cannot have this function in our text. Precisely when Moses identifies himself with the will of the Deity and proclaims the commandments as its representative, he removes the veil; and the same is true when he approaches the Deity directly in order to receive the commandments. The veil only covers his head when he is not active as mediator between God and the people. Between the lines one can read that the veil is to quench the fear of the Israelites before the divine splendor. But this means that distance from the Deity, not identification with it, is brought to expression with the motif of the veil.

Paul reinterprets both putting on the veil and removing it. Before one assumes the presence of arbitrary reinterpretations here, one should ask if attentive exegetical skill cannot in fact read out of the text what Paul reads into it.

The central point of the Pauline interpretation is the assumption that the brightness of Moses was corruptible. Paul emphasizes this corruptibility three times (3:9, 11, 14). And only because of the corruptibility of the splendor does Moses' veil fall into disrepute, as if a deceptive intent lay behind it. Now Exodus 34 speaks twice of Moses' being glorified. The first *dedoxasthai* stands in vv. 29–30, the second in v. 35. The first time Moses is glorified during the single moment of receiving the commandments; the second reference is a generalizing statement: " . . . whenever Moses went in before the Lord to speak with him, he took the veil off, till he went out. . . " (Exod. 34:34 LXX). In other words, Moses was "glorified" often. Unless one wishes to assume a constant increase of radiance at every direct

1. Cf. Noth, *Das zweite Buch Mose*, 220; Childs, *Exodus*, 609–10, 617–19, 620–24.

encounter with God, the following conception lies close at hand. At each encounter the radiance was renewed and freshened. But then the conclusion is necessary that after each encounter it gradually faded and that it was present to its full extent only when Moses came directly from God—when he handed on the revelation he had just received, the full aura of divine light surrounded him. Only after this did he don the veil—at a time, in other words, when the radiance began to fade. It must be underlined that none of this stands in Exodus 34, and that there is no evidence for a corresponding tradition of interpretation. Yet it is probable that an intelligent exegete like Paul could read something of the sort between the lines of the text.[2] One must, of course, have a distinctively broken relationship to Moses in order to view his splendor as corruptible and to impute deceptive intent to the veil.

Paul also gives a new meaning to the removal of the veil. Even the citation of the Septuagint in 2 Cor. 3:16 can be retraced to no known form of the text:[3]

Exod. 34:34 LXX	*2 Cor. 3:16*
henika d'an eiseporeuto Mouses	*henika de ean epistrepse*
evanti kyriou lalein auto	*pros kyrion*
periereito to kalymma	*periaireitai to kalymma*
heos tou ekporeuesthai	

First, Paul changes the concretely conceived "going in" into a "turning around" (cf. *epistrephein* in 1 Thess. 1:9; Gal. 4:9). Second, he changes the tenses. The narrative (iterative) imperfect becomes a promise, partly by use of the aorist subjunctive *epistrepse* (with resultative meaning), partly by use of the future *periaireitai*. Third and finally, he abbreviates the text, so that concrete circumstances recede. He drops

---

2. Hooker ("Beyond the Things," 300) is in my opinion correct in stating that Moses' splendor is "a glory which is presumably renewed when he speaks with God, and which could therefore well be understood—though Exodus does not say so—to fade at other times." A different opinion is held by Childs (*Exodus*, 621–22). According to Childs, since Paul does not advance reasons for the corruptibility of the splendor, this interpretation was already known to his readers and was based on tradition. Since Moses otherwise had no radiant countenance, the conclusion that his splendor was corruptible lay near at hand.

3. Hermann (*Kurios und Pneuma*, 39) wrongly denies that a citation is present here. First, the classical *henika han* occurs only here in the New Testament, a fact that is best explained by the influence of the Septuagint (cf. Blass et al., *Grammatik*, no. 105). Second, insofar as v. 17 may be understood as interpretation, v. 16 would be the text to be interpreted. On the problem, cf. Dunn, "2.Corinthians III.17," esp. 314 ff.

the explicit subject "Moses," and can neither use "speaking with God" as the goal of the "conversion" nor retain the temporal limitation of the unveiling (*heos tou ekporeuesthai*). It is futile to hunt for an Old Testament version in which one or another of these elements would already be present.[4] The abbreviations could not be explained by the history of the text. Rather, Paul changes the text. This is all the more true of the meaning he attributes to the text in the interpretation that follows. Here he equates the Lord with the Spirit. This is more than an exegetical equation, that is, an interpretation of the "Lord" mentioned in the text as the Spirit. In that case, one would have to expect a *to*, as in Gal. 4:25—the word "Lord" means the Spirit. Rather, an already established equation of Lord and Spirit is here read into the text, without there being any basis for this in the text.[5]

There can be no doubt that the interpretation of the Old Testament text can only be understood as a process of projection. A narrative of the glorification of Moses is "refunctioned" into a polemic against the law. Objectively, Paul does violence to the text. Must one therefore judge that "since . . . a mistake in memory on the part of the apostle, so familiar with the Bible, is not possible, one is forced to assume a *conscious* reinterpretation of the Old Testament text"?[6] Can one in all seriousness charge Paul with conscious manipulation of the Scriptures—Paul who adorns the Scriptures with divine predicates (Gal. 3:8, 22)? Paul, who grounds all important theological ideas on the Scriptures? Paul, for whom the Scripture is at all times the decisive basis of legitimation in development of his theology? Must we not presume an unconscious reinterpretation of the Scripture until the contrary is proved—objectively indeed an exegetical error, but subjectively an appropriate interpretation. Such an objective error would indeed only be intelligible if a powerful psychic dynamic stood behind it, an involvement that is no longer capable of objectivity but that sees everything in the light of a dominant experience.

4. Windisch (*Der zweite Korintherbrief*, 123) conjectures that there was a form of the text in which "Moses" was lacking as subject and in which *epistrephein* stood.

5. In v. 16, *kyrios* means Christ (cf. Herrmann, *Kyrios*, 17–57). First, a conversion of Moses to monotheism (i.e., to *kyrios* = God) would be meaningless. Second, in informal citations of the Old Testament without a citation formula, *kyrios* occasionally means Christ; cf. Phil. 2:11; Rom. 10:13; 1 Cor. 1:31; 2:16. Third, Paul had previously claimed that the veil was removed in "Christ"; now he brings the scriptural backing for this. Fourth, in the context that follows (v. 18), *kyrios* is rather certainly Christ, since the term "image" in 3:18 and 4:4 is to be related to Christ. Fifth, the term *eleutheria*, "freedom," refers to the Spirit of the Son (Gal. 4:6, 22ff.), in other words, to Christ as the mediator of freedom.

6. Vielhauer, "Paulus und das Alte Testament," 212.

TRADITIONS ABOUT MOSES

It would seem reasonable to begin immediately with assessment from the viewpoint of the psychology of religion. But we must first discuss the possibility that Paul read Exodus 34 in the light of a tradition about Moses that was available to him. The reinterpretation of the text would then be attributable to an exegetical tradition, not to Paul.

The thesis of a pre-Pauline Moses tradition is defended with minor variations by Siegfried Schulz and Dieter Georgi.[7] Both wish to reconstruct from the current text an earlier version in which Moses is evaluated positively but which was commented on critically by Paul. Both attribute this earlier version to Paul's opponents in Corinth, who are said to have appealed to Moses for support. Paul, then, is said to be attempting to get at his opponents through a critique of Moses.

But this thesis is not convincing. If we presume that the Corinthian opponents had appealed positively to Moses and Exodus 34, would Paul have been able to persuade them and their followers by forcibly reinterpreting the chief texts of their theology? Would he not have exposed himself all the more to the charges of falsifying the Word of God and twisting Scripture? The injustice to which Paul subjects the Old Testament text would have compromised him. The reality must have been just the opposite. Paul can afford a forced reinterpretation of the Old Testament text because he is sure from the start that the Corinthians also know themselves to be distant from the Old Testament. Each celebration of the Lord's Supper reinforced their consciousness of belonging to the new covenant (cf. 1 Cor. 11:25). That they belonged to the new covenant of Christ, and no longer to the old covenant of Moses, was part of their self-understanding. With regard to them, therefore, Paul could assess the old covenant negatively as "service of death" and of "condemnation" without establishing what death and condemnation consist in. In other words, Paul mobilized tendencies toward dissociation from the old covenant that were already present among the Corinthians. It is improbable that he struggled against a

7. In principle, three positions can be distinguished. (1) Behind 2 Corinthians 3, a written tradition about Moses is either postulated (thus Schulz, "Die Decke des Mose") or reconstructed in detail (thus Georgi, *Die Gegner*, 274–82). Paul is said to have commented critically on this tradition and sent it back to the Corinthians. (2) The assumption that Paul is criticizing a veneration of Moses that was present in Corinth is, however, not necessarily bound to the assumption of a fixed tradition prior to Paul. Cf. Rissi, *Studien*, 13–41; Collange, *Enigmes*. (3) Hickling ("The Sequence of Thought") accepts no confrontation with another theology, but only defense against personal charges.

veneration of Moses present among his enemies and in the community. His attack would have redounded upon himself.

Nevertheless, the thesis of Schulz and Georgi proceeds from a correct observation which requires explanation. In 2 Corinthians 3, Paul judges about Moses in a strikingly ambivalent manner. On the one hand, divine splendor is attributed to him and he becomes a type of the believer when he steps before God with unveiled face.[8] On the other hand, the new covenant is seen in sharp antithesis to Moses. A deceptive function is ascribed to Moses' veil. How can we explain this ambivalence toward the figure of Moses? Schulz and Georgi could have recognized something pertinent here. A different attitude toward Moses is visible behind the text as it now stands. This, however, would seem not to be the attitude of Paul's opponents in Corinth. Much more likely is the assumption that it is the attitude Paul himself once had toward Moses. Paul is not polemizing against a veneration of Moses present among those he is addressing; he is rather correcting his own veneration of Moses. Before his conversion he understood Exodus 34 in a completely different way; then light dawned on him. The veil fell from his heart. Moses was "exposed," but without the tie to him ever being completely abandoned. On the contrary, Paul even interprets him as a type of the convert. Since in 2 Cor. 4:6 Paul indirectly brings the removal of the "veil" into relationship with his conversion, our conjecture has from the start a certain probability in its favor. But how can it be established methodically? Here there are two ways. First, we must examine all the elements in the text that go beyond the Old Testament background and that could not possibly have come into the text through a Christian interpretation of Exodus 34. Second, we must show the presence in contemporary Judaism of traditions on the basis of which the presumed non-Christian elements and tendencies of interpretation may be explained.

Conclusions from the Text. The exegesis of Exodus 34 in 2 Corinthians 3 contains some tensions that indicate that originally everything was directed toward a glorification of Moses. Everything that is said about the splendor of the new covenant is dependent on what is still a presupposed positive evaluation of Moses. If, namely, the veiling of Moses was necessary because of the great divine splendor, then the

8. According to Schulz ("Die Decke des Moses," 21), in the Jewish-Christian tradition Moses is the "first Christian." Childs (*Exodus*, 624) states that "Moses is therefore an agent of both the old and the new."

lack of veiling in the Christian community could consistently be retraced to a lack of splendor; if, in other words, the splendor of the new covenant surpasses the glory of Moses, then this splendor would really have to be concealed. But for Paul, everything depends on the assertion that the splendor of the new covenant is unveiled. This positive assessment of being unveiled can only be explained by a continuing identification with the figure of Moses. Moses is unveiled in God's presence as a mediator of revelation. His glory is "graded": it must be concealed in public but is unconcealed before God. Paul takes over this system of gradation according to which being veiled relates to the lower level, being unveiled to the higher. But Paul no longer divides these levels among Moses' various functions and forms of appearance; he rather projects into them the opposition of old and new covenant. The gradualist system of levels that becomes visible behind 3:7ff. would then have originally served the following statement: If even the public service of Moses was glorious—so glorious that a veil had to conceal the divine splendor—how much more glorious is Moses' service in the immediate proximity of God. Behind an exoteric Judaism, an esoteric Judaism becomes visible; behind the veiled radiance, the unconcealed splendor; behind an imperfect preliminary stage, perfection—an immediate vision of the Deity, as is promised by the mystery cults, and also by apocalyptic visions of the throne room.[9] It is possible, then, that Paul presupposes an interpretation of Exodus 34 in which Moses is seen as mediator of the true vision of God, which exceeds what is accessible to all. The two stages, once both represented by Moses, are now reinterpreted, and Moses is completely limited to the preliminary stage. Christ mediates the true vision of God. Moses must turn to the Lord if he wishes to participate in this vision of God. An antithetical Moses-Christ framework is thus superimposed on a gradualist system of stages connected with Moses. Note that this is a conjecture. It would gain in historical probability if we could demonstrate the presence in contemporary Judaism of an interpretation of Moses in which Moses on Sinai represents a higher stage of faith.

Conclusions from Parallels. A picture of Moses of this sort can in fact be demonstrated. In Philo, Moses is a mystic and the hierophant of the true mysteries. The Old Testament is interpreted with the terminology of a cult mystery, which has an esoteric content as well as an exoteric

9. Paul also is acquainted with mystical experiences: he was assumed into the third heaven (2 Cor. 12:1ff.).

side. Philo's picture of Moses contains three elements that we can also sense behind 2 Corinthians 3: (1) a gradualist framework of levels of imperfect and perfect knowledge of God; (2) the conception of the transformation of Moses through the vision of God; and (3) the distinction of two groups of human beings.

1. *The gradualist framework of levels.*[10] In his *Allegorical Interpretation of Genesis* 3.100–102, Philo distinguishes two forms of knowledge of God. The lower level concludes from creation to God, while the higher level reaches immediate vision of God. The lower level is represented by Bezalel, who prepares the tent and the ark according to divine models (cf. Exod. 25:40; 31:1ff.). Moses represents the higher level:

> There is a mind more perfect and more thoroughly cleansed, which has undergone initiation into the great mysteries, a mind which gains its knowledge of the First Cause not from created things, as one may learn the substance from the shadow, but lifting its eyes above and beyond creation obtains a clear vision of the uncreated One, so as from Him to apprehend both the Word and this world. The mind of which I speak is Moses who says, "Manifest Thyself to me, let me see Thee that I may know Thee" (Exod. xxxiii. 13); "for I would not that Thou shouldst be manifested to me by means of heaven or earth or water or air or any created things at all, nor would I find the reflection of Thy being in aught else than in Thee Who art God. . . ." This is why God hath expressly called Moses and why He spake to Him. Bezalel also He hath expressly called, but not in like manner. One receives the clear vision of God directly from the First Cause Himself. The other discerns the Artificer, as it were from a shadow, from created things by virtue of a process of reasoning.[11]

This perfect knowledge of God is presented as a "mystery," with Moses as its hierophant. When Moses enters the "meeting tent" (Exod. 33:7ff.), he is introduced into the sacred mysteries (*On the Giants* 54):[12]

10. The most important texts of Philo are *Allegorical Interpretation of Genesis* 3.100ff., *Questions and Answers on Exodus* 2.40ff., *Moses* 2.69–70, *On the Posterity of Cain and His Exile* 13ff., *Moses* 1.158, and *On the Giants* 54. On these, cf. Pascher, *He basilike hodos*, 238ff.; Pascher seeks, surely incorrectly, to reconstruct a mystery ritual from these and other texts.

11. ET: F. H. Colson and G. H. Whitaker, *Philo*, vol. 1 of 10 vols. (LCL, 1929), 369.

12. The mystery vocabulary is not to be interpreted as reference to a real mystery cult (*pace* Pascher) but rather as a literary phenomenon. Cf. Wlosok, *Laktanz und die philosophische Gnosis*, 48–114, esp. 69ff.: mystery-like conceptions appear separated from the cult and precisely in this way "became free for religious speculation, and this means simultaneously that they became literary" (p. 113).

Entering the darkness, the invisible region, [Moses] abides there while he learns the secrets of the most holy mysteries. There he becomes not only one of the congregation of the initiated, but also the hierophant and teacher of divine rites, which he will impart to those whose ears are purified.[13]

2. *The transformation of Moses through the vision of God.* The motif of going in to God is to be found not only in Exod. 33:8, but also in Exod. 34:29ff., that is, in the pericope that Paul interprets in 2 Cor. 3:6ff. The text of the Septuagint speaks of "Moses' going in" in the same formulation in both texts: *henika d'an eiseporeuto Mousis* (Exod. 33:8 = 34:34). We may therefore assume that Philo understood both pericopes in the same sense—as reference to a divine mystery into which Moses introduces others. In fact, in *Moses* 2.69–70, Philo does assess Exod. 34:34 as witness to Moses' immediate vision of God. But in doing so he places the accent less on the knowledge of God than on the marvelous transformation wrought by the vision of God:

[Doubtless] he had the better food of contemplation, through whose inspiration, sent from heaven above, he grew in grace, first of mind, then of body also through the soul. . . . For we read that by God's command he ascended an inaccessible and pathless mountain, the highest and most sacred in the region, and remained for the period named, taking nothing that is needful to satisfy the requirements of bare sustenance. Then, after the said forty days had passed, he descended with a countenance far more beautiful than when he ascended, so that those who saw him were filled with awe and amazement; nor even could their eyes continue to stand the dazzling brightness that flashed from him like the rays of the sun.[14]

In Philo's commentary on Exodus this transformation is explicitly presented as apotheosis: "He is changed into the divine, so that such men become kin to God and truly divine" (*Questions and Answers on Exodus* 2.29, on Exod. 24:2).[15]

3. *Two classes of human beings.* What Moses experienced occurred to him as an exemplar, for not only Moses was called up the mountain. Moses' ascent can symbolically signify the ascent of every human being (*Concerning Noah's Work as a Planter* 23):

This is why those who crave for wisdom and knowledge with insatiable

13. ET: F. H. Colson and G. H. Whitaker, *Philo*, vol. 2 (LCL, 1929), 473.
14. ET: F. H. Colson, *Philo*, vol. 6 (LCL, 1935), 483, 485.
15. ET: Ralph Marcus, *Philo: Supplement*, vol. 2 of 2 vols. (LCL, 1953), 70.

persistence are said in the Sacred Oracles to have been called upwards;
for it accords with God's ways that those who have received his down-
breathing should be called up to him.[16]

In the following context (*Concerning Noah's Work as a Planter* 26), this
is grounded in the ascent of Moses:

Accordingly Moses, the keeper and guardian of the mysteries of the
Existent One, will be one called above; for it is said in the Book of
Leviticus, "He called Moses up above" (Lev. i. 1).[17]

But those who have been initiated into the true mysteries stand
opposite others. According to *Who Is the Heir of Divine Things* 76, those
who see and who look up toward heaven are on one side, while on the
other side is "the blind race, which has lost the sight which it thinks
it possesses [*ho blepein dokoun peperotai*],"[18] a race which has chosen evil
instead of good, the unjust instead of the just, the corruptible instead
of the incorruptible.

The parallelism is unmistakable when the three analogies between
Philo's picture of Moses and Paul's picture of Moses are juxtaposed:

Philo	*Paul*
Entrance to the Lord is perfect knowledge of God, which is to be distinguished from indirect knowledge of God.	Conversion to the Lord is perfect knowledge of God, which is to be distinguished from veiled knowledge of God.
The vision of God causes transformation and apotheosis in Moses.	Seeing the Lord causes transformation into the splendor and image of the Lord.
Those excluded from the vision of God are hardened (*peperotai*).	Listeners not transformed by the gospel are hardened (*eporothe*)

The comparison should not mislead to the premature conclusion
that Paul presupposes precisely the interpretation of Moses that is
attested in Philo. The parallels in Philo assure only the general historical
possibility that there was in Hellenistic Judaism an interpretation of

16. ET: F. H. Colson and G. H. Whitaker, *Philo*, vol. 3 (LCL, 1929), 225.
17. ET: ibid.
18. ET: F. H. Colson and G. H. Whitaker, *Philo*, vol. 4 (LCL, 1932), 321. For
further references to two classes of men, cf. *Who Is the Heir of Divine Things* 57, *Allegorical
Interpretation of Genesis* 3.104, *On the Unchangeableness of God* 142 ff.

Moses in which the transforming vision of God on Sinai played a particular role. In the variant present in Philo, this picture of Moses exhibits three elements that are also visible in 2 Corinthians 3: a gradualist structure of levels, transformation through the vision of God, and opposition to the hardened. Only one thing is lacking in Philo—the motif of the veil. Philo alludes only indirectly to this, when he emphasizes that the Israelites could not bear the sight of the divinized Moses. Since we have no other references to indicate that the veil of Moses was of major significance in Jewish exegesis,[19] the conjecture that Paul was the first to move this motif into the foreground lies close at hand. With the help of this motif he was able to carry out his Christian interpretation: what Philo attributes to Moses—mediation of true knowledge of God—is ascribed by Paul to Christ. Moses is replaced by Christ. By donning the veil, Moses devalued himself.

Note the following result. First, perceptible behind 2 Cor. 3:6–18 is a positive assessment of Moses, in which the public service of Moses is contrasted with his service immediately before God. Second, we find in contemporary Judaism, specifically in Philo, a picture of Moses that points in a similar direction. Third, Paul says of himself that a light that removed the veil dawned at his conversion—the veil that still lies over the hearts of his Jewish contemporaries. We may draw the following conclusion from these three observations. What Paul says in general about the Jews logically includes the Jew Paul and is based psychologically on his experience. Paul treats in this text in a generalized manner his own deception by the radiance of Moses. He himself once sought true knowledge of God from Moses. In this he knew himself to be superior to other erring men. He understood himself as a "light to those who are in darkness" (Rom. 2:19) and saw in Moses the "embodiment of knowledge and truth" (Rom. 2:20). But Christ took the place of Moses. In the light of the revelation of Christ, Paul radically reassessed Moses. The veil, once for him an indication of Moses' immediate service of God which surpassed all others, became for him a symbol of deceit and deception. Paul is correcting his own pre-Christian picture of Moses—not that of his foes.

Of course, in keeping with the nature of the material, we cannot go beyond founded conjectures in this field. If our conjecture is correct, it has an implication for the evaluation of the text from the perspective of the psychology of religion: the reassessment of Moses is not based

19. Cf. Billerbeck, *Kommentar* 3:516: "We have encountered no text in ancient rabbinic literature in which reference is made to the 'veil of Moses' in Exod. 34:33ff."

on tradition. On the contrary, Paul is not only projecting his theology into Old Testament texts but also correcting a traditional picture of Moses that he once shared himself. Here there is a wide-ranging restructuring of the field of perception, which can scarcely be understood unless one allows for a deeply rooted psychic dynamic that conferred on Paul's projections their plausibility and credibility.

Chapter 10

Psychological Analysis: 2 Corinthians 3:4—4:6

Aspects in Learning Theory: Moses as Model

In 2 Corinthians 3, Paul interprets the central symbolic model of Judaism—the figure of Moses. This figure had already been his person of reference in his pre-Christian days and still remained a point of reference for the self-understanding of the Christian apostle—and that not only in negative respect. Paul is not interested only in a sharp antithesis of Moses and Christ. To him, Moses is also exemplary in a positive sense: he is the basic type of the convert, in the midst of the Old Testament.

What is unmistakable at first, however, is the negative distinction from Moses: "Since we have such a hope, we are very bold, not like Moses" (2 Cor. 3:12–13).[1] The apostle's conduct consciously distinguishes itself from that of Moses. Paul rejects Moses as a model determining behavior. In doing so, he in no way denies Moses the divine splendor, that is, a specially distinguished status, which would be a favorable presupposition for the efficacy of models. He also criticizes none of the Mosaic commandments. He simply declares that the consequences of the Mosaic conduct are negative. The service of Moses leads to death and condemnation. His splendor is corruptible. Our problem is why Moses' service leads to such negative consequences. Why is Moses depreciated so strongly?

1. At this point the sentence is elliptical. Usually it is supplemented. "And [we act] not like Moses [who] put on a veil . . . " (thus Barrett, *A Commentary*, 118) or "And [it is] not as it was with Moses [who] . . . " (thus Bultmann, *Der zweite Brief an die Korinther*, 88). Rissi (*Studien*, 30) makes the original suggestion that *gegraptai* or a similar verb should be added: " . . . and not as the Scripture says that Moses put on a veil . . . " But that would make the critique of Moses into a critique of Scripture, which in my opinion is inconceivable for Paul.

Under the aspect of learning theory, the following thesis can be formulated: Moses is not criticized because of modes of behavior for which he is a model, but because of the inefficacious way in which he is a model. He is unable to anchor in the heart the norms of conduct he represents. His service is oriented on norms that are "carved in letters on stone" (3:7). Petrified laws cannot transform the human heart. But the divine norm demands the entire human being. It aims at a transformation of the heart and condemns one who does not come to such an inner transformation. For this reason, "the written code kills" (3:6).

Thus the criticism is directed toward Moses' relationship to the addressees of the old covenant. This relationship is characterized in principle by a distance that Paul illustrates with reference to different motifs in two parallel statements:[2] (a) that the radiant splendor of Moses prevents the Israelites from approaching (3:7); (b) that the veil of Moses prevents perception of the corruptible splendor (3:13). Whether Moses displays or conceals his "glory," the result in any case is a nonperception of reality and a distance between Moses and the Israelites. "But their minds were hardened" (3:14). The *alla*, "but," must be conceived in a strictly adversative fashion. Vision of the splendor and hardening within are opposed to each other. Behind this stands the conviction that the splendor really should penetrate into the interior. But this transformation that includes the interior occurs only in the Christian community. In 3:18*, Paul offers a formulation antithetical to 3:7 and 3:13:

> And we all, with unveiled face, behold [in a mirror][3] the glory of the Lord, and are changed into his likeness from glory to glory, as from the Lord who is Spirit.

Juxtaposition of the two texts may illustrate that this positive statement can only be understood against the background of negative statements about the old covenant, and even that the point of the train of thought lies in this antithesis:[4]

2. Rissi (*Studien*, 31) interprets the parallelism of 3:7 and 3:13 to the effect that in 3:7, Paul is citing his enemies, and in 3:13, he is correcting their statement "by exchanging the glowing countenance with the 'end of what fades.'" But there are many examples of Paul's "correcting" himself or making a statement more precise in parallel formulations; cf. Gal. 1:8 with 1:9; Rom. 7:8 with 7:11; and Rom. 2:1 with 2:3.

3. For the meaning "see in a mirror" rather than "reflect," see the extended consideration by Bultmann (*Der zweite Brief an die Korinther*, 93–97).

4. Striking 3:18 as a gnostic gloss deprives the text of its point—this against Schmithals, *Die Gnosis in Korinth*, 286ff.

2 Cor. 3:7, 13	*2 Cor. 3:18*
The Israelites behave like Moses:	Christians behave like the Lord:
A veil lies over Moses' face and their hearts.	All stand there with unveiled face.
They cannot see the glory of Moses.	All see the glory of the Lord as in a mirror.
The glory of Moses is fading.	All will be transformed into eternal glory: "from glory to glory."[5]

The decisive difference between the old covenant and the new is alluded to in the term *metamorphousthai*. Christ is a model who has the power to transform all human beings—and not only one chosen servant—into his image.[6] Moses was indeed transformed into a divine glory, but he had to conceal this from the community and thus increase the distance between himself and the community. He brought stone tablets of the law, whose content found no echo in human hearts (cf. the story of the golden calf). But Paul brought a gospel in which message and addressee merge: the community is the letter of Christ (2 Cor. 3:3). The community actualizes the new covenant, in which the norms of conduct are written in the heart and no one need instruct another (Jer. 31:31–34).

In the new covenant, the relationship of the forming model to the imitating human being is different from that in the old covenant. It is therefore not a jump in thought when Paul, in his defense of the apostolate, suddenly broadens the idea and includes all Christians: "*We all*, with unveiled face, behold the glory of the Lord" (3:18*). As in 2 Cor. 5:10, the *hemeis de pantes* means all Christians. In the new covenant, one individual is not exclusively "unveiled," but rather all in the same way. Servant and community are not distinguished from each other in the same way that Moses had to distinguish himself from the Israelites. When Paul, in 3:18, asserts the glory of all Christians, he did not "prove too much"[7] but rather drew attention to a decisive difference between the old covenant and the new, as he saw them.

The further train of thought confirms how decisive the transformation

5. According to Fridrichsen ("Scholia," 142–43), the expression means either a continuous process or an increase of the glory.
6. Larsson (*Christus als Vorbild*, 285–93) discusses the nature of the transformation. He says that it is (1) invisible, insofar as Christ is seen only in the Scriptures, and (2) visible, insofar as the outer man is destroyed and the inner renewed (2 Cor. 4:16). But the transformation involves more than an insight into Scripture.
7. Thus Lietzmann, *An die Korinther*, 115. Barrett (*A Commentary*, 126) is critical on this point.

of the social relation between "servant" and community is. Paul proceeds to draw a conclusion in 4:1–2: complete openness can reign between himself and the community. He commends himself by revelation of the truth to every human conscience before God (2 Cor. 4:2).

The same Moses who is at first judged so negatively is also a positive model of conversion: "As soon as he turns to the Lord the veil is removed" (2 Cor. 3:16*). Here Paul is thinking of Exod. 34:34: ". . . but whenever Moses went in before the Lord to speak with him, he took the veil off." It must have been a great discovery for Paul to find typologically, right in the middle of the Old Testament, "conversion to the Lord." Of course by our standards the exegesis is forced, but it is no more forced than the interpretation of the "rock which followed" as Christ in 1 Cor. 10:4. Just as that passage presupposes the hidden presence of Christ in Old Testament history at the time of the exodus, so too does our passage presuppose that Christ was there on Sinai.[8] Moses turned to him. In this way the veil was lifted. Now one can be transformed in one's innermost being by the Spirit. Insofar as Moses "corrected" his behavior and referred to another, superior model, he is a positive example. Thus in 2 Cor. 3:7–18, Paul depicts the exchange of two models, that is, a change in the external conditions of experience and behavior. The commitment to change is illustrated with the aid of the old model—Moses turned to the Lord.

The turn to a new model determining behavior has two results. First, there is a new type of motivation. Moses had to motivate man through norms imposed from without. His norms were letters etched in stone. Christ, on the contrary, confers the Spirit who transforms the heart. The model and those who live according to the model are conformed to one another. Second, a new social relationship between model and follower results from this. In the case of Moses, this relationship was marked by distance. Only one approaches the Deity, in a vicarious manner. Christians, however, all stand immediately before the Lord in the Spirit.

PSYCHODYNAMIC ASPECTS: CHRIST AS ACCESS TO THE UNCONSCIOUS

The material that could be described from the perspective of learning theory as a transition from one historically marked learning environment

8. Thus Bousset, *Kyrios Christos*, 101. A similar position is held by Rissi, *Studien*, 36–37.

to another historical world in which new models mark behavior can also be analyzed as an inner transformation of the human being. The section of 2 Corinthians from 3:1 to 4:6 itself suggests a view "from within." One can observe with regard to four central concepts how they are presented, in an interiorizing manner, as aspects of the human heart.

First, Paul places the community as a letter written in his (or its) *heart* in opposition to his opponents' letter of recommendation (3:2).

Second, he contrasts the stone tablets of the law with the "tablets of human *hearts*" (3:3).

Third, the veil of Moses appears not only over the reading of the law but also over the *hearts* of the listeners (3:15).

Fourth, the light of creation is interiorized and becomes the light that shines in the *hearts* of Christians (4:6).

This multiplication of interiorized conceptions cannot be a coincidence. Although the opposition of spirit and letter is not identical to the opposition of interiority and exteriority, the former does include the latter: where the Spirit works in Christian life, it transforms the human interior (cf. 2 Cor. 4:16). But what is changed in the human interior?

We now formulate our thesis: The veil symbolizes a boundary between consciousness and the unconscious. It is eliminated in Christ. When Christ opens access to the unconscious, the aggressive power of the historical norm comes (negatively) to light, but (positively) Christ as the image of God develops an "archetypal" power that transforms us. While the exposure of the aggressive norm can be well described with the concepts of Freud's psychoanalysis, categories of Jung's analytic psychology are more appropriate for the investigation of the transforming image.

An Interpretation as Symbolic of Conflict:
The Veil as Cover Over the Law

The symbol of the veil occurs three times in 2 Cor. 3:12–18: in connection with the lawgiver, in connection with the repeated imprinting of the law (the public reading of the old covenant), and finally, as an inner reality in those faithful to the law. This presents in an apt image the process of interiorization undergone by one who grows into the norms of one's historical environment. The norms represented by authoritative persons are imposed through constant repetition and eventually interiorized. The process is conscious only in part. We fully comprehend neither the origin of the norms nor their efficacy in ourselves. They are present within us, but aspects of their efficacy escape consciousness. Insofar as this is so, a "veil" lies over the heart of every individual. Here Paul touches on a universal human reality— a fact to which he himself alludes in this context. For Paul also uses the symbol of the veil a fourth time: "And even if our gospel is veiled, it is veiled only to those who are perishing" (2 Cor. 4:3). The gospel is directed to all. Those who are perishing are present among Jews and Gentiles. All interpretations, therefore, that relate the veil only to a specifically Jewish problematic fall short. Two such interpretations will be discussed here.[9]

Interpretation of 2 Corinthians 3 from a formal hermeneutical perspective holds that the reality hidden under the veil is the true meaning of the Old Testament.[10] In reading the Scripture, the Jews do not recognize that it has been fulfilled in Christ. The veil would then be symbol of a limit of understanding with regard to Scripture, but not (also) symbol of a limit of human understanding with regard to oneself and one's situation in view of the gospel.

Three arguments can be brought against this interpretation:

1. The formal hermeneutical interpretation of the motif of the veil fits well with its interpretation in v. 14. But Paul uses the motif several times. If he had said everything with the first interpretation, he could have contented himself with v. 14. The veil signifies not only limited insight into the Old Testament but also a general obduracy with regard to the message—something of which Paul can speak without any connection to the Old Testament in 4:4.

2. For Paul the old covenant is not only a "literary" but also a factual reality. The problem is not that the letter is unintelligible but that it kills (3:6). It is not the obscure meaning of Scripture but the threat of the condemning and destroying law which endangers existence that conceals itself behind the veil (cf. also the opposition of letter and spirit in Rom. 7:6).

3. The removal of the veil signifies not only increase in knowledge but also human transformation. The metamorphosis depicted in mystical language (3:18) far exceeds a deepened understanding of Scripture. It

9. A survey of research may be found in Hermann, *Kyrios*, 43ff.
10. Thus, among others, Allo, *Saint Paul*, 95. Käsemann's "Geist und Buchstabe" is not formal hermeneutical interpretation of 2 Corinthians 3. According to Käsemann, the Pauline hermeneutic of the Old Testament is determined in content by the eschatological transformation of the whole of existence through the justifying Christ-event.

signifies a new mode of existence in "freedom" and "glory," however much it also includes a new understanding of the Old Testament.

Most exegetes rightly go beyond a formal hermeneutical conception of 2 Corinthians 3. They envision the old covenant as a factual reality, not merely a literary one. A widespread interpretation holds that when the veil is removed from the old covenant, the fact that the old covenant has already reached an end becomes visible. Verse 14, then, is understood as follows: ". . . the veil remains over the reading of the old covenant. It [the veil] is not removed, for it [i.e., the old covenant] is taken away in Christ" (2 Cor. 3:14*). The subject of *katargeitai* would be the *palaia diatheke*.[11]

There are telling grounds against this interpretation.

1. The participle *me anakaluptomenon* certainly has the veil (neuter!) as its subject. The same subject is to be supposed for the following causal clause *hoti en Christo katargeitai*. Paul would have had to signal a change in subject clearly, especially since the alleged new subject previously stood in the genitive (*tes palaias diathekes*).

2. The verb *katargein* stands semantically in opposition to *menein*, as is seen from the opposition of *menein* and *katargein* in 2 Cor. 3:11 and 1 Cor. 13:8–13. Both verbs occur in v. 14; both are to be related to the same reality. The "remain" is from the start limited "until the present day"; what remains will, in other words, one day be removed. But in this case only the veil can be meant.[12]

3. The grammatical form *katargeitai* corresponds to the following verb forms *keitei* and *periaireitai*, in which "veil" is the subject of the sentence. These relationships are more clear from the grammatical form than is the relationship to the participle *katapgoumenon* (vv. 7, 11, 13).

4. If the topic were the end of the law through the death and resurrection of Jesus, one would expect an aorist or past tense, not the present *katargeitai*, for the old covenant would already have been abolished with Christ. [13] But the next sentence shows unmistakably that it is not at all a matter of objective elimination of a reality: it is a matter rather

---

11. Thus Lietzmann, *An die Korinther*, 113; Bultmann, *Der zweite Brief an die Korinther*, 89; Dunn, "2. Corinthians," 311 n. 7. Against this, Kümmel, *An die Korinther*, 200; Barrett, *A Commentary*, 120–121. Allo (*Saint Paul*, 91) offers an original interpretation: that the veil remains since it has not yet been revealed that it has in reality already been removed.

12. It is usually argued that in 3:7, 11, 13, *katargein* is said of the old covenant or of its splendor, and that the same subject is therefore to be presumed in v. 15; thus Bultmann, *Der zweite Brief an die Korinther*, 89.

13. Cf. Schlatter, *Paulus*, 517.

of the existing subjective disposition. The veil lies over the heart during the reading of the law; it is removed through conversion.

We can relate what hides behind the veil neither exclusively to the (christological) meaning of the Old Testament nor to the end of the old covenant. The point of departure is rather Paul's emphasis that the veil over the reading of the Old Testament is the *same* veil as that of Moses (*to auto kalymma*, v. 14); that is, what is concealed behind it is the same as in the case of Moses—the corruptibility of the splendor. The Israelites admire the splendor of the old covenant because they let themselves be deceived about its corruptibility. According to 3:7–11, this corruptibility results from the fact that the service of Moses was a service of death and condemnation. The summary heading in 3:6* shows what Paul is concerned with: "The letter kills, but the spirit gives life." What remained hidden from the Israelites is therefore ultimately the killing power of the law—in psychoanalytic terms, the aggressivity of the internalized norm. To all appearances, the Mosaic law is surrounded by splendor and glory, but its shadow sides had to be concealed from consciousness through a veil. Through Christ these shadow sides come to light. The hidden aggressivity of the law is revealed. The veil falls. Those aspects of the superego that had escaped consciousness and plagued and constricted human beings through their archaic severity come to light. A new freedom (*eleutheria*, v. 17) with regard to the unconscious aggressive power of the norm becomes possible.

We must again ask self-critically if we are imposing modern thoughts on Paul. Can an interpretation of this sort be made historically plausible? Does it correspond to analogies?

The idea that unconscious normative tribunals within us influence human experience and behavior is in principle not foreign to antiquity. Epictetus (*Discourses* 2.8.11–14) once spoke of the unknown god within man against whom everyone sins through misconduct:

> You are a fragment of God; you have within you a part of Him. Why, then, are you ignorant of your own kinship? Why do you not know the source from which you have sprung? Will you not bear in mind, whenever you eat, who you are that eat, and whom you are nourishing? Whenever you indulge in intercourse with women, who you are that do this? Whenever you mix in society, whenever you take physical exercise, whenever you converse, do you not know that you are nourishing God, exercising God? You are bearing God about with you,

you poor wretch, and know it not! Do you suppose that I am speaking of some external God, made of silver or gold? It is within yourself that you bear Him, and do not perceive that you are defiling Him with impure thoughts and filthy actions. Yet in the presence of even an image of God you would not dare to do anything of the things you are now doing. But when God Himself is present within you, seeing and hearing everything, are you not ashamed to be thinking and doing such things as these, O insensible of your own nature, and object of God's wrath![14]

In another passage (*Discourses* 1.14.12–13), Epictetus distinguishes the normative tribunal present within us from God. He says that God gave each individual as overseer a "demon" who never sleeps and cannot be deceived. This is always present—even when one is alone behind closed doors.

In Epictetus, the God unconsciously present "within us" appears chiefly as a positive tribunal. It is true that one who despises him attracts wrath upon oneself. But no deceptive glory surrounds him. The problem is not perceiving this inner tribunal falsely but rather paying attention to it at all. This is different in Paul. For him, the law that unconsciously has effects is a profoundly ambivalent reality. According to 2 Cor. 3:6, it kills. But the other texts in Paul also testify to a clear ambivalence.

1. Paul ascribes an unconsciously operative law to the Gentiles who have never heard of the Mosaic law (Rom. 2:14–15). In doing this, Paul makes use of the ancient conception of the "unwritten law." Antiquity knew a natural law in addition to "positive" law on the basis of social determination. Picking up this idea, Paul can say that a law is also written into the heart of the Gentiles. Their conscience and the inner process of self-accusation and defense are witnesses to this. This law written in the heart is an objective reality. It is not identical to conscience. Conscience, rather, is witness to the law and therefore cannot coincide with the law to which it bears witness. The "law of the Gentiles" is thus an internalized reality, which is not fully conscious. At least the fact that God has written this law into human hearts is unconscious.

2. Hellenistic Judaism had already drawn on the conception of the "unwritten law" in order to postulate the presence of the law before its revelation on Sinai.[15] Otherwise it would not have been possible to

---

14. ET: W. A. Oldfather, *Epictetus*, vol. 1 of 2 vols. (LCL, 1926), 261, 263.
15. Cf. Philo *On Abraham* 275. It is said of Abraham " 'that this man did the divine

present Abraham as a model of Jewish fulfillment of the law. Paul also knows the problem of a law prior to Moses. In Rom. 5:12ff., he develops the idea that death came into the world through Adam, life through Christ's obedience. Sin and law belong close together: "where there is no law there is no transgression" (Rom. 4:15). Now Paul has to explain how sin could exist before the coming of the law, before Moses. His explanation (Rom. 5:13–14) leaves an impression of help-lessness:

> . . . sin indeed was in the world before the law was given, but sin is not counted where there is no law. Yet death reigned from Adam to Moses, even over those whose sins were not like the transgression of Adam, who was a type of the one who was to come.

How should this be understood? Does death here exert a violent dominion over man, regulated by no law? A dominion without legal foundation in man's transgressions? But Paul speaks explicitly of transgression (*parabasis*) between Adam and Moses, precisely through emphasizing that it is not a matter of the same "transgression" as in the case of Adam. In each instance the punishment is the same— death. But if the rule that there is no transgression without law (Rom. 4:15) is valid, then there can be only one conclusion: although the law had not yet been revealed, it was already operative unconsciously.

3. Finally, in anticipation of the following chapter, let us refer to Rom. 7:7ff. As in 2 Cor. 3:7–18, here too the motif of deceit is connected with the law: "Sin, finding opportunity in the commandment, deceived me and by it killed me" (7:11). As in 2 Cor. 3:6ff., Paul here treats the opposition between service of the "letter" and in the "Spirit" (cf. Rom. 7:6). But whereas in 2 Cor. 3:6*, Paul simply declares that "the letter kills," in Rom. 7:7ff., he argues in a more differentiated manner. The law and its letter do not themselves kill; rather, sin kills with the help of the law. The aggressive power of the superego, which turns against the ego, comes not from the superego itself but from the flesh—psychologically speaking, from the id. Behind the back of the ego, the id has taken control of the superego and now as aggressive energy threatens the ego. Here too the law has unconscious aspects; otherwise the ego could not be deceived with its aid.

In reviewing the three texts that have been discussed, it should be

---

law and the divine commands.' He did them, not taught by written words, but unwritten nature . . . " (ET: F. H. Colson, *Philo*, vol. 6 of 10 vols. [LCL, 1935], 133, 135).

stressed that different contents enter the shadow of the unconscious. The Gentiles know nothing of the one God as originator of the law; the generations between Adam and Moses do not know the formulations of the law. The deceived ego in Rom. 7:7ff. is mistaken about the effects of the law. But the law always appears as something threatening. Among the Gentiles it manifests itself in a conflict of conscience. Between Adam and Moses it brings about death in an obscure manner. It opposes the ego as a destructive power. The aggressive trait of the law that Paul summarizes under the rubric "curse of the law" (Gal. 3:13) manifests itself everywhere. This curse is exposed through Christ. Christ himself becomes a curse (Gal. 3:13). In this way, the negative aspects of the law become conscious. The veil falls.

It is to be stressed once again that in order to interpret this aggressive element of the norm psychodynamically, there is, in my opinion, no need for belief that our experience and behavior are conditioned by the Oedipus complex. No father threatening castration stands behind the law that kills. The insight suffices that moral requirements can be experienced in an archaic level of man as signals that elicit anxiety. Instinctive direction through adaptations derived from the history of the race have indeed been replaced in us by social and moral systems of direction. But there is still within us an archaic level that is oriented toward activating the entire organism in response to certain signals through fear of death, in order to save it through flight or battle. On this level, moral commandments can be understood as "enemy signals," which elicit death anxieties—especially since real death threats were often joined to social and moral commandments. Even the mere existence of the demanding commandment can then be experienced as threatening: "the letter kills." Here it is not a matter of specific commandments. The norms are rather very varied in sociocultural respects. But all of them can be coupled to archaic death anxieties and become the law of sin and death. Paul was the first to articulate this recognition. What he analyzed in confrontation with the Mosiac law is representative for all human beings: all individuals must come to terms with their historical norms. All persons have within themselves the archaic readiness to react to demands that elicit anxiety. One is inclined to conceal from oneself what shadow sides normative mechanisms of direction can have. And one is inclined to obduracy when confronted with radically divergent norms. For one would like to take the corruptible splendor of one's norms and values for eternal "glory."

An Interpretation as Symbolic of
Integration: The Veil as Covering of the Image

The veil of Moses not only conceals the aggressive power of the law. It also conceals its positive counterpart—the true splendor of Christ that shines in the interior of human beings and so transforms them that they have escaped the dominion of the letter that kills. Only on the basis of this true splendor is the fragility of the corruptible splendor revealed: "Indeed, in this case, what once had splendor has come to have no splendor at all, because of the splendor which surpasses it" (2 Cor. 3:10). In three parallel statements, Paul describes this revelation of the true splendor that can be perceived only after removal of the veil:

> 2 Cor. 3:18*: But we all see [as in a mirror] with unveiled face the splendor of the Lord and are transformed into the same likeness from glory to glory, as by the Lord who is Spirit.
> 2 Cor. 4:3–4: And even if our gospel is veiled, it is veiled only to those who are perishing. In their case the god of this world has blinded the minds of the unbelievers, to keep them from seeing the light of the gospel of the glory of Christ, who is the likeness of God.
> 2 Cor. 4:6: For it is the God who said, "Let light shine out of darkness," who has shone in our hearts to give the light of the knowledge of the glory of God in the face of Christ.

The repetition of the same motifs and words is unmistakable. The motif of the veil occurs in 3:18 (unveiled face) and 4:3 (veiled gospel). "Seeing" is in both texts the opposite of being veiled (3:18; 4:4). The metaphor of light occurs in 4:4 and 4:6 in slightly varied linguistic expressions:

> ton photismon tou euaggeliou tes doxes tou Christou (4:4)

> pros photismon tes gnoseos tes doxes tou Theou (4:6)

The substitution of Christ and God in these parallel sentences points to their functional proximity.[16] While in 4:6 God is the creator God, who created the light, in 4:4 Christ is the "image" of God, according to which man was created. As the image of God he mediates the true glory (3:18; 4:4, 6). It is possible that here Paul is picking up general

---

16. In each case, a further portion of the sentence relates the glory of Christ to God, for Christ is the *eikon tou Theou* (2 Cor. 4:4); and the glory of God to Christ, for this glory appears *en prosopo Iesou Christou* (4:6).

Christian conceptions that are connected with conversion and baptism.[17] The sentences are overloaded. The concepts are not explained. As is often the case in liturgical language, their precise relationship remains unclear. What interests us is the process of illumination that is described in these parallel statements. Four elements may be noted.

First, the radiance of the image of Christ is operative even in the most interior part of human beings. In this regard, Paul is still thinking in 3:18 of the community assembled for worship (as contrast to the synagogue service). In 4:6, however, he is unmistakably describing an inner process: God lets light dawn in "our hearts." The darkness that is dispersed is a darkness within. Into this darkness the image of Christ shines. The illumination is identical in content to the dropping of the veil. While a critical light falls on the glory of Moses, the image of Christ is the source from which this light proceeds; the glory of Moses fades before its splendor. Put in psychodynamic language, illumination through the image of Christ is enlightenment of the unconscious.

Second, Paul portrays the process as renewal of the process of creation.[18] The God who once created light (Gen. 1:3) causes it to become bright once again within. The God who formed man according to his image (*eikon*) reveals himself in the image of Christ. The Creator God makes a new creature: a *kaine ktisis* (2 Cor. 5:17; Gal. 6:15) and a second Adam (1 Cor. 15:44–45). We always observe the same process: the concepts connected with primeval times—"light," "image," "creation," and "Adam"—are actualized anew. The primeval event is surpassed by a new act of creation. What once was determinative for the whole of creation becomes the goal and model of a new process. This aspect can be described psychodynamically by stating that regression to primeval images stands in the service of a progression toward new goals.

Third, the process of illumination has an enemy—the god of this world. Satan receives a predicate that brings him close to the Creator God. Presupposed is that the world created by God fell under the dominion of Satan and that "this world" is not eternal but will be replaced by a new world that begins with Christ. Christ has delivered us from this evil world (Gal. 1:4). But the old world presents opposition to the new. The ruler of this world makes men blind within so that they are not illuminated. In psychodynamic terms, the dominant

17. Jervell, *Imago Dei*, 196–97.
18. Jervell (*Imago Dei*, 173–76) considers 2 Cor. 3:18—4:6 an exegesis of Gen. 1:27.

consciousness places determined opposition to the enlightening of the unconscious.

Fourth, Paul twice uses the concept of image. In this way Christ is emphasized as revealer of God. As likeness of God he reflects the divine glory.[19] This aspect of the concept, which pertains to the theology of revelation, is often emphasized one-sidedly. The concept undoubtedly also has an anthropological accent, both on the basis of its derivation and in its Pauline usage. On the one hand, in Gen. 1:27 it designates the creation of man: "So God created man in his own image, in the image of God he created him." On the other hand, every time that Paul applies the concept of image to Christ[20] he emphasizes that human beings are destined to become like Christ. Christians are "to be conformed to the image of his Son" (Rom. 8:29). They are to bear the image of Christ as they have borne the image of Adam (1 Cor. 15:49) and are destined to be transformed into the image of the Lord (2 Cor. 3:18). As image, Christ reveals not only the Deity but also man; he is the true likeness of God, and simultaneously the true determination of man. If we seek to formulate this in psychodynamic terms, we could say that as the image of the goal of true humanity, Christ takes the place of the punishing superego. He unites in himself the opposition of God and man. He is a "coincidence of opposites."

Proceeding from the psychodynamic supposition that the metaphorical world of religious symbols represents psychic processes within us suggests the following interpretation. When one, against the resistance of the dominant consciousness, has found access to the unconscious, it is not only the side of historical systems of conviction which is hostile to life—rooted in, among other things, an archaic level of experience—that discloses itself. Simultaneously, a more comprehensive symbol of human determination replaces previous projections of goals—a symbol with a preexistent root prior to every historical culture, because it is anchored in creation itself. As image, Christ represents the archetypal goal of the self.

19. Thus esp. Wis. 7:25–26, where wisdom appears as emanation and likeness of God and where the metaphor of light is also present. Wisdom is the "reflection of eternal light" (7:26). It is therefore no coincidence that the concept of image in Gen. 1:26–27 becomes increasingly distant from the empirical human being. According to Philo, only the logos is the real image of God. The human being is created not as *eikon* but rather as *kat' eikon;* and even with this "likeness of the logos," not the whole human being is meant but only the *nous* (*Who Is the Heir* 230–32).

20. In this usage, the term "image" always refers to the Risen One; cf. Jervell (*Imago Dei*, 332): "Not the earthly Jesus, but the risen and exalted Lord who is the Spirit, is the true image of God."

Analysis of 2 Corinthians 3 from the perspective of learning theory interpreted the transition from Moses to Christ as replacement of an old model of conduct by a new model. Religious symbols were understood as representations of the external, historical learning environment. A psychodynamic reading of the texts, on the contrary, sees here an inner restructuring of our relationship to the unconscious. The integrative symbol of the self—Christ, the image of God—replaces the unconsciously operative aggressive norm. In distinction from the conception of learning theory, a doctrine of archetypes from the perspective of a psychology of religion would see in the new "model" not only the symbolic representation of a new historical learning environment but also the expression of a relatively open human tendency prior to all cultural determination, which does indeed articulate itself with the help of historically formed images but which is present in a preexistent manner in human nature. Precisely the crisis of culturally preprogrammed orientations of life is seen as constantly necessitating forays from the precultural region of archetypal structures. This region is seen as largely unconscious. An opening toward it functions like a revelation.

COGNITIVE ASPECTS: OVERCOMING OF DISSONANCE IN 2 CORINTHIANS 3

Psychodynamic change and orientation on new models are not a passive fate. A decision lies behind them. Of course we are often forced against our will into situations of decision, but how we assess and handle the situation depends on us. This is true also of Paul. He can depict his Damascus experience both as divine vocation (Gal. 1:15–16) and as personal decision (Phil. 3:7ff.). The impetus to change came from without. But Paul himself accepts the responsibility for the fact that as a result of his conversion, he sees as trash everything that he once considered gain (Phil. 3:7ff.).[21] Through a triple *hegeisthai* (count), he emphasizes this judgment as his own evaluation. He himself is responsible for the radical consequences he drew from his vocation to be an apostle, consequences that led to a far greater distancing from

21. Both aspects pertain to existential decision. Cf. Thomae (*Konflikt*, 180): "If we are justified in saying in the context previously alluded to that one, in being opened to meaning in an absolute manner, is free in decision, then it is now necessary to add that one is not free in regard to entering the state of decision. Freedom as openness for the background of meaning of one's own existence encounters us as the result of a possibly unique constellation and is afterwards in some circumstances irrevocably gone."

Judaism than was the case with other Jewish Christians and that were unusual within the framework of early Christianity.

Every decision leaves behind cognitive dissonance. In an acute situation of decision, we are not capable of doing justice to the excluded alternative. In the relaxed situation after the decision, on the contrary, we often see the attractive side of the excluded alternative more clearly. The postdecisional conflict confronts us with the task of restructuring the situation interpretively until it is once again consonant with the decision that has been made. It is well known that consonance with ourselves is often more important in this process than consonance with the facts.

The forced reinterpretation of the Old Testament in 2 Cor. 3:7–18 can in my opinion be understood as a reduction of dissonance at the cost of "objective" facts. Conscious manipulation of the Old Testament wording is excluded. It is rather a question of an unconscious restructuring of the Old Testament. Paul has to justify three points: first, his conversion from a Jewish form of life; second, his turning to Christ; and third, isolation from his former comrades in faith—the annoying fact that what seemed evident to him was not evident to them. He had to justify this in a postdecisional conflict in which the attractiveness of the once-abandoned form of life reasserted itself. Paul cannot avoid conceding to Moses an attractive splendor. The old covenant also had divine glory.

1. But how does he then justify his turning away from this glory? Paul legitimizes it with his exegetical "discovery" that the splendor of Moses was in reality fading. He does not deny its divinity but rather denies its eternity. It was most certainly justified to turn away from the fading splendor in order to turn toward the eternal splendor.

2. Did he not thus become unfaithful to the old covenant? Here Paul unambiguously says no! He discovers in the midst of the old covenant the requirement of conversion. Moses himself had already converted to the "Lord." Paul's conversion only follows the example of Moses. Certainly Paul cites the Old Testament very loosely in this passage. But what does pedantic convergence with the wording of the Old Testament mean if the newly interpreted Old Testament narrative corresponds to Paul's overall situation, if with its aid he can oppose the self-accusation that he, Paul, is a traitor to the ancestral traditions he once supported with great zeal (Gal. 1:14)?

3. But if turning away from the old covenant is justified and commanded by the Old Testament itself, why has it not been done

by everyone? Why do all not see that the splendor of Moses is fading? Paul names two explanatory causes—the veil of Moses and the "hardening of minds" (2 Cor. 3:13–14*). Both factors are subject to change. The veil of Moses was already removed in the Old Testament narrative. Hardening, for Paul and for antiquity in general, is something variable; the interpretation of behavior as hardening often even serves to defuse a social situation. One who is hardened and blinded need not attribute one's conduct to oneself. Causal attribution is referred to supernatural agents. Let us give some examples of the socially defusing effect of transsubjective causal attribution.[22]

(a) Agamemnon (*Iliad* 19.86ff.) traces the abduction of Briseis back to a blindness sent by the gods. He justifies himself with these words:

> It is not I that am at fault, but Zeus and Fate and Erinys, that walketh in darkness, seeing that in the midst of the place of gathering they cast upon my soul fierce blindness on that day, when of mine own arrogance I took from Achilles his prize. But what could I do? It is God that bringeth all things to their issue.[23]

Agamemnon does not for this reason seek to unload responsibility for the consequences; to the contrary, precisely because he does not retrace responsibility to himself, he has the freedom to offer compensation (19.137–38; cf. 9.119–20, 636–37): "I . . . could not forget Ate, of whom at the first I was made blind. Howbeit seeing I was blinded, and Zeus robbed me of my wits, fain am I to make amends and to give requital past counting."[24]

(b) Hardening through a demonic power can also be mentioned in a Jewish text as motive for God's mercy; those hardened, after all, are not themselves at fault for their condition. We read in the *Testament of Judah* (19.3–4):

> But the God of my fathers, who is compassionate and merciful, pardoned me because I acted in ignorance. The prince of error blinded me, and

22. Further references in Bultmann, *Der zweite Brief an die Korinther*, 106–8. One who has recognized the unburdening function of transsubjective causal attribution can hardly agree with Bultmann's statement that "the 'god of this world' is . . . not a causal power behind the human will but rather works in the evil decision of the will" (p. 106), insofar as this is meant to reflect the opinion of Paul. Bultmann does not cite *Iliad* 19.86ff. The explicit denial of the participation of one's own will (*ego d' ouk aitios eimi, alla Zeus*) would contradict his interpretation.

23. ET: A. T. Murray, *Homer: The Iliad*, vol. 2 of 2 vols. (LCL, 1925), 343.

24. ET: ibid., 347. On the entire question, cf. chap. 1 of Dodds, *The Greeks and the Irrational*.

I was ignorant—as a human being, as flesh, in my corrupt sins—until
I learned of my own weakness after supposing myself to be invincible.[25]

Here too the motif of hardening has unburdening character. The
prince of error, moreover, is none other than the "god of this world"
(2 Cor. 4:4).

(c) It could be objected against the cited examples that the motif of
hardening is unburdening only as long as it is not attributed to the
omnipotent God himself. In early Christianity, however, hardening is
also attributed to God himself. In 2 Cor. 4:4, Paul is clearly thinking
of Satan. But a few lines earlier, the *eporothe* in 3:14 has to be interpreted
as a divine passive, especially since Paul elsewhere traces back to God
the hardening of the Jews with regard to the message. In Rom. 11:8
he cites Deut. 29:4:

> God gave them a spirit of stupor,
> eyes that should not see and ears
> that should not hear,
> down to this very day.

In doing this, he changes the text of the Septuagint in an instructive
manner. In the Septuagint, Deut. 29:4 reads,

> Yet the Lord God has not given you a heart to know, and eyes to see,
> and ears to hear, until this day.

Paul replaces the "hardened heart" with the "spirit of stupor" of Isa.
29:10*. In addition, he underlines the temporal limitation of the
hardening through insertion of a *semeron*, "to the present day." The
decisive new accent is that a "stupor" is something passing, while the
heart, on the contrary, is something constant (despite the new heart
promised by God, Ezek. 36:26; 11:19). The unseeing eyes and deaf
ears are the consequences of the stupor; in contrast to the Septuagint,
here they are not juxtaposed by an "and" but must be understood in
apposition to the "spirit of stupor." Paul is concerned to retrace the
Jews' rejecting stance with regard to the gospel to a variable factor.
"Hardening" to him means no definitive judgment about other human
beings.[26]

If Paul is dealing with his own cognitive dissonance in 2 Corinthians
3, one cannot attribute an all-determining status to the polemic motif

---

25. ET: H. C. Kee, *The Old Testament Pseudepigrapha*, ed. Charlesworth, 1:800.
26. With this Paul sets a different accent than early Christianity. In him the idea of
hardening does not have the function of justifying the hopelessness of mission. Hardening
is not intended to make repentance impossible—an idea that is implied in Mark 4:12//
(= Isa. 6:9–10); John 12:40; and Acts 28:26.

in the text. Paul confronts above all himself, for his relationship to Judaism is always, among other things, a relationship to his own life. Paul leaves no doubt that his reflections refer to himself. The theme of the entire section is his apostolate, his task, his role. It is almost by way of excuse that he says, "What we preach is not ourselves, but Jesus Christ as Lord, with ourselves as your servants for Jesus' sake" (2 Cor. 4:5). But what does Paul intend with regard to himself?

Paul is seeking to overcome the cognitive dissonance between his decision against his former manner of life and his continuing estimation of the Old Testament—as the quintessence of this form of life. He succeeds in reading the Old Testament in such a way that it supports his decision, and even requires it, by restructuring cognitively the picture of the Mosaic service. This restructuring does not occur in the course of a distancing from Judaism. Just the opposite: in view of the distancing from Judaism that has already occurred, Paul seeks to preserve continuity with it.

Under the aspects of learning theory and psychodynamics, we stressed the change in Paul's outer and inner world; the analysis of cognitive aspects alerts us to the fact that despite this change Paul spontaneously sought a continuity that conferred coherence and meaning on life. The break with the old form of life placed him before the task of seeking what made possible identity in change. Paul sought to appropriate his past. This search for integration of the past cannot be interpreted only as disposing of a "disturbance" or as reducing dissonance. It also has a positive side. Conceptions that attribute to human beings a spontaneous tendency to self-realization will see here not only Paul's overcoming of a postdecisional conflict but also his positive striving to integrate resistant aspects of his own life. Christ as the image of God and symbol of the self places Paul positively before the task of integrating his Jewish past. With regard to existence in Christ, Paul writes in Gal. 3:28, "There is neither Jew nor Greek, there is neither slave nor free, there is neither male nor female; for you are all one in Christ Jesus." Even though Paul does not use the term "image," this concept is nonetheless presupposed, for the expression *arsen kai thelu* comes from Gen. 1:27*: "God created man in his own image, in the image of God he created him; *arsen kai thelu* he created them." To Paul, the unity of what otherwise dissolves into polarities pertains to the image of God. If the veil falls and man is transformed into God's image, this means not abandonment of the Jewish past but its incorporation into his own self-understanding. And this is true not only of Paul. Paul would not have described this process had he not considered it representative for all Christians. It is true of all Christians that as long as they have not integrated both their Jewish and gentile heritage, they are not yet transformed into the image of God. As long as they are not, a veil still lies on their hearts too.

EXCURSUS ON 1 COR. 11:3–16: THE VEIL ON THE HEAD OF WOMEN

The confrontation over the "veil" of Moses and the "veiled" gospel of Paul probably has a prehistory. At the very least, in reading 2 Corinthians 3, the Corinthians must have thought involuntarily of the dispute over women's head covering, which Paul had settled in 1 Corinthians 11 with such unusual arguments. In both cases, he starts from the same premises: the uncovered head symbolizes an immediate relationship to God. In both cases, the veil is placed in relationship to the divine glory and image. The man is the glory and image of God and must therefore wear no veil (1 Cor. 11:7). The unveiled Christians see the glory and image of God (2 Cor. 3:18). The veil on the head, on the contrary, symbolizes distance, whether in the case of women (1 Cor. 11:7) or of Moses (2 Cor. 3:7, 12). It is true that the terms are different— *kalymma* does not occur in 1 Corinthians 11[1]—but the terms are not the point. The function is comparable. Before we draw far-reaching conclusions from this to the symbolic content of the "veil" in 1 Corinthians 11, we must clarify three questions. First, what was the general practice in this regard in Hellenistic-Roman antiquity? Was wearing a veil required? Second, what motives stand behind the development in Corinth? Why do women appear "unveiled" there? Third, what motives determine Paul's reaction in 1 Corinthians 11? Only after we have clarified the historical context can we judge if, from a psychodynamic perspective, the covering on the head of women has a symbolic content similar to the veil of Moses—if it is a reference to the boundary between conscious and unconscious parts of human life.

The General Practice
Unfortunately, Paul leaves us unclear as to what sort of head covering he envisions in 1 Corinthians 11. If we abstract from the headband, the diadem, and the stephane, which leave the greater part of the head uncovered, we can distinguish three basic forms of female head covering.

1. *Kalymma* occurs as a variant reading to *exousia* (v. 10), especially in the Latin tradition. Instead, we find verbs and adjectives derived from the same root. *Kalymma* can designate a woman's veil (cf. Homer *Iliad* 24.93; Aeschylus *Agamemnon* 1178; Euripides *Iphigenia in Tauris* 372; Aristophanes *Lysistrata* 530ff.; Dicaearchus *De Graeciae urbibus* 18 [*Fragmenta Historicorum Graecorum* 2.259]). An association with 1 Corinthians 11 was therefore close at hand to someone reading 2 Corinthians 3.

1. The normal manner of "veiling" is draping something around the head. For this no special piece of clothing is needed. Rather, the himation is simply drawn over the back of the head. Innumerable women had themselves portrayed in this fashion on their family graves. There the countenance remains visible, but the himation can, if desired, also be drawn far forward. It is said in one text of the women of Thebes that the veil of the clothing on their heads covers almost the entire face, like a mask.[2] Something similar is surely meant by Dio Chrysostom (*Discourses* 33.48) when he praises the Tarsian practice regarding attire, "a convention which prescribes that women should be so arrayed and should so deport themselves when in the street that nobody could see any part of them, neither of the face nor of the rest of the body, and that they themselves might not see anything off the road."[3] Both passages speak explicitly of a himation. As a rule, however, the himation was worn open; otherwise, the deviant practice would not have been recorded so painstakingly.

2. Besides this, there is a shorter "veil" that reaches as far as the shoulders. In the frescoes of the synagogue of Dura Europos, this type can be distinguished clearly from the himation drawn over the head.[4] In Greek literature, a veil appears in Homer as *kredemnon*,[5] later as *kalyptre* and *kalymma*.[6] In the early Christian period it could perhaps also be called *mitra*.[7] This type is to be found in portraits much less frequently than the wrap around the head.[8]

3. A third type of head covering is the hood, usually wrapped from a cloth.[9]

---

2. Cf. Dicaearchus *De Graeciae* 18–19: "For the women of Thebes the head covering through clothing [*to ton himation epi tes kephales kalymma*] is constituted in such a way that one has the impression that the entire face is covered as by a small mask. For only the eyes appear through it; the rest of the face is completely covered by the clothing. The hair is blond and is bound up to the part, a style which the natives call 'lampidion [small torch]' " (*Fragmenta Historicorum Graecorum* 2:259).

3. ET: H. Lamar Crosby, *Dio Chrysostom*, vol. 3 of 5 vols. (LCL, 1940), 319. Conzelmann (*Der erste Brief*, 218 n. 40) thinks that Dio Chrysostom is lamenting the decay of the custom of veiling. The opposite is the case. Dio is recording the continuance of this custom during a period of general moral decay: "While they have their faces covered as they walk, they have the soul uncovered and its doors thrown wide open" (*Dio Chrysostom* 3:319).

4. Cf. Kraeling, *The Synagogue*, 159–60 n. 593. Kraeling is surely correct in considering the long veil the himation: "To bring the palla or the himation over the head was virtually the only form of 'veiling' used by women in Greece and Rome. Where 'veils' are referred to in literary texts, usually with a loose use of the term mitra, the allusion is often to Orientals."

5. *Iliad* 14.184; *Odyssey* 1.334, 4.623, among others.

6. Cf. Aeschylus *Agamemnon* 1178.

7. Cf. Brandenburg, *Studien zur Mitra*, 60 n. 32.

8. In Inan and Alföldi-Rosenbaum, *Römische und frühbyzantinische Porträtplastik*, I found only one 'veil' that was certainly not a himation—that worn by a priestess of Isis (no. 222)—but twenty-two instances of the himation as head covering.

9. Cf. Brandenburg, *Studien zur Mitra*, 53–66, 102–27. Since the miter was a headcloth, which could be bound as a hood or worn as a wrap, the cloth could also be used as a veil. Perhaps this explains the somewhat loose use of language (102–3).

One type of hood from Asia Minor was called a miter. The Septuagint and other Hellenistic Jewish writings use the same word for the "turban" of the high priest.[10] But a particularly festive woman's head covering is also called a miter; Judith puts one on in order to seduce Holofernes (Judt. 10:3; 16:8); Jerusalem is to put one on instead of mourning dress (Bar. 5:2). The festively adorned church appears to Hermes with a "miter" as veil.[11]

In my opinion, in 1 Cor. 11:3ff. Paul can only have been thinking of a himation pulled over the head. For in 11:15, he speaks in connection with women's head covering of a *peribolaion*, and the term *peribolaion* is largely synonymous with *himation* (cf. Ps. 101:27 LXX = Heb. 1:11–12). In addition, the himation was the usual way to veil oneself, in fact to a great extent the only way in Greece and Rome. If Paul had meant one of the more unusual forms of veiling he would have had to express himself more precisely. Yet he never uses a technical noun for the piece of clothing. This too is understandable with regard to the himation, for that is, after all, not specifically a veil but a piece of clothing that everyone wore over the chiton. It is not the presence or absence of the piece of clothing but rather its use that is under discussion— not a special *kalymma*, but the *katakalyptesthai*. Our hypothesis clarifies a further oddity of the text: The source of the problem in Corinth was the conduct of some women. Verse 13 relates only to women: "Is it proper for a woman to pray to God with her head uncovered?" But Paul discusses not only the conduct of women but also—purely hypothetically—the conduct of men: what if a man covers his head while praying, or lets his hair grow long (vv. 4, 14)? Only after this does he come to discuss the conduct of women (vv. 5–6, 15). To conclude, he even mentions himself and his collaborators as an example: they are unfamiliar with the practice he opposes (v. 16). One asks somewhat amazed where Paul and his collaborators would have had the opportunity to practice the disputed form of conduct; they certainly did not carry any specifically feminine articles of clothing in their baggage! But the juxtaposition of men and women becomes immediately intelligible if the issue is the use of the himation, for the himation was a part of dress for both men and women. It was only worn differently. The women used it to cover the head, the men left the head free. From this perspective, the thought has a certain logic: if women no longer veil themselves with the himation, what in principle is to prevent men from using their himation as head covering? To conclude, a final argument in favor of the himation: Veil, hood, and hairnet would have to be draped carefully and pinned in place. A himation, on the contrary, would simply be pushed over the head and could easily fall back on the shoulders.

---

10. Cf. Exod. 29:6; Lev. 8:9; Philo *Moses* 2.116, *Testament of Levi* 8.2, *The Letter of Aristeas* 98.

11. *The Shepherd of Hermas: Visions* 4.2.1. In addition to the three basic types that have been sketched, reference should also be made to the *kekryphalos*, in all probability a hairnet; cf. *Der kleine Pauly* 3:176, 1365.

The transition between veiling and unveiling could occur simply and undramatically in this case. Women could come veiled to the community assembly and take off the veil when they prayed or prophesied. I consider it improbable that women would have destroyed a carefully prepared head covering in praying or prophesying.

For the remaining argumentation we can therefore limit ourselves to the custom of veiling oneself with the himation. As far as this custom is concerned, an evident east-west tendency can be demonstrated. The archaeological findings are more informative than literary statements in this regard. Innumerable women had themselves portrayed in sculptures on graves. We can presume that what can be observed at the grave was permissible in life. People do not violate customs at the grave. As a rule, burial customs are far more conservative than the people who are buried. A sample comparison of grave sculptures from Palmyra, Asia Minor, Macedonia, and Rome yields the following picture. In Palmyra, adult women are almost without exception veiled. Unveiled women are young girls.[12] Of approximately one thousand eastern Greek grave reliefs from the Hellenistic-Roman period (mostly from Asia Minor) there were only fifteen unquestionably unveiled heads of adult women.[13] In Macedonia, the proportions in the imperial period are clearly different: of approximately one hundred grave reliefs only thirty-eight adult women are veiled, and sixty-three let themselves be portrayed unveiled.[14] The grave reliefs of freed Romans from the late republic and the imperial period, from whom we may presume an emphatic adaptation to "good manners," are interesting. In ninety-six group portraits, forty-three women are depicted with a himation drawn over the head, while thirty-five are depicted without head covering.[15]

12. Cf. Ingholt, *Studier*, pls. 10–16. Only in pl. 12 is the veil not placed over the shoulder, but it is still present. "The veil is apparently fastened behind the neck and falls down from there over the shoulders" (p. 64). In public the himation could be drawn so far forward that it veiled the whole head; cf. Seyrig, "Antiquités Syriennes," 160 and pl. 19. The grave reliefs I was able to see in the museums of Palmyra and Damascus show—apart from girls—almost exclusively veiled women.

13. Cf. Pfuhl and Möbius, *Die ostgriechischen Grabreliefs*, nos. 376, 379, 387, 452, 453, 549, 550, 556, 557, 581, 588, 596, 919, 929, 954. Portraits of children, e.g., 399, 524, 751, etc., were excluded.

14. Rüsch, "Das kaiserzeitliche Porträt." Group portraits of families in which some women are veiled and others in the same family unveiled are instructive; cf. nos. 10, 11, 26, 29, 34, 42, 75, 87, 94. It was, in other words, not the case that conservatively inclined families united in preserving the custom while liberal ones relinquished it. The question was obviously not a theme of conflict in the families depicted here. The problem was solved in a more tolerant fashion than was the case with the Christians in Corinth.

15. Kleiner, *Roman Group Portraiture*. This covers exclusively group portraits of freed slaves in Rome. If relatively many women are veiled, it must be remembered that those freed surely adapted themselves consciously to good old Roman customs (cf. pp. 184–88). But even the conservative style of these families did not prevent different behavior within the same family; cf. nos. 9, 60, and 91. Other families, on the contrary, behaved conformably—nos. 62 and 89 with a head covering, nos. 80, 84, and 92 without.

Life was probably even more liberal than the burial customs. Portraiture in Asia Minor yields a very different picture than grave reliefs in Asia Minor. Of eighty-five women's heads, forty-seven are unveiled, twenty-two have the himation drawn over the back of the head, and the rest are decorated with diadem, stephane, or hairband.[16] One cannot therefore claim that there was social pressure in Greece which made head covering a requirement for women.[17] When the veiling of women is required in some literary documents, a conservative ideal of women, not everyday reality, stands behind this.[18] In connection with 1 Corinthians 11, two questions in particular interest us. What was the custom specifically in Corinth? What can be determined about Jewish practices?

Archaeological discoveries make specific conclusions about Corinth possible.[19] Some unveiled women's heads are preserved from Roman times.[20] Otherwise we find women with a cap,[21] with diadem,[22] and with himation drawn over the head.[23] A clearly veiled woman is preserved on a relief from the time of Hadrian, which unmistakably shows barbarians, possibly prisoners of war.[24] In view of 1 Corinthians 11, two statues of men with togas drawn over their heads deserve special mention. The first statue represents Augustus. The head covering shows that he is offering sacrifice according to Roman custom.[25] A second male head, in which Nero, the son of Germanicus, is possibly depicted, is to be interpreted in a similar way.[26] That two of these unusual representations

16. Cf. Inan and Alföldi-Rosenbaum, *Porträtplastik*. Portraits with unveiled heads include, from the early imperial period, nos. 124, 174–76, 238, 277; from the second century, nos. 240, 270, 282, 288, 330, 339, 342. Portraits of women with drawn himation include, from the early imperial period, nos. 265, 281 (?), 310, 328, 329; from the second century, nos. 93, 167, 214, 225–27, 229, 239, 241, 257, 286, 311, 326. There are no striking regional differences within Asia Minor.

17. Thus most recently L. Schottroff, "Frauen," 120. According to Schottroff, the paranesis for women in 1 Cor. 11:2–16 is a "defensive stance imposed from without." But it cannot be a matter of adaptation to the pagan environment of Greece. Paul does appeal to custom—but to the custom of the Christian communities, not that of the environment.

18. Thus, correctly, L. Schottroff, "Frauen," 131–32 n. 83. According to Plutarch (*Quaestiones Romanae et Graecae* 14), it corresponds more to custom when a Roman woman covers her head in public. The comparative *synethesteron* speaks for itself. It was in no sense against custom to appear in public without a himation over the head. This was surely also true of the Roman colony of Corinth. Ovid (*The Amores* 1.31–34) is certainly not a witness to the general custom. It was an extraordinarily rigorous decision for C. Sulpicius Gallus to separate from his wife because she had been seen in public with her head unveiled (Valerius Maximus 6.3.10).

19. Cf. Johnson, *Corinth*, and Davidson, *Corinth*.

20. Johnson, *Corinth*, nos. 160, 163, 221, 222.

21. Ibid., no. 164.

22. Davidson, *Corinth*, nos. 399, 401, 402, 404—all from the Roman period.

23. Ibid., no. 391.

24. Johnson, *Corinth*, no. 224; cf. pp. 106–7.

25. Ibid., no. 134; cf. also p. 72.

26. Ibid., no. 137.

are preserved from Corinth precisely from the New Testament period may be coincidence. One is forced to think involuntarily of Paul's statement that for men a covered head is a disgrace. Would not the addressees in Corinth have had to think of the statue of Augustus, surely well known to them? In any case, it can at least be said that Corinth fits into the general east-west tendency. The scanty remains do not point to a social requirement of veiling.

The general east-west tendency is probably also valid for Judaism. In the frescoes of the synagogue at Dura Europos, nearly all women are veiled. The three exceptions can be explained relatively easily.[27] Preserved, to the contrary, is a family gravestone from Pannonia of an Anastasius, his wife Decusana, and their son Benjamin.[28] The menorah is shown between their heads. These are pious Jews. Yet they allowed themselves to be portrayed—and thus transgressed the second commandment. But they are also liberal in other respects: there is no sign of a head covering for the wife!

The Development in Corinth

How could the "veiling" of women become a problem at all? It is certainly not a general rejection of the practice of women wearing a head covering that is at stake. The problem is rather limited to the liturgy, more precisely to "praying and prophesying women," that is, to women in a pneumatic state. Did they lose control of their clothing in ecstasy, so that the shroud drawn over the head slid back over the shoulders? Did a conscious theology lie behind all this? Did some women orient themselves on the model of other cults?

We know little of other cults, but enough to make an explanation of the Corinthian conduct as adaptation to other cults appear very unconvincing. The cults of Dionysius, Demeter, and Isis come into question.

1. In Dionysian ecstasy, the women loosened their hair, but they were crowned with ivy. Their heads were not at all uncovered! In the frescoes of the Villa Item in Pompeii, which are often interpreted as a Dionysian initiation rite, the woman being initiated has loose hair. But the interpretation of this fresco as Dionysian mysteries is disputed. It could be a marriage ritual.[29]

2. We are well informed about clothing in the cult of Demeter by the inscription of Andania.[30] Here there are extensive prescriptions about the dress

27. The three are, first, Pharaoh's daughter, who is taking a bath and is therefore completely undressed (cf. Kraeling, *The Synagogue*, pl. 9); second, a woman standing behind Esther, probably a "maid or lady-in-waiting" (ibid., pl. 6; cf p. 160); and third, probably the mother of Moses, who exposes her child (ibid., pl. 9; cf. pp. 173–74). It should also be mentioned that the women's heads that serve more as ornaments, that are not a component of the biblical illustrations, are without veil.

28. Copy in Kanael, *Die Kunst*, no. 57. "This is the only known Jewish group depicted on a gravestone of the Roman period" (ibid., 70). According to Marmorstein ("The Veil"), a Jewess in the city was veiled.

29. Cf. Leipoldt, *Umwelt*, nos. 52–54. Winkes ("Zum Illusionismus," 931ff.) expresses doubts about the interpretation as mysteries.

30. Dittenberger, *Sylloge Inscriptionum Graecarum*, 736.

of the women participating in the rite. They amount to excluding demonstrative luxury: "No one shall wear golden jewelry, makeup, headband, braided hair, or sandals." A veil is not mentioned explicitly. Can one conclude from this that a veil was forbidden or that unveiled women participated in the cult?[31] This is not at all certain. The following four points must be taken into consideration.

First, the inscription (lines 12–16) explicitly mentions the women's himation. This could be drawn over the head at any time. A veil of this sort would certainly not fall under the prohibition of luxurious decoration![32]

Second, an inscription with comparable content is preserved from Lycosura in Arcadia.[33] This also forbids all ornamentation, for example, a purple himation or one with a flowered pattern. Here, beside the prohibition of braided hair stands explicitly *mede kekalummenos* (it is unclear whether this last regulation applies to women or to men).[34] If the *kekalummenos* refers to men, it could be concluded indirectly that women were permitted to appear veiled before the goddess Despoina (whose cult is involved here). If the expression refers to women, then one could conclude from the lack of a corresponding regulation in Andania that the women there could appear with head veil.[35]

Third, that the priestesses of Demeter in Asia Minor had themselves portrayed with a short veil is also to be considered. This veil is not identical to the himation.[36]

Fourth, a rejection of veils in principle in the cult of Demeter is excluded simply by the fact that the initiate is fully veiled during the initiation.[37] Yet one could also conclude from this that those already initiated are "unveiled."

3. Apuleius (*Metamorphoses* 11.10) relates that in the cult of Isis at Corinth, "the women had their hair anointed, and their heads covered with light linen; but the men had their crowns shaven."[38] But a devotee of Isis by the name of Isias from Smyrna had herself portrayed without head covering at the beginning of the second century C.E., while a priestess of Isis wore a short veil (but no himation).[39]

31. Thus above all Lösch, "Christliche Frauen," and Conzelmann, *Der erste Brief*, 218.

32. Lösch ("Christliche Frauen," 248–49) explains the prohibition of braided hair as rejection of any binding to another god. Nothing in the prescriptions regarding clothing supports this interpretation. The prescriptions are unambiguously directed against ornate clothing. The simple dress of archaic times perhaps became a sign of the sacred here.

33. Dittenberger, *Sylloge Inscriptionum Graecarum*, 939.

34. Cf. the discussion in Lösch, "Christliche Frauen," 241–42.

35. That the dress regulations of Andania apply to girls and to women is also to be considered. The veil is a sign of a married woman. Silence about head coverings that were perhaps possible enables a very general formulation of the dress regulations.

36. Cf. Pfuhl and Möbius, *Die ostgriechischen Grabreliefs*, nos. 403, 407, 409, 410.

37. Leipoldt, *Umwelt*, nos. 31, 32, 34.

38. ET: W. Adlington and S. Gaselee, *Apuleius* (LCL, 1915), 555.

39. Cf. Pfuhl and Möbius, *Die ostgriechischen Grabreliefs*, no. 376; Inan and Alföldi-Rosenbaum, *Porträtplastik*, no. 222.

Presuming an influence of strange cults is also improbable in view of Paul's manner of argumentation. We can observe clearly in 1 Corinthians how Paul uses analogies between Christian and pagan practices polemically or argumentatively (cf. 1 Cor. 10:14ff.; 12:2). Yet in 1 Cor. 11:2–16 he gives not the slightest indication of a connection between the questions of head coverings and pagan cults. How easily he could have taken advantage of such a connection. Would this not have saved him from all the argumentative weaknesses he himself seems to have sensed?

Independent of the question of to what influences the behavior of Christian women in Corinth is to be retraced historically, we can still make statements about the meaning of this conduct within the community. The removal of head covering must have been understood in an "emancipatory" manner, for the removal of the *kalymma* has precisely this meaning in Aristophanes' *Lysistrata* (530–32). Here the women intervene deliberately in politics and claim a right to a voice in public affairs—especially in the decision about war and peace. In this connection, the woman's *kalymma* becomes a symbol:

Magistrate: Silence for YOU?
              Stop for a wench with a wimple [*kalymma*] enfolding her?
              No, by the Powers, may I DIE if I do!
Lysistrata: Do not, my pretty one, do not, I pray,
              Suffer my wimple [*kalymma*] to stand in the way.
              Here, take it, and wear it, and gracefully tie it,
              Enfolding it over your head, and be quiet.
              Now to your task.[40]

The connection here between "silence in public" (i.e., with regard to public affairs) and the *kalymma* is noteworthy. I do not at all claim that the Christian women in Corinth consciously imitated Lysistrata. The analogy only illuminates how their action would have struck some people.

Their action can moreover be explained adequately from intrinsic causes. Since Paul himself had built up and formed the Corinthian community, it is possible that some Corinthian women drew the consequences of a specifically Pauline starting point. The radical sounding expression of Gal. 3:27–28 is well known: "For as many of you as were baptized into Christ have put on Christ. There is neither Jew nor Greek, there is neither slave nor free, there is neither male nor female; for you are all one in Christ Jesus."[41] Here the clothing symbolism is applied to baptism. The one baptized had taken off all clothes and put on Christ as a new garment. The new garment is not restricted to

---

40. ET: Benjamin Bickley Rogers, *Aristophanes*, vol. 3 of 3 vols. (LCL, 1924), 55.
41. That tradition is present here is probable in view of the broad distribution of the idea; cf. Col. 3:11; 1 Cor. 7:19; Gal. 5:6; 6:15; *Martyrdom of Peter* 9; *Gospel of Thomas* 22; *2 Clement* 12.2; Clement of Alexandria *Stromata* 3.13, 92.2. Cf. Paulsen, "Einheit," esp. 77ff.

one sex. Of course this was meant metaphorically. But did it not lie at hand to draw concrete conclusions and to refrain "in Christ" from certain symbols of sex roles? Did Paul perhaps have to correct consequences of his own preaching? This is possible. In 1 Cor. 11:2–3 Paul himself alludes to such a correction.[42] First he praises the Corinthians for maintaining the traditions (v. 2), but then he continues, "But I want you to understand . . ." (v. 3), as if he has to direct into the proper channel the adherence to tradition which in itself is commendable. This argument presupposes that the Corinthians in fact knew a tradition comparable to Gal. 3:27–28. Two factors point in this direction.

First, in 1 Cor. 12:13, Paul cites the tradition that stands behind Gal. 3:27–28 without indicating that he is introducing something new. The idea occurs as foundation for the symbolism of the body of Christ, as if Paul is appealing to a conception familiar to all: "For by one Spirit we were all baptized into one body—Jews or Greeks, slaves or free—and all were made to drink of one Spirit." In contrast to Gal. 3:28, here he does not mention the overcoming of sexual differences—understandably, if precisely this idea had caused problems in Corinth.[43]

Second, in 1 Corinthians 11 he also mentions an idea that stands close to Gal. 3:28 but that does not fit logically into the context.[44] First, Paul asserted the subordination of women; woman—man—Christ—God are related to each other respectively as the body to its head (v. 3). In v. 7, he reemphasizes this hierarchic order without mentioning Christ. But then he seems to retract it all: "Nevertheless, in the Lord woman is not without man nor man without woman" (v. 11*). Of course this formulation falls short of Gal. 3:28.[45] But

---

42. Thus Jervell, *Imago*, 292–95.

43. Cf. ibid., 294. However, one can also, conversely, bring the mention of the polarity male-female in Gal. 3:28 into connection with the Galatian situation. After all, the central Galatian problem, the requirement of circumcision, affected only the males. If there are no sexual differences in Christ, then the requirement of circumcision is also void. With the rejection of circumcision as a condition for gentile Christians, Paul, voluntarily or involuntarily, takes a step toward the religious equality of man and woman, however much he may otherwise think in a patriarchal fashion.

44. It is in my opinion unjustified to think for this reason of interpolations. This against Walker, "1 Corinthians 11, 2–16," and Cope, "1 Cor. 11, 2–16."

45. Galatians 3:28 argues against empirical reality with an idea inspired by Gen. 1:26–27. Christ is the image of God, in whom the differences between male and female are overcome. In 1 Cor. 11:7–8, 11–12, on the contrary, Paul draws on a tradition that distinguished between Genesis 2 and empirical reality. "Once Adam was created from Eve and Eve from Adam; since then [human beings are formed] through our image according to our likeness, not a man without a woman and not a woman without a man and neither without the *shekinah*" (Gen. Rab. 22 [14†]: Billerbeck, *Kommentar* 3:440). In vv. 8–9, Paul refers to the creation account (cf. *ektisthe*.) Verse 11 is then a correction of v. 8, where Paul had still claimed that man did not originate from woman. Verse 12 says the same as v. 11: all human beings originated *ek tou andros* and *dia tes gynaikos*. That man is not "without woman" and woman not "without man" (v. 10) must then be related to the natural process of generation and birth; for this reason, *choris* cannot be

even in its attenuated form, it does not at all fit the tendency of the argumentation in 1 Corinthians 11. Perhaps the Corinthian women had appealed to this idea that came from Paul. If Paul did not wish to become incredible, he had to recognize it—in principle.

The development in Corinth can be explained independently of external models. Perhaps the himation of praying and prophesizing women originally slid to their shoulders for trivial reasons. Then a fundamental problem developed from this. Theological arguments were found, Pauline traditions were cited, the connection between the stimulus "removal of the himation" and the reaction "praying and prophesizing" was smoothed and strengthened through more or less plausible cognitive acts of interpretation. In the course of this, the Corinthian women could have appealed to one of the most valuable characteristics of the young early Christianity—the equality in principle of the sexes.

Paul's Reaction

To us, Paul's reaction is a riddle. According to everything we know, women without head covering were no scandal in Corinth! Yet Paul argues against the practice. The terms *kataischunein* (vv. 4–5), *aischron* (v. 6), *opheilei* (vv. 7, 10), *prepon* (v. 13), *atimia* (v. 14), and *synetheia* (v. 16) speak of a clearer language than the unsuccessful theological efforts to justify dress customs. On what custom does Paul insist here? Certainly not on the Corinthian custom—more likely on oriental ones.[46] But even oriental custom does not explain everything. When, for example, Paul rejects head covering for males with sharp words, he is orienting himself more on "western" standards. In the east, head coverings for males were not found offensive;[47] in the west, on the contrary, it was considered a sign of effeminacy and generally traced back to oriental influence.[48]

---

translated as "different" (against Kürzinger, "Frau und Mann") but should be translated rather as "without cooperation of," as in John 1:3. Even Paul thus distinguishes between the unilateral creation of Eve from Adam (vv. 8–9) and the generation of all later human beings by two parents (vv. 11–12). But the distinction between Adam and following generations that stands behind vv. 8–9 and 11–12 is Christianized by "in the Lord." It is difficult to say what Paul was thinking of here. Is he playing Gen. 1:26–27 off against Genesis 2? For Christ is, after all, the image of God that is mentioned in Gen. 1:26–27, the image according to which man and woman were both created. In the light of this conviction, does he assess the empirically verifiable mutual dependence in propagation as an event "in the Lord"?

46. Thus Oepke, s.v. *kalymma*.

47. Cf. the caps of the Persians (Herodotus 7.61) and the miter of the Kissians and Babylonians (Herodotus 7.62, 1.195). For the Israelites, cf. the black obelisks of Salmanassar III (858–824): the Israelite depicted there wears a pointed cap (depicted in *Biblisch-historisches Handwörterbuch* 2:964). On male head covering in Israel in general, cf. Cornfeld, ed., *Pictorical Biblical Encyclopedia*, 325–26.

48. Virgil calls a man with a miter a *semivir* (*Aeneid* 4.215). Servius (*Aeneid* 4.215) comments with the words "quibus effeminatio crimini debatur, etiam mitra eius adscribebatur." For this reason the charge of wearing a miter can occur in polemic (e.g., Cicero *De Harispicum Responsis* 44). Further references in Herter, s.v. *effeminatus*, 631. It

The east-west tendency in dress customs does not sufficiently explain Paul's reaction. And even if the oriental Paul should be exercised in 1 Corinthians 11 at the more liberal customs of the west, there would still remain the riddle of why Paul demonstrates and demands adaptability elsewhere (cf. 1 Cor. 9:19–23) but in the insignificant question of dress argues with disturbing rigidity and "sub-Christian weakness."[49]

We should note first that Paul is insisting on a distinguishing symbol of the roles of the sexes. He is not interested in head covering in itself but is interested rather in the opposition of male and female behavior. For this reason, he always confronts female behavior with the corresponding male behavior, above and beyond the immediate occasion. The unveiled head and short hair of the man, and the veiled head and long hair of the woman, serve as symbols of the roles of the sexes. The vehemence with which he defends these conventional symbols of sex roles is intelligible only if these symbols are "overdetermined" for him. For Paul, the differentiation of sex roles depends totally on them. For this reason, he makes a question of theological principle out of a harmless symbol.

The Symbols of Male Sex Roles. Why does Paul really consider it a disgrace if men cover their heads? The Israelites often wore a cloth over their heads. The high priest even entered before Yahweh with his head covered (Lev. 16:4). But with all of this the boundary between the sexes was not confused. In Corinth, the head covering of men which Paul attacked (only hypothetically and prophylactically) would have been an assumption of female dress customs. The associations which that would have evoked in Greece are clear from a group of Attic vases from the fifth century B.C.E. Here symposiasts and revelers are represented in women's clothing, with head covering—among flute players, dancers, and hetarae.[50] Transvestism was practiced during revelry—a practice that was protected by custom and that existed for a long time further. Philostratus (*Imagines* 1.2) still writes in the third century C.E. that "the revel permits women to masquerade as men, and men to 'put on women's garb.' "[51] Things of this sort must have been an abomination to a Jew: "A woman shall not wear anything that pertains to a man, nor shall a man put on a woman's garment; for whoever does these things is an abomination to the Lord your God" (Deut. 22:5). The reaction against long hair is surely to be interpreted

---

is of course also offensive when the himation is drawn over the head of a man (Plutarch *Moralia* 200F).

49. Thus Weiss, *Der 1. Korintherbrief*, 270. But in Schlatter (*Die korinthische Theologie*, 311), one reads, "As for a man the basis and purpose of his life lie in God, so for a woman they lie in man."

50. Cf. Brandenburg, *Studien zur Mitra*, 76–86, pls. 1–5.

51. ET: Arthur Fairbanks, *Philostratus, Imagines; Callistratus, Descriptions* (LCL, 1931), 13.

in a similar way: any man with long hair was considered effeminate.[52] As *Pseudo-Phocylides* (210–14) shows, Jewish Hellenistic proverb literature sees—surely realistically—a connection between long hair and homosexuality:

> If a child is a boy, do not let locks grow on his head. Braid not his crown nor make cross-knots at the top of his head. Long hair is not fit for men, but for voluptuous women. Guard the youthful beauty of a comely boy; because many rage for intercourse with a man.[53]

Philo confirms such statements from another side. In *On the Contemplative Life* (48–56), he contrasts the luxurious banquets of his day (and his class) with the simple life of the therapeuts. Belonging to these banquets are beautiful boys, "recently pets of the pederasts" (52),[54] whose costume he describes in detail (50–51):

> Their faces [are] smeared with cosmetics and paint under the eyelids and the hair of the head [is] prettily painted and tightly bound. For they have long thick hair which is not cut at all or else the forelocks only are cut at the tips to make them level and take exactly the figure of a circular line. They wear tunics fine as cobwebs and of dazzling white. . . .[55]

On the basis of such evidence we can formulate the following hypothesis: Relativizing the symbolism of sex roles released such a "panic" reaction in Paul, because he believed that it threatened the whole order in the sexual realm. His overreaction is possibly a defense against homosexual tendencies.

The Symbols of Female Sex Roles. Of course, Paul treats male behavior only in passing. The central theme is women's headgear. Why is it a disgrace if a woman loses her hair? Probably he is thinking of social downgrading: the hair of female slaves was shorn. It is in this sense that Isaiah (Isa. 3:17*) announces to the fastidious daughters of Jerusalem that their hair will be shorn. A female slave is also socially devalued because she has become in sexual regard an object at the disposal of her master. For this reason, the loss of hair must have been demoralizing, even if absolutely no sexual exploitation followed. The *Testament of Job* (23—25) is instructive. Job's wife begs for bread for Job, who is afflicted with misery. Satan transforms himself into a bread seller. Since the wife has no money, he demands her hair. He shears her head in public and gives her three loaves of bread. The demoralized and humiliated woman comes to Job and relates, "Being remiss, I said to him, 'Go ahead, cut my hair.' So he arose and cut my hair disgracefully in the market, while the crowd

---

52. Cf. Herter, s.v. *effeminatus*, 632–33. But cf. also, on the contrary, the positive comments on long hair on men in Dio Chrysostom (*Discourses* 7.4); cf. also his "praise of hair."

53. ET: van der Horst, *The Sentences of Pseudo-Phocylides*, 101.

54. ET: F. H. Colson, *Philo*, vol. 9 of 10 vols. (LCL, 1941), 143.

55. ET: ibid.

stood by and marveled" (24.10).[56] The loss of her hair is the most extreme sign of humiliation, but there is still more. After the hair is cut, it is said that "Satan followed her along the road, walking stealthily, and leading her heart astray" (23.11).[57] Job's wife despairs of God. She advises Job to curse God and die. The loss of her hair made her receptive to the whisperings of Satan. Hair has an almost apotropaic significance.

Head covering can also have such apotropaic significance. According to *b.Sabb.* 156b, it protects both against the power of drives and the influence of the stars:

> R. Nahman b. Isaac's mother was told by astrologers, Your son will be a thief. [So] she did not let him [be] bareheaded, saying to him, "Cover your head so that the fear of heaven may be upon you, and pray [for mercy]." Now, he did not know why she spoke that to him. One day he was sitting and studying under a palm tree; the covering fell from his head, he raised his eyes and saw a date; temptation overcame him, he climbed up and bit off a cluster [of dates] with his teeth.[58]

In this story, the head covering is "determined" in two ways. It protects against the power of the stars and against tendencies toward kleptomania. The protection against internal drives is presented as protection against external (demonic) powers.

In Philo, the head veil of a woman appears in connection with the Israelites' law of jealousy (Num. 5:11–31). A woman suspected of adultery is to be brought before the priest with her head exposed (5:18) and she herself is to be subjected to an ordeal: she must drink cursed water that kills in the case of adultery. Philo interprets the removal of the head covering several times.[59] In *The Special Laws* (3.56), it occurs "in order that she may be judged with her head bared and stripped of the symbol of modesty, regularly worn by women who are wholly innocent."[60] Here the head covering is unambiguously a symbol of a sexual life corresponding to the prevailing norms. In *On the Cherubim* 14, Philo interprets Num. 5:18 as a symbol that God can probe even the unknown interior of man, including the motives of actions. Here the head covering becomes the symbol of an inner psychic region with motives and drives that lie prior to the action which is carried out.

In Paul we find a twofold motivation of head covering—with reference to males and with reference to angels. It is said that, because woman is created

---

56. ET: R. P. Spittler, *The Old Testament Pseudepigrapha*, ed. Charlesworth, 1:849.

57. ET: ibid.

58. ET: H. Freedman, *The Babylonian Talmud* 4:801. [The English translation has been modified in the light of Theissen's German text.]

59. Philo (*The Special Laws* 3.56) speaks of an *epikranon*. Josephus (*Jewish Antiquities* 3.270), on the contrary, paraphrases Num. 5:18 as *kai tes kephales to himation aphelon*, an indication that Jewish women in the Diaspora—Josephus is writing in Rome—probably veiled themselves like all other women, with a himation drawn over the head.

60. ET: F. H. Colson, *Philo*, vol. 7 (LCL, 1937), 511.

for *man*, she must wear a "power"[61] on her head (1 Cor. 11:10). A second *dia* follows the first: head covering is said to be necessary because of the *angels*. Logically speaking, the two foundations are juxtaposed,[62] but psychologically they coincide. The reference to the angels probably means the "lusting angels" of Gen. 6:1ff. who sought human wives—a story that enlivened the fantasy of apocalyptic circles in that period.[63] The woman's veil was, then, protection against the sexual desire of heavenly beings.[64] This is supported by the connection of decoration of the head and seduction by angels in a passage of the *Testaments of the Twelve Patriarchs, Reuben* 5.5–6. After a general warning against the beauty, the gazes, and the decoration of women, the passage cautions,

> Accordingly, my children, flee from sexual promiscuity, and order your wives and your daughters not to adorn their heads and their appearances so as to deceive men's sound minds. For every woman who schemes in these ways is destined for eternal punishment. For it was thus that they charmed the Watchers, who were before the Flood. As they continued looking at the women, they were filled with desire for them and perpetrated the act in their minds. Then they were transformed into human males, and while the women were cohabiting with their husbands they appeared to them. Since the women's minds were filled with lust for these apparitions, they gave birth to giants. For the Watchers were disclosed to them as being as high as the heavens.[65]

It could be objected that this passage is warning precisely against decoration of the head, while Paul demands head covering. Yet this is not a contradiction. A himation drawn over the head is not decoration; it rather conceals any decoration that is present, as may be seen in the grave reliefs of wealthy women in Palmyra.[66] Since the previous mention of angels in 1 Corinthians presupposes fallen angels—the Christians are to judge angels (1 Cor. 6:3)—one should think of lusting angels. Seen psychologically, a projection is present here. Sexual impulses are not ascribed to one's own person, but projected onto

61. The use of the term *exousia* for a head covering is singular. Four interpretations have been suggested: (1) The head covering is an apotropaic power—protection from the angels. (2) It is a sign of subordination to the male. (3) It is a sign of the authority of the woman to appear with equal standing to males in the liturgy. (4) At its base lies an Aramaic word that means both "power" and "head covering." The decision depends on how the "angels" are interpreted. If one thinks of fallen angels, then the apotropaic interpretation is most plausible. A survey of the discussion is offered by Leslie, *The Concept of Women*, 109–13.

62. Another possibility would be to relate the *dia touto* to "due to the angels."

63. Cf. *1 Enoch* 6ff.; *Jubilees* 5.1ff.; *2 Baruch* 56.10ff.; *Testament of Reuben* 5; Josephus *Jewish Antiquities* 1.73. Since one drew near to the angels in prayer (Ps. 138:1), the danger was particularly great at that time.

64. Thus Dibelius, *Die Geisterwelt*, 18, 233–34; Weiss, *Der 1. Korintherbrief*, 274–75.

65. ET: H. C. Kee, *The Old Testament Pseudepigrapha*, ed. Charlesworth, 1:784.

66. Cf. Böhme and W. Schottroff, *Palmyrenische Grabreliefs*, pl. 2.

demonic powers. The lusting angels are symptoms of an unintegrated sexuality. It is also unmistakable in the cited text from the *Testaments of the Twelve Patriarchs* that the Fall in Genesis 6 is an illustration and projection of male sexual concupiscence.

That Paul insists on a head covering precisely with regard to praying and prophesying women is not a point against this interpretation. Paul had previously, in 1 Corinthians 7, reflected quite openly on the relationship of sexuality and prayer. In 1 Cor. 7:5 he admonishes married couples, "Do not refuse one another except perhaps by agreement for a season, that you may devote yourselves to prayer; but then come together again, lest Satan tempt you through lack of self-control." It seems clear what is to be understood by the temptations of Satan—sexual fantasies that prevent concentration in prayer. In 1 Cor. 11:10 the angels have the function here attributed to Satan. The veil on the head serves to ward off sexual fantasies. It should be mentioned at least in passing that for overcoming such fantasies Paul not only insists on problematic head coverings but also considers sexual satisfaction in marriage an appropriate way (cf. 7:5).

As far as the prophesying women are concerned, we can adduce the report of Irenaeus (*Adversus Haereses* 1.13.3) about the prophetesses on whom the gnostic charismatic Mark conferred the gift of prophecy. He prayed over them and commanded several times, "Open your mouth and prophesy!" At this the women became agitated and, with pounding hearts, emitted unintelligible grunts. Mark took advantage of their emotionally confused state in order, among other things, to bind them sexually to himself.

The fact remains then, that in Paul, women's head covering is a symbol of defense against sexual impulses. It is for this reason that he insists on it almost compulsively. But the problem is not fully grasped with this. As 1 Corinthians 7 shows, Paul could argue more persuasively when sexual themes were broached. In 1 Corinthians 11 a new theme was added—the impending dissolution of the identity of sex roles.

Paul puts hair and head covering parallel to each other. Short hair is a sign of dissolution of the differentiation of sex roles. As Lucian (*Dialogues of the Courtesans* 5.3) attests, it is found among (lesbian) prostitutes. But asceticism can also lead to relativizing the symbolism of sex roles. Renunciation of the veil is based on ascetical grounds in *Joseph and Aseneth* 15.1.[67] Exceeding the command of the angel, Aseneth not only girded herself with the twofold belt of virginity but also covered her head with a veil (*katekalypse ten kephalen*, 14.17). When she came into the angel's presence, however, she was immediately commanded (15.1–2),

Remove the veil from your head, and for what purpose did you do this?

67. Appealing to *Joseph and Aseneth* 15.1, Scroggs ("Paul") holds that women in Corinth had postulated the overcoming of the boundary between man and woman on the basis of sexual asceticism.

For you are a chaste virgin today, and your head is like that of a young man.[68]

It is instructive that here too the veil is interpreted first of all as a symbol of sex roles. Without a veil, Aseneth's head is "like the head of a young man." In perfect asceticism the traditional symbols of sex roles can dissolve just as they do in sexually deviant behavior.

Paul opposes this dissolution of the symbols of sex roles. He seeks to emphasize the "natural" differences between man and woman. It is for this reason that he appeals to "nature" to regulate customs regarding dress and hair (1 Cor. 11:14–15). This appeal to "nature" is an error that even Paul could have seen through. On the basis of nature there is neither short nor long hair, neither veiled nor unveiled heads! Here Paul has another tradition in mind, one that argues on the basis of truly secondary sex characteristics—beards and masculine hair on the body in general. We find reflections of this sort in Epictetus (*Discourses* 1.16.9–14):

> Come, let us leave the chief works of nature, and consider merely what she does in passing. Can anything be more useless than the hairs on a chin? Well, what then? Has not nature used even these in the most suitable way possible? Has she not by these means distinguished between the male and the female? Does not the nature of each one among us cry aloud forthwith from afar, "I am a man; on this understanding approach me, on this understanding talk with me; ask for nothing further; behold the signs"? Again, in the case of women, just as nature has mingled in their voice a certain softer note, so likewise has she taken the hair from their chins. Not so, you say; on the contrary the human animal ought to have been left without distinguishing features, and each of us ought to proclaim by word of mouth, "I am a man." Nay, but how fair and becoming and dignified the sign is! How much more fair than the cock's comb, how much more magnificent than the lion's mane! Wherefore, we ought to preserve the signs which God has given; we ought not to throw them away; we ought not, so far as in us lies, to confuse the sexes which have been distinguished in this fashion.[69]

Epictetus is completely correct when he emphasizes the social function of secondary sex characteristics. They signal to other human beings expectations of behavior and thus contribute to security in conduct. In another passage (3.1.14), he seeks to convince a young man from Corinth that he ought not make himself like a woman through inappropriate hygiene, by removing the hair from his skin. This is said to contradict "nature" (3.1.25, 27, 30). With smooth skin, he would conduct himself like a pederast and could at most please licentious women (3.1.32–33).

---

68. ET: C. Burchard, *The Old Testament Pseudepigrapha*, ed. Charlesworth, 2:225–26.
69. ET: W. A. Oldfather, *Epictetus*, vol. 1 of 2 vols. (LCL, 1925), 111.

Epictetus has some grounds for appealing to nature. Secondary sex characteristics are naturally preprogrammed and simultaneously have a social function. Paul, on the contrary, appeals to unambiguously conventional symbols of sex roles, in which there is not even a compelling custom, in order to underline natural differences. He may have known types of argumentation like those which appear later in Epictetus, but he applies them in a completely disordered manner. The most plausible explanation is that he is really concerned with the "natural" differences, with the clearly identifiable sexual differences between man and woman. What is "natural" for him is heterosexual conduct. The only text in which he otherwise appeals to nature in order to legitimate human conduct is his condemnation of homosexual conduct in Romans. For him, homosexuality is *para phusin* (cf. Rom. 1:26). His intellectual mistake in 1 Cor. 11:13–14, the confusion of convention and nature, is to be explained by the fact that he is defending what for him is "natural" behavior in the roundabout way of defending dress customs—though it is possible that he was not even fully conscious of this connection. We must agree with C. K. Barrett: "It does seem probable that horror of homosexualism is behind a good deal of Paul's argument."[70]

Summary. The head covering in 1 Cor. 11:2–16 is an overdetermined symbol. It does not serve adaptation to the custom in Corinth but rather corresponds to the customs of the oriental Paul. Beyond its social function it has a psychic significance: it stabilizes the differentiation of sex roles. In doing this, it does not only emphasize the social superiority of the male; in vv. 11–12, Paul relativizes his statements on this point. What is more important is that it also symbolizes a defense against unconscious sexual impulses—in part heterosexual impulses, which in any case are more easily aroused by a hitherto unaccustomed view of the opposite sex, in part homosexual tendencies latently present in the community, which could have been aroused by a confusion in the differentiation of sex roles. It is a sign of a defensive stance against sexual impulses that have not been fully integrated.

Before one judges (and condemns) Paul from the perspective of an uninhibited modern sexual ethic, it should be remembered that 1 Corinthians 11 did not remain his last word. In 2 Cor. 3:18*, he stresses insistently that "we all, with unveiled face, behold the glory of the Lord and are changed into his likeness." Glory, likeness, and veil are here related in an entirely different manner than in 1 Corinthians 11. The situation is the same. Just as Paul is thinking in 2 Cor. 3:14–15 of the Jewish synagogue service, so too is he thinking of the Christian liturgy in 3:18: 1 Corinthians 11 requires the veiling of women during the liturgy; 2 Corinthians 3 presupposes for the liturgy—in principle— the removal of veils from *all*. In both texts the veil has symbolic significance; it symbolizes a boundary between consciousness and the unconscious, with

70. Barrett, *A Commentary*, 257.

the boundary being defended in one text and breached in the other. If Paul insists on a head covering in 1 Corinthians 11 and views its removal as a decisive symbol of Christian freedom in 2 Corinthians 3, this contradictory stance shows Paul's greatness and his limitations. With regard to the sexual impulses of the id he knows above all controlling, even repressing, forms of reaction. In this regard his theology has left a heavy heritage. Insisting on the head covering for a woman betrays a defect in inner freedom. In another direction, on the contrary, Paul was revolutionary: here the veil was to fall. Here—with regard to the contents and demands of the superego—a growth in freedom is to be registered. Thought through consistently, this freedom would have to have led also to a different relationship to the id. But we must take Paul as he is—with light and shadow.[71]

71. We should recall that even modern people are dependent on symbols of sex roles. Even as far as we are concerned, certain "fashions" are reserved to the female sex, and we react in a confused manner if conventional boundaries are suddenly breached. Enlightenment and sexual tolerance do not prevent irritation if, e.g., males use lipstick and eyebrow pencil.

PART FOUR

Law and Sin: Raising the Conflict to Consciousness According to Romans 7:7–23

So far we have noted that Paul knows of unconscious aspects of his own life and of the law. He knows of a conflict that could threaten his life. He senses behind the splendor of the law its killing power and sees beyond a good conscience the possibility in principle of unconscious guilt. This consciousness of the unconscious presupposes that the unconscious aspects of his life-world have to a degree become conscious; otherwise, we could say nothing about them. In Romans 7, Paul makes his theme the becoming conscious of a previously unconscious conflict between the flesh and the law. For this reason we must engage Romans 7 at length. It has played a central role in the history of psychological exegesis of Paul. For a long time it was understood as a biographical statement of Paul's, until in 1929 Werner Georg Kümmel prepared an end to all efforts at psychological interpretation with his article "Röm 7 und die Bekehrung des Paulus" ("Romans 7 and the Conversion of Paul").[1] There are three decisive arguments for Kümmel:

1. *The rhetorical fictive "I."* According to Kümmel, Paul uses "I" as a rhetorical means of illustrating a general train of thought. This "I" does not include the person of Paul.[2]

2. *The unbiographical statement of Rom. 7:9*.* "I lived once without law, but when the commandment came, sin revived." According to Kümmel, this statement cannot be related to Paul, since Paul could never have spoken of a life "without law" in reference to his pre-Christian period.[3]

---

1. Now in Kümmel, *Römer 7*. Its complete success can be observed only in German-speaking areas. To Packer ("The 'Wretched Man' "), on the contrary, it is beyond doubt that Paul is describing his own experience. But Buber (*Zwei Glaubensweisen*, 150) also considers the interpretation of the "I" in Romans 7 as rhetorical fiction "unacceptable"; for him, Romans 7 is "appropriated memory."

2. Kümmel, *Römer 7*, 67–90, 118–32.

3. Ibid., 78–84.

3. *The contradiction between Phil. 3:4–6 and Rom. 7:7ff.* In Phil. 3:6*,
Paul describes himself as one who fulfilled the law "blamelessly" before
his conversion. In Romans 7, however, the I who is speaking calls
itself a "wretched man" (7:24) who suffered under the impossibility of
fulfilling the law. According to Kümmel, since Phil. 3:4–6 is to be
understood biographically, and since Romans 7 stands in contradiction
to Philippians 3, it is impossible to assess Romans 7 as a statement of
Paul about himself.[4]

The result, for Kümmel, is that Romans 7 has no personal biographical background; it rather contains a "theory." Paul himself never
experienced the conflict analyzed in Romans 7. As a rule, doubts about
this conception proceeded from the liveliness and intensity of the
depiction present in Romans 7. But up to now no one has been
successful in refuting the arguments convincingly formulated by
Kümmel.

To quench false expectations, one should observe that the following
examination of Romans 7 does not seek to demonstrate that the text is
meant biographically. Instead it seeks to demonstrate that it has a
biographical background. What Paul says in general about man under
the law has its Sitz im Leben in his own experiences. Yet, demonstration
of a biographical background of this sort is not the chief concern of
the psychological exegesis presented here. What is decisive is the
objective statement of the text with its manifold psychological implications, which we could elucidate even if we knew nothing of the
author's life. Psychological exegesis is not necessarily dependent on
bits of information about the author's life; yet, it becomes more lively
if we are able to read texts against a personal background and trace
the transformation of personal experience into generally valid elements
of knowledge.

4. Ibid., 111–17.

Chapter 11

Text Analysis:
Romans 7

Romans 7:7–23 distinguishes itself from its context through the use of "I." For the first time after the beginning of the letter and an isolated passage in Rom. 3:7, Paul here again uses the first-person singular. We will therefore need to examine the "I" in Romans 7 at length. First, however, the position of the text in its context and the inner structure of the text must be worked out.

THE CONTEXT

In Romans 5—8, Paul portrays the soteriological change that transposes man from a state of nonsalvation to a state of salvation. In this description, the "law" seems almost to belong to those quantities that stand on the side of nonsalvation. Doubts are heard as to whether the soteriological turn preached by Paul does not in reality play into the hands of sin, if it encompasses a freedom from the law. The central section, Romans 6—7, is structured by a repeated anticipation of this doubt:

Rom. 6:1:   "What shall we say then? Are we to continue in sin that grace may abound?"

Rom. 6:15: "What then? Are we to sin because we are not under law but under grace?"

Rom. 7:7:   "What then shall we say? That the law is sin?"

These texts are an echo of real charges against Paul, to which he makes reference as early as Rom 3:8*. There he cites as slander against himself the slogan, "Let us do evil, that good may come from it!" Paul answers these charges in 6:1—7:6 with three trains of thought and three images.

1. In 6:1–14, he proceeds from the symbolism of baptism. Baptism

means dying with Christ. In baptism, the "body of sin" (6:6*) dies. One who is baptized has broken radically with the old. One lives in a new life, which differs from the old life as profoundly as resurrection from the dead differs from dying. It is therefore impossible to remain further in sin. A "boundary of death" lies between the Christian and sin.

2. In 6:15–23, the symbolism of a change in rule, which appears already in 6:12–14, is developed. As one has served sin, so now shall one serve justice. Grace does not mean amorality but means commitment to justice. One is always committed to a master. The new commitment excludes "remaining in sin."

3. In 7:1–6, a third symbolism occurs—the image of the twofold marriage, which combines elements of the two preceding trains of thought.[1] For one thing, it presupposes the discontinuity of life and death, the fact that Christians have died with Christ in baptism. Only death paves the way for a second marriage. Penetration of the boundary of death brings freedom from the law. At the same time, however, the image of a change of rule is drawn further. In the ancient world, marriage was a power relationship. The man was the "master." The woman was committed to the second husband just as she was to the first. Thus 7:1–6 forms a synthesis of 6:1–14 and 6:15–23.

If one considers the development of thought from 6:1 to 7:7ff., an increasingly sharp illumination of the past, that is, the time before the soteriological turn, becomes clear. The baptismal symbolism of death and life stresses exclusively the break with the past. What constituted this past is not developed in detail—apart from the fact that it was a matter of existence in the body of sin.

The symbolism of the change of rule goes one step further. Here the past appears a negative mirror image of the new state; as sin once enslaved and exercised a true reign of terror,[2] so does justice now take one into its service. The *hosper-houtos* in Rom. 6:19 places the periods before and after the soteriological turn in analogy with each other.

In the elucidation of the marriage image, the past is described even more precisely. The past marriage is presented pictorially as a rela-

---

1. Schnackenburg ("Römer 7," 288–89) wishes to make a break before 7:1. According to Schnackenburg, first, no objection is formulated as in 6:1 and 6:15; since the next objection does not occur until 7:7, that would be an argument in favor of connecting 7:1–6 to the preceding material. Second, the address *E agnoeite, adelphoi* is said to signal a new beginning; but cf. the *e agnoeite* in Rom. 6:3. The reference to the "rule of the law" (7:1*) unmistakably refers to 6:15*—"being under the law."
2. Cf. L. Schottroff, "Die Schreckensherrschaft."

tionship of dependence. But Paul interprets this relationship of dependence conceptually with the words "While we were living in the flesh, our sinful passions, aroused by the law, were at work in our members to bear fruit for death" (7:5). This expresses succinctly what Rom. 7:7–23 will analyze in detail.

To summarize the first result of our analysis of the context, we can say that Paul is answering the objections to his theology that he himself has anticipated. The objections revolve around the charge of antinomianism. In three symbols and images—the symbolism of burial, change in rule, and marriage—he refutes this objection and increasingly illuminates the time before his conversion as a contrast to the condition of redemption. This retrospective analysis, which expands in concentric circles, reaches its climax in Rom. 7:7ff.; here the past is brought "to concept" in a very abstract language. Romans 7:7ff. is therefore neither a digression nor an excursus but the goal of a larger complex of thought.

Yet Paul's glance in Rom. 6:1—7:6 is not directed only into the past. The old state, which is to be overcome, is constantly confronted with the new life. In the course of this confrontation, different aspects are emphasized. First the new state is "like life from the dead" (6:13*)—without a more detailed account of the quality of this new life. The symbolism of a change in rule conceives old and new life as service. The formal structure of life remains the same, so that the same terms and expressions can be applied to both states of life: "to yield one's members" (vv. 13*, 19*); "to be under" something (vv. 14*, 15*); "to obey" (v. 16*); "to be a servant" (vv. 16*, 20*); members as "weapons" (v. 13*) and "instruments" (v. 19*); the result as "fruit" (vv. 21*, 22*) and "goal" (vv. 21*, 22*). Within these formally stable structures, three things change: the master whom one serves, the result that one produces, and the consequences that the service entails. Here sharp antitheses dominate. If we put together all the correlative terms that stand in the same position syntactically and in opposition to each other semantically, the picture represented by figure 3 emerges.

Here the "law" stands on the same side as "sin" and "death"; even more oddly, it is on the same side as "lawlessness." How that is to make sense remains unclear. The extent to which the new life differs in principle from the old also remains unclear. Was it not described within the burial symbolism as a radical break with the old? Here, however, it has the same formal structure as the old life; only the contents change in a somewhat contradictory manner. Paul himself seems to sense the problematic of his statements when he stresses that

FIGURE 3

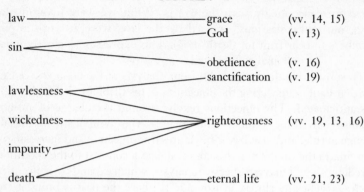

he speaks in a human way "because of the weakness of your flesh" (Rom. 6:19*).

The questions raised in chapter 6 are resolved only in the following chapter. The third section, Rom. 7:1–6, achieves an important precision: old and new life are each a service, but the old life is service "in the old nature of the letter," whereas the new service is "in the newness of the Spirit" (7:6*). What Paul juxtaposes antithetically in this text is developed in the following two chapters: service in the old letter, in 7:7–24; the present as life in the Spirit, in chapter 8. In the eighth chapter it then becomes finally clear that the new life is no new servitude that would be formally comparable to the old servitude; life in the Spirit signifies "sonship" (8:15) and "liberty" (8:21). Categories of servitude are ultimately inappropriate, for the essence of what is new is love from which nothing can separate (8:39). Only in chapters 7 and 8 does the contrast of old and new reach its goal. In the course of this, the review of the past life is formulated in the first-person singular, but the development of the new life in the Spirit is in the first-person plural (8:1ff.).

Yet there are constant efforts to challenge this clear structuring.[3] It is said that Paul speaks of the new life of the Christian from 7:14 on, not merely from 8:1 on, since the tense changes from past to present in 7:14. But there are important grounds against this conception.

---

3. Even the two most recent astute attempts (Cranfield, *A Critical and Exegetical Commentary*, 334–47, 355ff.; and Dunn, "Rom 7,14–25") are in my opinion unconvincing. The most important counterarguments may be found as early as Kümmel, *Römer 7*, 104–10; and Althaus, *Paulus und Luther*, 27–30.

1. It is only in 8:2 that Paul returns to the opposition of letter and spirit which is mentioned programmatically in 7:6. The juxtaposition of a "law of the Spirit of life" and a "law of sin and death" (8:2) is identical to the opposition of the letter which kills and the Spirit who gives life (2 Cor. 3:6). The liberation from the law of sin and death looks back to the state depicted in 7:14–24.

2. The statements in 7:14–24 represent in content the direct opposite of the statements about Christians in 8:1ff.:

7:14:	One is sold under sin.	8:2:	The Christian is liberated from the law of sin and death.
7:17:	Sin lives within one (cf. 7:20).	8:9:	The Spirit of God lives within one.
7:18:	Flesh and "I" are equated.	8:9*:	"You are no longer in the flesh."
7:23*:	The "other law" conducts war.	8:6:	The mind of the Spirit is life and peace.

3. The scissure in vv. 13–14 is marked too weakly to be considered the transition between pre-Christian and Christian periods of life; above all, it lacks a reference to Christ, without whom this transition is inconceivable. The formula-like expression *oidamen*, "we know," does refer to a knowledge of Christians (cf. Rom. 2:2; 3:19; 8:22, 26, 28; 1 Cor. 8:1, 4), but the object of this knowledge need not for this reason be the Christian life.[4]

Summary. Romans 7:6 sets the theme for chapters 7 and 8, through the contrast of letter and Spirit. In 7:7–25, the dark aspects of the law (the letter) are analyzed; in 8:1ff., life in the Spirit is presented. The two chapters are related to each other;[5] one can even ask if this relationship is not reflected in their composition. Two themes stand out in Romans 8: first, the overcoming of the flesh, and second, the sighing of creation. Each theme reflects as mirror image motifs of Romans 7. In 7:14–25, Paul depicted suffering under the flesh; in Rom. 8:1ff., he writes about overcoming the flesh through the Spirit. In Rom. 7:7–13, he analyzed the origin of sin, with clear allusions to the story of the Fall; in Rom. 8:18ff., he articulates the sighing of

4. E.g., Rom. 8:22 (the sighing of creation); Rom. 11:2 (Elijah); 1 Cor. 12:2 (prior pagan life).
5. The relationship of Romans 7 to Romans 8 is a variant of the "once-now" structure; cf. P. Tachau, *"Einst" und "Jetzt,"* 126–27, n. 163. Dupont ("Le problème," 389ff.) thinks that the antithetical sequence of 7:7–25 and 8:1–17 corresponds to the sequence of 1:18—3:20 and 3:21—4:25.

creation at the consequences of the Fall. While one ought not overestimate relationships of this sort, one can nonetheless recognize the recurrence of certain motifs and themes. But even the formal treatment is different. Romans 7:7ff. speaks emphatically of a lost and isolated I; Rom. 8:1ff., on the contrary, speaks in the first-person plural: a cosmic union has taken the place of isolation.

THE STRUCTURE OF ROM. 7:7–23

The "I" of Rom. 7:7ff. goes through a history. In this section, two parts of the text are clearly distinct from each other—a narrative part (vv. 7–13) and a descriptive part (vv. 14–23), which can be distinguished on the basis of formal criteria.[6]

1. The first part is formulated in the past tense—with the exception of the introduction in 7:7; the second part, on the contrary, is completely in the present tense. Up to now, there has been no satisfying interpretation of the change in tense.

2. Both parts are introduced by comments in the first-person plural. The first begins with the deliberative question "What then shall we say?" (7:7), the second with the declaration "But we know that . . ." (7:14*).[7] Both parts then immediately shift to the first-person singular.

3. In the second part, important statements are dependent on cognitive verbs: "we know" (v. 14), "I agree" (v. 16), "I know" (v. 18), "I find" (v. 21), and "I understand" (v. 15*); there are also major clauses with a cognitive verb and an object (vv. 22–23). It is clearly emphasized that this part is concerned with objects of knowledge, understanding, and conceiving. The first part is different. This part narrates how the I that is speaking achieved its knowledge and understanding. The way to achieving knowledge is depicted, not the knowledge that is present.[8]

Multiple repetitions and variations are striking in the first part. They shall be considered under the following methodological viewpoint:

6. Other divisions may be found in Michel, *Der Brief*, 222ff. (vv. 7–12, 13–17, 18–25); Wilckens, *Der Brief*, 72ff. (vv. 7–12, 13–25); and Schmithals, *Die theologische Anthropologie*, 25ff. (vv. 7–12, 13–16, 17–20; a tract formulated independently of the situation of the letter begins in v. 17).

7. The reading *oida men* is presumably adaptation to the first-person singular. On this, cf. Cranfield, *A Critical and Exegetical Commentary*, 355.

8. The stress on the interior realm in 7:14–24 could be adduced as a fourth criterion for distinction between the first and second parts of the text. In 7:7–13, there is only one mention of a covetousness "in me" (v. 8); in 7:14ff., the expression "in me" occurs three times and "in my members" twice. In addition, there is a mention of the "inner man" (7:22*); cf. Schlier, *Der Römerbrief*, 228–29; and Kuss, *Der Römerbrief*, 451–52.

where Paul repeats and varies an idea, the part of the idea that is more developed in the repetition often contains precisely what Paul is concerned with. It is as if he began twice, in order to express himself clearly, or as if he were not quite satisfied with the first formulation. In order to make repetitions and correspondences optically visible, the text of Rom. 7:7–13* is reproduced here:[9]

Thesis:
7 What then shall we say?
    Is the law sin?
    By no means!
    But I did not learn to know sin except through the law.
    First Argument:
    For [*gar*] even of covetousness I would have known nothing, had not the law said, "You shall not covet."
    8   But [*de*] sin found an occasion in the commandment and wrought in me all kinds of covetousness.
        Second Argument:
        For [*gar*] without the law sin is dead.   a
        9   Now [*de*] I once lived without law.   b
            But [*de*] when the commandment came, sin revived b
            and I died.   a
        10 And the commandment which should have led to
            life   b
            proved to be death to me.   a
    Third Argument:
    11 For [*gar*] when sin had found an occasion through the commandment, it seduced me and through it killed me.
Conclusion:
12 So the law is holy, and the commandment is holy and just and good.
13 Did the good, then, bring death to me?
    By no means!
    Rather [it was] sin
    (1) in order that it might be revealed as sin,
    (2) by working death in me through the good,
    (3) so that through the commandment sin might become sinful beyond measure.

The text can be described as a ring composition in structure. Two arguments that correspond almost literally (vv. 8, 11) encamp around the central section, which is based on the opposition of death and life.

9. The structuring took the connecting particles as its point of departure. In each case, an idea begins with *gar* and is pursued further with *de* and *kai*.

The whole is surrounded by rhetorical questions. The first (v. 7) inquires into the connection of sin and law, the second (v. 13) into the connection of law and death. All three quantities are joined as early as 7:5. The progress in thought should therefore not be overestimated.[10] It is clear that v. 13 offers a sort of summary of the preceding. The introductory question is picked up again, with variations, and the conclusion present in v. 12 is continued. The three statements in v. 13 correspond roughly to the three arguments of vv. 7b–11:

(1)	Sin became conscious through the law (vv. 7b–8).	(1)	Sin was revealed through the law (v. 13).
(2)	The sin awakened by the law effects death (vv. 8b–10).	(2)	Sin prepares death through the good (v. 13).
(3)	Sin deceived and killed through the commandment (v. 11).	(3)	Sin showed itself as sinful beyond measure through the commandment (v. 13).

The decisive point of the section seems to lie in the progress of thought from the first to the third argument. The repetitions, in part literal, attract attention, especially since they are joined with a clear variation. Sin not only becomes effective and conscious (v. 8), it also seduces and kills through the law (v. 11). One may presume that Paul lacked precisely this idea in the first formulation. The starting point of the train of thought is, after all, generally intelligible: law and covetousness are opposites. The law forbids covetousness. But if covetousness is aroused by the law, then the contrast of law and sin becomes shaky; this is even more the case if sin "seduces" and "kills" with the aid of the law, that is, if the enticing voice of sin conceals itself in the voice of the law and punishes with death those whom it has seduced on the basis of the prescriptions of the law. Then law and sin are no longer a contrast; although diametrically opposed by nature, they are tightly bound together in their effects.

The second part also displays an organic structure with striking repetitions. It begins with the thesis, "We know that the law is spiritual;

10. Michel (*Der Brief*, 222ff.) and Eichholz (*Die Theologie*, 255) structure the section into 7:7–12 and 13ff. because of the new idea ("death" in v. 13 instead of "sin" in v. 7). "After 7:7ff. it is a matter of the relationship of the Torah to sin; after 7:13ff., a matter of the relationship of the Torah to death." But the terms "kill" and "death" occur already in 7:10, 11, are missing in 7:14–23, and return only in the concluding lament of 7:24. That the terms "law," "sin," "death" belong together is clear from 1 Cor. 15:56; the connection of covetousness, sin, and death is clear from James 1:14–15.

but I am carnal, sold under sin" (v. 14), and the admission of a dead end, "I do not understand my own actions" (v. 15), which is developed in two parallel trains of thought, as this chart of Rom. 7:15–23* shows:[11]

First Train of Thought	*Second Train of Thought*
15 For [*gar*] not	19 For [*gar*] not the good
what I want,	that I want
is what I do,	I do,
but	but the evil
what I hate	that I do not want
I do.	is what I do.
16 But if [*ei de*] I	20 But if [*ei de*] I
do that	do that
which I do not want,	which I do not want
I agree with the law	
that it is good.	
17 So then [*vuni de*]	then
I no longer do it	I no longer do it
but rather sin	but rather sin
which dwells in me.	which dwells in me.
18 For [*gar*] I know	
that in me,	
that is, in my flesh,	
nothing good dwells.	
For [*gar*]	21 I find then [*ara*]
	the law valid
the willing is present in me,	for me, who wants to do the good,
but not the doing of the good.	that evil is present to me.
	22 For [*gar*] according to the
	inmost self I delight in the law
	of God.
	23 But [*de*] I see in my members
	another law,

11. There is no consensus among exegetes on the structure of Rom. 7:14–24. Käsemann (*An die Römer*, 191, 197) sees a sharpening of the idea between v. 20 and vv. 21ff.; the train of thought moves from the contradiction between willing and doing to the complete self-alienation of the creature. Michel (*Der Brief*, 222ff.) makes a division between v. 17 and v. 18, since from v. 18 on, Paul presents the idea that "man not only stands under the dominion of sin, but also knows of the lostness of this situation" (p. 232). Kuss (*Der Römerbrief*, 425ff.) structures according to formal perspectives; according to him, vv. 14–17 are repeated in vv. 18–20, and vv. 21–23 are a conclusion from what has been said. My own structuring again takes formal criteria (particles and repetitions) as its point of departure.

which resists the law of my
interior,
and makes me captive to the law
of sin which is in my members.

In the second part of Romans 7, which is formulated in the present tense, no progressing event is narrated; rather, the antithesis of law and sin, spirit and flesh, is drawn out in two trains of thought.[12] If there is progress here, it is not on the level of occurrence but on that of knowledge. In each instance, the starting point is a saying on the contradiction of willing and doing. The two trains of thought can be compared formally. In each case, there follows a conditional clause that draws conclusions (*ei de*), then clauses with conclusive particles (*nuni de*, v. 17; *ara*, v. 21) which are each supported through further statements attached by a *gar*. In the second development of the idea, the power of sin is evoked in connection with the repeated saying somewhat more briefly than in the first. But then the idea of assent to the law even and precisely in conflict with the law—an idea that had only been touched on in v. 16—is picked up again and treated at greater length. Assent to the law becomes delight in the law, and the *symphemi*, "I agree" (v. 16), is enhanced to a *synedomai*, "I delight" (v. 22). In a corresponding manner, the conflict with the powers that oppose the law is illuminated more sharply. It is here that the decisive new idea occurs. While the resisting power in v. 18 is identified with the flesh, in v. 23 it is termed "another law." The conflict between flesh and law becomes a clash between two laws and a conflict between two normative orientations. Since Paul introduces precisely this idea in his repetition, we may presume that the chief emphasis lies on this point.

Both parts of the text, that in the past tense and that in the present, have a comparable inner structure. Even in the second part Paul proceeds from a relatively evident statement—the sharp opposition between the spiritual law and the fleshly I. Once again, this opposition is relativized precisely in the expanded parts of the varied train of thought. The law fragments into a "law" in my members and a law that I serve with my reason. The apology for the law can be carried out only by fragmenting the law into a bright law of God and a dark, resisting law in the members. Both parts thus proceed from clear

12. Cambier ("Le 'moi,' " 17–18) seeks to establish a consistent antithesis in all details of the section.

oppositions, only to show that these oppositions are not after all as clear as seemed to be the case at first. Figure 4 will illustrate this.

FIGURE 4

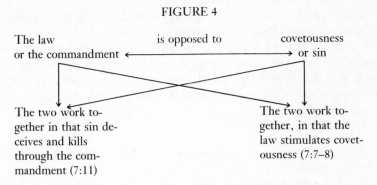

Point: Sin not only stands opposite the law but also becomes operative with the aid of the law. Sin and commandment work together despite opposing natures.

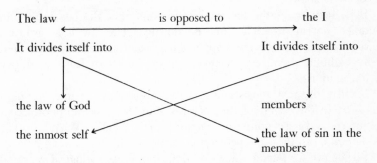

Point: The law not only stands opposite the inmost self but operates even in sinful man as law in his members. The division of law and I is depicted.

The point of both texts lies in the correction of dualistic patterns of thought. In doing this, Paul proceeds from two antagonistic tribunals that point beyond human beings: the law points to God, sin to the flesh that human beings share with all living things. Both tribunals are represented simultaneously in persons—the law of God in the *nous* (mind), the flesh in the members.[13] The human I—like the other tribunals not a purely "immanent" entity, much less an autonomous one—stands as a third tribunal between these two antagonistic tribunals. It is rather destined to be drawn in, either by the flesh (7:18) or by Christ (8:10). It is therefore completely legitimate to speak of a three-tribunal model in Romans 7, or to put it better, "behind" Romans 7. After all, in Romans 7 it is not Paul's intention to develop anthropological models. He intends rather to present soteriological dramatics with the aid of anthropological concepts. But the anthropological concepts used in this process point to three tribunals whose relationship is antagonistic and which are understood as the effects and as the stage of transsubjective powers.

To conclude the structural analysis, we can pose initial questions toward a psychological appraisal of the text.

The similarity between the psychoanalytic three-tribunal model and the anthropological-theological conceptuality of Paul has always been noticed. If this is a matter of factual parallels, where do the differences lie? How can it be explained historically that such formal parallels have come about?

Both sections of the text make the point that the law leads into conflict, not in principle, but functionally. The law is a historical entity. The lack of salvation appears here as grounded in culture, not only in human nature. Are there aspects here that learning theory could illuminate?

Finally, the text consists of repeated approaches to interpreting a conflict. In the course of this, accents shift. Can the shifts of accent be interpreted as a cognitive restructuring of the conflict? What historical situation led to this new perception of the conflict?

But before we pursue these questions in the psychological appraisal of the text, we must examine the "I" in Romans 7. The three questions that have been raised can be examined even if Paul did not include himself under this "I." But the text becomes incomparably more lively if we may read it against the background of personal experience.

THE "I" IN ROMANS 7

The accented use of "I" in Rom. 7:7ff. is singular in Pauline literature. To say "I" with emphasis seems to be a modern trait. Precisely for

---

13. Cf. Käsemann, *An die Römer*, 197: God and the power "sin" stand opposite each other as contestants. Each has a base in human existence—the inner man in one case, the members in the other.

this reason, the danger of misinterpretation is great. Every historian will be cautious when there is a question of ascribing traits of modern subjectivity to an ancient subject. Elements that point in this direction can without doubt be recognized in the *Confessions* of Augustine. Can it be that what achieves development there was already sown in early Christianity? We see that while the interpretation of the "I" in Romans 7 is initially only a special grammatical question—and it will be treated as a grammatical question in what follows—more than grammar is at stake in the interpretation of the "I." In principle, there are three possibilities of understanding the "I."

1. *As a personal "I"* by which Paul means himself in opposition to others. An example is 1 Cor. 15:8, where Paul distinguishes himself from the other apostles and Easter witnesses as one born out of due time.

2. *As a typical "I"* by which Paul means himself, yet not in opposition to others but rather in such a way that all Christians, Jews, or the human race in general are included. This typical "I" is present in Gal. 2:20, when Paul writes, "It is no longer I who live, but Christ who lives in me; and the life I now live in the flesh I live by faith in the Son of God, who loved me and gave himself for me."

3. *As a fictive "I"* with the aid of which Paul presents a general idea in a lively manner, but without including himself. A fictive "I" of this sort can be present especially in dialogical elements, when Paul in a sense slips into the role of another—such as that of the "strong man" who exclaims, "Why should my freedom be dependent on another conscience?" (1 Cor. 10:29b*).

Kümmel consciously excluded the first two possibilities: "For whether Paul speaks of himself alone or of himself as a type, in either case he is speaking of himself, and the text seems to me not to permit this."[14] Kümmel came to this decision on the only path that is methodically usable—through assessment of analogous linguistic practice in Paul and in antiquity. In this procedure it is naturally decisive that the analogies be appropriate, that they be analogies which contain the decisive characteristics of the text that is to be illuminated. Three criteria will be discussed here: the personal pronoun, the sentence form, and the tense. We will examine chiefly seventeen texts in Paul, which are discussed in Kümmel as witnesses to a fictive "I": Rom. 3:7; 3:8; 1 Cor. 6:12; 6:15; 10:29b; 10:30; 11:31–32; 13:1–3; 13:11–12; 14:11; 14:14–15; Gal. 2:18; 2:19; 2:20; Rom. 7:7a; 7:9; 7:14ff.[15]

14. *Römer 7*, 84.
15. Ibid., 121. In addition there are the references collected on 126–31: Demosthenes

(a) *The personal pronoun*. In Romans 7, Paul frequently emphasizes the first person through an explicitly placed *ego*, "I." This is found six times instead of the simple verb form, which is present chiefly in the presumably traditional saying in vv. 15 and 19 (i.e., in eight of nineteen total instances). Analogies that are adduced in the interpretation of Romans 7 should therefore if possible contain an explicit *ego*. This is attested about seventy-nine times in Paul.[16] The overwhelming majority of these texts must clearly be understood as personal. Some could be conceived as typical; only a few might be conceived as fictive. Among the seventeen Pauline attestations of a fictive "I" which are discussed by Kümmel, however, an explicit *ego* is found in only seven texts: Rom. 3:7; 1 Cor. 6:12; 10:29–30; Gal. 2:19; 2:20; Rom. 7:9; and Rom. 7:14ff. These are texts that are distinguished in part by their emphatic nature, in part by their dialogical character. Romans 3:5–7 refutes an objection; 1 Cor. 6:12 corrects a Corinthian thesis; 10:29–30 possibly reflects a fictive dialogue at table. The significance of the *ego* is probably accessible from the dialogical structure of the texts, especially since ancient rhetoric had little interest in the use of "I" as a stylistic device but rather treated the phenomenon of the fictive "I" together with other issues in the analysis of dialogical elements of style.[17]

(b) *The type of sentence*. In Romans 7, procataleptic questions, which raise the problem to which the text seeks to give an answer, are found in important places (vv. 7 and 13). The answer is given in declarative

Oration 9.17; Xenophon *Respublica Atheniensium* 1.11, 2.11; Horace *Ars poetica* 25–26, 86ff., 265ff.; Philo *On Dreams* 1.176–77. To be excluded (with the endorsement of Wilckens, *Der Brief*, 77 n. 293) are the rabbinic references, for these are narratives in the first-person singular in which the "I" means the narrating teacher—completely independently of whether the text is fictional or nonfictional. The fictive and the fictional "I" are to be distinguished. Speakers do not identify themselves with the fictive "I." With a fictional "I," one narrates to others something composed with which one wishes to identify oneself.

16. Not taken into consideration was an explicit *ego* in Old Testament citations of God's words; cf. Rom. 10:19; 12:19; 14:11; 2 Cor. 6:17. In the texts from outside the New Testament, the explicit *ego* is missing in Xenophon *Respublica Atheniensium* 2.11, and Horace *Ars Poetica* 24ff., 265ff. The *en emoi* of Philo *On Dreams* 1.176–77 is not to be counted here, since it always reads *en emoi* (instead of *moi*); cf. Blass, Debrunner, and Rehkopf, *Grammatik*, no. 279. An explicit *ego* is attested in Demosthenes *Oration* 9.17; Horace *Ars Poetica* 86ff.; and Xenophon *Respublica Atheniensium* 1.11.

17. Although ancient rhetoric reflected on all elements of style with great precision, the fictive "I" is not one of its themes; cf Lausberg, *Handbuch*. The phenomenon that interests us could be interpreted as a form of *aversio*, a turning away from the topic, from the speaker, or from the audience (nos. 848–51), or as an element of the *sermocinatio* (nos. 820–25). There are doubtless fictions in speech, when "something can be adduced which, if it were true, would clarify the question or at least contribute to its clarification" (Martin, *Antike Rhetorik*, 115; see, in addition, 191–92, 332).

sentences, only a few of which are conditional (vv. 7b, 16, 20). Above all, the important statement in v. 9 is formulated unconditionally. Analogies to the I-statements of Romans 7 should therefore as much as possible be unconditional declarative sentences, that is, not questions nor conditional sentences nor conditioned statements. Questions, after all, can contain a fictive "I" much more readily than statements; this is especially true of procataleptic questions, in which a possible objection is anticipated. The derivation of this stylistic element from dialogue can also be demonstrated in Paul. Within the parable of the wild and cultivated olive trees, he anticipates the objection of a gentile Christian with the words "You will say, 'Branches were broken off so that I might be grafted in' " (Rom. 11:19). "That is true," Paul answers, "they were broken off because of their unbelief . . ." (11:20). The "I" of the gentile Christian can naturally not be the "I" of the Jewish Christian Paul—not even if the introductory formula *ereis oun* were lacking. Such an introductory formula could easily be dropped, and the anticipated objection could be mentioned in the text without introductory words. Precisely this seems to have happened in Rom. 3:7ff. and 1 Cor. 10:29–30.

In Rom. 3:1–8, Paul refutes a list of theses, which first speak in the third-person plural, of the Jews (3:1, 3, 5), but then are formulated in the first-person singular with the explicit personal pronoun *emoi* or *kago:* "But if through my falsehood God's truthfulness abounds to his glory, why should I still be condemned as a sinner?" (3:7*). This is no doubt said from the perspective of the affected Jew, who has previously been threatened with judgment just like the sinful Gentile (Rom. 2:1ff.). Paul distances himself from this view. He repeats the objection again in sharper form, this time in the first-person plural: "And is what certain people attribute to us with blasphemous intent true: 'Let us do evil that good may come'? Their condemnation is just" (3:8*). This "we" is doubtless not only fictive. Here Paul speaks of himself. With regard to Romans 7, it is decisive that the fictive "I" in 3:7 is found in a rhetorical question, and especially that it is in a question with conditional structure. An analogy to this fictive "I" could therefore be sought only in the comparable rhetorical questions in Rom. 7:7 and 13, but not in the answers. On the contrary, when Paul refutes the rhetorical questions, he identifies himself with this refutation without reserve. The "By no means!" is not fictive!

It is also instructive to look at 1 Cor. 10:29–30. Here Paul gives the advice to refrain, in certain circumstances and for the sake of conscience, from eating meat that has been offered to idols. He makes this more precise: "But I mean not his own conscience, but that of another" (10:29a*). Here the first-person singular ("but I mean") is unquestionably to be related to Paul. There follow two emphatic questions, which can either be understood as the objection of a "strong person"[18] or as foundational rhetorical questions of Paul.[19] It is characteristic that the second of these questions (1 Cor. 10:29b–30*) is again dependent on a conditional clause:

For why should my liberty be determined by another's scruples?
If I [ego] partake of something with thankfulness,
why am I denounced for something
for which I [ego] speak a prayer of thanks?

The position formulated in these rhetorical questions is naturally not the position of Paul. His own opinion emerges from the following imperative sentences, in which he gives an answer to the questions that have been raised: "So, whether you eat or drink, or whatever you do, do all to the glory of God. Give no offense to Jews or to Greeks or to the church of God, just as I [kago] try to please all men in everything I do, not seeking my own [emautou] advantage, but that of many, that they may be saved. Be imitators of me as I [kago] am of Christ" (10:31—11:1). In this concluding statement of position, the twofold kago in two coordinated declarative sentences must in any case be related to Paul. It is a personal "I."

Romans 7:7ff. is to be judged analogously. Two procataleptic questions are raised here as well. The first personal pronoun occurring in them (in the plural in 7:7, in the singular in 7:13) is not the "I" of Paul, even if the rhetorical form betrays high personal involvement. But the greater part of the text that is of interest to us with respect to its possible biographical background (esp. vv. 7–13, in other words) is an answer to these questions in the form of declarative sentences. Corresponding answers and declarative sentences are to be adduced as analogies. Now in Rom. 3:1–9 and 1 Cor. 10:29ff., Paul identifies himself personally with his answers to questions that have been raised

18. Thus Lietzmann, *An die Korinther*, 52–53. According to this exegesis, Paul would identify himself fully with the reservation of the objection in v. 31.
19. Thus Bultmann, *Theologie*, 220. According to Bultmann, Paul bases his renunciation of flesh offered to idols on regard for the conscience of *others* and not on regard for *his own* conscience. Only the first of these is freedom (according to the principle of adaptation in 1 Cor. 9:19ff.); the second would be lack of freedom. According to Bultmann, Paul would include himself in the "I" of v. 29.

previously. One should therefore proceed from the idea that Paul also identifies himself very personally with the responsive declarative sentences in Rom. 7:7bff., however much his statements also bring to expression generally valid material. If questions in the first-person singular are advanced against this conception as references for a rhetorically fictive "I," one can fully recognize these references as rhetorically fictive, if it is clear that this is a matter not of analogies to the declarative sentences in Rom. 7:7ff., but of analogies to the questions in 7:7 and 7:13. But this eliminates some of Kümmel's references—specifically, Rom. 3:7; 3:8; 1 Cor. 6:15; 10:29–30; and Rom. 7:7a. Of the remaining declarative sentences, one could also eliminate 1 Cor. 11:31–32; 14:11; 14:14–15; and Gal. 2:18, since conditioned statements are present here. Of Kümmel's seventeen references, eight are still left.[20] The third criterion will thus be of decisive significance.

(c) *Tense.* Precisely those statements in Romans 7 with respect to which one is most tempted to seek a biographical background (7:8–11) stand in the past tense. The past tense individualizes more clearly than the present. The present tense often states what happens or can happen in general; the past states what has happened. The statement "Life is short" affects every individual; the statement "Life was short" is more suggestive of a particular person. Now, there are in Paul a number of statements in the first-person singular and in the past tense, including nineteen with an explicit *ego.*[21] But only two of the references adduced by Kümmel are in the past tense (1 Cor. 13:11–12 and Gal. 2:19); both texts are probably to be understood as typical. Is Rom. 7:7ff. supposed to be an exception?

In Romans 7 the tense changes in a striking way from past to present. Analogies with corresponding change in tense are naturally to be preferred. Two analogies will be adduced here. The first case is concerned with an autobiographical anecdote of Epictetus (*Discourses* 1.9.29–32). First there is a narrative in the past tense; then follows a general conclusion, itself subdivided into halves, in the present tense. The first half (*a*) is formulated in general terms in the third person,

20. Among the references of Kümmel, there are six conditioned statements or conditioned questions—Rom. 3:7; 1 Cor. 10:30; 11:31–32; 14:11; 14:14–15, and Gal. 2:18—in which the relationship to factual reality is more open from the start. I am grateful to F. Gnändinger, a student of theology, for this observation.

21. Cf. 1 Cor. 2:3; 3:1, 6; 4:15b; 5:3; 9:15; 11:23; 15:10; 2 Cor. 2:10; 12:13, 16; Gal. 1:12; 2:19; 6:14; Phil. 4:11; 1 Thess. 2:18; 3:5; Phlm. 13. Of the references outside the New Testament, only Horace *Ars Poetica* 267BC is in the past tense.

while the second (*b*) changes to the first-person singular with an explicit *ego:*

1. The part in the past tense:

   So likewise Rufus was wont to say, to test me, "Your master is going to do such-and-such a thing to you." And when I would say in answer, "'Tis but the lot of man," he would reply, "What then? Am I to go on and petition him, when I can get the same result from you?"

2. The part in the present tense:

   (*a*) For, in fact, it is foolish and superfluous to try to obtain from another that which one can get from oneself.

   (*b*) Since, therefore, I [*ego*] am able to get greatness of soul and nobility of character from myself, am I to get a farm, and money, or some office, from you? Far from it! I will not be so unaware of what I myself possess.[22]

The concluding rhetorical questions betray high personal involvement; it is, after all, a matter of the central Stoic doctrine of the independence of the inner self from external fate.[23] The doctrine is formulated in the present tense. The transition from past to present signals the step to a broader generalization. In this, the autobiographical "I" becomes a typical "I." In distinction from Rom. 7:7ff., the anecdote of Epictetus does offer concrete circumstances: Epictetus's teacher is mentioned by name, and his social status as slave is presupposed. Such concrete details are lacking in Romans 7. For this reason a second text shall also be adduced, one that is kept much more general: the "ideal biography" of King Solomon[24] in Wis. 7:1–13*:

1 I [*ego*] also am mortal, like all men,
   a descendant of the first-formed child of earth;
   and in the womb of a mother I was molded into flesh,
2 within the period of ten months, compacted with blood
   from the seed of a man and the pleasure of marriage.

22. ET: W. A. Oldfather, *Epictetus*, vol. 1 of 2 vols. (LCL, 1925), 73.

23. Epictetus likes to formulate central Stoic insights in the "I" form, a fact that may be interpreted as a sign of great personal involvement; cf. *Discourses* 1.1.21–25, 1.1.32, 1.6.29, 1.19.1ff., 1.21.2, 1.25.18ff. I would refer also to the change of tense in *Discourses* 1.28–32.

24. The term "ideal biography" stems from Georgi, *Weisheit Salomos*, 422. To the best of my knowledge, Berger (*Exegese*, 38) was the first to adduce Wis. 7:1ff. as an analogy to Rom. 7:7ff. He points out that the reference to Adam is to be found at once in v. 1.

3 and when I [*ego*] was born, I began to breathe
   the common air. . . .
12 But I rejoiced in all things, because wisdom leads them;
   but I did not know that she was their mother.
13 I learned without guile and I impart without grudging;
   I do not hide her wealth. . . .

The text fulfills all three criteria. It is a matter of declarative sentences with explicit *ego;* the tense changes in v. 13 from the past to the present. The change in tense signals the transition from the ideal biography of King Solomon to the communication of general insights. The *ego* is a typical "I," which includes Solomon, but means every wise person.

The closest parallel to Rom. 7:7ff., however, is to be found in Paul himself. There is a text in his writing as well that meets all three criteria. The parallel (Gal. 2:17–20) is all the more instructive because it is also closely related to Romans 7 in its formal structure:

> But if, in our endeavor to be justified in Christ, we ourselves were found to be sinners, is Christ then an agent of sin? Certainly not! But if I build up again those things which I tore down, then I prove myself a transgressor. For I through the law died to the law, that I might live to God. I have been crucified with Christ; it is no longer I who live, but Christ who lives in me. . . .

The structural similarity between Romans 7 and Galatians 2 may be clarified by figure 5.

FIGURE 5

	Romans 7	*Galatians 2*
Thesis:	vv. 4–6: first-person plural	vv. 15–16: first-person plural
Question:	v. 7a: absurd consequence: law = sin?	v. 17: absurd consequence: Christ = servant of sin?
Rebuttal:	*me genoito*	*me genoito*
Foundation:	(a) v. 7: Contrary-to-fact first-person singular	(a) v. 18: Contrary-to-fact (?) first-person singular
	(b) v. 9: Past tense with *ego*	(b) v. 19: Past tense with *ego*
	(c) vv. 14ff.: Present tense with *ego*	(c) v. 20: Present tense with *ego*

Of course, the two sections are not comparable in content: Romans 7 thematizes the origin of sin; Galatians 2, liberation from sin. But in each case a transition is depicted, first in the past tense, then in the present. What is decisive is that the sentences in Gal. 2:19–20 with an explicit *ego* indisputably include Paul[25] and—despite all typical traits—are also to be understood personally (vv. 20–21). Galatians 2:18, on the contrary, is disputed: "But if I build up again those things which I tore down, then I prove myself a transgressor." An *ei* with the indicative in the subordinate clause and with the indicative in the main clause signifies the real case.[26] But the statement does not apply to Paul, who after all refuses to reintroduce food taboos that he has abandoned, the reintroduction of which he holds against the Jewish Christians in Antioch. Is the "I" of Gal. 2:18 a fictive "I" then? An element of literary style? Or is it rather Peter who speaks here?[27] Or one of the Jewish Christians?[28] Or both?[29] But while the subordinate clause does apply to them—they have reestablished what they had abolished—the main clause does not, since they believe that they are fulfilling the law, not breaking it, by returning to the food taboos. In addition, the *ego* that follows in v. 19 is not separated by any adversative particle from the allegedly fictive "I" that precedes it. The solution presumably lies in the fact that the verse is contrary to fact as far as its meaning is concerned.[30] A corresponding instance may be found in Gal. 5:11: "But if I, brethren, still preach circumcision, why am I still persecuted?" Here the so-called real form unquestionably has a contrary-to-fact meaning. Thus, in Gal. 2:18 and 5:11, Paul is saying that if I—like my opponents—were to hold to food taboos and circumcision, which in fact I do not do, then I would be a transgressor and would be free of persecution. But even if one comes to another result in the exegesis of Gal. 2:18, it is possible to conclude from this passage to Rom. 7:7ff. only with difficulty. Galatians 2:18 is a conditional sentence,

25. This is conceded even by exegetes who do not relate Gal. 2:18 to Paul; cf Kümmel, *Römer 7*, 123 n. 1; Oepke, *Der Brief*, 93–94; and Mussner, *Der Galaterbrief*, 177–78.

26. Cf. Blass, Debrunner, and Rehkopf, *Grammatik*, no. 281. The difficulties of interpretation are discussed by Klein, "Individualgeschichte," 195.

27. So Mussner, *Der Galaterbrief*, 178; against this, Klein, "Individualgeschichte," 195–98.

28. So Kümmel, *Römer 7*, 123.

29. So Oepke, *Der Brief*, 93.

30. This use of the real form can also be observed elsewhere in the New Testament. In 1 Cor. 8:13, *ei* + indicative equals *ean* + subjunctive (cf. Blass, Debrunner, and Rehkopf, *Grammatik*, no. 372 n. 9); in Luke 17:2, *ei* + indicative is contrary to fact (no. 372.3).

not the sort of unconditioned declarative sentence that dominates in Romans 7 and that also follows in v. 19, where the *ego* unambiguously includes Paul.

Summary. As figure 6 shows, if we base ourselves on the three criteria that have been mentioned, only a few of the alleged parallels to Rom. 7:7ff. remain:

FIGURE 6

	1. Explicit ego	2. Declarative sentence	3. Past tense
Rom. 3:7	X	—	—
Rom. 3:8	—	—	—
1 Cor. 6:12	X	X	—
1 Cor. 6:15	—	—	—
1 Cor. 10:29b	—	—	—
1 Cor. 10:30	X	—	—
1 Cor. 11:31–32	—	X*	—
1 Cor. 13:1–3	—	X	—
1 Cor. 13:11–12	—	X	X
1 Cor. 14:11	—	X*	—
1 Cor. 14:14–15	—	X*	—
Gal. 2:18	—	X*	—
Gal. 2:19	X	X	X
Gal. 2:20	X	X	—
Rom. 7:7a	—	—	—
Rom. 7:9	X	X	X
Rom. 7:14ff.	X	X	—

* = conditional sentence structure

The sole formally convincing parallel to Rom. 7:9 is thus Gal. 2:19. The table could awaken the false impression that this is a matter of singular statements in Paul, as far as their form is concerned. The opposite is the case. Eighteen further statements in the first-person plural (with explicit *ego*, declarative structure, and past tense) are to be added: 1 Cor. 2:3; 3:1; 3:6; 4:15b; 5:3; 9:15; 11:23; 15:10; 2 Cor. 2:10 (two statements); 12:13; 12:16; Gal. 1:12; 6:14; Phil. 4:11; 1 Thess.

2:18; 3:5; Phlm. 13. The *ego* is unquestionably personal almost everywhere. Can these parallels that lie close at hand be brushed aside in the interpretation of Romans 7 in order to give preference to parallels that are formally and historically more distant? That would be methodically inadmissible.[31]

But the references outside the New Testament also point more in another direction. Only one of the eight references adduced by Kümmel for a fictive *ego* is formulated in the past tense (Horace *Ars Poetica* 267BC); no reference fulfills all three criteria. In the first book of Epictetus's *Discourses*, on the contrary, there are six texts with *ego*-statements in the past tense.[32] All these statements are unquestionably to be understood autobiographically. Saying this is not intended to deny the existence of a fictive "I" as an element of literary style. But as a fictive "I," it connected with dialogical signals[33] and occurs above all in questions[34] and in statements in the present tense.[35]

But in my opinion the content of Rom. 7:7ff. also speaks against the assumption of a purely fictive "I." The first explicit *ego* (v. 8) is provoked by the address of the divine law "You shall not covet."[36]

31. Cambier ("Le 'moi,' " 51) thinks that he can demonstrate in 1 Cor. 14:14–15 an "I" with which Paul describes conduct that is not his own—and which is not introduced only as a conditional case. But first, one must not forget the prior conditional structure of v. 14 in studying v. 15, and second, Paul says clearly in 14:18 that he too can speak in tongues. Thus the I of v. 15, which speaks in tongues, includes Paul.

32. *Discourses* 1.7.32, 1.9.27–28, 1.9.29ff., 1.10.2ff., 1.18.15, 1.29.21.

33. Among Kümmel's references from outside the New Testament only Demosthenes *Oration* 9.17 is a statement in the present tense with an explicit "I." But there a clear dialogical signal precedes the statement: "But you will not admit that . . . (ET: J. H. Vince, *Demosthenes: Olynthiacs; Philippics; Minor Public Speeches; Speech Against Leptines* [LCL, 1930], 225); cf. Epictetus *Discourses* 1.7.25, 1.9.8, 1.14.11, etc.

34. So Horace *Ars Poetica* 86ff., 265ff.; cf. Rom. 3:7; 1 Cor. 6:15; 10:30; Rom. 7:7a; Epictetus *Discourses* 1.12.8, 2.5.3.

35. Moule (in *The Law of the Spirit in Rom 7 and 8*, ed. de Lorenzi, 50–51) rightly raises the skeptical question "Is there any instance of the ego, of the Ich, any form, 'ni or ego, representing an individual or a class of persons collectively with which the speaker does not still identify himself?" I would adduce an example lacking in Kümmel, namely Epictetus *Discourses* 1.22.13–14: "For it is my nature to look out for my own interest. If it is my interest to have a farm, it is my interest to take it away from my neighbour; if it is my interest to have a cloak, it is my interest also to steal it from a bath" (ET: W. A. Oldfather, *Epictetus*, vol. 1 of 2 vols. [LCL, 1925], 147). Of course, the Stoic philosopher does not identify himself with such maxims. But the amorality of the statement is a clear signal to the reader of the fictive character of these sentences. It hardly requires a learned dissertation in order to recognize this! Perhaps one can also refer to Epictetus *Discourses* 1.17.16–17. Here Epictetus has a student speak in the first-person singular, without making it clear in the introduction to the address that the student is concerned.

36. So, rightly, Vergote ("Der Beitrag," 89): "The law provokes a consciousness of

The commandment addresses one in the second-person singular. This puts a response in the first-person singular close at hand. But where Paul is speaking of God's demands on human beings, he can hardly be thinking of a fictive "I" from which he excludes himself. That would contradict the gravity of the divine demand.

In addition, Paul picks up in Rom. 7:7ff. on what he had already summarized in 7:5: "While we were living in the flesh, our sinful passions, aroused by the law, were at work in our members to bear fruit for death." Paul also analyzes this cooperation of sin, law, and death in Rom. 7:7ff. Just as Paul did not exclude himself from the "we" of Rom. 7:6, so too is that inconceivable with respect to the "I" of Rom. 7:7ff.

There is in my opinion no doubt. Anyone who denies to Paul the *ego* in Romans 7 has to bear the burden of proof for this claim. What suggests itself most readily is to think of an "I" that combines personal and typical traits.[37] Without the contradiction to Philippians 3, which is still to be discussed, and the nonbiographical statement in Rom. 7:9, probably no one would ever have come up with the idea of considering the "I" fictive.

---

sin in the first person. Through its specific imperative form, the law has a dialogical character."

37. One could also refer to the "I" of the psalms as an analogy (cf. Wilckens, *Der Brief* 2:77–78; Michel, *Der Brief*, 225). In the Qumran psalms in particular, autobiographical and typical elements cannot be separated. In an older layer of these songs, the teacher of righteousness tells of perdition and salvation (e.g., 1QH 2.1–19; 4.5–29; 5.5–19; 5.20—6.36; 7.6–25; 8.4–40). Community songs (e.g., 1.5–39; cf. 21ff.) were later added, in which the "I" was meant typically, without distinction between the songs of the teacher and those of the community. "We have in other words in the Qumran texts both an autobiographical component and also a generalizing use of the 'I' " (E. Lohse, in the discussion following Cambier, "Le 'moi,' " 72). The analogy with the psalms is otherwise limited, for Rom. 7:7ff. is an argumentative text. Only the shift from lament to thanksgiving in Rom. 7:24–25a is reminiscent of the psalms. Yet there are analogies for this shift in argumentative texts (Philo *Who is the Heir* 309; Epictetus *Discourses* 4.4.7: "pos oun pausomai"; tote kai ego hemartanon nun d' ouketi, charis to theo). It is therefore not necessary to think of a liturgical Sitz in Leben for Rom. 7:24–25a (against Smith, "The Form"). The dialogue in Romans 7 is conducted precisely not with God but with an interiorized human dialogue partner who formulates objections in 7:7 and 7:13 and is addressed in 8:2. The "lostness" of the I who is speaking is illuminated precisely through the fact that it is alone with its "accusing and defending thoughts" (Rom. 2:15*).

Chapter 12

Tradition Analysis: Romans 7

Paul interprets the conflict with the law with the aid of two traditions: first, according to the model of the story of the Fall; second, by adducing a widespread ancient opinion. In this context, we must note, on the one hand, how Paul assumes these traditions and, on the other, how he assimilates them to the problematic of his life. Both are significant psychologically—both the given schemes of interpretation and their adaptation to the situation. The tradition analysis is therefore, here as elsewhere, in itself a decisive contribution to the psychological assessment of the text from a cognitive perspective.

THE FALL IN ROM. 7:7–13

The extent to which Adam's fall served as model for the "fall" depicted in Rom. 7:7–11 is disputed. The spectrum of exegetical opinion ranges from the assumption that Adam is speaking here[1] to the denial of any reminiscences of Adam.[2] There are three important objections to a reference to Adam:

1. The temporal location of the commandment. Paul cites the Decalogue and cannot possibly presuppose the later law of Sinai with regard to Adam!

2. The content of the commandment. The commandment in paradise is not to eat of the tree of knowledge. The term "covet," which is so important for Rom. 7:7ff., is lacking in Genesis 2 and 3.

3. The interiorization of the fall. There is not a single word in Rom.

---

1. The thesis is established in detail by Lyonnet: " 'Tu ne convoiteras pas,' " and "L'histoire du salut." Käsemann (*An die Römer*, 188) formulates it most accurately: "There is nothing in our verses that does not fit Adam, and everything fits only Adam." Cf. Schlier, *Der Römerbrief*, 223–24; Michel, *Der Brief*, 227–28; Leenhardt, *L'Épître*, 106–8.
2. Thus above all Kümmel, *Römer 7*, 85–87; Schrenk, S. V. *entole*,, 547.

7:7ff. about the snake, Eve, or the trees in paradise. It is a matter of inner processes.

In fact, one will have to assume that Adam is not the *subject* of the conflict in Rom. 7:7ff. but rather its *model*. In Rom. 7:7ff., the I assumes the role of Adam and structures it in the light of personal experience of conflict. Before we go into this restructuring, however, we must make sure that reference is made to Adam. To this end, we need to review the three objections.

1. *With regard to the temporal location of the commandment.* The law of Sinai came after Adam, as Paul himself stresses in Rom. 5:12ff. But precisely his observations there make possible a close connection of the commandment of paradise and the law of Sinai. In Rom. 5:14* Paul says, "Yet death reigned from Adam until Moses, even over those whose sins were not like Adam's transgression." Now the specifications of time "until Moses" (5:14*) and "until the law" (5:13*) are parallel both linguistically and in content. But if the law was lacking in the interim between Adam and Moses, then it follows that Adam's sin, in contrast to the sins of the lawless interim, was related to a "law" or to something similar. In other words, if, first, people in the interim period between Adam and Moses did not sin like Adam and if, second, they sinned without law, then the sin of Adam and the sin under the law must be comparable.[3] Above and beyond this, the varying terminology in Rom. 7:7ff. possibly contains a reference to the commandment of paradise. The text speaks of both *nomos* (law) and *entole* (commandment); *entole* frequently means the concrete commandment, and it therefore stands in the plural (cf. 1 Cor. 7:19; Eph. 2:15).[4] The term *entole* would be well suited to designate the individual commandment of the story

3. The equation of the commandment of paradise and the law of Sinai is historically possible, as Jewish traditions of interpretation show. In Targum Neofiti, Gen. 2:15 reads as follows: "And the Lord God took the man and caused him to dwell in the garden of Eden so that he do service according to the Law and keep the commandments" (ET: Martin McNamara and Michael Maher, *Neophyti l*, ed. A. Diez Macho, 501). Yet one must weigh the fact that Paul, in contrast to the rabbinic tendency to consider the law eternal, attributes great significance to its secondary and historical character (cf. Rom. 5:20; Gal. 3:17), and that retrojection of the law into paradise contradicts his theological interests. Yet 1 Cor. 10:1ff. should be recalled. Here Christ is already present in the Old Testament as the rock that followed—a contradiction to Gal. 4:4, according to which Christ came when the time was fulfilled.

4. The differences certainly must not be overemphasized. Both *philonomos* (cf. G. Horsley, *Heuremata*, no. 60) and *philentolos* (*Corpus inscriptionum Judaicarum* 1.132, 203, 482, 509) occur in Jewish inscriptions. It is, however, characteristic that *nomos* almost always stands in the singular (an exception in the Hebrew Bible is Ps. 105:45), whereas *entole* can stand in the plural.

of the Fall. Now in the Septuagint the commandment of paradise is introduced with the words *eneteilato kyrios ho theos to Adam* (Gen 2:16; cf. 3:11, 17). The affinity between *entellesthai* and *entole* was evident to those who used the language at that time.[5] In addition, on the occasion of the *eneteilato* in Gen. 2:17, Philo reflects on the term *entole* as distinguished from other terms.[6] Is it then a coincidence that Paul, in a place where one thinks most readily of Adam's fall, uses the term *entole* but, as far as *nomos* is concerned, only emphasizes its absence (Rom. 7:8–11)?

2. *With regard to the content of the commandment.* Although the commandment "You shall not covet" is not to be found literally in Genesis 2—3, it is extraordinarily appropriate to the story of the Fall: "So the woman saw that the tree was good for food, and that it was a delight to the eyes, and that the tree was to be desired [*horaios*] to make one wise" (Gen. 3:6*).[7] Here there is factually a mention of lust; one must remember that the eye is also connected with covetousness elsewhere (Prov. 6:25 LXX; Matt. 5:28). It is not surprising, then, that Jewish traditions designate the sin of Adam and Eve as lust. Eve laments, "He [the snake] went and poured upon the fruit the poison of his wickedness, which is lust, the root and beginning of every sin."[8] Here lust is presumably to be understood in a sexual sense, since a little later, sexual intercourse is designated a "sin of the flesh"[9] that emerged only upon expulsion from paradise; in paradise, Adam and Eve still lived apart from each other.[10] The *Apocalypse of Abraham* is even more clear. Here Adam and Eve consume the forbidden fruit

5. Compare *eneteilato* in John 14:31 with *entolen edoken* in v. 1 (B; L); in addition, compare *entole* in Mark 10:5 with the parallel *eneteilato* in Matt. 19:7.

6. Philo *Allegorical Interpretation* 1.92–93: "Now it is to this being [the earthly Adam of Genesis 2], and not to the being created after His image and after the original idea, that God gives the command [*entelletai*]. For the latter, even without urging, possesses virtue instinctively; but the former, independently of instruction, could have no part in wisdom. There is a difference between these three—injunction, prohibition, command accompanied by exhortation [*prostaxis, apagoreusis, entole kai parainesis*]" (ET: F. H. Colson and G. H. Whitaker, *Philo*, vol. 1 of 10 vols. [LCL, 1929], 209). In his paraphrase of Genesis 3, Josephus (*Jewish Wars* 1.43) speaks of an *entole*.

7. Thus, correctly, Lyonnet, " 'Tu ne convoiteras pas,' " 161.

8. *Apocalypse of Moses* 19; ET: L. S. A. Wells, *The Apocrypha and Pseudepigrapha of the Old Testament*, ed. Charles, 146. Here covetousness is not the cause but the consequence of the Fall. It is the eating of the fruit which causes desire. In Paul too the commandment awakens covetousness (Rom. 7:8). What precedes the commandment is not "dead covetousness" but "dead sin" (7:8b*). In James 1:15, on the contrary, desire precedes sin.

9. *Apocalypse of Moses* 25.

10. *Apocalypse of Moses* 15.

while they embrace.[11] The divine voice instructs the visionary (23.10), "This is the world of men, this is Adam and this is their desire on earth, this is Eve."[12] In 4 Macc. 18:8, there even seems to be a presupposition that the Fall consisted in sexual seduction. Thus the Fall is frequently interpreted with reference to desire, with a certain accent on sexuality. In Paul, however, the term *epithumia* is more comprehensive. It includes "all kinds of covetousness" (Rom. 7:8).

Independently of the story of the Fall, we can establish in the Judaism of that period a tendency to see the essential element of the law in the prohibition of covetousness. The Ten Commandments are summarized as *me epithumein* (4 Macc. 2:6). Covetousness is considered (in addition to avarice, idolatry, and ignorance) as the root of all evil:

> So great then and transcendent an evil is desire, or rather it may be truly said, the foundation of all evils [*hapanton pege ton kakon*]. For plunderings and robberies and repudiations of debts and false accusations and outrages, also seductions and adulteries, murders, and all wrongful actions, whether private or public, whether in things sacred or in things profane, from what other source do they flow? For the passion to which the name of originator of evil can truly be given is desire [*archekakon pathos estin epithumia*].[13]

The list shows the breadth of the spectrum of evils traced back to covetousness. It is for this reason that it appears as the basic evil, as in the *Apocalypse of Moses* 19, the *Apocalypse of Abraham* 24.10, and 1 Cor. 10:6.[14] This concentration on covetousness is also presupposed in Paul, when he summarizes the voice of the law in the command "You shall not covet." This corresponds, on the one hand, to the

11. *Apocalypse of Abraham* 23.6–7.
12. ET: R. Rubinkiewicz, *The Old Testament Pseudepigrapha*, ed. Charlesworth, 1:700. [The translation has been modified to reflect Theissen's German rendering of the passage.]
13. ET: F. H. Colson, *Philo*, vol. 8 (LCL, 1939), 59, 61. Cf. Philo *On the Decalogue* 173: "that fount of injustice, desire" (ET: F. H. Colson, *Philo*, vol. 7 [LCL, 1937], 91. Cf. also *On the Decalogue* 142: "for all the passions of the soul which stir and shake it out of its proper nature . . . hard to deal with, but desire is hardest of all" (ET: ibid., 77). According to *On the Special Laws* 4.130–31, desire is the greatest evil of the soul. That the text is not thinking only of sexual desire, nor even primarily of this, is clear from *On the Special Laws* 4.84–85, and also from the fact that avarice (*Pseudo-Phocylides* 42ff.; cf. 1 Tim. 6:10; *Polycarp to the Philippians* 4.1), idolatry (Wis. 14:27), and ignorance in general (Philo *On Drunkenness* 160) are named as archevils.
14. Here Paul is thinking of Num. 11:34. The *mnemata tes epithumias* that are named there also cause Philo (*On the Special Laws* 4.130–31) to speak of covetousness as the great evil of the soul.

Hellenistic environment,[15] in which Stoic philosophy elevated the overcoming of passion to the central ethical theme, and emphasizes, on the other hand, what distinguished Judaism from the environment— sexual discipline and food taboos. When Adam's sin, therefore, was interpreted as desire—desire for the forbidden food and sexual desire— this interpretation corresponded to the situation of Hellenistic Judaism.

Conclusion. If Adam's sin consisted in covetousness, and if the Ten Commandments can be summarized in the prohibition of covetousness, then it was easy to think of the entire law in connection with the commandment of paradise and to think of the commandment of paradise in connection with the law. All transgressions of the law then occur in "correspondence with the sin of Adam" (cf. Rom. 5:14). Even if Paul does not speak directly of Adam in Rom. 7:7ff., the figure of Adam stands clearly in the background.

3. *With regard to interiorizing the Fall.* Paul speaks of sin, covetousness, and the I; Genesis 2—3, on the contrary, speaks of Adam and Eve, the snake, and the trees of paradise. When Paul interiorizes motifs of the story of the Fall, he stands in a Hellenistic Jewish tradition of interpretation. Philo already interprets Adam as *nous* (mind) and Eve as *aisthesis* (sense).[16] The snake is considered a symbol of *hedone* (pleasure)[17] or of *epithumia* (concupiscence).[18] Naturally, Paul does not presuppose precisely these allegorical interpretations. But he does surely know comparable interpretations, and he is inspired by them. Two, possibly even three, motifs can be explained in this fashion: the motifs of deceit, death, and knowledge.

Paul speaks of sin's deceiving the I—*exepatesen me.* The words *epatesen me* stand in the Septuagint version of Gen. 3:13. The variation of the *apatan* to *exapatan* is neither linguistically nor in content of very great significance. *Exapatan* also occurs in 2 Cor. 11:3, in 1 Tim. 2:14, and in Theodoret (with regard to Gen. 3:13).[19] But Philo, above all, mentions the motif of deceit in allegorical exegesis of the Fall: "Pleasure, then, has cheated [*exepateken*] poor maimed sense of the power of

15. On what follows, cf. Berger, *Die Gesetzesauslegung Jesu* 1:343–49.
16. *Allegorical Interpretation* 2.5, 24, 38, and *passim.*
17. *On the Creation* 157, *Allegorical Interpretation* 2.72, 74, 76, 81, 87, and passim.
18. *Questions and Answers on Genesis* 1.47–48.
19. Cf. *Septuaginta,* ed. Rahlfs, vol. 1, *Genesis,* ed. Wevers, 92. The four references mentioned above which go back to Gen. 3:13 speak against Kümmel's assertion "that *exapatan* in Rom. 7:11 is not striking and one in no way needs to adduce Gen. 3:13" (*Römer 7,* 54). Josephus *Jewish Antiquities* 1.48, 49, where *exapatan* also stands, should be added.

apprehending matters."[20] Here the motif of deception is already interiorized.

The same is true of the motif of death. Paul writes, "But when the commandment came, sin revived and I died" (Rom 7:9). Just as sin's state of death is contemporaneous with the life of the I, so too must the revival of sin be simultaneous with the death of the I (v. 9). This striking trait can also be explained as an interiorized interpretation of the story of the Fall. The commandment of paradise—with particular clarity in the Septuagint version—contains the threat "On the day that you eat of it you shall die" (Gen. 2:17*)—a threat that did not come to fulfillment.[21] According to biblical information, Adam lived a good 930 years (Gen. 5:5). And elsewhere also, the coming of a commandment is not customarily connected with death; at most, death follows as punishment for a transgression. If the commandment of paradise nonetheless threatens immediate death, that, in Philo's opinion (*Allegorical Interpretation* 1.105–6), could only be due to its reference to an inner death:

> And further he says, "In the day that ye eat thereof, ye shall die the death" (Gen. ii. 17). And yet after they have eaten, not merely do they *not* die, but they beget children and become authors of life to others. What, then, is to be said to this? The death is of two kinds, one that of the man in general, the other that of the soul in particular. The death of the man is the separation of the soul from the body, but the death of the soul is the decay of virtue and the bringing in of wickedness. It is for this reason that God says not only "die" but "die the death," indicating not the death common to us all, but that special death properly so called, which is that of the soul becoming entombed in passions and wickedness of all kinds.[22]

That Rom. 7:7–13 contains so many reminiscences of the story of the Fall leads one to ask if a third motif in the introductory thesis, the motif of knowledge, does not also become intelligible on the basis of Genesis 2—3. "Yet, if it had not been for the law, I should not have known [*ouk egnon*] sin" (7:7). After all, the verb *ginoskein*, "know," also occupies a central place in Genesis 2—3. The prohibition in paradise

20. ET: Colson and Whitaker, *Philo* 1:375.
21. For this reason, the announced dying was soon reinterpreted into "being mortal"; cf. the *thnetos ese* in Origen *Hexapla Gen. 2:17*, and in Codex M, as well as the *mortalis eris* in Jerome (according to Wevers, *Septuaginta*, 86).
22. ET: Colson and Whitaker, *Philo* 1:217. Cf. also *Questions and Answers on Genesis* 1.16.

affects the tree of the knowledge *tou ginoskein kalon kai poneron* (Gen. 2:17; 3:22). Adam and Eve will become like God, *ginoskontes kalon kai poneron* (Gen. 3:6). They know (*egnosan*) their nakedness (Gen. 3:7). It could be that the knowledge of good and evil in the story of the Fall is modified into "knowledge of sin" (Rom. 7:7*) in adaptation to Pauline trains of thought (Rom. 3:20). Yet this is not certain. Unlike the references in Genesis 2—3 to *kalon* and *poneron*, Paul later speaks of *kakon* and *kalon* or *agathon* (cf. Rom. 7:16, 18, 19). The term *poneron* is missing.[23]

In sum, Paul unmistakably has the model of Adam in view in Rom. 7:7ff. He interprets his experience on the basis of this model. Some arguments also suggest that, conversely, he perceives the role of Adam in the light of his experience.

The revision of the assumed role could become clear in the striking repetition of 7:8 in 7:11. First Paul describes the conflict with the law in correspondence with the traditional role of Adam, as transgression of the norm. Within Pauline vocabulary, the terms *epithumia*, "covetousness," and *epithumein*, "to covet," can only be understood as antinomian, that is, as impulse against the law.[24] Zeal for the law, which is the nomistic sin, is never interpreted as a manifestation of covetousness. Even when Paul has "all" covetousness elicited by the commandment, he is hardly thinking of a nomistic striving, but more of a catalogue such as that in Gal. 5:19ff., where the covetousness of the flesh is concretized in many forms of conduct but not in zeal for the law. Above all, the model of Adam permits only an antinomian interpretation of "covetousness"; Adam was seduced to transgression of the law, not to its fulfillment.

Now, the structural analysis already showed that Paul sought to go

23. The pair of opposites *agathon/kakon* is found more frequently in the Septuagint and was surely the customary pair of antonyms (cf. Num. 14:23; 32:11; Deut. 1:39; 3 Kings 3:9 LXX; Ps. 33:15; Sir. 11:14, 25, 31; 12:3; 13:25; 17:7; 18:8; 33:14; 39:4). The oppositions *agathon/poneron* (cf. Eccl. 12:14; 2 Chr. 14:17) and *kalos/poneros* (cf. Lev. 27:10, 12, 14, 33; Num. 24:13) are much more rare. On the whole, there are only a few echoes of the story of the Fall in the part of Romans 7 that is in the present tense. Only two motifs could be mentioned. First, when Paul shoves responsibility for sin off onto the flesh or onto sin (7:18, 20), this recalls the attempts of Adam to attribute the guilt to Eve. Second, the term *katakrima* in 8:1 could be related to the same term in 5:12-21, in connection with Adam's transgression (so Schnackenburg, "Römer 7," 299-300).

24. Thus, correctly, Wilckens, *Der Brief* 2:80-81. In saying this, he opposes the nomistic interpretation of *epithumia*, which was defended above all by Bultmann and his school; cf. Bultmann, "Römer 7," 205-6; Braun, "Römer 7, 7-25," 101; Bornkamm, "Sünde," 55; Käsemann, *An die Römer*, 184, 188; and Schlier, *Der Römerbrief*, 223. An extended discussion may be found in Hübner, *Das Gesetz*, 65-69.

beyond the simple contrasting of law and covetousness. Not satisfied with his first statement, he varies it in 7:11. In doing so he no longer uses the term *epithumia* but replaces it with *hamartia*, "sin," a term that can also encompass nomist misconduct, for example, the persecution of Christians (1 Thess. 2:16). "The power of sin is the law" (1 Cor. 15:56). Four motifs indicate that Paul reads his own nomist conflict with the law into Adam's conflict with the law; in other words, he depicts his personal conflict with reminiscences of the Fall.[25]

1. *The motif of life.* According to Rom. 7:10*, the law in itself serves "toward life." Comparable statements about the connection of law and life may be found in Gal. 3:12 and Rom. 10:5, where Paul cites Lev. 18:5: life is promised to one who fulfills the law. Both texts think in this regard of a nomist stance. Galatians 3 warns against the desire to achieve salvation through circumcision and acceptance of the law, because commitment to the law is commitment to the entire law, which no one can fulfill and which therefore represents a curse for men. Romans 9:30—10:4 describes Israel's striving for its own right-eousness, in other words, the nomistic "zeal." It could therefore be that in 7:10 also, Paul is thinking of the nomist expectation that the law can confer life.

2. *The motif of death.* Romans 7:10 further states that this law, which should actually serve life, in fact draws death in its wake. The next sentence concretizes this: sin kills [*apekteinen*] through the command-ment. A corresponding statement in Paul may be found in 2 Cor. 3:6*: "The letter kills [*apokteinei*], but the Spirit gives life." For this reason, the office of Moses is a "service of death" and of "condemnation" (2 Cor. 3:7–11*). Here it is completely clear that the reference to the killing power of the law comes from the experience of the nomist misconduct that was fascinated by the splendor of Moses.

3. *The motif of deceit.* Paul can separate the law and sin only by imputing deceit to sin. Only on the basis of a deception can the voice of sin conceal itself in the voice of the law. Precisely this motif of deception also occurs in 2 Cor. 3:11ff. in connection with the veil of Moses. Against the clear statement of the Old Testament story, Paul

25. Although Bultmann ("Römer 7," 199) rejects the biographical interpretation of Romans 7, in a decisive place he nevertheless grounds his exegesis through recourse to Paul's biography: "However little Romans 7 is a confession of Paul, but rather a description of Jewish existence in general, still precisely this must therefore apply also to Paul's Jewish existence." But if Romans 7 can be applied to Paul in a deductive manner, why should the same text not have originated inductively from Paul's personal experiences?

accuses Moses of putting on a veil in order to deceive the Israelites about the passing character of service of the law. Those deceived, in other words, are precisely those who attend with the best intentions to the voice of the law. Romans 10:1–3 brings this idea to expression in a somewhat less sharp manner. Israel's zeal for the law occurs without insight (*ou kat' epignosin*). The Israelites seek their own righteousness because they do not know (*agnoountes*) the righteousness of God. Here too an illusion is ascribed to nomistic misconduct. In contrast to Rom. 7:11 and 2 Cor. 3:12–13, however, here this illusion is not traced back to a deception. It is considered objective ignorance, self-deception, not being deceived. What is attributed to Israel in 2 Corinthians 3 and Romans 10 is valid of every man, according to Romans 7. The conduct of all human beings can be understood according to the model of Adam, for all bear the image of Adam (1 Cor. 15:49).

4. *The motif of the "letter."* Against the above-mentioned arguments in favor of a nomistic accentuation of the originally antinomian conflict with the law in Rom. 7:9–10, one could object that this accent was determined through association of Pauline statements outside Romans 7 with this text. Yet Paul also refers to the nomistic problematic in the context itself. In 7:6*, he writes as the result of what has preceded and the heading of what follows: ". . . so that we serve not under the old nature of the letter but in the new nature of the Spirit." The service of the law is to be surpassed by the service of the Spirit. The opposition of letter and Spirit occurs elsewhere only in 2 Cor. 3:6 and Rom. 2:29. In 2 Cor. 3:6, the relationship to the nomistic service of the law is clear: the service of the new covenant is considered service of the Spirit; the old covenant, service of the letter.

That not only transgression of the law but even a particular way of wanting to fulfill the law is sin is also implied in 7:9. Merely the coming of the law lets sin revive. Here the presence of the commandment, not only disregard for it, seems to be threatening.

Summary. Four motifs could be determined by a nomistic problematic of the law. The role of Adam is structured anew on this basis. Since Paul speaks even in his introduction of "service in the old nature of the letter," one may surmise that he is aiming from the start at the nomistic conflict with the law. First, however, he offers the much more proximate illustration of an antinomian conflict. But the term *epithumia*, "covetousness"—as quintessence of impulses hostile to the law—is later replaced by the term *hamartia*, "sin"; and *epithumein*, "covet," is replaced by *thelein*, "to will" (starting with 7:15ff.). Terms that can also include the nomistic misconduct are thus selected for sinful behavior.[26]

THE SAYING IN ROM. 7:15 and 7:19

In Rom. 7:14ff., Paul has recourse to another tradition in order to develop the "knowledge of sin" (7:7*). Paul appends his thoughts to a proverbial formulation he repeats with slight variation. While in comparable repetitions he otherwise advances the thought (cf. Rom. 7:8 and 7:11; Gal. 1:8 and 1:9; 2 Cor. 3:14 and 3:15), here it is partly a matter of rhetorical variation—for example, in the chiastic ordering of *prasso* and *poio*—and partly one of greater integration into the Pauline context. The *agathon*, which appears as new in the repetition, picks up the *agathon* of Rom. 7:13:

7:15b	7:19
For not	For not the good [*agathon*]
what I want	that I want
is what I do [*prasso*]	do I do [*poio*]
but	but the evil [*kakon*]
what I hate [*miso*]	that I do not want
is what I do [*poio*].	is what I do [*prasso*].

The somewhat stereotyped repetition could indicate that here Paul is reproducing a preformed thought, from which he then twice draws conclusions that are attached by *ei de*. An investigation of the vocabulary at least does not tell against this conjecture. The word *miso*, which is present elsewhere in Paul only in a citation of the Septuagint in Rom. 9:13, occurs in this text. The verb *poiein* is used twice in the immediate context (vv. 16 and 20; cf. v. 21) but otherwise replaced by *katergazesthai* (7:17, 18, 20), a term that clearly stems from the context (7:8, 13, 15a).[27] The verb *prassein* occurs in Romans 7 exclusively in this saying, although it is certainly not an un-Pauline word. Last, an explicit *ego* is lacking in the saying, although the Pauline thought is quite concerned

---

26. Yet the term *hamartia* is associated with the nomistic problematic only in 1 Thess. 2:16. Paul's Jewish opponents fill up the measure of their sins when they impede his mission. The verb *thelein*, on the contrary, is found in Gal. 4:9; 4:21; 6:12–13 in connection with the nomistic requirement of circumcision.

27. Is Bultmann ("Römer 7," 207) then correct when he holds "that *poiein* and *prassein* must be interpreted with reference to *katergazesthai*"? In this way one would at least come closer to the specifically Pauline statement in distinction from the presumed tradition.

with this, for only the explicit *ego* that is added in the context makes
the juxtaposition of "I," sin, and flesh possible.

Yet, all of these observations are insufficient to conclude to a pre-
Pauline tradition. What is decisive is that the idea present in 7:15, 19
corresponds to a widespread ancient theme.[28] The starting point of
this tradition is a discussion from the age of the Sophist enlightenment.
Euripides (*Medea* 1074–80) had grounded the conduct of Medea, who,
overcome by feelings of revenge, had killed her children, with a general
anthropological insight: in everyone, not only in Medea, passion is the
cause of evil.[29] At the end of the decisive monologue, she dismisses
the children and says,

> Away, away! Strength faileth me to gaze
> On you, but I am overcome of evil.
> Now, now, I learn [*manthano*] what horrors I intend:
> But passion overmastereth sober thought;
> And this is cause of direst ills to men.[30]

It is possible that this statement is already a reaction to Socrates'
optimistic doctrine that right knowledge leads to right conduct.[31] The
discussion seems to have gone further. At least Euripides (*Hippolytus*
375–85) reiterates his opinion again, this time in a generalized form.
It appears no longer as reflexion in an acute conflict but as the result
of long consideration:

> Oft sleepless in the weary-wearing night
> Have I mused how the life of men is wrecked.
> 'Tis not, meseems, through inborn folly of soul
> They fare so ill,—discretion dwells at least
> With many,—but we thus must look hereon:
> That which is good we learn and recognise,

28. Cf. Hommel, "Das 7. Kapitel." His collection of references can be supplemented
(see below).

29. Dihle (*Euripides Medea*, esp. 12–16) gives an attractive interpretation of Medea's
statement which departs from the usual one: "My *thymos* [= my emotional tie to the
children] is greater than my reflections [= my rationally calculated plan for revenge
against Jason]." My great hesitancy to associate myself with this interpretation is due
to two considerations. First, the following generalization, that this is the cause of the
greatest evils among men, can hardly pick up on the superiority of maternal ties to plans
for revenge, and second, other foundational statements of Euripides correspond to the
traditional interpretation; cf. *Hippolytus* 375–85, and *Fragments* 840, 841.

30. ET: Arthur S. Way, *Euripides*, vol. 4 of 4 vols. (LCL, 1912), 367.

31. Thus Snell, "Das früheste Zeugnis." Probably, however, it is a matter of a
discussion that lay in the general atmosphere. Plato (*Protagoras* 352D) cites the pessimistic
opinion that men act against their better insight as the view of the "many."

> Yet practise not the lesson, some from sloth,
> And some preferring pleasure in the stead
> Of duty. Pleasures many of life there be;
> Long gossip, idlesse,—pleasant evils they;
> And sense of shame.[32]

Here the role of consciousness is emphasized even more strongly. We recognize and know the good (*epistametha kai ginoskomen*). Nonetheless, we do not do it. The cause is no longer seen in passion alone but is now seen also in *argia* (inactivity) and *hedone* (pleasure). While in other respects Euripides approached the Sophist picture of the human as susceptible of being formed through education,[33] he maintained throughout his life his thesis on the contradiction between drive and reason. One does have insight but nature compels one; one knows the good but makes no use of it; insight and the will separate under the influence of friends.[34]

Euripides' view is deeply rooted in the tradition. As early as Homer the *thymos* occurs as an independent voice that incites and moves man. Odysseus plans in his *thymos* to kill the cyclops immediately, but another *thymos* advises against this.[35] The voice of the *thymos* is not a component of the self. It is connected with the intervention of the gods in human life. According to one passage (*Illiad* 9.702–3), Achilles will fight "when the heart in his breast shall bid him, and a god arouse him."[36] The gods recede in Euripides and this clears the way for a deepened interpretation of the conflict with the *thymos* as an inner event.

Euripides either found support for his pessimistic thesis or brought to expression what many thought. Plato (*Protagoras* 352D) cites the corresponding opinion as the view of the multitude: "Now you know that most people . . . say that many, while knowing what is best, refuse to perform it, though they have the power, and do other things instead [*gignoskontas ta beltista ouk ethelein prattein*.]"[37] As we shall see, Euripides found many disciples for his "affective" interpretation of human misconduct.

But the opposing thesis was also not without resonance. It too may

32. ET: Way, *Euripides* 4:195.
33. Cf. Lesky, "Psychologie"; cf. 91ff. on Medea's conflict.
34. *Fragments* 840, 841, 220.
35. *Odyssey* 9.299ff.
36. ET: A. T. Murray, *Homer: The Iliad*, vol. 1 of 2 vols. (LCL, 1924), 433.
37. ET: W. R. M. Lamb, *Plato*, vol. 4 of 10 vols. (LCL, 1924), 227.

root deeply in Greek tradition.[38] Even Homer often interprets human
behavior "cognitively" as an expression of knowledge; for example,
Polyphemos "knows lawlessness" (*Odyssey* 9.189), and Nestor and
Agamemnon "know friendliness for each other" (3.277).[39] A path leads
from here to the Socratic thesis of knowledge as virtue, exemplified in
a text such as Xenophon's *Memorabilia* 3.9.4:

> Between Wisdom and Prudence he drew no distinction; but if a man
> knows and practises what is beautiful and good, knows and avoids what
> is base, that man he judged to be both wise and prudent. When asked
> further whether he thought that those who know what they ought to
> do and yet do the opposite are at once wise and vicious, he answered:
> "No; not so much that, as both unwise and vicious. For I think that all
> men have a choice between various courses, and choose and follow the
> one which they think conduces most to their advantage. Therefore I
> hold that those who follow the wrong course are neither wise nor
> prudent."[40]

Socrates' intellectualism was corrected and supplemented by his
belief in the "demon." This voice which comes from the depths of the
irrational does not contradict reason but advises against what is
unreasonable. In the *Protagoras* (351ff.), Plato followed Socrates' stance;
later he distanced himself from it by emphasizing more strongly the
irrational aspects in human beings, such as when he dissolved the soul
into three tribunals. In the *Protagoras* (358C), however, he defends the
opinion that evil goes back not to the effects of passion but to *amathia*
(ignorance), which consists in "having a false opinion and being deceived
about matters of importance."[41]

The Socratic conception was renewed magnificently by Chrysippus
(ca. 281–208). Against Plato, he firmly defended the unity of the soul.
The soul does not follow a foreign influence when it errs; rather it
always errs as a whole. In this, Chrysippus appeals explicitly to
Euripides' *Medea:*

> Medea declared before her infanticide: "I know what evil I intend to
> commit, I see it well; but passion is stronger in me than reason." But

---

38. Cf. Dodds, *The Greeks and the Irrational*, 17: "[T]he so-called Socratic paradoxes,
that 'virtue is knowledge,' and that 'no one does wrong on purpose,' were no novelties,
but an explicit generalised formulation of what had long been an ingrained habit of
thought."

39. ET: A. T. Murray, *Homer: The Odyssey*, vol. 1 of 2 vols. (LCL, 1919), 317, 89.
[The translations have been altered to reflect Theissen's more literal rendering.]

40. ET: E. C. Marchant, *Xenophon*, vol. 4 of 7 vols. (LCL, 1923), 225.

41. ET: Lamb, *Plato* 4:245.

this passion is not a sort of foreign power, which wrests dominion from the mind; it is Medea's mind, which in unhealthy agitation chooses the bad. It turns away from itself and from every reasonable reflection. Precisely this conscious turning away from calm reflection and from the mind itself is the essential characteristic of emotion.[42]

After the middle Stoics (with Posidonius, ca. 135–51 B.C.E.) returned to recognition of division between reason and emotion, the cognitive conception of human misconduct was renewed by Epictetus (ca. 50–120 C.E.); one can say that Epictetus was one of the first representatives of a cognitive psychology. With great intensity, he defended the thesis that human beings have control over their inner life but that this inner life is determined by their interpretations. One seeks what seems good and proper to one according to one's interpretation. Epictetus also poses for himself the counterquestion whether one cannot act against one's conviction, and cites Euripides in this context (*Discourses* 1.28.6–8):

"Cannot a man, then, think that something is profitable to him, and yet not choose it?" He cannot. How of her [Medea] who says,

Now, now I learn what horrors I intend:
But passion overmastereth sober thought?

It is because the very gratification of her passion and the taking of vengeance on her husband she regards as more profitable than the saving of her children. "Yes, but she is deceived [*exepatetai*]." Show her clearly that she is deceived, and she will not do it; but so long as you do not show it, what else has she to follow but that which appears to her to be true?[43]

It is clear that a pessimistic anthropological tradition is being reshaped here. Medea allegedly acted in conformity with her insight, not against it; it's just that she lacked the proper insight. This reshaping of the tradition takes place with the aid of the idea of deception: Medea deceived herself. For this reason one ought not reproach her but sympathize with her as with a blind or lame person.[44] The difference from Paul is obvious. It becomes even more clear if one compares the two authors' differing usages of the proverbial expression of the contradiction between willing and doing. Epictetus (*Discourses* 2.26.1–2) proceeds from the following thesis:

42. *Stoicorum Veterum Fragmenta* 3.473. Chrysippus had studied Euripides' Medea thoroughly. "Once he had cited almost the whole of Euripides' Medea in a piece, and when someone who had the book in his hand was asked what he was holding, he replied, 'Chrysippus' Medea' " (*Stoicorum Veterum Fragmenta* 2.1; cf. Pohlenz, *Stoa*, 22).
43. ET: Oldfather, *Epictetus* 1:179.
44. *Discourses* 1.28.9.

Every error involves a contradiction. For since he who is in error does
not wish to err, but to be right, it is clear that he is not doing what he
wishes [*ho men thelei ou poiei*]. For what does the thief wish to achieve?
His own interest.[45]

A little later (2.26.4–5) he again picks up the proverbial formulation:

He, then, who can show to each man the contradiction which causes
him to err, and can clearly bring home to him how he is not doing what
he wishes, and is doing what he does not wish [*pos ho thelei ou poiei kai
ho me thelei poiei*], is strong in argument, and at the same time effective
both in encouragement and refutation. For as soon as anyone shows a
man this, he will of his own accord abandon what he is doing. But so
long as you do not point this out, be not surprised if he persists in his
error; for he does it because he has an impression that he is right.[46]

The objective contradiction between intention and factual action can
be overcome through enlightenment. Misconduct is ultimately based
on cognitive grounds. It can therefore also be corrected by changing
cognitive interpretations.[47]

So far we have pursued the tradition that interprets the conflict
between willing and doing in a cognitive manner. But the opposition
did not remain mute.[48] It too appealed to Medea (with, in our judgment,

45. ET: Oldfather, *Epictetus* 1:431, 433.
46. ET: ibid., 433.
47. The difference between Paul and Epictetus emerges clearly in *Discourses* 2.17.19–
22. Medea does not know "where the power lies to do what we wish." It does not lie
in external factors but in ourselves. When we no longer want what we cannot achieve,
willing and doing correspond: "In a word, give up wanting anything but what God
wants. And who will prevent you, who will compel you? No one, any more than
anyone prevents or compels Zeus" (ET: Oldfather, *Epictetus* 1:343). One is free within.
But in Paul, one is also imprisoned with regard to one's interior. Epictetus knows the
"power to do what we wish" (2.17.21). Paul, on the contrary, knows that "I can will
what is right, but I cannot do it" (Rom. 7:18).
48. In the period that followed, Euripides *Medea* 1078–79 became the classical text
used to "illustrate the division of the soul into rational and irrational components and
to ground the possibility of emotionally motivated conduct against better knowledge"
(Dihle, *Euripides Medea*, 25 n. 14). This is probably the case as early as Posidonius (ca.
135–51 B.C.E.), as may be concluded from Galen. It is attested for the second half of the
first century and for the second century in Plutarch (*Moralia* 533D), Albinus (*Epistles*
24.3), Galen (*On the Doctrine of Hippocrates and Plato* 3.2), Aelios Aristeides (*Orationes* 50
[ed. Dindorf, 565]), and Clement of Alexandria (*Stromata* 2.63.3). Lucian (*Apology* 10)
offers a parody of the pair of verses. Such later authors as Synesios of Cyrene, Simplicius,
Stobaeus, Eustratios, Libanos, and Heirocles continue the tradition (listed in Dihle,
Euripides Medea, 25 n. 14). The mainstream of the tradition is thus determined by the
"affective" interpretation. Of course the idea also occurs independently of Euripides'
Medea. One example is Hecataios of Abdera (ca. 350–290 B.C.E.) in his presentation of

greater justification). Ovid (*Metamorphoses* 7.17–21) depicts her in conflict between love and reason. When seized by love for Jason, Medea struggles with herself to determine whether she shall value love for the stranger higher than ties to her homeland. It is in this situation that the famous words "video meliora proboque, detriora sequor" occur:

> Come, thrust from your maiden breast these flames that you feel, if you can, unhappy girl. Ah, if I could, I should be more myself. But some strange power [*nova vis*] holds me down against my will. Desire persuades me [*cupido*] one way, reason [*mens*] another. I see the better and approve it, but I follow the worse [*Video meliora proboque, detriora sequor*].[49]

To say that this is a platitude or merely a matter of weakness in carrying out good intentions[50] fails to recognize the depth of the conflict—here a conflict between two positive bonds, love for partner and love for homeland—while Medea is otherwise a paradigm of conflict between aggressive and loving impulses. She also occurs as a paradigm of this sort in Seneca. Seneca (*Medea* 938–44) gives a new accent to her conflict, in that he portrays it less as a conflict between passion and reason than as a battle between two emotions:

> Who do anger and love now hither, now thither draw my changeful heart? A double tide tosses me, uncertain of my course; as when rushing winds wage mad warfare, and from both sides conflicting floods lash the seas and the fluctuating waters boil, even so is my heart tossed. Anger puts love to flight, and love, anger: O wrath, yield thee to love.[51]

Seneca further dramatizes the conflict by having Medea kill the first

---

the Egyptians; Hecataios (cf. Diodorus 1.71.3) writes that the Egyptians judged about others "that while some frequently knew [*eidotas*] that they were on the verge of misconduct, they nonetheless did [*prattein*] what was bad." A second instance is Plautus (*Trinummus* 657–58): "I know what sort I ought to be, but I couldn't be it, poor fool. Getting in Venus' grip, growing enslaved to ease, I've fallen on evil days" (ET: Paul Nixon, *Plautus*, vol. 5 of 5 vols. [LCL, 1938], 161). The breadth of the tradition makes it probable that Paul is to be numbered among traditions of this sort. He is definitely to be considered capable of reminiscences of education. It also becomes clear that Chrysippus's and Epictetus's cognitive interpretation of the conflict stands isolated.

49. ET: Frank Justus Miller, *Ovid: Metamorphoses*, vol. 1 of 2 vols. (LCL, 1916), 343.

50. Thus Bultmann (*Theologie*, 248) and Käsemann (*An die Römer*, 193). Furthermore, the *deteriora sequor* is likely an ironic allusion to Virgil (*Aeneid* 3.188): "Let us yield to Phoebus and at his warning pursue the better course [*meliora sequamur*]" (ET: H. Ruston Fairclough, *Virgil*, vol. 1 of 2 vols. [LCL, 1932], 361). Thus Bömer, *Kommentar*, 204. A play of Ovid's about Medea is unfortunately not extant.

51. ET: Frank Justus Miller, *Seneca's Tragedies*, vol. 1 of 2 vols. (LCL, 1917), 307.

child first. Division overcomes her again before the murder of the second:

> Why dost thou delay now, O soul? Why hesitate, though thou canst do it? Now has my wrath died within me. I am sorry for my act, ashamed. What, wretched woman, have I done?—wretched, say I? Though I repent, yet have I done it! Great joy steals on me 'gainst my will [*invitam*], and lo, it is increasing.[52]

Not only poetry but also philosophical discussion appealed to Medea in order to address the nature of inner conflicts. Appealing to Plato and Posidonius, Galen (129–99 C.E.) argues against the cognitive interpretation of inner conflict in early and late Stoicism. Galen (*On the Doctrines of Hippocrates and Plato* 4.2.27) holds to different psychic tribunals and supports his conception with the well-known citation from Euripides:

> Medea . . . was not persuaded by any reasoning to kill her children; quite the contrary, so far as reasoning goes, she says that she understands how evil the acts are that she is about to perform, but her anger is stronger than her deliberations; that is, her affection has not been made to submit and does not obey and follow reason as it would a master, but throws off the reins and departs and disobeys the command, the implication being that it is the action or affection of some power other than the rational. For how could anything disobey itself or fail to follow itself?[53]

Somewhat further on (4.6.20–22), Galen directly attacks Chrysippus's appeal to Euripides. After citing *Medea* 178–79, he continues;

> If Euripides was to give evidence in support of the teachings of Chrysippus, he should not have said that she understands but the very opposite, that she is ignorant and does not understand what evils she is going to do. But to say that she knows this and yet is overcome by anger—what is that but the act of a man who introduces two sources for Medea's appetitions, one by which we recognize things and have knowledge of them, which is the rational power, and another irrational [power], whose function it is to be angry? This latter [power], then, coerced Medea's soul.[54]

Antiquity thought extensively and in a nuanced way about the conflict between willing and doing. Medea is the model of this conflict.

52. ET: ibid., 311.
53, ET: DeLacy, *Galen on the Doctrines of Hippocrates and Plato*, 245.
54. ET: ibid., 275.

In Rom. 7:15, 19, Paul picks up a widespread theme that is found in different variations. For example, the passions that cause the conflict can be tinged in a libidinous or in an aggressive manner; they can be called *ira* (Seneca) and *misos* (Hecataios), but also *eran*,[55] *eros* (Hecataios), *venus* (Plautus), and *cupido* (Ovid). Besides this, there appear sloth (*argia*, Euripides; and *otium*, Plautus)—and even generalizing references to *thymos*[56] or *pathos* (Galen). Usually the irrational drive is contrasted to insight, for example, to *mens* (Ovid) or to *ginoskein* (Euripides, Plato, Galen).

Paul is to be seen in connection with ancient reflection on the contradiction of willing and doing. His knowledge of the traditions of popular philosophy probably included the theme of the "inner conflict." He need not for this reason have read Euripides. Themes are not citations.

The decisive question is how Paul understood the theme. One could at first think that he favors the cognitive interpretation of human misconduct. The I is deceived when it does evil (Rom. 7:11). It does not understand what it performs (7:15). As in Epictetus, evil is a consequence of the *exapatasthai*. Yet the difference from the cognitive interpretation of human misconduct lies in the fact that in Paul the deception proceeds from sin, whereas in Epictetus sin is a result of deception, and the deception itself is ultimately self-deception of the rational soul, the *psyche logike*,[57] which falls into contradiction with itself. In Paul, self-deception becomes deception by a mythically appearing power—by sin.

Since sin is ultimately the fateful power, Paul stands closer to the "affective interpretation" of the inner conflict. In 7:5, the impulses evoking the conflict are designated *pathemata* and traced back to the flesh. These passions are tinged both libidinously and aggressively. The *epithumein* is a striving for the enjoyment of the things of others (cf. the Tenth Commandment), and the metaphors of war in 7:23 (cf. 8:7) suggest aggressive impulses.

The cognitive interpretation ultimately sees the conflict as a contradiction between a (subjectively) good intention and the (objectively) evil consequences. But in my opinion, after 7:14ff. at the latest, one can no longer speak of a conflict between intention and effect. By its very nature such a conflict would show itself only in retrospect. But then one would expect as early as the first formulation of the conflict

55. Euripides *Hippolytus* 358–59.
56. Euripides *Medea* 1079.
57. *Discourses* 2.26.3.

in vv. 15ff. "I hate what I do [i.e., what I have already done]." Yet, Paul writes, "I do what I hate" (7:15*). The saying is always formulated in such a way that its theme is not the (subsequent) evaluation of an action but the failure to do what has been evaluated (correctly from the start). On this point, compare the following six parallel formulations in Romans 7:

7:15b:	*ou gar ho thelo*	*touto prasso*
	all' ho miso	*touto poio*
7:16:	*ho ou thelo*	*touto poio*
7:19:	*ou gar ho thelo*	*poio agathon*
	ho ou thelo kakon	*touto prasso*
7:20:	*ho ou thelo*	*touto poio*

Only the preceding sentence (7:15a) has a different structure. Here the issue is a summarizing stance toward a deed that has (already) occurred:

7:15a:	*ho gar katergazomai*	*ou ginosko*

Can one conclude from this sentence that the I—like Adam—became aware of the reprehensibility of its conduct only in retrospect? Can it be that Paul then described this conflict with the aid of the ancient saying as if the reprehensibility of the conduct had been clear to the subject from the start?[58]

The second approach to formulating the conflict, in vv. 19–23, is completely unambiguous. By inserting an *agathon* (= *kalon;* v. 21) here, Paul refers to the divine law. For the I has agreed with the law, that it is good (*kalos*, v. 16), that the commandment is "holy and just and good" (v. 12). It is therefore the norm which is good (or evil), not the effect. What is good is not the life the law promises but rather the way to life (or to death), for otherwise Paul could not ask, "Did that which is good [the law], then, bring death to me?" (v. 13). Application of the war metaphor to a conflict between (prior) intention and (subsequent) effect would be completely impossible, for opponents in

58. Epictetus *Discourses* 2.26.1ff. would be a counterargument to these observations. The sentence there has the same structure as in Romans 7: *ho men thelei ou poiei.* But note that Epictetus uses the third-person singular. One can indeed determine from without that someone misses precisely what he (subjectively) seeks with the best intentions. But Paul writes here in the first-person singular. If an I says, "I hate what I do," then that I considers its deed reprehensible right at the moment of the act! On this, cf. Bader, "Römer 7," esp. 44ff.

war exist simultaneously. One must therefore hold that in 7:14–23 Paul is describing a consciously experienced conflict, in correspondence to most references to the theme of inner conflict (especially where that conflict is interpreted "affectively").

Paul gives new accents to the traditional saying. In its traditional content, it says that consciously held norms can be put out of force by a rush of emotions (or by sloth). Medea's example shows this. In Paul, however, it is a question not simply of the conflict between norm and emotion but of two laws that clash with each other. Thus at least linguistically he treats the conflict differently than as a simple conflict between duty and inclination, norm and emotion, knowledge and passion. It is clear from the start that this last conflict is to be resolved by decision for the normative side. Paul, on the contrary, speaks of an opposition of two normative systems—a law in the members and a law of the mind. The conflict is interpreted in a new way through this new linguistic designation even if the model of the "storm of emotions" that impose themselves against conviction and reason continues to stand in the background.

Thus the analysis of the tradition leads to a result that is important from the perspective of the psychology of religion. Differently accented structurings of the conflict with the aid of different models are present in the two parts of the text. At one point, Adam is the model for interpreting the conflict, at another, a judgment (often connected with Medea). The decisive difference is that Adam believes at the moment of his deed that he will achieve something positive for himself; he is deceived about the true consequences. Insight follows upon sin. In the case of Medea, however, the cognitive conflict is fully conscious at the moment of the crime. This suggests the hypothesis that in the first part of Rom. 7:7ff., the conflict before the decision is depicted, but in the second part, a postdecisional conflict is presented.[59]

59. This hypothesis will not be developed further later. Only this much will be noted. Romans 7:7–13 emphasizes temptation and deception as the decisive aspects of the conflict. Deception is a typical element of a predecisional conflict, inasmuch as under these circumstances, the situation is often cognitively distorted under the influence of motivational pressure. Thus the consequences are underestimated, bagatellized, and reinterpreted. The biblical story of the Fall gives good examples of such cognitive distortions. Death is threatened, but the tempting voice bagatellizes, "Of course you won't die!" (On the motif of deception, cf., above all, Cranfield, *A Critical and Exegetical Commentary*, 352–53.) From 7:14 on, however, it is no longer a deceived I which speaks but an I that is increasingly clear about its hopeless situation. As Adam in the postdecisional conflict seeks to shift all the guilt onto Eve, so too this I twice seeks to shift the guilt to transsubjective causes (flesh and sin; cf. 7:17, 20). The change in tense between 7:7–13 and 7:14–23 signals the transition between the presentations of predecisional and postdecisional conflicts.

Chapter 13

Psychological Analysis: Romans 7 and 8

Chapters 7 and 8 of the Epistle to the Romans are the most intense presentation in Paul of a transformation in human life. If any Pauline texts can be interpreted psychologically, it is these chapters. Here I want briefly to sketch in advance the aspects under which the two chapters can be analyzed psychologically.

From the perspective of learning theory, the transformations of behavior and experience that come to light here may be considered as a quenching of a culturally conditioned negative experience. The law has become a stimulus evoking anxiety, which maneuvers one into an impasse. Christ removes from this stimulus its power to evoke anxiety. He functions as a model.

Psychodynamically, the decisive transformation of behavior and experience lies in the unconscious becoming conscious. The encounter with Christ puts Paul in a position to deal with a repressed conflict. Christ functions as a reference person upon whom the unconscious aspects of the conflict are transferred.

Under a cognitive aspect, impulses in the direction of a change in human life occur through a new vision of the conflict. What originally seemed to be a normative conflict is reinterpreted as an existential conflict and solved by a comprehensive change of roles, in which causes that were previously seen as constant are experienced as mutable.

As this brief overview shows, the psychological analysis must in each case reach beyond Romans 7. Romans 7 is a retrospective on an unredeemed state. We understand this chapter only if we are clear about the meaning of redemption for Paul. Insofar as the transition from an unredeemed to a redeemed state is connected with transformations in experience and behavior, it is an object of psychological analysis.

ASPECTS IN LEARNING THEORY: THE
LAW AS STIMULUS TO SIN

Most psychological interpretations of Romans 7 proceed from a psychodynamic standpoint. The reason for this is the appealing analogy between the psychoanalytic three-tribunal model and the conflict between law, flesh, and "I" depicted in Romans 7. Yet these striking analogies ought not lead one to overlook the statements that directly contradict a psychodynamic doctrine of drives. According to this teaching, a drive is "autochthonous" from its origin. The environment can indeed reform it with commandments, channel, repress, or sublimate it. But the drive is present independently of such secondary handling. Paul, on the contrary, says, "Apart from the law sin lies dead" (7:8). With this, he means not only that the term "sin" presupposes relationship to a norm and that sin cannot be imputed without law (Rom. 4:15; 5:13) but also that only the law stimulates sin and awakens it to life. In other words, Paul says that the supposedly natural, carnal power of sin is in reality socioculturally conditioned. The norms and models contained in the law themselves evoke behavior contrary to the norm, even though their authentic purpose is to promote behavior corresponding to the norm. Such a conception of the stimulation and reinforcement of behavior contrary to the norm by the cultural environment itself no doubt corresponds more to an image of human beings based on learning theory than it does to a psychodynamic theory of drives.

There are of course many statements in Paul that one can interpret along the lines of a theory of drives. In Rom. 7:14ff., sin is traced back to the flesh, and flesh is a characteristic of all living things. The "drive" that contradicts the law appears as something rooted in nature. And as in some modern theories of drives, the drive contrary to the norm is hypostatized: sin lives within the human being and occupies the place of the I. Yet Paul modifies these statements in a second approach. What ultimately lives in the members is not a natural power but another law that lies in conflict with the law of God and of reason. It even seems to be the great discovery of Paul that the conflict he experienced is precisely not a conflict between nature and norm, but one between different aspects of the same historically pre-given norm system; it was a conflict between the law as spirit and as letter, between the law as life-giving Spirit and as death-bringing letter. In other words, the normative learning program of his environment itself

contained a stimulation and reinforcement of behavior contrary to the
norm.

Paul expresses this as follows: "I should not have known what it is
to covet if the law had not said, 'You shall not covet' " (Rom. 7:7).
Paul here picks up an insight that is also attested elsewhere in antiquity.
At the beginning stands again a word of Euripides: Nouthetoumenos
eros mallon piezei ("Love reproved more urgent grows").[1] Similar
formulations may be found in Ovid (The Amores 3.4.17; 2.19.3): "We
ever strive for what is forbid, and ever covet what is denied";[2] "what
one may not do pricks more keenly on."[3] Experience teaches that the
more one is warned, the more the warnings provoke contrary tendencies.[4] Limitations are precisely what make desire wild.[5]

Nor are comparable ideas completely foreign to Judaism. According
to the Life of Adam and Eve 19, the snake seeks to seduce precisely by
holding back the promised fruit at first: "I have changed my mind and
will not allow you to eat."[6] Similar ideas are alluded to in 4 Macc.
1:33–34. The meaning of the commandment lies in the renunciation
of what is desirable:

> Otherwise how is it that when we are attracted to forbidden foods we
> abstain from the pleasure to be had from them? Is it not because reason
> is able to rule over appetites? I for one think so. Therefore when we
> crave seafood and fowl and animals and all sorts of foods that are
> forbidden to us by the law, we abstain because of domination by reason.

Pride over self-control is indeed far greater here than insight into
the ambivalence of the prohibition. Later Augustine (Confessions 2.6;
cf. 2.4–6) bemoans at length this connection between prohibition and
desire: "Could anything please thee, that thou mightest not do lawfully;
and done too upon no other reason, but because it was not lawful?"[7]

Paul is to be seen in connection with such insights. In Rom. 7:7ff.,
he presents covetousness in its functional dependence on the law. It is
true that the law does not appear as the ultimate cause of covetousness.

1. Cited in Plutarch's Moralia 71A; ET: Frank Cole Babbitt, Plutarch's Moralia, vol. 1
of 14 vols. (LCL, 1927), 375. Luz (Das Geschichtsverständnis, 163–164 nn. 108–9) even
holds that "Euripides' saying was a winged word and was often cited."
2. ET: Grant Showerman, Ovid: Heroides and Amores (LCL, 1921), 461.
3. ET: ibid., 439.
4. Ovid Metamorphoses 3.566.
5. Livy 34.4.
6. ET: M. D. Johnson, The Old Testament Pseudepigrapha, ed. Charlesworth, 2:279.
7. ET: William Watts, St. Augustine's Confessions, vol. 1 of 2 vols. (LCL, 1912), 89.

But first, all covetousness is wrought by the commandment (v. 8); second, sin is dead without the law (v. 8b); and third, sin revives only with the coming of the commandment (v. 9). A latent disposition is surely already present, but it is only through the norm that it acquires direction and goal. Only through the norm is it identifiable as sinful conduct. Paul grasps this relationship conceptually with the term *aphorme*. Unfortunately, its precise signification cannot be determined. It can mean "point of departure," "point of connection," "foundation," "grasp," "pretext," "basis," "cause," "occasion," "possibility," "opportunity," "way," "chance," "backing," "support," or "help." If one wishes to determine more precisely its signification in Rom. 7:8 and 7:11, one will have to restrict oneself to the expression *lambanein aphormen* (with the accusative!). This expression almost never stands without more precise determination. Either the purpose is added with a genitive—for example, in *aphormen ton hamartematon*[8]—or with *pros* and *eis;*[9] or the occasioning reality is added with an *ek* or a *dia* or as a genitive.[10] Since *lambanein aphormen*, in contrast to the genitive expression *lambanein aphormes*,[11] almost never stands absolutely, it is likely to be specified more precisely in Rom. 7:8 as well. This consideration speaks in favor of drawing *dia tes entoles* to *aphormen labousa*.[12] There is a parallel in Polybius for the connection with *dia:* The historian must know *dia ti kai pothen hekasta ton pragmaton tas aphormas eilephen*.[13] The term *aphorme* would then be translated by "impetus" and "starting point," or even by "cause." This makes the law appear even more as the mediate occasion of sin than if one translates *aphorme* as "pretext."

8. Philo *Flaccus* 35. Cf. *ten aphormen tou telous* (Josephus *Jewish Antiquities* 8.409); *aphormen tou strategematos* (Josephus *Jewish Wars* 1.502); cf., in addition, Philo *On Abraham* 162.

9. Epictetus *Discourses* 3.24.3; and 2 *Clement* 16.1, respectively.

10. Polybius 3.32.7, 3.7.5; and Luke 11:54 v.1., respectively.

11. Cf. Philo *Moses* 1.46, *Flaccus* 34; Josephus *Jewish Antiquities* 10.256, *Life* 375.

12. This interpretation is rejected at length by Cranfield (*A Critical and Exegetical Commentary*, 350). He argues as follows: (1) The location of the words is analogous to v. 13b, where the adverbial determination with *dia* must be related to *katergazesthai*. But 7:5 may be cited as a counterexample: here the *dia*-expression refers to what precedes it. (2) The verb *katergazesthai* often stands with *dia* (cf., e.g., Rom. 15:18; 2 Cor. 9:11). But as a rule the expression *lambanein aphormen* with the accusative requires more precise specification; connection with *dia* is attested (see above). (3) The parallel in 7:11 speaks in favor of relating the *dia*-expression to the following verb. In fact, *dia tes entoles exepatesen me* and *kai di' autes apekteinen* do seem to stand parallel to each other, but the repetition of *di' autes* would be indispensable only if *dia tes entoles* is to be related to what precedes it. (4) Verse 13b is said to be the closest parallel. But this is even more true of 7:5.

13. Polybius 3.7.5.

But if the law is the impetus and stimulus of the conflict, and yet at the same time is retained as "holy, just, and good," then one can interpret the conflict depicted in Rom. 7:7ff. as the result of contradictory stimuli, reinforcers, and models, which proceed from the normative convictions of the cultural environment. In every culture there is beside the "official" learning program—or, more exactly, in it—an unofficial program of reinforcement whose effects stand in a painful relationship to the openly sought goals. If this is seen through, one can distinguish two aspects in the normative convictions of the culture. Paul does precisely this. In Rom. 7:6 he confronts these two aspects as the letter and the spirit. After the analysis of the conflict in Romans 7, however, he opposes them even more radically as the "law of the Spirit of life" and the "law of sin and death" (8:2). Romans 7:7–25 is to be understood within this parenthesis, since 7:6 is the announcement of theme for 7:7ff. and 8:2 is a résumé of chapter 7. Paul experienced the ambivalence of the official "learning program" so strongly that he sees in it the opposition of death and life. Psychologically, however, association with death means connection with fear of death. Through the constant connection of commandment and threat of death in the case of transgression, along with simultaneous stimulation of precisely those tendencies to which the threat of death is related, the law led to an inescapable conflict. It became a factor eliciting anxiety.

The Christ-event, which dominates all the ideas and fantasies of Paul, can be understood as "concealed behavior" with the aid of which irrational death anxieties in view of the demanding law are demolished. Christ serves as learning model for overcoming normatively conditioned anxieties. His effect is not based on denial of this anxiety; on the contrary, the anxiety is raised to an extreme. As in implosion therapy,[14] the endangered person is exposed once again and in a concentrated way to all stimuli that elicit anxiety, in order to experience that the threat of death is in fact not at all present with the stimuli that elicit anxiety. One can be exposed to the stimuli—and nevertheless survive. This experience puts one in a position to react confidently to the situation that formerly seemed to be life-threatening.

14. Good information on "implosive therapy" may be found in Kanfer and Goldstein, eds., *Helping People Change*, 277–83. This therapy seeks "to produce a frightening experience in the client of such magnitude that it will actually lessen his fear of the particular situation rather than heighten it" (p. 277). Anxiety is produced by linguistically bound fantasies. The method of "imaginal flooding" is related to this.

But one need not learn this with regard to one's own person. It can be learned with reference to a model. The condemning power of the law which elicits anxieties is exercised over the vicarious learning model Christ. The "wrath" of God, accumulated for centuries, pours over the crucified. The sins of all are punished in him. Flesh in an absolute sense is condemned in him (Rom. 8:21). The killing of Christ shows the full aggressive power of the law that threatens the sinner with death. But the resurrection of Christ shows that the killing power of the law was impotent with regard to him. The law that elicits anxiety had the opportunity to bring about its full effect. The threatening stimuli were raised to an extreme; nevertheless, the life-threatening stimuli proved to be powerless and without effect. Christ survives the penal judgment. He lives now in a form of existence in which the killing law has no part. The killing of Christ, then, was illegitimate. It affected an innocent one, the son of God. It also occurred "for our sins," not for his. Put briefly, Christ "was put to death for our trespasses and raised for our justification" (Rom. 4:25). There is therefore no longer condemnation for those who are in Christ (8:1). For who would still want to condemn? "Christ is here, who died, even more, who was raised" and who now participates in the power of God and intercedes for believers against the accusation of the law (8:34*). The decisive thing is that without being exposed immediately to the killing law, one perceives in the vicarious "model" that there is something stronger than all tendencies toward punishment; one recognizes that these tendencies are illegitimate. The same God who seems to function in the law as killing judge annihilates precisely this death.

What is constantly experienced with reference to the model in the symbolic actions of religious faith can be relived by everyone. Paul makes clear that every Christian lives through the same event that Christ lived through: "For I through the law died to the law, that I might live to God. I have been crucified with Christ" (Gal. 2:19–20). The law killed not only Christ but also the Christian with him (cf. Rom. 7:4; 2 Cor. 5:14). Every Christian was exposed to the unrestrained death threat of the law, but every one has survived this threat (with Christ). Now he is another man: "It is no longer I who live, but Christ who lives in me; and the life I now live in the flesh I live by faith in the Son of God, who loved me and gave himself for me" (Gal. 2:20).

But the imitative conduct of Christians is also connected with baptism: "We were buried therefore with him by baptism into death, so that as Christ was raised from the dead by the glory of the Father, we too might walk in newness of life" (Rom. 6:4). The event represented in the sacramental play means the same process depicted in Gal. 2:19–20. Whoever is buried with Christ is justified from sin (Rom. 6:7) and freed from the law (7:4–6).

Finally, there is also a third aspect of imitative and reliving behavior—suffering. In this the death of Christ appears in the life of the individual Christian (2 Cor. 4:10). Paul never interprets his suffering as punishment for sin—an undeceiving sign that the experience of suffering is free from intrapunitive tendencies.[15]

Through the Christ-event, anxiety before the threatening law is "quenched" by the symbolic actions of faith, which are equivalent to a "concealed learning process." In Pauline terms, the "curse of the law" is overcome, for the law strikes one individual vicariously (Gal. 3:13). For this reason Paul can speak of the demand of God without associating with it reactions that elicit or defend against anxiety. The divine demand becomes the "law of the Spirit of life" (Rom. 8:2). Death and life before God do not depend on this; it rather regulates interhuman conduct. All the demands of the law are summarized in the commandment of love (Gal. 5:14; Rom. 13:8–10). This changed attitude to the normative thematic is especially clear when Paul speaks of the "law of Christ" (Gal. 6:2). This law has its point less in the fulfillment of particular demands than in tolerable life together with those who do not correspond to the norms, that is, with those who are "overtaken in any trespass" (Gal. 6:1). "To be in the law of Christ [*ennomos Christou*]" means precisely this—to be able to adapt to differing sociocultural norms, to become a Jew to the Jews and a Gentile to the Gentiles (1 Cor. 9:19–23). This is a decisive increase in freedom. The new attitude to the normative thematic without doubt belongs to the most valuable contents of the New Testament.[16]

PSYCHODYNAMIC ASPECTS: THE UNCONSCIOUS CONFLICT WITH THE LAW[17]

The changed attitude to the normative thematic has aspects that escape analysis from the perspective of learning theory. Although the conflict

15. In 1 Cor. 11:30, however, he interprets instances of sickness and death among the Corinthians as the consequence of sins. Yet with regard to himself there is no interpretation of this sort. How close it would have been to say that he, the former persecutor of Christians, atoned for his offense through his suffering.

16. Only one work will be mentioned here as a summary presentation: Smend and Luz, *Gesetz*, esp. 89–112, on Paul.

17. Previous psychoanalytic exegeses are Créspy, "Exégèse"; Vergote, "Der Beitrag"; and Forsyth, "Faith."

with the law is evoked from without—through the demands of the law—the aggressive power of the law stems from within. The law's death threat does not proceed from its demands but from sin that has overpowered the law and concealed itself in the voice of the law. The factor that elicits anxiety is ultimately not the law but rather sin dwelling in the flesh. In Paul, the term *sarx*, "flesh," encompasses all the natural conditions of human life, everything human life has in common with other living things, even if each living thing has its own specific *sarx* (cf. 1 Cor. 15:39). We must therefore locate the cause of the anxiety produced by the law in the equipment one inherits from the history of the human race—in a latent readiness that could unfold only under the conditions of culture. For "apart from the law sin lies dead"; it revives only when the law comes (Rom. 7:8–9). Expressed in modern language: we must allow for a latent human readiness for anxiety, rooted in the history of the human race, which before the evolution of culture was elicited by specific hostile signals but which can also be coupled with moral demands after the replacement of the instinctive system of direction by cultural patterns of behavior. This connection is unconscious. To us, the law is holy, just, and good. We hear the law as a contradiction to the flesh. Unconsciously, however, we interpret it as a "hostile signal" and combine with it a fleshly energy that stems from our own interior—the unconditioned preparedness for activation that would be meaningful in life-threatening situations but that in confrontation with the moral demand leads to intolerance, distorted perception, mistaking of alternatives, in brief, to lack of freedom. It is the paradox of culture that the more intensely a person identifies with its requirements, the greater the danger becomes that these requirements will be joined to a destructive energy that can endanger the culture itself. Archaic "instincts" often unfold behind the façade of idealism; the works of the flesh often lurk behind above-average zeal for the law.

Our thesis is that Paul experienced this ambivalence of the law personally. Romans 7 depicts how the once-unconscious conflict with the law became conscious. We shall demonstrate this in three steps. First, we shall gather all the indices in Romans 7 that the conflict was once unconscious.[18] A second step then seeks to show that the

---

18. Käsemann (*An die Römer*, 184–204) polemizes with strong words against a psychological exegesis of Romans 7: "All of this indicates at least that every psychological interpretation is inappropriate, whether it relates to the person of Paul . . . or the origin of sin . . ." (p. 185). Paul transcends in principle the "level of the moral and of what can be experienced psychologically" (p. 192). Psychological and theological interpretations

contradiction between Phil. 3:4–6 and Romans 7 speaks in favor of a conflict that was once repressed. The final point to investigate is the significance of the figure of Christ for overcoming the conflict.

Raising the Conflict to Consciousness in Romans 7

That Paul attributes to the law precisely the function of making sin conscious speaks against the presumption of an unconscious conflict with the law: "If it had not been for the law, I should not have known [*ouk egnon*] sin. I should not have known what it is to covet [*ouk edein*] if the law had not said, 'You shall not covet' " (Rom. 7:7). The two cognitive verbs *ginoskein* and *eidenai* are almost synonymous; *ginoskein* signifies more the act of coming to know, while *eidenai* means more a state of knowledge.[19] A reinterpretation of the verbs into expression

---

are mutually exclusive: "The misery of a theology for which all cats are gray in the dark is covered up with the foolish formula 'psychology of sin' " (p. 193). Käsemann even says that anyone who sets the ethical conflict at the center of his exegesis completely misunderstands the text: "If the apostle contents himself here with such an evident truth of experience [namely, that one is not able to deal with oneself], then he is working with the wrong tools and doing a poor theology, or rather no theology at all but in reality a psychology oriented on the ethical problem" (p. 193). On the contrary, according to Käsemann, Bultmann's conception of the event depicted in Romans 7 as a transsubjective conflict leads "in a trailblazing way beyond a purely psychological and ethical interpretation" (p. 195). The conception of psychology that is present here is one-sided. First, psychology is identified with the investigation of conscious experience. This would not even apply to all phenomenological and hermeneutical approaches in psychology, much less to psychodynamic approaches that research precisely the "transsubjective," namely, that which escapes conscious experienceability and which places us in supra-individual contexts. Second, psychology is here reduced to the motivational-emotional aspects of human life. The analysis of cognitive acts—e.g., the interpretation of human conflict in Romans 7—is an equally important task. When Paul emphasizes repeatedly that it is not I but sin which dwells in me that does evil, he is carrying out a very specific causal attribution, which in itself is a significant psychic act.

19. The differences in accent are striking where the two verbs are used next to each other. In order to understand (*gnosthesetai*) what is spoken, one must know (*eido*) the significance of the sounds (1 Cor. 14:9–11); before their conversion, the Galatians knew nothing of God (*ouk eidotes Theon*), but now they have come to know him (*nun de gnontes Theon;* Gal. 4:8–9); Paul no longer knows anyone according to the flesh (*oidamen*). Even if he had come to know Christ according to the flesh (*egnokamen*), he would now no longer know (*ginoskomen*) him in this way (2 Cor. 5:16). One must therefore, paraphrasing, translate Rom. 7:7 as follows: "Apart from the law, I would not have come to know sin (at a particular time). And covetousness would not have become conscious to me (as lasting knowledge). . . ." The pluperfect *edein* underlines the permanent effect that perdures into the present (thus Cranfield, *A Critical and Exegetical Commentary*, 348). In Rom. 7:14, both verbs occur in reverse order. We know (*oidamen*) as lasting knowledge that the law is spiritual. But what I do, I do not grasp even though I make an effort to understand it (*ou ginosko*).

of a purely practical coming to know (without consciousness of the action) cannot be established sufficiently.[20] What is decisive is rather when recognition of sin begins.

Here one must attend to the fact that there are no cognitive verbs in 7:8–11. That sin "wrought" through the law all kinds of covetousness, that it revived, took advantage of the law, and deceived and killed man, does not include the idea that these events took place consciously. To the contrary, the motif of deception presupposes that the deceived I has only an incomplete consciousness of sin. Only after removal of the deception is it possible to speak of a "knowing" of sin. One will therefore have to locate recognition of sin at the end of the process.[21] Only the killing of the I removes its illusion about sin, enlightens it, and establishes recognition—just as Adam became a "knower" only after the Fall. Romans 7:13 confirms this view. According to this text, sin wrought death through what is good, in order that it might be revealed as sin—a revelation that coincides with the "recognition" of sin.

Thus there is an unconscious conflict with the law. Yet we must specify more precisely the content that remained unconscious. It is scarcely the case that there is a contradiction between norm and desire. What was revealed was rather that sin wrought death "through the good." The functional involvement of the law in the origin of sin was unconscious. The depth dimension of the conflict was unconscious. One could say in a word that what was unconscious was not sin as such but rather its "excess" (Rom. 7:13*). This is "revealed" only at the end of the process depicted in Rom. 7:7–13.

The second part of the text, which is in the present tense, sets in from the start with a "knowledge." This does not contradict the assumption of a once-unconscious conflict. For one thing, this knowledge does not touch the depth dimension of the conflict. That pneumatic law and carnal I are opposites is clear in any case. Second, however, in the continuation of the train of thought, Paul emphasizes that he had not understood what he was doing. Now it is important that the

20. It is not a matter of a practical coming to know sin (thus Michel, *Der Brief*, 172) but of insight into sin. De facto, men sin even without law (Rom. 2:12; 5:12–14), but only through the law do they recognize that their action is sin (3:20). Cranfield (*A Critical and Exegetical Commentary*, 348–49) interprets this correctly.

21. Bornkamm ("Sünde," 57) also argues in this vein: it is "premature to speak of this division as early as the interpretation of v. 11." Conversely, one can well say that "the *exepatesen me* is the basis of the *ou ginosko* (V. 15)" (p. 63). But then in 7:14ff., Paul gets beyond not understanding.

missing understanding of the conflict is replaced step by step with conscious insight. In place of the "I do not understand" of v. 15 comes a *sumpheimi*, "I agree," in v. 16 and an *oida*, "I know," in v. 18. From the division between willing and doing, it is concluded, first, that this division encompasses an assent to the law and, second, that nothing "good" dwells in the acting I. In other words, the knowledge of the contradiction in principle between the pneumatic law and the carnal I, anticipated in 7:14, is now applied to the conflict between willing and doing depicted in the saying of v. 15; this conflict is brought to conceptual expression. Behind the conflict of willing and doing stands the conflict of law and flesh, and this is formulated as a conscious recognition, for one can hardly deny cognitive content to the verbs *sumphemi* and *oida*.[22]

The reiteration of the saying in v. 19 makes allowance for this enhanced consciousness. It no longer speaks only of the conflict between willing and doing but now speaks of that between *agathon* and *kakon* (good and evil); in other words, it picks up terminologically on the conclusions drawn in 7:16 and 7:17–18. The ensuing train of thought brings further progress. Paul now formulates explicitly the "lawfulness" that dominates the conflict; *heurisko ara ton nomon*, "I find it to be a law" (7:21), stands in clear opposition to *ou ginosko*, "I do not know" (7:15*). What was still unintelligible at the beginning is now understood

22. The transsubjective interpretation of Rom. 7:14ff., inaugurated by Bultmann ("Römer 7") and defended by his students, is based, first, on identifying the good and evil in Rom. 7:18–19 with life and death (7:10, 13), i.e., identifying them not with the good and evil actions themselves but with their results, and second, on the position that the motif of illusion in Rom. 7:11 is also presupposed in 7:13–23. Observations with regard to verbal semantics, structure, and the history of tradition speak against this interpretation. (1) Verbal semantics: The equation of the "good" with "life" is not possible. If death is wrought by the good (v. 13), then the good is not the result but the causing means. The interpretation of *katergazesthai* as "bring something about as a result" is possible although not necessary (cf. Rom. 2:9, 10, and passim). (2) Structure: The text divides into two parts with clear progress in thought. Against the introduction of the motif of illusion from 7:11 speaks the fact that, according to v. 13, sin has already become "revealed." The subjective and conscious character of the conflict emerges for one thing from the emphasis on the I and the "inner event" (*en emoi*, three times; *en tois melesin mou*, twice; and *eso anthropos*, once), and also from the multiplication of cognitive verbs. (3) History of tradition: The theme present in vv. 15, 19 normally envisions a consciously experienced conflict between passion and reason. Critical comments on the transsubjective interpretation are made by Althaus (*Paulus*, 45–47), Kuss (*Der Römerbrief*, 469–72), and Wilckens (*Der Brief*, 88). Yet it is correct that the deception of the I in Rom. 7:11 presupposes ignorance of the consequences. Here Paul projects the conflict between good intention and evil consequence into Adam's conflict, which has a different structure. But in the course of the text, this "transsubjective" conflict is with increasing clarity "subjectivized," i.e., made conscious.

as a special instance of a "rule," a *nomos*, a principle. One can, after all, also react in a very different way to the contradiction of willing and doing—either with admonitions to carry out one's good intention or with a correction of intentions that may have been too far-reaching. In both instances, the conflict would be presented as capable in principle of being overcome. But Paul's thoughts amount to grasping the conflict that has been demonstrated as a conflict in principle, so that it must appear as insurmountable. The contradiction between willing and doing is ultimately a contradiction between the law of God and the law of sin. Both are perceived consciously: rejoicing in the law—a heightening of the agreement with the law mentioned in 7:16— and seeing the other law include a consciousness of this opposition. This opposition is experienced subjectively in the human interior. Whatever sort of uncomprehended unconscious conflict Paul departed from, in other words, in the end he achieves the sharpest consciousness of this conflict. The I that speaks in 7:21ff. is fundamentally different from the I of 7:11. The I of 7:11 lived in illusion and was deceived, while the I of 7:21ff. has lost all illusions. Thus the two parts of Rom. 7:7ff. depict in different ways the conflict becoming conscious; the first part proceeds from being deceived by sin to sin becoming revealed, and the second part moves from the nonunderstanding of the conflict to the uncovering of its "lawfulness."[23]

Yet the first part depicts this process as an objective event, whereas the second presents it as a process of understanding, as the many cognitive verbs in the first-person singular show. The first part says, "The very commandment which promised life proved to be death to me" (7:10; *heurethe* in the passive voice). The second part, on the contrary, says subjectively, "I find it to be a law. . ." (7:21; *heurisko* in the active voice). Not only does each of the parts show in itself an increase in consciousness, but an increase between the two parts in clarity, insight, and reflexivity is also to be noted.

In the earlier investigation of the *ego* ("I") in Romans 7, we found

23. That an intensification is present in the text is emphasized by Ellwein, "Das Rätsel," 262. It is the merit of Kertelge ("Exegetische Überlegungen") to have interpreted this intensification as a process of becoming conscious: "What he [Paul] presents in Romans 7 as the situation of the pre-Christian I was not experienced consciously, or not completely consciously, and was not written down as consciously experienced" (p. 113). The condition of unredeemed existence in the past is "to be described as *preconscious*." "Reflection of the believer on his pre-Christian I therefore serves the *becoming conscious* of precisely this I as one that comes to itself thanks to redemption through Jesus Christ" (p. 113; emphasis in part mine).

that there are no convincing linguistic or stylistic grounds to exclude
in principle the person of Paul from the *ego* ("I") of Romans 7. The
preceding analysis of a progressive process of developing consciousness
of a formerly unconscious conflict with the law does have validity
independently of a possible personal background. But inquiring into
such a background is inescapable. The chief argument against this is
the contradiction to Philippians 3.

The Contradiction of Rom. 7:7–23 and Phil. 3:4–6

The decisive argument against acceptance of a personal background
for Rom. 7:7ff. is Phil. 3:4–6. Although in Rom. 7:24, Paul calls
himself a "wretched man" who suffers under the law, in the other
passage he speaks of a man who was irreproachable in legal righteousness
(Phil. 3:6). Kümmel has formulated the problem pregnantly: "Either
the assumption is correct that Paul even as a Jew had despaired of the
law and experienced the inner division of Romans 7 (then Paul was
not *kata nomon Pharisaios* and *kata dikaiosunen ten en nomo amemptos*) or
Paul was, as he himself asserts, a genuine Pharisee (then this interpretation of Romans 7 and the location of the criticism of the law in his
pre-Christian period is incorrect)."[24]

In principle there are two possibilities for solving the problem. One
either denies the inner authenticity of one of the two texts for the sake
of ascribing it to the other—this is the classical solution—or holds to
the inner authenticity of both texts, in which case one must then relate
them to different periods or aspects of Paul's life.

The classical solution to the problem lies in denying the inner
authenticity of Romans 7 through a rhetorically fictive interpretation
of the "I." The inner authenticity of Philippians 3 is less frequently
called into question,[25] although the context is strongly polemical and
doubts could be raised whether Paul is characterizing his past in a
factually appropriate manner. But in Gal. 1:13–14, Paul speaks of his

24. Kümmel, *Römer 7*, 113.
25. Cf. Kuss, *Der Römerbrief*, 480. The polemical context does not permit Paul to
depict a conflict with the law here. The whole argumentation amounts to parallelizing
Paul's opponents with the pre-Christian Paul, in order to move the community to
distance itself from these opponents just as clearly as Paul has distanced himself from
his past. Cf. Hyldahl, *Loven*. If Paul in this context had admitted a failure with regard
to the law, then he could easily have been charged with "ressentiment." But "he will
not let it be said of him that he is rejecting the Jewish grounds for fame in principle
because he was not able to achieve them in practice; oh no!" Dibelius, *An die Thessalonicher,
I.II. An die Philipper*, 58).

past in comparable expressions. The repetition of comparable state-ments in different contexts suggests that these statements are to a certain degree independent of their context. We can therefore proceed from the fact that Paul was a Pharisee who was proud of the law.

Must one then interpret Romans 7 and Philippians 3 with reference to different things—for example, Philippians 3 with reference to Paul's pre-Christian period; Romans 7, to his Christian period or to a time of inner temptation after the Damascus experience?[26] This solution is also impossible to carry out. Romans 7:13–24, in my opinion, is all too clearly concerned with unredeemed humanity. There remains a possibility that has not been weighed up to now. It could be a matter of different aspects of one and the same period of life. Logical contradictions can coexist psychologically; recognitions of depth psy-chology often proceed from the fact that the unconscious aspects of our life can stand in opposition to its conscious intentions. The thesis defended here, therefore, is that Phil. 3:4–6 reflects the consciousness of the pre-Christian Paul, while Romans 7 depicts a conflict that was unconscious at the time, one of which Paul became conscious only later.

This thesis must not be confused with other attempts to attribute to Paul an unconscious preparation for his conversion. In such attempts, an unconscious positive attraction to the Christian faith is usually postulated, and one simultaneously allows for a conscious conflict with the law, of the sort that comes to expression in Romans 7. Oddly, none of the previously presented psychodynamic interpretations of the conversion of Paul has made use of the contradiction between Philip-pians 3 and Romans 7.

According to Oskar Pfister, Paul suffered from a religious compulsion, which is distinguished from an individual compulsive neurosis by its social embedding, but is comparable to such a neurosis in other respects. Law and religion served Paul by unburdening the tensions that had accumulated through the confrontation of law and libido—just as a compulsive neurotic seeks relief from psychic tensions in neurotic ritual. Paul's conflict with the law was conscious: "Paul came into contact with the Christians and their teaching as an unsatisfied man, torn by inner needs."[27] His hatred for Christians is to be explained by the fact that the Christians called into question his attachment to the law—his compulsive ritual. They devalued precisely the means by

26. Thus Goguel, *"kata dikaiosunen."* Similarly Zahn, *Der Brief,* 337–71. According to Zahn, in Rom. 7:14ff. Paul speaks as one who is converted but not yet reborn!
27. O. Pfister, "Die Entwicklung," 277.

which Paul wanted to overcome his inner tensions. But at the same time Paul felt himself attracted to them: "Thus the persecutor found in the persecuted some great things which he could not deny. He sought to deny them, and probably talked himself into the idea that the Christians were nevertheless foes of God and despisers of the law. . . . The secret fear of sinning against the innocent and hating the legate of God had to be repressed from consciousness ever more strongly and with greater violence."[28]

In Pfister it is above all Christians by whom an unconscious fascination is exerted on Paul; in Jung it is Christ—not, indeed, the "historical Jesus" but the archetypal Christ who, in the Damascus vision, is held to have suddenly illumined and transformed Paul's consciousness from the depths of the collective unconscious. "Saul had already been a Christian unconsciously for an extended time, which explains his fanatical hatred for Christians; for fanaticism is always to be found in people of this sort who have an inner doubt to drown out. It is for this reason that converts are the worst fanatics. The vision of Christ on the way to Damascus merely signifies the moment when the unconscious Christ-complex associated itself with the I of Paul. That Christ confronted him in a quasi-objective manner is explained by the circumstance that the Christianity of Paul was a complex of which he was unconscious."[29] C. G. Inglis accepted this interpretation and enriched it with the element of a simultaneous conscious conflict with the law—oddly enough, with an appeal to Phil. 3:6: "He [Paul] was conscious, before his conversion, of profound dissatisfaction with the righteousness to which he had attained under the Law (Ph 3,6)."[30]

Both interpretations envision an unconscious turning toward Christ but not an unconscious turning away from nomism. This is also true of H. Fischer, who nonetheless takes one step further. His thesis is that Paul had to repress, with the aid of the law, libidinous impulses with a clearly homosexual component, in order to keep these from his consciousness. He identifies himself consciously with the law: "The law is evoked as the preserving power of order against the threatening chaos within him."[31] The Christians' freedom from the law calls into question his internal mechanisms of suppression: "Paul must not admit to himself that in the depths of his being he envies the Christians for the freedom from the law; he therefore needs to respond to the secret sympathy for Christians with an even stronger hatred for them."[32] The Christians thus addressed positively an unconscious side of Paul that had previously been

---

28. Ibid., 279.
29. Jung, "Die psychologischen Grundlagen," 348–49.
30. Inglis, "The Problem," 228. The claim that an unconscious inclination of the pre-Christian Paul toward Christianity is evident simply from the fact that Paul never mentions such an inclination (p. 228) is characteristic of some types of argumentation in depth psychology. Anything can be proved in this fashion!
31. H. Fischer, *Gespaltener christlicher Glaube*, 56. On Paul, cf. 44–76, esp. 56ff.
32. Ibid., 57.

repressed: "The contradiction against the law finds in his deep layers an ally that constantly attempts anew to overcome rational reflection with the unconscious power of a drive."[33] Here Fischer approaches recognition of an unconscious conflict with the law. He writes, "This passionate rejection of the law from the depths of his being will later be able to express itself freely in a struggle carried out by the I against the law, which Paul, after his conversion, is able to designate in the way he experienced it already before his conversion but without being able find the proper expression for it—as 'paidagogos,' which Luther appropriately translated as 'penal master.' "[34] The formulation still remains somewhat open to misunderstanding. That Paul "experienced" an insufficiency in the law implies a consciousness of this insufficiency. Thus Fischer remains on the whole within Pfister's tradition of exegesis. An unconscious fascination by Christians is postulated—here enriched with the position that it was freedom from the law that caused this unconscious fascination.

We admit that we can say nothing about an unconscious Christianity of the pre-Christian Paul. The sources point to an unbroken identification with the law. Yet it is legitimate to ask if the two most important texts on Paul's pre-Christian life, Phil. 3:4–6 and Gal. 1:13–14, suggest the possibility of an unconscious conflict with the law.[35] Even though differences in accent are to be observed in details, three motifs occur in each of these two texts: a motif of persecution, a motif of personal standing, and a motif of norm.

1. In almost identical formulations, Paul refers in both texts to his persecution of the Christian community: *diokein ten ekklesian (tou Theou)* (Gal. 1:13; Phil. 3:6; cf. 1 Cor. 15:6). Here there is aggressive behavior against a small minority that deviated from the norms of the majority. The verb *porthein* (in Gal. 1:13 and 1:23; cf. Acts 9:21) even includes an element of violence.

2. In addition to this, in both texts Paul specifies his position within his people more precisely. He emphatically numbers himself among his *genos* in both texts (Gal. 1:13; Phil. 3:5). Within the people, he names the Pharisees and his contemporaries as a closer circle of reference. The motive is comparable in each instance. Paul wishes to single himself out, whether it be that as a Pharisee he surpassed all

33. Ibid., 59.
34. Ibid., 56–57.
35. On the interpretation of both autobiographical texts, see esp. Blank, *Paulus*, 214–22, 231–38; on Paul's activity as persecutor, see 238–48. A psychological analysis of Phil. 3:2ff. may be found in Gremmels, "Selbstreflexive Interpretation."

other compatriots in piety or that as a young man he sought to exceed
all his contemporaries.

3. Finally, Paul stresses his relationship to the norms of Judaism.
The two statements "I was an extreme zealot for the traditions of my
fathers" (Gal. 1:14*) and "As to righteousness under the law I was
blameless" (Phil. 3:6*) correspond to each other. Since Paul was a
Pharisee, the "traditions" as well as the law belonged for him to the
valid norms. In this regard Paul unmistakably ascribes to himself an
overidentification with these norms, when he writes that he was an
extreme zealot (Gal. 1:14) or when he exclaims *ego mallon*, "I all the
more," before he enumerates his former distinctions, among them his
commitment on behalf of the law (Phil. 3:4).

The three motifs occur in different sequence in the two "autobiographical" texts, yet they belong close together, whether they are
reduced to the theme of an illusory "confidence in the flesh" and put
in parallel through statements using *kata* (Phil. 3:4–6) or summarized
under the heading "my former life in Jerusalem" (Gal. 1:13). It is
characteristic that while the term "zeal" occurs in both texts, it does
so in connection with different motifs. In Gal. 1:14, Paul calls himself
a zealot for the traditional norms; in Phil. 3:6, he characterizes his
activity as persecutor as "zeal." This indicates a factual connection
between persecution and consciousness of norms. Overidentification
with the norms of one's own group and aggression against outside
groups are closely connected; the only thing disputed is how they are
connected. As far as I can see, interpretation can proceed from either
the motif of norm or that of personal standing.

According to the first interpretation, the overidentification with the
norms of one's own group could be the formation of a reaction to an
unperceived inability to fulfill the norms and a resistance to these
norms because of this inability. Since one is unwilling and unable to
perceive this resistance in oneself, it is in part repressed, in part
projected onto other groups. Suitable victims are above all minorities
that seem to correspond to the projections in some behavior traits. In
rejecting or opposing these minorities, the executors struggle against
what they are unwilling to perceive in themselves or in their own
group. The outside group assumes the role of a scapegoat, which
simultaneously represents one's own misconduct and offers the opportunity to reject it demonstratively.[36]

Another interpretation proceeds from the motif of personal standing.

36. On the scapegoat theory of social prejudices, see Heintz, *Soziale Vorurteile*, 109ff.
and passim.

One who pursues esteem and influence within a group can often do so at cost to others who stand outside the norms prevailing within the group. By devaluing them, one exalts oneself. By exercising power with regard to them, one secures one's own power internally. Since rejection of the "stranger" is in some circumstances an adaptation inherited from the history of the race, and since its presence within human beings can be taken for granted, there is no need for the assumption that one is unconsciously identifying the rejected minority with negative aspects of oneself. Here one can expect unmitigated persecution.[37] Naturally, unconscious conflicts can play a role here. Striving for power can originate from an unadmitted conflict with one's own impotence—such as a traumatically experienced inferiority of a social or physical sort.

It should also be emphasized that mistreatment of other people and other groups as "scapegoats" or as a jumping board for one's own will to power are phenomena of normal life, with regard to which one need envision neither abnormal inclinations nor neurotic conflicts. Pathological elements can play a role. Yet the modern inclination to sniff pathological elements behind every inhuman persecutorial activity is more likely a defensive claim of our culture, with which we preserve ourselves from insight into the appalling "normality" of evil. The Third Reich showed sufficiently the degree to which a normal human being is ready to degenerate.

We therefore have to weigh the two possibilities that have been sketched. Does the aggression directed by the pre-Christian Paul against the Christian community stem from a repressed conflict with the law or from a striving oriented on power? In order to make a well-founded decision, we must draw on Paul's general statements about the life of Jews under the law. In doing so, we base ourselves on the methodical assumption that general statements about the Jews logically include the Jew Paul, but that psychologically they are colored by the problematic of the Jew Paul—and that they therefore must not be assessed as objective statements. If an overidentification with the law, joined to an aggressive stance toward others, can be demonstrated in

37. Kümmel (*Römer* 7, 157–58) rightly stressed this possibility against Pfister. Not every fanaticism is the product of defense mechanisms: "There can spring from an authoritative faith without any second thoughts the consciousness that a rejected religious opinion attacks the honor of God, of the church, etc., or that it destroys the divinely willed purity of a religious community and must therefore be eradicated" (p. 157). It is important that this is not a contrast of a psychological interpretation with a nonpsychological interpretation, but rather two different attempts at psychological interpretation of Paul's persecutorial activity.

these general statements, then that would be a clear indication in favor of the "scapegoat interpretation."

Now in Rom. 2:17–23, we find in the general statements about the Jews a caricatured—and unjust—criticism of the overidentification of the Jew with the law, an overidentification that will not recognize in itself behavior contrary to the law. This is one of the major Pauline anacoluthons, which illustrates even stylistically the contradiction between pride in the law and unperceived transgression of the law.[38] Romans 2:17–20* reads,

> But if you call yourself a Jew
> and rely upon the law
> and boast of your relation to God
> and know his will
> and know how to test what is important,
>   because you are instructed in the law,
> and if you trust yourself
> to be a guide to the blind,
> a light to those who are in darkness,
> a corrector of the foolish,
> a teacher of the immature,
>   because you have in the law the embodiment of
>   knowledge and truth . . .

The self-praise has two parts. The first thematizes with five parallel finite verbs the relation of the Jew to God on the basis of the instruction received (passively) in the law; the second speaks in four infinitives of the Jew's superiority over others. Here the one who is instructed becomes the instructor, who raises a claim to leadership of others. After this introduction, five questions follow (Rom. 2:21–23*), separated by an anacoluthic break from the preceding:

You who teach others—do you not teach yourself?
You who preach to others against stealing—do you steal?
You who say not to commit adultery—do you commit adultery?
You who abhor idols—do you rob temples?
You who boast in the law—do you dishonor God by breaking the law?

The first part (2:17–20) would seem to correspond to the self-consciousness of the Pharisee Paul.[39] Reference might be made to the

38. Cf. Bornkamm, "Paulinische Anakoluthe," 76–92; on Rom. 2:17–23, cf. 76–78.
39. Cf. Goguel, *"kata dikaiosunen,"* 262. Perhaps it is a matter of a "retrospective polemic of Paul the Christian against Paul the Jew." Yet this would seem to apply only to the first part of Rom. 2:17ff. Paul hardly committed the crimes listed in Rom. 2:21ff.

fact that the term *pepoithenai* occurs in Rom. 2:19 as well as Phil. 3:4. One can even determine a comparable sequence of themes. First, the ethnic belonging is emphasized (Rom. 2:17; Phil. 3:5); then, the efforts for the law; after that, the relationship to other groups—just that in Rom. 2:19* it is the "blind, unwise, and immature" but in Phil. 3:6 it is the Christians. But though Phil. 3:6 leads to an emphatic stress on the legal righteousness of the pre-Christian Paul, what follows in Rom. 2:21ff. is just the opposite! Here the topic is suddenly the violation of the law by one proud of the law. In other words, in Rom. 2:17ff., Paul combines a demonstrative pride in the law with an inability to perceive his own violation of the law. That this inability was "repressed" is the most likely explanation, not only from a psychological perspective but also from the context. The whole section, Rom. 1:18—3:20, is after all directed toward recognition of sin—and presupposes that there is no complete consciousness of sin in the groups that are discussed. Rather, recognition of sin is attained only on the basis of a revelation from heaven of the wrath of God, a revelation that encounters human resistance (Rom. 1:18).

Paul also gives us indications of the usual projection mechanisms, on the basis of which we find in others precisely the negative things we do not wish to recognize in ourselves. After criticizing pagan behavior in Rom. 1:25ff., he extends his criticism to encompass both those who assent to such actions (Rom. 1:32) and those who criticize it. The latter can only refer to Jews, although the address speaks generally of "man" (Rom. 2:1):[40]

> Therefore you have no excuse, O man, whoever you are, when you judge another; for in passing judgment on him you condemn yourself, because you, the judge, are doing the very same things.

Paul literally says here only that we condemn in others what we do ourselves. Clear recognition of the projection mechanism, that we condemn others *because* we see in them what we do not want to see in ourselves, is still lacking. But he is not far from this recognition.

We can conclude that Paul's general statements about the Jews point clearly in the direction of that inner connection between overidentification with the law, projection, and aggressive prejudice that we presumed behind Phil. 3:4–6 (and Gal. 1:13–14). It is in my opinion legitimate to insert these general statements about the Jews into the

40. If one isolates 2:1 as a gloss (thus Bultmann, "Glossen," 281), reference could be made to 2:3.

personal statements of Paul about his pre-Christian life. For this much is certain: in these statements Paul does not say all that he could. In Phil. 3:4–6, he enumerates his good qualities, which he considers disadvantage and harm in the light of the revelation of Christ. He sees them in a completely new way. Yet he does not develop his new recognition but only emphasizes that he has turned radically from his past—as if he wanted to forget it (Phil. 3:13). What he nevertheless says about his past is written completely from the perspective of the Pharisee, as is clear from three points:[41]

1. Only as a Pharisee could he claim that he was "blameless" in righteousness under the law (Phil. 3:6). As a Christian such a statement was for him impossible (cf. Gal. 3:11; Rom. 3:23).

2. Nor does he depict his activity as persecutor from a Christian perspective. In contrast to Gal. 1:13 and 1 Cor. 15:9, here he characterizes the Christian community simply as *ekklesia*, not as *ekklesia tou Theou*. For the Paul who persecuted Christians they simply could not be the community *of God*.

3. Last, in the description of Paul's origin, one could also think of a self-presentation formula of the pre-Christian Paul: "I, Paul, of the people of Israel, of the tribe of Benjamin, Hebrew of Hebrews, as to the law a Pharisee" (Phil. 3:5*). As is well known, Paul's Christian self-presentation reads differently (cf. the prescripts of the letters).

From all of this we draw the conclusion that what Paul conceals in Philippians 3—namely, how he sees his pre-Christian period in the light of the "knowledge of Jesus Christ" (Phil. 3:8*)—is precisely what he develops in Romans 7; in doing so he gives his personal fate generally valid form, yet betrays high self-involvement through the typical *ego*. Only together do Philippians 3 and Romans 7 give an accurate picture. The demonstrative pride in the law of Paul the Pharisee was the formation of a reaction to an unconscious conflict with the law, in which the law became a factor eliciting anxiety. At the time Paul could not admit to himself his suffering under the law. But when the veil fell from his heart through his encounter with Christ, he recognized the shadow side of his zeal for the law. Romans 7 is the result of a long retrospective bringing to consciousness of a conflict that had once been unconscious. Paul considers this conflict to be universally human. He imputes a hidden conflict with the law even to Gentiles (Rom. 2:14–15). In order to postulate this, he did not need to restrict himself

---

41. As Gnilka (*Der Philipperbrief*, 191) rightly says, "*Amemptos* is not meant ironically. The conviction is not feigned; it was genuine. Paul drew back before the great shift."

to human consciousness. He had experienced in his own life that conflict with the law can also be present unconsciously.

Faith as Treatment of Conflict

The last reflections pose a question. What role does faith in Christ play in making the conflict conscious and dealing with it? The available psychodynamic interpretations usually see in the breakthrough of faith in Christ the becoming conscious of a previously existing unconscious attachment to Christ. Insofar as we can actually come to a controllable interpretation in this area, I would like to propose a differently accented interpretation.

If Paul's aggressive prejudices against the Christian minority that transgresses the norm represent a scapegoat projection, then this means that in the Christians he unconsciously persecuted himself. Christ became for him a symbol of his negative identity, that is, of all those aspects he did not wish to perceive in himself and from which he consciously wished to distance himself. Instead of seeing and addressing in himself repressed incapacity to fulfill the law and anxiety at the demands of the law, he persecutes them in a small group that deviated from the law. The central point of this group was one cursed by the law, one who represented openly what Paul experienced unconsciously in an archaic level of himself—that the law became a factor hostile to life, a factor evoking anxiety. How the shift from persecutor of Christians to Christian missionary came about will always remain hidden from our psychological knowledge: Paul saw the one wrongly thought to be cursed as a divine figure. Yet we can surmise what this shift meant psychologically. It was equivalent to the appropriation of a repressed negative identity—of everything, in other words, that Paul up to then had been unwilling to perceive in himself. For if the persecution of Christians—on the basis of an unconscious projective equation of the persecuted with his own "shadow"—was fundamentally self-persecution and self-punishment, then the shift to being a Christian missionary was self-appropriation, integration of the shadow, and overcoming of the destructive inner-directed punitive tendencies.

It is possible that Paul brought this reality to expression in a universally valid symbolism. He took this symbolism over from the Christians, yet it is only in him that it moves into the center of reflection on the redemptive effect of Christ. Paul understood Christ as the atoning victim for our sins, and even as the scapegoat of the Old Testament day of atonement (Rom. 3:25). All sin was laid and "projected" on Christ. For in himself he was innocent. But, unlike the scapegoat in Leviticus 16, he was not driven into the wilderness in order to die far from men and free the community of its sins. He rather became the central person of reference for the community, present in mystical fashion in their hearts during their assemblies. With this the process of projection was made transparent. All recognize their sins in the vicarious scapegoat. And all were convinced that these sins were overcome. Is not the recognition of the scapegoat as the center of the community equivalent to an appropriation of the "shadow"?

In Romans 7, Paul presents the intellectual result of this process of appropriation. The hostile relationship between the I and the law, once unconscious, is now articulated openly. Here Paul comes to statements whose proximity to psychoanalytic insights is astonishing. The relationship of law, self, and flesh corresponds in some respects to the relationship of superego, ego, and id.[42] It would of course be inappropriate to expect complete correspondence between Pauline and psychoanalytic anthropologies. The interpretive framework differs in the two cases, not to mention that there is a great historical distance. But the similarities stand out all the more sharply against the background of indisputable difference.

Neither in Paul nor in psychoanalysis is it a matter of purely immanent tribunals. The id rather represents an archaic heritage, which binds an individual with the entire history of the race—just as the flesh binds one to all living beings. The superego is the deposit of cultural traditions, as mediated by parents to the child. It stands for all "internalized" norms, anxieties, and ideals—just as the law is the quintessence of the divine norms and values transmitted from without. The ego is sovereign in neither case, although it is destined for autonomy. It is subordinated to other tribunals that in their structure point beyond themselves. The human being is the stage of a conflict with cosmic tribunals. In psychoanalysis, these are transsubjective biological and social powers; in Paul, on the contrary, they are mythical tribunals and theological entities.

The functional relationship of the three tribunals is even more

42. Cf. Créspy, "Exégèse," 169ff.; and Hofstätter, "Tiefenpsychologische Persön-lichkeitstheorien," 545. Reservations are registered by Vergote ("Der Beitrag," 100), who holds that the law is not identical to the superego: the superego is rather the interiorized law; the law is an entity that comes from without. This is correct! But what is interiorized must at one point have come from without; even the superego is the deposit of an objective reality. Conversely, what moves one from without must be present within; even the law has a base within one in the *nous* and the *syneidesis!*

important than their structure. Both Paul and psychoanalysis specify it as antagonistic. A "civil war" rages within us.

Here the analogy yields a decisive point. In Paul, the point of Romans 7 is the relativizing of oppositions that have been imagined in far too static fashion. Sin makes use of the voice of the law; as an obscure, rebellious power, the law dominates human beings. This clearly calls into question every division of the human being into a higher and a lower part—the basic scheme of every idealist anthropology. Even what is lofty and good, even law and commandment, exhibit an irritating ambivalence. This corresponds precisely to the psychoanalytic recognition that the superego is not only a reality that directs the ego positively but one that contains archaic, aggressive components that threaten the ego with irrational guilt feelings and ultimately derive from the dark potential of the id for aggression (as, I would surmise, a relic of adaptation to life-threatening situations in the history of the race). On the other hand, it is often equipped with libidinous portions that fascinate the ego through what is (often) an unrealistic ideal of the ego; these too are drives that have broken off from the id. To put it briefly: Destructive and libidinous drives of the id overpower the superego and influence the ego from above in threatening and promising manners. Paul expresses this by saying that sin deceives (= promises) and kills (= threatens) by means of the commandment.[43]

Paul brings the ambivalence of the superego to expression in the somewhat contradictory metaphors he adduces to describe the relationship to the law. On the one hand, he uses the image of marriage. Unredeemed man is bound to conscience as the wife is bound to her husband (Rom. 7:1–3). This postulates a libidinous link to the law, a link Paul no doubt once possessed (Phil. 3:4–6; Gal. 1:13–14). On the other hand, Paul describes the conflict with the law in drastic martial metaphors. A law in one's members fights against the law of reason and holds one captive (Rom. 7:23). Here an aggressive stance with regard to the superego comes to expression. Both aspects of this ambivalent stance are connected with the flesh and with the law. As long as Christians lived in the flesh, they were bound to the first

43. On this, cf. Forsyth, "Faith," 476ff. Forsyth compares Romans 7 less with Freud's three-tribunal model than with his "drive mythology," the antagonism of the life and death drives as seen by the later Freud. In order to allow the life drive to come to bear, suppression of the destructive drive is necessary. The latter is transformed into guilt feelings. Paul's solution is that in fact there is no culture (= no law) that could confer life without guilt feeling (= death). True life lies beyond the law and is given by God.

husband, or to the law of the man (Rom. 7:1ff.). But the rebellion
against this link was located in the "members" (7:18, 23). In the same
way an ambivalent effect proceeds from the law. By virtue of its
attractive-libidinous power it seduces; and by virtue of its aggressive-
destructive energy it kills. In reality, however, it is not the law that
deceives and kills through the commandment, but rather the libidinous
and destructive energy of sin that works unconsciously in it (Rom.
7:11).

One decisive difference remains. In psychoanalysis, conflicts are
overcome through making them conscious; in Paul, they are overcome
through the saving intervention of Christ. In one case, the individual
activates his own powers; in the other, one trusts in the power of God.
Yet this difference is relativized when one looks at it more closely. All
modern therapies proceed from the position that the disturbed individual needs assistance from without; the individual needs a therapist.
Nowhere else is such decisive value attributed to the therapist as in
psychoanalysis. According to this school, the once-unconscious conflict
is "transferred" to a therapist, "acted out" in interaction with the
therapist, and raised to consciousness. The therapist comes to the aid
of the weakened ego in order to strengthen it against the demands of
the superego and the id. Even here, in other words, alteration of
behavior does not occur "autonomously"; it is, rather, dependent on a
"heteronomous" relationship to another person. Is something comparable not also the case with regard to faith in Christ? Can the effects
of changing behavior and experience, which faith in Christ certainly
had on Paul, be described with the psychodynamic categories of
transferral, becoming conscious, and dealing with conflict?

An unconscious conflict is also acted out in one's relationship to
Christ. One who suffers under the conflict with the law transfers
hostility against the law—and that means against the demanding God—
onto Christ. This hostility extends to a hidden death wish, which can
still be sensed in two texts in Paul. Twice in his writings there occur
images that in their internal logic presuppose the death of God and
even make this appear desirable. Each image seeks to illustrate freedom
from the law. But in each image the death of God, implicitly
presupposed, remains unexpressed or, more exactly, is replaced by
the vicarious death of Christ. The passages in question are the testament
symbolism of Galatians 3—4 and the marriage symbolism of Rom.
7:1–6.

Galatians 4:1–7 compares redemption to an heir's coming of age.

Through a will, the father had established a time at which the son would enter upon the inheritance. Up to that point, he is subject to guardians and administrators. Within this image, the death of the father is the presupposition of the emancipation of the heir. However, in the use of the image—introduced by *houtos kai hemeis*, "so with us" (Gal. 4:3)—no reference is made to the death of the father; on the contrary, when the time was fulfilled, God sent his Son to redeem those suffering under the law. In the metaphorical half, the death of the father is presupposed; in the factual half, it is denied or, more exactly, replaced by the death of Christ, who came "to redeem us from the law" (Gal. 4:5*).[44]

In Rom. 7:1–6 the issue is an image that is introduced as a model example. Paul states in advance the thesis to be defended: "The law is binding on a person only during his life" (Rom. 7:1). As an illustrating example, Paul chooses the widow who is bound to her husband only during the husband's lifetime. After his death, she is free to marry another. The same situation is said to pertain to the Christian and the law. Exegesis has long puzzled about who could be meant by the first husband. The law? Sinful passions? The flesh?[45] The solution does not lie in adding another conjecture to these. The question must not be, What was Paul thinking about? but must rather be, What did Paul not want to think about under any circumstances? What ideas did he wish to avoid so thoroughly that he was willing to accept as a price a completely confused image? For freedom from the law is first demonstrated with regard to the deceased man (v. 1), then with regard to the surviving widow (vv. 2–3), and finally with regard to the relationship of two deceased persons who have returned to life (v. 4). The answer lies at hand. Within the traditional religious vocabulary the husband can only be God.[46] Paul's image actually tends toward the idea that

44. Against this, cf. Oepke (*Der Brief*, 113): "That a testament comes into force only after the death of the testator, while God does not die, is a minor error in the similitude, which one can ignore." But for Paul the association of testament and death seems to be quite firm; cf. "the new testament in my blood" (1 Cor. 11:25*), with regard to which one must of course allow for the double meaning of *diatheke* (= "covenant" and "testament").

45. Cf. Kümmel, *Römer 7*, 36–42.

46. Hosea 1—3 compares Israel's relationship to God, to a marriage. Israel is an unfaithful wife. She chases other men, the gods. Idolatry is therefore adultery (cf. Jer. 3:1—4:4; Hos. 4:12–14). After the destruction of Jerusalem, the city is accused as an unfaithful wife (Isa. 57:7–13; Ezek. 16:32). Paul knows this tradition. In 2 Cor. 11:2*, he compares the community to a bride: "For I have betrothed you to one man, in order to present you as a pure virgin to Christ." In order to refute an application of this

the God of the law has died. But Paul must, of course, suppress this thought. It would be blasphemy. Even worse, if we read Rom. 7:1–4 in connection with the preceding reflections on the change in rule (Rom. 6:12ff.) and still have in our ear what is said there about "sin's reign of terror," the first marriage slips into a bad light from the start. The wish to dissolve it would be understandable. But entering a new marriage during the husband's lifetime would be adultery. The plagued wife therefore "longs" for his death. But what if the husband is the God of the law? Paul could never, under any circumstances, admit the thought that man under the law has a death wish for God. For this reason he makes a logical jump. It is not the husband who dies (as foreseen in the image) but Christ—and in him all Christians (Rom. 7:4). The death wish is no longer directed against God but is now vicariously against Christ. Christ represents God. The hidden death wish against the God of the law finds fulfillment with regard to him. But Christ also represents men. All Christians die with him—and are thus withdrawn from the realm of the law (Rom. 7:4–6).

Assuming a hidden death wish against the God of the law seems at first glance monstrous.[47] Paul himself, however, confirms the hostile relationship between God and us prior to redemption: we were "enemies of God" (Rom. 5:10*). A profound hostility toward God is rooted in the flesh (Rom. 8:7). But hostility tends toward death: Paul places parallel to each other "The thought of the flesh is death" (8:6*) and "The thought of the flesh is hostility toward God" (8:7*). It lies in the logic of the martial metaphors present in Rom. 7:23 to accept the idea of a hidden hostility against God in unredeemed humanity—a hostility expressed openly in Rom. 5:10; 7:23; and 8:6–7.

Paul's clear statements about the hostility of unredeemed humanity toward God show that the conflict is not only acted out but also made conscious. This is not a matter of a gradual transition to greater clarity, as if the conflict had previously already been conscious to a certain degree. At least in Paul himself, it was not only unconscious but repressed, as Phil. 3:4–6 shows. Overidentification with the law served

---

metaphor to Christ, Kümmel (*Römer 7*, 41) objects that in 2 Cor. 11:2 Paul is thinking of the community, whereas in Rom. 7:1ff. he is speaking of the individual Christian. But this argument is hardly convincing. In 1 Cor. 6:16, Paul is able to apply the image of marriage both to the relationship of the individual to Christ and to the community as a whole. Until the contrary is proved, we must assume that the marriage image awakened religious associations—i.e., that it suggested thinking of relationship to God.

47. Even O. Pfister ("Die Entwicklung," 272) believes he can conclude, "With regard to hidden death wishes, however, nothing can be demonstrated in Paul."

to block from consciousness the hostile relationship between law and flesh. It became conscious suddenly. A veil fell from the heart. The aggressiveness of the killing letter was exposed. The unconscious interpretation of relationship to the norm in the light of archaic enemy patterns was seen through. The deceptive splendor of the law faded. But becoming conscious is the first presupposition of handling conflict. Here Christ shows a new way. He overcomes the conflict between flesh and law by unifying in himself the two antagonistic tribunals.

According to Rom. 8:2–3, Christ takes the place of the flesh. God sent him in the "likeness of sinful flesh." Christ himself became "sin" (2 Cor. 5:21). But at the same time Christ takes the place of the law. He mediates the "law of the Spirit of life" (Rom. 8:2), which liberates the believer from the law of sin and death. Christ is thus *telos nomou* (Rom. 10:4)—simultaneously fulfillment and end of the law. He takes the place the law had previously occupied. For after Paul designates Christ as the *telos* of the law in Rom. 10:4, he is able to cite an Old Testament text (Deut. 30:11ff.) about the law and insert Christ where previously, in the Old Testament, the law had been mentioned.[48] The same process can be observed in 2 Cor. 3:12ff. According to the Old Testament story, Moses received God's commandment when he turned to the Lord. According to the Pauline interpretation, however, he encountered Christ when he "converted." In psychodynamic terms, because Christ takes the place of both the flesh and the law, the id and the superego, he becomes the symbol of an integration of originally antagonistic tribunals. Christ becomes a "coincidence of opposites."

The psychodynamic interpretation of faith in Christ is more complex than its analysis in learning theory. Faith in Christ is not only hidden learning from the symbolic model. It is that too. But not only is immunity from the anxiety-eliciting stimuli of the law learned from the model; rather, the symbol is what makes the situation of man with regard to the law conscious for the first time—namely, the unconscious structuring of the situation according to archaic enemy patterns. The figure of Christ not only has effects summoning forth imitation, though these are not excluded; the relationship to Christ also encompasses projection, distancing, and identification. The negative identity of man is projected onto Christ. He becomes both

---

48. According to Vielhauer (*Paulus*, 215), Paul "by means of interspersed interpretive comments replaces the law by Christ and interprets 'the Word' [of the law] as the Christian message of faith."

whipping boy and scapegoat.[49] He is whipping boy insofar as he
becomes the vicarious object of an aggressiveness that is actually
directed toward God, and scapegoat insofar as hostility toward God
is also ascribed vicariously to him as subject, so that he also bears the
punishment for it: in him God condemns the hostility of the flesh
(Rom. 8:3). It is precisely for this reason that Christ as integrating
symbol can represent both the demands of the law and human flesh.
He transforms both. Now the situation with regard to the law can
only be interpreted as "love." The entire law is contained in love. The
flesh can be replaced by the Spirit.[50]

So far, we have always interpreted the texts on two different levels
that, however, do not contradict each other. Paul presents in the texts
general processes, but his own life stands in the background. The
personal element is often difficult to grasp even when it makes its
presence felt. But the interpretations that are present in the texts
themselves are clearly recognizable. Here it is a matter of cognitive
acts with which Paul interprets his experience and behavior and that
of all Christians. We shall now once again devote our attention to these
separately.

COGNITIVE ASPECTS: ACCEPTANCE OF ROLES
AND STRUCTURING OF CONFLICT

Transformations of human experience and behavior are always changes
in self-understanding; in fact, the manner in which one perceives and
assesses oneself is in many respects a decisive factor in lasting

49. The difference between whipping boy and scapegoat lies in the fact that received
aggression is passed on to the whipping boy, and one's own aggressiveness is projected
onto the scapegoat.

50. By way of conclusion we shall discuss the question of how the striking agreements
between Freud and Paul with regard to some very formal characteristics can be explained.
On this point, I would present the following conjecture. Both Freud and Paul were
Jews who had emancipated themselves from the Jewish tradition. A lifelong confrontation
with Moses and the law played a prominent role in both of their lives. Both, therefore,
had a superego thematically marked by similar contents. In both instances, separation
from the "law" did not lead to libertinism, although both were declared heretics in this
regard. Both sought a new, "more humane" relationship to the law. In both of them,
love played a central role in this. In brief, it could be that the agreements between
Freud and Paul—despite different frameworks of interpretation—correspond to a
comparable cultural and historical situation, namely, the boundary between Judaism
and a movement emancipating itself from the prior religious traditions. In Paul a new
religion originates from this movement; in Freud it is connected with a decided turning
away from any type of religion. On this problem, cf. also J. Schreiber, "Sigmund
Freud," and Scharfenberg, *Sigmund Freud*, 60–61.

transformations. In transformations that involve far-reaching changes, we not only interpret one thing or another in a new way but change the comprehensive patterns of interpretation that lie at hand in the "supply of roles of religions and philosophies of life." The change depicted in Romans 7—8 can also be described as a change in the assumption of roles. Unredeemed humanity is interpreted in the light of the role of Adam, redeemed humanity in the light of the role of the new Adam.

The Role of Adam

It has already been demonstrated in the tradition analysis that Paul interprets the conflict of the I with reference to the role of Adam. Here it will be shown that this is an active process of restructuring which serves to make the transition from unredeemed to redeemed humanity intelligible. Recognition of an active restructuring process of this sort can solve one of the classical problems of Romans 7—the problem of the unbiographical statement of 7:9. This is a chief argument against the thesis that Romans 7 has a personal background, for Paul could never say of himself, "I once lived without the law" (Rom. 7:9*). It is true that Judaism did recognize a stage in which one growing up was not yet fully responsible for fulfillment of the law. But becoming gradually accustomed to the individual commandments took place as early as possible—even before the commitment to the entire Torah at the age of thirteen. Philo can therefore rightly assert that the child learns the law from early childhood on.[51] It was possible to designate a child (*nepios*) as *philonomos* (lover of the law) on a Jewish gravestone.[52] The statement of Rom. 7:9, therefore, fits neither Paul nor any other Jew. Is Paul then speaking of people in general? But who is he supposed to be thinking of here? Of the Gentiles? One could never say of them that the law came to them and "killed." Is Adam speaking? But who in the Roman community would have understood that? Adam is indeed the model of the statements in Rom. 7:7ff., but not their subject. In other words, one who rejects relationship of the statement to Paul has not yet solved the problem by doing this.

Now it is one of the central insights of a psychology of religion that

51. *On the Embassy to Gaius* 210.
52. On this inscription from Rome, cf. 203 n. 4. The inscription reads, "Enthade keitai Eukarpos nepios, hosios, philonomos. En eirene koimesis sou" ("Here lies Eukarpos—a child, hallowed, a friend of the law. Your sleep is in peace"). The "friend of the law" (*philonomos*) is still a child.

is concerned with role theory that identification with traditional roles makes possible a restructuring of perception. In other words, role and experience, tradition and experience, do not stand in opposition; on the contrary, received roles are conditions of the possibility of contemporary experience. The restructuring of experience and perception can definitely lead to tensions with empirical reality. We must therefore ask if the nonbiographical statements in Rom. 7:7 are not explained in this way—the role of Adam presupposes a state without law. If Paul interprets his life in the light of the role of Adam, he must with intrinsic necessity attribute to himself a state free of law—even contrary to his actual biography.

This hypothesis can be tested only by demonstrating on historical-critical grounds, that is, on the basis of analogies, the possibility of such a reinterpretation of one's own life in the light of received roles. Three examples of this will be adduced from the Pauline corpus.

1. In Gal. 1:15–16, Paul interprets his Damascus experience by reference to the role of the servant of God in Isa. 49:1*: "The Lord called my name from my birth."[53] Now, as far as Paul is concerned, there could certainly be no question of continuity in his life from the womb on. The former persecutor of Christians had rather undergone a 180-degree change. Nonetheless, he relates the Old Testament role to himself, while formulating his statement in a way that corresponds better to biographical reality. Using two parallel participles, he speaks of God "who set him apart from the womb and called him through his grace" (Gal. 1:15*). Paul separates here between birth and vocation (on the way to Damascus). But even so he preserves against his biographical discontinuity a continuity that is no longer empirically supportable.

2. In Phil. 3:12ff. the situation is just the opposite. Here Paul assumes the role of the athlete (cf. 1 Cor. 9:24–27) in order to illustrate his break with the past and his orientation toward the future. Paul turns toward the past no more than a runner looks behind him. Paul has forgotten what lies behind him and reaches out toward what lies ahead of him. Yet we know quite well that Paul had not at all forgotten what lay behind him.[54] He had not forgotten the Old Testament nor the rabbinic method of interpreting it nor his tie to the history of Israel.

3. In the third instance, it is a question not merely of tension with

53. Cf. Holtz, "Zum Selbstverständnis."
54. Thus, correctly, Gremmels, "Selbstreflexive Interpretation," 44ff.

biographical reality but of a clear contradiction. In 1 Cor. 9:19–23*, Paul assumes the role of Christ in order to underline his renunciation of privileges and his adaptability in all directions:

> For though I am free from all,
> I have nonetheless made myself a slave to all,
>   that I might win the majority.
> To the Jews I became as a Jew,
>   that I might win Jews.
> To those under the law
>   I became as one under the law—
>   although I myself do not stand under the law—
>   that I might win those under the law. . . .

Just as in Romans 7, Paul speaks here in the first-person singular in statements in the past tense (yet without an explicit *ego*). Although the name Christ does not occur, it is clear that Paul is interpreting his life according to the role of Christ. For Christ also became a "slave" (Phil. 2:7*) like Paul. Christ also was "placed under the law" (Gal. 4:4*)— just as Paul places himself under the law. Christ is "weakness on God's part" (1 Cor. 1:25*)—just as Paul intends to be weak with the weak. In all of this, he is an imitator of Christ (1 Cor. 11:1). Now, the name of Adam does not occur in Rom. 7:7ff. any more than Christ is explicitly mentioned in 1 Cor. 9:19ff., although Adam and Christ stand respectively in the background. But just as the "I" of 1 Cor. 9:19ff. is not for this reason the "I" of Christ, so too one cannot speak of the "I" of Adam in Rom. 7:7ff. In both texts, rather, Paul himself speaks, whether the accent is placed on the typical (Rom. 7:7ff.) or on the exemplary (1 Cor. 9:19). What is decisive is that the statements in both texts come into tension with biographical reality. Strictly speaking, Paul could not say that he had become a Jew (or like a Jew) to Jews. He was from the start a Jew, "circumcised on the eighth day, of the people of Israel, of the tribe of Benjamin, a Hebrew born of Hebrews" (Phil. 3:5; cf. 1 Cor. 11:22). Nor does the aorist *egenomen* permit a durative interpretation, such as "I was (once) a Jew to the Jews." The text speaks rather of a transition. Translation as "I showed myself to the Jews as a Jew" would not remove the difficulties. It is true in any case that Paul did not become a Jew to the Jews in the same way that he became one without the law to those without the law, or weak to those who were weak—namely, in voluntary adaptation, and not owing to his origin. One must rather accept the fact that here Paul is interpreting his life in the light of the role of Christ and in the process comes to statements that biographically are not correct. The idea of sovereign adaptation to each addressee demands independence with regard to them, so that the assumed equality with them is voluntary— just as Christ assumed the form of man freely.

It can therefore be established that acceptance of traditional roles can lead to reinterpretations of one's own life. Modern psychology itself provides examples of this. It has incorporated ancient roles such as those of Oedipus and Narcissus in order to interpret in their light problems of its own life; and there is much to be said for the idea that this did not occur only in correspondence with empirical reality but was rather its creative reinterpretation. But if the possibility of such new interpretation exists in principle, there is nothing to be said against relating Rom. 7:9 to Paul despite the contradiction to biographical reality.

This naturally does not exclude the possibility that there were elements in Paul's life that justified such an interpretation. But the pre-Christian life of Paul largely escapes our knowledge.[55] Conjectures about a "fall" of the young Paul are idle. Yet one can ask if Paul was always the fanatic for the law that he showed himself to be in the persecution of Christians.[56] Does he not speak in Gal. 1:15* of a "being set apart" from his mother's womb, which is continued in his vocation as apostle to the Gentiles? Does not the previous account of zeal for the law interrupt this continuity? It is after all unthinkable that the election from his mother's womb on had as its goal the persecution of Christians! Was there then perhaps a period before this zeal for the law which could be devalued by a nomistic zealot as a "time without the law"? Could not a member of the Qumran community have characterized the period before his entrance as a period without obedience to the law? And did there not exist from the perspective of the Pharisees people "who do not know the law" (cf. John 7:49)? Did Paul perhaps experience two changes in his life? Similar to Luther, who was first driven into the monastery, then driven out of the monastery? Or like Augustine, who first became a Manichaean, then a Christian? Or Buddha, who first sought his salvation in strict asceticism, but then in meditation? It could then be the case that one day fanaticism for the law seized possession

55. Oepke, "Probleme," is still foundational.

56. Modalsli ("Gal 2,19–21," 32) could be understood in this way: "Because of the strongly personal thrust of chapter 7, however, the idea that Paul is even speaking here of a decline that took place in his own life, from a life in childlike faith to the spiritual death of the righteousness of the law, is perhaps not entirely to be rejected." Even Josephus (*Life* 10–12) experimented successively with different faith directions. A "conversion" to zeal for the law is more probable than conjectures such as those of O. Pfister ("Entwicklung," 272), who relates Rom. 7:9 to transgressions and "impermissible fantasies" of a sexual sort, or of Deissmann (*Paulus*, 64–65), who thinks of childhood disobedience to the commandment to honor parents.

of Paul. But we can only raise questions. The sources deny us the possibility of an answer.

It is easier to answer the question about the psychic significance that the role of Adam had for Paul in looking back at his unredeemed past. It without doubt served him as a way of presenting his personal conflict with the law as a general human conflict. The conflict was thus classified and integrated into Paul's symbolic world—no longer a personal oddity, but the fate of every human being. This insight was so valuable to him that he could easily overlook the contradiction between empirical reality and interpretation.

But Paul did not stop here. In his conflict with the law, something new was contained, something to be grasped neither by reference to Adam nor by reference to timeless human structures. Paul pushes the analysis of the conflict further. The second part, in the past tense, betrays hardly any reminiscences of Adam. The point of the text, constantly emerging more clearly, is that the conflict with the law is not only a conflict between norm and drive but also the conflict between two normative orientations. In each part of Rom. 7:7ff., one can note two efforts toward correction of the "popular" confrontation of law and covetousness and of law and flesh.

The initial thesis of the first part is that the law forbids covetousness. This is corrected in two ways: first, the commandment itself awakens covetousness; second, the commandment is an instrument of sin (7:8 and 7:11).

The initial thesis of the second part is that the law is opposed to the carnal I. This also is corrected in two ways. For, first, the I is not identical to the flesh (7:18), and second, in reality two "laws" clash (7:23).

Each section contains a clear progress. The first part ends with the recognition that the law is an instrument of sin. The second part leads to the more radical insight that the law splits into two laws that combat each other. The climax of the Pauline analysis is 7:22–23: "For I delight in the law of God, in my inmost self, but I see in my members another law at war with the law of my mind and making me captive to the law of sin which dwells in my members."

Against the interpretation that the issue here is a conflict of two normative powers, one could object that the term "law" is being used here in a loose sense.[57] Paul can, after all, also designate the fact of

57. According to Käsemann (*An die Römer*, 197), the issue here is a play on the term

the clash of two laws as a *nomos* and have in mind the meaning "principle" or "rule"? Is it then a play on words? Hardly! On the contrary, the new linguistic labeling of the conflict gives it a fundamentally new interpretation. The following observations speak against a mere play on words.

First, the opposition between two aspects of the law, which is intensified after 7:22–23 to an antagonism of two laws, is foundational to the entire train of thought in Rom. 7:7ff.:

7:6:	service in the new Spirit	service in the old letter
7:22ff.:	the law of God according to the inner man	"another law" in my members
	law of my Spirit	law of sin in my members
7:25:	to serve the law of God with the Spirit	to serve the law of sin with the flesh
8:2:	the law of the Spirit of life	the law of sin and of death

Romans 7:6 is an announcement of the theme of 7:7ff. and 8:1ff. There can be no doubt that the old letter refers to the Mosaic law (2 Cor. 3:6), and that the "service in the new Spirit" is also related to the law, for the law is spiritual (Rom. 7:14) and the Spirit is the power that enables its fulfillment (Rom. 8:4). Something preestablished by the announcement of the theme can hardly be a mere play on words: the new orientation on the norm becomes a conflict of two normative systems.

Second, the association of the law with metaphors of captivity is well attested. It occurs in different nuances. According to Rom. 7:23a, the law is the party that takes one captive; according to 7:23b, it is the prison; according to Gal. 3:24, it is the jail's custodian. The law also appears as a prison in Rom. 7:6. Now, the Mosaic law is clearly meant in Rom. 7:6 and Gal. 3:23–24. It is thus impossible not to think of the Mosaic law with regard to the law that takes captive in v. 23.

Third, the association of the Mosaic law with one's "members" is also preestablished. Romans 7:7–23 is an unfolding of the thesis of 7:5: the passions of sin that are evoked by the law work in one's "members"

"law." Similar positions are held by Lietzmann (*An die Römer*, 77) and Schlier (*Der Römerbrief*, 234). According to Smend and Luz (*Gesetz*, 153 n. 173), the "other law in my members" is in no case the Mosaic law which has been perverted by sin. Cranfield (*A Critical and Exegetical Commentary*, 364) accepts a purely metaphorical use of language, in order to designate the compulsive power of sin. In my opinion, Wilckens (*Der Brief*, 90) is correct: *nomos* must "be related consistently in its various meanings to the Torah."

and lead to death. Again, there is no doubt that the Mosiac law is meant here. Here it is already brought into functional connection with the "members." On the basis of 7:5, the reader can only think of the Mosiac law in reference to the "law of sin in my members" (7:23*).

Fourth, even where Paul separates himself from the Old Testament law in his use of the term *nomos*, the association with the Mosaic law is never excluded. The law of the Gentiles replaces the Mosaic law (Rom. 2:14–15) and is presented as a "written" law—analogous to the Mosaic law and in contradiction to the conception of an *agraphos nomos*. When Paul says that he is *ennomos Christou* (under the law of Christ), he is at the same time thematizing his relationship to the Jewish law (1 Cor. 9:20–21). Even the "law of Christ" in Gal. 6:2 cannot be separated from the fulfillment of the Old Testament law in the commandment of love of Gal. 5:14. Therefore, even if one were to assume for Rom. 7:22–23 a loose and transferred meaning, the idea of the Mosaic law would still impose itself.[58]

Romans 8:2 picks up once again the two laws of 7:23. Christ has liberated us "from the law of sin and death," that is, from the killing letter of the law of Sinai (2 Cor. 3:6), in order to give us a new normative orientation through the "law of the Spirit of life," in which the law is fulfilled pneumatically. Paul speaks of this foundational change in attitude toward the norm as if it is a conflict between two normative orientations. But linguistic designations are not secondary processes. They determine how we see and evaluate a problem. Paul confers a new cognitive structure on the conflict. If his statements remain contradictory, it is to be remembered that he is entering new territory in the history of experience and behavior. The conflict he analyzes cannot be grasped according to traditional patterns of inter-pretation. It is neither a departure from the law (as, for example, in a transition from Judaism to paganism) nor a struggle with oneself about its fulfillment (within Judaism). These variants of a normative conflict are restructured by Paul into an existential conflict.

The distinction between normative and existential conflicts goes back to Hans Thomae.[59] Normative conflicts are concerned with applying an already existing system of convictions to the current situation.

58. Thus, correctly, A. von Dülmen (*Die Theologie*, 118), who does conclude to a fourfold use of the term *nomos* in Rom. 7:21ff. but holds that Paul consciously chose the ambiguous term in order to make possible association with the Mosaic law, "which as such shrouds within itself the possibility of salvation and nonsalvation."
59. H. Thomae, *Konflikt*.

Resolution of the conflict occurs by cognitively restructuring the perception of the situation and its consequences until it coheres with a dominant conviction. In normative conflicts, the general orientation of life remains undisputed. What is disputed is the course one must pursue in order to correspond to this general orientation. The situation in existential conflicts is different. Here the system of convictions is itself affected. Two different normative orientations and projections of the future stand irreconcilably opposite each other. One cannot choose between them with the aid of existing convictions. The general orientation of life must change, in order for a projection of the future coherent with one's own convictions to come into being.

Both forms of decision are historically and socially conditioned. Thomae rightly raises the question "whether in these forms of decision a historical structuring of psychic processes does not become tangible, according to which it is only in a world that has been secularized and to a large extent emancipated from both philosophical and political norms that such processes [namely, existential decisions] become visible, while previously decisions were always merely 'good' or 'bad.' . . ."[60] Would it then be an ahistorical anachronism to speak of existential decision already in antiquity? Existential decisions presuppose a pluralistic world with competing systems of norms. Or, put more cautiously, pluralistic societies require existential decisions of their members more frequently than closed societies with a unified system of values and norms. But pluralism in world views is not only a characteristic of European modernity. On the contrary, Greco-Roman antiquity (especially in late Hellenism and in the early imperial period) was the first culture with a vital pluralism in world views, in which different conceptions of human existence, philosophies of life, and systems of norms competed with one another.[61] The existence, in principle, of religious tolerance made the juxtaposition of religious cults easy to bear. One either equated the alien gods with familiar

60. Ibid., 130. Yet Thomae himself (pp. 145–46) offers Augustine as an example of an existential decision—in other words, an ancient example!

61. A. D. Nock, *Conversion*, is foundational. Nock (p. 7) distinguishes adhesion to new cults from an existential reorientation, which he finds above all in Judaism, Christianity, and philosophy. Adhesion means "having one foot on each side of the fence which was cultural and not credal. They led to an acceptance of new worships as useful supplements and not as substitutes, and they did not involve taking a new way of life in place of the old. This we may call adhesion, in contradistinction to conversion. By conversion we mean the reorientation of the soul of an individual . . . a turning which implies a consciousness that a great change is involved, that the old was wrong and the new is right."

gods or integrated them into the existing pantheon. Pluralism became problematic only when groups that raised claims to absoluteness, like Judaism and Christianity, competed with one another and appealed for adherents. Early Christianity in particular undertook missionary activity. It raised a clear claim to absoluteness. It did not limit itself to the higher class, like the philosophical schools that competed with one another, but rather addressed the man in the street. It demanded for the first time existential decisions on a broad social basis—even if conversions to philosophical schools[62] or transitions to Judaism are comparable. The historical conditions for existential decisions were present in Greco-Roman antiquity for the first time in history. Such existential decisions in no way belong to the timeless repertoire of human behavior, as existential interpretation assumed a priori. This type of human decision came about historically. It emerges clearly in Paul. Paul is a missionary of an alternative, subcultural movement, which required of each new entrant a restructuring of the entire orientation of life.

One could object that there had already been the call to repentance—by the prophets, by the Baptist, and by Jesus. Undoubtedly the evolution of existential decision, as it is present in early Christianity, begins here. But even the term "repentance" indicates that this is a matter of a radical normative decision. For, practically, repentance means return to the traditional systems of norms and values, now understood in a new way. Movements of repentance are movements of renewal that want to activate all or part of the traditional system of values. The various movements of repentance in contemporary Judaism therefore demanded in principle no existential decision in the sense of a new fundamental orientation. They remained within the biblical tradition. But the identity crisis of Judaism in this period, that is, the development of mutually competing conceptions of Jewish identity, doubtless conferred on the call to repentance the accent of an existential decision. The various conceptions in fact differed so much from one another that the decision between them could become a new existential orientation.

Early Christianity had begun at first as a renewal movement within Judaism. It became a new religion—or should we say a new form of life?—which demanded of each new member an existential decision only when it crossed the boundaries of Judaism. Whoever joined it as a Jew could perhaps be contented with reinvigorating certain elements

62. Ibid., 164–86.

of his own tradition, while allowing others to recede. But whoever joined it as a Gentile had, like Paul, to hold what he had valued as loss. Paul's historical significance consisted in the fact that he not only experienced and underwent this existential decision but that he formulated it in such a way that it became a generally valid paradigm of a psychic event that affected many.[63] For this reason he is in the right when he lets his person become visible behind his theology, or when he formulates in his theology in a generally valid fashion what stems from his own life. He was a representative person in whose individual fate a new pattern of experience and behavior showed itself. Augustine is perhaps comparable. But his conversion took place against the background of a Christian church and family influences.

We therefore understand Romans 7 as a historically conditioned cognitive restructuring of the conflict with the law. Paul first interprets it according to the model of Adam as general human destiny. In doing this, he proceeds from patterns of interpretation that are suited to normative conflicts. With increasing clarity, however, he sees behind the normative conflict an existential conflict between two fundamentally different orientations of life. Of course, this occurs tentatively. Historically, Paul was entering virgin land. It is therefore no surprise that he constantly has recourse to statements that would fit normative conflicts better. But Phil. 3:2ff. leaves no room for doubt that his turn was not a revivification of traditional values and norms.

The Role of Christ

What significance did the figure of Christ have for the restructuring of Paul's self-perception? Someone trapped in a profound conflict is no longer capable of preserving a positive self-image. He is dependent on another's taking over the role of the "self" and offering him the unconditional estimation he can no longer offer himself. The partner becomes a "mirror" of the self or, better, its representative. He intervenes in the inner dialogue in order to give a constructive direction to destructive monologues. He is thus more than a "symbolic learning model" or the object of projection; he is the mediator of a transformed self-perception.

Romans 7:7–23 can in fact be construed as an inner dialogue that

---

63. Luz (*Das Geschichtsverständnis*, 159) rightly states that "the arguments of the apostle would not be probative if what was under discussion were experiences that had affected only the individual Paul, who was after all not known in Rome, and that did not in some form or other affect other people."

leads more and more deeply into a destructive self-condemnation. The I is alone with itself. We look into the inner process of mutually accusing and defending thoughts that Paul already mentioned in 2:15. There is no prospect for improvement, for in the first part the conflict is depicted as general human fate. No one can escape the model of Adam; all are marked by him. In the second part, however, the misery is ascribed emphatically to transsubjective causes: "It is not I that cause evil," the text says, "but sin which dwells in me" (cf. 7:17*, 20*). The I is even completely relativized: "For I know that nothing good dwells within me, that is, in my flesh" (7:18). To infer from such transsubjective attributions of causality that the I which is speaking here wishes to shirk responsibility would be to misunderstand the intention of the statement.[64] With regard to causal attributions, two possibilities must be considered. They retrace behavior to either permanent or mutable factors. When the factors are mutable, there is a prospect of change for the good. But Paul is thinking of permanent factors: the sin that dwells in him is no transient guest, as even the verb "dwells" shows. Above all, however, the flesh is something that pertains to the permanent equipment of the human being. The transsubjective causal attributions are thus not efforts to shirk responsibility; they rather illumine the hopelessness of the situation.

Redemption occurs when a new partner intervenes from without in one's destructive monologue and replies to the lament "Wretched man that I am! Who will deliver me from this body of death?" (7:24). This partner brings a law of the Spirit and of life without condemning, absolutist demands; on the contrary, the partner shares the "groaning of creation" (Rom. 8:23*) over the inadequacy of the world and intercedes before God against every condemning tribunal (Rom. 8:26, 34). In Rom. 8:31–39*, a constructive inner dialogue takes the place of the destructive inner dialogue of 7:7–23. The questions are raised in a challenging manner: Who is against us? Who shall accuse God's elect? Who shall condemn? Who shall separate us from the love of God? And the answer in each case is, No one! There is no tribunal in heaven or on earth that possesses the right to drive one again into the destructive monologue at which Paul looks back in Rom 7:7ff. The inner forum before which one had lost oneself in despair is transformed into a heavenly forum (Rom. 7:7–23) in which the harshness of reality is indeed present but despair is overcome (Rom. 8:31–39).

64. For the opposite opinion, cf. Stendahl, "The Apostle Paul," esp. 211ff.

How does it come about that one can evaluate and judge oneself in an entirely new fashion? Paul gives the answer in Rom. 8:3ff. Christ appeared in the "form of sinful flesh" (8:3*) and began to dwell in believers. Christians are destined to the same form as the Son of God (8:29). They too are to be called "sons of God" (8:15, 23). But, since the resurrection, Christ lives "according to the Spirit" (Rom. 1:4). Similarly, Christians can live and exist "according to the Spirit" (Rom. 8:5ff.). Christ came into the world in order to make possible a new, pneumatic form of life. Paul had already expressed in compressed form in Gal. 4:4–7 what he says about this in Romans 8. There, as in Romans 8, we find a connection of mission and redemption, conferral of the Spirit and the cry "Abba," sonship and inheritance:

Gal. 4:4–7*	*Romans 8**
1. Mission and Redemption	
4 But when the fullness of time had come, God sent his Son, born of a woman, subject to the law,	3 God sent his Son in the form of sinful flesh and for sin and he condemned sin in the flesh,
5 that he might redeem those subject to the law, that we might achieve acceptance as sons.	4 that the justice required by the law might be fulfilled in us, who walk not according to flesh, but according to the Spirit.
2. Conferral of the Spirit and the Cry of "Abba"	
6 But because you are sons, God has sent the Spirit of his Son into our hearts, who cries, "Abba! Father!"	14 For all who are led by the Spirit of God are sons of God, 15 for you have not received the Spirit of slavery so that you would again have to fear, but you have received the Spirit of sonship, in whom we cry, "Abba! Father!"

3. Sonship and Inheritance

7 Thus you are no longer slave	16 This Spirit bears witness with our spirit that we are children of God.
but son; and if son, then also heir through God.	17 But if we are children, then we are also heirs of God and co-heirs with Christ.

Some common Christian traditions such as the mission formula and the cry of "Abba" would seem to lie at the basis of the Pauline train of thought.[65] Otherwise, it is likely a matter of a train of thought developed by Paul himself, which he had presented several times and had constantly varied and deepened. In Romans he develops it at particular length. He expands it with two thematically closed amplifications—first, with fundamental thoughts on the relationship of flesh and Spirit (8:4–13), and second, with an impressive evocation of the "groaning of creation" in 8:18–27. It cannot be a coincidence that precisely these two parts contain the decisive perspectives that lead beyond Romans 7. The organization here is chiastic. The amplification about flesh and spirit has recourse to the second part of Romans 7; the presentation of the cosmic groaning refers to the first part. We may assume that Paul carried out the expansion of the train of thought with which he was already familiar in conscious adaptation to the context.

1. In Rom. 7:14–23, Paul had already illumined the irresolvability of the conflict with the law by tracing sin back to the flesh, that is, to a factor that was constant from the perspective of unredeemed man. As an overcoming or leaving of the flesh only death was conceivable. But the appearance of Christ enabled a new view here. In Romans 8, flesh is no longer invincible to Paul. Christians no longer walk according to the flesh (8:4); they no longer even exist "according to the flesh" (8:5) and "in the flesh." Even in 7:5*, the thematic introduction to the depiction of the soteriological change in Romans 7—8, Paul was able to say in retrospect, "While we *were* in the flesh . . ." Here Paul carries out a decisive change in the causal attribution of human hopelessness. It is still attributed to the flesh but now as a changeable factor, not a constant one. The new interpretation of the human situation is made possible by the appearance of Christ. Christ appeared in the form of

---

65. Cf. von der Osten-Sacken, *Römer 8*, 144–145, 129ff.; Paulsen, *Überlieferung*, 40ff., 88ff.

the flesh, but he was a pneumatic being, who was not bound to the limits of the flesh. Death could therefore not affect him. Rather, since the resurrection, he lives "according to the Spirit of holiness" (Rom. 1:4). If it is permissible to employ a modern expression, one can say that Christ is a mutation of human existence in which the previous limits of the human condition are transcended. Paul calls the new way of life, which surpasses the carnal—that is, biological-natural—conditions of man, spirit. But he knows a creative dying with Christ that makes possible the transition to a new existence even under the conditions of this life. But all who believe in Christ are destined to this new existence; all shall be conformed to the image of the Son of God (8:29). One is no longer determined definitively by the flesh.

2. The second expansion of the train of thought that was already present in Galatians 4 is the section on the "groaning of creation." The cognitive restructuring of human self-understanding which occurs here is just as radical as that in Rom. 8:5–13. The human being appears here as someone who is no longer determined finally by the role of Adam, however much he may still suffer under the existing Adamitic being. It is rather true that "just as we have borne the image of the earthly [man], we shall also bear the image of the heavenly man" (1 Cor. 15:49*). Here Paul formulates the process that can be described in the modern psychology of religion as a change of roles on the basis of a new stock of symbolic roles in the Christian preaching. One can distance oneself from the Adamitic role because the second Adam has appeared and lets the world appear in a new light. In Rom. 5:12–21, Paul had prefaced this foundational change in roles to his discussions of the soteriological shift, before developing it in Rom. 6:1—7:6 with the aid of the symbolism of burial, change of rule, and marriage. In Romans 7 and 8 we then find the most intensive reflection on the foundational change of roles. Romans 7:7–13 interprets the conflict with the law in the light of the role of Adam, while Rom. 8:18–27 depicts the waiting for the revelation of the new role the Christians may even now ascribe to themselves. This waiting is still determined by Adam's deed. The entire creation groans under the consequences of his fall. In Christians this cosmic sigh joins the sighs of the divine Spirit, who is himself a "pledge" of overcoming Adamitic existence. The Spirit makes distancing from the role of Adam possible.

Summary. Christian preaching's stock of roles offers us a new self-understanding. We need no longer understand ourselves according to the role of Adam but can rather orient ourselves on the role of Christ and judge and assess ourselves anew in its light. The cognitive restructuring of the self-image takes place through changed causal attribution of sin. Sin is attributed to the flesh and to the one who vicariously took on flesh. In this way, a new hope of overcoming human finality and finitude become possible. One may—despite all mistakes—evaluate oneself in an unconditionally positive manner. One may understand oneself anew as son of God, who may trustfully say "Abba" to one's father.

A review of the psychological evaluation of Romans 7 and 8 shows that the change of experience and behavior depicted in the Pauline texts can be illumined from different perspectives. But a common thread also becomes visible: the decisive impulses for change in behavior and experience derive from the Christ symbolism.

Christ appears as a vicariously acting and suffering model. The aggressive power connected with the law strikes him without damaging him seriously. God condemns him, but revises the judgment. The crucified is exalted. Believers constantly reenact this event in their interior. Through this "hidden behavior" they learn to approach the demanding God without anxiety.

Christ, the symbolic model of behavior which is brought to man from without by Christian preaching, becomes according to the psychodynamic conception the catalyst of an inner transformation. As one's person of reference, Christ takes on one's negative identity. The unconscious aggressivity against the demanding God finds in him its vicarious object. It is acted out and becomes capable of reaching consciousness and subject to being treated.

But Christ does not affect one only as a model mediated from without or as a symbol arising from within; rather, he offers one a pattern of interpretation according to which one can address oneself to external and internal influences. One is not committed to the role of Adam. Christian preaching brings about a change in roles, through which one can understand oneself in an entirely new manner. Neither flesh nor sin is definitive. They can be judged and evaluated anew, so that one can achieve a realistic—yet unconditionally positive—self-image.

It is impossible to miss the fact that the past is retrospectively made conscious on the basis of the change to the positive that has already occurred. Only the overcoming of anxiety makes possible the interpretation of anxiety as anxiety before the demanding God. Only the reappropriated identity illumines the preceding conflict. Only from Christ is light shed on Adam's hopelessness.

PART FIVE

Glossolalia—Language of the Unconscious?

In the preceding chapters, it has chiefly been aspects of the unconscious which are burdensome to man that have come to speech—the possibility of unconscious antinomian impulses, the archaic severity of the killing law, the repressed conflict with the law. All these aspects may be summarized under the concept of the "forensically unconscious": one always stands as if in a court process one does not fully see through. But it throughout became clear that, for Paul, the confrontation with the unconscious brought positive things to light as well. He exhibits calm and confidence with respect to possible antinomian impulses within himself. When the veil of Moses is lifted, the killing law is transformed into a transforming light within. The conflict with the law is overcome. In the course of this, the positive aspects of the unconscious are always opened by the Spirit. The transformation of the forensic situation of accusation into confidence occurs through the vicarious intercession of the divine Spirit before the inner forum (Rom. 8:26–27). The removal of the veil lets the image of Christ shine and makes possible service of the "life-giving Spirit" (2 Cor. 3:6*). The conflict with the law is overcome in a life "according to the Spirit" (Rom. 8:2ff.). It is always the Spirit that expands human consciousness and opens new possibilities of behavior and experience. In a word, what is forensically unconscious is transformed into a pneumatic unconscious. The pneumatic person is condemned by no one (1 Cor. 2:15). He transcends the limits of human existence. In the following two chapters we want to investigate two aspects of the pneumatically unconscious: glossolalia as pneumatic speaking and "wisdom teaching" as pneumatic insight.

The interpretation of the Spirit as a power transcending normal human limits goes back to H. Gunkel, whose epoch-making work, *Die*

Wirkungen des heiligen Geistes, appeared in 1888. It contained the demonstration that the "Spirit" in early Christianity had nothing to do with the spirit of the modern world and of philosophy but was rather a power, envisioned as a fluid, that broke through the customary context of life and expressed itself in miracles and speaking in tongues. Ten years after publication of the book, Gunkel judged in retrospect as follows: "When I now go through my work again, what strikes me above all is that the pneumatic manifestations are there often described from the standpoint of an outside observer who joins the group; but it would be more correct and more profound to conceive them first as the pneumatic person himself finds them." He challenges subsequent research to recognize "that this is a matter of real psychological events, not of phrases or of superstition."[1] Gunkel thus posed the task of making glossolalia and other pneumatic manifestations intelligible in terms of a psychology of religion. Up to now, New Testament exegesis has failed in this task. Yet glossolalia would be a thankful object of analysis from the perspective of the psychology of religion; after all, even theologians opposed to psychology are quite willing to admit the necessity of psychological reflections on this subject, perhaps with the opinion that psychological analysis exposes religious phenomena but that glossolalia is among those phenomena one could abandon to psychological exposure without self-denial. After all, even Paul does not relate to it without criticism. Discomfort with psychology can here easily join discomfort with glossolalia. The following investigations are free of this attitude. Psychology serves the unprejudiced under-standing of human experience and behavior. It is not its task to condemn deviant linguistic behavior. Glossolalia must rather be ex-amined without constraints in a scientific manner; perhaps precisely the scientific investigation of glossolalia is an example that one can in this way come to substantially more benevolent and tolerant attitudes with regard to the strange phenomenon of glossolalia.

In what follows, the structure of the most important text on glossolalia—1 Corinthians 14—will first be described. Next, traditions and historical analogies to speaking in tongues will be discussed. Finally, the phenomenon of glossolalia will be analyzed with regard to the psychology of religion from three approaches. In this, we shall also have recourse to Rom. 8:18–30 as a specifically Pauline interpre-tation of pneumatic speaking.

1. Gunkel, *Die Wirkungen*, 2d ed., iv–v.

Modern analogies can also serve to illuminate Corinthian glossolalia. They have the inestimable advantage of being much more readily accessible to scientific investigation than historical phenomena. Rich linguistic, sociological, and psychological research on glossolalia has developed parallel to the new Pentecostal movement (especially in the United States). Although its results cannot serve as support for historical theses, they can serve as a heuristic starting point and as illustration. Hypotheses about glossolalia in Corinth can originate from observation of contemporary phenomena, but they must be verified exclusively on the basis of the historical sources.

Yet one should not underestimate the weight of the modern analogies. Linguistically, it is a question of the same phenomenon—a paralanguage whose expressions exhibit phonetic structure but no semantic content, at least not in the sense that one could "translate" word for word, sentence for sentence. It occurs in a religious context and is assessed controversially by insiders and outsiders. As deviant linguistic behavior it is an important group characteristic. The extent to which universal, interculturally valid human possibilities are realized in this deviant linguistic behavior is disputed. One who joins Noam Chomsky in postulating universal linguistic structures for normal linguistic behavior—despite its immense cultural variability—will have to do this all the more for glossolalia. Its form is much less variable culturally than normal linguistic behavior, even if there are, within glossolalia, traditions, special developments, and dialects. In each case there is a historical continuity from Corinthian to modern glossolalia: in most cases, modern glossolalia is determined by biblical texts. It belongs to the effective history of the New Testament, even though this effect first became visible in modern times—a phenomenon that gives pause.

Chapter 14

Text Analysis:
1 Corinthians 14

In 1 Corinthians 12—14, Paul answers an inquiry (written?) of the Corinthians on the theme of the "gifts of the Spirit" (12:1, cf. 7:1), to which prophecy, miracle working, and gnosis, among other things, belong.[1] Some people in Corinth attributed a special status to glossolalia; to them, glossolalia was a heavenly language (13:1), or a visible proof that God was present in the ecstatic speaker (14:25). Others preserved a greater distance from this phenomenon.[2] These were probably the ones who turned to Paul.

Paul replies very diplomatically. He consistently expresses a high regard for the gifts of the Spirit (cf. 12:31; 14:1), commits himself to speaking in tongues (14:18), and concludes with the warning not to suppress it (14:39); but in reality he strives to correct its high evaluation in Corinth.

In a first train of thought (1 Corinthians 12), he avoids any critical remark on speaking in tongues. He relativizes it only in a very general way, by postulating the equality of all pneumatic gifts: they all have a common origin. All go back to the same divine Spirit (12:4–11); all are dependent on one another like the members of an organism

1. Holtz ("Das Kennzeichen") surmises that the community had asked about the "pneumatics," but that Paul answers as if he had been asked about "pneumatic gifts." It is for this reason, according to Holtz, that, in 1 Corinthians 12, Paul speaks of *charismata* rather than *pneumatika*. But for Paul the two terms are synonymous (cf. 1 Cor. 12:31 and 14:1). Perhaps he chooses the term "charisms" because it is more general and because it is not connected so closely with ecstatic phenomena.

2. That a "polarization" occurred in the community owing to glossolalia (thus, Stendahl, "Glossolalia," 112) is something we must infer from, first, the question addressed to Paul; second, the mention of a impending "schism" in the body of Christ (1 Cor. 12:25), an idea foreign to the body metaphor; and third, the fact that in 14:37 Paul speaks exclusively to a group of prophets and pneumatics, but understands under the latter term only those who speak in tongues.

(12:12–26). That at this point he already has speaking in tongues in mind is evident from the three catalogues of charisms in 1 Cor. 12:8–10, 12:28, and 12:29–30: each breaks off when he has mentioned speaking in tongues (and the interpretation that accompanies it). A certain evaluation is already given implicitly by this; it becomes explicit only toward the end of the chapter, when Paul enjoins, "Strive after the greater gifts" (1 Cor. 12:31).

In chapter 12, Paul shows the equal value of all pneumatic gifts in a positive manner; in chapter 13, he demonstrates this in negative terms. All are of equally little value if they are lacking in love; when compared with love, they are worthless. Even here there is still no critical word aimed specifically against glossolalia. Rather, all the gifts of the Spirit—prophecy, glossolalia, and knowledge—stand on the same level.[3]

What Paul is aiming at becomes clear only in the next chapter. In 1 Corinthians 14, a clear hierarchy is established among the pneumatic gifts. The first critical words against glossolalia come here. It is subordinated to prophecy. Paul takes the criterion for this hierarchy from the previous chapter: love appears within the community as the will to *oikodome*, or "constructive cooperation."

Chapter 14 is carefully structured. Reflections in principle on glossolalia (14:1–25) are followed by practical instructions (14:26–36). Comparable imperatives stand at the beginning and the end: "Earnestly desire the spiritual gifts, especially that you may prophesy" (14:1) and "Earnestly desire to prophesy, and do not forbid speaking in tongues" (14:39). Here is a detailed outline of 1 Corinthians 14:[4]

> 14:1–5: Paul postulates the superiority of prophecy over glossolalia. He deduces from the criterion of *oikodome* the requirement that ecstatic speech be intelligible or that it be translated. In what follows (14:6–25), he shows in three respects the superiority of intelligible speech. It is superior when the addressees are members of the community (vv. 6–12), God (vv. 13–19), and outsiders (vv. 20–25).

---

3. In this context, 1 Corinthians 13 is necessarily pertinent and ought not be separated on the basis of literary criticism (for the opposite view, cf., most recently, Schenke and K. M. Fischer, *Einleitung* 1.93).

4. Dautzenberg (*Urchristliche Prophetie*, 226ff.) divides on the contrary into 14:1–11; 12–19; 20–25. Two points speak against this: first, the address "brothers" in 14:6, 20, and 26, which suggests a division between vv. 5 and 6; and second, the parallelism of *houtos kai humeis* in 14:9 and 14:12, which orders v. 12, like v. 9, to what precedes it. It is correct that the transition between vv. 6–12 and vv. 13–24 is fluid. The train of thought slides from a prayer for intelligibility (v. 13) to the intelligibility of prayer (v. 14).

14:6–12: The community as addressee of ecstatic speech. Different forms of intelligible speech (apocalypse, knowledge, prophecy, teaching) are opposed to glossolalia. To demonstrate their superiority, Paul offers himself as example: "If I came to you . . ." (v. 6*), but then grounds the requirement of intelligibility in a general fashion:

(*a*) Through a double metaphor (vv. 7–8). The first image, that of the flute and the harp, is directed toward clarity of speech, and the second, that of the bugle signal, is directed toward its efficacy. Both metaphors are formulated as rhetorical questions. The interpretation is appended with *houtos kai humeis*, "so with yourselves."

(*b*) The second argument makes use of the analogy between a foreign language and glossolalia (vv. 10–12). In both cases, speaker and listener stand opposite each other as "aliens." This social aspect is of particular interest to Paul. He signals his personal involvement through the use of the first-person singular. As in the double metaphor, the interpretation is appended with *houtos kai humeis*.

14:13–19: God as addressee of ecstatic speech. Various forms of prayer (petition, singing, thanksgiving) are opposed to prayer in tongues. Paul again grounds his statements through the example of his person (vv. 15, 18–19). The requirement that a prayer be intelligible cannot factually be established solely by appeal to the *oikodome*. That interhuman communication should be intelligible is evident. But the question is why communication with God should not make use of another language. Does God not understand every language, even "inexpressible groans" (cf. Rom. 8:26–27)? Paul therefore brings a new criterion into play: the requirement of human totality. The speaker should participate in prayer with spirit and mind. As a further basis, two instances are mentioned in which glossolalia appears as a form of interhuman communication:

(*a*) The case of the "outsider," who cannot reenact another's prayer in tongues and who is therefore not edified (vv. 16–17). Here Paul switches to the second-person singular.

(*b*) The model of Paul, who privately practices glossolalia more than all others but who wishes not to make use of it in the community, serves as a second argument. Here Paul returns to the first-person singular. In addition, he leaves the theme of "prayer," which is not so well suited to give emphasis to the requirement of intelligibility. He speaks of "instruction" (14:19*).[5]

5. It is now often claimed one-sidedly that glossolalia is communication with God (e.g., Stendahl, "Glossolalia," 113; Best, "The Interpretation," 46). But in 1 Corinthians 14, Paul mentions three different addressees. Is this only to emphasize the requirement of intelligibility? This requirement is evident above all with regard to human addressees.

14:20–25: The unbeliever as addressee of ecstatic speech. Paul begins anew with the address "brother" but without the transitional particle found in vv. 6 and 39. At first he offers an anthropological argument: speaking in tongues is childish behavior. Then Paul reflects on the social function of speaking in tongues:

(a) A biblical citation (Isa. 28:11) is interpreted in an appended conclusion: prophecy, not glossolalia, is a sign for unbelievers.

(b) A contrast example (vv. 23–25) is intended to support this. Glossolalia repels outsiders. But through prophecy outsiders are converted. Above all, prophecy makes possible a reliable judgment of the faith of new entrants: it exposes the secrets of the heart. Inasmuch as it does this, it is a sign for believers—namely, for the community.[6]

14:26–36: Practical regulations for community life follow the reflections in principle (vv. 1–25). They begin with a general admonition that, once again, mentions the criterion of *oikodome* (14:26). Then Paul continues with concrete community rules:

(a) In the rules on glossolalia, the instructions for speaking in tongues (v. 27) are followed by a conditional commandment of silence: without a translator, the speaker in tongues shall be silent (v. 28).

(b) The admonitions on prophecy are structured in similar fashion. The positive rules are followed by a conditional commandment of silence (v. 30) with appended reasons (vv. 31–33a).

(c) The admonitions to the women, on the contrary, follow a deviating sequence. First there is an unconditional commandment of silence (v. 34), then an instruction that limits this command of silence: the women may inquire at home (v. 35). The admonitions to the women fall formally outside the train of thought. With regard to content they stand in tension with 1 Cor. 11:2 and 14:26 and presuppose a liturgy concentrated on doctrine. They are either pre-Pauline tradition that is inserted here or later interpolation.[7]

14:37–40: Paul reinforces what has been said:

(a) By emphasizing his authority over the pneumatics. He first addresses prophets and speakers in tongues, whom he here calls *pneumatikoi* (vv. 37–38).

(b) After this, he appeals to the entire community. He summarizes the foundational part of his admonitions in 14:39, and the practical part in v. 40.

This structural analysis already gives some pointers for an analysis from the perspective of the psychology of religion. From a psycho-

---

6. On the problematic of 1 Cor. 14:20–25, cf. above, 74–80.
7. For the most recent extended treatment, cf. Dautzenberg, *Urchristliche Prophetie*, 257–73.

dynamic perspective, it is easy to attribute to glossolalia a function similar to prophecy. It is true that often both merely appear with a whole group of different charisms (cf. 14:6, 13–14, 26; also 12:8–11, 28; 13:1–3, 8), but they are directly confronted with one another in emphasized places—namely, in the admonitions framing the passage (14:1–5) and 14:37–40) and in the section on the effect of charismatic speech on outsiders (14:20–25). The difference between the two charisms lies in intelligibility. Paul writes in 14:5,

> Now I want you all to speak in tongues, but even more to prophesy. He who prophesies is greater than he who speaks in tongues, unless some one interprets, so that the church may be edified.

It is literally true that Paul says only that prophecy is of equal value to speaking in tongues when the latter is accompanied by an intelligible exegesis. The equivalence of two phenomena does not follow from their equal value. Yet this is suggested in our case, for there are also parallels between the two phenomena elsewhere. One who speaks in tongues speaks of mysteries (14:2); one who prophesies has knowledge of mysteries (13:2). One who practices glossolalia edifies oneself; whoever prophesies edifies the community. What glossolalia achieves with respect to the speaker, prophecy does with respect to others. This suggests the following conclusion. While prophecy reveals the "hidden things of the heart" in other people, glossolalia has the same function with respect to the speaker. It reveals the deep layers of the speaker's psychic life, without being able to introduce them into public communication. Our hypothesis, therefore, is that glossolalia is the language of the unconscious; prophecy and interpretation make this conscious.

But initial points of contact are also present from the standpoint of "social learning." Speaking in tongues is reinforced by social estimation and elicited by models; if one speaks, others feel themselves driven to imitation (14:27). But glossolalia does not achieve acceptance in the entire community. Although the concrete background remains obscure to us, we may formulate the hypothesis that with his position on glossolalia, Paul is intervening in a struggle for influence and prestige within the community.

Finally, from the perspective of cognitive psychology, one will direct interest toward the great significance Paul attributes to "interpretation." It is only interpretation that makes speaking in tongues a worthwhile expression of life. We must seek to reconstruct the interpretation Paul gives to speaking in tongues.

Chapter 15

Tradition Analysis:
1 Corinthians 12—14

In connection with the gifts of the Spirit, Paul reminds the Corinthians of their pagan past: "Now concerning spiritual gifts, brethren, I do not want you to be uninformed. You know that when you were heathen, you were led astray to dumb idols, however you may have been moved" (1 Cor. 12:1–2). Paul compares being moved by the Spirit to pagan religiosity. The Christians were once led astray by dumb idols (*egesthe apagomenoi*) as they are now driven by the Holy Spirit (*pneumati agesthe*, Gal. 5:18; cf. Rom. 8:14).[1] Paul himself thus suggests something that studies in the history of religions confirm: the ecstatic phenomena in early Christianity are to be seen in connection with comparable occurrences in antiquity.[2]

The analogies important for us may be divided into three groups: Bacchanalian frenzy, Platonic inspiration, and apocalyptic heavenly language. Bacchanalian frenzy is a collective phenomenon of motoric ecstasy, whereas Platonic inspiration is a matter of insights in a paranormal condition. In the case of apocalyptic heavenly language, linguistic behavior itself is transformed ecstatically. All three analogies can illuminate aspects of early Christian glossolalia.

---

1. Maly ("1.Kor 12, 1–3") denies the existence of an analogy between pagan and Christian phenomena. According to him, Paul is thinking of an opposition between slavery and freedom. In my opinion, Weiss (*Der l. Korintherbrief*, 296) is correct in saying that it is precisely the analogy that is stressed.
2. Analogies to the phenomenon of speaking in tongues are collected in Currie, " 'Speaking in Tongues.' " Most of the analogies stem from the Jewish-Christian realm and are often not identifiable precisely as glossolalia. But there are many analogies to the general phenomenon of ecstasy and ecstatic speech. These will be discussed in what follows to the extent that the pattern of interpretation and modes of behavior that are connected with them can illuminate aspects of early Christian glossolalia. Dautzenberg, "Glossolalie," is a good overview.

BACCHANALIAN FRENZY

The most forceful literary depiction of Bacchanalian frenzy is found in the *Bacchae* of Euripides (ca. 485–407 B.C.E.).[3] The Theban king Pentheus seeks to combat the Dionysian ecstasy that is rampaging among the women in his country. It has already made inroads at the royal court. His mother and grandmother, as well as the aged visionary Teiresias, have been seized by it. Only Pentheus resists the irrational flood. He has the god, who appears incognito, placed in chains, and is further strengthened in his aversion when the god miraculously frees himself and performs further wonders. Pentheus's fate is sealed when he allows himself to be persuaded to observe the unrestrained behavior camouflaged as a Maenad. The Maenads discover him and tear him to shreds in the madness that he is a predatory animal—his own mother being in the forefront. Triumphantly, she bears his head to Thebes. When the crime is exposed, the god exiles her to a distant land. The drama (1386–87) ends with the mother's hope that there "memorial is none of the thyrsus-spear! Be these unto other Bacchanals dear."[4]

The drama is a puzzle. Euripides took a skeptical stance with regard to the traditional world of the gods. Did he, in this work of his old age, nonetheless return to the archaic belief in the gods which he otherwise criticized so sharply? Or does he intend only to expose the inhumanity of religion in order to take the gods ad absurdum? The only thing certain is that he presents the hopeless situation of the human being, who seeks to assert the self against irrational powers, but precisely in doing so succumbs to them. For it is precisely Pentheus, the committed battler against driven frenzy, who is infected by this when he yields to uncontrolled fantasies of a great "slaughter"[5] among the ecstatic women (*Bacchae* 796–97) and even accepts in an externally visible way the premises of his foe by camouflaging himself in women's clothing. In this he repeats the fate of his mother, who once also was skeptical about the god. But she too is punished. She becomes the symbol of a readiness for corruption that lies unconscious within us and that can destroy even the mother-child relationship. Unconscious aggressive impulses develop in the ecstatic state and overcome deeply rooted moral inhibitions. There can be no doubt that the Bacchanalian frenzy is a breakthrough of unconscious drive dynamics. Or, more

---

3. Cf. Dodds, ed., *Euripides Bacchae*, esp. xi–l.
4. ET: Arthur S. Way, *Euripides*, vol. 3 of 4 vols. (LCL, 1912), 121.
5. ET: ibid., 67.

precisely, the Dionysian cult is the ritualization of unconscious drives and is as such also a socially recognized way of channeling them, dealing with them, and overcoming them.[6]

The saga of Pentheus is structurally comparable to the saga of the Minyades. In contrast to other women, the daughters of Minya of Orchomenos refuse to join in Dionysian ecstasy and prefer to fulfill their domestic duties, but they are punished by the god with madness and in ecstasy kill one of their children. Rejected by the other ecstatic women because of this offense, they are transformed into birds.[7]

Again it is precisely those who—according to one version of the saga, out of love for their husbands[8]—refrain from ecstatic madness who succumb in the worst way to its destructive forces. The conscious world, symbolized by the fulfillment of domestic duties, is destroyed through a rebellion of the unconscious. We know from Plutarch how little such frenzy was a purely literary motif. Even in Plutarch's time, a feast of Dionysus was celebrated in Boötihian Orchomenos, the city of Minya, during which a priest once killed with a sword one of the women of the race of Minyades.[9] The feelings of anxiety with regard to forces of the irrational, which burden the whole society, are here symbolically repressed. In the one woman, the readiness of all to degenerate is "killed." But significantly, the victim is one of those who have closed themselves to the ritualized ecstasy. Resistance to the irrational powers is more dangerous than an arrangement with them.[10]

Even antiquity had a clear sense of the appalling side of Dionysian ecstasy. Among other things, the Bacchanalian scandal in Rome (185

6. This interpretation of the cult of Dionysus is based on Dodds, *The Greeks and the Irrational*, 76–80, 270–80. Early Dionysian ritual "purged the individual of . . . infectious irrational impulses . . . by providing them with a ritual outlet" (p. 76). But release does not free one from the pressure of drives. The Dionysian myths constantly tell of punishment of crimes committed while in Bacchanalian frenzy. It was necessary to warn against them.

7. The saga is given here according to Aelian (*Varia Historica* 3.42). The women kill the child, as they mistake the child for a fawn. According to Plutarch (*Moralia* 299E–F), on the contrary, the women cast lots for the child who is to be killed. Ovid (*Metamorphoses* 4.1–40, 390–415) omits the motif of infanticide entirely. The saga belongs to the feast of Agronia. On its psychological interpretation, cf. Burkert, *Homo necans*, 194ff.

8. Thus in the version of Aelian (*Varia Historica* 3.42).

9. Plutarch *Moralia* 299E–F. The custom said only that a woman could be killed. But this usually did not happen in Plutarch's day. When a priest did in fact kill a woman, this led to withdrawing the priesthood from the priest's family.

10. The myth of the Proitides is also comparable. The three daughters of Proitos despise the cult of Dionysus and are therefore struck with madness and kill their children. Melampus heals them of their madness. Yet in the process one of the women meets her death (Apollodorus 2.2).

B.C.E.) shows this. The cult of Dionysus, newly introduced from the East, had in Rome soon opened itself to males and had led, if we may believe Livy's report (39.13), to excesses of a sexual and aggressive nature:

> From the time that the rites were performed in common, men mingling with women and the freedom of darkness added, no form of crime no sort of wrong-doing was left untried. There were more lustful practices among men with one another than among women. If any of them were disinclined to endure abuse or reluctant to commit crime, they were sacrificed as victims. To consider nothing wrong . . . was the highest form of religious devotion among them. Men, as if insane, with fanatical tossings of their bodies, would utter prophecies. Matrons in the dress of Bacchants, with dishevelled hair and carrying blazing torches, would run down to the Tiber, and plunging their torches in the water (because they contained live sulphur mixed with calcium) would bring them out still burning.[11]

Of course, one will have to ask critically how much these statements of the witness Hispala before the court exaggerate. Yet the tendency is clear. The identity of sex roles is dissolved, the overcoming of moral inhibitions is experienced as liberating, and ecstasy is experienced as being gifted with prophetic power. The Senate prohibited the mysteries.[12] The first attempt to introduce in Rome a ritualization of the unconscious readiness for degeneration had failed. The readiness for degeneration had indeed been strongly stimulated, but its social control had failed in the new environment. At one time, the social sanctions had worked.

Although the cult of Dionysus was ancient, it won significance only over the course of time. The aristocratic society of the Homeric epics hardly took notice of it.[13] Dionysus did not belong to the Olympic gods of the ruling class but to the chthonic gods of the peasant subjects,[14] quite apart from the fact that his cult was a foreign import (from Thrace or Phrygia). The career of this god requires all the more explanation for this reason: a god of the underclass is accepted by the whole of society, despite initial resistance.[15] E. R. Dodds's explanation

---

11. ET: Evan T. Sage, *Livy*, vol. 11 of 13 vols. (LCL, 1936), 255.
12. Dessau, *Inscriptiones Latinae Selectae*, no. 18.
13. But cf. *Iliad* 6.130ff.
14. Cf. Guthrie, *The Greeks*, 34–35, 301–4.
15. The motif of resistance is found in several sagas of Dionysus, in the myths of the Proitides, the Minyades, and Pentheus, and also in Homer (*Iliad* 6.130ff.). Is

is still worth considering.[16] The more the structuring of society proceeded according to rules, the more societal norms were interiorized. In other words, the more an outer-directed culture of shame became a culture of guilt, so much the greater must the need for liberation from the burden of social norming have become. Dionysus may originally have been a nature god; now he became a social god in whom the society brought to expression and dealt with its antinomian impulses—everything that we experience within ourselves as "nature," although in its naturalness it is always socially marked. In the Hellenistic age Dionysus was a beloved god.[17] His cult gradually changed. In the second century B.C.E., we find in Athens a Dionysian cultic group that is distinguished by strict discipline and order.[18] The ecstatic cult is petrified. But the need for ecstatic liberation from the pressure of social norming had not lessened. What would be more likely than that new religions had entered upon the role of the Dionysian cult? Why should not early Christianity offer what Dionysus had lost in momentum?

The ecstatic phenomena in the Corinthian community cannot be derived genetically from the cult of Dionysus. But the two religious manifestations have comparable functions from the viewpoint of social psychology.[19] In both instances, a new cult makes missionary advances. In both instances, ecstasy is an important element of the new movement. There are prophetic gifts, a vague indication that the identity of sex roles is being dissolved (1 Cor. 11:2–16), and the liberating experience of distancing from social and religious rules: "All things are permitted!" (1 Cor. 6:12*). Extraordinary linguistic utterances play a role in each case, even if there was no glossolalia in the cult of Dionysus.[20] But it

---

resistance to the foreign cult reflected in this? Cf. Nilsson, *Geschichte* 1:565, 611–12. Are social tensions, and also processes of integration, reflected in this? Cf. the sociological analysis of the motif of resistance in McGinty, "Dionysos's Revenge."

16. Dodds, *The Greeks and the Irrational*, 76–80. On the transition from a "shame-culture" to a "guilt-culture," cf. pp. 28–63. In this transition help was received from two parties—Apollo and Dionysus. "Each ministered in his own way to the anxieties characteristic of a guilt-culture. Apollo promised security. . . . Dionysus offered freedom" (p. 76).

17. Cf. the survey in Köster, *Einführung*, 185–89.

18. Dittenberger, *Sylloge Inscriptionum Graecarum*, 1109.

19. Thus Hengel, *Der Sohn Gottes*, 48–49 n. 56: "Since in the imperial age the Dionysian Thiasoi had largely become traditional civil associations . . . in which ecstatic experience receded, people sought such experiences in new cults such as early Christianity." Hengel considers the Bacchanalian scandal in Rome to be the closest parallel to Corinthian enthusiasm.

20. It was not for nothing that Dionysus had the sobriquet *ho Iakchos*, "the screamer" (e.g., Euripides *Bacchae* 725) and *ho Bromios*, "the noisemaker" (ibid., 375, 411, and

is above all noteworthy that both Bacchanalian ecstasy and the pneumatic doings in Corinth were manifestations of a collective ecstasy. "If, therefore, the *whole* church assembles and *all* speak in tongues, and outsiders or unbelievers enter, will they not say that you are mad [*mainesthe*]?" (1 Cor. 14:23*). Admittedly, Paul is only depicting a hypothetical case. In fact, all did not speak in tongues (1 Cor. 14:30). But there must have been tendencies in the direction of an uncontrolled collective ecstasy (14:27). In Greece, the closest analogy to this would have been the Dionysian cult.[21] An outsider would involuntarily have had to ascribe to the Christians a ritual *mania*. And Paul is well aware of this. For this reason he insists on restricting states of collective ecstasy, in order to create a hearing for individual pneumatic speakers.

In conclusion, reference should be made to some aspects of Bacchanalian frenzy that have to do with the psychology of religion. On the one hand, this frenzy is the breakthrough and ritualization of an irrational dynamic of drives. Precisely because this interpretation is so plausible, let it be stressed that the modes of conduct in which this dynamism of drives expresses itself are socially learned and based on preestablished roles of conduct that spread through imitation. As strange as it may sound, even ecstasies occur in fads and can be positively or negatively influenced by social reinforcers; it is even true that without mutual reinforcement of ecstatic conduct in the Bacchanalian group, the paranormal experience would not even be conceivable. For this reason, Dionysus is not simply a cipher for socially reinforced paranormal states.[22] He has a relationship to reality. Paranormal states afford a view of unusual aspects of reality. Dionysus symbolizes captivation by the ambivalence of destructive and creative force in nature and society. Yet this relationship to an "objective" reality is not automatically given with ecstatic behavior. It must rather be stressed that only specific cognitive interpretations of reality confer on Dionysian captivation a relation to objective reality. Only interpretations confer stability on the experience. Only they make a psychic state an answer to a reality.

---

elsewhere). The Bacchanalian cry *euoi, euoi,* was perceived as a Phrygian sound (ibid. 156). Prophecies were expressed in madness (ibid., 286–89). When Livy (39.8) writes "viros, velut mente capta, cum iactatione fanatica corporis vaticinari," this hardly points toward clearly articulated expressions. But none of this was speaking in tongues.

21. On the relatedness of Dionysian and Corinthian ecstasy, cf. Delling, *Der Gottesdienst*, 45–47.

22. Cf. the interesting study of McGinty (*Interpretation*), who rightly stresses the need for an interpretation that does justice to the various aspects.

PLATONIC INSPIRATION

If Paul prefers individual forms of ecstasy to collective frenzy, he stands near the tradition of the Platonic doctrine of inspiration.[23] Plato once distinguished four types of divine madness (as distinguished from pathological madness): the prophetic madness that Apollo confers; the cultic madness of Dionysus; the poetic madness of the Muses; and the erotic madness produced by Eros and Aphrodite.[24] According to *Phaedrus* 265A, all forms of divine madness are caused by a "divine release from the customary habits."[25] Even antiquity, in other words, distinguished between Dionysian ecstasy and other forms of inspiration, which we can group together here since their result is always a linguistic utterance—an oracle, a poem, a thought! The models of inspiration are women—above all, the Delphic Pythia, then the priestesses of Dodona and the Sibyl.[26]

In what follows we can concentrate on the question of the extent to which the self-understanding of Platonic inspiration contains indications that creative impulses emerge from unconscious depths within human beings. The question may be made more precise. It is constantly said that prophets, poets, and philosophers do not know what they say in the state of inspiration. Is this theme of ignorance an indication that inspiration surfaces from the unconscious? Are interpretations from the viewpoint of learning theory therefore out of place? Is what is traced back to inspiration precisely what one cannot learn (through conscious effort)?

The motif of ignorance occurs first in Socrates's *Apology*. Socrates has received from the Delphic oracle the message that he is the wisest of all men. In his conversations with other wise men he tests the truth of this saying. He constantly comes to the conclusion that the others know as little as he. But in addition he knows that he knows nothing, and is in this sense wiser than all others—wiser than statesmen, poets, and handworkers. The ignorance of the poets is brought into connection with the ecstatic state of inspiration. Socrates (*Apology* 22B–C) comes to realize

> that what they composed they composed not by wisdom, but by nature
> and because they were inspired, like the prophets and givers of oracles;

23. On the following, cf. F. Pfister, "Ekstase"; Oepke, s.v. *ekstasis*; Dodds, *The Greeks and the Irrational*, 64–101, 207–35. Specifically on Plato, cf. Gundert, "Enthusiasmos."
24. *Phaedrus* 265B.
25. ET: Harold N. Fowler, *Plato*, vol. 1 of 10 vols. (LCL, 1914), 351.
26. *Phaedrus* 244A.

for these also say many fine things, but they know none of the things they say [*isasin de ouden hon legousi*].[27]

To Socrates, ignorance is a defect. There is not yet much to note as far as a positive evaluation of inspiration is concerned.[28] But the motif of ignorance is assessed much more positively as early as *Ion* 533D–35A. The poet could not compose

> until he has been inspired and put out of his senses [*ekphron*], and his mind is no longer in him [*ho nous meketi en auto ene*]: every man, whilst he retains possession of that, is powerless to indite a verse or chant an oracle.[29]

This has a positive side. According to *Ion* 534C–D, God deprives the poets of reason in order to make the listeners certain

> that it is not they who utter these words of great price, when they are out of their wits, but that it is God himself who speaks and addresses us through them.[30]

A paradoxical connection exists between one's ignorance and one's being filled by God. The "enthusiasm" now no longer establishes one's ignorance as something to be evaluated negatively, as in Socrates; rather, one's "ignorance" in an ecstatic state establishes that one is filled by God. According to *Ion* 534E, in order to show that the poets are spokesmen of the deity, "the god of set purpose sang the finest of songs through the meanest of poets."[31] The same idea occurs in the *Meno* (99C–D). Here, against the Socratic teaching that good conduct rests on knowledge, Plato asserts that virtue is a divine gift and that it is exercised unknowingly:

> Then we shall be right in calling those divine of whom we spoke just now as soothsayers and prophets and all of the poetic turn; and especially we can say of the statesmen that they are divine and enraptured, as

27. ET: Fowler, *Plato* 1:85.
28. This devaluation of ignorance is even clearer in Xenophon (*Memorabilia* 3.9.6): ". . . but not to know yourself, and to assume and think that you know what you do not, he put next to Madness" (ET: E. C. Marchant, *Xenophon: Memorabilia and Oeconomicus* [LCL, 1923], 225, 227). We are here still far from the conception of a divinely given madness, whose divine origin is confirmed by human ignorance.
29. ET: W. R. M. Lamb, *Plato*, vol. 3 (LCL, 1925), 423.
30. ET: ibid., 423.
31. ET: ibid., 425. This paradox is reminiscent of the "treasure in earthen vessels" in 2 Cor. 4:7.

being inspired and possessed of God when they succeed in speaking many great things, while knowing nought of what they say.[32]

One would be inclined to assume that at least philosophers know what they do and say. But in the *Phaedrus* (250A), Plato casts doubt on this too. Those seized by the philosophical *eros* fall into a divine madness when they are overcome by the remembrance of the preexistent world of ideas and by longing for this world:

> Few then are left which retain an adequate recollection of them; but these when they see here any likeness of the things of that other world, are stricken with amazement and can no longer control themselves; but they do not *understand* their condition because they do not clearly perceive.[33]

But Plato would not have been a philosopher had he not insisted in principle on a rational appropriation of what was experienced in ecstasy. He therefore (*Timaeus* 72A–B) demands an interpretation of what is said in ecstasy, whether it be by the ecstatic person who has in the meantime again become sober or by someone else:

> But it is not the task of him who has been in a state of frenzy, and still continues therein, to judge the apparitions and voices seen or uttered by himself; for it was well said of old that to do and to know one's own and oneself belongs only to him who is sound of mind. Wherefore also it is customary to set the tribe of prophets [*propheton*] to pass judgment upon these inspired divinations; and they, indeed, themselves are named "diviners" [*manteis*] by certain who are wholly ignorant of the truth that they are not diviners [*manteis*] but interpreters [*hupokritai*] of the mysterious voice and apparition, for whom the most fitting name would be "prophets of things divined" [*prophetai de manteuomenon*].[34]

Here Plato probably has in view the practice at Delphi, where prophets or poets interpreted the oracle's unintelligible statements.[35] For Plato, such interpretation stands on the same level as the interpretation of dreams.[36] If we recognize that the interpretation of dreams has the effect of making unconscious content conscious, then we can surmise the same about the interpreters of ecstatic expressions.

Hellenistic Judaism accepted the doctrine of inspiration and applied

32. ET: W. R. M. Lamb, *Plato*, vol. 4 (LCL, 1924), 369.
33. ET: Fowler, *Plato* 1:483, 485. My emphasis.
34. ET: R. G. Bury, *Plato*, vol. 7 (LCL, 1929), 187, 189.
35. On Plato's views of manticism and prophecy, cf. Fascher, *PROPHETES*, 66–70.
36. Cf. *Timaeus* 71E.

it to the Old Testament prophets. Recourse to Plato is unmistakable in Philo.[37] In Philo, the more transcendent God is over the entire world—including Plato's world of ideas—so much the more is being filled ecstatically by God irrational, strange, and distant from normal experience. This is reflected in a passage from *Who Is the Heir* (263–65) which takes as its point of departure a reference to Moses in Gen. 15:12:

> Admirably then does he describe the inspired when he says "about sunset there fell on him an ecstasy." . . . "Sun" is his name under a figure for our mind. . . . So while the radiance of the mind [*nous*] is still all around us, when it pours as it were a noonday beam into the whole soul, we are self-contained, not possessed. But when it comes to its setting, naturally ecstasy and divine possession and madness fall upon us. For when the light of God shines, the human light sets; when the divine light sets, the human dawns and rises. This is what regularly befalls the fellowship of the prophets. The mind is evicted at the arrival of the divine Spirit [*exoikizetai men gar en hemin ho nous kata ten tou Theou pneumatos aphesin*], but when that departs the mind returns to its tenancy. Mortal and immortal may not share the same home. And therefore the setting of reason and the darkness which surrounds it produce ecstasy and inspired frenzy.[38]

The radicalization of the Platonic idea of inspiration could be illustrated by reference to the symbol of the sun. In Plato, the sun is the symbol of the idea of the good, of the deity itself.[39] The path of the philosopher leads from the dark shadows of the cave to the clarity of light. But in Philo, the sun can be the symbol of human reason.[40] Darkness must rule for the deity to make entrance into the soul. Apart from this, the two have the same basic ideas. Both emphasize the replacement of the I (of reason) by another subject. The motif of ignorance occurs in Philo (*Special Laws* 4.49) as it does in Plato:

> For no pronouncement of a prophet is ever his own; he is an interpreter prompted by Another in all his utterances, when knowing not [*en agnoia*] what he does he is filled with inspiration, as the reason withdraws and surrenders the citadel of the soul to a new visitor and tenant, the Divine

37. Cf. esp. *Who Is the Heir* 68–70; *On the Creation* 71. On the general characterization of Philonic ecstasy, cf. Bousset, *Die Religion*, 449.
38. ET: F. H. Colson and G. H. Whitaker, *Philo*, vol. 4 of 10 vols. (LCL, 1932), 417, 419.
39. *Republic* 508A–509B.
40. Yet the sun can also be a symbol of God, who probes everything; cf. *On Dreams* 1.90.

Spirit which plays upon the vocal organism and dictates words which clearly express its prophetic message.[41]

Philo also emphasizes in another text (*Special Laws* 1.65) that "he that is truly under the control of divine inspiration has no power of apprehension when he speaks."[42] He is a passive organ of an alien will.[43] His body is in a state of agitation.[44] He has no power over himself. Being determined by an alien power can reach the point of overriding a conscious intention. In *Moses* 1.274, Philo illustrates this by Balak, who has to prophesy good to the Israelites against his will. The angel tells him,

> I shall prompt the needful words without your mind's consent, and direct your organs of speech as justice and convenience require. I shall guide the reins of speech, and, though you understand it not, employ your tongue for each prophetic utterance.[45]

Josephus describes the inspiration of Balak in similar terms. The Spirit of God speaks through Balak,[46] but the prophet is not conscious of his words (*ouden hemon eidoton*).[47]

The Platonic-Philonic tradition of inspiration was taken over by the ancient church from Hellenistic Judaism. The prophets were considered the instrument of God,[48] the flute[49] or harp[50] of the divine power. According to Epiphanius, Montanus sees man in complete passivity when the Spirit speaks through him:

> Behold, man is like a lyre, and I hasten by like a plectrum. Man sleeps

41. ET: F. H. Colson, *Philo*, vol. 8 (LCL, 1939), 37, 39.
42. ET: F. H. Colson, *Philo*, vol. 7 (LCL, 1937), 137.
43. The prophet says nothing of his own; cf. *Special Laws* 1.65; *Who Is the Heir* 259; *On Rewards and Punishments* 55; *Moses* 1.281, 286.
44. Cf. *On Drunkenness* 147: "For with the God-possessed not only is the soul wont to be stirred and goaded as it were into ecstasy but the body also is flushed and fiery, warmed by the overflowing joy within which passes on the sensation to the outer man, and thus many of the foolish are deceived and suppose that the sober are drunk" (ET: F. H. Colson and G. H. Whitaker, *Philo*, vol. 3 [LCL, 1930], 395, 397). On the theme of "sober intoxication," cf. Lewy, *Sobria ebrietas*.
45. ET: F. H. Colson, *Philo*, vol. 6 (LCL, 1935), 417.
46. The *pneuma Theou* is considered the divine power in the prophet in Philo also (*Who Is the Heir* 265, *Moses* 1.175, 201, 277). The prophet is even considered divinized (*Questions and Answers on Exodus* 2.29).
47. *Jewish Antiquities* 4.119.
48. Theophilus *Ad Autylochum* 2.9.
49. Athenagoras *Apology* 9.
50. Hippolytus *The Antichrist* 2.

and I watch. Behold, it is the Lord who arouses the hearts of men and gives to man a [new] heart.[51]

But precisely with respect to the theme in which we are interested, that of ignorance, there is a decisive change.[52] In the confrontation with Montanist prophecy, it becomes the criterion between true and false prophecy. While one's "ignorance" was once a proof of one's having been seized by a god, in Christianity it becomes a sign of demonic possession, as Origen (*Contra Celsum* 7.3) clearly states:

> It is not the work of a divine spirit to lead the alleged prophetess into a state of ecstasy and frenzy so that she loses possession of her consciousness. The person inspired by the divine spirit . . . ought to possess the clearest vision at the very time when the deity is in communion with him.[53]

Is this new development only a consequence of anti-Montanist polemic? Or did tendencies that were previously present become visible in the course of this polemic? This question will concern us later.

At this stage, a quick look at Paul suffices to attest the presence of the Platonic tradition of inspiration. The opposition of *pneuma* and *nous* derives from this tradition. For Paul, as for the Corinthians, ecstatic speech is talking without *nous* (1 Cor. 14:14–15), speech that is dependent upon interpretation. The theme of ignorance does not occur in 1 Corinthians 11—14, although it appears constantly in the tradition. Yet, as Rom. 8:26–27* shows, Paul is familiar with the tradition. Christians moved by the Spirit do not know how to pray as they ought. The divine Spirit therefore intercedes for them, "with inexpressible sighs."

From the perspective of the psychology of religion, the Platonic tradition of inspiration is instructive in many respects. The constantly recurring theme of ignorance permits the conjecture that unconscious contents break through in ecstasy. Yet it would be premature to underestimate the influence of social learning in favor of such psychodynamic interpretation. As the following text (Longinus, *On the Sublime*

51. *Refutation of All the Heresies* 48.4.1.
52. The motif of ignorance is found in Christian and pagan authors of the second and third centuries. Cf. Tertullian (*De Anima* 21); Aelius Aristides (*In Defence of Oratory* 43). After the process of revelation, the prophetesses in Dodona know nothing of what they had said: husteron ouden hon eipon isasin. Aristides then generalizes this observation to all divinely inspired predictions.
53. ET: Chadwick, *Origen: Contra Celsum*, 397.

13.2) makes clear, the power of models is especially unmistakable in
poetic inspiration:

> For many men are carried away by the spirit of others as if inspired,
> just as it is related of the Pythian priestess when she approaches the
> tripod, where there is a rift in the ground which (they say) exhales
> divine vapour. By heavenly power thus communicated she is impregnated
> and straightway delivers oracles in virtue of the afflatus. Similarly from
> the great natures of the men of old there are borne in upon the souls of
> those who emulate them (as from sacred caves) what we may describe
> as *effluences*, so that even those who seem little likely to be possessed are
> thereby inspired and succumb to the spell of the others' greatness.[54]

Again we encounter the phenomenon of an "ecstasy according to
pattern." But even this does not exhaust the subject. The idea of
inspiration by divine spirit occurs in antiquity in very different
frameworks of interpretation. Whether one utters prophecies in ecstasy,
achieves a vision of the world of ideas, is incited to poetic works, or
participates in the language of angels is not an interpretation added
secondarily to the psychic event but rather a cognitive framework that
determines human experience and behavior from the start.

The Platonic tradition of interpretation is instructive precisely for
illuminating the cognitive aspect of early Christian ecstasy. The
reactions that Paul anticipates from outsiders can be explained from
the Dionysian tradition of collective ecstasy. The Platonic tradition of
interpretation, on the contrary, is able to illumine the self-understanding
of early Christian speakers in tongues. Yet essential characteristics of
glossolalia are not yet ordered historically by this. A decisive difference
to Platonic inspiration consists in the fact that Platonic inspiration
leads to intelligible expressions, whereas glossolalia is unintelligible.

APOCALYPTIC HEAVENLY LANGUAGE

An analogy to the linguistic phenomenon of glossolalia is first found
in Jewish apocalyptic conceptions of a heavenly language which is not
accessible to human beings. In the Slavonic version of *Enoch* (*2 Enoch*

---

54. ET: Roberts, *Longinus on the Sublime*, 81. Similarly, Plato *Laws* 719C. Like the
Muse on the tripod, the poet is beside himself, "and since his art consists in imitation,
he is compelled often to contradict himself, when he creates characters of contradictory
moods; and he knows not which of these contradictory utterances is true" (ET: R. G.
Bury, *Plato*, vol. 9 [LCL, 1926], 305). Here too inspiration and mimesis (though not as
the imitation of models) are connected.

19.6; cf. *2 Enoch* 17), Enoch is transposed into heaven, where he hears the song of the angels, "having but one voice and singing in unison. And their song is not to be reported."[55] Paul knows comparable traditions. He was caught up into the third heaven and there heard *arreta rhemata* (inexpressible words; 2 Cor. 12:4). To him, glossolalia is the tongue of angels (1 Cor. 13:1). Elsewhere too, early Christianity knows something of heavenly language. In the Apocalypse of John, there resounds in heaven a "new song" that no one can learn except those who have practiced strict sexual asceticism on earth (Rev. 14:3).

In the majority of references, the issue is indeed only a passive listening to an unintelligible heavenly language. 1 Corinthians 13:1 is an exception. In the *Testament of Job*, however, we find the desired reference that those in an ecstatic state speak this heavenly language even on earth. Before his death, Job bequeaths to his daughters a miraculous belt. Job had been cured by it (47.6–8), and it has prophetic power (47.9). When the daughters put it on, it transforms their heart and enables them to speak in a heavenly tongue (48.1–3):

> Thus, when the one called Hemera arose, she wrapped around her own string just as her father said. And she took on another heart—no longer minded toward earthly things—but she spoke ecstatically in the angelic dialect, sending up a hymn to God in accord with the hymnic style of the angels. And as she spoke ecstatically, she allowed "The Spirit" to be inscribed on her garment.[56]

The other two daughters are also transformed ecstatically; in the language of the "archons" (49.2) and the "cherubim" (50.2), they extol the work of the heavens and the glory of the heavenly powers. Here too there are, then, different "kinds of tongues" (1 Cor. 12:10). And here too—just as in 1 Corinthians 14—there follows an interpretation in the presence of the Holy Spirit (51.3–4).

There are further analogies between Corinthian glossolalia and the apocalyptic heavenly language in the *Testament of Job*. In Corinth too the angels were known to be near in the liturgy (1 Cor. 11:10). The relationship to them was influenced by a piece of clothing—in Corinth, by women's headcovering; in the *Testament of Job*, by a miraculous belt. In both instances, women play a special role. In both cases paralinguistic occurrences are conceived as "angelic language." No genealogy can be deduced from such analogies. The external presup-

55. ET: F. I. Andersen, *The Old Testament Pseudepigrapha*, ed. Charlesworth, 1:134.
56. ET: R. P. Spittler, ibid., 1:865–66.

positions necessary for this are lacking. The *Testament of Job* can be neither dated nor located with certitude.[57] Language and style point more toward the post–New Testament period. Whether there were manifestations of glossolalia within Judaism prior to early Christianity escapes our knowledge.[58]

Yet the *Testament of Job* can be assessed as a factual parallel. In this respect it gives clear indications that the heavenly language is spoken in a transformed psychic state. Job's daughters receive a new "heart." References to unconscious processes, however, are lacking. Only Paul alludes to these. Whether his rapture occurred "in the body or out of the body I do not know, God knows" (2 Cor. 12:2–3). The heavenly language leads into a realm that everyday human consciousness does not penetrate but that the omniscient God probes. He knows more about the human state than human beings themselves know. This combination of a human limit to consciousness and divine omniscience is a decisive presupposition in the history of religion for the uncovering of the unconscious.

While some things thus speak in favor of a psychodynamic conception of the "heavenly language" as the language of the unconscious, there are also points of departure for an approach from learning theory. The heavenly language is tied to a material stimulus, the miraculous belt. It understands itself as imitation of the language of angels, but it is also imitation in a much more proximate sense: one daughter imitates the other.

Summary. The Dionysian tradition explains possible patterns of interpretation for outsiders of tendencies toward collective ecstasy in Corinth. The social aspect of glossolalia is especially addressed here. The Platonic tradition of inspiration illumines the self-understanding of those who speak in tongues: their speaking is an expression of the divine Spirit, which excludes human reason. Fundamental anthropological aspects of ecstasy are reflected on here. The tradition of an apocalyptic heavenly language, on the other hand, is able to shed light

---

57. On these questions, cf. Schaller, *Das Testament Hiobs*, 309–12.

58. Harrisville ("Speaking in Tongues") believes that he can establish that the concept of "speaking in tongues" goes back to the Qumran community and that glossolalia was probably already practiced there. But the correspondence of the citation of Isa. 28:11 in 1QIsa[a] with 1 Cor. 14:21 and Aquila is far too meager a basis for this, especially since in 1QH 2.18 and 4.16, one sees that Isa. 28:11 is cited in a manner similar to the Septuagint and related to false prophets. On this problem, cf. Betz, "Zungenreden."

on the linguistic phenomenon of glossolalia: the unintelligible language is the language of angels.

Indications that unconscious processes come to expression in ecstatic speaking were found in all three areas of tradition. The motif of ignorance was found everywhere. Crimes committed during Bacchanalian frenzy occur without knowledge (i.e., without conscious direction and under the influence of distorted perception). Prophets, poets, and philosophers do not know what happens to them during inspiration; they are dependent on subsequent interpretation. Apocalyptic heavenly language presupposes a transformed heart. Something that escapes our everyday consciousness always comes to light, whether it be archaic tendencies toward degeneration or heavenly bliss. But it would be premature to interpret ecstatic phenomena for this reason exclusively from the perspective of psychodynamic approaches. We saw rather that ecstasy follows patterns that are learned socially. It occurs according to a model. What is decisive is that ecstatic states have entirely different significance depending on their interpretation. They always occur in an interpreted world.

It is now our task to discuss the phenomenon of glossolalia systematically on the basis of the three approaches to the psychology of religion we have sketched: as learned behavior, as the language of the unconscious, and as interpreted event.

Chapter 16

Psychological Analysis:
1 Corinthians 12—14

Aspects of Glossolalia in
Learning Theory

Glossolalia is socially learned behavior, which is acquired upon entrance to a new religious community.[1] From the perspective of learning theory we must raise the questions, Which stimuli, reinforcers, and models evoke glossolalic behavior? and, Which ones restrict it? In the Corinthian situation, three factors come into question as determinative of behavior: Paul, the non-Christian environment, and groups formed within the community. In what follows, all three factors will be studied with regard to their social-psychological significance for glossolalia.

Paul as Model?

Paul's Corinthian correspondence is in itself a valuable document on influencing behavior. In 1 Corinthians 12—14, Paul wishes to restrict speaking in tongues. His central problem is not glossolalia itself but a system of social reinforcement, developing in Corinth, that attributes exaggerated value to glossolalia and thus requires this behavior more than is appropriate.

Paul first attempts to influence the stimuli of glossolalic behavior.

---

1. According to Samarin ("Glossolalia"), glossolalia, on the one hand, cannot be learned like a foreign language. "But in another sense there is learning; there must be, because the acquisition is generally associated with becoming a member of a social group with its own pattern of behaviour and values" (pp. 60–61). Samarin accents the direct stimulation of behavior by commands and encouragement. Holm ("Das Zungenreden," esp. 234–38) stresses the significance of symbolic models for learning to speak in tongues; it is stimulated and reinforced by biblical texts. Kildahl (*The Psychology*, 41, 45, 50) emphasizes the significance of real models. Glossolalia almost always develops in dependence on an authoritative person of reference.

He associates them with the "dumb idols" that also evoke ecstatic behavior in paganism (1 Cor. 12:2). Not only the Spirit but also demons can cause ecstatic speech. This brings into disrepute all stimuli of ecstatic speaking. What stimuli were concretely operative escapes our knowledge. Yet Paul mentions one example—women's headcovering. According to 1 Cor. 11:2ff., removal of the headcovering is a stimulus to prayer and prophecy. Paul suspects demonic powers here; the headcovering is thought to serve as a "power" to protect the woman from demonic angels. But if the woman who prays and prophesies is open to demonic powers, who can be sure that the Spirit of God and not a demon is speaking in her? We see how Paul reinterprets existing stimuli to ecstatic behavior through more or less intelligible association.

But Paul's chief goal is to reduce through argumentation the social reinforcement of glossolalia. To this end he pursues two strategies. First, he introduces a clear hierarchy. Prophecy is superior to glossolalia, but love surpasses all charismatic gifts. In this way glossolalia is relativized but also integrated into the community. The second proposal stands in tension to this. It amounts to privatization of glossolalia. Glossolalia is without constructive value in the community, however worthwhile it may be for the individual (1 Cor. 14:4, 19). It should therefore be excluded as much as possible from community life. Here Paul has recourse to a model of problem solving that he had also applied elsewhere in 1 Corinthians. If problems that burden the common life of different groups in the community occur, he transposes them to the private realm of individual members of the community. Thus, the rich are to eat at home, so that there are no tensions between them and the poor at the Lord's Supper (1 Cor. 11:34). Or they may with good conscience participate in private meals with flesh that has been sacrificed (1 Cor. 10:23ff.); only public meals in the temple are problematic (1 Cor. 8:7–13). Something similar holds for speaking in tongues. Individuals can be as active as they wish in this regard. But in the private realm all social reinforcers are lacking. Thus the likelihood of the occurrence of glossolalia is clearly reduced.

Last, Paul develops two models. The first is symbolic: even God spoke to people in strange language. But this was in vain (Isa. 28:11 = 1 Cor. 14:21). This biblical citation could once have been used in the sense of a positive apology for speaking in tongues against outsiders who do not understand.[2] But here it seeks to restrict speaking in

2. According to Sweet ("A Sign," esp. 243–44), the scriptural citation was once intended to defend Christian glossolalia against Jewish attacks.

tongues. The second model—Paul himself—also functions along this line. Paul speaks in tongues more than all others, but within the community he prefers intelligible speech (1 Cor. 14:19). He would be of no value to anyone if he were to express his message in tongues (1 Cor. 14:6).

We see how Paul seeks to influence stimuli, social reinforcements, and models in accordance with his intentions, in order to suppress speaking in tongues. Only indirectly do we learn something about the factors that promote it. We shall now turn our attention directly to these factors.

Distinction from the Environment

Glossolalia is a kind of conduct, specific to a group, that distinguishes early Christianity from its environment. It creates among the members of the community an emotional bond, not least through the fact that only Christians possess the gift of glossolalia. The decisive social reinforcement of speaking in tongues is that it is—or can be—a symbol of belonging to the group.

This suggests the following hypothesis. Must not belonging to the community be symbolized visibly upon entrance to the community? One may surmise that wherever a particular form of behavior has a high social value and distinguishes clearly from the environment, formal or informal initiation rites will develop in which the particular form of behavior plays a role.[3] Applied to the Corinthian community, this means that the conditions for a tendency to make glossolalia the decisive criterion of belonging to the group were present in Corinth. Some surely must have said that those who wish to join the community are fully received and accepted when they display glossolalic behavior (or let it be known that they understand it). Glossolalia would then be in this sense a "sign for the believers" (1 Cor. 14:22*). One could recognize with reference to glossolalia that new entrants had really found the path to the community. Paul, on the contrary, wants to assign this task to prophecy. It reveals the "secrets of the heart" of the new entrants and thus makes possible a judgment about them.

The following arguments may be offered in favor of this hypothesis.

1. In Acts, glossolalia does in fact have a legitimating function. It is a visible sign of possession of the Spirit and legitimizes the acceptance

3. Gerlach and Hine (*People*, 119–35) interpret glossolalia as a "commitment act" that promotes group identity and cohesion. Assumption of socially deviant behavior is "a bridge-burning act" (pp. 125–26).

of Samaritans (Acts 8:14–24),[4] Gentiles (10:44–48; 11:15–17), and disciples of John (19:1–7) into the community. Now "Luke" doubtless stems from the realm of Pauline Christianity. He could reflect views that were popular in some Pauline communities and that were possibly also widespread in Corinth.

2. The disunified use of the terms *pneuma*, "spirit," and *pneumatikos*, "spiritual," becomes intelligible. On the one hand, only speakers in tongues were considered pneumatics (1 Cor. 14:37); on the other hand, each baptized person possessed the Spirit (12:13). Everyone who confessed Jesus as Lord belonged to the community and was a pneumatic (12:1–3). Here a dispute over the boundary of the community becomes visible. Some tended to attempt to introduce glossolalia as the criterion of the "true Christian." We can leave unanswered the question whether an inconsistent concept of the Spirit promoted this tendency or was its expression.

3. It also becomes understandable that entrance to the community seems to occur in stages. Paul distinguishes believers, outsiders, and unbelievers.[5] Outsiders already belong to the community in a certain sense. It can theoretically be expected of them that they participate in prayer through a responsorial Amen (1 Cor. 14:16). This distinguishes them from unbelievers, who do not appear next to the outsider in v. 16. On the other hand, outsiders lack something essential. They appear in 14:23–24 next to unbelievers. Now, the difference between the

4. There is nothing in Acts 8:17 that permits one to conclude directly to glossolalia. But v. 18 presupposes that one can establish reception of the Spirit tangibly. This suggests thinking of speaking in tongues here as well.
5. Thus, above all, Weiss, *Der 1. Korintherbrief*, 329–31. For a different interpretation, cf. Conzelmann, *Der erste Brief*, 286; and Schlier, s. v. *idiotes*, 217. Lietzmann (*An die Korinther*, 71ff.) argues that in v. 16 "outsider" means all members of the community who do not possess the gift of glossolalia but in vv. 23–24 "outsider" is a synonym for "unbeliever": the term "outsider" is a self-designation; "unbeliever" is a designation used by others. Two arguments speak against this interpretation. First, the formulation "to fill the place of the outsider" in v. 16* suggests either a particular seat or a role that can be filled by different persons. On *topos* in the sense of a social role, cf. Acts 1:25; Ignatius *Letter to the Smyrnaeans* 6.1; *1 Clement* 40.5; and Epictetus *Discourses* 2.4.5. The term *idiotes* is attested in inscriptions for cult participants who are not members of the association (*Orientis Graeci Inscriptiones Selectae* 90.52; Dittenberger, *Sylloge Inscriptionum Graecarum*, 1013.6, 736.16ff.). Second, the varied sequence in vv. 23 and 24 is likely to be explained by the fact that the content of the main clause which follows applies in a particular way to the one mentioned last. It is especially the unbeliever who sees madness in speaking in tongues; it is especially the outsider who is "convicted and tested" (14:24*). Paul assumes as self-evident that even one who sympathizes with Christianity (the outsider) can be repelled by glossolalia and that even the unbeliever can come to faith directly through prophecy.

believer and the outsider that becomes visible in the text lies in their stance toward speaking in tongues. The outsider does not understand speakers in tongues (14:16–23). But everyone among those gifted with the Spirit has a chance to understand them. We therefore propose the hypothesis that the outsider is one who already belongs to the community but has not yet delivered proof of possession of the Spirit— a proof that some understand as speaking in tongues. Verse 16 is then formulated from the perspective of those who wish to make speaking in tongues or other pneumatic gifts the decisive criterion of belonging to the community. In vv. 23–24, however, Paul wishes to deny that speaking in tongues is the sign for believers. Everyone who truly worships God (v. 25) belongs to the community. From this perspective, there is no threefold division—unbelief, joining of the community, belief—but only a twofold division between unbelief and belief. The outsider and the unbeliever can therefore appear juxtaposed in vv. 23–24.

4. If Paul is opposing the tendency to conceive of glossolalia (or another visible pneumatic gift) as the criterion of authentic belonging to the community, the contradiction between 1 Cor. 14:22 and 14:24–25 becomes intelligible. According to v. 22, prophecy exists for the sake of believers, but according to vv. 24–25, it is precisely among unbelievers that it functions positively. Paul understands the statement to mean that prophecy takes the place of glossolalia as "sign of recognition for believers" (i.e., for the community). Prophecy makes it possible to judge with certitude whether an unbeliever has come to faith (vv. 24–25). It is not a sign of recognition in the sense that all prophesy (instead of speaking in tongues) and thus demonstrate their possession of the Spirit, but rather in the sense that new entrants are judged by prophets. Paul therefore does not say directly in v. 22 that prophecy is a sign in the same sense as glossolalia. In the remarks on prophecy, he does not repeat the term "sign" but rather says in general that prophecy exists for the sake of believers.

5. Last, that the significance of glossolalia as a criterion of belonging to the community was the disputed point in Corinth also emerges from 1 Cor. 12:1–3. Here Paul makes clear that the decisive criterion is the confession of the Lord Jesus. This confession guarantees possession of the Spirit, who can manifest himself in various ways, not only in the form of speaking in tongues.

Summary. In Corinth there existed a tendency—not undisputed— to make speaking in tongues the criterion of possession of the Spirit and of belonging to the community. As a distinctive language, speaking in tongues created an unambiguous distinction from the environment and could strengthen the group's emotional feeling of cohesiveness. One may doubt that it necessarily repelled outsiders; the stimulus of something strange always attracts, especially in a culture that knew of the blessing of divine *mania*. The Corinthian thesis was probably that glossolalia is a sign of recognition for believers. If this tendency had become established, glossolalia would have been socially reinforced more than all other behavior.[6] Paul argues, against this, that although speaking in tongues is indeed a (negative) characteristic distinguishing Christians from the environment, it is not for that reason a positive criterion of belonging to the community. The emotional tie in the community does not depend on a single characteristic type of behavior present in all community members. The Spirit manifests itself in various ways. Prophecy is better able to decide if someone really belongs to the community or not. The reaction to prophecy should therefore be the decisive criterion in the judgment of new entrants.

Groupings Within the Community

Speaking in tongues serves to distinguish from outside. In this function it was disputed in Corinth. All did not possess the gift of speaking in tongues. "Do all speak with tongues?" Paul asked (1 Cor. 12:30). In the Corinthian community, in other words, there were groups besides the groups that spoke in tongues. Glossolalia distinguished within, not only from without. We would like to know more about these groups but must content ourselves with surmises.

Groups Bound to Persons? In the modern Pentecostal movement, dependence on charismatic leaders and on a like-minded group is a decisive condition for the origin, stabilization, and ending of speaking in tongues. J. P. Kildahl sees in this dependency syndrome the key to psychological interpretation of glossolalia. Again and again, he encountered exaggerated expectations of their community leader on the part of those who spoke in tongues; often he could not even distinguish whether they spoke of the community leader or of Christ.[7]

6. Martin ("Glossolalie," 127) accurately describes the social reinforcement of speaking in tongues: "The converts thereby gained prestige, honor, and power, and consequently desired to 'speak in tongues' in the hope of securing divine power and favor among men."

7. Kildahl, *The Psychology*, 44. He speaks of a "dependency syndrome" (p. 50). "We found no tongue-speaker who was unrelated to a glossolalia authority figure whom he esteemed. When glossolalia was an important life goal there was always a relationship to a leader and/or to a group which conveyed a feeling of acceptance and belonging"

Similar dependency structures seem to have existed in early Christianity as well. In Acts, the Holy Spirit is usually poured out in the presence of charismatic authorities; Peter and John bring the Spirit to Samaria (8:14–17). Cornelius and his household begin to speak in tongues in the presence of Peter (10:44–48). Paul mediates the gift of speaking in tongues in Ephesus through laying on of hands (19:1–7). Irenaeus (*Adversus Haereses* 1.13.3) gives a descriptive account of the suggestive influence of charismatic authorities in his description of the practices of Marcus:

> It appears probable enough that this man possesses a demon as his familiar spirit, by means of whom he seems able to prophesy, and also enables as many as he counts worthy to be partakers of his Charis themselves to prophesy. He devotes himself especially to women, and those such as are well-bred, and elegantly attired, and of great wealth, whom he frequently seeks to draw after him, by addressing them in such seductive words as these: "I am eager to make thee a partaker of my Charis, since the Father of all doth continually behold thy angel before His face. Now the place of thy angel is among us: it behooves us to become one. Receive first from me and by me [the gift of] Charis. Adorn thyself as a bride who is expecting her bridegroom, that thou mayest be what I am, and I what thou art. Establish the germ of light in thy nuptial chamber. Receive from me a spouse, and become receptive of him, while thou art received by him. Behold Charis has descended upon thee; open thy mouth and prophesy." On the woman replying, "I have never at any time prophesied, nor do I know how to prophesy"; then engaging, for the second time, in certain invocations, so as to astound his deluded victim, he says to her, "Open thy mouth, speak whatsoever occurs to thee, and thou shalt prophesy." She then, vainly puffed up and elated by these words, and greatly excited in soul by the expectation that it is herself who is to prophesy, her heart beating violently [from emotion], reaches the requisite pitch of audacity, and idly as well as impudently utters some nonsense as it happens to occur to her, such as might be expected from one heated by an empty spirit. . . . Henceforth she reckons herself a prophetess, and expresses her thanks to Marcus for having imparted to her of his own Charis. She then makes the effort to reward him, not only by the gift of her possessions (in which way he has collected a very large fortune), but

---

(pp. 80–81). If the relationship to the charismatic leader was disturbed, the glossolalic behavior often ceased also. Kildahl therefore assumes a close connection between glossolalia and the ability to be hypnotized (pp. 54ff.). Vivier ("The Glossolalic," 163, 170), on the contrary, found less suggestibility in glossolalics than in an "orthodox" control group that rejected glossolalia.

also by yielding up to him her person, desiring in every way to be united to him, that she may become altogether one with him.[8]

The dependency syndrome is unmistakable. We may surmise a similar dependence in the relationship of the Montanist prophetesses Prisca and Maximilla to Montanus. But is it also true of Corinth?

Paul criticizes a Corinthian dependency syndrome with clear words: "Each one of you says, 'I belong to Paul,' or 'I belong to Apollos,' or 'I belong to Cephas,' or 'I belong to Christ' " (1 Cor. 1:12). Paul proposes the counterthesis that "all are yours" (1 Cor. 3:22)—all apostles, even the entire world—but everything is subordinated to Christ and God. Does this dependency syndrome have anything to do with the glossolalia in Corinth? T. W. Manson thinks that Paul had introduced glossolalia to Corinth; later, Paul affirms that he too possesses this gift but does not esteem it very highly.[9] J. C. Hurd argues that Paul himself had been the great model for speaking in tongues; only regard for new influences stemming from Palestine into Corinth moved him to relativize the significance of glossolalia.[10] H. M. Schenke and K. M. Fischer think of Apollos as the decisive model of pneumatic behavior.[11] Unfortunately, it is impossible to reach a well-founded conclusion. Paul does not associate the problem of glossolalia with personal questions. He alludes only quite indirectly to a connection.

Twice Paul introduces himself as a model. In 14:6 he denies the missionary value of speaking in tongues. If he came to the Corinthians speaking in tongues he would be of no value to them. Here glossolalia is associated with the apostolic office. Is it a concealed jab at other apostles? That too is not demonstrable.

The second time he presents himself as model is in 1 Cor. 14:18; he speaks in tongues more than the Corinthians do, but he wishes to refrain from speaking in tongues in the community. What is striking here is Paul's need to attribute to himself the first place in a mode of behavior that in principle he wishes to relativize. The inclination to be the first and the greatest is

8. ET: Alexander Roberts: ANF 1:334–35. At issue here is prophecy in the form of glossolalia; cf. Lietzmann, *An die Korinther*, 69; and Weinel, *Die Wirkungen*, 72ff.

9. Manson, "The Corinthian Correspondence," esp. 203–5.

10. Hurd, *The Origin*, 243–44, 281. According to Hurd, Paul first appeared with "demonstration of the Spirit and of power" (1 Cor. 2:4), i.e., as one who spoke in tongues, but he now distances himself from such childish speech (1 Cor. 13:11). Against Hurd, cf. Sweet, "A Sign," 249ff.

11. Thus Schenke and K. M. Fischer, *Einleitung*, 92, 95; and Hyldahl, "Den korintiske situation."

unmistakable in Paul.[12] He is the last apostle—but also the most successful (1 Cor. 15:9–10). He surpasses "superapostles" with whom he is in competition (2 Cor. 11:21ff.). He could be prouder than others of his Judaism (Phil. 3:2ff.). Once he surpassed all his contemporaries (Gal. 1:14). The motif of dominance emerges in Paul particularly when he has to defend himself against the influence of competing missionaries. This is quite clear in the cited texts. Does he also wish to get the better of other missionaries in 1 Corinthians 14 when he describes himself as the greatest in speaking in tongues? This is not certain.

The only certain thing is that for Paul the decisive problem is not the personal tie to charismatic authorities but the social function of glossolalia. He is less interested in the origin of the phenomenon than in its effects. No matter who "introduced" glossolalia to Corinth, it must have been a process within the community through which glossolalia became the criterion of internal and external demarcation. Paul opposes this. We must therefore ask, In what circles in Corinth could glossolalia achieve such weight?

Groups Specific to Social Strata? We make some progress if we link up glossolalia with Corinthian problems other than that of the Corinthian parties. It is striking that of the five parts of 1 Corinthians that are introduced by *peri*, the first three treat the foundational questions of interpersonal relationships—sexuality (chap. 7), table fellowship (chaps. 8—10), and language (chaps. 12—14). Two tendencies in the Corinthian community can be distinguished with regard to these themes. On the one hand, there is a stance aiming toward separation. Marriages with non-Christians can be dissolved; all table fellowship using ritually slaughtered meat is forbidden to a Christian; the esoteric special language of glossolalia is to be preferred to intelligible communication. On the other hand, there are indications of a countercurrent that insists on a relative openness toward the outside. Mixed marriages are to be assessed positively; meat offered to idols is not taboo; intelligible communication is superior to glossolalia. Paul mediates. He has understanding for the tendencies pushing toward separation but fundamentally supports the other current.

It is a plausible assumption that the separatist tendencies which have been sketched have the same social location, that is, that ascetic inclinations, anxiety about ritual meat, and glossolalia were prevalent in the same groups as were rejection of asceticism, of food taboos, and

12. As Stendahl ("Glossolalia," 110) accurately remarks, Paul has "a tendency—an annoying one at that—to claim that he is the greatest in everything."

of overestimated glossolalia. Then one could draw the following conclusion by way of analogy. The "strong" who were free with regard to ancient food taboos probably belonged to the higher classes in Corinth, which were comparatively well integrated into the "world" and which were reluctant to refrain from contacts and invitations.[13] The critics of glossolalia should probably be sought in the same classes; one who favored openness to the world in eating would probably also feel repelled by an esoteric group language. Conversely, glossolalia could have exerted great attraction precisely for the less educated and the weak.[14] For this is, after all, an ability that is not tied to educational presuppositions but that, according to the conclusions of modern linguists, is present universally in a latent manner independently of social stratification.[15] Anyone can product unintelligible utterances. Danger of embarrassment does not exist, since the clear criteria necessary for that are lacking. Higher evaluation of glossolalia would then be a higher evaluation of the groups and strata active in speaking in tongues. A confrontation about authority in the community becomes visible behind the question of glossolalia: by which values and groups is the community to be formed?

In keeping with his "patriarchalism of love," which aims at balance, Paul seeks to retain the high estimation of glossolalia but would rather see the leadership of the community in other hands: in the hands of those with greater self-control, of prophets "to whom the spirits are subject" (14:32*), of interpreters who possess the gift of translating irrational contents into intelligible speech—in general, of those members of the community who are distinguished in providing services and in performing leadership tasks, the two gifts Paul consciously incorporated into the list of charisms in 1 Cor. 12:28. When Paul supports these persons and wishes to give them a greater authority within the

13. Cf. my reflections in "Die Starken."
14. Thus Hollenweger, "Narrativité," esp. 211. According to Hollenweger, there were, on the one hand, "illetrés et illuminés" who made use of speaking in tongues, and on the other hand, cultivated circles who appealed to the Scripture and to the letters of Paul. Thiselton ("The 'Interpretation' of Tongues," 34) agrees. Stendahl ("Glossolalia," 122) rightly refers to the democratizing effects of glossolalia: "It has been one of the expressions through which in a certain sense 'the last have become the first.' " One cannot use against this the correct sociological observation that glossolalia can also be found today in higher circles and on the university campus (cf. Best, "The Interpretation," 52). It is a characteristic of our age that those who belong to upper classes take on modes of behavior of the lower classes.
15. The thesis that glossolalia is a universal human capability is represented especially by Samarin, *Tongues*.

community, he is probably intervening in disputes about internal community authority. He promotes precisely those circles on whom he also relies otherwise—the strata somewhat more open to the world and more prosperous, on whose sense of responsibility, initiative, and experience the stable development of the communities depended.

Groups Specific to Gender? A third surmise must be appended. In the midst of the admonitions on speaking in tongues within the community stands the famous, and infamous, "women should keep silence in the churches" text (1 Cor. 14:33b–36). Even though it could be an interpolation, it is hardly coincidental that it stands in this place. One may surmise that glossolalia occurred more frequently in women, in other words, in a group that in all strata was socially disadvantaged but that in principle had equal rights in the early Christian communities (Gal. 3:28). It cannot be coincidence that ecstatic phenomena are attested precisely for women in early Christianity. Think of the soothsaying girl (Acts 16:16), the prophesying daughter of Philip (Acts 21:9), the prophetess Jezebel in Thyatira (Rev. 2:20), the Montanist prophetesses Priscilla and Maximilla,[16] the prophetess Amma in Philadelphia,[17] or the prophetesses of the Gnostic Marcus.[18] Ecstatic phenomena were also connected with women elsewhere in antiquity. Bacchanalian frenzy first seized women. The manticism of inspiration made use of female mediums, the Pythia of Delphi, the priestesses of Dodona, or the sibyl. The apocalyptic heavenly language was spoken by the daughters of Job. Prophetic women are well attested in Corinth (1 Cor. 11:2ff.). It is therefore possible that glossolalia was widespread among the Corinthian women. Yet the direct discussions of glossolalia make no reference to this. The phenomenon was certainly in principle independent of sexual boundaries.

To conclude from the perspective of learning theory, glossolalia is dependent on a particular social and historical learning situation—on entrance into a new religious community that distinguishes itself sharply from the environment in its values. This community is the decisive stimulus, reinforcer, and model of glossolalic behavior. Glossolalia is released by assemblies of the community (1 Cor. 14:23),

16. Epiphanius *Refutation of All the Heresies* 48.1.2–3.
17. Eusebius *Ecclesiastical History* 5.17.3.
18. Irenaeus *Adversus Haereses* 1.13.3. Reference may also be made to a charismatically gifted Christian woman who in ecstasy had visions, conversed with angels, read minds, and prescribed medicine (Tertullian *De Anima* 9.4) and to an inspired prophetess who in the third century C.E. predicted an earthquake (Cyprian *Epistles* 75.10.74).

becomes a model for imitative behavior (1 Cor. 14:27), and receives enormous social reinforcement from the conviction that in it an immediate effect of the Holy Spirit is present. Functionally, glossolalia serves to promote the emotional coherence of the group, partly through distinction from without, partly through integration of disadvantaged groups that are able to join in speaking in tongues independently of their social status and degree of education. Paul exposes the possible ambivalent effects of glossolalia. It can have the effect of repelling outsiders; within, it can call into question the cohesiveness of the group, if there form glossolalic subgroups inclined toward seeing in glossolalia the decisive criterion for possession of the Spirit and full membership in the community.[19] Paul reacts in a contradictory manner. First he establishes a clear hierarchy. Glossolalia and the groups that stand behind it are shunted to the second place, and the authority of rationally inclined group is strengthened. With this, glossolalia is relativized but in its relativity incorporated into the community. Second, he tends toward privatization of speaking in tongues, that is, to its exclusion from community life. But in doing so he deprives glossolalia of its basis of existence. Without social stimuli, models, and reinforcers, it is bound to wither. Outside a glossolalic community it is condemned to extinction.[20] No wonder that in the realm of Pauline Christianity we hear nothing more of an ability to speak in tongues.

But Paul's confession that he himself speaks in tongues and his attempt to privatize glossolalia are instructive in another respect as well. Must not glossolalia have had a personal value for Paul over and above the social value which he disputes? The idea that an interpretation of glossolalia as socially learned behavior is not sufficient to illuminate the phenomenon psychologically imposes itself almost automatically on the basis of the Pauline texts.

PSYCHODYNAMIC ASPECTS OF GLOSSOLALIA

The result thus far is that glossolalia is socially learned behavior, which, however, seems to be motivated even independently of social

19. Socially disintegrative effects of glossolalic behavior can also be observed in modern instances. Boundaries are formed between an in-group speaking in tongues and an out-group (Kildahl, *The Psychology*, 66–75). Yet that is true of every new and deviant behavior. It burdens the group if it evokes polarizations.

20. Samarin ("Glossolalia," 62) adduces three instances in which glossolalia emerged spontaneously outside a community that speaks in tongues. But with Christians one must always allow for symbolic models from the Bible in this matter.

reinforcements. It has a personal value for the individual. One who speaks in tongues edifies oneself (1 Cor. 14:4). Of course one can also analyze the individual value of speaking in tongues from the perspective of learning theory: glossolalia is reinforced by inner ("concealed") processes within the human being, for example, by feelings of happiness and similar things. The positive inner consequences are then a motive for repetition of the behavior. But this simply poses the problem. For what reason can speaking in tongues be experienced as something positive? What needs are satisfied here? What problems are solved? In addressing these questions, we are considering glossolalia from a psychodynamic perspective—as an expression of a conscious or unconscious psychic intention. In what follows, three hypotheses toward explaining the individual value of speaking in tongues will be discussed on the basis of the Pauline texts. The positive value of glossolalia could lie, first, in its affording access to unconscious dimensions; second, in its allowing repressed impulses access to consciousness; and third, in its being a regressive reassumption of childish forms of behavior and experience.

Glossolalia—Language of the Unconscious?

Glossolalia is unintelligible language. But it would be language of the unconscious only if it were unintelligible to its very speaker, not only to others—that is, if it contained an intrapersonal limit to understanding, not only an interpersonal one. Two arguments may be brought against this hypothesis. First, Paul compares glossolalia with a foreign language (1 Cor. 14:10–11). In the case of a foreign language, the meaning of the words is known to the speaker; only the listener understands nothing. Second, Paul presupposes that those who speak in tongues can interpret what they say (1 Cor. 14:4). Hans Conzelmann therefore holds, "Unlike the Greek theory [namely, of the inspiration of Pythia] Paul does not think that the glossolalia is unintelligible to the speaker himself."[21] Our thesis that glossolalia is language of the unconscious must therefore be made more precise: glossolalia is language of the unconscious, but language capable of becoming conscious. Those who speak in tongues do not understand what they say, but they could understand it. Three arguments speak in favor of this thesis.[22]

21. Conzelmann, *Der erste Brief*, 276.
22. Fathers of the church were also of the opinion that glossolalics do not understand what they say; cf. John Chrysostom *Homilies on the Two Epistles to the Corinthians* 35.3: The one speaking in tongues is "without fruit" for himself, not only for others—*ho nous ouk edei to legomenon.*

1. Paul presupposes as the normal case that the speakers in tongues do not understand their own utterances. To this Paul opposes his ideal, which amounts to an understanding of the unconscious, and that not only by an interpreting listener but by the speaker himself. In assessing the comparison of glossolalia with a foreign language, he makes a logical jump. The foreign language is unintelligible to the listener but intelligible to the speaker (1 Cor. 14:11). To be consistent, Paul would have to insist that the listener must learn the meaning of the words. Yet he appeals to the speaker, not the listener: "Therefore, he who speaks in a tongue should pray for the power to interpret" (14:13). In other words, he localizes the problem of understanding in the speaker. For the speaker to pray for understanding of his own speech is meaningful only if he does not understand it. This is also confirmed by 14:5*. Here Paul does not say that all who speak in tongues understand their own words but only that "he wishes" that all understood their own utterances. His wish shows that the reality is different.

2. Glossolalia and interpretation are two different charisms conferred on different people, "to another various kinds of tongues, to another the interpretation of tongues" (1 Cor. 12:10). One who speaks in tongues is not automatically an interpreter. Not all speakers in tongues understand what they say. Of course one and the same person can possess both gifts. But it is precisely the text (1 Cor. 14:27–28*) that presupposes a combination of both gifts which clarifies the independence of glossolalia and interpretation:

> If any speak in a tongue, let there be only two or at most three, and each in turn; and let one interpret. But if he is not an interpreter [or, But if no interpreter is present], let him keep silent; he speaks for himself and for God.

The text is obscure. Does it presuppose that the translator is one of those who speak in tongues? Or can it be anyone? Is one permitted to speak in tongues only if one can oneself give a translation?[23] The only thing clear is that there is one translator for several speakers in tongues.

23. Weiss (*Der 1. Korintherbrief*, 340) states that the one who speaks in tongues could not know if an interpreter was present, yet one could judge whether one possessed the hermeneutic gift oneself. But if only those capable of interpretation are permitted to speak in tongues, why does Paul not demand that all speakers in tongues interpret themselves? Thistleton ("The 'Interpretation' ") translates *diermeneuein* as "to put into words." But for one (according to 1 Cor. 14.27) to put into words what another says unintelligibly is interpretation.

In case this translator had himself previously acted as a speaker in tongues, he would have to interpret the utterances of others in tongues as well as his own glossolalia. This confirms the assumption that as a rule glossolalia and interpretation were not joined. Otherwise, it would be a pure tautology to make the activity of speakers in tongues dependent on the presence of hermeneutic abilities. What is decisive from the perspective of social psychology is that the translation is centralized. One person announces the directives. Paul betrays a good sense of necessary authority structures.

3. As a third argument in favor of retracing glossolalic utterances to unconscious impulses, we adduce the anthropological terms in which Paul describes the process of speaking in tongues. He assigns glossolalia to the spirit but interpretation to the mind (1 Cor. 14:15-16); that is, glossolalia does not encompass the entire human being. At least it does not encompass the tribunal Paul calls *nous* and which in relationship to the *pneuma* is without doubt of a rational nature. Glossolalia, therefore, is not only a problem of interpersonal understanding but a problem of intrapersonal integration.[24]

In conclusion, glossolalia is language of the unconscious—language capable of consciousness. What otherwise escapes everyday consciousness comes to light here. Put differently, glossolalia makes unconscious depth dimensions of life accessible. What becomes accessible here escapes us just as it escaped the consciousness of most of those who spoke in tongues. Some psychodynamic theories seek to learn even more. We shall now turn to them.

Glossolalia—Language of the Repressed?

The classical psychoanalytic interpretation of glossolalia is appealing: glossolalia enables the expression of impulses that are incompatible with the prevailing sociocultural norms but that may venture into the light of day in a form unintelligible to consciousness. Glossolalia is said to rest on a compromise between conscious norms and drives contrary to the norm. It should be assessed on analogy with a neurotic symptom—as an expression of unresolved tensions.[25]

---

24. Tugwell ("The Gift," 140) paraphrases in modern language, The whole man should pray, "not excluding his subconscious." Tugwell rights notes that in Paul this would have to read, The whole man should pray, without excluding his consciousness! The problematic is different in modern man and in early Christian man.
25. Thus, first, O. Pfister: "Behind all speaking in tongues . . . we found painful thoughts that repressed thoughts analogous to themselves . . . , which usually revivified infantile experiences and brought them to veiled expression." ("Die psychologische Enträtselung," 781). This thesis has recently been defended by Laffal: "Speaking in

This interpretation had a certain plausibility as long as glossolalia was a relatively unusual phenomenon that one hardly ever encountered in one's own circles. But when the Pentecostal movement grasped the educated middle class and the established churches in the United States in the middle of the twentieth century, it became increasingly difficult to interpret glossolalia as a pathological phenomenon.[26] Increased contact with those who speak in tongues caused the conviction to grow that it concerns people without psychic deficits.[27]

What is difficult to evaluate in modern glossolalia would seem to be even more difficult to decide as far as early Christian glossolalia is concerned. Yet there is a text in Paul—one that has caused much puzzlement—that could shed a little light on the assumption of a process of repression. In 1 Cor. 12:2–3*, Paul writes,

> You know that when you were heathen, you let yourselves be led irresistibly to dumb idols, just exactly as you were drawn. Therefore I make known to you that no one who speaks in the Spirit of God says "Anathema Iesous" and no one can say "Kurios Iesous" except in the Holy Spirit.

Since Paul introduces with these words a section aimed at an evaluation of glossolalia (1 Corinthians 12—14), they would seem to have a relationship to glossolalic behavior, even though the cited utterances are brief grammatically correct sentences. The point of comparison is that in each case it is a matter of speaking in the Spirit, of ecstatic speech. But precisely that is occasionally doubted. Does Paul perhaps only intend to underline that the confession of Jesus Christ is not bound to an ecstatic state? Every Christian could speak it, whether or not equipped with special pneumatic gifts.[28] The following arguments speak against this conception.

The Corinthians had inquired regarding the pneumatic gifts and had understood under this term ecstatic phenomena. They read the

---

tongues serves to provide verbal form to a conflicted wish while at the same time hiding the wish by stripping the verbalization of communal meaning. Some degree of conscious expression is allowed to the conflicted wish, but the wish itself escapes conscious recognition" (*Pathological and Normal Languages*, 88). In this version of the theory it is not necessary to think of repressed *childhood* experiences.

26. Mosiman, *Das Zungenreden*, and Cutten, *Speaking with Tongues*, are older historical surveys. Sketches of Neo-Pentecostalism may be found in Kelsey, *Tongue Speaking*, 95ff.; and Hollenweger, *Enthusiastisches Christentum*.

27. The presumption that people who are active in speaking in tongues are psychically disturbed people is a prejudice; cf. Kildahl, *The Psychology*, 48ff.; Gerlach and Hine, *People*, xxi–xxii; and Goodman, *Speaking in Tongues*.

28. Thus Dautzenberg, *Urchristliche Prophetie*, 143–46; similarly, Holtz, "Das Kennzeichen," 373–74.

text with this pre-understanding. To them, "speaking in the Spirit" was ecstatic speech. They could not anticipate what Paul would develop only in 12:4–31, namely, that even such sober phenomena as "helping" and "leadership tasks" belonged to the pneumatic charisma.

Paul further calls to mind the ecstatic phenomena of paganism, which, as the choice of words shows, he parallels to the pneumatic phenomena in Christianity (cf. "were driven" in 1 Cor. 12:2*; Rom. 8:14*; Gal. 5:18*).

Above all, one must not imagine the confession *Kurios Iesous* as a routine liturgical occurrence. It is the cosmic confession of all powers. Every tongue (*pasa glossa*) joins in this confession (Phil. 2:19–20)— including the denizens of heaven and of the underworld, the angels and the demons. We may include those who spoke in tongues together with the entire community in this cosmic "public"; they did, after all, speak the language of angels. The expression "every *glossa*" includes glossolalia, *the glossa* in an absolute sense (cf. 1 Cor. 14:26). The confession itself is an ecstatic phenomenon. J. Weiss has therefore rightly noted that 1 Cor. 12:2–3 is concerned "with ecstatics, not with people in a normal state."[29] "Anathema to Jesus" and "Lord Jesus" were ecstatic utterances and are as such analogies to glossolalia.

A second disputed problem is whether an anathema was really expressed, or whether Paul constructed an anathema that was never really spoken in this form.[30] The danger exists again here that we judge incidents that are inconceivable in modern communities to have been inconceivable in early Christianity as well. Had Paul only wanted to say that no one would come to the idea of cursing Jesus, that all recognize him as Lord and that all therefore have the Spirit of God, he could simply have written, "None of you curses Jesus!" or "Do you curse Jesus? By no means!" Precise observation of the structure of the sentence perhaps offers the key to understanding the phenomenon. Paul does not write, "Whoever says anathema to Jesus does not speak in the Spirit"; he writes conversely, "No one who speaks in the Spirit of God says 'Anathema to Jesus.' " Speaking in the Spirit is presupposed. What is disputed is only what one who speaks in the Spirit can say. Glossolalic utterances always contain, among other things, cryptosemantic elements—allusions to biblical names and

29. Weiss, *Der 1. Korintherbrief*, 296.

30. The first alternative is defended by, among others, Weiss (*Der 1. Korintherbrief*, 295) and Beare ("Speaking," 241–42). Cf. also nn. 32–34 below. The second position is defended by Conzelmann (*Der erste Brief*, 241), Hurd (*The Origin*, 193), Sweet ("A Sign," 241), Maly ("1.Kor 12,1–3," 90–93), and de Broglie ("Le texte fondamental").

liturgical formulas. That people heard the name Jesus in them is rather
certain; reference to Jesus was, after all, already established by the
liturgy. Was it not possible to hear an "anathema" as well?[31] How
quickly could a "Maranatha, Maranatha Jesus" become a "Mar ana-
thamar" through different intonation and accentuation! How easily
could one hear an anathema from what was said! Or the one speaking
in tongues could involuntarily transform the familiar syllables of the
maranatha into an "anathema," so that the others—and the speaker—
would be shocked to attention, as if an evil demon had twisted the
words on the tongue! Speakers in tongues are no more immune to
linguistic mistakes than other people; and it would seem that their
mistakes and misstatements are not to be explained differently from
those of a normal speaker.

Finally, that an anathema was really spoken also emerges from the
location of the section. In all the sections beginning with *peri*, Paul
first takes a position on real problems of the community, often while
picking up on formulations of the community's letter that had been
delivered to him. Just as he first cites the Corinthians in 8:1 (and
possibly in 7:1), so too it would seem that in 12:2 he first cites actual
utterances; one can even surmise that such blasphemous utterances
were an occasion for the inquiry. The circles in Corinth that were
reserved toward ecstatic activity would have had an understandable
reason to request Paul to take a position.

We proceed therefore from the position that the curse upon Jesus
was in fact spoken. In this regard one need not think of Jews,[32] or of
persecuted Christians,[33] or of Gnostics.[34] The utterances took place in
the community. They must have raised among the Christians the

31. A somewhat different position is represented by Albright and Mann, "Two
Texts." They hold to a misunderstanding within the history of the text and argue that
an Aramaic text is to be assumed as original.
32. Schlatter, *Paulus*, 333. The assumption that non-Christian Jews had cursed Jesus
fails on the fact that Paul would hardly have needed to instruct the community that
non-Christians do not possess the Holy Spirit.
33. Cullmann (*Die ersten christlichen Glaubensbekenntnisse*, 23–24) argues as follows: The
Holy Spirit had been promised to persecuted Christians (Mark 13:11; Matt. 10:19–20);
if they cursed Jesus before the court, they could later say that it was not they who had
cursed but the Holy Spirit, to whom according to Mark 13:11 they were to entrust
themselves, had put the words in their mouths. Derrett ("Cursing Jesus") argues
differently: Christians were seduced to the anathema by Jews in the synagogue, so that
they could continue to belong to the synagogue. The fact that the ecstatic pull that Paul
adduces as a comparison does not fit the situation of persecution speaks against both
interpretations. But there is certainly no thought of Jewish Christians. Paul reminds his
addressees of their own pagan past.
34. Thus Schmithals, *Die Gnosis*, 45–52.

question of how one could reliably judge members of the community. In 1 Cor. 14:24–26, Paul gives an answer: prophecy reveals what is hidden within us.

One could say the same thing of ecstatic speech. In such speech one loses control over what one says. It is possible that—as in everyday misstatements—unconscious orientations come to light in this fashion.[35] Proceding from this idea, H. Weinel interpreted 1 Cor. 12:2–3 through categories that anticipated psychoanalytic insights. In glossolalia, the vocal organs are

> placed in vigorous motion completely independently of the will of the subject. In the course of this, unarticulated individual sounds, meaningless combinations of sounds, but also correct words and combinations of words come into existence. These words or brief sentences are taken from the consciousness of the human subject. Yet sometimes they come from the suppressed consciousness. For when in Corinth the words, "Jesus [is] a curse!" (1 Cor. 12:3) escape from those who speak in tongues, this is to be placed in the same category with the sudden emergence of sexual-sensual images in the visions of persons who in awakened consciousness are characterized by a powerful suppression of their sensual drives. In ecstasy, as in dreams, the most secret things sometimes emerge with force from the dark depths of the nightsides of consciousness into the light. And not only monks but also more recent visionaries have then with repugnance attributed such experiences to demonic powers, because they are incapable of acknowledging such frightful things as components of the life of their own souls.[36]

This statement was published in 1899, one year before the appearance of Freud's interpretation of dreams—a sign that no esoteric psychoanalytic secret knowledge is necessary in order to interpret aspects of religious life as an expression of unconscious dynamics. We can, then, conclude that repressed things can express themselves in ecstatic speech. This is not excluded in glossolalic behavior. Are we therefore compelled to accept the psychoanalytic interpretation of glossolalia?

In our example, what is suppressed is precisely not suppressed and repressed in ecstatic speech, but rather expressed openly. An analogy

35. Weiss, Der 1. Korintherbrief, 295: "in enthusiasmo veritas."
36. Weinel, Die Wirkungen, 72. According to Beare, "A modern teacher would perhaps think of such 'spirits' as evidences of a subconscious hostility to Christ and the gospel breaking out in words when the control of the conscious mind were removed in a state of ecstasy" ("Speaking," 241–42). Schmithals (Die Gnosis, 47) considers such reflections a questionable application of modern psychoanalysis to 1 Cor. 12:3. As far as Weinel is concerned, however, it is hardly a matter of applying psychoanalysis but is rather a matter of everyday human knowledge.

to ecstatic speaking would, then, lie less in neurotic symptoms than in free association during therapy. Ecstasy would not be a continuation of repression but a step toward overcoming it. Uncontrolled break-through of unconscious stances is certainly not identical with their integration, but it would be the first sign of an opening toward previously unconscious impulses.

According to orthodox psychoanalytic doctrine, these would have to be impulses placed under taboo by the general sociocultural norms. There can be no talk of this in regard to 1 Cor. 12:2–3. On the contrary, the negative assessment of Jesus as one who was executed and crucified which expresses itself in the anathema corresponds extremely well with the norms of the wider society (cf. 1 Cor. 1:23; Gal. 3:10, 13). The convictions of a small subcultural group are the repressing factor.

Last, it is not traumatic events of the distant past that are repressed but rather attitudes that in the case of new converts were quite conscious not too long ago.

These reflections lead to the following interpretation of the phenom-enon. In the "Anathema Jesus," attitudes that had been repressed in the converts as a result of a "postdecisional" conflict are revealed. Their conversion to Christianity was a profound existential decision. Every decision leaves behind cognitive dissonance. In order to reduce the dissonance between our decision and the attractiveness of the excluded alternative, we either emphasize the positive aspects of the chosen alternative—seek, in other words, elements consonant with our deci-sion—or suppress from our consciousness the dissonant aspects of the excluded alternative. The Corinthian Christians also had a decision behind them. They had decided against the generally accepted system of values, according to which one who is crucified is a criminal. They had chosen a radically different normative orientation of their lives. But they had not reenacted this decision with all the levels of their person. In the postdecisional conflict, they had suppressed the judgment "Jesus is cursed!" which corresponded to the general system of values, in order not to fall into contradiction with themselves. But under reduced self-control, the value stance that had been excluded by the decision in favor of Christianity and that had been suppressed again broke through and led to the cry "Jesus is cursed!"[37]

We offer this preliminary result. All that has been established is the

---

37. I could not find contemporary analogies. Yet the reference of Samarin (*Tongues*,

possibility that individual pneumatic utterances could be an expression of a conflict. But psychoanalytic theory goes further; it sees speaking in tongues as a whole, not only specific glossolalic aberrations, as symptoms of conflict. Beyond this, it locates this conflict in early childhood experiences. Speaking in tongues—like religious behavior and experience in general—is said to be recourse to early childhood modes of behavior.

Glossolalia—Regressive Behavior?

The psychoanalytic thesis cannot be completely false. Glossolalia does in fact exhibit regressive traits in linguistic, social, and psychological aspects.

From a linguistic perspective, the experience of glossolalia presupposes a reactivation of childhood abilities to learn speech. The different language traditions of glossolalia can scarcely be explained without reference to an unusual gift for imitation.[38] There are, in addition to this, specific characteristics: The inventory of phonemes is reduced.[39] The unity of the linguistic sign as a conventional combination of sign and what is signified disintegrates. Of the three dimensions of language—the expressive, semantic, and appellative—the semantic dimension is lost. In this, glossolalia regresses to the level of childhood sounds, which as yet signify nothing but are merely expression and appeal. Saying this is not intended to imply that glossolalia is a repetition of early childhood babbling. Anyone who has once achieved linguistic competence can later become active only on the foundation of this competence and can regress only within the framework of a linguistic competence.[40] But no doubt can exist that glossolalia is a return to more primitive forms of speech.

This regression becomes even clearer if we observe the social relationship of speaker and listener. The first babbling monologues of

---

206–7) to two ministers in whom strong aggressive impulses came to view while they spoke in tongues, so that they gave up speaking in tongues, is interesting.

38. Kildahl (*The Psychology*, 53) holds that dependence on charismatic models leads to different traditions of glossolalic style.

39. Samarin ("Glossolalie as Regressive Speech," 79) notes four formal characteristics: "1. echoism . . . , 2. a tendency toward regularity of cadence . . . , 3. a reduced inventory of sounds and 4. a preference for open syllables." In general, he finds a primitivization of speech, which he explains by stating that "the speaker returns to processes that characterized his language learning in early childhood, at a time when he was first learning the part of language most obvious to a child—its phonetic representation. It is in this sense only that I use the term 'regressive' for glossolalia" (p. 85).

40. Samarin (*Tongues*, 127) notes that glossolalia is based "on the linguistic competence and knowledge of each speaker."

the child are completely egocentric. They are not yet directed to an addressee. In three- to six-year-olds, dialogues are frequently "collective monologues," in which each speaks to himself, without listening to the other.[41] The ability of decentered speaking, which abstracts from one's own person and can depict content for every possible addressee, develops only gradually. Paul confirms the egocentric character of glossolalic speech in early Christianity. One who speaks in tongues edifies oneself (1 Cor. 14:4); no one hears such speakers (14:2), who speak for themselves and for God (14:28). The return to egocentric speaking is itself an indicator of psychic regression. To this is added a further regressive trait in the transformation of consciousness. With regard to modern glossolalia, it may be disputed whether it occurs in normal or deviant consciousness. As far as early Christianity is concerned, the question can be settled definitively: Paul presupposes a deviation from normal consciousness, an exclusion of the mind. In this paranormal state, the human subject is either replaced by the divine Spirit or absorbed into it. God is the subject and the addressee of the glossolalic utterances. Thus a psychic state is brought about in which the subject-object relationship is not yet developed, in which the I and the environment rather merge with one another. In other words, glossolalia is connected with the a-dual experience of the world that is characteristic of early childhood, which revives in religious mysticism and can also be experienced in an intense state of being in love.[42]

From a linguistic perspective, glossolalia is therefore reassumption of a more primitive level of speaking; socially, it is a return to egocentric use of language; psychically, it is a regression to a-dual experience of the world. The ancient sources confirm these traits. Paul explicitly formulates the thesis that glossolalia is a matter of childish conduct. After his admonition on intelligible speech in the community, he proceeds, "Brethren, do not be children in your thinking; be babes in evil, but in thinking be mature" (1 Cor. 14:20). And he is surely also thinking of glossolalia in 1 Cor. 13:11: "When I was a child, I spoke

41. Cf. Piaget and Inhelder, *The Psychology of the Child*, 120–21.
42. Cf. ibid., 22. Psychoanalytic theorists speak somewhat confusingly of primary narcissism in this connection. But it is a narcissism without a Narcissus. Freud ("Das Unbehagen," 197ff.) saw in this early childhood narcissism a root of the "oceanic feeling," a religious experience of a somewhat more sublime sort. Sundén finds this feeling alive in the Pentecostal movement: "The conceptions of the Holy Spirit that are present among its members could possibly be those of unlimitedness and of unity with the universe, which Freud spoke of with regard to the oceanic feeling" ("Regression," 59).

like a child, I thought like a child, I reasoned like a child; when I became a man, I gave up childish ways."[43]

But is glossolalia for this reason exclusively regression? It is well known that a shift has occurred in the psychological evaluation of regression, inasmuch as the possibility of a creative regression is conceded in principle;[44] in view of the high estimation that recourses to a-dual modes of experience enjoy at the moment, one will even have to warn against overestimation of regressive behavior and experience. A creative regression is present only when the recourse to what are in principle surpassed modes of behavior and experience leads to a broadening of the repertoire of behavior, when one-sided elements of the process of socialization that has occurred are corrected without creating new and perhaps even greater one-sidedness. Glossolalia in itself is neutral. It can be a retreat from more mature modes of behavior, but it can also signify a broadening of psychic competence. If the regressive and egocentric traits dominate, the result is disintegrative effects on the individual and on the community. Everything depends on the extent to which it is possible to integrate glossolalic behavior into the conscious life of the individual and of the group. Here Paul works with different criteria. He sees opportunities where the unconscious impulses that express themselves in glossolalia are raised to consciousness, become communicable, and serve the positive connection of the members of the group with one another. From him, the connection of glossolalia with interpretations is decisive.

We can provisionally summarize our interpretation of glossolalia from a psychodynamic perspective. Glossolalic behavior is not dependent only on social stimuli, reinforcers, and models. It is also reinforced and motivated by inner processes. It leads, first, to a broadening of consciousness, in that it affords access in a very diffuse fashion to unconscious contents. These, second, can stand in tension to everyday consciousness, and even be suppressed. Third, glossolalia is a broadening of the repertoire of behavior through recourse to childish behavior traits that lie prior to socialization with its one-sidedness. It is connected with a return to non-dual experience of the world. But these partial interpretations simply pose the problem of an

43. Different motives are suggested for Paul's reference to childish behavior in 1 Cor. 14:20. Grant ("Like Children") thinks that the glossolalics had appealed to Mark 10:15. Stendahl ("Glossolalia," 114 n. 5) points out that reference is made to children in the context of Isa. 28:10–11 (cf. 28:9). Probably Paul proceeds simply from the phenomenon of aberrant linguistic behavior. Childish speech is then appropriate as an image.
44. Cf. Heimbrock, *Phantasie*, esp. 80ff.; 46ff.; 57ff.

overall psychodynamic interpretation of the phenomenon. Can the three observations be brought together meaningfully into one context?

Attempt at an Overall Interpretation with the Aid of Rom. 8:18–30

An overall psychodynamic interpretation of the phenomenon of glossolalia would have to say that glossolalic experience and behavior open depth dimensions of an unconscious conflict whose roots lie in the past. Romans 8:18–30 contains precisely these three elements: the unconscious becoming conscious; expression of a profound conflict; recourse to a prior event (although this is not a matter of early childhood experiences). Before we interpret the text as a Pauline interpretation of glossolalia, we must establish that glossolalia is actually the issue here.[45] In what follows, the four chief arguments against this hypothesis will be discussed.

1. The first argument is that when Paul speaks of "inexpressible sighs" in Rom. 8:26, these are by definition inaudible;[46] glossolalia, however, consists of perceptible sounds. Romans 8:26 is therefore said to be thinking rather of the general human phenomenon of an accusation in one's inner dialogue with oneself. In fact, linguistically, the expression *stenagmoi alaletoi* can be translated as "inexpressed and dumb sighs."[47] Yet in connection with ecstatic phenomena the adjective *alalos* means not "dumb" but rather "unintelligible." When the oracle in Delphi was possessed by an *alalon kai kakon pneuma*, she did not become mute but rather spoke with an unusually rough voice.[48] The epileptic boy of Mark 9:25 is possessed by a *pneuma alalon*. When he sees Jesus, he cries aloud. In addition to this, there is a little-noted difficulty in Rom. 8:23ff. It is said twice of Christians that they sigh: they sigh in

45. Käsemann, "Der gottesdienstliche Schrei," is foundational for the interpretation as a reference to glossolalia. According to Käsemann, Paul is correcting early Christian enthusiasm through a view of glossolalia that is determined by a *theologia crucis*. This interpretation has been followed above all by Balz (*Heilsvertrauen*, 69–92).

46. Niederwimmer, "Das Gebet." Wedderburn ("Romans 8,26," esp. 371ff.) pleads emphatically for an inaudible inner speech comparable to the nonverbal communication between lovers. He thus does not interpret 8:26 as a reference to glossolalia but seeks even so to develop from this verse criteria for the theological judgment of glossolalia.

47. This is discussed at length by Balz ("Heilsvertrauen," 78–80). "Inexpressible" need mean "unexpressed" no more than "not hear" in 1 Cor. 14:2 can mean "inaudible." Moreover, an interpretation with reference to unexpressed inner speech (among other things) would not necessarily contradict relating the text to glossolalia, since glossolalia (nowadays) also occurs as inner speech; cf. Kildahl, *The Psychology*, 4. Such inner glossolalia is perhaps thought of in the *Acts of Peter* 39.

48. Plutarch *De defectu oraculorum* 51.2.

themselves (8:23) and the Spirit sighs in them (8:26–27). The first sigh can be understood as a general human groan in the inner dialogue with oneself, for it merely continues the sighing of creation and occurs "in oneself." But if the "inexpressible sighing" of the Spirit is also understood as the nonverbal sighing of Christians, it remains unclear how the sighing of the Spirit is distinguished from the general sighing of Christians.

2. The second argument is that the inexpressible sighs are understood only by God. Glossolalia, on the contrary, is susceptible of translation.[49] We saw, however, that while Paul does insist that glossolalia be intelligible and capable of being translated, this is an ideal condition, not the reality. In fact most of those who speak in tongues do not understand what they say, unless they have at their disposal the additional charism of interpretation. In itself, therefore, glossolalia too is unintelligible and is immediately accessible only to God. Conversely, however, it is also true that the inexpressible sighs of the Spirit are not completely unintelligible. Romans 8:18ff. is an attempt to understand and interpret them.

3. A further argument points out that the inexpressible sighs are a collective prayer and maintains that glossolalia, on the contrary, is private prayer.[50] It is correct that in Rom. 8:36 Paul states, "We do not know how to pray as we ought." That indicates collective prayer— a conception that, moreover, hardly fits the assumption that the issue is one of sighing in inner dialogue. It is decisive that one must not imagine glossolalia as a private matter. Within the liturgy, glossolalia expresses something that moves everyone. Otherwise Paul could not formulate the expectation that another person should speak amen to prayer in tongues or to its translation (1 Cor. 14:16).

4. A difficulty is often seen in the fact that the "inexpressible sighs" are an expression of suffering with the whole of creation but glossolalia is said to be ecstatic rapture.[51] The atmosphere is said to be entirely different in the two cases. But it is a prejudice to associate glossolalia a priori with specific atmospheres. In Origen (*Contra Celsum* 7.9), glossolalia is enveloped by a dark penitential atmosphere. Celsus reports on ecstatic prophets who wander about Syria and Palestine begging and who preach as follows:

49. Thus von der Osten-Sacken (*Römer 8*), who speaks emphatically against interpretation with reference to glossolalia (272–75). Cf. also Wilckens, *Der Brief*, 162.
50. Thus von der Osten-Sacken, *Römer 8*, 272.
51. Ibid., 274.

"I am God [or a son of God, or a divine Spirit]. And I have come. Already the world is being destroyed. And you, O men, are to perish because of your iniquities. But I wish to save you. And you shall see me returning again with heavenly power. Blessed is he who has worshipped me now! But I will cast everlasting fire upon all the rest, both on cities and on country places. And men who fail to realize the penalties in store for them will in vain repent and groan [stenaxousin]. But I will preserve for ever those who have been convinced by me." Then after that he [Celsus] says: Having brandished these threats they then go on to add incomprehensible, incoherent, and utterly obscure utterances, the meaning of which no intelligent person [echon noun] could discover; for they are meaningless and nonsensical, and give a chance for any fool or sorcerer to take the words in whatever sense he likes.[52]

The prophets caricatured by Celsus would have been wandering early Christian charismatics, who could certainly have been seen from outside as beggars and prophets.[53] Their prophecy is connected with glossolalia, for nothing other than that can be meant by "incomprehensible, incoherent, and utterly obscure utterances." Unlike the situation in Paul, however, we do not find here the sequence glossolalia-interpretation; rather, the intelligible words precede the utterances in tongues. Probably glossolalia was considered a sign of the end time (as in Acts 2:14ff.). Paul's eschatological interpretation is incomparably deeper, but it remains within the framework of what we can recognize historically as possible.

Anyone who cannot be convinced by these arguments in favor of identifying the "inexpressible sighs" as glossolalic utterances can nevertheless follow the further reflections. In 1 Corinthians 14, after all, Paul is seeking precisely to make the boundary between glossolalic and intelligible speech more fluid. What the Spirit inspires is to be understood simultaneously with the mind. Sharp distinctions between glossolalic and normal linguistic "sighs" tend to disappear for him as long as it is a matter of utterances caused pneumatically—and that is the case in Rom. 8:26.

Back to the psychodynamic interpretation of glossolalia! The three

52. ET: Henry Chadwick, *Origen: Contra Celsum*, 402–3.
53. So, correctly, Lietzmann (*Geschichte*, 2:45). The Trinitarian formula, the imminent expectation, and the call for repentance speak in favor of wandering Christian preachers. The threat of a judgment in fire for places that reject them may also be found in Luke 10:12. It is also to be assumed that the Exalted One and the Spirit speak in the first-person singular through the prophets. Against the interpretation as wandering Christian preachers, cf. Weinel, *Die Wirkungen*, 90–91.

elements of its psychodynamic interpretation—the unconscious becoming conscious, the expression of conflict, and regression—are found in the Pauline interpretation of pneumatic speaking in Rom. 8:18ff.

1. Glossolalic speaking occurs in Romans 8, as it does elsewhere, as the language of the unconscious. The sighing of the Spirit stems from the depth of the human heart, which is probed only by him "who searches the hearts of men" (Rom. 8:27). But man has no complete insight into the origin and goal of glossolalic sighing. For "we do not know how to pray as we ought" (8:26). The theme of ignorance is combined with the theme of God's knowledge of the heart. Together, the two conceptual elements produce the conception of an unconscious dimension within man.

2. Paul relates glossolalic sighing to a primeval conflict whose negative outcome subjected all creation to corruptibility (8:20). There is no doubt that Paul is thinking of the Fall, the conflict of Adam according to which Paul has interpreted the human conflict under the law in general (Rom. 7:7ff.). This fall recurs in each individual. It is simultaneously primeval event and individual fate. Even for Paul, then, it is not only this or that utterance in tongues that is an expression of a conflict; rather, glossolalia as such is a "symptom" of a traumatic event that lies over human life like a dark shadow from both mythic and individual past.

3. Regression is the third rubric of a psychodynamic interpretation of glossolalia. This trait is also to be found in the Pauline interpretation. Glossolalic experience not only harks back to a primeval event; it corresponds to a sigh in the whole of creation. A tendency we share with nonhuman creation—in other words, an archaic heritage within us—comes to expression here. Associations with childhood are also unmistakable. For the glossolalic sighing (8:26) is expression of the Spirit, just like the community's cry of "Abba" (8:15). At the time of Paul, the use of "Abba" still clearly bore early childhood associations. It was the child's familiar address to the father, which later did become increasingly broadened.[54] Paul himself lets these associations become

54. In "Abba," esp. 58–67, Jeremias has rightly corrected his earlier thesis that *Abba* is in every case an early childhood expression for one's father, since both the circle to whom this address was directed and the circle of those who used it in speech were extended beyond the relationship of father and child. Yet some of his sources for the expansion of the linguistic usage continue to show clearly its origin in early childhood. For—with regard to the first point—though people other than one's father were addressed as Abba, the oldest source for this expanded linguistic usage attributes it to schoolchildren (*b.Ta 'an.* 23b = Billerbeck, *Kommentar* 1:375). And—with regard to the second point—

clear when he replaces the term "sons of God" (Rom. 8:14) with the term "children of God" after the cry of "Abba" (8:17); associations of the latter term with early childhood are demonstrable.[55] The metaphors having to do with birth are even more clear. It is true that the image, as so often is the case, is somewhat askew: the sons whose birth and appearance are awaited themselves sigh in labor pains.

The psychodynamic analysis of glossolalia searches for the inner function of glossolalic behavior—especially for the "inner reinforcers" that make it a value for the individual. Proceeding from the comments of Paul, one comes to the following conjectures.

Glossolalia is quite certainly a stimulating experience that affords man access to new and previously unconscious dimensions; one can even interpret glossolalia, with Jung, as a breakthrough of unconscious energy.[56] The strangeness of glossolalic speech is then explained as follows. A collective unconscious that is strongly estranged from conscious life has to express itself at first in a strange manner.[57] Integration of the unconscious impulses is not achieved immediately; the first result is an inflation-like flooding of consciousness by the unconscious. That can have destructive effects, but it is also an opportunity.[58] To take advantage of this opportunity positively, it is decisive that glossolalic utterances correspond to the value system of a group; the experience of such correspondence could even constitute a

---

though adults do also speak of their abba, it is not coincidental that they do so when speaking of their childhood: "While I was still a boy, I saw while riding on Abba's shoulders . . ." (*t.Sanh.* 9.11). In addition, Christian fathers of the church attest the early childhood use of "Abba" as a form of address as late as the fourth century (cf. the references to Theodore of Mopsuestia, John Chrysostom, and Theodoret of Cyrus in Jeremias, "Abba," 61 n. 41).

55. Cf. 1 Thess. 2:7 ("like a nurse taking care of her children"); 1 Thess. 2:11; 2 Cor. 12:14; Gal. 4:19; Rom. 9:8–9.

56. Jung commented on glossolalia only in passing. In "Das Wandlungssymbol," 311, he states that the cross as a symbol of psychic order appears precisely in times of psychic disorder, "while the latter is usually provoked by the entrance of unconscious content." In a footnote he refers to glossolalia in early Christianity.

57. Kelsey (*Tongue Speaking*, 197) cites from a letter Jung wrote in 1955: "Speaking with tongues (glossolalia) is observed in cases of ecstasies. . . . It is probable that the strangeness of the unconscious contents not yet integrated in consciousness demands an equally strange language."

58. The comments of people active in speaking in tongues which have been collected by Samarin (*Tongues*) point in this direction. Glossolalia is said to have "a profound effect on the deep feelings and attitude which the mind cannot always directly control" (p. 206). It is said to bring to expression "the heights and depths of what one feels" (p. 206), to be "an opening and releasing of the deeper centers of life" (p. 208). One who speaks in tongues "has dropped the facade of logical flesh and is on a plateau of privacy with our Father beyond the subtle influence of accepted social niceties" (p. 209).

part of the inner reinforcement psychodynamic theories seek. Instead of division between private impulses and social norms, instead of antagonism between consciousness and the unconscious, the consonance of these elements is experienced. Paul expands this consonance to the whole of creation. When one yields to the pneumatic impulses that come from the unconscious, one may believe that one is in harmony with the whole cosmos—including the highest norm-giving tribunal, God himself.

Glossolalia would thus be both expression of a tension between unconscious contents and the everyday world and reduction of this tension. When Paul interprets glossolalic experience and behavior eschatologically in Rom. 8:18–30, he confers on them a new function: glossolalia is an impulse toward human transformation. All glossolalic groaning aims toward the "appearance of the children of God," who are "destined to conformity with the Son of God." With this interpretation, Paul integrates the inflation of consciousness by the unconscious into his symbolic world. The central symbol is sonship, and the Son. The tendency toward him would correspond to a preexistent orientation grounded in creation. Expressed in the language of an archetypal theory of religion, sonship is the symbol of the self in whom the conflict between the unconscious archaisms within us and their cultural requirements has been overcome. Glossolalia is a longing for the appearance of the self, for "individuation," which assumes form through suffering. The regressive tendency of glossolalic behavior and experience would thus receive a progressive orientation.

With this conception we have modified the psychodynamic approach in a cognitive manner. The transformation of regressive energy into a progressive tendency occurs through interpretation of glossolalia, through its integration into the symbolic world of the community. Here the symbols are not only an expression of psychic processes; they determine their orientation. As certain as it is that glossolalia is incited by the external learning world and that it is motivated by inner processes, its function is still always dependent on the interpretation that is ascribed to it.

COGNITIVE ASPECTS
OF GLOSSOLALIC BEHAVIOR

At first glance, glossolalic behavior seems extremely resistant to cognitive efforts at psychological interpretation, for in glossolalia reason is excluded in favor of a scarcely differentiated emotional current. But the legitimacy of the cognitive perspective is grounded in the phenomenon itself; in early Christianity, hermeneia—that is, the gift of interpretation—belongs to glossolalia. We assume that Paul was one of those who possessed it. He identifies himself with speaking in tongues (1 Cor. 14:18) but attributes to it value for the community only when it is joined to an interpretation. His instruction "He who speaks in a tongue should pray for the power to interpret" (14:13) applies also to himself. Beyond this, interpretation was an important instrument of community leadership. It conferred social recognition on the speakers who were interpreted and could also set theological accents. It is hardly conceivable that Paul renounced this instrument of influence. At the time when the Epistle to the Romans was composed, he was in Corinth, in a community that was active in speaking in tongues. The community no doubt raised the expectation that he practice himself what he had recommended so emphatically in his letter. We therefore assume that Paul stepped forward in community assemblies as an interpreter of glossolalic utterances. Presumably he uses in Rom. 8:18ff. the images, word fields, and patterns of expression on which he also drew in other contexts when interpreting glossolalia during the liturgy.[59] But before we investigate the cognitive structuring of glossolalic experience in Romans 8 we must first clarify what took place in an interpretation. How was glossolalic behavior interpreted in Corinth? What new interpretation does Paul give to the social environment of glossolalic behavior in 1 Corinthians 12? But it is in Romans 8 that Paul presents the summation of his theological reflection on pneumatic speech. We shall therefore turn to this chapter again at the end (pp. 332–41 below).

The Cognitive Structuring of Glossolalic Behavior in Early Christianity in General

The most striking characteristic of glossolalic speech is its lack of semantic content. No specific content can be ordered to the phonetic

59. In 1 Cor. 14:26*, Paul lists different forms that have their Sitz im Leben in the early Christian liturgy: psalm, teaching, revelation, glossolalia, interpretation. In Phil. 2:6–12, he cites an early Christian psalm (or one he composed himself). First Corinthians 15:3–5 could be an early Christian teaching. In 2 Cor. 12:1–9, he reports on a revelation. That he does not communicate any glossolalic utterances is understandable. But it is surely conceivable that he has preserved for us an interpretation. Von der Osten-Sacken, on the contrary, comes to the conclusion that Rom. 8:19–27 is not "composed in a specific form with corresponding Sitz im Leben" (*Römer 8*, 97). He postulates an earlier version behind the text. But the stylistic characteristics he adduces as foundation can be explained just as well by proximity to oral linguistic form.

elements, although the structure of speaking in tongues, which is similar to language, suggests a content and is experienced within the glossolalic community as significant. "Mysteries" (1 Cor. 14:2) are communicated. But how are they communicated?

Semantically, the problem can be formulated as follows. Glossolalia is speech without denotative content, in which communication is limited almost exclusively to the connotative associations. The emotional-associative outer sphere of utterances becomes the semantic core. The problem can be formulated more precisely. How can emotional connotations be communicated without denotatively significant words? To early Christianity, that was a miracle. To us, however, it is not inexplicable; rather, those who spoke in tongues made use of means of communication we all use.[60]

Glossolalia contains, first, cryptosemantic elements, that is, fragments of language that involuntarily evoke significant associations. Expressions like "Yezu," "Yeshua," and "Yay-so" are reminiscent of Jesus;[61] utterances such as "satana," "amen," and "kristu" are identifiable by everyone.[62] Ancient magical texts with cryptosemantic names of gods offer analogies.[63] As far as primitive Christianity is concerned, one could think of elements from foreign languages such as "Abba"[64] (Rom. 8:15–16; Gal. 4:6) and "Maranatha!" (1 Cor. 16:22), and possibly also of short acclamations such as "Kyrios Iesous."[65]

Secondary means of linguistic expression like intonation, tempo, and tone are to be mentioned in the second place. We can tell from these whether someone is questioning, narrating, admonishing, or commanding. General emotional atmospheres are deposited in them. Thus it could be that the different "kinds of tongues" (1 Cor. 12:10) are distinguished through such secondary linguistic means.

Third, nonverbal means of communication—posture, mimicry, and gestures—are very important. In almost every cultural region one can recognize from posture whether someone is praying or not. It is clear

60. Osser, Ostwald, et al. ("Glossolalic Speech," 10) refer to social factors and patterns of intonation as bearers of meaning. Cf. Williams, "Glossolalia," 18.

61. Examples in Samarin, *Tongues*, 89.

62. Examples in Holm, "Das Zungenreden," 230.

63. Cf. Lietzmann, *An die Korinther*, 69.

64. Moffatt, *The First Epistle*, 213, holds that expressions like "a-b-a-b" could have been understood as "abba."

65. Every tongue (*pasa glossa*) shall confess Jesus as Lord (Phil. 2:10–11). Speaking in tongues (*glossa*) can then hardly be excluded, especially since it is the language of angels (1 Cor. 13:1) and the angels as heavenly powers are to join in the acclamation (Phil. 2:10–11).

from 1 Corinthians 14, for example, that it was possible to distinguish in Corinth between glossolalic messages and prayers.

Last, reference may be made to situative means of communication. As soon as a group is present in a space with sacral symbols, a preliminary element of communication is established by its location and by its common convictions.

The communication of emotional-connotative contents probably occurred in glossolalia through cryptosemantic, secondary linguistic, nonverbal, and situative means of communication. Certainly, no precise messages can be sent in this way. What is sent here is diffuse and general.

A further problem consists in how the interpreters could render such diffuse messages into intelligible language. Their interpretations had to be accepted by the group (and also by the speaker). Before one thinks of suggestion or self-deception, one should take into consideration a much more proximate explanation—that psychological experiments show us that emotional states are ambivalent.[66] A state of corporal excitement brought about by one and the same drug can be experienced both as fear and as joy, depending on whether one is in a social milieu evoking fear or in a friendly setting. How the emotional excitement is colored depends on the processes of cognitive interpretation. But if individuals interpret their condition in correspondence to the perceived social situation, it is possible in principle that the emotional condition of a group could also be subsequently interpreted and steered by an interpreter. Such interpretations can be experienced as evident. The condition to be interpreted is in itself, after all, ambiguous, global, and diffuse.

Of course, we cannot verify this hypothesis on the basis of Pauline texts. Investigations of contemporary glossolalia do confirm it. Three American researchers had a preacher of the Pentecostal movement record utterances on ten themes (severity, softness, emptiness, death, beginning, fullness, leadership, end, consequences, weakness) on a tape that was then played to different test groups under differing conditions. The results may be summarized in two points. First, the answers of the evaluators exhibited an astonishing agreement among themselves, but seldom captured the point the one speaking in tongues wished to express. Second, the agreement related to emotional aspects. All nonverbal and situative possibilities of communication were absent

66. Schachter and Singer, "Cognitive, Social, and Physiological Determinants"; summarized in Oerter, *Psychologie*, 444ff.

in this experiment. The assessment of glossolalic utterances had to be restricted completely to the tape recording. Nonetheless, a type of emotional communication did occur.[67] If that is possible in the artificial situation of the laboratory, how much more is it possible in real life, where the speaker and the listener are joined through prior communication and where the interpreter is not a blank page. If the interpreter is an influential person with sensitivity, it will not be difficult for that person to sense and to articulate the emotional condition of the group.

These reflections on the semantic aspects of glossolalic speech confirm what other contemporary investigations of glossolalia show in general: glossolalia is no supernatural phenomenon; it can be explained naturally. It is true that the natural phenomenon of glossolalia, like everything natural, can attain symbolic character. Comparison with related paralinguistic phenomena shows how dependent this is on the framework of interpretation. Numerous linguistically meaningless utterances are preserved from antiquity (esp. from the 3d and 4th cents.) as magical formulas. Of course one must distinguish between glossolalia and such formulas. It would seem that magical formulas were often forcibly constructed. They had to be learned by heart. Glossolalia, on the contrary, is a spontaneous stream of phonemes.[68] But despite such differences, ancient magical formulas exhibit to some extent linguistic traits similar to modern glossolalic utterances. A comparison of randomly selected magical formulations of a length of one thousand letters with a corresponding normal text shows that some of the linguistic characteristics of glossolalia that have been demonstrated by W. J. Samarin can also be demonstrated in magical formulas:[69]

> 1. Echolike phenomena are far more frequent in magical formulas than in normal texts. Some examples from Greek papyri will illustrate this: "tazo zon tazo tazo ptazo . . . souori . . . souo oous . . . saraptoumi sarachti . . . zouzo arrouzo . . . chachach chachach charcharachach . . . acha achacha chach charchara chach."[70] In normal text, echolike phenomena originate from the requirements of grammatical congruence. In

---

67. Lafall, Monahan, and Richman, "Communication."
68. Manson ("The Corinthian Correspondence," 204) rightly stresses the difference. The combination of sounds in the magical papyri are the "product of perverted ingenuity rather than religious ecstasy. It is not glossolalia, whatever else it may be." Dautzenberg ("Glossolalie," 231) expresses himself more positively on possible connections.
69. Samarin, "Glossolalia," 79ff. The sample test comes from Preisendanz, *Papyri*, 10–13. I am grateful to M. Hoffmann for preparation of the statistics.
70. Preisendanz, *Papyri*, 135ff.

nonsemantic utterances, they can develop simply on the grounds of phonetic play.

2. In addition, a preference for open syllables can be recognized in magical formulas. In large part, these are due to lengthy multiplication of vowels. In an equal number of letters, magical formulas contained 381 open syllables (91 closed), while the normal texts contained 339 open syllables (107 closed).

3. Certain differences in the use of vowels and consonants are also present. In the magical formulas there were 543 vowels; in the normal texts, 539. The differences emerge when one compares the different vowels. The vowels *a* and *o* were preferred in magical formulations (*a:* 190 in magical formulas, 123 in normal texts; *o:* 68 in magical formulas, 43 in normal texts).

Yet, despite some comparable linguistic traits, the self-understanding of ancient magicians and that of early Christian speakers in tongues are diametrically opposed. The magicians apply their paralinguistic utterances instrumentally to manipulate the secret "sympathies" between things, but the attitude of speakers in tongues toward their language is not at all instrumental. What streams from their mouths is not even their work but an utterance of the Holy Spirit. They transform no object. The accent lies rather on change of the subject. The language is not an instrument but a charism.

The differing experience of comparable paralinguistic phenomena is certainly not dependent on possible linguistic differences, but rather on socially supported processes of interpretation. Three traits will be emphasized as far as early Christianity is concerned. First, the transsubjective causal attribution of glossolalic behavior, which gives the speaker in tongues a feeling of being filled with a divine Spirit. Second, the social assessment of exclusivity. Only a few possessed the gift of glossolalia. The early Christian community distinguished itself from its environment through this gift. Third, positive self-perception on the basis of the glossolalic gift. If the charism is conferred only on a few and if it joins one immediately with the Deity, then those who speak in tongues can ascribe to their lives an unconditioned value. A cognitively oriented psychology will see in this positive self-experience the decisive key to the positive effects of glossolalic behavior. Here lies the determinative "inner reinforcement" of glossolalia. Even conflicts and tensions can be borne more easily, treated and overcome with the help of a positive self-image—and such treatment need not always be adapted to reality. The result can be the exclusion of resistant aspects of reality because they are not compatible with one's own self-image.

The three traits that have been emphasized are intended to illustrate that it is not the inner and outer world in itself but rather its interpretation that determines religious experience and behavior. That unconscious tendencies come to expression in glossolalia can hardly be denied. But it depends on the interpretation whether one sees in them negatively evaluated "repressions," collective archetypes that function positively, or inspiration by the Holy Spirit. The same is true of the learning environment. Glossolalia is dependent on a reinforcing and stimulating social environment. But again it depends on its interpretation whether one sees in glossolalic groups psychically dependent people, representatives of an alternative culture, or the elect of the last days. The self-image of those who speak in tongues and their image in the eyes of others will be colored differently in a manner corresponding to such interpretations.

The Cognitive Restructuring of the Social Environment: 1 Corinthians 12

We have already seen how Paul seeks to influence glossolalic behavior through influencing stimuli, reinforcers, and models of the social environment. As the founder of the community, Paul is a decisive factor in the social environment of the Corinthian communities. Yet the greatest weight is to be attributed to a consistent cognitive restructuring, through which community and glossolalia are placed in a new relationship to each other, not to transformation of individual elements of this environment. This will be shown with regard to two points. First, Paul emphatically expands the transsubjective causal attribution of Christian conduct, its retracing to the Holy Spirit, to all the activities of Christians. This occurs with the aid of a modified concept of the Spirit. Second, Paul transforms the functional evaluation of Christian activities through the image of the "body of Christ," in which all activities are functionally dependent on one another.

Besides the conception that special charismatics have received the Spirit and exercise the Spirit in extraordinary gifts (cf., e.g., 1 Cor. 3:1; 14:37), there was another conception in early Christianity, according to which all Christians had received the Spirit with baptism (1 Cor. 12:13). Paul is able to actualize this more general conception in order to understand the whole Christian life as effect of the Spirit.

He lists the charisms of the Christian life three times in 1 Corinthians 12. These lists contain a variety of activities in addition to speaking in tongues but are chiefly interested in relativizing glossolalia. Each time the list breaks off after mention of speaking in tongues (cf. 12:8–10; 12:28; 12:29–30). If one also takes into consideration the later catalogue of charisms in Rom. 12:6–8, the receding of irrational gifts of the Spirit is impossible to overlook.[71] Even in 1 Cor. 12:28–30 Paul no longer mentions the wonder-working faith and the discernment of spirits which are found in the first list of charisms; instead he adds "helpers" and "administrators"—representing very down-to-earth activities. In Rom. 12:6–8, healings, speaking in tongues, and the gift of interpretation are also dropped from the catalogue of charisms. Above all, however, this catalogue of charisms shifts into very general admonitions (12:9ff.) directed to every Christian. What Paul is seeking may be formulated psychologically as follows. He wishes to achieve a cognitive restructuring of social perception with the aid of a more general concept of the Spirit. The personal gift is to be understood as the effect of precisely that power which is at work in all members of the community.[72]

This cognitive restructuring of social perception becomes even more clear in the image of the body of Christ. The general image of the body and its members was frequently applied to social and political relationships in antiquity. The Pauline usage of the image has some particular traits with regard both to scope and to content.[73]

The scope of the community encompassed by the body metaphor was specified in different ways in antiquity. The image occurs in three ways.

1. It is used to interpret the polis as an organic body. The classical example of this is the fable of Menenius Agrippa.[74] The fable of the rebellion of the members against the stomach serves to overcome the conflict between plebeians

71. Cf. the table in Kuss, *Der Römerbrief,* 554.
72. In his review of Weinel's book on the effects of the Holy Spirit, Bousset worked out clearly the significance of cognitive interpretations for the experience of the Spirit. In Paul the conception of the Spirit is based not only on experiences but also on reciprocal influence of experience and theory.
73. On the social use of the body imagery, cf. Nestle, "Die Fabel," and Knox, "Parallels." In what follows we abstract from mythical use of the body imagery which interprets the cosmos as the body of the deity. This imagery could be connected with the social body imagery. The fact that the world had always been conceived as a large organism contributed to facilitating the transfer of the social imagery from the polis to the cosmos as a large polis. K. M. Fischer (*Tendenz,* 52–78) gives a good overview.
74. Livy 2.32; Dionysius of Halycarnassus 6.86; Zonaras *Epitome of History* 7.14; cf. also Plutarch *Coriolanus* 6; Babrius 134; Romulus 66.

and patricians. The Sitz im Leben of this image is the class struggle that threatens the polis, which is met with appeals for harmony. A divided polis is considered a sick body.[75] The best state is one in which the citizens all rejoice and suffer with one another—just as the fate of one member calls the entire body into joint suffering.[76]

2. Through the conquests of Alexander, the foundations for the expansion of the image in the Hellenistic age were created. The entire cosmos could be understood as a polis, and every person could be understood as a citizen of this polis. The transference of the body imagery to the cosmos lay at hand, though there was awareness of the tensions between the polis imagery and the body imagery in transferring the imagery to the cosmos.[77] The most impressive development of the image may be found in the Stoics of the imperial period, for example, in Seneca: "All that you behold, that which comprises both god and man, is one—we are parts of one great body. Nature produced us related to one another, since she created us from the same source and to the same end. She engendered in us mutual affection, and made us prone to friendships. She established fairness and justice; according to her ruling, it is more wretched to commit than to suffer injury. Through her orders, let our hands be ready for all that needs to be helped."[78] How an individualistic element can be combined with this universalist expansion of the image is instructive. If the world is a fatherland with everyone a citizen, then one may no more harm an individual than one may harm the fatherland, for the individual is a part of the whole.[79]

3. In comparison with this, the Pauline use of the image is a constriction. Not the world or the polis is the body but a small group within society—the Christian community. Possibly the Jewish community in the Diaspora had already understood itself in this way. According to Philo (On the Virtues 103), the Jews should accept proselytes as full-fledged members "by having the same griefs and joys, so that they may seen to be the separate parts of a single living being which is compacted and unified by their fellowship in it."[80] A new element here is that the body is not pre-given but rather originates through historical process. A transformation in human beings through conversion is presupposed. In early Christianity, the Spirit led to overcoming the boundaries between Jews and Greeks, free and slave (1 Cor. 12:13). The body of Christ is also more than an image. Since the Risen One lives in Christians, the body is a mystical reality. One may criticize the early Christian usage of the image

75. Plato Laws 1.62D. Cf. the metaphor of illness in Plato Republic 2.372E, 426A–C; Josephus Jewish Wars 4.406–7.
76. Plato Republic 462; cf. 1 Cor. 12:26.
77. Cf. Dio Chrysostom Discourses 36.30.
78. ET: R. M. Gummere, Seneca: Ad Lucilium Epistulae Morales, vol. 3. of 3 vols. (LCL, 1925), 91); cf. Epictetus Discourses 2.20.1ff.; Marcus Aurelius 2.1; 7.13.
79. Seneca De Ira 2.31.7.
80. ET: F. H. Colson, Philo, vol. 8 of 10 vols. (LCL, 1939), 227.

as a restriction in comparison with its cosmopolitan function in the Stoa: as the body of Christ, the church separates itself from all present communities. But the body imagery again achieves cosmic breadth in the Deutero-Pauline epistles. Yet even then it is a matter of a body that comes into being, not a naturally preestablished body (cf. Col. 2:19).

A second characteristic of the Pauline use of the image lies in the specification of interhuman relationships within the body. The content of the image is changed just like its scope.

1. The social body imagery is usually used to draw out the inevitable superiority of one of the members. That is the point in Menenius Agrippa. Romulus, a composer of fables, gives the same material the ingenuous moral "This fable admonishes the servant to be faithful."[81] In Babrius, an educator of princes, the fable of the rebellion of members against the head has an antidemocratic point.[82]

2. Yet the body imagery is also frequently used to underline the mutual connection of the members, without attributing precedence to a particular member. Seneca, for example, states that the body politic is preserved inviolate by the alertness and love of its members.[83] "Mutual affection" is given to members of a body.[84] All are destined to cooperate as members.[85] This mutual solidarity also includes the weaker ones. Thus Solon is said to have given to each citizen the right to file suit for another, in order to accustom citizens to feeling like "members of one body."[86] The duty to help those in need of aid follows from the unity of men.[87] With this we come quite close to the early Christian employment of the image.

3. In Paul this idea of solidarity is sharpened. In the body of Christ all are to care for one another (1 Cor. 12:25). In this, one member has a prominent place, yet this is not the dominating member but the weakest. If one member is specially emphasized elsewhere within the body imagery, it is, for example, the head or the stomach, that is, the members on which the other members depend. In Paul this position is taken by the weakest member; the "least honorable" members are accorded special honors (1 Cor. 12:23–24*). Here Paul is thinking of the lower part of the body with the sexual organs, which are covered by clothes. To express this without the image, we may say that the weakest members in the Christian community become the decisive criterion for the conduct of all. Even Christ is not the dominating part in the "body of Christ." He forms the entire body. He is just as present in the weakest

81. Romulus 66.
82. Babrius, no. 134.
83. Seneca *De Ira* 2.31.7.
84. ET: Gummere, *Seneca: Ad Lucilium Epistulae Morales* 3:91.
85. Marcus Aurelius 2.1, 7.13.
86. ET: Bernadotte Perrin, *Plutarch's Lives*, vol. 1 of 11 vols. (LCL, 1914), 453.
87. Seneca *Epistles* 95.52.

members as in the strongest. With this, all efforts to establish precedence in principle for specific charisms are criticized.

The new causal attributions and functional evaluation of glossolalic behavior that become evident in Paul have the same intention: the multiplicity of Christian activities have the same origin in the Spirit and the same value in the body of Christ. The Corinthian interpretation of glossolalia was determined by a theme of separation: glossolalia is the sign of the elect with reference to which one recognizes believers in distinction from the world. Paul, on the contrary, restructures the interpretation of glossolalia on the basis of a theme of social connection: it is part of a diversity held together by the Spirit and the body of Christ.

The Cognitive Restructuring of Psychic Dynamics: 1 Corinthians 14

Paul also offers new patterns of interpretation for the self-perception of those who speak in tongues. These also affect, first, the causal attribution of glossolalic behavior and, second, its evaluation.

For the Corinthian community, the subject of speaking in tongues was the Spirit of God. The human subject is excluded during the glossolalia; the mind is silent. Here Paul sets new accents. The element in us that drives toward glossolalia is ascribed to the human subject to a greater degree than it was in the tradition. What speaks in tongues is "my spirit." One may dispute whether this refers to the participation in the divine Spirit which is accorded to each individual,[88] or whether it is the human spirit that gives witness to the revelation of the divine Spirit. Romans 8:16, where God's Spirit bears witness to our spirit that we are God's children, speaks in favor of the second alternative. 1 Corinthians 14:32, where mention is made of the "spirits of prophets," in other words, of many individual "spirits," could be adduced in favor of the first assumption. In any case, however, it is a tribunal which is ascribed to the individual human being and for which the individual is responsible. Otherwise it would be meaningless to state that the prophetic spirits are subject to the prophets. One cannot simply claim that a strange pneumatic stream is pouring through the speaker. One reveals oneself in pneumatic speaking.

Only on the basis of this relativizing of the transsubjective causal

---

88. Thus Weiss, *Der I. Korintherbrief*, 327–28. But in Rom. 1:9, *en to pneumati mou* means simply "in my spirit," i.e., the individual human spirit.

attribution of glossolalic behavior is it understandable why the relationship of *nous* and *pneuma* is so completely different here from what it is in the Platonic tradition of inspiration. There the *nous* leaves one in order to make room for the divine *pneuma*.[89] In Paul, however, both are to be active together. "I will pray with the spirit and I will pray with the mind also" (1 Cor. 14:15). In Paul the opposition between spirit and mind is not an unbridgeable contradiction between human reason and divine Spirit but (also) an inner opposition between different human aspects which is in no sense unbridgeable. Philo says that divine Spirit and human mind cannot dwell next to each other, but Paul claims the opposite. Spirit and mind can be joined to each other and complement each other.

One could object that in Rom. 8:26 Paul recognizes an ecstatic prayer in which the Spirit takes the place of the subject. This text doubtless stands near to the Platonic tradition of inspiration. This is shown not least by the theme of ignorance:

> Likewise the Spirit helps us in our weakness; for we do not know how to pray as we ought, but the Spirit himself intercedes for us with sighs too deep for words.

But precisely this text makes clear the difference from the Platonic tradition of inspiration. According to this tradition, the inspired person is an instrument of the divine will. Inspired persons say nothing of their own. Only the deity speaks through them. But in Paul just the opposite is true. The divine Spirit comes to the aid of human weakness. In pneumatic ecstasy, one does not say what the Deity wishes to say; rather, the divine Spirit articulates what one would like to say but cannot. It supplies words vicariously. What one says is the continuation of the cosmic sigh that is alive in all creatures. The theme of ignorance is revised correspondingly. It is a matter not of one's ignorance of what the divine Spirit spews forth, but of ignorance about oneself. We do not know what *we* should pray!

The visible transformations of the Platonic tradition of inspiration complement one another. First, the human being is not God's instrument; rather, God's Spirit is the promoter of human desire for expression. Second, the mind is not excluded when the Spirit becomes active; rather, both work together. In both cases the tendency is the same. Ecstatic speech is not attributed without mediation to transsub-

89. Philo *Who Is the Heir* 265; cf. Plato *Ion* 534B.

jective causes; it is rather the language of the subject, whether a human subject, moved by God, articulates its impulses with the aid of the mind (1 Cor. 14:14ff.) or the divine Spirit vicariously formulates unconscious human impulses as inexpressible sighs. In both cases it is intended that one be placed in a position to communicate what moves one in one's inmost being. Here we can establish a clear tendency toward subjectivizing ecstatic experience: such experience is attributed to the subject to a greater extent than it was in the tradition. When the ancient church later emphasized against the Montanists that inspiration does not exclude the human subject but rather strengthens it, this argument pursued a tendency that goes back to Paul.

The modified causal attribution of glossolalic behavior necessarily leads to a new evaluation. If the human subject also brings itself to expression in glossolalia, then glossolalia participates in human transitoriness and inadequacy. We can infer from 1 Cor. 14:37 that the Corinthian speakers in tongues called themselves *pneumatikoi;* they probably also considered themselves, as *pneumatikoi*, to be "perfect" (1 Cor. 2:6*, 15*; 3:1*). Here Paul revalues: one should seek perfection in another area—in understanding (1 Cor. 14:20). One who has the glossolalic gift is not already perfect; the perfect person is rather one who can communicate it intelligibly. But even in this case it is a matter of something provisional. For intelligible prophecy and knowledge will also one day cease, along with unintelligible glossolalia, when the perfect comes. Then only love will remain (1 Cor. 13:10–13).

Glossolalic Experience and the Whole of Reality in Rom. 8:18–30

In 1 Corinthians 12—14, Paul is completely determined by the immediate problematic of integrating overflowing pneumatic activity into the community life and into the entire person; in Romans 8 he addresses the phenomenon from a changed perspective. Immediate problems are no longer to be detected. Paul is able to assess glossolalia more positively than in 1 Corinthians. Three aspects will be emphasized. First, glossolalic experience and behavior become the first sign of overcoming the conflict of flesh and spirit. Second, glossolalia is retraced to a universally present cosmic tension; Paul undertakes a new causal attribution. Third, a new evaluation is based on this. Even more strongly than in 1 Corinthians 13, glossolalia here appears as a transitory phenomenon and as an expression of suffering. These three aspects will be discussed in order.

1. The appearance of Christ served to overcome the conflict between flesh and spirit (Rom. 8:2–3). But the portrayal of the redeemed in Rom. 8:1–16 is at first still determined by this opposition. The flesh seeks hostility; the spirit peace. The flesh is rejected by God; the Spirit makes one pleasing to God. The fleshly works of the body must be killed; the Spirit gives life.

In Rom. 8:18–30 something new takes the place of this antagonistic train of thought. The longing of creation, of the community, and of the Spirit form together a melancholy accord. A threefold sigh streams through the cosmos. Everything joins in this sighing. The new tone, in comparison to the first section with its antagonism of flesh and spirit, becomes even more clear when one considers that the term *ktisis*, "creation," in scope though not in content roughly encompasses the same sphere of objects that the term "flesh" covers—that is, all living things, even absolutely everything that is subjected to corruption.[90] Whereas elsewhere Paul always emphasizes the contradiction between nature and the new man, here he uncovers a profound correspondence—a common longing that joins "nature" and the spirit. The many terms with the prefix *sun* are characteristic of this section— *summarturei* (v. 16), *sugkleronomoi, sumpaschomen, sundoxasthomen* (v. 17), *sustenazei, sunodinei* (v. 22), *sunantilambanetai* (v. 26), *sunergei* (v. 28), and *summorphous* (v. 29). All these statements with the prefix *sun* characterize the new basic tone: the correspondence between creation, community, and Spirit.

A third section of the text (Rom. 8:31–39) brings a further change in the structure of the thought. Four challenging questions structure the text: "Who is against us?" (v. 31), "Who shall bring any charge against God's elect?" (v. 33), "Who is to condemn?" (v. 34), "Who shall separate us from the love of Christ?" (v. 35).[91] These are challenges to an opponent of the Christians in court. The answer is clear from the start: there no longer exists any hostile power that could threaten the redeemed. No enemy makes its presence known; rather, all hostility is overcome through "love," a term that occurs three times (vv. 35, 37,

90. On the old dispute as to what *ktisis* includes, cf. Wilckens, *Der Brief*, 152–53. The *ktisis* must include everything that is subjected to the *phthora* (8:21), but *phthora* is synonymous with *sarx* and *haima* (1 Cor. 15:50). Beyond this, the accented mention of the "entire" creation lets the scope of creation be drawn quite broadly.

91. On the formal structure, cf, the analysis of von der Osten-Sacken, *Römer 8*, 14–60. The indicators of pre-Pauline tradition are in my judgment too weak. Paul is hardly formulating ad hoc. He is reflecting ideas with which he works constantly. Slight shifts of accent and inconsistencies can easily be explained in this way.

39). This love overcomes not only all accusing voices before the forum of God but also all external sufferings. The last part of the text can be characterized formally as "contradiction overcome by love." It thus forms a synthesis between the first two sections of the text—the contradiction of flesh and spirit and the consonance of the cosmic sigh. In each case a contradiction is evoked, but only in order to establish that there is no longer any contradiction. A cosmic consonance is evoked, yet not a consonance of sighing and suffering but one of a love uniting all things.

It is important to be clear that in this text glossolalia is not criticized. It serves as a positive argument. The "pledge of the Spirit," the first experiential sign of an overcoming of the contradiction, shows itself in glossolalia. All interpretations that seek to establish here only "antien-thusiastic" tendencies overlook this trait.[92] The view of reality as a whole is undoubtedly influenced by "enthusiastic" behavior and ex-perience, among other factors. Yet the converse is also true: pneumatic experience is integrated into the whole of reality in a new manner.

2. Integration of pneumatic experience into the whole of reality occurs through a new causal attribution of glossolalic behavior. Glos-solalia is not retraced only to the divine Spirit. It is an expression of a longing inherent in the whole of creation, which joins us with all living beings. The Spirit vicariously articulates this longing which comes from within one and even from the whole of nature. The deeper cause of glossolalic behavior is an obscure event that exposed all creation to nothingness. The corruptibility of creaturely life is not an inevitable fact but rather slavery under which life came through the Fall. Creation was subjected to corruptibility by God.[93] Here Paul undertakes a

92. The antienthusiastic interpretation was founded by Käsemann, *Der gottesdienstliche Schrei*, 231 and passim. He is followed by Balz, *Heilsvertrauen*, 69–72. Wilckens, on the contrary, rejects the idea of an antienthusiastic tendency (*Der Brief*, 156). Von der Osten-Sacken (*Römer 8*, 78–104) argues for a mediating position. He holds that Paul's (written) source had an antienthusiastic tendency but that Paul wished to establish the certainty of hope.

93. Wilckens (*Der Brief*, 154) leaves open the question of who does the subjecting. In my judgment, four points speak in favor of God. First, the probability that *hupetage* and *hupotaxanta* have the same subject. Second, the parallel in 1 Cor. 15:27–28, where the *hupotaxon* is definitely God. Third, the analogy in Rom. 1:18ff. All men become nothing and are delivered by God to their punishment (cf. *emataiothesan*, 1:21, with *mataiotes*, 8:20). Fourth, the inner cohesion of the train of thought. The punishment for an offense is followed by lament at the punishment that has been imposed and intercession with the one who imposed it. Bauer (*Griechisch-deutsches Wörterbuch*, 360) attests that the cause can also be designated with an accusative. But the problem does doubtless lie here: no unambiguous instance can be established in Paul. Romans 3:25 is disputed.

typically mythical causal attribution. A contemporary phenomenon is retraced to a primeval event from which all else follows.

In order to interpret the present on the basis of the mythical primeval event, Paul makes use of two different fields of imagery: sociomorphic and physiomorphic metaphors, forensic and natal images.[94]

The forensic imagery of the court joins the negative experiences of the present with the primeval age. Suffering is punishment. The inexpressible sigh in the glossolalics is lament before God's court[95] and simultaneously intercession before his forum. Negotiations about human beings are conducted in heavenly language. One may be certain that one has a reliable advocate, although one cannot probe heaven, where the negotiation takes place. In other words, one may be certain that in glossolalia one has access even to the spheres inaccessible to consciousness, where absolute norms judge and condemn conduct. The killing threat of the superego is definitively overcome. The flesh is set on death, but the spirit is set on "peace and life" (Rom. 8:6*). But glossolalia is the "mind of the Spirit" (8:27), and thus overcoming of hostility against God. In glossolalia, unconscious interpretation of the normative and demanding tribunals according to the pattern of hostility is overcome.

The sociomorphic imagery is overlaid by a physiomorphic imagery. The utterances of the Spirit are the expression of the pains of birth.[96] The groans of creation (8:22) are directed not toward the intervention of an extrinsic power but rather toward the emergence of the new creatures from within the whole creation. The anxious waiting of the creature is directed toward the "revealing of the sons of God" (8:19), the birth of a new form of life. The natal imagery brings to expression that human beings not only are judged differently before God because of the Spirit who has grasped them; they also experience in themselves a profound metamorphosis, a process that is connected with sufferings and pains but that has within itself the hope that in the end the "liberty

94. Cf. my attempt to order the most important soteriological images systematically, "Soteriologische Symbolik."

95. Schniewind ("Das Seufzen") interprets our entire text on the basis of the juridical imagery (and thus on the basis of the doctrine of justification). The Spirit's intercession for us is grounded in the intercession of Christ.

96. This is a question of the woes of the last days; cf. Mark 13:8; *4 Ezra* 4.40ff.; *1 Enoch* 62.4; and surely also 1QH 5.30–32; 2.7–12. The general image of the woes has as its point of comparison only the "pain" that precedes a turn to the good; cf. John 16:21. But in Rom. 8:18ff., the image is reinforced by further traits. The birth imagery is alluded to anew when mention is made of the appearance of the sons of God, who are said to be similar in form to the "first-born."

of the glory of the children of God" (8:21*) will be realized. In this way the mythical causal attribution of the current state through recourse to a primeval event is corrected; the ban of the primeval event is penetrated. Up to now, this event determined reality. But where the Spirit is at work, a metamorphosis of the human being occurs. One is no longer committed to Adamitic nature.

Through joining mythical causal attribution with the imagery fields of judgment and of birth, glossolalic experience and behavior attains a central position in the "interpreted world." This results in a self-contained context: the sigh of the creature is lament over the primeval doom, a moaning under the punishment that follows upon the Fall. It is simultaneously appeal to the condemning tribunal to avert the disaster—an appeal formulated vicariously for human beings by the divine Spirit. God's Spirit becomes the intercessor before God. Above all, however, the glossolalic sigh is an expression of hope for the final overcoming of disaster. The birth pains of the new human being find expression in it. Lamenting, vicarious, and hoping sighs have the same direction. They wait for the overcoming of the Fall, for the appearance of the sons of God who will have the form of the image of Christ—in other words, that form which human beings had before the Fall (Gen. 1:27) and which the new human being will have (1 Cor. 15:49).

One who is inclined to take mythical texts at their word will come to the following interpretation of Romans 8. The sigh of the creature is a reaction to the loss of the security of paradise, over which humanity grieves in its myths of origin. This loss is connected with the coming of the commandment. The supplanting of instinctive systems of direction by moral requirements destroyed the security that adaptations in the history of the race were once able to provide. The transition to cultural evolution is experienced in retrospect as exile from paradise, although life before the cultural evolution was certainly not paradisiacal. Retrospect transfigures. We are conscious that we are the only living beings that have undergone the step to cultural evolution (even if other living beings are close to it). Through humanity, insecurity has come into creation; with this step, the whole evolution is even at stake. We are responsible for it—and it can be subjected to "corruptibility" for our sake. Humanity has attained the power to destroy the conditions for the life of other creatures as well. But humanity also formulates the hope most clearly. Only in us does the vague remembrance of the time before the conflict become a source of renewal; only in us does mute suffering become the "birth pains" of a new existence. All living things are dependent on our achieving a new stage of our existence. All await longingly our transformation into a more free form of existence. We are a transition with regard to the whole of reality.

3. We have seen that Paul integrates pneumatic experience into his interpretation of reality as a whole. But it would be equally correct to say that by interpreting pneumatic experience as "inexpressible sighing," he integrates into it dark aspects of reality that had until then not been perceived. In this way glossolalic experience receives a negative coloring that was foreign to it in Corinth, where it was considered a proof of God's presence. Paul does not dispute this, but unlike the Corinthian glossolalics, he sees the presence of God in suffering. The interpretation of glossolalia as "sighing" is a conscious cognitive restructuring of ecstatic experience. The following arguments speak in favor of this position.

First, it should be pointed out that the term "sigh" does not do justice to the phenomenon of glossolalia from a linguistic perspective. It is true that glossolalia can give expression to sadness.[97] But glossolalia is not a "sigh"; it is based on the phonemes of the native tongue—at times enriched by phonemes of a foreign language—whereas groans are formed from sounds that are excluded from the given phonological system. Sighing is unarticulated speaking; glossolalia, on the contrary, is an unsemantic speaking that, however, is articulated in such a way that it is usually taken to be a foreign language. Glossolalia, therefore, also does not immediately give the impression of being a "sigh."[98]

The linguistic use of *stenazein* and *stenagmoi* yields a further argument. These words are indeed attested for the groaning and sighing of human beings but not for God or the Holy Spirit. Thus the people in Egypt send "sighs" to God (Acts 7:34). The Christians "sigh" (2 Cor. 5:2*, 4) in their body, just like the souls imprisoned in human bodies in the Hermetic writings.[99] In Virgil (*Eclogue* 4) even countries can sigh.[100] Parallels are therefore to be found for the first two forms in which cosmic sighing appears—the sighing of creation and that of human

97. Positive, even euphoric, frames of mind are chiefly connected with glossolalia (cf. Samarin, *Tongues*, 202ff., 210), but it can also give expression to sad frames of mind (ibid., 93). At the present time, the breakthrough to glossolalia frequently occurs in or after a life crisis; Kildahl (*The Psychology*, 57) was able to determine with his collaborators that in eighty-five percent of those who spoke in tongues a "clearly defined anxiety crisis" preceded the assumption of the new mode of conduct.

98. Cf. Samarin, *Tongues*, 207–8.

99. *Corpus Hermeticum* 23.33.

100. Cf. Hommel, "Das Harren."

beings. But they are lacking for the third form of appearance—the inexpressible sighing of the Holy Spirit. Here Paul would seem to have coined a new linguistic practice, in doing which he was able to pick up on the idea of intercession: mediators bring our prayers before God (Tob. 12:12–15). Even the Holy Spirit can appear before God's court, but if he does, it is as an accuser.[101]

A third argument in favor of a conscious correction of glossolalic experience through its interpretation as "sighing" derives from the context. A self-correction of Paul is clearly present here. For according to 8:15 the Christians have already received the "sonship" for which, according to 8:23, they long while "sighing." In the spirit of sonship the Christians cry "Abba" in 8:15–16, but in 8:26–27 the only thing they can produce is an inarticulate "sighing." How is this self-correction to be understood? The first section (8:1–17) treats the overcoming of flesh and sin. Here the Christian has in the present the certainty of being redeemed, since there is no longer any condemnation for those who are "in Christ" (8:1). The second section (8:18–30), on the contrary, treats the overcoming of suffering, which according to the Pauline understanding can even be encountered where there was no sin—in nonhuman nature. With respect to suffering, the Christian is still exposed to negative reality in all its severity. Paul's self-correction corresponds to the *theologia crucis* that can also be found elsewhere in his writings; the corrected statement stands close to general Christian conceptions.

A final argument in favor of a conscious correction is the situation in which the Epistle to the Romans was composed. It was written in Corinth and pursues further many ideas of 1 Corinthians.[102] If Paul assesses the "sighing of the Spirit" as a consequence of our weakness in Rom. 8:26*, one will have to take into consideration that the term "weakness" had already played an important role in the confrontation with the Corinthians. The Corinthians expected signs and wonders of an apostle (2 Cor. 12:2). But Paul insisted to them that the Christian charismatic can demonstrate strength precisely in "weakness" (2 Cor. 12:9), since there is the model of Christ, who "was crucified in weakness, but lives by the power of God" (2 Cor. 13:4). Now if Paul earlier contradicted the expectations of the Corinthians with the term "weakness," it is probable that he was able to correct with the same

---

101. *Testament of Judah* 20; on this, cf. Balz, *Heilsvertrauen*, 77–80, 87ff.
102. Cf. 1 Cor. 1:21//Rom. 1:18ff.; 1 Cor. 8—10//Rom. 15; 1 Cor. 12.4ff.//Rom. 12:3ff.; 1 Cor. 15:44ff.//Rom. 5:12ff.

term the assessment of glossolalia that dominated in Corinth. To him
glossolalia did not signify being filled with heavenly strength but rather
participation in "weakness." Ecstatic experience thus becomes a vehicle
to make one sensitive to the sufferings in all creatures. The model of
Christ stands in the background in Rom 8:26–27 as well. The section
is introduced with the declaration that being co-heirs with Christ
means suffering with him in order to be glorified with him (Rom.
8:17).

The Pauline interpretation of glossolalic behavior as "sighing" sets
a new accent. Yet it would be premature to understand Rom. 8:18–27
as "antienthusiastic polemic" for this reason. Enthusiastic experience
has rarely been interpreted as imposingly as it is in Rom. 8:26–27.
Rarely has such a key function in understanding the world been
attributed to it. Paul is concerned not with polemics against enthusiasm
but rather with the integration of reality as a whole—including its
negative aspects—into the ecstatic experience, and with a new view of
reality on the basis of ecstatic experience. Romans 8:18ff. integrates
glossolalic experience and behavior cognitively into the symbolic world
of Paul.

By way of conclusion, emotional and motivational effects of the
cognitive interpretation of glossolalic experience and behavior which
Paul presented will be studied briefly. Psychodynamic theories see
these effects in dealing with inner conflicts; approaches from the
perspective of learning theory see them in social integration. Cognitive
interpretations seek the decisive "inner reinforcement" in glossolalics'
positive self-evaluation. If the divine Spirit speaks from them, then
they have become the dwelling of God. Their life is filled with power,
value, and significance. They will experience this all the more intensely
the less they can attribute power, value, and significance to themselves
on the basis of their social status—and, as Paul attests (1 Cor. 1:26ff.),
very few in the Corinthian community could do that. The feeling of
positive self-value contributes to reducing conflicts with oneself and
with the environment, but it also carries with it the danger that real
problems will no longer be perceived realistically, because they do not
correspond to the new, positive self-image. If in the Corinthian
community poor slobs mutually reinforced each other in thinking they
were "filled, rich, and powerful" (1 Cor. 4:8*), Paul could confront
that ironically with the real severity of his own life—perhaps in order
to remind some in Corinth of the facts of life. Glossolalia makes
possible an enhanced, if not even exaggerated, positive self-image.

Here Paul begins in Romans 8. What rises from the depth of the heart is not only the pneumatic current in which Christians immediately experience their unconditioned value, but also a sighing of the whole creation. In psychodynamic terms, glossolalic experience should not only be "enjoyed" as a reduction of tensions; it should also function in making one sensitive to tensions. In cognitive terms, suffering should be assumed into the self-image of the pneumatic—not only on the fringe but at its center. It is precisely the ecstatic gift of glossolalia that connects one with all those in creation who suffer.

How is the cognitive restructuring of glossolalic experience brought about? There can be no doubt that the decisive impulses emerge from the figure of Christ. In his figure the negative aspects of reality are joined to the positive experience of redemption. As Son of God he is the model for every Christian. All have received the Spirit and sonship. All will be glorified with Christ. As the crucified, he is the model of suffering. All should expose themselves with Christ to negative experience of reality. To this extent, the transformation of glossolalic experience can be explained by learning theory—with the aid of the concept of model.

A psychodynamic interpretation would describe this occurrence as an inner transformation, not only as a learning process caused from without. Paul uses the metaphor of birth in its description. The whole creation lies in labor. Something new will be born from the depth of reality; the freedom of the children of God will appear. These images suggest the idea that there exists a tendency toward wholeness which comes from within, an archetypal tendency toward integration of even dark aspects of the world and the self, a tendency that merges with the figure of Christ who comes from outside.

Perhaps the difference between the psychodynamic view of "pneumatic transformation" and the view of learning theory is only a question of perspective. It could be that the model "Christ," coming from without, activates and brings to consciousness a preexistent structure within believers—an open "program" that lets the organism strive for wholeness and fulfillment. Conversely, it could be that the historical figure of Christ achieves a significance surpassing what is historically pre-given only in the light of such open archetypical structures, with the result that a historical man is believed as the appearance of the Son of God. Perhaps historical figures remain ineffective in the history of religion unless they address preexistent psychic structures and form them anew. Perhaps these structures would remain permanently hidden if they were not activated contingently by figures approaching them from without. The function of religious images and symbols would then consist in establishing a connection between the historically mediated learning experiences and an inner psychic dynamic by means of cognitive processes. An experience achieves permanence, stability, clarity, and communicability only if it is integrated cognitively into a symbolically interpreted world.

This applies also to our interpretation of glossolalia. Emerging from within, from impenetrable archaic layers of human existence, it is nonetheless without doubt conditioned by historical factors. This deviant linguistic behavior achieves significance only when it is cognitively placed in relationship to reality as a whole. Perhaps the way Paul interprets it is not so wrong after all. Perhaps it is really to be brought into connection with the Fall—as a reminder of an unsemantic phonetic play of primitive man that is not as yet constricted by the demands of cultural evolution and used socially and instrumentally in different languages.

PART SIX

Wisdom for the Perfect as Higher Consciousness: 1 Corinthians 2:6–16

There are formal correspondences between the forensic and the pneumatic unconscious. What is unconscious forensically has two aspects—unconscious sin and unconscious norm, the first originating in human beings, the second originating in God. What is unconscious pneumatically is similar. Glossolalia is, on the one hand, speaking to God (as prayer), on the other hand, revelation of God to human beings (as glossolalic message). Both dimensions of the unconscious thus have an anthropological aspect and a theocentric aspect. From this there result, in total, four dimensions of the unconscious in Paul, as figure 7 shows.

FIGURE 7

	Forensically Unconscious	*Pneumatically Unconscious*
theocentric aspect	the unconscious norm: God's demand on human beings	pneumatic message: God's revelation to human beings
anthropological aspect	the unconscious guilt: human action before God	pneumatic prayer: human speaking before God

Paul is familiar with, besides pneumatic speech, a pneumatic knowledge that surpasses natural human possibilities but that is expressed in clear language rather than being communicated in glossolalic sounds. The classic text of such an ecstatic revelation is 1 Cor. 2:6–16.

Chapter 17

Text Analysis: 1 Corinthians 2:6–16

One can recognize the problem that is decisive in the interpretation of the text by proceeding from a structural analysis of the context. The parallelism is striking between 1:18—2:5, the section on the preaching of the cross as foolishness, and 2:6—3:23, the section on the preaching as wisdom. This formal parallelism poses the most important problem in the exegesis of 1 Cor. 2:6–16. What is the relationship of the preaching of the cross to the wisdom teaching? Juxtaposition illustrates the parallelism:

The preaching as foolishness	*The preaching as wisdom*
1 Cor. 1:18–25: The word of the cross as foolishness in the world	1 Cor. 2:6–16: The preaching as wisdom among the perfect
(*a*) is unrecognizable by the world in its wisdom (vv. 18–21);	(*a*) is unrecognizable by the rulers of this world (vv. 6–8);
(*b*) is scandal and foolishness to Jews and Gentiles, power and wisdom for believers (vv. 22–25).	(*b*) is foolishness to the psychics, wisdom for the pneumatics (vv. 9–16).
1:26–30: Application to the community:	3:1–4: Application to the community:
The foolishness of the message of the cross shows itself in its social composition.	The conflict in the community shows that its members are not yet "perfect."
2:1–5: Application to the apostle:	3:5–23: Application to the apostles:
Paul did not preach the message of the cross as wisdom teaching.	No one should boast of his wisdom.

In principle there are two possibilities for determining the relationship of the preaching of the cross to the wisdom teaching. Either one conceives the wisdom teaching as a higher level for the advanced, or one conceives the two as a dialectical unity. Under the first supposition, foolishness and wisdom would relate to each other as initial teaching relates to doctrine for the perfect; 2:6–16 would be a surpassing of the preaching of the cross.[1] Under the second supposition, the preaching of the cross is foolishness with respect to the world, but wisdom in God's view. It is a matter not of two successive contents of preaching but rather of the same content under two aspects—as foolishness for those who reject it, as wisdom for those who concur with it.[2]

Which conception is correct—the gradualist or the dialectical? Each can appeal to weighty arguments—the gradualist chiefly to observations about the form, the dialectical to observations about the content. As we shall see, the key to understanding the text lies precisely in this tension between form and content.

THE FORM OF THE WISDOM DISCOURSE IN 1 COR. 2:6–16

Paul speaks in the style of a revelation discourse and in doing so makes use of a threefold "revelation pattern" (2:6–8).[3] What (1) was hidden (vv. 6–8) has been revealed (2) to the pneumatic (vv. 10–12), so that (3) he can proclaim it further among pneumatics (vv. 13–16). A comparable pattern is found in Col. 1:26–28. The hidden mystery (v. 26a) has now been revealed (vv. 26b–27) and been preached to all men (v. 28). In a similar manner, secrecy, revelation, and further communication of revelation through the preaching follow upon one another in Eph. 3:5–8; 2 Tim. 1:9–11; and Tit. 1:2–3. The last part can be abbreviated (Tit. 1:2–3) or can even be lacking (1 Pet. 1:20). What is striking in comparison is that nowhere except in 1 Corinthians 2 is the passing on of revelation restricted to a particular circle of Christians; on the contrary, passing on of revelation is identical with the mission

1. Thus, among others, Bauer, "Mündige," and Winter, *Pneumatiker*, 275–76. Cf. also Winter's survey of research, *Pneumatiker*, 3–55; and Dautzenberg, "Botschaft."
2. Thus, among others, Schlier, "Kerygma"; according to Schlier, "Sophia says nothing other than what the kerygma also says" (p. 229). See also L. Schottroff, *Der Glaube*, 217, 219; Wilckens, "Zu 1.Kor 2,1–16"; and most recently, Sellin, "Das 'Geheimnis.' "
3. Cf. Lührmann (*Das Offenbarungsverständnis*, 113–40), according to whom Paul takes over a pre-given model. According to Conzelmann (*Der erste Brief*, 75), on the contrary, the model was developed in the internal school activity that surrounded Paul.

of preaching. It is directed to "every man" (Col. 1:28), encompasses Jews and Gentiles (Eph. 3:2–8; Rom. 16:26) and is public preaching, as the terms *kerygma* (Rom. 16:25) and *kerux* (2 Tim. 1:11) show. Paul, on the contrary, restricts the passing on of revelation to the circle of the perfect. The perfect human is not the goal of the preaching (Col. 1:28) but its presupposition (1 Cor. 2:6; 3:1ff.). Was Paul here varying a traditional pattern? Was the Corinthian situation the occasion for a polemical variation of the pattern? Did Paul want to correct a false darkness that was overly impressed with the state of knowledge already reached? Or was an originally esoteric revelation pattern later "universalized" in the Pauline school on the basis of the mission experience— that is, broadened to everyone as possible recipient of revelation? We do not know.

Yet we can with good reasons surmise that Paul is using a form of discourse that was known in the Christian liturgy. Three times he characterizes the text as a *lalein* (2:6, 13; 3:1). The majority of references to *lalein* point to the situation of oral discourse; think only of the twenty-four references in 1 Corinthians 14.[4] In 1 Cor. 2:6–16 there would then be the literary deposit of a form of oral communication, an example of one of the manifold oral forms Paul presupposes in 1 Corinthians 12—14.

This thesis is supported by the fact that Paul links the wisdom discourse to the "perfect." The limitation to a particular circle in the community would not have been possible in the letter, since the letter was read to all in the liturgy, at which both outsiders and unbelievers could be present (1 Cor. 14:16, 23ff.). The announcement that "we speak wisdom among the perfect" (1 Cor. 2:6*) is meaningful only in the situation of oral discourse, where the speaker can know all addressees and where his speech occurs only once; through being fixed in a letter it becomes potentially accessible to all.

Finally, we may also infer that the oral form presupposed in 1 Cor. 2:6–16 is a "pneumatic" form of discourse. It is imparted by the Spirit, taught by the Spirit, and intelligible only to "spiritual" people. We therefore assume that the Sitz im Leben of the wisdom teaching lay in assemblies of an inner circle in the communities or around the apostle, in which one heard higher wisdom as inspired speech. In such

---

4. Of the total of fifty-two references to *lalein* in Paul, twenty-four are in 1 Corinthians 14 alone. Written communication can also occasionally be designated as *lalein* (cf. Rom. 7:1), but the connection of the word on the whole to oral communication is unmistakable.

small circles (in his circle of collaborators? in select house communities?),
Paul spoke as to the perfect.[5]

It is more difficult to identify 1 Cor. 2:6–16 with one of the pneumatic
forms of discourse mentioned in 1 Corinthians 12—14. The three
listings in 1 Cor. 12:8–10, 14:6, and 14:26 do not correspond:

12:8	*14:6*	*14:26*
wisdom discourse	revelation	psalm
knowledge discourse	gnosis	didache
gift of healing	prophecy	revelation
miraculous powers	didache	speaking in tongues
prophecy		interpretation
discernment of spirits		
speaking in tongues		
interpretation		

The listing in 1 Cor. 12:8–10 is clearly the most systematic, especially
since the context in itself already thematizes the relationship of unity
and multiplicity. In 14:6, on the contrary, the purpose is only to
confront intelligible and unintelligible forms of discourse; here some
examples of intelligible forms of discourse, in arbitrary order, suffice.
The same is true of 14:26, where Paul wishes to characterize the
confusion in the Corinthian community and where he does not even
mention the important gift of prophecy. Thus it is only in 12:8–10, if
at all, that we have a systematic indication of different pneumatic gifts;
the arrangement of the charisms in pairs also speaks in favor of this
interpretation.

If we had to choose among the oral "forms" that are mentioned, we
could exclude glossolalia and interpretation along with prophecy.[6] The
first of these must be translated, the latter two judged. But in 2:15,
Paul says with self-esteem; "The spiritual man judges all things, but
is himself to be judged by no one." Further, in 1 Cor. 14:30, he depicts
prophecy as the consequence of an actual revelatory process. Even
while one of the prophets is speaking, another can receive a revelation.

5. Much speaks in favor of a "school operation" with Paul as the center. Cf.
Conzelmann, "Paulus," and Judge, "The Early Christians as a Scholastic Community."
6. Dautzenberg ("Botschaft," 139ff.) considers 1 Cor. 2:6–16 to be an early Christian
prophecy, on the basis of the terms "mystery" (cf. 1 Cor. 13:2; 14:2), *sugkrinein* (cf.
diakrinein in 14:29; 12:10), and *eidenai* (cf. 13:2). But one could conclude with equal right
from the term *apokaluptein* to an apocalypse, from *gignoskein* to a gnosis, from *didaktos* to
a didache, and from the central concept of *sophia* to a *logos sophias* (1 Cor. 12:8).

In 1 Cor. 2:6–16, on the contrary, Paul writes about a wisdom over which he has long disposed: he could have communicated it to the Corinthians even during his stay in Corinth, but they were not yet mature enough for that. The only one of the forms of oral discourse that remains is the *logos sophias* or *gneoseos*. Three points speak in favor of this possibility. First, the theme of 1 Cor. 2:6–16: the passage is concerned with *sophia* (vv. 6–7, 13). Second, the significance of the process of knowledge: it is a matter of *gnosis*, as the repetition of the verb *gignoskein* in vv. 8, 11, and 14 shows. Third, the indirect characterization of the passage as a *logos:* it is the counterpart to the *logos tou staurou* (1:18; 2:4).[7]

In any case, the literary form of the text presupposes that Paul is here communicating a special revelation that exceeds what is already known. Corresponding to this is the image of "milk" and "solid food" (3:2), which is also used in the Epistle to the Hebrews and which there illustrates the sequence of initial teaching and doctrine for the perfect.[8] As in 1 Cor. 2:6ff., it is connected with the antonyms *nepios* and *teleios* (Heb. 5:12ff.). Of course there is no thought of an institutionalized religious curriculum in 1 Corinthians 2. The form of pneumatic discourse, which occurs spontaneously, speaks against this. Yet one should ask if such wisdom teaching for the perfect does not have a tendency toward informal social separation, inasmuch as Paul develops in a narrower circle theological doctrines that were not intended for the ears of all. Paul does, after all, constantly let it be known that he could report "pneumatic" experiences beyond what is intended for the community. He has received "revelations" that he would yield only against his principles (2 Cor. 12:1ff.). He speaks for himself in tongues (1 Cor. 14:18ff.). He is in ecstasy for God, but for the community only what he says in a sober state is of significance (2 Cor. 5:13). He

7. If one accepts the idea that in formal respects 1 Cor. 2:6–16 is the literary deposit of a form that was once oral, then assumption of a pre-Pauline source that Paul is said to have commented on critically (so Lührmann, *Das Offenbarungsverständnis*, 115ff.), and even more the hypothesis of a non-Pauline origin of the text with an anti-Pauline tendency and its secondary interpolation into 1 Corinthians (so Widmann, "1.Kor 2,6–16"), are superfluous. One should think rather of Pauline school tradition (with Conzelmann, *Der erste Brief*, 75–76).

8. The image of milk and solid food occurs twice in Philo in connection with the opposition of *nepios* and *teleios;* cf. *On Husbandry* 9, and *On Sobriety* 8–9. Further references are *On the Preliminary Studies* 19, *On the Migration of Abraham* 29, *On Dreams* 2.10, and *Every Good Man Is Free* 160. The context of thought is usually the education of man. Since the pair of opposites also occurs in Epictetus (*Discourses* 2.16.39, 3.24.9), one could also assume a connection with a theological "school operation" as far as Paul is concerned. Cf. Thüsing, " 'Milch.' "

disposes over a wisdom revelation that he does not wish to communicate to everyone (1 Cor. 2:6–16). It could be the case that something of this hidden "wisdom" has been preserved for us by the school of Paul in the Deutero-Pauline letters (Colossians; Ephesians). But what is the content of this higher wisdom?

THE CONTENT OF THE WISDOM DISCOURSE IN 1 COR. 2:6–16

On the basis of form, style, and theme, one should assume that in 1 Cor. 2:6–16 Paul is communicating previously unknown contents. But he does not write much beyond what he had already said in the preaching of the cross in 1:18ff.; in reality, he only unfolds what he had already implicitly presupposed there.

Even in 1 Cor. 1:18ff. Paul had confronted a "wisdom of God" (v. 24) with the "wisdom of the world" (v. 20). The wisdom of the world has been made into foolishness by God; the wisdom of God is despised by men as foolishness. There are in other words two types of wisdom, just as there are two types of foolishness. When Paul assures in 2:1–5 that he has not preached in Corinth with "wisdom," he obviously means the "wisdom of men" (2:5), in other words, the wisdom God has destroyed (1:19). When he then nonetheless speaks of "wisdom among the perfect," beginning in 2:6*, that is the "wisdom of God," a point Paul underlines so clearly through the twofold negation that it is "not the wisdom of this world or of the rulers of this world" (2:6*), that there can be no doubt of the opposition of the "wisdom of men" (v. 5) and the "wisdom of God" (v. 7). Paul therefore undertakes no about-face.[9] While the form of the text may awaken expectations of an entirely new content, as far as content is concerned the train of thought suggests development of the divine wisdom hidden in the cross.[10] A more precise analysis of the text structure in 2:6–16 shows in fact that not much points beyond the preaching of the cross in 1:18ff. The greater part of the revelation discourse offers no new

---

9. Thus, earlier, Wilckens, *Weisheit*, 60. In the meantime Wilckens himself has performed an about-face (cf. "Zu 1.Kor 2,1–16," 506).

10. The decisive counterargument is that if the wisdom were hidden dialectically in the foolishness, then Paul would already have proclaimed it with the preaching of the cross. But the wisdom proclaimed in 2:6ff. is something new to the Corinthians. Therefore a different concept of wisdom underlies 2:6ff. than 1:18ff. Thus, most recently, Winter, *Pneumatiker*.

revelation as far as content is concerned;[11] it is rather reflection on the possibility of receiving revelation and passing on revelation.

The first part (vv. 6–9) speaks of the objective event of revelation, of the hidden wisdom that was crucified by the archons (rulers) of this age. The preexistence of wisdom, and especially the mention of the archons, go beyond 1:18ff. but are present there implicitly. For the archons represent the world,[12] and that is already mentioned in 1:18ff. The wisdom of God has long been ignored—even independently of the crucifixion of Jesus. Thus it is preexistent. In both instances wisdom runs into "nonrecognition." The *oudeis . . . egnoken* in 2:8 corresponds to the *ou egno* in 1:21. In both texts the cross is also discussed emphatically (1:18, 23; 2:8).

The second part (vv. 10–16) thematizes the subjective aspect of the event of revelation—first its acceptance, then its mediation to others. The two sections of text are structured parallel to each other, as this chart shows:

1 Cor. 2:10–12	*1 Cor. 2:13–16*
Revelation occurs through the Spirit (v. 10a)	The handing on of the revelation is directed to pneumatics (vv. 13ff.)
Question: *tis gar oiden* (v. 11)	Question: *tis gar egno* (v. 16a)
Application in first-person plural: *hemeis de . . .* (v. 12)	Application in first-person plural: *hemeis de . . .* (v. 16b)

Verses 10–12 speak first of the human reception of revelation. Verse 9* had already prepared this theme, when it was mentioned that God's revelation "had entered the heart of no man."[13] A presupposition of

11. According to Scroggs ("Paul"), Paul emphasizes in 1 Cor. 2:6–16 only *that* he disposes over a perfect wisdom but conceals its content since the Corinthians are not yet mature enough for the reception of perfect wisdom (cf. 37, 47). But in 3:1 Paul does not say, "I *can* not address you as spiritual men"; rather he says, "I *could* not."

12. In both texts, *aion* (1:20; 2:6, 8) and *kosmos* (1:20–21; 2:12) are juxtaposed as synonyms.

13. 1 Corinthians 2:9 is first of all scriptural proof of what precedes it. The *kathos gegraptai*, "as it is written," always relates, as it does in Rom. 1:17, 2:24, 3:10, 4:17, 8:36, and in many other texts, to the preceding sentences. This is also true of 1 Cor. 2:9 despite the adversative *alla*, as *alla kathos gegraptai* in Rom. 5:21 shows. The logic is clear: if the mystery of God has been seen and heard by no one, then it has also not been seen and heard by the archons of this world. Yet 2:9 is also a transition to what follows. The citation consists of two parallel relative clauses without a main clause. The main clause belonging to this could be 1 Cor. 2:10*: "What no eye has seen . . . this God has revealed to us through the Spirit." Otherwise the *apokaluptein* lacks an object in v. 10. Elsewhere it stands with an object (cf. Rom. 8:8; Gal. 1:6; 3:23; Phil. 3:15). Yet the citation and application (vv. 9, 10) form no fixed grammatical unit, as the new

the reception of revelation is the Spirit; the goal of conferral of the Spirit is a knowledge, namely, a grasping of what God has given (v. 12).

Verses 13–16 hark back formally to the beginning. *Sophian de laloumen* and *ha kai laloumen* stand parallel to each other. Now it is developed why the perfect wisdom can be expressed only among the "perfect" or among "pneumatics." This is connected with the nature of revelation. The last section is therefore parallel in thought to vv. 10–12: there the Spirit searches all (2:10), here the pneumatic judges all (2:15). There the axiom that "like knows like"[14] appears in the form that only the Spirit knows what is in man, and that only the divine Spirit knows what is in the depths of the deity. Here, on the contrary, it is said that pneumatic things are made intelligible only by pneumatic things.

Summary. In the preaching of the cross and in the wisdom teaching the same symbol stands materially at the center—the cross. But it is shifted into a new context through the wisdom revelation. In the course of this, new accents are set as far as content is concerned. Beyond the preaching of the cross in 1:18ff., there appear, first, the mysterious figures of the "archons of this world," as if with them the deeper causes of the cross were exposed. Beyond the communication of the objective event of revelation there is, second, reflection on the subjective conditions of the reception of revelation. The event of revelation becomes conscious of itself. As far as content is concerned, in other words, the same reality stands at the center in each text, but as far as the form is concerned, 2:6ff. is clearly a further development of the preaching of the cross.

In conclusion, we propose a hypothesis to solve this classic problem of exegesis. The higher wisdom of Paul consists not in new contents but rather in a higher stage of consciousness in which the same contents are reflected upon. In the "initial preaching," Christians are seized by the symbol of the cross. But it is only through the "doctrine of perfection" that they grasp what seizes them. Both the immature and the perfect are affected by the same revelation, but only the perfect penetrate what happens to them and in them. In brief, perfect wisdom consists in making conscious a previously unconscious content.

---

beginning with *gar* and *de* (v. 10) shows. Lührmann (*Das Offenbarungsverständnis*, 116–17, 136) thinks that with vv. 8b and 9 Paul introduced the relationship to the cross into an already existing revelation model. This surmise is difficult to verify.

14. This is an old theme; cf. Müller, *Gleiches*.

Chapter 18

Tradition Analysis:
1 Corinthians 2:6–16

At first glance, 1 Cor. 2:6–16 fits only poorly into the intellectual world of Pauline theology. For this reason it is all the more important to insert the text into a development in the history of the tradition that leads from Old Testament wisdom up to gnostic speculation on Sophia. For Paul unmistakably draws on Jewish wisdom traditions,[1] and some things—the hostile archons, the "depths of the deity," the abrupt opposition between psychic and pneumatic man, and the opinion that the pneumatic man will not be known or judged by others—are reminiscent of later gnostic texts.[2] Paul is to be located somewhere

---

1. 1 Corinthians 2:6–16 exhibits many points of contact with the wisdom tradition: the preexistence of wisdom; the parallelism of Sophia and Pneuma (Wis. 9:10–17); the linking of being "perfect" with wisdom (Wis. 9:6); the assertion of omniscience (Wis. 7:23; 9:11); the instruction through the Spirit or through wisdom (Wis. 8:7; 9:18); the strict notion of revelation, according to which divine things cannot be known without God's Spirit (Wis. 9:16–17); the idea of incorporation, in which wisdom enters the interior of the human being (Wis. 9:27). Paul also demonstrates acquaintance with sapiential motifs elsewhere. Cf. the sapiential natural theology in Rom. 1:18ff. and Wisdom 13, the idea of image in 2 Cor. 4:4 and Wis. 7:16, the assertion of mission in Gal. 4:4, 6, and Wis. 9:10, 17 (here in particular the juxtaposition of wisdom and pneuma or of Christ and the Spirit), and the preexistent salvific intervention of wisdom in 1 Cor. 10:1ff. and Wis. 10:18–19; 11:4. It is possible that the so-called Christ mysticism is also marked by sapiential material: wisdom dwells in the hearts of the wise as Christ dwells in the hearts of believers. Other points of contact with the wisdom tradition are polemical. The Wisdom of Solomon associates wisdom with *eugeneia* (8.3), wealth (8.5), and power: the wise man is the true king (6.20). The relationships are in any case so numerous that it is understandable when 1 Cor. 2:6–16 is derived by Scroggs ("Paul," esp. 48ff.) from sapiential traditions.

2. The connections with Gnosticism are just as numerous as the relationships to wisdom. (1.) With regard to the archons, cf. e.g., *The Hypostasis of the Archons (Nag Hammadi Codices* 2.86.20—97.23) and *The Apocryphon of John (Berlin Gnostic Codex* 53.20ff.; 63.10). (2.) On the "depths of the deity," cf. Hippolytus *Refutatio omnium haeresium* 5.1.4: "They have styled themselves Gnostics, alleging that they alone have sounded the depths of knowledge" (ET: J. H. MacMahon, ANF 5:47). Cf. also Hippolytus

between traditional wisdom and gnostic Sophia; he would even seem to have been an important factor in this evolution.[3]

THE JEWISH WISDOM TRADITION

Wisdom is an international phenomenon. Experience is reflected upon in proverbs and maxims, in order to track down a constant regularity in the often contradictory and baffling phenomena, without systematizing them. One rather contents oneself with formulating in a pointed fashion the connections that are discovered, juxtaposing them, and collecting them in accordance with loose material perspectives. Underlying this lies—more implicitly than explicitly—the belief that behind the multiplicity of life and of the world stands an order that is transparent to God's will and that makes meaningful action possible.

In the late Old Testament period, this confidence falls into a crisis.[4] Skepticism as to whether God is at all visible through the world expresses its presence (Ecclesiastes). The experience of suffering causes doubt whether God's wisdom is at all accessible. As Job (28:12–13) laments, this wisdom is considered to have disappeared:

> But where shall wisdom be found?
>   And where is the place of understanding?
> Man does not know the way to it,
>   and it is not found in the land of the living.

The crisis of experiential wisdom led to a change in sapiential thinking. Wisdom became revealed wisdom, which is no longer legible from the phenomena but rather rests on the special self-revelation of God. In itself it is hidden. Only beyond the familiar everyday world may it perhaps be found. In antiquity, speculations about everything

---

Refutatio 6.30.6; *The Gospel of Truth* (Nag Hammadi Codices 1.22, 25; 35.15; 37.8; 40.26); Theodotus 29. (3.) The opposition of psychics and pneumatics is attested in this fashion only in gnostic texts, in Valentianism, among other places; cf. Irenaeus *Adversus Haereses* 1.5.1–2, 4–5; 6.1–2, 4; 7.1–2, 5: "They conceive, then, of three kinds of man, spiritual, material and animal" (ET: ANF 1:350). (4.) On the nonrecognizability of the pneumatic, cf. Basilides, in Irenaeus *Adversus Haereses* 1.24.6: " 'Do thou,' they say, 'know all, but let nobody know thee' " (ET: ANF 1:350). Derivation from gnostic texts was carried out most thoroughly by Wilckens (*Weisheit* but later corrected in "Zu 1.Kor 2,1–16."

3. The tendency of wisdom to Gnosticism is unmistakable. Cf. Koester, "One Jesus"; Schenke, "Die Tendenz"; Colpe, "Gnosis II," esp. 573–81.

4. Of the extensive literature we shall mention only von Rad, *Weisheit*. On the transformation of sapiential thought in the Hellenistic age, see Mack, *Logos*. On the social background of this transformation and crisis of wisdom, see Crüsemann, "Die unveränderbare Welt."

lying beyond the accessible world of experience occur in the form of myth. Wisdom, already a mythical being in Proverbs 8, now becomes even more the subject of a mythical drama, in which three aspects constantly recur.[5] Preexistent wisdom seeks a dwelling place (1), fails at first in this endeavor (2), but finally takes up residence in a small circle of the elect (3), whether it be in Israel (Sir. 24:3–8; Bar. 3:37), among the angels in heaven,[6] among the "children of wisdom" (Matt. 11:18–19*), or in the circle of elect pneumatics (1 Cor. 2:6–16). As the following chart shows, the three aspects of the wisdom myth can also be recognized behind 1 Cor. 1:18ff. and 2:6ff., no matter whether Paul is thinking of a hypostatized attribute of God or of an independent mythical figure:

	1 Cor. 1:18ff.	*1 Cor. 2:6ff.*
Preexistent wisdom	The world could have known God through God's wisdom (1:21; cf. Rom. 1:18ff.).	God destined wisdom for our salvation before the word (2:7).
Wisdom's failure	The world did not recognize God through its wisdom (1:21).	None of the archons of this world knew the wisdom of God (2:8).
Acceptance of wisdom	The faithful (1:21) and the called (1:24) accept the foolishness of the cross as God's wisdom; the others reject it.	The pneumatics accept among themselves God's revelation; but the psychics cannot receive it (2:10ff.).

Because of these formal analogies, it is worthwhile to compare the sapiential thinking in the Wisdom of Solomon with the Pauline statements. Doing so shows significant differences with respect to the social, anthropological, and cosmological aspects of wisdom.

Social Aspects of Wisdom

The Wisdom of Solomon belongs to the category of revealed wisdom. Yet, according to its own self-understanding, it seeks to perpetuate the traditional experiential wisdom, by means of which one oriented oneself in this world. It is characteristic of this that it circulates under the name of King Solomon (cf. esp. chap. 9)—the prototype of the wise man, to whom the major traditional books of wisdom (Proverbs,

5. On the wisdom myth and its reception in the New Testament, cf. Wilckens, s.v. *sophia*, esp. 497ff., 508–10.
6. *1 Enoch* 42.1–2.

Ecclesiastes) were attributed. The addressees suggested by the composer correspond to the royal author. Wisdom addresses the kings of this earth several times: wisdom confers a royal consciousness and is the most important quality of the ruler. "The desire for wisdom leads to a kingdom. Therefore if you delight in thrones and scepters, O monarchs over the peoples, honor wisdom, that you may reign forever" (6:20–21; cf. 6:1). Of course this is a fiction. In reality the wise are often powerless and persecuted (2:10ff.). But the retention of the fiction of the powerful ruler is then all the more remarkable. The wise person is the true king (5:16). The wise do not belong to a future world in this regard. According to 6:24, it is already true of this world that

> A multitude of wise men is the
> salvation of the world,
> and a sensible king is the stability
> of his people.

It is true that one should prefer wisdom to scepters and thrones, but characteristically it is King Solomon himself who makes this statement. How differently Paul judges about the wisdom that is hidden in the foolishness of the cross. It has nothing to do with the rulers of this world either literally or metaphorically.

Anthropological Aspects of Wisdom

In the Wisdom of Solomon, wisdom is closely connected with Adam. Solomon, the ideal wise man, calls himself an offshoot of the "earth-born patriarch" (7:1*). God made Adam by his "wisdom" (9:2). Even in the Fall wisdom protected man and helped him (10:1–2). In brief, wisdom is ordered to natural man. Of course it stems from God. But it enters the soul and body of man, without any need for human nature to be transformed. It is frequently ordered explicitly to the *psyche* (soul):

> She entered the soul [*psyche*] of a servant
> of the Lord.
>
> (Wis. 10:16)

> In every generation she passes into holy souls [*psychas*]
> and makes them friends of God, and prophets.
>
> (Wis. 7:27)

Here "soul" is not conceived in contrast to "body." The latter is indeed mortal, the former immortal (16:14), but both occur in synonymous parallels:

> Because wisdom will not enter a deceitful soul [*psychen*],
> nor dwell in a body [*somati*] enslaved to sin.
>
>   (Wis. 1:4)

Similarly, the wise King Solomon "received a good soul [*psyche*]" and "entered an undefiled body [*soma*]" (Wis. 8:19–20).

While *psyche* and *soma* are used parallel to each other, the two terms *psyche* and *pneuma* largely overlap. Yet, as in Paul, the anthropological concept of the *pneuma* is to be distinguished from *Pneuma* in the sense of the Holy Spirit. The Wisdom of Solomon polemizes that an idolater

> failed to know the one who formed him
> and inspired him with an active soul [*psychen energousan*]
> and breathed into him a living spirit [*pneuma zotikon*].
>
>   (Wis. 15:11)
>
> A man . . . cannot bring back the departed spirit [*pneuma*],
> nor set free the soul [*psychen*]
> that has been received [by the underworld].
>
>   (Wis. 16:14*)

Only in one passage (Wis. 9:13–17) could one sense an incipient opposition between "soul" and (Holy) "Spirit":

> For what man can learn the counsel of God?
> Or who can discern what the Lord wills?
> For the reasoning of mortals is worthless,
> and our designs are likely to fail,
> for a perishable body [*soma*] weighs down
>   the soul,
> and this earthy tent burdens the
>   thoughtful mind [*nous*].
> We can hardly guess at what is on earth,
> and what is at hand we find with labor;
> but who has traced out what is in the heavens?
> Who has learned thy counsel,
>   unless thou hast given wisdom
> and sent thy holy Spirit [*pneuma*] from on high?

Here *psyche* and *nous*, on the one hand, and the mortal *soma*, on the other hand, stand in opposition to each another. God himself has to communicate wisdom. Mind and soul are not of themselves able to achieve wisdom. The step from experiential to revelatory wisdom is unmistakable.[7] Yet, in the light of parallel statements on the dwelling of wisdom in the soul, one will not be able to read even Wis. 9:13ff. in a dualistic manner. According to Wis. 9:18*, the Spirit that comes from above does not exclude the human *nous* and *psyche*, but places them in their true function:

> And thus the paths of those on earth were set right,
> and men were taught what pleases thee,
> and were saved [or preserved] by wisdom.

A brief glance at Paul again shows the great differences. To him, "natural man" is excluded from the higher wisdom. Wisdom does not enter the human *psyche*; rather, the *psychikos anthropos* is in principle incapable of receiving the Holy Spirit.

The Cosmic Aspect of Wisdom

In the Wisdom of Solomon, wisdom is the "architect of all things" (7:21*) and remains permanently present in its works. It is omnipresent and can be operative everywhere. It can do everything, sees everything, and penetrates everything (7:22–26). "It reaches mightily from one end of the earth to the other, and orders all things well" (8:1*). It is the spirit of this world, even though it also affords outlooks to another world (10:10). This world is fully affirmed: "The generative forces of the world are salvific [*soterioi*]" (1-14*); the world perceptible to the senses is so beautiful that those who venerate created things religiously are to be excused. They are "misled by appearance, for the things that are seen are beautiful" (13:7*). Yet wisdom is also present in history, not only in nature. It helps the chosen people in "wonders and signs" (10:16). The difference from Paul is evident. In Paul, the higher wisdom does not belong to this world; it is radically opposed to the "spirit of this world." It points to a new world.

THE DEVELOPMENT TO WISDOM TEACHING IN PAUL

Paul unmistakably presupposes wisdom traditions of the type of the Wisdom of Solomon. This is tangible even in Rom. 1:18ff., and all

---

7. This is not yet the step to gnosis, unless one uses the term "gnosis" in such a broad sense that it becomes historically imprecise, as it does in Georgi (*Weisheit*, 394): "Wisdom is a gnostic text, . . . the oldest that we possess."

the more so in 1 Cor. 1:18ff. Yet the possibility of understanding self
and world that is presented positively in the wisdom traditions appears
in him only as a culpably squandered possibility. The somewhat
mysterious sentence, ". . . in the wisdom of God, the world did not
know God through wisdom . . ." (1 Cor. 1:21) registers the failure of
sapiential piety. The relationship of *en te sophia* and *dia sophias* is
probably to be understood in the sense that "wisdom of God" means
the objective aspect of wisdom. The whole world is penetrated by
omnipresent wisdom. It is "in" wisdom. Nonetheless, human beings
did not know God with the aid of their wisdom—in the sense of a
subjective quality. But God does not now send—as in Wisdom 9—the
divine Spirit from above in order to aid imperfect human intellectual
power. He chooses instead an entirely different path of revelation—
the cross.

Instead of speaking simply of wisdom, Paul therefore speaks antithetically of human and divine wisdom. Instead of one world, he
speaks of two worlds; instead of one person with a *psyche*, he speaks of
two opposed persons—the psychic and the pneumatic. And he no
longer attributes this wisdom to the ruling groups, but he attributes it
to the lower classes. There can be no doubt that in Paul a profound
transformation of sapiential thinking has occurred. From the viewpoint
of the history of tradition, the riddle of 1 Cor. 1:18ff. and 2:6ff.
consists in making his step historically intelligible. We shall therefore
investigate in order the same aspects we also analyzed in the sapiential
thinking of the Wisdom of Solomon.

Social Aspects of Wisdom

Even in traditional wisdom thinking, there is the conception that
wisdom found a dwelling in a small group after it had vainly sought
a dwelling among others. Sirach 24:6–8 is an example:

> In every people and nation
>   I have gotten a possession.
> Among all these I sought a resting place;
>   I sought in whose territory I might lodge.
> Then the Creator of all things
>   gave me a commandment,
> and the one who created me
>   assigned a place for my tent.
> And he said, "Make your dwelling in Jacob,
>   and in Israel receive your inheritance."

A similar text is found in the Ethiopian version of *Enoch* (1 *Enoch* 42.1):

> Wisdom could not find a place in which she could dwell; but a place was found [for her] in the heavens.[8]

Here there is indirect reference to a rejection of wisdom, but the motif does not emerge clearly. This changes for the first time in Christian texts. The messengers of wisdom are killed and persecuted (Luke 11:49–51); the incarnation of wisdom is crucified by the archons (1 Cor. 2:6ff.). The traditional motif that wisdom finds no resting place is sharpened on the basis of historical experiences. This sharpening can scarcely be made intelligible apart from Jesus' crucifixion.

That wisdom now turns precisely to those who are not wise according to normal standards would also seem to go back to historical experience. Wisdom is withdrawn from the "wise and understanding" (Matt. 11:25), from the "educated, powerful, and wellborn" (1 Cor. 1:26*). It reveals itself to the immature, the uneducated, and the powerless. Paul refers to the social composition of the community in order to show that there is no connection between God's wisdom and the ruling class. In doing so, he contradicts the opinion that one could (in some transferred sense) "achieve rule" (1 Cor. 4:8*) with the aid of wisdom. This restructuring of a traditional framework of interpretation corresponds to the social reality of the first community. It was a subcultural movement of unimportant people. It can understand the wisdom that has been given it only as antiwisdom.[9]

---

8. ET: E. Isaac, *The Old Testament Pseudepigrapha*, ed. Charlesworth, 1:33.

9. Stegeman (*Das Evangelium*, 26–27, 30–31) disputes the existence of a few members of the upper class in Corinth. According to him, 1 Cor. 1:26 is meant ironically since a *eugenes*, a nobleman, could not have belonged to the Corinthian community. But, first, *eugeneis* certainly does not mean members of the politically ruling class. In Philo (*Flaccus* 64), respected Jews who were killed by the Alexandrian people while making purchases at the market are termed noble. Philo (*On the Virtues* 198) defines "noble" in the literal sense as "born of highly excellent parents," *hostis an kalon kai agathon genetai goneon* (ET: F. H. Colson, *Philo*, vol. 8 of 10 vols. [LCL, 1939], 285). In 1 Cor. 4:10, Paul varies the term to *endoxoi*. Second, it is to be considered that the connection of power, wealth, and nobility with wisdom stems from the sapiential tradition; cf. Wis. 8:3ff., and Philo *On Sobriety* 55–57 (the wise man is "noble," rich, respected, and sole king). The adjectives in 1 Cor. 1:26 are probably determined in part by the antithesis to the metaphorical sapiential linguistic practice. Third, according to Paul, the election of members of the lower class corresponds to creation ex nihilo (1 Cor. 1:28). The existence of upper-class members is mentioned against this model of theological interpretation. A complete lack of those who are wise, powerful, and wellborn according to the flesh would suit Paul's argumentation so well that he leaves room for their existence only in contrast to the tendency of his argumentation. On the problem, cf. Wuellner, "Ursprung," 165–84.

It is scarcely a coincidence that wisdom and antiwisdom are confronted with each other precisely in the Epistle of James. The community that stands behind the Epistle of James also counts itself among the poor (James 2:5–7); in 3:15–17, it too opposes the wisdom it has been given to another wisdom:

> This wisdom is not such as comes down from above, but is earthly, unspiritual, devilish. For where jealousy and selfish ambition exist, there will be disorder and every vile practice. But the wisdom from above is first pure, then peaceable, gentle, open to reason. . . .

In some respects this passage is reminiscent of 1 Cor. 2:6ff., but the expression "wisdom from above" and the attributes *epigeios*, *psychike*, and *daimoniodes* have no direct analogies in Paul. Conversely, the term "Spirit" is lacking in James. Probably both texts go back to early Christian wisdom traditions independently of each other. Both document the sharpening of revelatory wisdom to a dualism of wisdom, and allow the social background of this process in the history of the tradition to become visible.

Anthropological Aspects of Wisdom

The most striking characteristic in 1 Cor. 2:6ff. is the opposition of "psychic" and "pneumatic"; up to now this has resisted derivation from the history of the tradition. The gnostic parallels are chronologically later and often even presuppose 1 Corinthians 2,[10] and before Paul the opposition is nowhere demonstrable. But Paul himself gives an indication. In 1 Cor. 15:44 he connects the opposition of psychic and pneumatic with the speculation about two primeval humans, which was doubtless inspired by the juxtaposition of two creation accounts in Genesis 1 and Genesis 2. In doing this, Paul corrects the sequence. The heavenly and pneumatic human (from Genesis 1) follows the earthly and psychic human (from Genesis 2). Paul's correction could presuppose an interpretation that corresponded to the biblical sequence.

Now, speculations about two primeval humans—a heavenly model

---

10. For the Book of Baruch, cf. Hippolytus *Refutatio omnium haeresium* 5.26.9, 26.32–33, and the citation of 1 Cor. 2:9 in 5.26.16. For Basilides, cf. Hippolytus *Refutatio* 7.27.6 and the citation of 1 Cor. 2:13 in 7.16.3. For Valentinianism, cf. Irenaeus *Adversus Haereses* 1.5.1 and the citation of 1 Cor. 2:14, 15 in 1.8.3; Hippolytus *Refutatio* 6.34.1 and the citation of 1 Cor. 2:14 in 6.34.8. For the Naassenes, cf. Hippolytus *Refutatio* 5.6.6–7, 8.26, 34, 44, and the citation of 1 Cor. 2:13–14 in 5.8.26. Does this not speak against a derivation of the antonyms *psychikos-pneumatikos* from gnosis, as is proposed in Wilckens, *Weisheit*, 89–90, and Winter, *Pneumatiker*, 169ff.? Cf. now Wilckens, "Zu 1.Kor 2,1–16," 528ff., esp. 534ff.

(Genesis 1) and an earthly replica (Genesis 2)—are well attested in Philo, and in the sequence that is presupposed and corrected by Paul.[11] The problem is only that efforts to derive the opposition of *psychikos* and *pneumatikos* from speculations of this sort are unsuccessful.[12] On the contrary, the creation account does not suggest such an opposition, nor was it interpreted along these lines.

The Septuagint renders Gen. 2:7 as follows: "And God . . . breathed upon his face the breath of life [*pnoen zoes*], and the man became a living soul [*psychen zosan*]."[13] The contemporary texts often render *pnoe* as *pneuma*, so that pneuma often appears as the cause of the psyche, but not as its opposite. Josephus (*Jewish Antiquities* 1.34) writes: "God fashioned man by taking dust from the earth and instilled into him spirit [*pneuma*] and soul [*psychen*]."[14] According to Wis. 15:11, God gave us an active soul and a spirit full of life (*pneuma zotikon*). In one passage, Philo renders *pnoe* as *pneuma*.[15] One must, in other words, already know in advance the opposition of *pneumatikos* and *psychikos* if one wishes to impose it on Gen. 2:7.

Now, one could attempt to explain this opposition through the juxtaposition of the two creation accounts. In Gen. 1:1 there is in fact mention of the *pneuma Theou*, whereas Gen. 2:7 refers to the *psyche*, which is closely bound to the earthly human. Yet in Philo there is not much that points in this direction, and the little that is there is obscure. First, Philo in one text ascribes the *pneuma* explicitly to the heavenly primeval man of Gen. 1:26, while he recognizes the *pnoe* of Gen. 2:7 only as its reflection.[16] But it is a long way from a reflection to an apodictic contradiction. Second, Philo characterizes the earthly human

11. Cf. Philo *Allegorical Interpretation of the Law* 1.31; *On Creation* 134.

12. A derivation of the *psychikos-pneumatikos* terminology from the Jewish Hellenistic exegesis of Gen. 2:7 is found in Dupont (*Gnosis*, 172–80) and Pearson (*The Pneumatikos-Psychikos Terminology*, esp. 11–12, 17–21). But only some important presuppositions for the contrast of two types of men, mature and immature, and the foundation of such contrasts from the creation narrative can be derived from Philo—not the terminological opposition of *psychikos* and *pneumatikos*. Thus rightly R. A. Horsley ("Pneumatikos") and Wilckens ("Zu 1.Kor 2,1–16," 528ff.). That we, e.g., have preserved in the "Hypostatis of the Archons" (*Nag Hammadi Codices* 86.20—97.23) a gnostic speculation on Gen. 1— 2 in which there are no Christian traits—apart from the introductory citation of Eph. 6:12—and in which the opposition psychic-pneumatic plays an important role could speak in favor of a connection of the antonyms with speculation about the creation account independently of Paul.

13. ET: Brenton, *The Septuagint Version*, 3.

14. ET: H. Thackeray, *Josephus*, vol. 4 of 8 vols. (LCL, 1930), 17.

15. Philo *Allegorical Interpretation of the Law* 3.161.

16. Ibid. 1.42.

of Gen. 2:7 as *soma* and *psyche*, but he describes the heavenly human with attributes like *noetos*, *asomatos*, and *aphthartos*;[17] but here the antonym *pneumatikos* is lacking. In other words, where Genesis 1 is connected with the term *pneuma*, the antonym *psyche* is lacking. Where *psyche* is connected with Genesis 2, the contrasting term *pneumatikos* is lacking. The fact remains that it has up to now been impossible to derive the opposition of *pneumatikos* and *psychikos* from pre-Pauline sources.[18] The interpretation of the two creation accounts with these antonyms is a step beyond the known Jewish Hellenistic exegesis. How was this step possible?

Even the devaluation of the term *psyche* in trichotomic anthropological models does not explain much.[19] Where the threefold division of *soma*, *psyche*, and *nous* takes the place of the twofold division of *soma* and *psyche*,[20] the soul comes into proximity with the body and becomes the link between a higher and a lower part within the human being.[21] But the trichotomy *soma*, *psyche*, *pneuma* is never found before Paul (cf. 1 Thess. 5:23). Beyond this, devaluation of the *psyche* never occurs consistently. Even when it is associated with evil powers, as in Plutarch,[22] it can simultaneously be seen as an instrument of God.[23]

Independently of Paul, mention is made of an opposition of man to a spirit that overcomes him only in texts reflecting an ecstatic experience. The reflection of such experience is to be distinguished in principle from anthropological models: inspiration and ecstasy are paranormal

17. Philo *On the Creation* 134.
18. Winter (*Pneumatiker*, 150–51) adduces two references from Philo for the opposition of *psyche* and *pneuma*. (1) In *On Dreams* 1.119, the divine Logos replaces the human *nous* and the human *aisthesis* and in the course of this is said to be "forward to meet and greet at once the practising soul, whose willing champion he is when it despairs of itself" (ET: F. H. Colson and G. H. Whitaker, *Philo*, vol. 5 [LCL, 1934], 361). But if the *pneuma* is the champion of the soul, then no opposition in principle is present here. (2) In *Who Is the Heir* 55–56, *pneuma* and *psyche* are not simply opposed; rather, the entire soul is subdivided into a higher psychic life and a psychic life that is joined to the flesh, a *psyche psyches* and a *psyche pases sarkos*. There can be no question of a dualism—as Winter (*Pneumatiker*, 156) maintains. Philo is acquainted with dualistic schemes of thought, but he does not apply them to the terms *pneuma* and *psyche*.
19. Schweizer, "Zur Trichotomie."
20. E.g., Plato *Timaeus* 30B; Mark Antony *Meditations* 3.16.1, 12.3.1.
21. Cf. Dihle, "Psyche," 612: "As far as the overall picture is concerned, we see that in the philosophical language of the Hellenistic-Roman age *psyche* does indeed still designate the whole of intellectual and spiritual functions, but that a certain devaluation of the word comes in, especially through distinction of the *nous* from the *psyche*, insofar as it is no longer able to signify pure spirituality."
22. *De Genio Socratis* 591D–F; *De Iside et Osiride* 371A–B.
23. Plutarch *De Pythiae Oraculis* 404B.

experiences; anthropological models seek to capture the "normal" human structure. Furthermore, it is a characteristic of ecstasy that it confronts the divine with the entire human essence—in other words with the human being's highest organs and tribunals as well as all else—while anthropological models aim at intrahuman stratification. Thus, according to Strabo, a *pneuma enthousisiastikon* filled the Pythia in Delphi.[24] Lucan opposes this *spiritus* to the "total human being" of the prophesizing Pythia.[25] According to Philo, the *theion pneuma* overcomes one in ecstasy, while one's *nous* departs.[26] Even in Paul, the threefold division *soma, psyche, pneuma* occurs first in 1 Thess. 5:23 after he has evoked pneumatic experiences in early Christianity: "Do not quench the Spirit, do not despise prophesying" (1 Thess. 5:19–20). The opposition *pneumatikos-psychikos* would therefore seem to be retraceable to the interpretation of ecstatic experiences in early Christianity. It is probably an early Christian linguistic innovation that existed even before Paul, as James 3:15 and Jude 19 indicate.

We can now summarize our reflections. The Pauline opposition of *pneumatikos* and *psychikos* was prepared by the devaluation of the *psyche* in the Roman-Hellenistic period, derives primarily from reflection on pneumatic-ecstatic experience in early Christianity, and was brought secondarily into contact with Gen. 2:7. It is to be noted that Paul goes beyond all three recognizable traditions.

1. Paul has in common with the anthropological models of his time that he structures the human interior in an incipiently topical manner. To him the *psyche* is not everything; the human interior can include more. But what goes beyond the *psyche*? Is it the human spirit (*pneuma*), which Paul mentions in 2:11? Or is it the divine Spirit (2:10–11)? The only thing certain is that it is only through conferral of the divine Spirit that an expansion of consciousness beyond the limits of the *psyche* can occur. Only the divine Spirit opens access to a new inner dimension. Without him there would be an immovable limit to understanding. For the psychic does not understand the revelation; indeed, the psychic simply cannot understand it (1 Cor. 2:14). Such an abrupt opposition of the *psyche* to the expansion of human consciousness cannot be demonstrated prior to Paul.

2. But there is also a weighty difference with regard to the ecstatic tradition. In Paul the divine Spirit is indeed contrasted radically to

24. Strabo 9.3.5.
25. *Pharsalia* 5.161ff.
26. *Who Is the Heir* 265.

human capability, but not in such a way that human knowledge and understanding are excluded. The theme of ignorance is lacking in 1 Cor. 2:6–16. In Plato and Philo the ecstatic person does not know what he experiences in ecstasy, but just the opposite is true in 1 Cor. 2:6ff.: conferral of divine Spirit makes one capable of knowledge, understanding, and recognition. The Spirit is a "consciousness-forming power."[27]

3. In contrast to the presumed tradition of argumentation that Paul corrects in 1 Cor. 15:44–45,[28] Paul stresses that the pneumatic is to be understood as goal, not as origin—that is, that the pneumatic human being is not the primeval one of Genesis 1—2 but rather Christ, the new man. The psychic human being precedes him temporally. This shift of accent is important from the perspective of the psychology of religion. If the conferral of the Pneuma signifies an expansion of consciousness beyond the familiar "psychic" limits, this, according to Paul, is not an expansion of consciousness that points only to the depths of our origin but rather one that points into the future. Or more precisely, what according to the interpretation of others is information about our archaic derivation Paul interprets in such a way that it becomes a reference to the future. What could be understood as "regression" becomes "progression." The *pneuma* points to a new world. With this observation, we reach the final aspect of the matter.

The Cosmic Aspect of Wisdom

For Paul, the original unity of cosmos and wisdom has decayed. Yet wisdom is not for this reason radically a-cosmic. It belongs not to the old world but to the new creation. Even before Paul this development began to emerge in *1 Enoch* 42:1. There wisdom leaves the earth in order to take residence among the angels in heaven. In the context of the apocalyptic text, this means that wisdom will become accessible only in the new world, unless one already has access to this new world in visions (or visionary texts). Paul presupposes the opposition of two worlds. Yet he speaks explicitly only of the existing world (1 Cor. 1:20; 2:6; 3:18), not of the new age. While he does use the term "new creation" occasionally in his writings (Gal. 6:15; 2 Cor. 5:17)—a term, in other words, that could be related to the new age at least as far as meaning is concerned—he relates the new creation to contemporary

27. Goppelt, *Theologie*, 450.
28. Agersnap (*Paulusstudier*, 7ff.) denies that Paul is correcting a given conception here.

phenomena. A comparable tendency toward rendering present eschatological salvific goods is also recognizable in 1 Cor. 2:6ff. In 2:9, Paul
cites from an apocryphal text that can no longer be identified: "What
no eye has seen, nor ear heard, nor the heart of man conceived, what
God has prepared for those who love him." The citation reflects a
widespread theme.[29] What is withdrawn from human senses and
thought is in most cases the heavenly world that the apocalyptic
visionary already sees now but that all who do God's will on earth
will later receive as reward. Some examples will suffice:

According to the *Biblical Antiquities* 26.13, after God had hidden the tablets
of the law and twelve precious stones in heaven, he said,

> And they shall be there until I remember the world, and visit the
> dwellers upon earth. And then I will take them and many other better
> than they, from that *place* which *eye hath not seen nor ear heard neither hath
> it come up into the heart of man*, until the like cometh to pass unto the
> world.[30]

The *Testament of Jacob* 8.8 relates that, on a journey to heaven, God showed
Jacob the place of the blessed in contrast to the place of the damned:

> And he showed me all the resting-places and all the good things prepared
> for the righteous, and the things that eye has not seen nor ear heard,
> and have not come into the heart of men, that God has prepared for
> those who love him and do his will on earth.[31]

Similarly, *2 Clement* 11.7 teaches,

> If then we do righteousness before God we shall enter into his kingdom,
> and shall receive the promises "which ear hath not heard, nor hath eye
> seen, neither hath it entered into the heart of man."[32]

The texts could be multiplied.[33] Here it is always a matter of future
salvific goods. In Paul, however, the revelation is related to a present
reality. What God reveals through the Spirit is nothing other than the
"depths of God" (1 Cor. 2:10). God does not reveal some thing, but

---

29. This is the convincing result of the work of Berger ("Zur Diskussion"), who in
this respect has placed research on a new foundation through evaluation of an extensive
collection of material. Cf. von Nordheim, "Das Zitat"; Hofius, "Das Zitat"; and Sparks,
"1.Cor 2,9."

30. ET: James, *The Biblical Antiquities of Philo*, 157–58.

31. ET: K. H. Kuhn, *The Apocryphal Old Testament*, ed. Sparks, 444. [This passage
is to be found only in the Coptic (Bohairic) text.]

32. ET: Kirsopp Lake, *The Apostolic Fathers*, vol. 1 of 2 vols. (LCL, 1912), 145, 147.

33. Cf. the collection of material from apocryphal writings in Berger, "Zur Diskussion," 271ff.; on the patristic references, cf. Prigent, "Ce que l' oeil n'a pas vu."

himself—just as the spirit of a man opens itself of its own accord to another (v. 11). The expansion of consciousness beyond human boundaries is in itself communication of salvation. One achieves participation in the "inner life" of another person—in the Pneuma of God and the Nous of Christ. But the orientation toward a new world remains. This distinguishes Paul from later gnostic speculation, where wisdom seeks to return to the heavenly home. Creation has come about only because of a disaster; the goal of redemption is the reversal of this disaster. In Paul, on the contrary, redemption is directed toward fulfilling God's creative intention in a "new creation." The transition to the new creation begins already, in small Christian groups that demonstrate through their social composition that God has chosen the "things that are not" (1 Cor. 1:28) to destroy what exists. Wisdom reveals itself among them as counterwisdom to the wisdom of this world.

In conclusion, if we read 1 Cor. 2:6–16 against the background of Jewish Hellenistic wisdom tradition, then it is precisely deviations from this tradition that can best be explained by specifically Christian impulses. The revaluation of traditional wisdom, the conception of a counterwisdom, its connection with the lower classes—all this presupposes the message of the cross and the social reality of the Christian communities. Paul neither adapts himself to foreign ideas nor polemizes in a covert fashion against the ideas he describes. Paul rather reflects his own convictions. We should believe that he means his words to be taken seriously. For they do witness to an overwhelming expansion of consciousness beyond human limits, which draws in its wake a radical revaluation of traditional Jewish wisdom theology.

Chapter 19

Psychological Aspects:
1 Corinthians 2:6–16

ASPECTS OF 1 COR. 2:6–16
IN LEARNING THEORY

Paul himself describes the reception of revelation as learning. "And we impart this in words not taught by human wisdom but taught by the Spirit" (1 Cor. 2:13). He contrasts two learning processes: the learning process by which one is "socialized" into the world, and an opposed learning process that confers entirely new possibilities of behavior and experience. Paul is aware that these are processes stimulated and influenced from without: one receives either the spirit of the world or the Spirit from God (2:12). Here "spirit" means a formative influence from without.[1] A change takes place within the formative environment. Or, formulated more cautiously, we observe the attempt to free oneself from the existing learning environment (the world and its spirit). But the new environment is by definition not accessible to outsiders. It does not impinge upon the eye and the ear. It is inaccessible to natural "psychic" experience. Despite this inaccessibility we can make some statements about the stimuli, reinforcements, and models that lead to the new learning process.

Paul connects the "perfect" wisdom with a specific social situation. Only among the perfect does he speak wisdom. In 1 Cor. 2:13, *en teleiois* does not mean "to (the) perfect"; for that a simple dative would suffice (cf. Rom. 3:19; 7:1; 1 Cor. 3:1; and many other texts). The words are rather to be understood, like *lalein en ekklesia*, "speak in

---

1. Does Paul understand the "spirit of the world" as a demonic being that blinds believers (thus Weiss, *Der 1. Korintherbrief*, 63) or is it a matter of forming an analogy to the Spirit of God?

church" (1 Cor. 14:19), as an indication of the social framework.[2] For each pneumatic discourse there is a situation that stimulates it; Paul gives us a sample of this in 1 Cor. 2:6–16—the group of the "perfect." He specifies them more precisely in 3:1–3. Harmony is a presupposition of wisdom discourse. As long as conflict and rancor rule, Paul cannot communicate his wisdom.

The homogeneous group of the perfect with its positive emotional climate is not only the stimulus of the wisdom discourse but also its most important reinforcement. Only in this group does the higher wisdom find positive resonance. Paul's inability to communicate (*edunethen* = first-person singular, 1 Cor. 3:1) it to the Corinthians is grounded in the inability of the Corinthians to receive it (*oupo gar edunasthe* = second-person plural, 1 Cor. 3:2). Paul presents this state of affairs in generalized form in 2:14: the psychic man does not receive what is of the divine Spirit. To him it is foolishness, and he cannot (*ou dunatai*) recognize it, for it must be judged pneumatically. Here one can note a certain imbalance in the estimation of the reinforcing consequences. On the one hand, Paul binds the perfect wisdom to positive resonance in the group; on the other hand, he claims that "the spiritual man judges all things, but is himself to be judged by no one" (2:15), as if he were completely independent of the reaction of others, no matter whether they are pneumatics or psychics.

What Paul says in 2:13ff. about the social relationship of pneumatics and psychics has a model in the relationship of Christ to the archons of this world. By reference to this model it becomes clear which "reinforcement system" Paul wishes to separate himself from. Just as the pneumatic person moves among those who reject his wisdom and misunderstand him, so too Christ appeared in a world that rejected him. In both cases the wisdom of God was misunderstood. The *oudeis egnoken* (v. 11) and the *ou dunatei gnonai* (v. 14) correspond to the *oudeis . . . egnoken* (v. 8). The archons are models of the psychic person who cannot grasp divine wisdom, who even stands opposed to it in hostility. But Christ is the model of the pneumatic who proclaims the same eternal wisdom of God that is the cause of the Christ-event.

But who are the mysterious archons? Whether or not Paul thought of mythic figures in this regard, the recipients of the letter must also have thought of the earthly rulers who were responsible for Christ's

2. Thus Barrett, *A Commentary*, 68–69. A different position is held by Conzelmann (*Der erste Brief*, 78 n. 31).

crucifixion.[3] They did, after all, know important parts of the Passion tradition, as Paul himself attests (1 Cor. 11:23–26). They probably knew more about the circumstances of the crucifixion than the fact that Jesus was "betrayed" and "handed over" (1 Cor. 11:23*), for a tradition of this sort would necessarily have awakened questions about those who betrayed Jesus, handed him over, and crucified him.[4]

Yet not only the recipients but the author as well thought of historical rulers in connection with the archons. In Rom. 13:3, the sole Pauline reference apart from 1 Cor. 2:6ff., civil officials are meant by *archontes;* and the train of thought in 1 Cor. 1:18ff. points more to human figures. For divine wisdom is opposed to *human* wisdom, the wisdom of the wise, of the scribes and of debaters (1:20), of the educated, powerful, and wellborn (1:26ff.). Paul generalizes in view of the situation in Corinth. God will destroy not only the wisdom of the wise (1:19) but absolutely everything that represents something in the world—all the "things that are" (1:28). The association among human wisdom, power, and corruptibility that is established here is presupposed in 2:6ff.,[5] when Paul speaks of the wisdom and the rulers of this world and characterizes them as "transient" (*katagroumenon*, 2:6, and *katargese*, 1:28). On the basis of this chain of associations, the archons in 2:6 are primarily earthly rulers—not merely the concrete rulers of Palestine, Pilate and Antipas, but earthly rulers in general, in Corinth and Judea.[6]

---

3. Thus Schniewind ("Die Archonten"), Miller ("*ARCHONTON*"), Carr ("The Rulers"), and Wilckens ("Zu 1.Kor 2, 1–16").

4. Luke calls the Jewish authorities that were co-responsible for the execution archons (Luke 24:20; cf. 23:13, 35; Acts 3:17; 13:27). Since the Corinthian community had a tradition of the Last Supper that was related to the Lukan tradition (cf. 1 Cor. 11:23ff. with Luke 12:19ff.), it is conceivable that it was also acquainted in other respects with a Passion tradition with Lukan tinges and that the "archons" were familiar to it on that basis. But this is only a vague conjecture.

5. Precisely the connection of the "archons" with wisdom and power is frequently adduced in favor of a demonological interpretation. Yet these associations are already present in the wisdom literature. (1) Lietzmann (*An die Korinther*, 12) thinks that it is not a characteristic sign of earthly rulers to spread wisdom. But the ideal is that the wise man be king and that the king be wise; cf. Wis. 6:20–21. (2) Dibelius (*Die Geisterwelt*, 90) thinks that it would not have been necessary to stress the transitoriness of the rulers with regard to earthly rulers. The earthly rulers of Palestine were probably already deceased by the time of the composition of the Letter to the Corinthians. Yet the sapiential text in Bar. 3:16–19 emphasizes, "Where are the princes of the nations [*archonton ton ethnon*] and those who rule over the beasts of the earth . . . ? They have vanished and gone down to Hades, and others have arisen in their place." Cf. Feuillet, "Le 'Chefs de ce siècle' et la Sagesse divine d'après 1 Cor 2,6–8."

6. A further argument for the interpretation of the archons as men is the citation in 2:9, which serves as biblical proof of the preceding statements. The archons did not

The rejection of Christ by these archons corresponds to the rejection of wisdom among human beings. But it is then clear from which system of reinforcement Paul wishes to be independent: it is the system of reinforcement represented by the dominant classes and the leading groups. The assertion that no one can judge the pneumatic is pointed against those who otherwise have the power to judge others. If these powerful people have opposed with hostility the wisdom of God in Christ, and if Christ has overcome their resistance, then Christ becomes a model of behavior and experience that has made itself independent of the negative sanctions of the dominant system of convictions. This is not only a purely formal independence. The wisdom of this world is characterized by its link with social and political power; the foolishness of the preaching is characterized by its link with a crucified man. If this "foolishness" is recognized as superior wisdom, then the principle of dominance that rules the world is itself called into question. A struggle for power and influence would contradict this perfect wisdom. The divided Corinthians are thus not mature enough for it. They are still "fleshly" (1 Cor. 3:1–3).

Paul still conceals what he opposes positively to the fleshly struggle. At the beginning of 1 Corinthians the accent lies wholly on the fact *that* a system of reinforcement independent of the old world has appeared with Christ. In the citation in 2:9, Paul implies that this system of reinforcement is operative among those who love God. But none of this is developed. Only later does Paul become more concrete: all pneumatic experience is directed toward love (1 Corinthians 13). In 1 Cor. 3:1*, he reproaches the Corinthians as "immature." In 1 Corinthians 13, he shows them the way to maturity: "When I was a child, I spoke like a child, I thought like a child, I reasoned like a child; when I became a man, I gave up childish ways" (1 Cor. 13:11). The *teleioi* of 1 Cor. 2:6 are those who know the *teleion* of 1 Cor. 13:10. What is "perfect" is love.[7]

From 1 Corinthians 13 we thus come to know the new "reinforcement system" of Paul, which is only imperfectly operative even among Christians. One characteristic is striking here. As a rule, Paul motivates love and solidary behavior extrinsically. He appeals to authorities like

---

recognize the wisdom of God, for it is written that what God has prepared for his elect has not entered the heart of *man*. It will be shown below that the demonic conception is also not entirely unjustified: the earthly archons are in fact shrouded in a mythical aura.

7. On 1 Corinthians 13, cf. Wischmeyer, *Der höchste Weg*.

the law (Gal. 5:14; Rom. 13:8–10)—to moral stimuli, in other words. He threatens negative consequences in case of unloving behavior (cf. Gal. 5:21). He invokes the model of Christ (Rom. 15:7). But in 1 Corinthians 13, he leaves behind all these extrinsic forms of motivation. Love is commanded without reference to an authority. Every allusion to the Old Testament is lacking, as is every appeal to a word of the Lord, or argumentation on the basis of authoritative tribunals. If there is a demand of love—if, in the language of learning theory, there is anything that "stimulates" love—then this occurs through presentation of loving behavior and through nothing else. The same is true of motivation with the aid of positive and negative consequences. No positive consequences are promised. In the end there remain faith, hope, and love. Love is the greatest among them. It is in itself reward for all eternity. Paul does not even promise that it will be "rewarded" by disappearing negative consequences; on the contrary, love bears all, believes all, hopes all, endures all. Once again Paul motivates in a purely intrinsic manner. For this reason he can also renounce all models. He refers neither to himself nor to Christ as models of loving behavior. Rather, he speaks of love as of an acting person: "Love is patient and kind; love is not jealous or boastful; it is not arrogant or rude. Love does not insist on its own way; it is not irritable or resentful; it does not rejoice at wrong, but rejoices in the right. Love bears all things, believes all things, hopes all things, endures all things . . ." (1 Cor. 13:4–7). Here love appears as an example of itself. It is its own model. It is from love that one learns what love is. From the perspectives of learning theory, the new reality Paul experienced as overpowering revelation and as "perfection" can be described as intrinsically motivated love: love is experienced as a value in itself. It unfolds itself among the perfect, those who are driven by the Spirit of God, without appeal to external authorities, without reference to reinforcing consequences, without dependence on exemplary models.

In sum, from the perspective of learning theory, Paul wishes to desensitize with regard to the dominant reinforcement system in society through development of the preaching of the cross as "foolishness for the world" and as "wisdom for the perfect." The dominant system is to lose its power over Christians. The preaching is to make one independent from every external judgment. The decisive condition for learning is the model of Christ. In him the impotent is shown as powerful, and the powerful as weak. With a view to him one need not be impressed by the claims of the powerful, the respected, and the wellborn. In 1 Cor. 2:6–16, Paul does not yet develop the new "reinforcement system" for the perfect. Only later does he concretize materially what for him is perfect, something that points far beyond the everyday reality of the community: what is perfect is intrinsically motivated love. Only love has completely overcome the reinforcement system based on domination. Only love has emancipated itself from all external authorities, consequences, and models, from all the extrinsic reinforcements whose functioning is inconceivable without power. Such wisdom is for those who are perfect.

PSYCHODYNAMIC ASPECTS: THE CENSORSHIP OF THE DOMINANT CONSCIOUSNESS

The transformation of the Christian is not only an event evoked from without. The Spirit transforms within. The linguistic use of *pneuma* encompasses both aspects—both the gift conferred from without and the inner tribunal. Each individual has a *pneuma*.[8] But pneumatic persons have in addition participation in another person—in the Pneuma of God (v. 12) and the Nous of Christ (v. 16). They have opened their individual spirits to the more comprehensive Spirit of God. Only now does "what no eye has seen and no ear heard, what has entered the heart of no man" (v. 9*) become accessible to them. Only as transformed do they become receptive to new impulses, reinforcements, and models. This inner transformation can be described more readily with psychodynamic categories than with those of learning theory.

Our structural analysis has already yielded an initial conjecture. Tensions between form and content—between a form of revelation discourse that points beyond the initial preaching and its material correspondence with the initial preaching—suggested the idea that the higher wisdom consists in grasping what was received unconsciously in the initial preaching. Every Christian possesses the Spirit of God, but only the pneumatic in the stricter sense "understands the gifts bestowed on us by God" (2:12*). Paul depicts this process of something becoming conscious first as an "objective" event (2:6–9), then as a subjective process (2:10–16). The key to psychodynamic interpretation

8. Romans 8:16 is generally considered the best proof that human and divine spirit are to be separated sharply. Yet one can certainly read it as follows: the Spirit himself witnesses together with our spirit. This corresponds both to the meaning of *summarturein* in Rom. 2:15 and 9:1 and to the following context, where the sighing resounds both in Christians and in the divine Spirit (8:23, 26). If the Christian can become "one Spirit" with the Lord (1 Cor. 6:17), then excessively sharp theological distinctions disappear.

of the text lies in the homology between "objective" and "subjective" depiction. The objective depiction could be the symbol of an inner transformation. Conversely, the symbols suggested to an individual by Paul's preaching effect a profound subjective process of transformation.

The Objective Depiction of the Process of Revelation: 1 Cor. 2:6–8

We ask first if the depiction of the Christ-event is transparent for something else. Does it have additional symbolic value that points beyond an external event? Whether it thus points to an inner event will be clarified in a second step. The question is to be addressed above all to the "archons of this world." People have always surmised that these are not historical rulers but rather demonic powers.[9] The two interpretations are not sharp alternatives.[10] The historical rulers could be heightened symbolically to mythical powers. They are doubtless shrouded with a mythical aura in 1 Cor. 2:6ff., inasmuch as they participate in a dramatic event that encompasses heaven and earth.

Such mythical heightening is possible within the world of Pauline thought. Even the archons in Rom. 13:3 are not only secular officials but "servants of God" (v. 4*). Whoever obeys them obeys God's command (v. 2). While the state is not a demonic reality—the passage is rather directed against too negative an assessment of the state—a mythical aura does surround it. It is something both empirical and superempirical! Another example is 1 Cor. 11:2–16. The factual subordination of a wife to her husband is veiled with a mythical aura. Just as Christ is subordinated to God, so too is the wife subordinated to the husband. The earthly relationships have correspondences in heavenly relationships. In this regard Paul can also invoke Satan, if the events on earth are repugnant to him. That his opponents have found response in his own communities can lie only in the appearance of false apostles as apostles of Christ. Just as Satan transformed himself into an angel of light, so too have his servants (2 Cor. 11:13–15). Even the sufferings to which Christians are exposed in the world are more than "natural" events. Suffering cannot separate Christians from God (Rom. 8:35). For no mythical power—neither death nor life, neither

9. The demonological interpretation, which goes back to Origen, was renewed by Everling (*Die paulinische Angelologie*, 11–12) and Dibelius (*Die Geisterwelt*, 88–99), and defended but later abandoned by Wilckens (*Weisheit*, 62–63).

10. Thus, correctly in my estimation, Cullmann, *Der Staat*, 45, 75ff.

angels nor powers—can separate them from the love of God. The parallelism of the catalogues of forces and powers in Rom. 8:35–39 illustrates the parallelism of earthly and mythical events, in which one cannot distinguish sharply between simple correspondence and causal involvement. Should not something similar be true of the archons of this world? It is unmistakable that Paul takes his point of departure from the historical rulers. Yet, in my opinion, they are transparent to a "mythical" connection that exceeds the historical connections. Four arguments will be mentioned in favor of a mythical interpretation of this sort which heightens the historical interpretation.

1. Paul speaks of "rulers of this age," not simply of rulers. After *archontes*, the genitive *tou aionos toutou* must be conceived as an objective genitive.[11] It is a question of the rulers over this world (not only of worldly rulers). But the Jewish and Roman authorities in Palestine could never be called rulers over the entire world. Lukan linguistic usage confirms this. Where Luke speaks of "archons," he always specifies more precisely. He speaks of "your archons" (Acts 3:17), "their archons" (13:27), "archons of the people" (4:8). They stand beside the high priests (Luke 23:13; 24:20), the elders and the scribes (Acts 4:5), or the people (Luke 23:35); in brief, it is always a matter of specific archons limited in their realm of power. In Paul it is different. Since in 2 Cor. 4:4* he calls Satan "the god of this age," one must also relate the term "archons of this age" to cosmic powers, in other words, to those *theoi* (gods) in heaven and on earth whose existence Paul does not call into dispute (1 Cor. 8:5), even if through Christ they have lost their power.[12]

2. The archons are specified as corruptible powers, which would be superfluous with regard to human rulers. Human beings are by definition mortal. It is true that this argument is not compelling.[13] The attribute *katargoumenoi* is reminiscent of *katargein* in 1:28. There Paul

11. Cf. the *archontes tou laou* (Acts 4:8) or the *archon ton basileon tes ges* (Acts 1:5), as well as the *archontes ton ethnon* (Bar. 3:16).

12. That *archontes* can designate mythical powers is shown by Dan. 10:13 LXX; Ignatius *Letter to the Smyrnaeans* 6.1; and Justin *Dialogue with Trypho* 36.5. The *archon* in the singular is a mythical power in the *Testament of Simeon* 2.7; *Testament of Judah* 19.4; Eph. 2:2; *Barnabas* 4:13; *Martyrdom of Polycarp* 19.2. There are numerous references for later Gnosis: see, among others, Origen, *Contra Celsum* 6.27, 31, 33, 35 (on the Ophites); *The Hypostatis of the Archons* (*Nag Hammadi Codices* 2.87–89; 92—93; 96.15; 97.23), the *Apocryphon of John* (*Berlin Gnostic Codex* 53–54, 63). Martin Dibelius's observation (*Die Geisterwelt*, 93) is still valid: "The line that leads from him [Paul] to gnosis is present, and the only question is the point at which one begins to use the name Gnosticism."

13. Cf. n. 4 of this chapter.

says that God "destroys" what exists, that no flesh might boast before God; here the *katargein* unmistakably affects even respected and highly placed people. But in 1:26ff. it is also placed in a cosmic context. The highly placed among the Corinthians become transparent to being in general, to all "flesh" that seeks to boast of itself before God. If the lowly are chosen and the highly placed lose their significance, then the creator God is at work, the one who calls into being what is not (Rom. 4:7). But if the socially powerful become transparent to a mythical background in 1 Cor. 1:28, must this not also be true of the "archons of this world" in 1 Cor. 2:6ff.? Could one not understand the attribute *katargoumenoi* on the basis of 1 Cor. 15:24ff.? According to this text, at the end Christ will destroy (*katargese*) all rule (*archen*) and all might and power that resists the rule of God—with death itself as the last enemy. The mention of death shows that this is a matter of mythic powers. Yet they cannot be separated sharply from earthly powers. Obviously, these too will lose their power in the end.

3. The mention of the crucifixion is often considered the decisive argument for a historical interpretation of the "archons," since here reference is made to an unambiguously historical event.[14] Yet 1 Cor. 2:8 brings the archons into connection not only with the historical cross but also with the mythically conceived preexistence of divine wisdom. The subordinate clause in which the archons are mentioned (v. 8*) stands parallel to a subordinate clause that relates to preexistent realities (v. 7*):

> hen proorisen ho Theos pro ton aionon eis doxan hemon
> hen oudeis ton archonton tou aionos toutou egnoken
>
> which God decreed before the ages for our glory
> which none of the rulers of this age understood

Both relative clauses elucidate what is meant by the hidden wisdom of God. They say, first, positively, that it was chosen before the world and, second, negatively, that none of the archons recognized it.[15] If the two clauses are read in context, one must relate the nonrecognition by the archons to preexistent wisdom, not only to the historical Jesus; the feminine relative pronoun is unambiguously dependent on the "hidden wisdom," and wisdom was hidden in its preexistence. Are

14. Thus Wilckens, "Zu 1.Kor 2,1–16," 508.

15. The perfect *egnoken* designates a state. But if the ignorance of the archons is a state—and not only a single act—then the reference to the Passion narrative is less suggested.

not the archons then also preexistent beings? Or, put more cautiously, do not the historically unique archons in Palestine become transparent for all earthly rulers in general?

Now, one could object that on only one other occasion does Paul speak of persons who are responsible for the killing of Jesus. There he is unmistakably thinking of the Jews (1 Thess. 2:15) who killed the Jew Jesus. But this analogy is, in my opinion, not convincing. 1 Thessalonians 2:15 stands in a different tradition, the Deuteronomic tradition of the murder of the prophets.[16] The term "crucify" does not occur in this tradition; the verb used is "kill" (cf. Luke 13:34; 11:49ff.). For only in this way can a continuity to the murders of the prophets be established. The killing of Jesus is, after all, only one link in a long chain of assaults. According to Luke 11:49ff., wisdom sent many prophets and apostles, and many were killed. This successive mission of many messengers would contradict the scheme of revelation in 1 Cor. 2:6ff.: what has long been hidden has finally and uniquely come to light.

A second observation may be added. Precisely if one does not wish to exclude the historical rulers from the "archons of this world" in 1 Cor. 2:8, one must register a contradiction to 1 Thess. 2:15. There it is only the Jews who kill Jesus. But the Roman rulers without doubt belong to the "archons" responsible for his crucifixion. Even the term "crucify" must have suggested this association in the world of that day: the cross was a Roman death penalty. The unilateral mention of the Jews in 1 Thess. 2:15 is explained both by the prior tradition of the murder of the prophets and by the context of thought in 1 Thessalonians: Paul wishes to find an analogy for the persecution of Christians by members of their own clan, whether they are Jews or Gentiles. Since 1 Thess. 2:15 stands in a different context of thought from 1 Cor. 2:8, one may not conclude without further ado from one text to the other.

4. On the basis of other Pauline texts it is impossible to exclude Paul's connecting the crucifixion with mythical powers. According to the hymn of Philippians the preexistent one takes on the form of a slave. It is clear that the exalted one triumphs over all mythical powers (Phil. 2:6–11). Could not these mythical powers already stand in connection with the cross? Could they not be the "lords" to whom the "form of a slave" of the humbled one is related? One of Paul's students

16. Steck, *Israel*.

later speaks of triumph over the powers through the cross (Col. 2:15).
It is therefore not inconceivable that Paul already understood the cross
as expression of a battle between Christ and the mythical powers, but
that he spoke of this only in the circle of the "perfect"—something
that could explain the singularity of the conception in 1 Cor. 2:6ff.

The interpretation of the archons proposed here rejects the widespread alternative "historical or demonic." The archons are historical
rulers who are heightened symbolically to demonic powers. This
conception finds support in the *Testimony of Truth*,[17] where unambiguously historical figures such as Pharisees, scribes, and John the Baptist
are viewed as "archons" (9.9–21):

> For many have sought after the truth and have not been able to find it;
> because there has taken hold of them [the] old leaven of the Pharisees
> and the scribes [of] the Law. And the leaven is [the] errant desire of the
> angels and the demons and the stars. The Pharisees and the scribes are
> those who belong to the archons who have authority [over them].[18]

John the Baptist also becomes an archon (31.2–5):

> The water of the Jordan is the desire for sexual intercourse. John is the
> archon of the womb.[19]

That these archons are really mythical realities is clear from the
Testimony of Truth 42.24–25, where "the archons and the powers and
the demons"[20] are mentioned together. In the *Testimony of Truth* 29.17–
18, they appear beside angels, demons, and stars. There can be no
doubt that the cited references assure the historical possibility that
historical figures could simultaneously be conceived as mythical powers.

Summary. The esoteric doctrine for the perfect in 1 Cor. 2:6ff.
deepens the historical event of the crucifixion to a mythical event. The
historical events are heightened mythically. In the historical archons,
the mythical power of this age in general becomes visible. In a sense,
we experience in 1 Cor. 2:6ff. the birth of a myth. But mythification
occurs when there is brought to expression something that has occurred
not only once but constantly since its archetypal occurrence and that
can occur further.

---

17. Koschorke, "Der gnostische Traktat."
18. ET: Søren Giversen and Birger A. Pearson, *The Nag Hammadi Library*, ed.
Robinson, 406–7.
19. ET: ibid., 407.
20. ET: ibid., 410.

The Subjective Aspect of the Event
of Revelation: 1 Cor. 2:9–16

As we have seen, the rejection of Christ by the "archons of this world" is a model for the resistance the divine counterwisdom finds in society. From a psychodynamic perspective we must deepen this view further. The archons of this world do not represent only the external resistance of society, in other words, an external system of reinforcement; in addition, they are symbols of the inner resistance that has its locus in the human being—symbols of the interiorized censorship of the historical system of convictions. It is precisely for this reason that they receive mythical character. They represent something lying ready in everyone, beyond what is unique and historical. They are the symbol of an inner limit to understanding, which the ancients articulated in mythical images just as self-evidently as we articulate it in psychological language.

A first indication of this inner limit to understanding is given by v. 9, which mediates between the objectively and subjectively formulated sections of the text. With the apocryphal citation, Paul wishes to establish why the archons misunderstood the wisdom of God and crucified Christ—why, in other words, they gave him no place in their realm. The foundation reads, "But, as it is written, 'What no eye has seen, nor ear heard, nor the heart of man conceived, what God has prepared for those who love him' " (2:9). Here the issue is suddenly no longer that Christ has no place in this world but that in him one encounters a reality which in principle has no place in any human heart. The interiorization of the objective mythical event is unmistakable; it becomes even more clear if one takes into consideration the tradition history of the apocalyptic theme present in 2:9. For this history, as a rule, is concerned with future salvific goods that lie prepared as reward for the just.[21] The idea of reward recedes in Paul. It does echo in the citation, for the love of God is a presupposition for attaining salvific goods, but Paul does not pick up on this idea. Nor does he distinguish between current revelation of the (future) salvific goods and their (later) mediation. The current revelation is already mediation of salvation. It mediates access to the depths of God and expands consciousness beyond human limits.

Thus Paul's train of thought is as follows. Something that was

---

21. According to Berger ("Zu Diskussion," 279), Paul is no longer concerned with the reward of the just but is concerned with the "question of the true revelation." The apocalyptic conceptual framework of the citation is attenuated.

accessible to no one has penetrated into the heart of Christians. God has revealed it to them—against the embittered resistance of the archons of this world. The archons thus become hostile guards in front of the human heart. Formulated in our language, this means that the kerygma forced its way into the unconscious human depths against an inner resistance.

In this context, the archons symbolize three things. First, they symbolize a resistance on the border between what is conscious and what is unconscious; they are the censorship on the threshold between consciousness and what transcends consciousness. Second, they make the form of this resistance transparent by exposing it as a censorship that admits the kerygma only in the deformed figure of the cross. Third and finally, they make transparent the origin of the resistance. The rulers of the world represent the dominant consciousness of society, which is experienced as a compulsive power. We shall consider these theses in order.

1. The archons symbolize the resistance against the redeeming power of the kerygma—precisely as psychic resistance on the threshold of consciousness and the unconscious. Put mythically, the archons defend their world. They annihilate the redemptive manifestation that is threatening to them. But they deny it access not only to their realm but also to the human heart. Only in this way does the connection between vv. 8 and 9–10 become intelligible: the revelation to believers corresponds positively to the nonrecognition of the archons. The parallel statement in 2 Cor. 4:4ff. confirms this. The archons of this age are identical in function to the "god of this age," whose function consists in "blinding the minds [*noemata*] of unbelievers, to keep them from seeing the light of the gospel of the glory of Christ, who is the likeness of God" (2 Cor. 4:4*). Here too it is a matter of blindness to glory (cf. 1 Cor. 2:7, 8); here too it is a matter of inner blinding, of a "veil over the heart"—in brief, of the resistance of a hardened consciousness to the redeeming alternative. Overcoming this resistance occurs through a miracle. In 2 Cor. 4:6, it is described in analogy to the creation of light—as the shining of a light in the heart. In 1 Cor. 2:6ff., it is depicted as conferral of the Spirit.

Precisely in connection with the conferral of the Spirit the theme of God's omniscience occurs twice (1 Cor. 2:10, 15). "For the Spirit searches everything, even the depths of God" (2:10). The *panta erauna*, "searches everything," has its closest parallel in Rom. 8:27 in *eraunon tas kardias:* " . . . he who searches the hearts of men knows what is in the mind of the Spirit." Omniscience and knowledge of hearts belong together. One therefore associates involuntarily: the Spirit searches everything, not only the depths of God but also the depths of the human heart.[22] Of course, at first that is only an associative connection. But it is suggested by the facts. After all, to search the depths of the Deity means to achieve insight into what has now finally penetrated into the human heart and left traces deep within.

This relationship of the theme of omniscience to the human interior is also suggested by the second text (1 Cor. 2:15). Here the theme is carried over from the Spirit to the spiritual man: "The spiritual man judges all things [*panta*], but is himself to be judged by no one" (2:15).[23] This "all things" doubtless also encompasses the spiritual man's own self—precisely that which can be judged by no one else; this is especially evident since in v. 11 the ability of self-knowledge is ascribed explicitly to the Spirit.[24]

Can we not conclude from this that the depths of the Deity have their counterpart in the depths of the human interior? Or, in other words, that what comes from the depths of the Deity also opens new depths within man—though only after a powerful resistance within him has been overcome.

2. The archons symbolize the psychic resistance as deforming censorship. They are responsible for the crucifixion. The crucifixion had its final ground in the fact that they did not recognize the preexistent wisdom of God, which is directed toward the salvation of

22. Cf. *1 Clement* 21.2–3: " 'The Spirit [*pneuma*] of the Lord is a lamp searching [*ereunon*] the inward parts.' Let us observe how near he is, and that nothing escapes him of our thoughts or of the devices which we make" (ET: Kirsopp Lake, *The Apostolic Fathers*, vol. 1 of 2 vols. [LCL, 1914], 47). Here the Spirit searches the depths of the human interior. Cf. also Jdt. 8:14: "You cannot plumb the depths of the human heart [*bathos kardias*], nor find out what a man is thinking."

23. The statement that the spiritual person judges everything but is judged by no one would seem to be a transferral of divine attributes to humanity. This transferral is still tangible in Philo *On the Creation* 69: "For the human mind evidently occupies a position in men precisely answering to that which the great Ruler occupies in all the world. It is invisible while itself seeing all things, and while comprehending the substances of others, it is as to its own substance unperceived" (ET: F. H. Colson and G. H. Whitaker, *Philo*, vol. 1 of 10 vols. [LCL, 1929], 55).

24. In later gnostic texts this connection—that omniscience is primarily self-knowledge—comes clearly to light. Cf. *The Book of Thomas the Contender* 138.15–20: "You will be called 'the one who knows himself.' For he who has not known himself has known nothing, but he who has known himself has at the same time already achieved knowledge about the Depth of the All. So then, you, my brother Thomas, have beheld what is obscure to men, that is, that against which they ignorantly stumble" (ET: John D. Turner, *The Nag Hammadi Library*, ed. Robinson, 189).

believers. They are responsible for the fact that God's intention, directed toward salvation, appears on earth as foolishness—in the form of the cross. Through their resistance, they bring it about that the redeeming message presents itself to consciousness only in a deformed, distorted, even destroyed form, in the form of the most discriminatory type of execution. It is precisely in this form, unacceptable to the dominant consciousness—one can even say, in this "eliminated" form, in which according to human judgment it can have no sort of powerful effect—that the kerygma demonstrates its liberating power. Passing the censorship of consciousness it penetrates into the human depths and opens new dimensions.

This process can be illumined by a comparison from the history of religion. In connection with 1 Cor. 2:6ff., people have always referred to certain analogies in gnostic texts, namely, to the descent of the redeemer through the planetary spheres, in the course of which the redeemer disguises himself.[25] In the *Martyrdom and Ascension of Isaiah* (10.7–12), God commands the redeemer as follows:

> Go out and descend through all the heavens. You shall descend through the firmament and through that world as far as the angel who (is) in Sheol, but you shall not go as far as Perdition. And you shall make your likeness like that of all who (are) in the five heavens, and you shall take care to make your form like that of the angels of the firmament and also (like that) of the angels who (are) in Sheol. And none of the angels of that world shall know that you are Lord with me of the seven heavens and of their angels. And they shall not know that you (are) with me when with the voice of the heavens I summon you, and their angels and their lights, and when I lift up (my voice) to the sixth heaven, that you may judge and destroy the princes and the angels and the gods of that world, and the world which is ruled by them.[26]

Although from the perspective of the history of tradition, one cannot derive 1 Cor. 2:6ff. from conceptions of this sort, a factual comparison can still elucidate what is characteristic of 1 Corinthians 2. During the descent into the world the redeemer disguises himself in order not to be recognized. He is able to pass the demonic guards unrecognized.

25. Cf. Dibelius, *Die Geisterwelt*, 92ff. In *The Second Treatise of the Great Seth* 56.24–27, the redeemer says, "For as I came downward no one saw me. For I was altering my shapes, changing from form to form. And therefore when I was at their gates I assumed their likeness" (ET: James Brashler, Peter A. Dirkse, and Douglas M. Parrott, *The Nag Hammadi Library*, ed. Robinson, 332).

26. ET: M. A. Knibb, *The Old Testament Pseudepigrapha*, ed. Charlesworth, 2:173.

According to this myth, the result is not a conflict between the redeemer and the powers but rather a compromise. The redeemer conceals his true form and appears in such a way that he is acceptable to the angelic powers. The "censorship" causes a change of form, a disguise, hidden behind which the initially rejected content can enter consciousness—that is, enter the realm of this world. Here the censorship works exactly in the way classical psychoanalysis has analyzed it—as a compromising power that forces the unacceptable content to disguise itself. But in Paul things are different. A compromise is not possible. The result is conflict. The archons misunderstand the wisdom of God. They pose themselves openly for defense. What emerges from the realm transcendent to consciousness is precisely not admitted on the basis of a compromise but suppressed, killed, and destroyed. But the archons thus call themselves into question. They shall be annihilated. The censuring compulsion is thus not circumvented but eliminated. Paul appears as more radical than the gnostic statements about the descent of the redeemer that are often adduced for comparison.

3. In addition, the archons symbolize the historical causes of psychic resistance to the redeeming message. In Paul the archons are historical rulers, though with a mythical aura. Their resistance to the message is resistance of the ruling classes—and has its effect in the social composition of the Corinthian community, in which the upper classes were scarcely represented, though not completely lacking. Now the consciousness of the rulers is usually bound up with the dominant consciousness—the collective convictions and evaluations that inescapably mark every member of a society. It often appears as a compulsive power marking the individual. To put it in ancient language, it often appears as something demonic; for this reason, the archons are heightened to cosmic powers present everywhere that the message is contradicted on the basis of the dominant consciousness. Whoever with the preaching of the cross recognizes an execution as access to salvation has separated himself radically from the standards of this consciousness, that is, from the values, norms, and standards of the existing society.

So far we have interpreted psychodynamically the negative side of the process of transformation—the liberation from the censorship of the historical system of convictions. But what about its positive side? If the archons represent an inner censorship, what does the figure of Christ, who falls into conflict with them, represent?

Just as the historical rulers of Palestine became mythical realities, so too did the historical Jesus. He becomes the embodiment of preexistent wisdom. Even if one understands wisdom as a gift conferred on the pneumatic, one ought not deny that the *sophia* myth shimmers through the preexistent wisdom of 1 Cor. 2:6ff. Here there is no sharp either-or. Even in the wisdom literature, wisdom is both mythical figure and human quality. Now Paul makes the following statements about wisdom. It is preexistent. The world could have known God through it (1:21). But it was revealed only through Christ. What Paul formulates now—in 2:6ff.—is "wisdom," precisely this preexistent, hidden wisdom revealed in Christ that is rejected by the rulers of this age. What imposes itself against their resistance is in other words a preexistent tendency. It stems from a realm whose temporal dimension is sketched with the words "before the ages" (2:7) and whose spatial dimension is sketched as the "depths of God" (2:10). Something has penetrated into the human heart from a primeval depth dimension of reality—a cosmic tendency that is programmed into creation and that already existed before people fell under the power of the rule of the archons. Up to now it was hidden, but it became manifest in the figure of Christ—just as a concrete symbol can be a manifestation of an invisible preexistent structure, an "archetype." In fact it lies close at hand to think here of a psychic tendency, programmed into us by evolution, which achieves consciousness of itself in the figure of Christ— even against the resistance of the given cultural system of convictions.

Such a connection of a cosmic event with an inner process is not a retrojection of modern ideas into the Pauline world of images. Rather, this connection has its precursors in the history of the tradition in Jewish Hellenistic sapiential thinking. For wisdom is first of all a cosmic power. It formed the world (Wis. 7:21), is present everywhere (7:24), knows and can do everything (9:11; 7:27). It incarnates itself in friends of God and in prophets (7:27). The wise pray that it also take up dwelling in their hearts. Solomon begs for the sending of wisdom from heaven (9:10) and of the "holy Spirit" from on high (9:17). If wisdom takes a place in his heart, he imitates its mystic marriage with God (8:2–3). His *symbiosis* with wisdom (8:16) is imitation of its *symbiosis* with God (8:3). In the history of tradition, this "wisdom mysticism" is the precursor of the Pauline Christ mysticism. For Paul also knows the marriage imagery. He too sees the relationship to Christ as a kind of "marriage" (Rom. 7:1ff.; 1 Cor. 6:16–17). He too speaks of the "dwelling" of the Spirit in us, and even of Christ in us (8:9–10*). In him too a cosmic reality becomes the object of mystical experience, for the transcending of human consciousness through opening for the divine Spirit is without doubt a mystical experience (1 Cor. 2:10ff.).

Of course, Paul deviates in many respects for the traditional wisdom thinking. In the Wisdom of Solomon the sending of wisdom and of the Spirit is one act. In Paul, wisdom incarnates itself only in one man. At first only Christ is the image of God (2 Cor. 4:4)—like wisdom (Wis. 7:26). At first only he is sent by God (Gal. 4:4)—like wisdom (Wis. 9:10, 17). Just like wisdom, he was already salvifically present at the exodus (cf. 1 Cor. 10:1ff. and Wis. 10:18–19; 11:4ff.). But the incarnation of wisdom in Christ is separated from the general incarnation in human beings. The latter is predicated only of the Spirit, even though Paul in individual borderline statements can speak of "Christ in us" (Rom. 8:10*; Gal. 2:20*). The exclusive binding to one historical person is connected with the reestimation of wisdom; it is true that wisdom always wanted to be recognized, but it is only in the paradoxical form of the cross that it achieved its aim. The traditional wisdom piety had gone astray. The cosmic intentions of divine wisdom, present with creation, had to be realized against the dominant cultural system of convictions.

At what do these tendencies which arise from creation and from one's own interior aim? Paul never develops this more tangibly than in Romans 8. If the Spirit of Christ dwells in Christians, if even Christ himself is present in them, then from this follow overcoming of fleshly nature, solidarity with suffering and sighing creation, but above all, the deep feeling of solidarity with the central reality that Paul calls love and that overcomes the separations created by guilt, suffering, and hostile powers (Rom. 8:31–39).

Now a summary of our psychodynamic analysis of 1 Cor. 2:1–16. The problem with which we began was the distinction of an initial preaching from the wisdom teaching for the perfect. Since the cross is the central content for every stage of faith, the difference lies not in faith in new contents but in a more profound consciousness of the Christian symbols. Both simple believers and "advanced" pneumatics are grasped by the symbol of the cross. But only the latter penetrate the unconscious connections in which the preaching of the cross functions. Only they penetrate the inevitable psychic and social resistance against the symbol of the cross; only they emancipate themselves consciously from the compulsive standards of this world. Their consciousness has opened itself into unknown depths, so that they think they have grown beyond human consciousness. The sudden expansion of consciousness achieved by the kerygma is experienced as ecstatic absorption into a greater divine consciousness to which even the depths of the Deity do not remain concealed. On the one hand, the message of the cross affects the unconscious, bypassing the censorship of societal consciousness; on the other hand, hitherto hidden tendencies from the human depths, which become conscious with the aid of the cross, come to meet it. They penetrate into the heart, fill it with spirit, and confer freedom with respect to the world's system of sanctions—and simultaneously a new solidarity with the whole creation.

COGNITIVE ASPECTS: THE RESTRUCTURING OF FOOLISHNESS INTO WISDOM

As obvious as simply combining the approaches of learning theory and psychodynamics would be in the interpretation of 1 Cor. 2:6–16, this would underestimate the significance of interpretive procedures for the processes depicted in 1 Cor. 2:6ff. The theme of the section is the "wisdom of God." The term "wisdom" always contains a cognitive element. Wisdom includes knowledge, reflection, "theory." This is also true of "perfect wisdom." It can be understood and misunderstood (vv. 8–9, 11, 14). It leads to a knowledge (vv. 11, 12), to a *sugkrinein* (v. 13) and an *anakrinesthai* (v. 14). All these cognitive verbs indicate a process of understanding, conceiving, and interpreting. The goal of the wisdom discourse is a radical restructuring of judgment and evaluation. What is "foolishness" from the perspective of the world is to appear as "wisdom" through the Spirit. One who has the "mind" of the Lord (v. 16) judges differently from a "psychic." The central purpose of the text is thus a cognitive restructuring. We must therefore deepen our previous interpretations. In 1 Cor. 2:6–16, Christ is not only behavior model for desensitizing with regard to the dominant system of reinforcement. He is not only the symbol of liberation from an inner censorship. Christ is the cause of a radical restructuring of the internal and external world. The psychological problem is where the figure of Christ receives its restructuring power. Where does the cause for the transformation of the interpreted world lie?

An impetus toward restructuring the interpreted world lies in the cognitive dissonance that came into the world through Christ. This dissonance was triggered by the cross. Where an executed man is presented as mediator of salvation, the interpreted world formed by Jewish and Greek traditions must appear disturbed. The cross is a scandal to the Jews since it contradicts the expectation of powerful signs in which God intervenes salvifically. It is foolishness to the Greeks since it contradicts the standards of wisdom. Strong cognitive conflicts force one either to defend the received system of interpretation through reinforcement of elements consonant with it or to restructure it to such an extent that originally dissonant elements appear as consonant in a more comprehensive or transformed framework. Seen retrospectively, abrupt dissonances can have liberating effects because they necessitate restructuring and open new perspectives.

The transition from the preaching of the cross (1:18—2:4) to the wisdom preaching (2:6ff.) is not a "change of front" or polemic adaptation to the addressees or a protest against Paul subsequently ascribed to Paul himself; rather, in this transition there occurs a cognitive restructuring of the interpreted world. The cross was foolishness in the world as traditionally interpreted. In it the cross was cognitively dissonant. It is wisdom in the world, newly interpreted symbolically, that is created by the preaching. In this new world it affords access to a more profound consonance. This restructuring takes place with regard to both the internal and the external world.

Cognitive Restructuring of the Environment

As we have seen, Paul links perfect wisdom to a social group, to the "perfect." This social environment is not only the stimulating and reinforcing condition of the transformation; it is itself interpreted as part of a comprehensive process of transformation. For if one who had according to normal standards failed became a world ruler, then those who are otherwise defeated according to normal standards are to be evaluated differently. It is precisely the foolish, the weak, and the lowly who are the "wise" within the new frame of reference. They experience a total transformation of their evaluation. Paul, after all, does not merely register the fact that in the Corinthian community only a few belong to the higher classes. That is correct. But Paul goes beyond this fact by active restructuring. Decisive significance is attributed to the lower classes. They are chosen by God as that which is not. The few members of the upper class, on the contrary, are completely neglected. They do not fit into the framework of interpretation in which Paul places the social situation of the community. Paul sees this situation in analogy to creation. As God then called into being that which is not (Rom. 4:17), so too has he chosen that which is not— groups that are "nothing" within the social hierarchy. The accent falls completely on these groups. In fact, community members from the higher classes had a much greater significance for life in the Corinthian community; with their greater material possibilities, they were, after all, indispensable for it. But that does not count before God. God chooses that which is nothing.

What is true of the social world is true of the world in general. Its structure is not definitive. In speaking of "this world," Paul presupposes the existence of a new world. Prior to all "worlds," God had a plan that leads beyond "this world." This plan was realized in Christ. But since Christ did not fit into this world—he was rejected by it—he can be ordered into a meaningful context only as the beginning of a new world. This too is treatment of a cognitive conflict. The contradiction to this world which is articulated in the cross is interpreted as a meaningful event in a more comprehensive context, one that encompasses eternity and a new world. It then no longer appears as a meaningless contradiction but rather opens a more comprehensive horizon of meaning. How much all that Paul says about the world in general is the mirroring of experiences with the social world need not be specially emphasized.

On the basis of a cognitive interpretation of this sort, what we said about Christ as a model of behavior can be deepened. Christ is indeed a learning model for self-assertion with respect to the sanctions of "this world." But this model becomes effective only if it is placed in a larger cognitive framework—if the contradiction to this world is interpreted as a foreshadowing of another reality, not merely as a futile protest. Reinforcements perceived from the model have influence that determines behavior only if they "fit" into the entire cognitive world of the learner. If they contradict this world, then the behavior shown in the model can even have opposite effects.

Cognitive Restructuring of the Inner World

Just as the external world is restructured cognitively, so too is the internal world seen in a new light. The opposition *psychikos-pneumatikos* stems from the confrontation of two types of human beings, as present in 1 Cor. 15:44–49. This is not (only) a matter of juxtaposed groups. Rather, all bear initially the image of the earthly man. All have a *soma psychikon*. Faith in Christ transforms one into a new form of existence; Christians transformed by the resurrection have a *soma pneumatikon*. But in 1 Cor. 2:6ff., the antonyms *psychikos-pneumatikos* are connected with the present reception of revelation, not with the future resurrection. The pneumatic is already extant in the present and is not distinguished by a transformed body. The term *pneuma* means, rather, an inner dimension of human existence. Only for this reason can the spirit within (*to en auto;* v. 11) be adduced as image and analogy to the Spirit conferred by God. In the same way, the antonym *psychikos* is connected with psychic acts. That the "psychic" does not receive God's truth is identical to the inability of eye, ear, and heart to push forward to this truth on their own (2:9). The antonyms *psychikos-pneumatikos* thus relate to different inner aspects, of which the pneumatic aspect is not already present on the basis of nature but must be conferred upon human beings. The event that also characterizes the external world repeats itself in this internal "space." Just as the cross is foolishness for the human world outside (1:23), so too is it foolishness for the "psychic" (2.14). In both the external world and the internal world, the cross evokes cognitive dissonances. These dissonances are a stimulus not only to the restructuring of the interpreted external world but also to the restructuring of the interior. Just as one must relativize this world in order to experience the scandal of the cross as meaningful in a broader context, so too must one open up a new dimension—the pneumatic dimension—beyond the given psychic capabilities in order to overcome the cognitive dissonance of the cross. Only then does "foolishness" appear to one as "wisdom," that is, as an element of a self-coherent structure.

The restructuring of the "inner man" can be analyzed with the categories of psychodynamic theories. But these categories change their original character in the framework of a cognitive approach. For if religious symbols are no longer seen exclusively as representations but are rather conceived as active cognitive structuring of inner-drive dynamism and unconscious archetypes, then psychodynamic theories of religion are decisively modified. This will be demonstrated with reference to both the interpretation of the archons within the framework of classical psychoanalysis and the interpretation of the figure of Christ within the framework of the doctrine of archetypes.

As we saw, one can interpret the archons as symbols of the inner censorship which deform impulses arising from the unconscious. Yet precisely through application of the psychoanalytic categories "censorship," "deformation," and "unconscious," one places oneself in opposition to the psychoanalytic theory of religion. According to the classic formulation of that theory, religious symbols are (neurotic) compromises between the censorship of the superego and impulses contrary to norms, whose functioning depends in part on the resultant compromises' remaining unconscious. Are the archons symbols in this sense? Only if one places entirely new accents. For, first, in 1 Cor. 2:6ff. no unconscious process is presented in a coded manner; rather, its basic elements are made transparent. The archon symbolism is not the result of a process of repression but the presentation of such a process. The psychomythic parallelism between 2:6–8 and 2:9–16 is even an indication that the psychic aspect of this process was conscious. Second, the result is not a compromise between censorship and contradictory impulses but rather an open confrontation. What—third—arises into the center of the person and penetrates into the heart is not an impulse contrary to norms but rather something liberating, the Spirit. If one were permitted to generalize on the basis of the Pauline texts exegeted here, one would have to say that religion is not (only) collective compulsory neurosis but therapy with collective symbols. Its symbols are not symptoms but symbolic actions in which a transformation of behavior and experience occurs. The task of theology consists in making conscious what is contained unconsciously in these symbolic actions, a task in which it pursues further a tendency contained in these symbols and images.

We now inquire into the archetypal interpretation of the figure of Christ. The psychology of religion presented by the doctrine of archetypes offers the advantage that it allows from the start for the possibility that had to be demonstrated against classical psychoanalysis—that religious symbols can have a positive effect in transforming behavior and experience. But does this effect really consist in giving ourselves over and entrusting ourselves to the archetypal tendencies of the collective unconscious through orientation on religious images? Precisely the wisdom myth lends itself well to interpretation on the basis of the doctrine of archetypes: here the myth itself depicts how a preexistent tendency seeks a "dwelling" within. But even here, precise investigation of the myth leads to important corrections of the doctrine of archetypes.

We begin with the presence within human beings of a genetically preprogrammed tendency to self-realization, individuation, form, or totality. The assumption may be somewhat speculative, but it has a foundation in the observation that all organisms seek to preserve an inner equilibrium. A corresponding tendency probably also regulates our psychic life. But by assuming a tendency of this sort we do not yet have the key to the history of religions. Where human beings, in each case, seek self-realization is highly disputed within this history. Where salvation lies is unknown. Even whether it is to be sought in religious forms at all is today more than ever the object of skepticism and discussion. Even though the entire history of religion witnesses to the vitality of this tendency toward realization of the "successful self," it also demonstrates the multiple and contradictory forms the realization takes. If preformed programs lies at the basis of the religions, they must be "open programs."

Take the example of the wisdom myth. Wisdom long sought a dwelling before it found acceptance in a small circle of the elect. Yet where this circle of the elect was to be sought remained controversial. Within Judaism wisdom was identified with the law; within Christianity, with Christ. The question as to who took account in an appropriate manner of the preexistent tendency people thought they were able to sense in the entire cosmos remained open between Jews and Christians. The wisdom myth suggests the assumption that there is indeed a general tendency to "salvation" and self-realization, an open program, but that this tendency is interpreted in different ways in individual historical environments. In one historical environment it is structured on the basis of the idea of the law: one who wishes to attain true life must face up to the demands of God. These requirements confer freedom, dignity, and self-consciousness, but they also allow recognition that everyone remains imperfect and is dependent on God's mercy. But in another historical environment the tendency to "self-realization" is "structured" by the figure of Christ. One attains truth only after conflict with the law, a conflict in which the law loses its absolutist character.

Against a doctrine of archetypes that is naive in view of the historical multiplicity of religious symbolism, it must therefore be emphasized that there is no "natural" connection between salvation and Christ symbolism, much less a connection with the repelling symbol of the cross—neither from an archetypal tendency nor from the symbol of the cross. There were many crosses in the Roman Empire. And they were in the first place a triumph of the dominant system over rebels and deviants. The connection between the archetypal longing for wholeness and the symbol of the cross was learned historically. It came into existence only through the framework in which the cross of Jesus was embedded. It is an example of structuring learning, in which a pre-given readiness to react, the tendency to wholeness and to salvation that is assumed here, is joined in a meaningful structure with a symbol—the cross of Christ—which is in itself repulsive. The striving for salvation can be realized only in a paradoxical manner, namely, through liberation from the compulsion of the prevailing system of convictions.

Again we come to the same result. Precisely in the application of psychodynamic categories it is necessary to allow at decisive points for cognitive processes of interpretation. Religious symbols are not representatives of timeless archetypes but rather the cognitive structuring and restructuring of archetypes. Even the striving for "individuation" is not simply present as given by nature; rather, it can unfold itself only when it is interpreted by cognitive systems. These cognitive systems are historically variable. They belong to the tradition and are preserved by learning processes.

Once again 1 Cor. 2:6–16 illuminates a theme that has run through these investigations—the expansion of the Pauline life-world through incorporation of regions that were previously unconscious and that transcended consciousness. Four dimensions of the unconscious have been uncovered in the course of this: antinomian impulses and normative requirements as forms of the forensically unconscious; ecstatic speech and revelation as forms of the pneumatically unconscious. One could also describe the expansion of the Pauline life-world as follows. What otherwise is the hardly perceived or denied background of the everyday life-world emerges in religious experience as decisive reality. This restructuring can be grasped in the sense of Gestalt theory as a change in ground and background. Religious experience and thought thematize the depth dimensions of the life-world. Here what is otherwise background becomes the ground. The everyday life-world fades in significance. It becomes the background until a change in phase allows it to step into the foreground again.

This change in phase can lead to paradoxical insights. Foolishness appears as wisdom, weakness as power, a defeat as victory. The range of behavior and experience is enlarged by cognitive restructurings of this sort. The ability to see reality in an entirely different way means freedom.

Religious symbolism's potency for the cognitive restructuring of reality displays its power not only with regard to the everyday life-world but also with regard to the religiously interpreted world. Early Christianity built a new symbolic "world" from elements of the Jewish and Hellenistic tradition. But even the early Christian "initial preaching" can be experienced as insufficient; there are even deeper insights for the perfect. Later gnostic movements surpass one another in constantly sketching new interpretations of the world, all of which amount to saying that reality in itself is completely different from what "natural man" perceives. Even "natural man" is completely different at the innermost core from that person's experience of self: the person is an exploded spark of that completely different reality. "Gnosis" is the religious potency for radical cognitive restructuring that has become conscious of itself. Fascination with the insight that suddenly transforms everything becomes the dominant motif. In 1 Cor. 2:6–16 we sense something of this "gnostic" fascination. Yet Paul is no Gnostic. For in him pleasure in the cognitive restructuring of the entire life-world finds a counterbalance in the binding of religious symbolism to a pre-given reality to which all human action—from the most sublime cognitive operations up to straightforward mutual aid—is an imperfect attempt to answer.

Epilogue

The Effects of the Pauline
Preaching in
Transforming Behavior
and Experience

Our investigation proceeded on the basis of few texts, and this concentration was necessary. Only in this way can psychological analyses be conducted in such a methodically disciplined manner that they became plausible; they do not contradict the tested historical-critical methods of exegesis but rather make them more profound. They have the same goal: to make texts intelligible on the basis of their connection with life. They are based on historical-critical research and encourage the posing of new historical questions.

The whole of Pauline theology always came into view from the individual texts—something that is self-evident to a hermeneutically oriented psychology, for parts become intelligible only within the framework of the whole. But it was not possible to treat everything. Further themes for a psychological analysis of Pauline texts would be Paul's self-understanding as apostle, his confrontation with alien expectations of the role, his relationship to sexuality, the significance of the sacraments, the motivation of ethical admonitions, and so forth. But a closed picture is yielded even by the few texts that have been treated.

By way of conclusion, instead of recording the many individual results, we shall sketch an answer to the basic question of exegesis from the perspective of the psychology of religion, the question of the extent to which the religious symbolism contained in the Pauline texts could have effects in transforming experience and behavior. In doing this, we shall again work through the three psychological approaches—learning theory, psychodynamic approaches, and cognitive approaches—but work out a common denominator under two aspects. First an aspect intrinsic to Pauline theology: within the Pauline life-world, the figure of Christ is the decisive factor for the modification of experience and behavior. To this is added an external aspect: the modifications of experience and behavior which become visible are to be seen in the overall context of ancient society in the first and second centuries after Christ, even though we do not yet have sufficient clarity about these connections.

From the perspective of learning theory, we see that the gospel is the offer of an unconditioned positive system of reinforcement, which not only stands in competition to the social system of reinforcement but also stands structurally in tension with it. From the model of Christ one can learn that one condemned by the social system of sanctions can represent the truth. The "system of reinforcement" demonstrated in him does not introduce as a means anxiety at negative consequences but rather offers overcoming of this anxiety. God's demand does indeed encounter us as a commandment threatening death. But the death meted out to Christ is revised. God himself overcomes the consequences of his killing demand. The killing law shows itself to be powerless in view of the model of Christ. Through learning from the model, anxiety with regard to the normative thematic of life is "extinguished." The same is true, mutatis mutandis, for one's stance toward suffering. The connection of an extremely negative symbol, execution on the cross, with the most positive symbols of salvation and redemption makes it possible to reduce avoidance reactions with respect to suffering—a presupposition of help for the weak, ill, and those in need of aid and of the constructive handling of suffering in themselves. But this point could not be developed.

The result of the analysis on the basis of learning theory can also be carried over partially into psychodynamic categories. Yet there are also new aspects. Christ replaces both the id and the superego; he overcomes the shadow and embodies the ideal self. He is the new Lord—but also the scapegoat. Because he is both simultaneously (and in this way bridges the tension that underlies all repressions), he enables previously unconscious aspects of life to become conscious.

The previously repressed conflict with the law, in which both partners to the conflict had unconscious sides, becomes conscious. A "veil" lay over the killing law. This was removed in Christ. He takes the cover that lay over the sacredness of normative systems and reveals their aggressive power. Simultaneously, the unconscious rebellion of the flesh against the law becomes conscious—a rebellion that was so difficult to see through because the flesh made use of the most sacred norms to deceive and threaten human beings.

Yet the unconscious does not reveal itself only as a sphere pregnant with conflict; rather, integrating tendencies also rise from unconscious depths—a longing for wholeness and salvation, which is formed anew by connection with the historical figure of Christ. Wholeness and salvation are not conceivable without incorporation of dark aspects of world and self. Glossolalia does connect with the unconscious depths of the heart, but it connects with the suffering of creation and not only with heavenly bliss.

We recognize in Paul the same ambivalence with regard to the unconscious that characterizes the modern age, for the unconscious is experienced both as threatening conflict event and as healing power.

On one point, however, Paul distinguishes himself profoundly from modernity. The opening with regard to the unconscious is not total. With regard to sexual impulses, Paul exhibits an accepting stance only to a limited degree. His ideal is asceticism. Before one condemns this aspect of Pauline theology, one should weigh the possibility that control of sexuality is the inevitable price of interhuman relations in the community, of great emotional intensity, yet free from sexual competition. But this too could not be investigated here.

It is certain that the inner transformation of human beings through confrontation with previously unconscious aspects of life is an expansion of the sphere of behavior and experience chiefly with respect to the normative thematic. Christ is an avenue of access to the unconscious. He lifts the veil from the heart. As judge and judged, he unites in himself superego and id, ideal I and shadow. But he also directs the libidinous energies of the id in a new direction. In the body of Christ, one experiences the overcoming of the limit of the person—toward which sexual union also leads (cf. 1 Cor. 6:15ff.).

From the cognitive perspective, Christ appears as the central "role offer" of early Christian religion, in the light of whom reality is perceived anew. In the role of the incarnate Son of God, who assumes the human role which had been alien to him, he makes it possible to adapt and relativize different sociocultural norms (1 Cor. 9:19ff.). As the Crucified, he transposes one into a distance in principle from this world; what appears in this world as foolishness opens a more comprehensive horizon of meaning in divine wisdom. As the Risen One, he is alive in the members of the community and thus enables a new assessment of interhuman solidarity: through him all are members of the one body. In the role of the judge he transforms one's relation to oneself: he makes possible self-assessment without self-condemnation. What is decisive is that he is incorporated into the inner dialogue of believers and forms their self-image. No one is any longer committed definitively to the flesh; the Spirit dwells in every Christian. A positive self-image is thus maintained against the empirical reality of guilt and suffering.

It is immaterial whether one conceives the figure of Christ as a model, a symbol, or a role; in any case, it is the decisive factor in the transformations of behavior and experience that enter for Paul with the soteriological turn. In this the turning away from the old forms of experience and behavior sometimes emerges more sharply than the turn toward new ones. Yet the heart of Pauline theology also beats here. Christ makes possible new forms of behavior and experience. If the censorship of the prevailing system of convictions is overcome and the deceptive veil over the sacred norms has fallen, then one experiences a mystical ecstatic transformation. The archetypal image of Christ shines within. Preexistent wisdom takes possession of one's heart. One is transformed. Paul's language becomes mystical and warm when he speaks of this transformation. It is of so much value to him that he will speak of it only before the "perfect." The reality of Christian communities shows all too clearly that they are still far removed from what for Paul is "perfect" in an absolute sense— intrinsically motivated love (1 Corinthians 13).

What Paul sketches in his images and symbols far exceeds the actual reality. But it is deeply rooted in reality. The new forms of behavior and experience that are made possible by the figure of Christ are the inner aspect of a more comprehensive historical process—the origin of a subcultural form of life in a pluralist society.

Two perspectives emerged during the investigation. First, it was a form of life "from below." It interpreted itself as a contradiction to the "rulers of the world" (1 Cor. 2:8*). Although there were in it members from the higher classes, the orientation on what is "below" remained determinative for all. The body imagery widespread in antiquity thus received a new accent: the weakest member is the criterion of behavior for the community.

A more horizontal structuring is joined to this vertical social stratification. Early Christianity is a form of life standing between Jews and Greeks. Only the tension between different sociocultural systems makes possible the discovery of the unconscious—because what each group denies in itself is seen more clearly from the perspective of the other. Only the competition of systems of conviction leads to the formation of existential decisions in which the entire orientation of life is at stake, not merely the fulfillment of undisputed norms. It is possible that only in the field of tension between different cultures could glossolalic behavior, which gives the impression of being "pre-cultural," achieve such central significance. Only here could the replacement of historical systems of conviction be experienced as liberation.

One cannot emphasize often enough that psychic processes are historically formed. The symbolic actions of religion stand with all human actions and their conditions in mutual influence. They take place within a social framework that makes possible and limits human action. We do not yet grasp what historical forces brought forth and determined early Christianity. Were class tensions transformed into religious images in the symbols of early Christianity, as Erich Fromm once thought? Did an astonishing high level of civilization make possible for the first time the origin of a society that could renounce conformity to a much greater degree than other societies that were exposed more severely to the pressure of life? Was it in a position to "stand" very different subcultures, among them early Christianity, which recruited its members from the lower urban classes and forced its way upwards? Was only this world able to tolerate to a limited extent a subcultural movement that had emigrated interiorly from "this world" and its "wisdom," in order to proclaim in its midst the start of the new world? A society within which even its own rejection could be developed into a practicable form of life is a noteworthy phenomenon among known societies.

But beside and within this external history there is an inner history of humanity. It becomes accessible to us in religious images and symbols, in works of art and philosophies. This internal history is no less important than the external. Here early Christianity plays an important role; it determined human experience and behavior perma-nently. Anyone who thinks that this religion can be illumined histor-ically and factually without psychological reflection is just as much in error as one who pretends that everything about this religion can be said in this fashion.

Abbreviations

ANF	Ante-Nicene Fathers
ATD	Das Alte Testament Deutsch
AThANT	Abhandlungen zur Theologie des Alten und Neuen Testaments
BEvTh	Beiträge zur evangelischen Theologie
BFChTh	Beiträge zur Förderung christlicher Theologie
BHTh	Beiträge zur historischen Theologie
BWANT	Beiträge zur Wissenschaft vom Alten und Neuen Testament
BZNW	Beihefte zur Zeitschrift für die neutestamentliche Wissenschaft
EKK	Evangelisch-katholischer Kommentar zum Neuen Testament
EtB	Etudes bibliques
FiBü	Fischer Bücherei
FRLANT	Forschungen zur Religion und Literatur des Alten und Neuen Testaments
GTA	Göttingische Gelehrte Arbeiten
HM	Hallische Monographien
HNT	Handbuch zum Neuen Testament
HThK	Herders theologischer Kommentar zum Neuen Testament
ICC	International Critical Commentary of the Holy Scriptures
JSHRZ	Jüdische Schriften aus hellenistisch-römischer Zeit
KEK	Kritisch-exegetischer Kommentar über das Neue Testament
KNT	Kommentar zum Neuen Testament

KPS	Klassich-philologische Studien
LCL	Loeb Classical Library
MThSt	Marburger theologische Studien
NTA	Neutestamentliche Abhandlungen
RAC	*Reallexicon für Antike und Christentum*
RVV	Religionsgeschichtliche Versuche und Vorarbeiten
SBLDS	SBL Dissertation Series
SHAW.PH	Sitzungsberichte der Heidelberger Akadamie der Wissenschaften—Philosophisch-historische Klasse
SNTSMS	Society for New Testament Studies Monograph Series
StANT	Studien zum Alten und Neuen Testament
StNT	Studien zum Neuen Testament
StUNT	Studien zur Umwelt des Neuen Testaments
TDNT	*Theological Dictionary of the New Testament* (ET of *TWNT*)
TEH	Theologische Existenz heute
ThHK	Theologischer Handkommentar zum Neuen Testament
TWNT	*Theologisches Wörterbuch zum Neuen Testament*, ed. G. Kittel and G. Friedrich
WdF	Wege der Forschung
WMANT	Wissenschaftliche Monographien zum Alten und Neuen Testament
WUNT	Wissenschaftliche Untersuchungen zum Neuen Testament

Bibliography

Agersnap, S. *Paulusstudier, 1. Kor 15 og Rom 2.* Tekst og Tolkning 7. Kopenhagen: Gyldendal, 1979.

Albright, William F., and C. S. Mann. "Two Texts in 1. Corinthians." *New Testament Studies* 16 (1970): 271–76.

Allo, Ernest B. *Saint Paul: second épître aux Corinthiens.* 2d ed. EtB. Paris: Gabalda, 1956.

Allport, Gordon W. *The Individual and His Religion: A Psychological Interpretation.* New York: Macmillan Co., 1950.

———. *Personality: A Psychological Interpretation.* New York: Henry Holt & Co., 1937.

Althaus, Paul. *Paulus und Luther über den Menschen.* Gütersloh: Bertelsmann, 1938.

d'Aquili, E. G. "The Neurological Bases of Myth and Concepts of Deity." *Zygon* 13 (1978): 257–75.

Arndt, M., and H. Schulz. "Individualpsychologische oder kollektivistische Interpretation? Jahweinthronisation und Ich-Konstitution (Ps 93)." In *Doppeldeutlich,* ed. Y. Spiegel, 189–211. Munich, 1978.

Avi-Yonah, Michael, ed. *The Encyclopedia of Archaeological Excavations in the Holy Land.* London: Oxford Univ. Press, 1975–78.

The Babylonian Talmud. Ed. I. Epstein. Vol. 4. Ed. H. Freedman. London: Soncino Press, 1938.

Bader, G. "Römer 7 als Skopus einer theologischen Handlungstheorie." *Zeitschrift für Theologie und Kirche* 78 (1981): 31–56.

Balz, H. R. *Heilsvertrauen und Welterfahrung: Strukturen paulinischer Eschatologie nach Römer 8, 18–39.* BEvTh 59. Munich: Chr. Kaiser, 1971.

Barrett, C. K. *A Commentary on the Second Epistle to the Corinthians.* New York: Harper & Row, 1973.

Bauer, Walter. *Griechisch-deutsches Wörterbuch zu den Schriften des Neuen Testament und der übrigen urchristlichen Literatur.* 5th ed. Berlin: Töpelmann, 1963.

———. "Mündige und Unmündige bei dem Apostel Paulus." In *Aufsätze und kleine Schriften*, ed. Georg Strecker, 122–54. Tübingen: J. C. B. Mohr [Paul Siebeck], 1967.

Beare, F. W. "Speaking with Tongues: A Critical Survey of the New Testament Evidence." *Journal of Biblical Literature* 83 (1964): 229–46.

van den Berg, Jan H. *Metabletica: Über die Wandlung des Menschen: Grundlinien einer historischen Psychologie.* Göttingen, 1960. ET of Dutch original: *The Changing Nature of Man: Introduction to a Historical Psychology.* New York: W. W. Norton & Co., 1961.

Berger, Klaus. *Exegese des Neuen Testaments.* Heidelberg, 1977.

―――. *Die Gesetzesauslegung Jesu I.* WMANT 40. Neukirchen: Neukirchener Verlag, 1972.

―――. "Zur Diskussion über die Herkunft von IKor. II 9." *New Testament Studies* 24 (1978): 270–83.

Best, E. "The Interpretation of Tongues." *Scottish Journal of Theology* 28 (1975): 45–62.

Beyerlin, Walter, ed. *Near Eastern Religious Texts Relating to the Old Testament.* Philadelphia: Westminster Press, 1978.

The Biblical Antiquities of Philo. Trans. M. R. James. New York: Ktav, 1971.

Biblisch-historisches Handwörterbuch. Ed. B. Reicke and L. Rost. 4 vols. Göttingen: Vandenhoeck & Ruprecht, 1962–79.

Billerbeck, Paul. *Kommentar zum Neuen Testament aus Talmud und Midrasch.* Munich: Beck, 1922– .

Bishop, J. G. "Psychological Insights in St. Paul's Mysticism." *Theology* 78 (1975): 318–24.

Blank, J. *Paulus und Jesus: Eine theologische Grundlegung.* StANT 18. Munich: Kösel, 1968.

Blass, Friedrich W., Albert Debrunner, and Friedrich Rehkopf. *Grammatik des neutestamentlichen Griechisch.* 14th ed. Göttingen: Vandenhoeck & Ruprecht, 1976. ET of 9th German ed.: *A Greek Grammar of the New Testament and Other Early Christian Literature.* Chicago: Univ. of Chicago Press, 1961.

Böhme, A., and W. Schottroff. *Palmyrenische Grabreliefs.* Liebighaus Monographie 4. Frankfurt, 1979.

Bömer, Franz. *P. Ovidius Naso, Metamorphosen: Buch VI–VII.* Kommentar von Franz Böhme. Heidelberg: Winter, 1976.

Bommert, H. *Grundlagen der Gesprächstherapie.* Stuttgart, 1977.

Bornkamm, Günther. "Paulinische Anakoluthe." In *Das Ende des Gesetzes: Gesammelte Aufsätze* 1:76–92. BEvTh 16. Munich: Chr. Kaiser, 1952.

―――. "Sünde, Gesetz und Tod." In *Das Ende des Gesetzes: Gesammelte Aufsätze* 1:51–69.

―――. "Die Vorgeschichte des sogenannten zweiten Korintherbriefes." In *Geschichte und Glaube zweiter Teil: Gesammelte Aufsätze* 4:162–94. BEvTh 53. Munich: Chr. Kaiser, 1971.

Bousset, Wilhelm. *Kyrios Christos.* Göttingen: Vandenhoeck & Ruprecht, 1913.

6th ed., 1967. ET: *Kyrios Christos: A History of the Belief in Christ from the Beginnings of Christianity to Irenaeus*. Nashville: Abingdon Press, 1970.

————. *Die Religion des Judentums in späthellenistischen Zeitalter*. 4th ed. Tübingen: J. C. B. Mohr [Paul Siebeck], 1966.

————. Review of H. Weinel, *Die Wirkungen des Geistes*. *Göttingische Gelehrte Anzeigen* 163 (1901): 753–76.

Brandenburg, Hugo. *Studien zur Mitra*. Fontes et Commentationes 4. Münster, 1966.

Braun, Herbert. "Römer 7,7–25 und das Selbstverständnis des Qumran-Frommen." In *Gesammelte Studien zum Neuen Testament und seiner Umwelt*, 100–119. 2d ed. Tübingen: J. C. B. Mohr [Paul Siebeck], 1967.

Bredenkamp, K. I. "Was ist Lernen?" In *Pädagogische Psychologie*, ed. F. Weinert, C. F. Graumann, et al., 2:607–30. FiBü. Frankfurt, 1974.

Brenton, Lancelot C. L. *The Septuagint Version: Greek and English*. Grand Rapids: Zondervan Pub. House, 1970.

de Broglie, G. "Le texte fondamental de Saint Paul contre la foi naturelle (1.Cor. XII,3)." *Recherches de Science Religieuse* 39 (1951–52): 253–66.

Brun, L. "Um der Engel willen 1. Kor 11,10." *Zeitschrift für die neutestamentliche Wissenschaft* 14 (1913): 298–308.

Buber, Martin. *Zwei Glaubensweisen*. Zurich: Manesse, 1950. ET: *Two Types of Faith*. London: Routledge & Kegan Paul, 1951.

Bultmann, Rudolf. "Glossen im Römerbrief." In *Exegetica: Aufsätze zur Erforschung des Neuen Testaments*, 278–84. Tübingen: J. C. B. Mohr [Paul Siebeck], 1967.

————. "Römer 7 und die Anthropologie des Paulus." 1932. In *Exegetica: Aufsätze zur Erforschung des Neuen Testaments*, 198–209. Tübingen: J. C. B. Mohr [Paul Siebeck], 1967.

————. *Theologie des Neuen Testaments*. 4th ed. Tübingen: J. C. B. Mohr [Paul Siebeck], 1961. ET: *Theology of the New Testament*. New York: Charles Scribner's Sons, 1951–55.

————. *Der zweite Brief an die Korinther*. Ed. Erich Dinkler. Göttingen: Vandenhoeck & Ruprecht, 1976. ET: *The Second Letter to the Corinthians*. Trans. Roy A. Harrisville. Minneapolis: Augsburg Pub. House, 1985.

Burhoe, R. W. "Religion's Role in Human Evolution: The Missing Link Between Ape-Man's Selfish Genes and Civilized Altruism." *Zygon* 14 (1979): 135–62.

Burkert, Walter. *Homo necans: Interpretation altgriechischer Opferriten und Mythen*. RVV 32. Berlin: Walter de Gruyter, 1972.

Cambier, J. M. "Le jugement de tous les hommes par Dieu seul, selon la vérité, dans Rom. 2,1—3,20." *Zeitschrift für die neutestamentliche Wissenschaft* 67 (1976): 187–213.

————. "Le 'moi' dans Rom 7." In *The Law of the Spirit in Rom 7 and 8*, ed. L. de Lorenzi, 13–127. Rome: St. Paul's Abbey, 1976.

Carr, W. "The Rulers of This Age—I Corinthians II, 6–8." *New Testament Studies* 23 (1977): 20–35.

Carrez, M. "Le 'Nous' en 2 Corinthiens." *New Testament Studies* 26 (1980): 474–586.

Chadwick, Henry. *Origen: Contra Celsum.* Cambridge: At the Univ. Press, 1953.

Charles, R. H., et al., eds. *The Apocrypha and Pseudepigrapha of the Old Testament.* London: Oxford Univ. Press, 1913.

Charlesworth, James H., ed. *The Old Testament Pseudepigrapha.* 2 vols. Garden City, N.Y.: Doubleday & Co., 1983–85.

Childs, Brevard S. *The Book of Exodus: A Critical, Theological Commentary.* Philadelphia: Westminster Press, 1974.

Collange, J. F. *Enigmes.* SNTSMS. Cambridge: At the Univ. Press, 1972.

Colpe, Carsten. "Gnosis II (Gnostizismus)." In *RAC* 11:537–659.

Conzelmann, Hans. *Der erste Brief an die Korinther.* KEK. Göttingen: Vandenhoeck & Ruprecht, 1969. ET: *1 Corinthians: A Commentary on the First Epistle to the Corinthians.* Hermeneia. Philadelphia: Fortress Press, 1975.

———. "Paulus und die Weisheit." In *Theologie als Schriftauslegung,* 177–90. BEvTh 65. Munich: Chr. Kaiser, 1974.

Cope, Lamar. "1 Cor 11,2–16: One Step Further." *Journal of Biblical Literature* 97 (1978): 435–36.

Cornfeld, Gaalyahu, ed. *Pictorial Biblical Encyclopedia.* New York: Macmillan Co., 1964.

Corpus inscriptionum Judaicarum. Vol. 1. Vatican City: Pontificio Istituto di Archeologia Christiana, 1936.

Cox, D. *Jung and St. Paul: A Study of the Doctrine of Justification by Faith and Its Relations to the Concept of Individuation.* New York: Association Press, 1959.

Cranfield, C. E. B. *A Critical and Exegetical Commentary on the Epistle to the Romans.* ICC. Edinburgh: T. & T. Clark, 1975.

Créspy, G. "Exégèse et psychoanalyse: Considérations aventueuses sur Romains 7,7–25." In: *L'évangile, hier et aujourd'hui* (Festschrift F. J. Lienhardt), 169–79. Geneva, 1968.

Crüsemann, Frank. "Die unveränderbare Welt: Überlegungen zur 'Krisis der Weisheit' beim Prediger (Kohelet)." In *Der Gott der kleinen Leute,* ed. W. Schottroff and W. Stegemann, 1:80–104. Munich, 1979. ET: *God of the Lowly.* Maryknoll, N.Y.: Orbis Books, 1984.

Cullmann, Oscar. *Die ersten christlichen Glaubensbekenntnisse.* Zurich: Evangelischer Verlag, 1943.

———. *Der Staat im Neuen Testament.* Tübingen: J. C. B. Mohr [Paul Siebeck], 1956. ET: *The State in the New Testament.* New York: Charles Scribner's Sons, 1956.

Currie, S. " 'Speaking in Tongues': Early Evidence Outside the New Testament Bearing on 'Glossais Lalein.' " *Interpretation* 19 (1965): 274–94.

Cutten, George B. *Speaking with Tongues: Historically and Psychologically Considered*. New Haven: Yale Univ. Press, 1927.

Dautzenberg, Gerhard. "Botschaft und Bedeutung der urchristlichen Prophetie nach dem ersten Korintherbrief (2:6–16;12–14)." In *Prophetic Vocation in the New Testament and Today*, ed. J. Panagopulous, 131–61. Leiden: E. J. Brill, 1977.

———. "Glossolalie." In *RAC* 11:225–46.

———. *Urchristliche Prophetie*. BWANT 104. Stuttgart: Kohlhammer, 1975.

Deissmann, G. Adolf. *Paulus: Eine kultur- und religionsgeschichtliche Skizze*. Tübingen: J. C. B. Mohr [Paul Siebeck], 1911. ET: *Paul: A Study in Social and Religious History*. New York: Harper & Row, 1957.

DeLacy, Phillip, ed. *Galen: On the Doctrines of Hippocrates and Plato*. Berlin: Akademie, 1981.

Delling, G. *Der Gottesdienst im Neuen Testament*. Göttingen: Vandenhoeck & Ruprecht, 1952. ET: *Worship in the New Testament*. Philadelphia: Westminster Press, 1962.

Derrett, J. Duncan M. "Cursing Jesus (I Cor. XII,3): The Jews as Religious Persecutors." *New Testament Studies* 21 (1975): 544–54.

Dessau, Hermann, ed. *Inscriptiones Latinae Selectae*. 2 vols. Berlin: Weidmann, 1892–1906.

Dibelius, Martin. *Die Geisterwelt im Glauben des Paulus*. Göttingen: Vandenhoeck & Ruprecht, 1909.

———. *An die Thessalonicher I,II. An die Philipper*. HNT 11. Tübingen: J. C. B. Mohr [Paul Siebeck], 1913. 3d ed., 1937.

Diels, H. *Die Fragmente der Vorsokratiker*. 3d ed. Vol. 2. Berlin: Weidmann, 1912.

Diez Macho, Alajandro. *Neophyti 1: Vol. 1: Genesis*. Madrid: Consejo Superior de Investigaciones Cientificas, 1968.

Dihle, Albrecht. *Euripides Medea*. SHAW.PH. 1977/5. Heidelberg: Winter, 1977.

———. "psyche." In *TWNT* 9:605–14. ET: *TDNT* 9:608–17.

———. "Das Satyrspiel 'Sysiphos.' " *Hermes* 105 (1977): 28–42.

Dilthey, Wilhelm. "Ideen über eine beschreibende und zergliedernde Psychologie." 1894. In *Gesammelte Schriften* 5: 139–240. Leipzig: Teubner, 1924 ET: *Descriptive Psychology and Historical Understanding*. The Hague: Martinus Nijhoff, 1977.

Dindorf, W., ed. *Aelios Aristeides: Orationes*. 1829.

von Ditfurth, Hoimar. *Wir sind nicht nur von dieser Welt*. Hamburg: Hoffman & Campe, 1981. ET: *The Origins of Life: Evolution as Creation*. San Francisco: Harper & Row, 1982.

Dittenberger, W. *Sylloge Inscriptionum Graecarum*. 3d. ed. Leipzig, 1915–

Dodds, Eric R., ed. *Euripides Bacchae*. Oxford: At the Clarendon Press, 1944. 2d ed., 1960.

————. *The Greeks and the Irrational*. Berkeley and Los Angeles: Univ. of Calif. Press, 1951.

Donfried, Karl P. "Justification and Last Judgment in Paul." *Zeitschrift für die neutestamentliche Wissenschaft* 67 (1976): 90–110.

von Dülmen, Andrea. *Die Theologie des Gesetzes bei Paulus*. Stuttgart: Katholisches Bibelwerk, 1968.

Dunn, James D. G. "2. Corinthians III,17—The Lord Is the Spirit." *Journal of Theological Studies* 21 (1970): 309–20.

————. "Rom 7,14–25 in the Theology of Paul." *Theologische Zeitschrift* 31 (1975): 257–73.

Dupont, J. *La connaissance religieuse dans les Epîtres de Saint Paul*. Brugge: Desclée, 1949.

————. "Le Problème de la structure littéraire de l'Epître aux Romains." *Revue biblique* 62 (1955): 365–97.

Eibl-Eibesfeldt, Irenäus. *Der vorprogrammierte Mensch*. Munich, 1976.

Eichholz, Georg. *Die Theologie des Paulus im Umriss*. Neukirchen: Neukirchener Verlag, 1972.

Eliade, M. *Patterns in Comparative Religion*. New York: Sheed & Ward, 1958.

Ellwein, E. "Das Rätsel von Römer 7." *Kerygma und Dogma* 1 (1955): 247–68.

Everling, O. *Die paulinische Angelologie und Dämonologie: Ein biblisch-theologischer Versuch*. Göttingen: Vandenhoeck & Ruprecht, 1888.

Faber, Heije. *Religionspsychologie*. Gütersloh, 1973. ET of Dutch original: *Psychology of Religion*. London: SCM Press, 1976.

Falkenstein, Adam, and W. von Soden. *Sumerische und akkadische Hymnen und Gebete*. Zurich, 1953.

Fascher, Erich. *PROPHETES: Eine sprach- und religionsgeschichtliche Untersuchung*. Geissen: Töpelmann, 1927.

Festinger, L. "Die Lehre von der 'kognitiven Dissonanz.' " In *Grundfragen der Kommunikationsforschung*, ed. W. Schramm, 27–38. Munich, 1964.

Fetscher, R. *Grundlinien der Tiefenpsychologie von S. Freud und C. G. Jung in vergleichender Darstellung*. Problemata 69. Stuttgart, 1978.

Feuillet, André. "Le 'Chefs de ce siècle' et la Sagesse divine d'après 1 Cor 2,6–8." In *Studiorum Paulinorum Congressus Internationalis Catholicus 1961* 1:383–93. 2 vols. Analecta Biblica 17–18. Rome: Pontifical Biblical Inst., 1963.

Fischer, H. *Gespaltener christlicher Glaube: Eine psychoanalytische orientierte Religionskritik*. Hamburg: Reich, 1974.

Fischer, Karl M. *Tendenz und Absicht des Epheserbriefes*. FRLANT 111. Göttingen: Vandenhoeck & Ruprecht, 1973.

Flückiger, F. "Die Werke des Gesetzes bei den Heiden (Röm 2,14ff.)." *Theologische Zeitschrift* 8 (1952): 17–42.

Forsyth, James J. "Faith and Eros: Paul's Answer to Freud." *Religion and Life* 46 (1977): 476–87.

Fragmenta historicorum Graecorum. Ed. K. and T. Müller. 2 vols. Paris: Didot, 1841–48.

Freeman, Kathleen. *Ancilla to the Pre-Socratic Philosophers.* Cambridge: Harvard Univ. Press, 1966.

Freud, Sigmund. "Eine Kinderheitserinnerung des Leonardo da Vinci." 1910. In *Gesammelte Werke* 8:128–49. Frankfurt, 1945. ET: "Leonardo da Vinci and a Memory of His Childhood." In *The Standard Edition of the Complete Psychological Works of Sigmund Freud* 11:63–137. London: Hogarth Press, 1957.

————. *Der Mann Moses und die monotheistische Religion.* 1939. In *Studienausgabe* 9:455–581. Frankfurt, 1974. ET: *Moses and Monotheism.* In *Standard Edition* 23:7–137. 1964.

————. *Neue Folge der Vorlesung zur Einführung in die Psychoanalyse.* 1932. In *Studienausgabe* 1:448–608. 1969. ET: *New Introductory Lectures on Psycho-Analysis.* In *Standard Edition* 22:5–182. 1964.

————. *Totem und Tabu.* 1912–13. In *Studienausgabe* 9:287–444. 1974. ET: *Totem and Taboo.* In *Standard Edition* 13:1–161. 1953.

————. *Das Unbehagen in der Kultur.* In *Studienausgabe* 9:191–270. 1974. ET: *Civilization and Its Discontents.* In *Standard Edition* 21:64–145. 1961.

————. *Vorlesungen zur Einführung in die Psychoanalyse.* 1916–17. In *Studienausgabe* 1:34–445. 1969. ET: *Introductory Lectures on Psycho-Analysis.* In *Standard Edition*, vols. 15–16. 1961–63.

Fridrichsen, A. "Scholia in Novum Testamentum." *Svensk exegetisk arsbok* 12 (1947): 140–47.

————. "Der wahre Jude und sein Lob: Röm 2,28f." *Symbolae Arctoae* 1 (1927): 39–49.

Friedrich, G. "Ein Tauflied hellenistischer Judenchristen: 1. Thess 1,9f." *Theologische Zeitschrift* 21 (1965): 502–16.

Friesen, Isaac I. *The Glory of the Ministry of Jesus Christ Illustrated by a Study of 2 Cor. 2:14—3:18.* Basel: Reinhardt, 1971.

Fromm, E. "Die Entwicklung des Christusdogmas: Eine psychoanalytische Studie zur sozialpsychologischen Funktion der Religion." *Imago* 16 (1938): 305–73. (= E. Fromm, *Religio*, 11–68. Stuttgart, 1980).

Gager, John G. *Kingdom and Community: The Social World of Early Christianity.* Englewood Cliffs, N.J.: Prentice-Hall, 1975.

Georgi, Dieter. *Die Gegner des Paulus im 2. Korintherbrief.* WMANT 11. Neukirchen: Neukirchener Verlag, 1964. ET: *The Opponents of Paul in Second Corinthians.* Philadelphia: Fortress Press, 1986.

————. *Weisheit Salomos.* JSHRZ 3.4. Gütersloh, 1980.

Gerlach, Luther P., and Virginia M. Hine. *People, Power, Change: Movements of Social Transformation.* Indianapolis: Bobbs-Merrill, 1970.

Gnilka, Joachim. *Der Philemonbrief.* HThK 10.4. Freiburg: Herder & Herder, 1982.

Goguel, M. *"kata dikaiosunen ten en nomo genomenos amemptos* (Phil. 3,6): Remarques sur un aspect de la conversion de Paul." *Journal of Biblical Literature* 53 (1934): 257–67.

Goodenough, Erwin R. *Jewish Symbols in the Greco-Roman Period.* Vol. 9. New York: Pantheon Books, 1964.

Goodman, Felicitas D. *Speaking in Tongues: A Cross-Cultural Study of Glossolalia.* Chicago: Univ. of Chicago Press, 1972.

Goppelt, L. *Theologie des Neuen Testaments.* Göttingen, 1978. ET: *Theology of the New Testament.* 2 vols. Grand Rapids: Wm. B. Eerdmans, 1981–82.

Görlitz, P., et al. *Bielefelder Symposium über Attribution.* Stuttgart, 1978.

Görres, Albert. *Methode und Erfahrungen der Psychoanalyse.* Munich, 1958. ET: *The Methods and Experience of Psychoanalysis.* New York: Sheed & Ward, 1962.

Grant, R. M. "Like Children." *Harvard Theological Review* 39 (1946): 71–73.

Gremmels, C. "Selbstreflexive Interpretation konfligierender Identikationen am Beispiel des Apostles Paulus (Phil. 3,7–9)." In J. Scharfenberg et al., *Religion—Selbstbewusstsein—Identität,* 44–57. TEH 182. Munich, 1974.

Gressmann, H. *Altorientalische Texte zum Alten Testament.* 2d ed. Berlin, 1966.

Gundert, H. "Enthusiasmos und Logos bei Platon." *Lexis* 2 (1949): 25–46.

Gunkel, H. *Die Wirkungen des heiligen Geistes.* Göttingen: Vandenhoeck & Ruprecht, 1888. ET: *The Influence of the Holy Spirit: The Popular View of the Apostolic Age and the Teaching of the Apostle Paul.* Philadelphia: Fortress Press, 1979.

Guthrie, W. K. C. *The Greeks and Their Gods.* Boston: Beacon Press, 1955.

Gutmann, Joseph. "Programmatic Painting in the Dura Synagogue." In *The Synagogue: Studies in Origins, Archaeology, and Architecture,* ed. J. Gutmann, 210–32. New York: Ktav, 1975.

Hardy, Alister C. *The Biology of God: A Scientist's Study of Man the Religious Animal.* London: Jonathan Cape, 1975.

Harrisville, R. A. "Speaking in Tongues: A Lexicographical Study." *Catholic Biblical Quarterly* 38 (1976): 35–48.

Heckhausen, H. "Lehrer—Schüler—Interaktion." In F. E. Weinert et al., *Funk-Kolleg Pädagogische Psychologie* 1:549–73.

Heimbrock, H. G. *Phantasie und christlicher Glaube.* Mainz: Grünewald; Munich: Chr. Kaiser, 1977.

Heintz, P. *Soziale Vorurteile.* Cologne, 1957.

Hengel, Martin. *Der Sohn Gottes: Die Entstehung der Christologie und die jüdisch-hellenistische Religionsgeschichte.* Tübingen: J. C. B. Mohr [Paul Siebeck], 1975. ET: *The Son of God: The Origin of Christology and the History of Jewish-Hellenistic Religion.* Philadelphia: Fortress Press, 1976.

Héring, J. *La première épître de Saint Paul aux Corinthiens.* Neuchatel: Delachaux & Niestlé Spes, 1949. ET: *The First Epistle of Saint Paul to the Corinthians.* London: Epworth Press, 1962.

Hermann, Ingo. *Kyrios und Pneuma: Studien zur Christologie der Paulinischen Hauptbriefe*. STANT 2. Munich: Kösel, 1961.

Herter, H. "Effeminatus." In *RAC* 4:620–50.

Heusser, H., ed. *Instinkte und Archetypen im Verhalten der Tiere und im Erleben des Menschen*. Darmstadt: Wissenschaftliche Buchgesellschaft, 1976.

Hickling, C. J. A. "The Sequence of Thought in II. Corinthians, Chapter Three." *New Testament Studies* 21 (1975): 380–95.

Hofius, O. "Das Zitat 1Kor 2,9 und das koptische Testament des Jakob." *Zeitschrift für die neutestamentliche Wissenschaft* 66 (1975): 542–86.

Hofstätter, R. "Tiefenpsychologische Persönlichkeitstheorien." In *Handbuch der Psychologie* 4:542–86. Göttingen: Hogrefe, 1960.

Hollenweger, W. J. *Enthusiastisches Christentum: Die Pfingstbewegung in Geschichte und Gegenwart*. Zurich: Wuppertal: Brockhaus, 1969. ET: *The Pentecostals*. Minneapolis: Augsburg Pub. House, 1977.

———. "Narrativité et théologie interculturelle: Un aspect négligé de 1Cor 14." *Revue de Théologie et de Philosophie* 110 (1978): 209–23.

Holm, N. S. "Das Zungenreden bei Anhängern der Pfingstbewegung im schwedischsprachigen Gebiet Finnlands." *Archiv für Religionsphilosophie* 13 (1978): 224–38.

Holtz, T. "Das Kennzeichen des Geistes (1Kor XII 1–3)." *New Testament Studies* 18 (1971–72): 365–76.

———. "Zum Selbstverständnis des Apostels Paulus." *Theologische Literaturzeitung* 91 (1966): 321–30.

Hommel, H. "Das Harren der Kreatur." In *Schöpfer und Erhalter*, 5–23. Stuttgart, 1956.

———. "Das 7. Kapitel des Römerbriefs im Licht antiker Überlieferung." *Theologia Viatorum* 8 (1961–62): 90–116.

Hooker, Morna D. "Beyond the Things That Are Written? Saint Paul's Use of Scripture." *New Testament Studies* 27 (1980–81): 295–309.

Horsley, G. H. R. *New Documents Illustrating Early Christianity*. Vol. 1. North Ryde, N. S. W.: Ancient History Documentary Research Centre, 1981.

Horsley, R. A. "Pneumatikos vs. Psychikos: Distinctions of Spiritual Status among the Corinthians." *Harvard Theological Review* 69 (1976): 269–88.

van der Horst, P. W. *The Sentences of Pseudo-Phocylides*. Leiden: E. J. Brill, 1978.

Hübner, H. *Das Gesetz bei Paulus*. FRLANT 119. Göttingen, 1978. ET: *Law in Paul's Thought*. London: T. & T. Clark, 1985.

Hurd, John C. *The Origin of I Corinthians*. New York: Seabury Press, 1965.

Hyldahl, Niels. "Die Frage nach der literarischen Einheit des zweiten Korintherbriefes." *Zeitschrift für die neutestamentliche Wissenschaft* 64 (1973): 289–306.

———. "Den korintiske situation—en skitse." *Dansk teologisk tidsskrift* 40 (1977): 18–30.

————. *Loven og Troen: En analyse of Filipperbrevets tredie kapitel.* Acta Jutlandica 11.6. Copenhagen: Munksgaard, 1968.

Inan, J., and E. Alföldi-Rosenbaum. *Römische und frühbyzantinische Porträtplastik aus der Türkei, Neue Funde.* 2 vols. Mainz, 1979.

Inglis, C. G. "The Problem of St. Paul's Conversion." *Expository Times* 40 (1928–29): 227–31.

Ingolt, H. *Studier over palmyrensk skulptur.* Copenhagen, 1928.

Jacobi, Jolande. *Komplex, Archetypus, Symbol in der Psychologie C. G. Jung.* Stuttgart, 1957. ET: *Complex/Archetype/Symbol in the Psychology of C. G. Jung.* Princeton: Princeton Univ. Press, 1959.

Jastrow, M. *Die Religion Babyloniens und Assyriens* 2.1. Giessen, 1912.

Jeremias, J. "Abba." In *Abba: Studien zur neutestamentlichen Theologie und Zeitgeschichte,* 15–67. Göttingen, 1966. ET in *The Prayers of Jesus,* 11–65. Philadelphia: Fortress Press, 1978; London: SCM Press, 1967.

Jervell, Jacob. *Imago Dei: Gen. 1,26f. im Spätjudentum, in der Gnosis und in den paulinischen Briefen.* FRLANT 58. Göttingen: Vandenhoeck & Ruprecht, 1960.

Johanson, B. C. "Tongues, a Sign for Unbelievers? A Structural and Exegetical Study of I Corinthians XIV 20–25." *New Testament Studies* 25 (1979): 180–203.

Johnson, F. P. *Corinth: Results of Excavations IX: Sculpture 1896–1923.* Cambridge, Mass., 1931.

Judge, Edwin A. "The Early Christians as a Scholastic Community." *Journal of Religious History* 1 (1960): 4–15, 125–37.

Jung, C. G. *Aion.* 1951. In *Gesammelte Werke* 9.2. Olten, 1976. ET: *Aion.* In *The Collected Works of C. G. Jung* 9.2. New York: Pantheon Books, 1959.

————. "Die psychologischen Grundlagen des Geisterglaubens." 1919. In *Die Dynamik des Unbewussten: Gesammelte Werke* 8:339–60. Zurich, 1967. ET: "The Psychological Foundations of Belief in Spirits." In *Collected Works* 8:301–18, 1960.

————. "Versuch einer psychologischen Deutung des Trinitätsdogma." 1942–48. In *Gesammelte Werke* 11:121–218. Zurich, 1963.

————. "Das Wandlungssymbol in der Messe." In *Gesammelte Werke* 11:219–323. Zurich, 1976.

Kanael, B. *Die Kunst der antiken Synagoge.* Munich, 1961.

Kanfer, Frederick H., and Arnold P. Goldstein, eds. *Helping People Change: A Textbook of Methods.* 2d ed. New York: Pergamon Press, 1980.

Käsemann, Ernst. *An die Römer.* 3d ed. HNT 8a. Tübingen: J. C. B. Mohr [Paul Siebeck], 1974. ET: *Commentary on Romans.* Grand Rapids: Wm. B. Eerdmans, 1980.

————. "Geist und Buchstabe." In *Paulinische Perspektiven,* 237–85. Tübingen: J. C. B. Mohr [Paul Siebeck], 1969. ET: *Perspectives on Paul.* Philadelphia: Fortress Press, 1971.

————. "Der gottesdienstliche Schrei nach Freiheit." In *Paulinische Perspektiven*, 211–36.

Kelsey, Morton. *Tongue Speaking: An Experiment in Spiritual Experience*. Garden City, N.Y.: Doubleday & Co., 1964.

Kertelge, Karl. "Exegetische Überlegungen zum Verständnis der paulinischen Anthropologie nach Römer 7." *Zeitschrift für die neutestamentliche Wissenschaft* 62 (1971): 105–14.

Kildahl, John P. *The Psychology of Speaking in Tongues*. New York: Harper & Row, 1972.

Kittel, Gerhard. *Die 'Macht' auf dem Haupte 1. Kor. 11,10*. Arbeiten zur Religionsgeschichte des Urchristentums 1. Leipzig, 1920.

Klein, Günter. "Individualgeschichte und Weltgeschichte bei Paulus." In: *Rekonstrucktion und Interpretation*, 180–224. Munich: Chr. Kaiser, 1969.

Der kleine Pauly. 4 vols. Stuttgart: Druckenmüller, 1961–

Kleiner, Dianna E. E. *Roman Group Portraiture: The Funerary Reliefs of the Late Republic and Early Empire*. New York: Garland, 1977.

Knox, W. L. "Parallels to the N.T. Use of *soma*." *Journal of Theological Studies* 39 (1938): 243–46.

Koch, Klaus. "Sühne und Sündenvergebung um die Wende von der exilischen zur nachexilischen Zeit." *Evangelische Theologie* 26 (1966): 217–39.

Koester, Helmut. *Einführung in das Neue Testament*. Berlin: Walter de Gruyter, 1980. ET: *Introduction to the New Testament*. 2 vols. Philadelphia: Fortress Press, 1982.

————. "One Jesus and Four Primitive Gospels." In James M. Robinson and Helmut Koester, *Trajectories Through Early Christianity*, 158–204. Philadelphia: Fortress Press, 1971.

Kraeling, Carl H. *The Excavations at Dura-Europos: Final Report VIII, Part I*. London, 1956.

Kraiker, C. *Psychoanalyse, Behaviorismus, Handlungstheorie: Theorienkonflikte in der Psychologie*, Munich, 1980.

Krauss, Samuel. *Synagogale Altertümer*. Berlin and Vienna: Harz, 1922.

Kümmel, Werner G. *An die Korinther I, II*. 5th ed. Erklärt von Hans Lietzmann. Ergänzt von W. G. Kümmel. Tübingen: J. C. B. Mohr [Paul Siebeck], 1969.

————. *Einleitung in das Neue Testament*. 20th edition. Heidelberg: Quelle und Meyer, 1980. ET of 17th ed.: *Introduction to the New Testament*. Nashville: Abingdon Press, 1975.

————. *Römer 7 und das Bild des Menschen im Neuen Testament*. Munich: Chr. Kaiser, 1974.

Kürzinger, J. "Frau und Mann nach 1.Kor 11,11f." *Biblische Zeitschrift* 22 (1978): 270–75.

Kuss, Otto. *Der Römerbrief, 1.–3. Lieferung*. Regensburg: Pustet, 1957–1978.

Laffal, Julius. *Pathological and Normal Language*. New York: Atherton Press, 1965.

————, J. Monahan, and P. Richman. "Communication of Meaning in Glossolalia." *Journal of Social Psychology* 92 (1974): 277–91.

Langer, Susanne K. *Philosophy in a New Key: A Study in the Symbolism of Reason, Rite, and Art*. Cambridge: Harvard Univ. Press, 1951.

Larsson, Edvin. *Christus als Vorbild*. Uppsala: Lund, 1962.

Lausberg, H. *Handbuch der literarischen Rhetorik I/II*. Munich: Hueber, 1960.

Leenhardt, F. J. *L'Epître de Saint Paul aux Romains*. Neuchatel: Delachaux & Niestlé Spes, 1957. ET: *The Epistle to the Romans: A Commentary*. Cleveland: World Pub., 1961.

Leipoldt, Johannes. *Umwelt des Urchristentums*. 3 vols. Berlin: Evangelische Verlagsanstalt, 1965–67.

Lesky, A. "Psychologie bei Euripides." In *Euripides*, ed. E. R. Schwinge, 79–101. Darmstadt: Wissenschaftliche Buchgesellschaft, 1968.

Leslie, W. H. *The Concept of Woman in the Pauline Corpus in Light of the Social and Religious Environment of the First Century*. Ann Arbor, Mich.: University Microfilms, 1976.

Lewy, H. *Sobria ebrietas: Untersuchungen zur Geschichte der antiken Mystik*. BZNW 9. Giessen: Töpelmann, 1929.

Lietzmann, H. *An die Korinther I.II*. HNT 9. Tübingen: J. C. B. Mohr [Paul Siebeck], 1923. 4th ed., 1949.

————. *An die Römer*. 3d ed. HNT 8. Tübingen: J. C. B. Mohr [Paul Siebeck], 1928.

————. *Geschichte der alten Kirche II*. 3d ed. Berlin: Walter de Gruyter, 1961. ET: *A History of the Early Church*. New York: Charles Scribner's Sons, 1949–52.

Long, George, ed. *The Discourses of Epictetus*. London: Bell, 1909.

Lorenzer, A. *Kritik des psychoanalytischen Symbolbegriffs*. Frankfurt: Suhrkamp, 1970.

de Lorenzi, L., ed. *The Law of the Spirit in Rom 7 and 8*. Rome: St. Paul's Abbey, 1976.

Lösch, S. "Christliche Frauen in Corinth." *Theologische Quartalschrift* 127 (1947): 216–61.

Lührmann, Dieter. *Das Offenbarungsverständnis bei Paulus und in den paulinischen Gemeinden*. WMANT 16. Neukirchen: Neukirchener Verlag, 1965.

Luz, Ulrich. *Das Geschichtsverständnis des Paulus*. BEvTh 49. Munich: Chr. Kaiser, 1968.

Lyonnet, Stanislaus. "L'histoire du salut selon le ch. 7 de l'épître aux Romains." *Biblica* 43 (1962): 117–51.

————. " 'Tu ne convoiteras pas' (Rom VII, 7)." In *Neotestamentica Patristica* (Festschrift Oscar Cullmann), 117–51. Leiden: E. J. Brill, 1962.

McGinty, Park. "Dionysos' Revenge and the Validation of the Hellenic World-View." *Harvard Theological Review* 71 (1978): 77–94.

———. *Interpretation and Dionysos: Method in the Study of a God.* Religion and Reason 16. The Hague: Mouton, 1978.

Mack, B. L. *Logos und Sophia: Untersuchungen zur Weisheitstheologie im hellenistischen Judentum.* StUNT 10. Göttingen: Vandenhoeck & Ruprecht, 1973.

Mahoney, Michael J. *Cognition and Behavior Modification.* Cambridge, Mass.: Ballinger, 1974.

Maly, K. "1. Kor 12,1–3 eine Regel zur Unterscheidung der Geister." *Biblische Zeitschrift* 10 (1966): 82–95.

Mann, U. *Einführung in die Religionspsychologie.* Darmstadt: Wissenschaftliche Buchgesellschaft, 1973.

Manson, T. W. "The Corinthian Correspondence (1)." In *Studies in the Gospels and Epistles,* 190–209. Manchester: Manchester Univ. Press, 1962.

Marmorstein, J. "The Veil in Judaism and Islam." *Journal of Jewish Studies* 5 (1954): 1–11.

Marshall, P. "Enmity and Other Social Conventions in Paul's Relation with the Corinthians." Diss., Macquarie University (Australia), 1980.

Martin, I. J. "Glossolalie in the Apostolic Church." *Journal of Biblical Literature* 63 (1944): 123–30.

Martin, Josef. *Antike Rhetorik: Technik und Methode.* Munich: Beck, 1974.

Mattern, Lieselotte. *Das Verständnis des Gerichtes bei Paulus.* AThANT 47. Zurich: Zwingli, 1966.

Maurer, C. "sunoida." In *TWNT* 7:897–918. ET: *TDNT* 7:898–919.

Meichenbaum, Donald. *Cognitive-Behavior Modification: An Integrative Approach.* New York: Plenum, 1977.

Meyer, E. *Einführung in die lateinische Epigraphik.* Darmstadt: Wissenschaftliche Buchgesellschaft, 1973.

Michel, Otto. *Der Brief an die Römer.* 5th ed. KEK. Göttingen: Vandenhoeck & Ruprecht, 1978.

Miller, G. "*ARCHONTON TOU AIONOS TOUTOU*—A New Look at 1 Corinthians 2,6–8." *Journal of Biblical Literature* 91 (1972): 522–28.

Modalsli, O. "Gal 2,19–21; 5,16–18; Röm 7,7–25." *Theologische Zeitschrift* 21 (1965): 22–37.

Moe, O. "Zur Frage der sittlichen Selbstbeurteilung des Apostels Paulus." *Zeitschrift für Systematische Theologie* 16 (1939): 483–91.

Moffatt, James. *The First Epistle of Paul to the Corinthians.* London: Hodder & Stoughton, 1938.

Mosiman, Eddison. *Das Zungenreden geschichtlich und psychologisch untersucht.* Tübingen: J. C. B. Mohr [Paul Siebeck], 1911.

Moule, C. F. D. "2 Cor. 3,18b. *kathaper apo kuriou pneumatos.*" In *Neues Testament und Geschichte* (Festschrift Oscar Cullman), 231–37. Tübingen: J. C. B. Mohr [Paul Siebeck], 1972.

Müller, Carl W. *Gleiches zu Gleichem: Ein Prinzip frühgriechischen Denkens.* KPS 31. Wiesbaden: Karrassowitz, 1965.

Mussner, Franz. *Der Galaterbrief.* HTKNT 9. Freiburg: Herder & Herder, 1974.

Nase, E., and J. Scharfenberg, eds. *Psychoanalyse und Religion.* Darmstadt: Wissenschaftliche Buchgesellschaft, 1977.

Nestle, W. "Die Fabel des Menenius Agrippa." *Clio* 21 (1927): 350–60.

Niederwimmer, K. "Das Gebet des Geistes, Röm 8,26f." *Theologische Zeitschrift* 20 (1964) 252–65.

———. "Kerygmatisches Symbol und Analyse: Zur Kritik der Tiefenpsychologischen Bibelinterpretation." *Archiv für Religionsphilosophie* 7 (1962): 203–33. Also in *Psychoanalyse und Religion*, ed. Nase and Scharfenberg, 264–91.

———. "Tiefenpsychologie und Exegese." *Wege zum Menschen* 22 (1970): 257–72.

Nilsson, Martin P. *Geschichte der Griechischen Religion*, 2d ed. Vol. 1. Munich: Beck, 1955. ET of Swedish edition: *A History of Greek Religion*. New York: W. W. Norton & Co., 1964.

Nock, Arthur Darby. *Conversion: The Old and the New Religion from Alexander the Great to Augustine of Hippo.* Oxford: Oxford Univ. Press, 1933.

von Nordheim, E. "Das Zitat des Paulus in 1Kor 2,9 und seine Beziehung zum koptischen Testament Jakobs." *Zeitschrift für die neutestamentliche Wissenschaft* 65 (1974): 112–20.

Noth, Martin. *Das zweite Buch Mose.* ATD 5. Göttingen: Vandenhoeck & Ruprecht, 1965. ET of 1st edition: *Exodus: A Commentary.* Philadelphia: Westminster Press, 1962.

Oepke, Albrecht. *Der Brief des Paulus an die Galater.* 3d ed. ThHK 9. Berlin: Evangelische Verlagsanstalt, 1973.

———. "ekstasis." In *TWNT* 2:447–57. ET: *TDNT* 2:449–58.

———. "kalupto." In *TWNT* 3:563–65. ET: *TDNT* 3.556–58.

———. "kalymma." In *TWNT* 3:564. ET: *TDNT* 3:557.

———. "Probleme der vorchristlichen Zeit des Paulus." *Theologische Studien und Kritiken* 105 (1933): 387–404. Also in *Das Paulusbild in der neueren deutschen Forschung*, ed. K. H. Rengstorf, 410–46. WdF 24. Darmstadt: Wissenschaftliche Buchgesellschaft, 1964.

Oerter, R. *Psychologie des Denkens.* Donauwörth, 1971.

———. *Struktur und Wandlung von Werthandlungen.* Munich: Oldenbourg, 1978.

Osser, H. A., et al. "Glossolalic Speech from a Psycholinguistic Perspective." *Journal of Psycholinguistic Research* 2 (1973): 9–19.

von der Osten-Sacken, Peter. *Römer 8 als Beispiel paulinischer Soteriologie.* FRLANT 112. Göttingen: Vandenhoeck & Ruprecht, 1975.

Packer, J. I. "The 'Wretched Man' in Romans 7." In *Studia Evangelica* 2 (1964): 621–26.

Pascher, Joseph. *He basilike hodos: Der Königsweg zur Wiedergeburt und Vergottung bei Philon von Alexandreia*. Paderborn: Schöningh, 1931.

Paulsen, Henning. "Einheit und Freiheit der Söhne Gottes—Gal. 3,26–29." *Zeitschrift für die neutestamentliche Wissenschaft* 71 (1980): 74–95.

————. *Überlieferung und Auslegung in Röm 8*. WMANT 43. Neukirchen: Neukirchener Verlag, 1974.

Pearson, Birger A. *The Pneumatikos-Psychikos Terminology in 1 Corinthians: A Study in the Theology of the Corinthian Opponents of Paul and Its Relation to Gnosticism*. SBLDS 12. Missoula, Mont.: Nag Hammadi Seminar, 1976.

Pettazoni, Raffaele. *The All-Knowing God: Researches Into Early Religion and Culture*. London: Methuen, 1956.

Pfister, F. "Ekstase." In *RAC* 4:944–87.

Pfister, Oskar. "Die Entwicklung des Apostels Paulus: Eine religionsgeschichtliche und psychologische Skizze." *Imago* 6 (1920): 243–90.

————. "Die psychologische Enträtselung der religiösen Glossolalie und der automatischen Kryptographie." *Jahrbuch für psychologische und psychopathische Forschungen* 3 (1911): 425–66, 730–94.

Pfuhl, Ernst, and H. Möbius, *Die ostgriechischen Grabreliefs*. 4 vols. Mainz, 1977–79.

Piaget, Jean, and Bärbel Inhelder. *The Psychology of the Child*. New York: Basic Books, 1969.

Pohlenz, Max. *Stoa und Stoiker*. Zurich: Artemis, 1950.

Portmann, Adolf. "Das Problem der Urbilder in biologischer Sicht." In *Biologie und Geist*, 133–49. Frankfurt, 1956.

Preisendanz., Karl. *Papyri Graecae Magicae*. vol. 1. Leipzig, 1928.

Prigent, P. "Ce que l'oeil n'a pas vu, ICor 2,9: Histoire et préhistoire d'une citation." *Theologische Zeitschrift* 14 (1958): 416–429.

Prümm, Karl. *Diakonia Pneumatos: Der 2. Korintherbrief als Zugang zur apostolische Botschaft*. Rome: Herder & Herder, 1960–67.

von Rad, Gerhard. *Weisheit in Israel*. Neukirchen: Neukirchener Verlag, 1970. ET: *Wisdom in Israel*. Nashville: Abingdon Press, 1972.

Reese, James M. *Hellenistic Influence on the Book of Wisdom and Its Consequences*. Rome: Pontifical Biblical Institute, 1970.

Reumann, John. " 'Stewards of God': Pre-Christian Religious Application of *oikonomos* in Greek." *Journal of Biblical Literature* 77 (1958): 339–49.

Ricoeur, Paul. *The Conflict of Interpretations: Essays in Hermeneutics*. Evanston: Northwestern Univ. Press, 1974.

————. "Fatherhood: From Phantasm to Symbol." In *The Conflict of Interpretations*, 468–97. Evanston: Northwestern Univ. Press, 1974.

————. *Freud and Philosophy: An Essay on Interpretation*. New Haven: Yale Univ. Press, 1970.

Rissi, Mathias. *Studien zum zweiten Korintherbrief: Der alte Bund—der Prediger—der Tod*. AThANT 56. Zurich: Zwingli, 1969.

Roberts, P. "A Sign—Christian or Pagan?" *Expository Times* 90 (1978–79): 199–203.

Roberts, W. Rhys. *Longinus on the Sublime*. Cambridge: At the Univ. Press, 1899.

Robinson, James M., ed. *The Nag Hammadi Library*. New York: Harper & Row, 1978.

Rubenstein, Richard L. *My Brother Paul*. New York: Harper & Row, 1972.

Rüsch, A. "Das kaiserzeitliche Porträt in Makedonien." *Jahrbuch des deutschen Archaeologischen Instituts* 48 (1969): 59–196.

Saake, H. "Echtheitskritische Überlegungen zur Interpolationsthese von Röm 2,16." *New Testament Studies* 19 (1972–73): 486–89.

Samarin, William J. "Glossolalia as Learned Behaviour." *Canadian Journal of Theology* 15 (1969): 60–64.

———. "Glossolalie as Regressive Speech." *Language and Speech* 16 (1973): 77–89.

———. *Tongues of Men and Angels: The Religious Language of Pentecostalism*. New York: Macmillan Co., 1972.

Schachter, S., and J. E. Singer. "Cognitive, Social, and Physiological Determinants of Emotional State." *Psychological Review* 69 (1962): 379–99.

Schaller, B. *Das Testament Hiobs*. JSHRZ 3.3. Gütersloh, 1979.

Scharfenberg, J. *Religion zwischen Wahn und Wirklichkeit*. Hamburg: Furche, 1972.

———. "Religiöses Bewusstsein als Narzissmus?" In *Religion—Selbstbewusstsein—Identität*, 10–16. TEH 182. Munich: Chr. Kaiser, 1974.

———. *Sigmund Freud und Seine Religionskritik als Herausforderung für den christlichen Glauben*. Göttingen: Vandenhoeck & Ruprecht, 1968.

———, and H. Kämpfer. *Mit Symbolen leben*. Olten, 1980.

Schenke, Hans-Martin. "Die Tendenz der Weisheit zur Gnosis." In *Gnosis* (Festschrift Hans Jonas), ed. B. Aland, 351–72. Göttingen, 1978.

———, and K. M. Fischer. *Einleitung in die Schriften des Neuen Testaments*. Vol. 1. Berlin: Evangelische Verlagsanstalt, 1978.

Schlatter, Adolf. *Die Korinthische Theologie*. BFChTh 18. Gütersloh: Bertelsmann, 1914.

———. *Paulus, der Bote Jesu: Eine Deutung seiner Briefe an die Korinther*. Stuttgart: Calwer, 1934.

Schlier, Heinrich. "idiotes." In *TWNT* 3:215–17. ET: *TDNT* 3:215–17.

———. "Kerygma und Sophia—zur neutestamentlichen Grundlegung des Dogmas." In *Die Zeit der Kirche: Exegetische Aufsätze und Vorträge*, 206–32. Freiburg: Herder & Herder, 1956.

———. *Der Römerbrief*. HThK 6. Freiburg: Herder & Herder, 1977.

Schmidbauer, Wolfgang. *Mythos und Psychologie: Methodische Probleme, aufgezeigt an der Ödipus-Sage*. Munich: Reinhardt, 1970.

Schmithals, Walter. *Die Gnosis in Korinth: Eine Untersuchung zu den Korinther-*

briefen. FRLANT 66. Göttingen: Vandenhoeck & Ruprecht, 1956. ET: *Gnosticism in Corinth: An Investigation of the Letters to the Corinthians.* Nashville: Abingdon Press, 1971.

————. *Die theologische Anthropologie des Paulus.* Stuttgart: Kohlhammer, 1980.

Schnackenburg, Rudolf. *Die Johannesbriefe.* HThK 13. Freiburg: Herder & Herder, 1953.

————. "Römer 7 im Zusammenhang des Römerbriefes." In *Jesus und Paulus* (Festschrift Werner Georg Kümmel), 283–300. Göttingen, 1975.

Schniewind, Julius. "Die Archonton dieses Äons: I.Kor 2,6–8." In *Nachgelassene Reden und Aufsätze,* 104–9. Berlin: Töpelmann, 1952.

————. "Das Seufzen des Geistes, Röm 8,26.27." In *Nachgelassene Reden und Aufsätze,* 81–103. Berlin: Töpelmann, 1952.

Schottroff, Luise. "Frauen in der Nachfolge Jesu in neutestamentlicher Zeit." In *Frauen in der Bibel,* ed. W. Schottroff and W. Stegemann, 91–133. Munich, 1980.

————. *Der Glaubende und die feindliche Welt: Beobachtungen zum gnostischen Dualismus und seiner Bedeutung für Paulus und das Johannesevangelium.* WMANT 37. Neukirchen: Neukirchener Verlag, 1970.

————. "Die Schreckensherrschaft der Sünde und die Befreiung durch Christus nach dem Römerbrief des Apostels Paulus." *Evangelische Theologie* 39 (1979): 497–510.

Schottroff, W., and W. Stegemann. *Der Gott der kleinen Leute.* Vol. 1. Munich, 1979. ET: *The God of the Lowly.* Maryknoll, N.Y.: Orbis Books, 1984.

Schreiber, Alfred. *Die Gemeinde in Korinth: Versuch einer gruppendynamischen Betrachtung der Entwicklung der Gemeinde von Korinth auf der Basis des ersten Korintherbriefes.* NTA 12. Münster: Aschendorff, 1977.

Schreiber, J. "Sigmund Freud als Theologe." In *Psychoanalyse und Religion,* ed. Nase and Scharfenberg, 233–63.

Schrenk, G. "entole." In *TWNT* 2:542–53. ET: *TDNT* 2:545–56.

Schulz, Siegfried. "Die Decke des Mose." *Zeitschrift für die neutestamentliche Wissenschaft* 49 (1958): 1–30.

Schwarz, G. "*exousian echein epi tes kephales?* (1. Korinther 11, 10)." *Zeitschrift für die neutestamentliche Wissenschaft* 70 (1979): 249.

Schweizer, Eduard. "Zur Trichotomie von 1.Thess. 5,23 und der Unterscheidung des *pneumatikon* vom *psychikon* in 1.Kor 2,14; 15,44; Jak. 3,15; Jud. 19." *Theologische Zeitschrift* 9 (1953): 76–77.

Scroggs, R. "The Heuristic Value of Psychoanalytic Model in the Interpretation of Paul." *Zygon* 13 (1978): 136–57.

————. "Paul and the Eschatological Woman Revisited." *Journal of the American Academy of Religion* 42 (1974): 532–37.

————. "Paul *SOPHOS* and *PNEUMATIKOS.*" *New Testament Studies* 14 (1967–68): 33–55.

Sellin, G. "Das 'Geheimnis' der Weisheit und das Rätsel der 'Christuspartei' (zu 1Kor 1—4)." *Zeitschrift für die neutestamentliche Wissenschaft* 73 (1982): 69–96.

Septuaginta. Ed. A. Rahlfs. Vol. 1, *Genesis.* Ed. J. W. Wevers. Göttingen: Vandenhoeck & Ruprecht, 1974.

Seyrig, Henri. "Antiquités syriennes 17: Bas-reliefs monumentaux du temple de Bêl à Palmyre." *Syria* 15 (1934): 155–86.

Siebeck, Hermann. *Geschichte der Psychologie.* I.1.2. Gotha: Perthes, 1880–84.

Smend, Rudolf, and Ulrich Luz. *Gesetz.* Stuttgart: Kohlhammer, 1981.

Smith, E. W. "The Form and Religious Background of Romans VII 24–25a." *Novum Testamentum* 13 (1971): 127–35.

Snell, Bruno. "Das früheste Zeugnis über Sokrates." *Philologus* 97 (1948): 125–34.

Sparks, H. F. D. "1. Cor 2,9—A Quotation from the Coptic Testament of Jacob?" *Zeitschrift für die neutestamentliche Wissenschaft* 67 (1976): 269–76.

———, ed. *The Apocryphal Old Testament.* Oxford: At the Clarendon Press, 1984.

Spiegel, Y., ed. *Doppeldeutlich.* Munich, 1978.

Steck, Odil Hannes. *Israel und das gewaltsame Geschick der Propheten: Untersuchungen zur Überlieferung des deuteronomistischen Geschichtsbildes im Alten Testament, Spätjudentum und Urchristentum.* WMANT 23. Neukirchen: Neukirchener Verlag, 1967.

Stegemann, W. *Das Evangelium und die Armen: Über den Ursprung der Theologie der Armen im Neuen Testament.* Munich: Chr. Kaiser, 1981. ET: *The Gospel and the Poor.* Philadelphia: Fortress Press, 1984.

Steinleitner, F. S. "Die Beichte im Zusammenhang mit der sakralen Rechtspflege in der Antike." Diss., Munich, 1913.

Stendahl, Krister. "The Apostle Paul and the Introspective Conscience of the West." *Harvard Theological Review* 56 (1963): 199–215. Also in *Paul Among Jews and Gentiles*, 78–96. Philadelphia: Fortress Press, 1976.

———. "Glossolalia—The New Testament Evidence." In *Paul Among Jews and Gentiles*, 109–24.

Stollberg, D. "Tiefenpsychologie oder historisch-kritische Exegese? Identität und der Tod des Ich (Gal 2,19–20)." In *Doppeldeutlich*, ed. Y. Spiegel, 215–26. Munich, 1978.

Sundén, Hjalmar. *Gott erfahren: Das Rollenangebot der Religionen.* Gütersloh, 1975.

———. "Regression und Phasenwechsel." *Archiv für Religionsphilosophie* 13 (1978): 51–60.

———. *Die Religion und die Rollen.* Berlin: Töpelmann, 1966.

Sweet, J. P. M. "A Sign for Unbelievers: Paul's Attitude to Glossolalia." *New Testament Studies* 13 (1966–67): 240–57.

Synofzik, E. *Die Gerichts- und Vergeltungsaussagen bei Paulus.* GTA 8. Göttingen: Vandenhoeck & Ruprecht, 1977.

Tachau, Peter. *"Einst" und "Jetzt" im Neuen Testament.* FRLANT 105. Göttingen: Vandenhoeck & Ruprecht, 1972.

Tarachow, S. "St. Paul and Early Christianity." *Psychoanalysis and the Social Sciences* 4 (1955): 223–81.

Taubes, J. "Religion und die Zukunft der Psychoanalyse." 1957. In *Psychoanalyse und Religion,* ed. Nase and Scharfenberg, 167–75.

Theissen, Gerd. *Argumente für einen kritischen Glauben.* Munich: Chr. Kaiser, 1978. ET: *A Critical Faith: A Case for Religion.* Philadelphia: Fortress Press, 1979.

———. "Soteriologische Symbolik in den paulinischen Schriften: Ein strukturalistischer Beitrag." *Kerygma und Dogma* 20 (1974): 282–304.

———. "Die Starken und die Schwachen in Corinth." *Evangelische Theologie* 35 (1975): 155–72. Also in *Studien zur Soziologie des Urchristentums,* 272–89. ET: "The Strong and the Weak in Corinth: A Sociological Analysis of a Theological Quarrel." In *The Social Setting of Pauline Christianity: Essays on Corinth,* 121–43.

———. *Studien zur Soziologie des Urchristentums.* WUNT 19. Tübingen: J. C. B. Mohr, 1979. Partial ET: *The Social Setting of Pauline Christianity: Essays on Corinth.* Philadelphia: Fortress Press, 1982.

Thistleton, A. C. "The 'Interpretation' of Tongues: A New Suggestion in the Light of Greek Usage in Philo and Josephus." *Journal of Theological Studies* 30 (1979): 15–36.

Thomae, Hans. *Das Individuum und seine Welt: Eine Persönlichkeitstheorie.* Göttingen: Hogrefe, 1968.

———. *Konflikt, Entscheidung, Verantwortung: Ein Beitrag zur Psychologie der Entscheidung.* Stuttgart: Kohlhammer, 1974.

———. *Psychologie in der modernen Gesellschaft.* Hamburg, 1977.

———, and H. Feger. *Hauptströmungen der neueren Psychologie.* Bern, 1969.

Thüsing, Wilhelm. " 'Milch' and 'feste Speise' (1.Kor 3,1f. und Hebr 5,11—6,3)." *Trierer Theologische Zeitschrift* 76 (1967): 223–46, 261–80.

Tugwell, Simon. "The Gift of Tongues in the New Testament." *Expository Times* 84 (1972–73): 137–40.

van Unnik, W. C. " 'With unveiled face': An Exegesis of 2. Corinthians III. 12–18." *Novum Testamentum* 6 (1963): 153–69.

Vergote, Antoine. "Der Beitrag der Psychoanalyse zur Exegese: Leben, Gesetz und Ich-Spaltung im 7. Kapitel des Römerbriefs." In *Exegese im Methodenstreit,* ed. Xavier Léon-Dufour, 73–116. Munich, 1973.

———. *Religionspsychologie.* Olten, 1970. ET of original French: *The Religious Man: A Psychological Study of Religious Attitudes.* Dayton: George A. Pflaum, 1969.

Vielhauer, Philipp. *Geschichte der urchristlichen Literatur.* Berlin: Walter de Gruyter, 1975.

————. "Paulus und das Alte Testament." In *Oikodome: Aufsätze zum Neuen Testament* 2:196–228. Munich: Chr. Kaiser, 1979.

Vivier, L. M. "The Glossolalic and His Personality." In *Beiträge zur Ekstase*, ed. T. Spoerri, 153–75. Basel, 1968.

Walker, W. O. "1. Corinthians 11, 2–16 and Paul's Views Regarding Women." *Journal of Biblical Literature* 94 (1975): 94–110.

Watanabe, Y. "Selbstwertanalyse und christlicher Glaube." *Evangelische Theologie* 40 (1980): 58–75.

Wedderburn, A. J. M. "Romans 8,26—Toward a Theology of Glossolalia." *Scottish Journal of Theology* 28 (1975): 369–77.

Weinel, Heinrich. *Die Wirkungen des Geistes und der Geister*. Tübingen: Laupp, 1899.

Weiss, Johannes. *Der 1. Korintherbrief*. Göttingen: Vandenhoeck & Ruprecht, 1970 [1910].

Wendel, C. *Der Thoraschrein im Altertum*. HM 15. Halle, 1950.

Wetzel, F. G. *Kognitive Psychologie: Eine Einführung in die Psychologie der kognitiven Strukturen von Jean Piaget*. Weinheim, 1980.

Widmann, M. "I.Kor 2,6–16: Ein Einspruch gegen Paulus." *Zeitschrift für die neutestamentliche Wissenschaft* 70 (1979): 44–53.

Wiesenhütter, E. *Grundbegriffe der Tiefenpsychologie*. Darmstadt: Wissenschaftliche Buchgesellschaft, 1969.

Wilckens, Ulrich. *Der Brief an die Römer, Röm 1—5*. EKK 6.1. Neukirchen: Neukirchener Verlag, 1978.

————. *Der Brief an die Römer, Röm 6—11*. EKK 6.2. Neukirchen: Neukirchener Verlag, 1980.

————. "sophia." In *TWNT* 7:497–529. ET: *TDNT* 7:496–528.

————. *Weisheit und Torheit: Eine exegetisch- religionsgeschichtliche Untersuchung zu 1. Kor. 1 und 2*. BHTh 26. Tübingen: J. C. B. Mohr [Paul Siebeck], 1959.

————. "Zu 1.Kor 2,1–16." In *Theologia Crucis—Signum Crucis* (Festschrift Erich Dinkler), 501–37. Tübingen: J. C. B. Mohr [Paul Siebeck], 1979.

Williams, C. G. "Glossolalia as a Religious Phenomenon: Tongues at Corinth and Pentecost." *Religion* 5 (1975): 16–32.

Windisch, Hans. *Der zweite Korintherbrief*. Ed. G. Strecker. Göttingen: Vandenhoeck & Ruprecht, 1970 [1924].

Wink, Walter. *The Bible in Human Transformation: Toward a New Paradigm for Biblical Study*. Philadelphia: Fortress Press, 1973.

Winkes, Rolf. "Zum Illusionismus römischer Wandmalerei der Republik." In *Aufstieg und Niedergang der Römischen Welt* 1.4:927–44. Berlin: Walter de Gruyter, 1973.

Winter, Martin. *Pneumatiker und Psychiker in Korinth: Zum religionsgeschichtlichen Hintergrund von 1. Kor. 2,6—3,4*. MThSt 12. Marburg: Elwert, 1975.

Wischmeyer, O. *Der höchste Weg: Das 13. Kapitel des 1. Korintherbriefes*. StNT 13. Gütersloh, 1981.

Wlosok, Antoine. *Laktanz und die philosophische Gnosis*. Heidelberg: Winter, 1980.

Wuellner, W. "Ursprung und Verwendung der *sophos-, dunatos-, eugenes*-Formel in 1.Kor 1,26." In *Donum Gentilicium: New Testament Studies in Honour of David Daube*, ed. E. Bammel et al., 165–84. Oxford: At the Clarendon Press, 1978.

Wyss, Dieter. *Die tiefenpsychologischen Schulen von den Anfängen bis zur Gegenwart*. Göttingen, 1961. ET: Psychoanalytic Schools from the Beginning to the Present. New York: Jason Aronson, 1973.

Zahn, Theodor. *Der Brief des Paulus an die Römer*. KNT 6. Leipzig: Deichert, 1910.

Zumkley-Münkel, Cordula. *Imitationslernen*. Düsseldorf, 1976.

Index of Passages

422

Polycarp
To the Philippians
4.1—205n.
4.3—85n.

Psalms of Solomon
14.6 (17.25)—87n.
17.24ff.—101n

Pseudo-Phocylides
42ff.—205n.
210-14—169

Qumran
1QH
1.1-19—201n.
1.5-39—201n.
2.7-12—335n.
2.18(-19)—74n., 290n.
4.5-29—201n.
4.16—74n., 290n.
4.29-40—108n.
5.5-19—201n.
5.20-6.36—201n.
5.30-32—335n.
7.6-25—201n.
8.4-40—20in.
12.34—87n.
18.20—70n.
18.24—87n.
1QIsa—74n., 290n.
1QM 16.15—87n.
1QS V, 5—70n.

Romulus
66—327n., 329n.

Second Treatise of the Great Seth
56.24-27—382n.

Seneca
Ad Lucilium Epistulae Morales
3:91—329n.
De Ira
2.31.7—328n., 329n.
Epistles
95.52—329n.
Medea
178-79—218
938-44—217
On Anger
3.36.1-2—109
3.36.3—110

Shepherd of Hermas
Mandates
4.3.4—84n., 86n.
4.34—87n.
Visions
4.2.1—160n.

Sirach
1:30—85n., 89
11:14, 25, 31—208n.
12:3—208n.
13:25—208n.
15:18—84n.
16:17—85n.
17:7—208n.
17:15, 20—85n.
18:8—208n.
23:18-20—84
24:3-8—355
24:6-8—359
33:14—208n.
39:4—208n.
39:19—85n.
42:18-20—86, 87n., 89
42:19—85n.

Socrates
Apology
22B-C—282
Ion
533D-35A—283
Meno
99C-D—283

Sophocles
Antigone
184—85n.
Susanna
42-43—86
42—85n.

Strabo
9.3.5—364

Sylloge Inscriptionum Graecarum
736.16ff.—295n.
1013.6—295n.

Tertullian
De Anima
21—287n.

Testaments of the Twelve Patriarchs
Testament of Abraham
10—92
Testament of Jacob
8.8—366
Testament of Job
23-25—169
23.11—170
24.10—170
47.6-9—289
48.1-3—289
49.2—289
50.2—289
51.3-4—289
(Testament of) Judah
19.3-4—155
19.4—375n.
20—72n., 90, 338n.
Testament of Levi
8.2—160n.
(Testament of) Reuben
1.4—88
4.3-4—110
5.5-6—171
Testament of Simeon
2.7—375n.

Testimony of Truth
9.9-21—378
29.17-18—378
31.2-5—378
42.24-25—378

Theophilus
Ad Autylochum
2.9—286n.

Tobit
12:12-15—338

Vergil
Aeneid
3.188—217n.
4.215—167n.
Eclogue
4—337

Wisdom [of Solomon]
1:4—357
1:6—87n.
2:10ff—356
5:16—356
6:1—356
6:20-21—356, 370n.
6:20—353n.